Augustine and Modern Law

Philosophers and Law
Series Editor: Tom Campbell

Titles in the Series:

Aquinas and Modern Law
Richard O. Brooks and James Bernard Murphy

Aristotle and Modern Law
Richard O. Brooks and James Bernard Murphy

Augustine and Modern Law
Richard O. Brooks and James Bernard Murphy

Cicero and Modern Law
Richard O. Brooks

Plato and Modern Law
Richard O. Brooks

Locke and Law
Thom Brooks

Rousseau and Law
Thom Brooks

Kant and Law
B. Sharon Byrd and Joachim Hruschka

Marx and Law
Susan Easton

Hobbes on Law
Claire Finkelstein

Foucault and Law
Ben Golder and Peter Fitzpatrick

Derrida and Law
Pierre Legrand

Hume and Law
Ken Mackinnon

Gadamer and Law
Francis J. Mootz III

Nietzsche and Law
Francis J. Mootz III and Peter Goodrich

Wittgenstein and Law
Dennis Patterson

Hegel and Law
Michael Salter

Augustine and Modern Law

Edited by

Richard O. Brooks

Vermont Law School, USA

and

James Bernard Murphy

Dartmouth College, USA

Routledge
Taylor & Francis Group
LONDON AND NEW YORK

First published 2011 by Ashgate Publishing

2 Park Square, Milton Park, Abingdon, Oxfordshire OX14 4RN
711 Third Avenue, New York, NY 10017

Routledge is an imprint of the Taylor & Francis Group, an informa business

First issued in paperback 2018

British Library Cataloguing in Publication Data
Augustine and modern law. – (Philosophers and law)
1. Augustine, Saint, Bishop of Hippo–Political and social views. 2. Augustine, Saint, Bishop of Hippo–Influence.
3. Political science–Philosophy–History–To 1500.
4. Jurisprudence–History.
I. Series II. Brooks, Richard Oliver. III. Murphy, James Bernard, 1958–
340.1'1–dc22

Library of Congress Control Number: 2010937378

ISBN 978-0-7546-2894-1 (hbk)
ISBN 978-1-138-37856-8 (pbk)

Contents

C Marriage

Acknowledgements

The editors and publishers wish to thank the following for permission to use copyright material.

American Journal of Jurisprudence for the essay: Anton-Hermann Chroust (1973), 'The Fundamental Ideas in St Augustine's Philosophy of Law', *American Journal of Jurisprudence*, **18**, pp. 57–79.

Cambridge University Press for the essay: R.A. Markus (1979), 'Coge Intrare: The Church and Political Power', in *Saeculum*, Cambridge: Cambridge University Press. pp. 133–53. Copyright © 1979 Cambridge University Press.

Georgetown Law Journal for the essay: Francesco Lardone (1933), 'Roman Law in the Works of St Augustine', *Georgetown Law Journal*, **21**, pp. 435–56.

Johns Hopkins University Press for the essay: Eugene Vance (1978), 'Augustine's *Confessions* and the Poetics of the Law', *Modern Language Notes*, **93**, pp. 618–34.

Oxford University Press for the essays: Gaylon L. Caldwell (1960), 'Augustine's Critique of Human Justice', *Journal of Church and State*, **7**, pp. 7–25; R.A. Markus (1965), 'Two Conceptions of Political Authority: Augustine, *De Civitate Dei* xix, 14–15, and Some Thirteenth–Century Interpretations,' *Journal of Theological Studies*, **16**, pp. 68–100.

Philosophy Documentation Center for the essays: D.J. MacQueen (1973), 'The Origin and Dynamics of Society and the State According to St Augustine', *Augustinian Studies*, **4**, pp. 73–101; Eric O. Springsted (1998), 'Will and Order: The Moral Self in Augustine's *De Libero Arbitrio*', *Augustinian Studies*, **29**, pp. 77–96.

Random House, Inc. for the essay: Whitney J. Oates (1948), 'The Life and Religion of Saint Augustine', in Anton Charles Pegis (ed.), *Basic Writings of Saint Augustine Volume I*, New York: Random House, pp. ix–xl.

Rowman & Littlefield Publishers, Inc. for the essay: Ernest L. Fortin (1996), 'Augustine and the Problem of Christian Rhetoric', in J. Brian Benestod (ed.), *The Birth of Philosophic Christianity*, New York nd London: Rowman & Littlefield Publishers, Inc., pp. 79–93. Copyright © 1996 Rowman & Littlefield Publishers, Inc.

Society of Christian Ethics for the essay: John R. Bowlin (1997), 'Augustine on Justifying Coercion', *Annual of the Society of Christian Ethics*, **17**, pp. 49–70.

Society for the Promotion of Roman Studies for the essay: P.R.L. Brown (1964), 'S. Augustine's Attitude to Religious Coercion', *Journal of Roman Studies*, **54**, pp. 107–116.

University of California Press for the essay: Rüdiger Bittner (1999), 'Augustine's Philosophy of History', in Gareth B. Matthews (ed.), *The Augustinian Tradition*, Berkleley, CA: University of California Press, pp. 345–61. Copyright © 1999 The Regents of the University of California.

University of Dayton for the essay: Michael J. White (1994), 'Pluralism and Secularism in the Political Order: St Augustine and Theoretical Liberalism', *University of Dayton Review*, **22**, pp. 137–53.

University of Missouri for the essay: John von Heyking (2001), 'The Coercion of Heretics', in John von Heyking, *Augustine and Politics as Longing in the World*, Columbia, MO: University of Missouri Press, pp. 222–57.

University of Pennsylvania Press for the essays: Rex Martin (1972), 'The Two Cities in Augustine's Political Philosophy', *Journal of the History of Ideas*, **33**, pp. 195–216; Peter Burnell (1993), 'The Problem of Service to Unjust Regimes in Augustine's *City of God*', *Journal of the History of Ideas*, **54**, pp. 177–88. Copyright © 1993 Journal of the History of Ideas; Theodor E. Mormmsen (1951), 'St Augustine and the Christian Idea of Progress: The Background of the *City of God*', *Journal of the History of Ideas*, **12**, pp. 346–74; Richard Shelley Hartigan (1966), 'Saint Augustine on War and Killing: The Problem of the Innocent', *Journal of the History of Ideas*, **27**, pp. 195–204.

University of St Thomas for the essay: Charles J. Reid, Jr (2009), 'Marriage in its Procreative Dimensions: The Meaning of the Institution of Marriage Throughout the Ages', *University of St. Thomas Law Review*, **6**, pp. 454–83.

Wm. B. Eerdmans Publishing Co. for the essay: Robert Markus (1999), 'Life, Culture and Controversies of Augustine', in Allan D. Fitzgerald (ed.), *Augustine Through the Ages: An Encyclopedia*, Grand Rapids/Cambridge: William B. Eerdmans Publishing Co., pp. 498–504. Copyright © 1999 Wm. B. Eerdmans Publishing Co.

Every effort has been made to trace all the copyright holders, but if any have been inadvertently overlooked the publishers will be pleased to make the necessary arrangement at the first opportunity.

Series Preface

The series *Philosophers and Law* selects and makes accessible the most important essays in English that deal with the application to law of the work of major philosophers for whom law was not a main concern. The series encompasses not only what these philosophers had to say about law but also brings together essays which consider those aspects of the work of major philosophers which bear on our interpretation and assessment of current law and legal theory. The essays are based on scholarly study of particular philosophers and deal with both the nature and role of law and the application of philosophy to specific areas of law.

Some philosophers, such as Hans Kelsen, Roscoe Pound and Herbert Hart are known principally as philosophers of law. Others, whose names are not primarily or immediately associated with law, such as Aristotle, Kant and Hegel, have, nevertheless, had a profound influence on legal thought. It is with the significance for law of this second group of philosophers that this series is concerned.

Each volume in the series deals with a major philosopher whose work has been taken up and applied to the study and critique of law and legal systems. The essays, which have all been previously published in law, philosophy and politics journals and books, are selected and introduced by an editor with a special interest in the philosopher in question and an engagement in contemporary legal studies. The essays chosen represent the most important and influential contributions to the interpretation of the philosophers concerned and the continuing relevance of their work to current legal issues.

TOM CAMPBELL
Series Editor
Centre for Applied Philosophy and Public Ethics
Charles Sturt University

Introduction

No thinker seems as remote from the concerns of modern jurisprudence as does Augustine. After all, he wrote no treatise or even dialogue on the topic of law.[1] Moreover, at a time when jurisprudence and legal philosophy are dominated by an instrumental pragmatism, Augustine's heavily theological and metaphysical approach to law seems hopelessly outmoded in our allegedly post-Christian, post-metaphysical age. And yet, for precisely these reasons, Augustine has never been more urgently relevant. Augustine was deeply aware of the tacit presuppositions that underlie all theorizing: he famously said 'I believe in order that I might understand' (Sermo 43, 7, 9: PL 38, 257–8). Augustine is crystal clear that his presuppositions are rooted in his Christian faith.[2] Many leading contemporary philosophers, such as Richard Posner, John Rawls, and Jurgen Habermas, claim to theorize about law and politics without metaphysical presuppositions. But Augustine would have no trouble showing that modern legal pragmatism, political liberalism, and discourse theory all rest on deep tacit assumptions about human nature, the hierarchy of goods, and the reality of divine purpose. Augustine frankly grounds his account of human law in the eternal law of God and in the law of nature. The main difference between Augustine and these contemporary theorists is that Augustine forthrightly owns up to his own presuppositions. He invites us to do so as well.

Augustine turns out to be deeply illuminating of our contemporary predicament. Not only because of the stark contrast between his metaphysical depth and modern pragmatism, but also because his theological and metaphysical premises led him to some seemingly 'modern' conclusions. In his reluctant but resolute advocacy of the legal suppression of heresy,[3] Augustine helped to lay the foundations for some of the worst abuses of medieval theocracy. Yet, with the rising spectre of Islamic theocracy, the theocratic elements of Augustine's thought are now more relevant than ever. What is less well understood is how Augustine's Christian idealism led him to views of politics that are even more grimly realistic than those

---

[1] Perhaps his discussion of 'On Order' and sections of his 'On Free Will' are his most specific jurisprudential works. In Part III of this book, the essays by Anton-Hermann Chroust, Robert Markus and Francesco Lardone (Chapters 7, 8 and 9, respectively) describe the jurisprudential aspects of Augustine's theory. See also Fortin (1978). Section IV of our bibliography lists a number of other sources which pertain to Augustine's view of law.

Of course, Augustine is not the only ancient author who has not penned a treatise on jurisprudence. Aristotle also gives us no such treatise (unless one counts his Athenian Constitution and his last treatise on justice. Perhaps Augustine did not write specifically on the law because, in the time he lived, a complex system of law had emerged in Rome. For one of many accounts, see Matthews (2000).

[2] The primacy of the Christian faith is best articulated in *On Christian Doctrine*, where the act of interpretation and the supportive liberal arts are premised upon adherence to faith. See also Burton (2005).

[3] See the essays in Part V by John Bowlin, Peter Brown and John van Heyking on the coercion of heretics (Chapters 20, 21 and 22, respectively).

of Machiavelli[4] or how Augustine's theology led him to affirm the essential secularity of politics and law in the post-biblical epoch.[5] According to Augustine, we cannot understand the sinful reality of human law and politics apart from the ideals of divine creation; similarly, the secularity of the realms of politics is intelligible only against the claims of the Christian Church. Augustine never confused the heavenly city with the earthly city; but he also asserted that we cannot understand our fallen, sinful and secular world except by contrast to our ultimate heavenly destiny.

According to Augustine, our human nature is complex: we have a good created nature but also a fallen corrupted nature that is prone to sin.[6] The trait most characteristic of such a mixed creature is hypocrisy, the tribute that vice pays to virtue. If we were simply good or simply bad, we would have no resort to hypocrisy. To use the language of the later scholastics, law has a directive function in leading us to the good and a coercive function in restraining us from evil. The directive function of law appeals to our good, created nature while the coercive function of law is necessary only because of our fall into sinfulness. Most legal theorists emphasize either the directive or the coercive functions of law. Aristotle, Cicero, Aquinas, Suarez, Grotius, Locke, Raz, Dworkin and Habermas emphasize how law guides the practical reasoning of human agents who seek the good. By contrast, Callicles, St. Paul, Hobbes, Madison, Austin and Schmidt emphasize how law violently constrains the wicked. With his complex view of human nature, Augustine alone is able to do justice to both the directive force of human law, as rooted in the divine and natural law,[7] and to the coercive force of human law, regretfully necessary after Adam's expulsion from Paradise. Because of our complex nature, human law must both offer us rational guidance and threaten us. More generally, political theorists also tend to regard government in general as either a force for good (Plato, Aristotle, Aquinas, Marsilius, Machiavelli, Hegel, Rawls) or as a necessary evil (Gorgias, St Paul, Hobbes, Madison, Hayek). Augustine's attitude is again complex: some aspects of government are necessary even in Paradise, while other aspects are necessary only because of our Fall from grace.[8]

Why Augustine and Why Now?

We live in an age of disillusioned idealism and Augustine is the great theorist of disillusionment. As Americans we are especially prone to the dangers of political disappointment because we tend to harbour such high hopes. The Puritans dreamed of a New Israel, a purified Christian City on a Hill, only to awaken to the trauma of heresy, schism and witch burning. The new

[4] For a discussion of Augustine's realism, see Part IV A and the essays by Eric Springstead (Chapter 12) and Reinhold Niebuhr (Chapter 13). For a list of other sources, see Section VA of the Selected Bibliography.

[5] Augustine's secularity is outlined in Markus (1988).

[6] Augustine's account of sin and the fallen nature of mankind is illustrated in his history of Rome in Book I in his *City of God*. It is also reflected in his view of history. (See the essays in this volume by Theodor Mommsen (Chapter 14) and Rüdiger Bittner (Chapter 15).

[7] Although Augustine identifies in passing 'natural law', it remained for Aquinas to articulate a full theory of natural law. See the essay by Robert Markus in Part III of this volume (Chapter 10); see also, Chroust (1946).

[8] The role of government is carefully outlined in *City of God*.

American nation saw itself as a symbol and instrument of freedom and democracy but nearly foundered on slavery and wars of conquest. In the twentieth century, many Americans invested dearly in the dream of a Christian nation, while many other Americans confidently expected the triumph of atheist humanism and the death of religion: both groups are struggling to reconcile themselves to the disappointment that American society is neither Christian nor atheist but permanently divided. When the Soviet Union collapsed, we talked about a Pax Americana and the End of History, only to immediately greet genocide in the Balkans and world-wide Islamic jihad.

Over the course of his long life, Augustine embraced many kinds of idealism and then succumbed to many kinds of disillusionment.[9] As a young man, full of intellectual arrogance, he searched for modes of spiritual redemption based on the acquisition of special kinds of knowledge: salvation for the intellectual elite. To his crushing disappointment, none of these elite sects offered him the nourishment that he found in the simple faith of the mostly illiterate followers of Jesus. Then, converting to Christianity, he was instantly disappointed in his own and other Christians' conduct: instead of becoming humble and chastened, the new Christians often became proud and smug; celibacy, he noticed, often made people stingy. Augustine believed that Catholic Christian faith was so intrinsically noble and beautiful that it would attract adherents by force of argument with no need for any external compulsion; but his hopes foundered on the reality of the Donatist heretics. Augustine patiently spent decades attempting to persuade the Donatists of what he saw as their errors; but eventually, and with deep regret, he finally enlisted the secular powers to apply legal 'pressure' on the Donatists. As a new Christian in the fourth century, when Christianity was the official religion of the Roman Empire, Augustine initially embraced the common hope that God had chosen Rome to create a universal Christian Empire, with peace, justice and the one true faith extending over the whole world. The Pax Romana was to become the Pax Christiana. But during the fifth century, as Rome succumbed to internal collapse and external invasion, Augustine grew disillusioned with the whole idea of a Christian empire. He began to accept the idea that Christians would always have to share the political community with non-Christians, so that the challenge was to work out the terms of cooperation in conditions of permanent political pluralism.[10] What could be more relevant for American law and politics today?

The danger of disillusioned idealism is, of course, cynicism. And Augustine does occasionally slip into cynicism. But in general Augustine realizes that the key to avoiding disappointment is to scale back one's expectations of human life. Political disillusionment comes from expecting too much from politics: if we hope to see our highest ideals embodied in our political institutions and in our law, we are headed for a bitter disappointment. The twentieth century witnessed the apex of extravagant political hope in the history of the world, from 'the war to end all wars' and 'making the world safe for democracy' to the Thousand-Year Reich and World Communism.[11] The human race barely survived this orgy of idealism. We must now massively scale back our expectations for politics and there is no better guide to this chastened idealism than Augustine. Ever since Reinhold Niebuhr, Augustine has been

---

[9] For accounts of Augustine's life and world, see the essays in Part I of this volume by Whitney Oates (Chapter 1) and Robert Markus (Chapter 2). The definitive biography of Augustine is Peter Brown's *Augustine of Hippo* (1967, rev. 2000). See also Section II of the Selected Bibliography.

[10] See Part II.C, especially Michael White's essay (Chapter 8). See also Cochrane (1944).

[11] For a modern history, see Glover (1989).

called the classic theorist of political realism.[12] But much of what we call 'realism' today is merely cynicism or the amoral celebration of force. Augustine is better understood as a chastened idealist, who puts his treasure in Heaven and works for modest amelioration of our suffering here on Earth.

Augustine as a Source of Modernity.

Augustine is one of those rare thinkers who transformed the sensibilities of an entire civilization. His unlikely modern counterpart is Jean-Jacques Rousseau. Charles Taylor, for example, begins his influential study of modern culture, *Sources of the Self*, with a chapter on Augustine (Taylor, 1989, pp. 127–43). Rene Descartes is often said to have launched modern philosophy with his answer to his own radical skepticism 'Cogito ergo sum'; but 1,200 years earlier Augustine had already said 'Si fallor, sum'. Augustine is the great champion of interiority, of the exploration of the self: he pioneered a religious form of modern existentialism by saying 'I am a question to myself.'[13] Nothing is more mysterious than the depths of the human soul. Augustine wrote the world's first autobiography, his *Confessions*, and what could be more characteristically modern than writing an autobiography? Augustine was also one of the first people in the Western world to read silently: he tells us that when he once observed Ambrose in his study, to his utter amazement he saw Ambrose reading without moving his lips. We now believe that the ancients always read aloud as recitation and that Ambrose and Augustine championed the new culture of silent, meditative reading. Finally, Augustine was essential in creating our modern view of linear history: we no longer believe that history is cyclical, like the seasons.[14]

Although Augustine lived his whole life in the later days of the ancient Roman empire, he is often described as a medieval thinker. If the project of medieval philosophy is to reconcile the claims of Athens and Jerusalem, to harmonize philosophy and biblical faith, then Augustine is a medieval philosopher. As a Christian Platonist, Augustine is the very emblem of one medieval synthesis of Athens and Jerusalem; as a Christian Aristotelian, Aquinas is the other leading emblem. If Matthew Arnold is right that Western civilization is a dynamic compound of Hebraism and Hellenism, then Augustine is one of the founders of our civilization. Augustine sought to revise philosophy in the light of revelation and to articulate biblical faith in the light of reason. He said both 'I believe in order that I might understand' and that 'faith seeks understanding'. He defended the truths of the Christian faith, as developed by philosophical analysis and argument. Christian belief provided Augustine with the principles of his whole approach to morality, politics, and law.

---

[12] See Part IV.A, in particular Chapter 13 by Reinhold Niebuhr. Section V.A. of the Selected Bibliography lists other treatments of Augustine's realism.

[13] For a discussion of Augustine's 'interiority' see Cochrane (1944), pp. 441–503.

[14] One 'modern cyclical historian' is Nietzsche; see Lowith (1997). The notion of return may also be found in Vico's notion of 'ricorso' (1744), and echoed in those historians such as Toynbee (1947) who see the cycle of rise and decline in many civilizations.

Augustine's Realism as a Critique of Plato's Idealism.

Perhaps the best way to understand Augustine's political realism (or chastened idealism) is to consider his relation to Plato, the greatest idealist of our civilization. Because Augustine was a Platonist, they have enough in common to make their disagreements profound and important. Plato, for example, also contrasts the heavenly city with the earthly city at the end of book nine of the *Republic*. Augustine is both a Platonist and perhaps Plato's most profound critic. Through Augustine, Plato is Christianized and Christianity is Platonized. Indeed, Nietzsche defines Christianity as 'Platonism for the masses.'

In the *City of God*, Augustine describes why he is a Platonist:

> If Plato says that the wise man is the man who imitates, knows, and loves God, and that participation in this God brings man happiness, what need is there to examine the other philosophers? There are none who come nearer to us than the Platonists. (Book XIX, chap. V)[15]

Augustine claims that Plato could have easily adopted the Christian faith. After all, Clement of Alexandria said in this vein: 'What, after all, is Plato but Moses in Attic Greek?' Both Plato and Augustine understand philosophy as what Kant would later call 'ontotheology': this means that ultimate reality (*ontos*), ultimate rationality (*logos*) and God (*theos*) all converge. Augustine was clearly an astute student of Plato: 'It is well known that Socrates was in the habit of concealing his knowledge, or his beliefs; and Plato approved of that habit. The result is that it is not easy to discover his own opinion, even on important matters.' Augustine's own views are also often very difficult to pin down, for several reasons: some of his works take the form of dialogues, in which Augustine does not speak *proprie voce*; he is not always analytically precise in his formulations[16] (much of scholastic philosophy was devoted to reconciling the seeming inconsistencies in his thought); and his views changed over the course of his long life. A measure of Augustine's ambiguous legacy is the astonishing fact that he is the theological father both of Roman and Protestant Christianity.

Although Protagoras famously said that 'man is the measure of all things,'[17] Plato explicitly rejects this view in the *Laws* and says that 'not man, but God is the measure of all things'. Plato goes on to say: 'So he who would be loved by God must just himself become like God as much as possible' (*Laws*, 716C). This is why Augustine approves of Plato's proposal to censor the depictions of the gods in poetry: both thinkers believe that true knowledge of ethics, law and politics is impossible without true knowledge of God. But Augustine's appropriation of Plato is always qualified by Augustine's commitment to the fundamental truths of the Bible. Thus he judiciously concludes that 'sometimes Plato's views support the true religion, which

---

15 The reference to 'Planonists' is likely a reference to Plotmus. Augustine was reputed to have read primary Plotinus. See O'Meara (1958).

16 Augustine was a dialectic not a logistic thinker. As a consequence, the preliminary settled definition of terms was not important. Terms became defined through his dialogue, autobiography or his historical narrative. See McKeon (1952), pp. 43–57.

17 Aristotle set forth a more nuanced view of the relation of the body and soul; proper bodily functions and the pleasures which derive from them are an important part of the good life. Augustine does not appear to have read Aristotle and we do not discuss the relations of Aristotle's thought to Augustine.

our faith has received and now defends; sometimes they seem to show him in opposition to it' (*City of God*, Book VIII).

Augustine broke with Plato's philosophical anthropology. According to Augustine, Plato grasped neither the true dignity nor the true evil of man. Man's great dignity derives from his creation in the image of God; man's evil stems from his misuse of his freedom. Man's radical and creative freedom gives him a different dignity than Plato allowed; but man's misuse of freedom by denying his dependence on God makes all men (even philosophers) more prone to evil than Plato allowed. Augustine has a complex view of human nature: we have a good created nature, but our fallen nature inclines us to evil. On Plato's view, most human beings are too irrational and prone to evil to make democracy viable; the masses are governed by appetite rather than by right. A few philosophers, however, are rational enough to transcend evil and their superior knowledge of justice gives them the right to rule. Augustine was not himself a proponent of democracy, or of any particular regime; but the great twentieth-century Augustinian Reinhold Niebuhr said that the capacity of human beings for justice makes democracy possible while the inclination of human beings for injustice makes democracy necessary. Plato, in short, underestimated the common human capacity for justice and, at the same time, overestimated the philosophers' ability to avoid injustice. Of course, Augustine's critique of Plato is not entirely fair: in the *Statesman*, Plato acknowledges the fragility of justice, even under philosopher-kings, and he recommends the rule of law as a second-best regime; Plato's *Laws* develops that second-best regime at length.

To see how Plato underestimated human goodness, let us compare Plato's and Augustine's views of God and creation. Both Plato and Augustine see man as made in the image of God, but they have very different views of God and, hence, of man. Plato's god of *Timeaus* and the *Republic* is a divine craftsman (*demiourgos*). Plato's demiurge, when constructing the universe, looks to the eternally given forms and incorporates then into the eternally pre-given matter. As M.B. Foster says: 'His activity is that of realizing the forms by embodying them in matter, but neither the forms nor the matter in which they are embodied, are the product of his activity' (1935, p. 181; see also Watson (1985)). Plato's god does not create, he merely informs. By contrast, Augustine's God creates the universe from nothing. His radical creative freedom is such that, instead of shaping pre-given material to conform to the eternal forms, God creates both the matter and the forms of everything. The creative activity of God is free from both of the limitations to which Plato's demiurge is subject: God is neither limited by a given matter, nor determined by a given form. God creates, not according to a rational blueprint like Plato's divine craftsman, but out of love, like a parent. God's creation, like human procreation, does not merely shape a given matter into a given form, but rather gives birth to both matter and form. God creates; the demiurge merely informs.

Plato's and Augustine's views of human creativity, whether in the arts, politics, or law, flow from their understanding of divine creative activity. For Plato, every craftsman is like the divine craftsman: the shoemaker invents neither the form of a shoe nor the matter from which it is crafted; he merely informs the matter (*Republic*, 596B). Plato calls the guardians of his ideal republic 'the best possible craftsmen' who attempt to shape the members of a community according to the form of justice. The guardians obviously create neither the matter of the community (its members) nor the form of justice. For Augustine, following St Paul, the Christian does not achieve goodness mainly by conforming to some pre-given form or law. Jesus laid down two very general commandments, to love God and neighbour; there is an infinite variety of ways to obey these commandments. Each Christian obeys the general law of love in a unique vocation. Ethics and politics are more like the fine arts, which aim at a unique creation, than like a craft that imitates an existing ideal. Although Paul and Augustine do not deny the reality of a moral law, there is an invitation to moral creativity in Christianity unlike anything in Plato. As St Paul said: 'we are rid of the law, free to serve in a new spiritual way' (Romans 7:6). Or as Augustine says: 'Love and do what you will' (1 John 4).

Where Plato articulates a particular set of customs and laws as the eternal form of the good, Augustine argues that the law of love[18] can be articulated in an infinite number of different social customs and laws: 'She [the City of God] takes no issue with that diversity of customs, laws, and traditions whereby human peace is sought and maintained' (*City of God*, Book 19, chap. 17). In short, Augustine welcomes human creativity in law and politics where Plato asks us to imitate, so far as conditions allow, the specific ideals discovered through dialogue in the *Republic* and legislated within the *Laws*.

Plato and Augustine offer revealingly contrasting answers to the question: What is the best way of life? Plato believes that the life that most closely conforms to the eternal idea of the good is the philosophical life: the life of the mind, by communing with the heavenly forms, most nearly escapes the evils of the body. Obviously, such a life is open only to a few people. Augustine also asks which is the best way of life and he considers three options: the philosophic, the political, and the ideal of 'Romanitas' – that is, the political life tempered by philosophy. But, instead of picking one ideal, Augustine reframes the whole question by arguing that 'a man can like the life of faith in any of these and get to heaven' (*City of God*, Book 19, chap. 18). The issue for him is not whether one is a politician or a philosopher (as the pagans endlessly debated), but whether one obeys the law of love. Augustine's implicit maxim is 'God loveth adverbs': it doesn't matter what substantive noun we choose (tinker, tailor, soldier, sailor) but what adverbial conditions we honour in living out any legitimate human calling (lovingly, prayerfully, conscientiously, humbly, compassionately). Since Plato's god is supremely rational, only a few philosophers can become supremely excellent; Augustine's God is love, so that every human being is capable of supreme excellence, which is why saints have come from every occupation.

What are the political consequences of Plato's view that the highest good for an individual is to conform as perfectly as possible to the general form of the good? First, since only philosophers attain knowledge of the good, all other human beings are merely instruments used to enable the few guardians to live in the light of the good. The guardians are the craftsmen and the other classes are the material to be shaped. For Augustine, this use of most human beings as mere instruments for the perfection of the few reveals an appalling contempt for individual human dignity. Second, even the individual philosophers are merely parts of the whole republic and, as parts, are inferior to the whole. When Adeimantus asks Socrates how the guardians could be happy without families or property, Socrates answers, ominously that 'in founding the city we are not looking to the exceptional happiness of any one group among us but, as far as possible, that of the city as a whole' (Plato, *Republic*, 420 B). This radical subordination of the individual to the community is, history shows, fraught with danger. Augustine, with his doctrine than man is created in the image of God, refuses to completely

[18] The editors have not included essays on love and its relation to law in Augustine; see, Arendt (1996).

subordinate an individual person to any human regime. The political community must respect the dignity of each person because the person, and not any state, is an image of God.

If Plato underestimated the spark of divine creativity in every human being, then he also overestimated man's capacity to transcend evil and realize true human good. The reason why Plato overestimated man's capacity to transcend evil is that he identified the body as the source of evil. This is why Plato insists that 'the philosopher's occupation consists precisely in the freeing and separation of soul from body' (*Phaedo*, 67 D); or, in the language of the *Republic*, the freeing of the rational part of the soul from the irrational bodily parts of the soul. Reason, in Plato's view, is fundamentally oriented toward the good, the true and the beautiful. But the rational soul is imprisoned in the body and must be freed from bodily corruption. In the *Republic*, Plato says that bodily appetite is an evil that maims the soul. The many are ruled by their bodies while only the few live by reason. Plato designs his ideal republic to enable an elite group of philosophers to renounce the pleasures of the body and ascend to the rational contemplation of the good. Indeed, the *Republic* opens with Cephalus's story illustrating the wisdom of Sophocles: When asked whether, in old age, he could still enjoy intercourse with a woman, Sophocles answered: 'Most joyfully did I escape it, as though I had run away from a sort of frenzied and savage master' (*Republic*, 329 C). This observation anticipates Plato's view that sexual desire is both the tyrant of the soul and the soul of the tyrant (*Republic*, 572–5).

Augustine agrees that, if the body were the source of human evil, then Plato's *Republic* is a profound and rigorous diagnosis and remedy for the human condition. But Augustine denies that the body is the source of human evil; human evil is much deeper and pervasive than Plato allows. Therefore, the *Republic*, because of its naive diagnosis of human evil, prescribes a remedy that is profoundly dangerous. For Augustine, the ultimate source of evil is the human soul, not the body, therefore attempts to transcend evil through reason will fail because reason itself is prone to evil, especially the evil of rationalization. Augustine became convinced that bodily appetite is not the source of evil when he reflected on the source of his own sins. He relates in the *Confessions*, for example, that as a teenager he and his friends would steal pears from a neighbour's orchard. If appetite were the source of evil, then why, Augustine later asks, did we not even eat those pears? What led Augustine to this theft was nothing bodily, but a spiritual perversity – a kind of pride that made him feel superior to others and to basic moral norms. Augustine noted the parallel between his own sin and the biblical account of the origin of sin. Adam and Eve did not taste the forbidden fruit because they were hungry: they were tempted by pride, by the promise of the serpent that they could become like God.

Although Augustine (and Christians in general) are often accused of a hatred of the body, Augustine emphasizes that evil stems from the depths of the soul. 'It is an evil will that makes the holy body evil' (*City of God*, Book 14, chap. 4). Augustine argues that it is clear that the body could not be the source of evil, because Satan, being a fallen angel, has no body. Moreover, to blame the body for evil is to blame God: 'We ought not, therefore, to blame our sins and defects on the nature of the flesh, for this is to disparage the Creator' (*City of God*, Book 14, chap. 5). True, a disordered soul can then corrupt the body by enlisting its cooperation, as we see in gluttony and other addictive behaviours. But, according to Augustine, these bodily evils have their origin in the soul. Mircea Eliade comments on this contrast between Plato and Augustine:

> What a paradox: The Greeks, who loved life, existence in the flesh, the perfect form, had, as an ideal of survival, the survival of the pure intellect. Christians, who are apparently ascetics and scorn the body, insist on the necessity of the resurrection of the body, and cannot conceive of paradisiac blessedness without the union of the soul and the body.

If the soul is the origin of evil, then the powerful rational discipline of Plato's guardians is no real protection from the spiritual evil of pride: these guardians are all too likely to use their reason to rationalize their selfish domination of society. As that great nineteenth-century Augustinian Lord Acton said: 'Power tends to corrupt, and absolute power corrupts absolutely'. No governing class could possibly have more power than Plato's guardians, who control education, sexuality, the family, the economy and religion, and who are constrained neither by law nor by custom. Augustine thinks it naive to think that any rational discipline could prevent the abuse of this power. Indeed, the ability of philosophers to rationalize evil makes them in some ways even more dangerous than non-philosophers. As we noted above, Plato himself acknowledged some of these dangers, which is why, in the *Statesman* and in the *Laws* he defends a 'second-best' regime based, not on the rule of reason, but on the rule of law. Augustinian realism led James Madison to insist on dividing sovereign power in the American constitution between the branches of the national government as well as between national and state governments. Madison was grimly realistic about human motivation and his checks and balances depended upon the clash of egos, so that 'ambition would counteract ambition'.[19]

Augustine on Personality and History[20]

In his classic study, *Christianity and Classical Culture*, Charles Norris Cochrane says of Augustine: 'The discovery of personality was, at the same time, the discovery of history' (1944, p. 503).[21] Let us see how Augustine's theory of human personhood relates to his understanding of human history. Augustine was certainly not the first historian but he is the first philosopher to see history as an important source of truth. Aristotle, for example, placed history even below poetry, on the grounds that even poetry is more universal than history, which is just the record of 'one damn thing after another.' But since the Bible is the history of God's relationship to his people and because the Bible insists upon the historicity of its claims, Augustine had to make history central to the human quest for truth.

The ancient appraisal of the superiority of the universal over the particular is precisely what Augustine seeks to transcend with his new notion of personality. For the defining marks of human personality – namely, uniqueness and freedom – will turn out to be for Augustine the defining marks of human history. Yet, for the Greeks, the Bible embodied the scandal of particularity: how could unique events have universal significance? To see what Augustine means by personality, let us consider what Plato and Aristotle say about individuality, since they have no term or concept for personality. For them, human nature is defined by the formal property of rationality, which is common, while we are individuated by our matter (including

19 For other discussions of the relationship of Plato and Augustine, see de Vogel (1985) and Jaspers (1962).

20 For articles dealing with history, see the essays in this volume by Mommsen (Chapter 14) and Bittner (Chapter 15). For a more extended list, see Section V.B of the Selected Bibliography.

21 To be sure, some later histories were to ignore the role of individuals in history.

our bodily appetites and affects). So what is most valuable about us is what we have in common with others, to a greater or lesser degree. Yet no individual is complete or self-sufficient, so we need to be part of a whole; indeed, for Plato and Aristotle, the individual relates to the polity precisely as a part to a whole. The part may be temporally prior to the whole, but the whole is logically prior to the part, as Aristotle says in the *Politics*.

Indeed, for the Greeks, what belongs to the individual is 'idia' or literally idiotic; while what belongs to the polity is 'koine' or common. This implies a radical subordination of the good of individuals to the good of the polity, for the common good is universally judged superior to individual good. Even Aristotle, who does say that the good of the polis can only mean the good of each citizen, radically subordinates not only non-citizens, but also citizens themselves to the good of the polis, permitting involuntary abortion, infanticide and colonization, tight controls on marriage and religion, etc. All of this follows inexorably from the concept of an individual as a part of the whole.

People wonder why the modern epoch is characterized by both a culture of individualism and by mass societies. But the rise of individualism and of mass societies is not really a paradox: for individuals are by definition the components of a mass and masses are made of individual parts. Individualism and mass society are both the by-products of the eclipse of communities. A biblical faith must take issue with the classical priority of the common over the individual, since Genesis tells us that each individual, and not the state, is made in the image of God.

God is not an individual, obviously, because he is no part of any larger whole; God is a person and indeed, in Trinitarian theology, a community of persons. Once we grasp why God is a person and not an individual we can begin to understand human personhood. As it happens, we get our term and concept of person (*hypostasis*, *prosopon*, *persona*) from Trinitarian theology. The enduring mystery of God is that he is a whole who is made up of wholes, the three Persons of the Trinity. Augustine will use these theological reflections to argue that we abandon the classical contrast of individual part to social whole in favour of the new contrast of the person to the community, for a community is a whole composed of wholes, just as God is a community of persons. In this Augustinian understanding, persons are in some ways subordinated to the community, in the sense that each of us can be involuntarily taxed or drafted, but, at a deeper level, each person is inviolable in the sense that no person ought to be prevented from Christian worship by any political community.

In the classical psychology, individuals have a universal reason, subject to the laws of logic, and particular passions, subject to the laws of psychology. A few highly educated and virtuous people can attain the rational self-mastery that Aristotle calls freedom. Freedom is not a given in the human condition, but rather the achievement of a few. In Augustine's Christian psychology, by contrast, freedom is given *in* the human condition; evil is essentially the abuse of that freedom. We exercise this freedom, not through reason or passion, which are not free, but through the will: the will is the basic source of energy in the person and can direct either reason or passions toward various ends. What I will is what I love and I am free to love good or evil. Love is to the mind what weight is to the body. If our will, if our loves, express our freedom they also express our uniqueness. For our reason and our passions are subject to general laws, of logic or psychology, but the pattern of each person's will or loves is wholly free and unique.

We can predict where reason or passion might lead someone, but we cannot predict what they will, what they love. Knowledge and virtue are not ultimates any more, for the quest for knowledge and for virtue might well embody the evil will to power, the '*libido dominandi*'. God, says the Bible, is love; and we are made in his image, meaning that we are essentially what we will, what we love: Quid sumus, nisi voluntates?

Cochrane notes (1944, p. 386) that, in the thousand years of literary history preceding Augustine, the Greco-Roman world had not produced a single autobiography until Augustine's *Confessions*. Although we are full of interest in the details of people's lives and in their spiritual journeys, the classical philosophers saw things quite differently.

It would never occur to Plato and Aristotle to write, let alone publish, the details of their lives; to them all that matters is the truth, which is common, not in the individual trivialities of those who seek truth. All they reveal about themselves is usually in letters to intimate friends.[22]

Returning to Cochrane's profound connection between Augustine's views of personality and of history, we shall see that his view of history centres on precisely the values of freedom and uniqueness that also constitute human personality. If, for Augustine, human personality is the free and unique quest of each human being toward God, so is human history. To see why human freedom should loom so large in Augustine's conception of history, Cochrane looks at the historiography of his eminent predecessor. Herodotus (1952, 1994) is often called the 'father of history' and his search for the causes (*aitia*) of history embody the Ionian philosophical investigation of nature from Thales to Heraclitus.

Ever since Anaximander, Ionian natural philosophers have described a natural justice governing the cosmos: Anaximander interpreted the cycle of the day and of the seasons as a pattern of transgression and retribution: winter goes too far and is punished by spring, night does too long and is punished by dawn. Heraclitus says that if the sun strays from its path, the Furies will find him out and punish him. For the arbitrary interventions of the Homeric gods, Heraclitus offers instead an impersonal deity of natural necessity. Herodotus applies this cosmic necessity, this law of balance and compensation, to human history: He uses it to explain the ebb and flow of the Nile, the expansion and contraction of empires, the ebb and flow of East and West.

This raises the question: what is the relation of these cosmic processes to deliberate human choice? The Ionian scientists analysed human psychology in the same materialist terms: they describe desire and aversion in terms of physical attraction and repulsion. Herodotus sets for a law of moral cosmic balance when he says that the penalties men suffer are directly proportional to their own wrongdoing. Those who overreach the divine allotment are checked by Nemesis. This process, whereby the principle of expansion is ever checked by the principle of limitation, is an endless, eternal oscillation of a pendulum; there is no hope for alteration of this fate: 'brief and powerless is man's life; on him and on all his race the slow, sure doom falls pitiless and dark'; or in Herodotus's words: 'That which is destined to come to pass as a consequence of divine activity it is impossible for man to avert … Of all the sorrows which afflict mankind, the bitterest is this, that one should have consciousness of much, but control over nothing' (Cochrane, 1944, p. 468).

22 To be sure, Plutarch wrote biographies, but these were studies of the public actions of his subjects – not their interior thoughts.

Thus, classical historiography deployed a set of concepts designed, it seems, to remove all human agency and freedom from historical causation: concepts of necessity, fate, chance, and fortune. Although we might think of fortune as the opposite of necessity, fortune is actually just the flip-side of necessity. Even the Greek understanding of happiness, as in the terms '*eudaimonia*' and '*eutuchia*', means good fortune, as if our own happiness were not the product of our own deliberate conduct. Now Augustine mounts a radical attack on these ideas of necessity, fate, and chance. He sees these appeals as a '*fantastica fornicatio*' – fatal both to intellectual integrity and to moral responsibility. Whatever we do not understand we ascribe to some imaginary cosmic force, rather than just admit that we do not understand. And ascribing our own lives and history to chance and necessity, nicely frees us from any responsibility.

True, sometimes Augustine does not live up to his own principles, as when he tries to 'explain' the rape of innocent Christian women by marauding barbarians; but at his best, he simply confesses that 'we have no idea why God permits these evils' (*City of God*, Book I).

Classical historiography is closely related to classical astrology, and Augustine is withering in his attacks on astrology, which is an obvious denial of human freedom.

For Augustine, human freedom does not contradict the order of nature, any more than miracles contradict that order: for all order stems from Divine providence. There is neither impersonal necessity nor blind chance in the cosmos; rather, all embodies the rational will and mysterious purposes of divine providence: 'Omnia revocanda ad divinam prudentiam'.

Augustine's pun here on providential and prudential reflects an actually etymological relation between *pronoia* and *phronesis* in Greek: human free agency guided by prudential reason is but the image of divine free agency known as providence. There, for Augustine, is thus perfect continuity between the divine governance of the cosmos and history and human self governance. What is the difference between ascribing the order of the cosmos and of human history to divine providence as opposed to fate, fortune, or necessity? Let us look at the word providence (*pronoia*): it means fundamentally foresight rather than manipulation. According to Augustine, God's perfect foreknowledge of history does not undermine our freedom and responsibility; he foresees but does not manipulate the outcome. Put differently, God governs history, not despite human freedom, but precisely through our freedom (*On Order (De Ordine)*, 2007). God foresaw, but presumably regretted, Adam's misuse of his freedom; and even redemption by Jesus was mediated by Mary's free decision to accept the angel's invitation to bear the Lord. Compare the free moral responsibility of Adam and of Mary to Aeneas's frequent lament, which he uses to avoid marriage to Dido: 'non sponte sequor Italiam'.

What the Bible teaches us about history, says Augustine, is that the record of God's saving work is always mediated by free human choice; history is not a blind, impersonal force, but the creation of individual men and women freely responding to God's invitations. Augustine famously distinguishes two narratives within the larger unity of human history: his work is a tale of two cities. The City of God begins with man's friendship with God in paradise and the City of Man begins with man's misuse of his freedom.

Abel chooses the City of God, and Cain the City of Man. Israel represents the City of God, while Babylon and Rome represent the City of Man. But the distinction between these two cities is ultimately nothing more than the moral choice facing every human person; these two cities ultimately reside in every human heart. For we cannot escape our responsibility for choosing to love God or love self; we must choose the love of power or the power of love.

The drama of history is nothing more than the drama played out in the heart of every human person: we are what we love, and we are free and responsible for what we love. Thus, he says, a political community is defined by the shared loves of its members: typically, this shared love is of domination and wealth, meaning that kingdoms are large mafias and mafias are small kingdoms. It is not scale, but the kind of love that defines a community.

Many Christians to this day retain a pagan or astrological view of biblical history: they see the Bible as a code or as an almanac that, once interpreted, will predict the future. Thus, when the Psalmist says that in the eyes of the Lord, a thousand years are like a day, this was interpreted in light of the six days of creation to mean that history would last seven days, the seventh being the Millennium of Revelation. Of these readings of the Bible Augustine says: 'What amazes me is the presumption of those who hazard such opinions'. True, Augustine himself often avers to the six ages of history, though he confesses that he has no idea how long each age lasts. At a deeper level, he sees such readings as profound misreadings. A Greek scientist famously complained to Augustine that the account of creation in Genesis is not compatible with science, and Augustine famously replied that the Bible does not tell us how the Heavens go, but how to go to Heaven. Similarly with history, the Bible does not tell us what are the laws of history or how to predict history, as if we were bystanders. The Bible tells us that we are free to accept or reject God's invitation, and the Bible records the story, the meaning and consequences, of those myriad free decisions. The Bible tells us how to make proper use of our freedom; history is but the by-product of the use and abuse of that freedom. The classical view of history as a closed system of natural necessity, fortune or fate led inevitably to a denial of uniqueness. In other words, the two defining dimensions of personality – freedom and uniqueness – are deeply interrelated.

As we saw in the case of Herodotus, classical historiography adopted the explanatory model of the Ionian natural philosophers. These philosophers believed the cosmos was eternal or at least very old, and the only change comprehensible to them for eternity was cyclical: the cycles of days, seasons, and generations were transposed to cycles of expansion and contraction, cycles of growth and decline, cycles of the rise and fall of civilizations. Aristotle said that all of the discoveries of Greek philosophy had been known and lost countless times in the past. Plato and Aristotle thought that every epoch has been repeatedly destroyed by a cataclysm innumerable times and every time only a remnant survived to begin civilization again from scratch. For the classical historians, there is no direction, or growth, or goal to history, just the eternal return of the same: thus Thucydides (1952, 1994) tells us that the lessons he discerns from the Peloponesian war are of permanent value to mankind, since the human condition is ever the same.

These cycles involve the endless reiteration of typical situations; a belief, says Augustine, that does the grossest injustice to the unique character and significance of the individual historical event. According to Augustine, if the Bible tells us anything, it tells us that history follows the unique path of a person's journey toward God, not some endless cycle. History has a unique beginning (*exortus*), a unique linear path (*processus*) and a unique end (*finis*). History cannot move in cycles because, Augustine insists, Christ died once for all men. Nor, for Augustine, is history a matter of progress (not a *procursus*): he says that it is not progress toward a fixed or known goal but rather a procession or excursion (*excursus*). Again, to understand the order of history we must reflect upon the order of human personality in the journey of life. We all know that we must die, just as we know history will end; but we do not know much about the time, place and manner – meaning that each person's life is not so much a journey to a known destination, but more a genuine adventure into the unknown. The same is true of human history as a whole. As individuals and as the human family, we are called like Abraham out of Ur and led by faith we know not where.

As persons, our experience has continuity over time and is cumulative; we do not live in discontinuous cyclical stages; we do not start from scratch, reinvent the wheel and make the same mistakes over and over. We have one unique path and all of our experiences are unique and never to be repeated. The same is true of history: the human community has one unique path involving myriad unique events, and history is never truly repeated. History may, as Leibniz supposed, spiral, but it never cycles. Every new event in incorporated into the whole of what has gone before; the new part changes the whole, and the whole changes the significance of each new part. Personal and historical time thus has a structure, namely the structure of cumulative continuity.

Thus, for Augustine, the discovery of personality, of free will and uniqueness, was the key to the discovery of the shape of history. Rather than interpret history in categories foreign to personal experience, in categories of impersonal necessity, chance and fate, Augustine sees history in personal terms, as the story of God's personal invitation and every human being's personal response. It is a story, not about the abstract relation of divinity to humanity, nor about types, classes, nations, or even rational animals; it is rather the story of the continuous and cumulative experience of a love relationship between two unique persons, between the one God of Abraham and every single irreplaceable man or woman whom he invites into his kingdom.

Law and jurisprudence today reflect Augustine's views of personality and history in myriad ways.[23] Our legal system assumes that virtually all adult human beings are free and responsible moral agents, whether making contracts or committing torts or crimes. We worry about the 'moral hazards' of various insurance schemes that shield persons from the consequences of their own moral choices. Our commitment to inviolable human rights assumes that individual persons have a dignity surpassing the claims of any political community. Even purely secular champions of human rights such as Jurgen Habermas concede that these rights have their origin in the Christian doctrine of the person. And, especially in common law jurisdictions, lawyers use historical methods to discover the law in past judicial decisions and commentaries. Indeed, early in the nineteenth century, the jurist Karl Frederich von Savigny founded the Historical School of Jurisprudence by claiming that law is nothing more than the historically-specific consciousness of each nation, a view later developed by Henry Sumner Maine and James C. Carter. Today, historical approaches to law are very common in legal doctrine, legal sociology, and legal anthropology.

Augustine and Secular Politics.

Before Augustine, no one had ever envisaged a non-religious political and legal order. It was an axiom of all Western political thought, whether stemming from Athens or from Jerusalem, that political unity rested upon religious unity. Plato and Aristotle do not believe in the gods of the public cult, but they insist that every polity enforce uniform public worship. And

[23] For a somewhat different view see Bittner's essay in this volume (Chapter 15).

ancient Israel waged unceasing war upon idolatry and paganism in the name of the one true God. To put the contrast bluntly, for the Greeks and Romans, Caesar was god, while for Israel, God was Caesar; in both Athens and Jerusalem, political order was assumed to require religious uniformity. But Augustine imagines Christians and pagans sharing the same political community and cooperating in the fostering of a minimal level of law, order and peace, upon which every person, no matter what his religious beliefs, depends (White, Chapter 8).

Although Augustine is often thought to be a champion of theocracy, during the fifth century he abandoned his hopes for a Christian empire and came to accept that Christians would always live essentially as strangers or pilgrims (*peregrini*) amidst the political societies in which they lived. Like the Jews of the Diaspora, Christians would be in the secular world but not of it. As Robert Markus argues in his influential book *Saeculum: History and Society in the Theology of St Augustine* (1988), Augustine is the pioneering theorist of the 'secular', by which he means the epoch between the Ascension of Jesus and the Last Judgment. During this period of history, the City of God and the City of Man are inextricably intermixed—only Jesus himself will separate them in the Last Judgment. Augustine frequently reminds us not to identify Rome with the City of Man and the Church with the City of God: just as some outside of the visible Church belong to the City of God, so some inside of the visible Church belong to the City of Man. There are no visible, sociological institutions that demarcate the saved from the damned: only God can make that judgment. In our secular age, both pagan Rome and the Christian Church are irreducibly mixed societies. What this means is that, in their temporal dimension, both the political community and the Christian Church are secular: they both depend upon a common set of temporal goods. As Markus puts it: 'Sacred and profane, for him, interpenetrate in the *saeculum*; the 'secular' is neutral, ambivalent, but no more profane than it is sacred' (1988, p. 122).

What are these temporal goods that form the basis for political cooperation between the two cities? They are the most basic good of political life, such as law and order within a polity and comity between polities – in a word, what Augustine calls 'peace'. As he says: 'She [the City of God] takes no issue with that diversity of customs, laws, and traditions whereby human peace is sought and maintained' (*City of God*, Book 19, chap. 17). Christians can thus cooperate in good faith with non-Christians within a shared political community for the promotion of a limited and temporal peace. Augustine uses the notion of peace in both minimal and maximal senses. The full peace of the City of God is found only in Heaven; here on earth, we must aim lower at a minimal peace, a peace that makes possible the evangelical work of the Church, just as the Pax Romana facilitated the spread of Christian doctrine.

Of course, until the Enlightenment, no actual historical polity ever embraced fully this ideal of a secular and religiously pluralistic political community. Both Catholic and Protestant rulers enforced religious orthodoxy. Even after the Enlightenment, good faith cooperation across religious allegiances has been rare: many states continued either to enforce religious orthodoxy (Spain until 1975) or to suppress all religion (the many communist states). There is always a great danger of anachronism when discussing Augustine's concept of the '*saeculum*' in light of modern ideals of secularity. Our term 'secular', as any dictionary will attest, connotes a realm of activity that is non-religious, whereas Augustine's *saeculum* refers to the epoch of history in which temporal goods are shared by religious and non-religious citizens. Our 'secular' often becomes anti-religious, while Augustine's is religiously neutral.

But John Rawls' image of the 'overlapping consensus' is helpful in understanding Augustine's vision of political pluralism. According to Rawls' theory of political liberalism, secular liberals and religious believers can cooperate in good faith in a political community by affirming some principles and goods that they have in common. After all, the rule of law provides individuals with rights and liberties that are essential for the pursuit of any conception of a good life, whether religious or not. Each of us, no matter what our ultimate allegiances, has good reason to affirm these 'secular' political principles. Secular politics is thus limited to the temporal goods common to any religious or non-religious ideal. Here is how Markus describes Augustine's theory of peace as the overlapping consensus between all kinds of believers:

> The *res publica* will inevitably embrace among its members people with a variety of different ultimate allegiances. But these allegiences fall outside the sphere of *the res publica*. So far as these are concerned, within its restricted sphere the state is inherently 'pluralistic', being the sphere in which the concerns of individuals with divergent ultimate loyalties coincide. (1988, p. 69)

Like today's theorists of political liberalism, Augustine seeks to scale back the aspirations of politics: if the political community can desist from pressuring anyone into a ultimate faith, then we can all cooperate in good faith to secure the order and the liberties necessary for the pursuit of any ultimate faith. For Augustine, Christians should put their faith and allegiance in the one genuinely Christian society on Earth, namely the Church. Since there are no other Christian societies, to try to create a Christian polity will inevitably lead to idolatry, corruption, disappointment and scandal. Of course, in theory but especially in practice, the notion of a religiously neutral secular state is very controversial: many religious believers, for example, see the alleged neutrality of the secular state as just a rhetorical cover for an anti-religious agenda. And, as we shall see, Augustine's conception of tolerable religious pluralism is not the same as that of today's political liberals.

Augustine's theory of the *saeculum* is only one strand in his political thought and it is difficult to square with, for example, his support for the use of legal coercion against the Donatist heretics. But even his tentative and merely suggestive forays into the notion of a secular politics are profoundly innovative and epoch-making. Although this notion of a principled political pluralism implies a realm of autonomy both for the state and for the Church, there is no doubt that Augustine himself emphasized the autonomy of the Christian Church rather than the autonomy of politics. And his historical legacy in Western Europe centred upon the claims of the Church to immunity from civil political coercion, rather than on the claims of the State to be free from religious authority.

Augustine and Interpretation

Augustine was a child of classical thought and continued its tradition. To be sure, as we said above, his work transcended and transformed classical tenets and embodied unique principles of historical secularism and personality which are now foundations of modern law. But he also hung on to his classical education, an education which included classical rhetoric which he studied and taught (Brown, 1997, 2000). In his youth, as he abandoned his teaching and practice of rhetoric, he moved towards classical philosophy, crafting a series of dialogues which were clearly influenced by Plato and subsequent Platonic thought as well as Cicero. So when he finally converted to Christianity, he not only transcended classical thought by his newly found Christian beliefs. He also held on to the classical liberal arts, which he found to be useful in the reading and interpreting the New and Old Testaments, and he adopted a classical rhetoric in his sermons and debates with other religious sects. As one philosopher has put it, Augustine 'baptized' classical thought (Rist, 1996).

In finding new ways to interpret the Old and New Testament (as well as some Roman code law),[24] Augustine advanced a theory of reading and teaching as well as interpreting and arguing about texts, which helped to lay the basis for these arts in the modern age. All of these activities are central to the understanding and practice of modern law. To understand these practices, we can benefit from Augustine's views of these matters. The deepest discussion of Augustine's treatment of reading and its allied disciplines, Brian Stock's recent book, *Augustine the Reader* (1996), is invaluable. In the following section, we shall set forth what Augustine has to contribute.

Augustine was an avid reader. His *Confessions* record the innumerable ways in which reading informed each major stage of his life. His early education, his teaching and practice of rhetoric, and the transition period of his life when he turned to Plotinus or other neo-Platonists. He was deeply impressed by Ambrose's silent reading and his conversion was marked by the selection and reading of a key passage from the Bible. Many of his works – for example, *Concerning the Teacher*, *The Letter and the Spirit*, *On Christian Doctrine* – contained discussions of the nature and meaning of words and their interpretation. On his death bed, he pasted on the wall phrases from the Bible to remind him of God's words.

Reading, at least for the Church leadership, was the central part of the Christian faith, since the Old and New Testaments formed the core of this religion of 'the Book'. (Later, the Koran was to become the third religion of the Book). The Bible required attention to the text, since it was regarded as setting forth God's word. The Old and New Testaments were written at different times and yet these accounts were treated as interrelated parts of the Christian faith. Since the New Testament was a compilation of several different accounts of Christ's time on this earth, these different accounts required interpretation to be reconciled. The Bible also contains figurative and metaphorical speech as well as stories and parables, all of which require interpretation.[25] For these reasons, there was considerable debate about the meaning of the testaments, and careful exegesis and interpretation was required. Augustine was a participant in the debates over these interpretations.

Just as Augustine's Christianity was a religion of the book, modern law is also dependent upon 'the book'. Written constitutions, statutes, law codes, regulations, court opinions are all written and require interpretation. The modern state has been described as a 'republic of statutes'. Jaroslav Pelikan's comparison of the Bible and the Constitution (2004) points out the many parallels between understanding the two texts. Law is taught through the reading of legal materials. The practice of legal rhetoric relies upon written sources for the materials for its arguments.

---

[24] See the essay by Lardone on Augustine and Roman Law in this volume (Chapter 11).

[25] For one recent account of the reading of the Bible, see Kugel (2007).

Augustine offered a theory of reading which preceded his approach to interpretation. He viewed words or syllables, on their own, as meaningless. Thus a text, on its own, did not have a 'plain meaning'. Only when words were treated as signs either of other signs, thoughts or 'cognizable objects' did they acquire meanings. Insofar as words were signs of other signs or cognizable things, one must track their relationship to those signs or things in order to determine their meaning (*Concerning the Teacher*).

Thus, Augustine's theory of words was a theory which began with Aristotle, extended through Aquinas, and John of Poinsot. Modern theorists include Husserl, Mortimer Adler and John Deely. Adler has traced the outlines of this 'semantic' argument, comparing it with the syntactical theory of Russell and the ordinary language of Wittgenstein (Adler, 1976). What is important about the semantic theory of language in general, and Augustine's theory of language in particular, is that it refers, at least in part, to cognizable things to find the meaning of words. This approach provides the basis for Augustine's theory of interpretation as set forth in his *On Christian Doctrine.* This theory of interpretation is, in part, the search for cognizable things indicated by signs. The search for cognizable things, in turn, opens up the relevance and importance of liberal and other arts in the interpretive process.

Augustine's *On Christian Doctrine* is a handbook on interpretation of the Bible. The starting point is faith and Book I is devoted to outlining the tenets of the Catholic faith. In Book II, Augustine turns to the problems of interpreting unknown signs in the Bible and, in Book III, to the interpretation of figurative language. In his account of unknown signs (which may include reference to other signs or to things), he suggests that knowledge of languages, history, dialectic, rhetoric, arithmetic and natural science may be employed. (He also includes the non-liberal mechanical arts and rejects astrology). In Book IV, on rhetoric, Augustine expects religious speakers to be trained in rhetoric during their early childhood and he cites Cicero for a definition of the purposes of rhetoric. In Augustine's words, 'Whatever has been rightly said by the heathen, we must appropriate it to our use'. Hence, Augustine is able to reintroduce the classical studies indirectly into the interpretation and teaching of the Bible.

These liberal arts subjects help in learning things which in turn advance the interpretation of the Bible. But they are limited in purpose to the knowledge of the Bible – not to be engaged in for their own sake. In this sense, Augustine replaces 'liberal studies' with 'religious studies'. This focus upon the Bible is illustrated in Book III, where Augustine is concerned with the interpretation of figurative language. Here, rather than employ the liberal arts to determine when figurative or literal language is used and what the meaning of figurative language might be, Augustine turns to faith, as the test of the appropriateness of interpretation of literal and figurative language.[26] Similarly, when he discusses rhetoric, he looks to its guidance by Christian ethics and finds the best examples of rhetoric to be studies in the Christian writers.

Augustine's approach to interpretation and rhetoric has relevance to the practice of law. Although there are some modern judges and scholars who find the meaning of law only on the face of law itself and in its literal meaning, there are many others who find relevant the liberal arts in the task of understanding constitutions, statutes and legal opinions.[27] To be sure, Augustine limited the contributions of the liberal arts by his faith as articulated in the Catholic

[26] For a discussion of Augustine's approach to interpretation and its relationship to the disciplines, see Pollmann and Vessey (2006).

[27] One example of an elegant statement is Bobbit (1984); another is Posner (1987).

creed; similarly, the relevance of the liberal arts in interpretation and rhetoric within law is cabined by its relevance to the legal materials at hand.

Augustine's Law and Order, and the Modern Welfare State

Much of modern jurisprudence views law as an instrument to achieve order. Beginning with an early work, *de Ordine* (illustrated and modified throughout subsequent writings), Augustine challenges the modern view – human law for him is part of a larger order, revealed by faith and understood by the arts and sciences.[28] It is this vision of order– an order of the universe, an order in history, an order in the life and destiny of each individual, an order of shared love and peaceful relations within political communities. All orders were to be grasped by the arts and sciences ordered in the service of faith. Such an Augustinian vision expands the scope of jurisprudence – linking law to the world and to a faith beyond the world.

For Augustine, God created the order. Even if one were to abandon Augustine's faith, his vision of order encompassing nature, history, law, and the order of the sciences might remain. And if a shared notion of order were accepted as a foundation,[29] the law of peaceful communities might find deep connection to nature and history, as well as the sciences which study nature and history. Such connections lay an alternative basis for a modern jurisprudence.[30] Such a 'jurisprudence' of order requires inquiries in scope and depth equivalent to those which modern jurisprudence has devoted to the notion of 'justice'.[31]

Augustine recognized that order as the foundation of law, creates fundamental problems for any satisfactory jurisprudence. For jurisprudence must make room for freedom within the realm of order. And such freedom can lead to moral evil.[32] And how moral evil fits within the realm of order is a central issue. Hence, a central problem for Augustine is the relationship between order and freedom. It perhaps is not surprising that Augustine's most extensive discussion of the law is in *On Free Will.*

Augustine offers a deep and difficult view of freedom.[33] It includes volition, the unimpeded human activity. However, it extends beyond volition to include the undetermined freedom of choice. This freedom of choice includes both the choice among alternatives (which may be a choice between goods), and moral choice – the choice between good and evil. Evil

---

28 In *de Ordine*, Augustine laid bare the order of the arts and sciences and viewed them as revealing order directly. Later, in *On Christian Doctrine*, he viewed the arts and sciences as vehicles to understanding words and things as a way of understanding the Bible.

29 Accepting order as a foundational principle without God may be based in philosophy or in a form of secular faith.

30 In one sense, such a vision of modern jurisprudence echoes the earlier vision of legal realism in which natural and social laws were to be uncovered in the scientific study of law. But the underlying role of order itself was ignored in legal realism. Such order merely served to facilitate practical solutions to legal problems.

31 There has been a literal explosion of works on justice in modern jurisprudence, perhaps due to the seminal work of John Rawls.

32 I will use the term 'moral evil' to identify evil results from human responsibility as opposed to 'cosmic evil' – great harms created by nature.

33 A good summary of Augustine's view of freedom is set forth by Oates in Chapter 1 in this volume. A more analytic view can be found in Adler (1958–61).

choice is not the product of bad character or ignorance or of irrational forces alone. Evil can be rationally chosen by anyone. A person who chooses good rather than evil is informed by God's grace. God's grace is limited to the few.

The capacity to choose either good or evil is part of being human. Adam, the first human, made that choice in Eden. Hence, moral evils in the world are the product of the fact that God granted humans the power to choose evil. Augustine documents these evils in history during the first part of his monumental *City of God.* For secular moderns, even if one were to reject the religious source of free will, one might embrace free will as part of the nature of man and accept the possibility that one might choose evil.

But the story of the Garden of Eden has other implications for Augustine. God punished Adam and Eve, expelling them from Eden. A train of consequences followed for their descendants. Although retaining our freedom of choice, we were now mortal and susceptible to the pains of mortal life including death. God's punishment of Adam and Eve and their descendants restores the order either in this world or the next. But that order now includes the evils of the human condition.

For Augustine, the punishment of the sins of Adam and Eve and their descendants is followed not only with the later opportunity of salvation through Jesus Christ but also through punishments by natural rulers within the family and the punishments of some evil acts by political authorities. In this sense, some kinds of human law help to restore the eternal order in history, as well as exhibiting the eternal, natural and human order. Order is the proper relation between God and his creations, the hierarchy of beings, and man and his goals. For Augustine, it is also the proper relation between men and their common pursuit of the shared necessities of life. In this view, human law is part of a larger order of the universe and the life of beings, securing them 'in an earthly peace ... the *well ordered* concord of civil obedience and rule' (*City of God*, Book XIX, chap. 17).

The well-ordered concord of Augustine is not the just republic of Cicero. Augustine rejects justice as the central norm for understanding the bond of men in states. He concludes that the public weal 'is not secured through justice, but through common agreement as to the objects of their love' (*City of God*, Book XIX, chap. 24). This rejection of 'justice' and the adoption of shared love is a radical rejection of the Roman republican and Justinian notion of rights. It is a precursor to the future modern notion of a welfare state, bound in the common pursuit of shared necessity. To be sure, this shared necessity is not based upon the utilitarian principles of the modern welfare state. Augustine rejects utility and the pursuit of pleasure for its own sake. The justification of the pursuit of earthly goods is that 'it makes earthly peace bear upon the peace of heaven ... [and can be called and esteemed] the peace of reasonable creatures, consisting as it does in the perfectly ordered enjoyment of God and one another in God' (*City of God*, Book XIX, chap. 17). To be sure, Augustine reserves or carves out protections for Christian beliefs – an implicit rights-based recognition of rights. But, even with these reservations, Augustine's foundation of republic based upon a shared love offers an alternative rationale for our modern welfare state.

Conclusion

Augustine's approach to law offers both a critique of ancient views and the adoption and modification of them. In so doing, he provides a bridge from the ancient world of law to our modern legal jurisprudence. In some cases, he has given us fundamental concepts of the individual personality, freedom of choice and secular history. He offers the first formulation of the art of interpretation of texts. He has recognized that order rests beneath the workings of the law and that even evil is within whatever order is to be found. He challenges modern jurisprudence to find some comparable notion of freedom, evil and order for the legal systems of our world. In this book, we have selected articles which we believe to admirably illustrate many of these contributions.

Acknowledgements

The Editors would like to acknowledge the assistance of Professor Carl Yirka in the difficult task of finding relevant articles among the myriad of publications by and on St Augustine. Professor Yirka also prepared an extensive and detailed bibliography – the only extensive bibliography which deals with materials pertaining to Augustine and modern law. The editors also wish to thank Michele La Rose, librarian at Vermont Law School, for her unflagging efforts to secure copies of articles in the bibliography – only a few of which appear within this volume. Professor Yirka would like to thank Tom Paul, Alicia Cordero and Natalia May for their assistance. Professor Brooks wishes to both acknowledge and thank Laura Gillen, who not only retyped major portions of the text, but also organized and edited the materials. Finally, Professors Brooks and Yirka would like to acknowledge the considerable support which Vermont Law School provides in this effort.

James Bernard Murphy and Richard Oliver Brooks

References

Adler, M. (1958–61), *The Idea of Freedom: A Dialectical Examination of the Conceptions of of Freedom*, Garden City, NY.: Doubleday and Company, Inc.

Adler, M., (1976), *Some Questions About Language: A Theory of Human Discourse and Its Objects*, Chicago, IL: Open Court Publishing.

Arendt, H. (1996), *Love and Saint Augustine*, ed. J.V. Scott and J.C. Stark. Chicago and London: University of Chicago Press.

Bobbit, P. (1984), *Constitutional Fate, A Theory of the Constitution*, Oxford: Oxford University Press.

Brown, P.R.L. (1967, 2000), *Augustine of Hippo: A Biography*, Berkeley, CA: University of California Press.

Burton, P. (2005), 'The Grammarian's Spoils: *De Doctrina Christiana* and the Contexts of Literary Education', in K. Pollmann and M. Vessey (eds), *Augustine and the Disciplines: From Cassiciacum to Confessions*, Oxford: Oxford University Press, pp. 167–83.

Chroust, A.-H. (1946), 'The Philosophy of Law from St Augustine to Thomas Aquinas', *New Scholasticism*, **20**, pp. 26–71.

Cochrane, C.N. (1944), *Christianity and Classical Culture: A Study of Thought and Action from Augustus to Augustine*, New York: Oxford University Press.

de Vogel, C.J. (1985), 'Platonism and Christianity: A Mere Antagonism or a Profound Common Ground?', *Vigiliae Christiane*, **39**, pp. 1–62.

Fortin, E. (1978), 'Augustine, Thomas Aquinas and the Problem of Material Law', *Mediaevalia*, **4**, pp. 179–208.

Foster, M.B. (1935), *The Political Philosophies of Plato and Hegel*, Oxford: Oxford University Press.
Glover, J. (1989), *Humanity: A Moral History of the Twentieth Century*, New Haven: Yale University Press.
Herodotus, trans. R. Waterfield (1952, 1994), *The History of Herodotus*, Oxford, NY: Oxford university press.
Jaspers, K. (1962), *Plato and Augustine*, New York: Harvest.
Kugel, J.L. (2007), *How to Read the Bible: A Guide to Scripture, Then and Now*, New York: Free Press.
Lowith, K. (1997), *Nietzsche's Philosophy of the Eternal Recurrence of the Same*, Los Angeles: University of California Press.
Markus, R.A. (1988), *Saeculum: History and Society in the Theology of St Augustine*, Cambridge: Cambridge University Press.
Matthews, J.F. (2000), *Laying Down the Law: A Study of the Theodosian Code*, New Haven, CT, and London: Yale University Press.
McKeon, R. (1952), *Freedom and History: The Semantics of Philosophical Controversies and Ideological Conflicts*, New York, NY: Noonday Press.
O'Meara, J.J. (1958), 'Augustine and Neo-Platonism', *Recherches Augustiniennes*, **1**, pp. 91–111.
Pelikan, J. (2004), *Interpreting the Bible and the Constitution*, New Haven: Yale University Press.
Pollmann, K. and Vessey, M. (eds) (2006), *Augustine and the Disciplines: From Cassiciacum to Confessions*, Oxford: Oxford University Press.
Posner, R. (1987), 'The Decline of Law as an Autonomous Discipline 1962–1987', *Harvard Law Review*, **100**, pp. 761–80.
Rawls, J. (1971), *A Theory of Justice*, Cambridge, MA: Harvard University Press.
Rist, J.M. (1996), *Augustine: Ancient Thought Baptized*, Cambridge: Cambridge University Press.
Stock, B. (1996), *Augustine the Reader: Meditation, Self-Knowledge, and the Ethics of Interpretation*, Cambridge, MA, and London: Belknap Press.
Taylor, C. (1989), *Sources of the Self: The Making of the Modern Identity*, Cambridge, MA: Harvard University Press.
Thucydides, trans. R. Warner (1952, 1994), *The History of the Peloponesian War*, London: Penguin Books.
Toynbee, A.J. (1947), *A Study of History*, in D.C. Somervell (abridgment of Vols. I–VI), New York: Oxford University Press.
Vico, G. (1730/1744), 'Scienza Nuova Seconda', in T. Goddard Bergin and M.H. Fisch (rev. trans. 3rd edn), *The New Science of Giambattista Vico*, Ithaca, NY: Cornell University Press, 1948/1976.
Watson, W. (1993), *The Architectonics of Meaning: Foundations of the New Pluralism*, Chicago, IL: University Of Chicago Press.

Bibliography

Augustine and Modern Law: A Selected Bibliography

Compiled by Carl A. Yirka

I AUGUSTINE'S WRITINGS

A Collected Works

A Library of Fathers of the Holy Catholic Church, Anterior to the Division of the East and West. Translated by members of the English Church. Edited by E.B. Pusey. Oxford: John Henry Parker and London: J. Rivington, 1838–1881.

Available on Google books.

Augustine. *The Confessions of S. Augustine*. Revised from a former translation by E.B. Pusey. A Library of Fathers of the Holy Catholic Church, vol. 1. Oxford: J.H. Parker, 1838.

———. *Expositions on the Book of Psalms, translated with notes and indices*. 6 vols. Oxford: John Henry Parker and London: J. Rivington, 1847–53.

vol. 1. Psalms 1–36. Translated in part by J. Tweed; A Library of Fathers of the Holy Catholic Church, 24. Oxford: John Henry Parker and London: J. Rivington, 1847.

vol. 2. Psalms 37–52. Translated by T. Scranton; A Library of Fathers of the Holy Catholic Church, 25. Oxford: John Henry Parker and London: J. Rivington, 1848.

vol. 3. Psalms 53–75. Translated by T. Scranton and H.M. Wilkins; A Library of Fathers of the Holy Catholic Church, 30. Oxford: John Henry Parker and London: J. Rivington, 1849.

vol. 4. Psalms 76–101. Translated by T. Scranton and H.M. Wilkins; A Library of Fathers of the Holy Catholic Church, 32. Oxford: John Henry Parker and London: J. Rivington, 1850.

vol. 5. Psalms 102–125. Translated by H.M. Wilkins; A Library of Fathers of the Holy Catholic Church, 37. Oxford: John Henry Parker and London: J. Rivington, 1853.

vol. 6. Psalms 126–150. Translated by H. Walford; A Library of Fathers of the Holy Catholic Church, 39. Oxford: John Henry Parker and London: J. Rivington, 1857.

———. *Homilies on the Gospel According to St John, and his First Epistle*. 2 vols. Oxford: John Henry Parker and London: J. Rivington, 1848–49.

vol. 1. *Homilies 1–43, St John 1–8*. Translated by H. Browne. A Library of Fathers of the Holy Catholic Church, 26. Oxford: John Henry Parker and London: J. Rivington, 1848.

vol. 2. *Homilies 44–124, St John 9–21 and Homilies 1–10, 1 St John* (1849) Translated by H. Browne. A Library of Fathers of the Holy Catholic Church, 29. Oxford: John Henry Parker and London: J. Rivington, 1849.

———. *Sermons on Selected Lessons of the New Testament*. 2 vols. Oxford: John Henry Parker and London: J. Rivington, 1844–45.

vol. 1. *S. Matthew, S. Mark, S. Luke* (1844). Translated by R.G. Macmullen. A Library of Fathers of the Holy Catholic Church, 16. Oxford: John Henry Parker and London: J. Rivington, 1844.
vol. 2. *S. John, Acts, Romans, I Corinthians, Galatians, Ephesians, Philippians, I Thessalonians, I Timothy, Titus, James, I John* (1845). Translated by R.G. Macmullen. A Library of Fathers of the Holy Catholic Church, 20. Oxford: John Henry Parker and London: J. Rivington, 1845.
———. *Seventeen Short Treatises of St Augustine, Bishop of Hippo*. Translated by C.L. Cornish and H. Browne. A Library of Fathers of the Holy Catholic Church, 22. Oxford: John Henry Parker and London: J. Rivington, 1847.

Loeb Classical Library series

Augustine. *The City of God Against the Pagans. Volume I, Books I–III*. Translated by George E. McCracken. Loeb Classical Library 411. Cambridge, MA: Harvard University Press, 1957.
———. *The City of God Against the Pagans. Volume II Books IV–VII*. Translated by William M Green. Loeb Classical Library 412. Cambridge, MA: Harvard University Press, 1963.
———. *The City of God Against the Pagans. Volume III, Books VIII–XI*. Translated by David S. Wiesen. Loeb Classical Library 413. Cambridge, MA: Harvard University Press, 1968.
———. *The City of God Against the Pagans. Volume IV, Books XII–XV*. Translated by Philip Levine. Loeb Classical Library 414. Cambridge, MA: Harvard University Press, 1966.
———. *The City of God Against the Pagans. Volume V, Book XVI – Book XVIII, Chapters I–XXXV*. Translated by Eva Matthews Sanford. Loeb Classical Library 415. Cambridge, MA: Harvard University Press, 1965.
———. *The City of God Against the Pagans. Volume VI, Book XVIII, Chapter XXXVI – Book XX*. Translated by William Chase Green. Loeb Classical Library 416. Cambridge, MA: Harvard University Press, 1960.
———. *The City of God Against the Pagans. Volume VII, Books XXI–XXII*. Translated by William M. Green. Loeb Classical Library 417. Cambridge, MA: Harvard University Press, 1972.
———. *Confessions, Volume I, Books I–VIII*. Translated by William Watts. Loeb Classical Library 26. Cambridge, MA: Harvard University Press, 1912.
———. *Confessions, Volume II, Books XI–XIII*. Translated by William Watts. Loeb Classical Library 27. Cambridge, MA: Harvard University Press; London: W. Heinemann, 1912.
———. *Select Letters*. Translated by James Houston Baxter. Loeb Classical Library 239. Cambridge, MA: Harvard University Press; London: W. Heinemann, 1965.

A Select Library of the Nicene and Post-Nicene Fathers of the Christian Church Series. Edited by Philip Schaff. Grand Rapids, MI: Eerdmans, 1886–1890.

Available on the Internet at Christian Classics Ethereal Library http://www.ccel.org.

Augustine. *The Confessions and Letters of St Augustin, with a Sketch of His Life and Work*. A Select Library of Nicene and Post-Nicene Fathers of the Christian Church, edited by Philip Schaff, 1st series, vol.1. Grand Rapids, MI: Eerdmans, 1886.
———. *St Augustin's City of God and Christian Doctrine*. A Select Library of the Christian Church, Nicene and Post-Nicene Fathers, edited by Philip Schaff, 1st series, vol. 2. Grand Rapids, MI: Eerdmans, 1993.

———. *On the Holy Trinity, a Doctrinal Treatises, Moral Treatises*. A Select Library of the Christian Church, Nicene and Post-Nicene Fathers, edited by Philip Schaff, 1st series, vol. 3. Grand Rapids, MI: Eerdmans, 1980.

———. *St Augustin: The Writings Against the Manichaeans and Against the Donatists*. A Select Library of the Christian Church, Nicene and Post-Nicene Fathers, edited by Philip Schaff, 1st series, vol. 4. Grand Rapids, MI: Eerdmans, 1974.

———. *St Augustin: Anti-Pelagian Writings*. A Select Library of the Christian Church, Nicene and Post-Nicene Fathers, edited by Philip Schaff, 1st series, vol. 5. Grand Rapids, MI: Eerdmans, 1991.

———. *St Augustin: Sermon on the Mount, Harmony of the Gospels, Homilies on the Gospels*. A Select Library of the Christian Church, Nicene and Post-Nicene Fathers, edited by Philip Schaff, 1st series, vol. 6. Grand Rapids, MI: Eerdmans, 1974.

———. *St Augustin: Homilies on the Gospel of John, Homilies on the First Epistle of John, Soliloquies*. A Select Library of the Christian Church, Nicene and Post-Nicene Fathers, edited by Philip Schaff, 1st series, vol. 7. Grand Rapids, MI: Eerdmans, 1986.

———. *St Augustin: Expositions on the Book of Psalms*. Vol. 8. A Select Library of the Christian Church, Nicene and Post-Nicene Fathers, edited by Philip Schaff. Grand Rapids, MI: Eerdmans, 1979.

B Specific Works Related to the Law

Augustine. *Against the Academics: Contra Academicos*. Translated and annotated by John J. O'Meara. Ancient Christian Writers, 12. Westminister, MD: The Newman Press, 1951.

———. 'Answer to Maximinus the Arian.' In *Arianism and Other Heresies*. Translated by Roland J. Teske. Edited by John. E. Rotelle, Book II:XIV.3, Part 1, vol. 18. The Works of Saint Augustine: A Translation for the 21st Century. Hyde Park, NY: New City Press, 1995.

———. *St Augustin: Anti-Pelagian Writings*. A Select Library of the Christian Church, Nicene and Post-Nicene Fathers, edited by Philip Schaff, 1st series, vol. 5. Grand Rapids, MI: Eerdmans, 1991.

———. *Augustine on the Romans: Propositions from the Epistle to the Romans and Unfinished Commentary on the Epistle to the Romans*. Translated by Paula Fredriksen Landes. Chico, CA: Scholars Press, 1982.

———. *Basic Writings of St Augustine*. Vols. I & II, Edited by Whitney Oates. New York: Random House, 1948.

———. *The City of God*. Translated by Marcus Dods. Great Books of the Western World vol. 16. Chicago: Encyclopedia Britannica, 1953.

———. *City of God against the Pagans*. Edited and translated by R.W. Dyson. Cambridge: Cambridge University Press, 1998.

———. *De Civitate Dei (City of God)*. Translated by G. E. McCracken, et al. Bilingual ed. 7 vols. Loeb Classical Library. Cambridge, MA: Harvard University Press, 1957–71.

———. *De Dialectica*. Translated with introduction and notes by Darrell B. Jackson from the text newly edited by Jan Pinborg. Boston: Reidel, 1975.

———. *The Confessions*. Translated by R.S. Pine-Coffin. Great Books of the Western World vol. 16. Chicago: Encyclopedia Britannica, 1953

———. *On Christian Doctrine*. Translated by J.F.Shaw. Great Books of the Western World vol. 16. Chicago: Encyclopedia Britannica, 1953.

———. *On Order (De Ordine)*. Translated and introduction by Silvano Borruso. South Bend, IN: St Augustine's Press, 2007.

———. *Political Writings*. Translated by Michael W. Tkacz and Douglas Kries; Introduction by Ernest L. Fortin. Indianapolis: Hackett, 1994.

———. *The Political Writings of St Augustine*. Edited with introduction by Henry Paolucci; Interpretive Analysis by Dino Bigongiari. Washington, DC: Regnery, 1962.
———. *The Rule of Saint Augustine.* With an introduction and commentary by Tarsicius J. van Bavel. Translated by Raymond Canning. New York: Doubleday, Image Books, 1986.
———. *St Augustine Against the Academics.* Translated and annotated by John J. O'Meara. Ancient Christian Writers: The Works of the Fathers in Translation, edited by Johannes Quasten and Joseph C. Plumpe. Westminster, MD: Newman Press, 1950.
———. *St Augustine on Education.* Edited and translated by George Howie. Chicago: Regnery, 1969.
———. *Saint Augustine's Childhood: Confessions Book 1.* Translated by Garry Wills. New York: Viking, 2001.
———. *Saint Augustine's Memory: Confessions Book 2.* Translated by Garry Wills. New York: Viking, 2002.
———. *Saint Augustine's Sin: Confessions Book 3.* Translated by Garry Wills. New York: Viking, 2003.
———. *Saint Augustine's Conversion.* Translated by Garry Wills. New York: Viking, 2004.
———. 'Three articles on legislation against the Donatists.*' Bibliothèque Augustinienne, Oeuvres de saint Augustin* . Translated by Guy Finaert; edited by Yves Congar. *(i) 28, .731–733; (ii) 30, 792–794; (iii) 31, 810–814.* Paris-Bruges: Desclée, de Brouwer et Cie, 1963

II AUGUSTINE: HIS LIFE AND HIS WORLD

Adams, Jeremy DuQuesnay. *The Populus of Augustine and Jerome: A Study in the Patristic Sense of Community*. New Haven, CT: Yale University Press, 1971.
Aland, K. 'The Relations between Church and State in Early Times: A Reinterpretation.' *Journal of Theological Studies* 19 (1968): 15–27.
Armstrong, Arthur Hilary, and Robert A. Markus. *Christian Faith and Greek Philosophy.* London: Darton, Longman & Todd, 1960.
Augustine. *The Catholic and Manichaean Ways of Life.* Edited by Donald Arthur Gallagher and Idella J. Gallagher. Fathers of the Church 56. Washington, DC: Catholic University of America Press, 1966
Bardy, Gustave. 'Saint Augustin et Tertullien.' *L'Année théologique Augustinienne* 13 (1954): 145–50.
Barker, Ernest. *Social and Political Thought in Byzantium*. Oxford: Oxford University Press, 1957.
Barnes, Timothy D. 'Aspects of the Background of the *City of God*.' *Revue de L'Université d'Ottawa* 52 (1982): 64–80.
———. *Constantine and Eusebius*. Cambridge, MA and London: Harvard University Press, 1981.
Beskow, Pex. *Rex Gloriae: The Kingship of Christ in the Early Church.* Translated by Eric J. Sharpe. Stockholm: Almquist & Wiksell, 1962.
Bettenson, Henry, ed. *Documents of the Christian Church.* 2nd ed. Oxford: Oxford University Press, 1963.
Bonner, Gerald. *Saint Augustine of Hippo: Life and Controversies*. London: Westminster Press, 1963.
Brisson, Jean-Paul. *Autonomisme et christianisme dans l'Afrique romaine: de Septime Sévère a l'invasion vandale.* Paris: Editions E. de Boccard, 1958.
Brown, Peter Robert Lamont. *Augustine of Hippo: A Biography.* Berkeley, University of California Press, 1967.
———. *Augustine of Hippo: A Biography*. New edition, with an epilogue. Berkeley: University of California Press, 2000.
———. *Authority and the Sacred: Aspects of the Christianization of the Roman World.* Cambridge: Cambridge University Press, 1995.
———. 'The Later Roman Empire.' *Economic History Review*, n.s. 20, no. 2 (August 1967): 327–43.

———. 'Political Society.' In *Augustine: A Collection of Essays*, edited by R.A. Markus, 331–35. New York: Anchor Books, 1972.

———. *Power and Persuasion in Late Antiquity: Towards a Christian Empire*. Madison, WI: University of Wisconsin Press, 1992.

———. *Religion and Society in the Age of Saint Augustine*. New York: Harper and Row, 1972.

———. 'Religious Coercion in the Later Roman Empire: The Case of North Africa.' *History* 48 (1963): 283–305.

———. 'Religious Dissent in the Later Roman Empire: The Case of North Africa.' *History* 46 (1961): 83–101.

Buckland, William Warwick. *The Roman Law of Slavery: The Condition of the Slave in Private Law from Augustus to Justinian*. 1908. Reprint, Cambridge: University Press, 1970.

Burns, J.P. 'Augustine's Role in the Imperial Action against Pelagius.' *Journal of Theological Studies*, n.s. 30 (1979): 67–83.

Bury, John Bagnell. *History of the Later Roman Empire: From the Death of Theodosius I to the Death of Justinian*. London: Macmillan, 1923.

Cadoux, C.J. *The Early Church and the World*. Edinburgh: T. & T. Clark, 1925.

Cameron, Alan. 'Cicero and St Augustine.' *Hermes: Zeitschrift für klassische Philologie*. Bd. 95 (1967): 256.

Chadwick, H. *Early Christian Thought and the Classical Tradition*. New York: Oxford University Press, 1966.

Cochrane, Charles N. *Christianity and Classical Culture: A Study of Thought and Action from Augustus to Augustine*. Oxford: Oxford University Press, 1944.

Congar, Yves. 'L'Interprétation historique du donatisme', In *Bibliothèque Augustinienne. Oeuvres de saint Augustin* 30. Translated by Guy Finaert; introduction and notes by B. Quinot. 25–48. Paris-Bruges: Desclée, de Brouwer et Cie, 1963.

———. Introduction: Traités antidonatistes, volume 1. In *Bibliothèque Augustinienne. Oeuvres de saint Augustin* 28, translated by Guy Finaert and edited by Yves Congar. 7–133. Paris-Bruges: Desclée, de Brouwer et Cie, 1963.

Cranz, F. E. 'Kingdom and Polity in Eusebius of Caesarea.' *Harvard Theological Review* 45 (1952): 47–66.

———. 'St Augustine and Nicholas of Cusa in the Tradition of Western Christian Thought.' *Speculum* 28 (1953): 297–316.

Daube, David. *Roman Law: Linguistic, Social, and Philosophical Aspects*. Edinburgh: Edinburgh University Press, 1969.

de Ste Croix, Geoffrey 'Early Christian Attitudes to Property and Slavery.' In *Christian Persecution, Martyrdom, and Orthodoxy*, edited by Michael Whitby and Joseph Streeter, Chapter 7. Oxford and New York: Oxford University Press, 2006.

Duchesne, Louis. *Early History of the Christian Church, from Its Foundation to the End of the Fifth Century. Vol. 3, The Fifth Century*. London: John Murray, 1924.

Dvornik, Francis. *Early Christian and Byzantine Political Philosophy: Origins and Background*. 2 vols. Dumbarton Oaks Studies 9. Washington, DC: Dumbarton Oaks Center for Byzantine Studies, 1966.

Frend, William H.C. 'Augustine and State Authority: The Example of the Donatists.' In *Orthodoxy, Paganism, and Dissent in the Early Christian Centuries*. Chapter 12. Aldershot, UK and Burlington, VT: Ashgate/Variorum, 2002

———. *The Donatist Church: A Movement of Protest in Roman North Africa*. Oxford: Clarendon Press, 1952.

———. 'The Gnostic-Manichean Tradition in Roman North Africa.' *Journal of Ecclesiastical History* 4 (1953): 13.

———. *Martyrdom and Persecution in the Early Church: A Study of a Conflict from the Maccabees to Donatus*. New York: New York University Press, 1967.

———. *The Rise of Christianity.* Philadelphia: Fortress Press, 1984.

———. 'The Roman Empire in the Eyes of Western Schismatics in the Fourth Century.' In *Miscellanea Historiae Ecclesiasticae*: *congrès de Stockholm, août 1960*, 9–22. Bibliothèque de la revue d'histoir ecclésiastique 38. Louvain: Publications Universitaires de Louvain, 1961.

Greenslade, S. L. 'Heresy and Schism in the Later Roman Empire.' In *Schism, Heresy and Religious Protest*, edited by Derek Baker. 1–20. Studies in Church History 9. London: Cambridge University Press, 1972.

———. *Schism in the Early Church.* London: SCM Press Limited, 1952.

Harries, Jill. *Law and Empire in Late Antiquity*. New York: Cambridge University Press, 1999.

Humphreys, Edward Frank. *Politics and Religion in the Days of Augustine*. PhD Thesis, Columbia University, 1912.

Kligerman, Charles. 'A Psychoanalytic Study of the Confessions of St Augustine.' *Journal of the American Psychoanalytic Association* 5, no. 3 (1957): 469–84.

Ladner, Gerhart B. *The Idea of Reform: Its Impact on Christian Thought and Action in the Age of the Fathers*. Cambridge: Harvard University Press, 1959.

Lambiris, Michael. *The Historical Context of Roman Law*. North Ryde, Australia: LBC Information Series, 1997.

Lamirande, Emilien. 'Augustine and the Discussion of the Sinners in the Church at the Conference of Carthage (411).' *Augustinian Studies* 3 (1972): 97–112.

———. *L'Église céleste selon Saint Augustin*. Paris: Études augustiniennes Château-Gontier, Imprint de l'Indépendant, 1963.

———. *La situation ecclésiologique des donatistes d'après saint Augustin: Contribution à l'histoire doctrinale de l'oecuménisme*. Ottawa: Éditions de l'Université d'*Ottawa*, 1972.

Lamotte, J. 'Le mythe de Rome "ville éternelle" et saint Augustin.' *Augustiniana (Leuven)* 11 (1961): 225–60.

Madec, Goulven. 'Tempora christiana: expression du triomphalisme chrétien ou recrimination païenne.' In *Scientia Augustiniana: Studien über Augustinus, den Augustinismus und den Augustinerorden: Festschrift Adolar Zumkeller zum 60. Geburtstag*, edited by Cornelius Petrus Mayer, Willigis Eckermann, 112–36. Würzburg: Augustinus Verlag, 1975.

Mandouze, André. 'L'Afrique chrétienne, le donatisme et saint Augustin.' In *Le Mystère d'unité*. Vol 1, *Découverte de l'oecuménisme*. 279–97. Cahiers de la Pierre-qui-vire, nouv. série 17. Paris-Bruges: Desclée, de Brouwer, 1961.

Mann, William, ed. *Augustine's Confessions: Critical Essays.* Lanham, MD: Rowman & Littlefield, 2006.

Markus, Robert A. 'Christianity and Dissent in Roman North Africa: Changing Perspectives in Recent Work.' In *Schism, Heresy and Religious Protest*, edited by Derek Baker. 21–36. Studies in Church History 9. London: Cambridge University Press, 1972.

———. *The End of Ancient Christianity*. Cambridge: Cambridge University Press, 1990.

———. *From Augustine to Gregory the Great*. London: Variorum Reprints, 1983.

———. *Saeculum, History and Society in the Theology of St Augustine*. Cambridge: Cambridge University Press, 1970.

Marrou, Henri-Irénée. *Saint Augustin et la fin de la culture antique.* Paris: De Boccard, 1938.

Martroye, François. 'La repression du donatisme et la politique religieuse de Constantin et de ses successeurs en Afrique.' *Mémoires de la Société Nationale des Antiquaires de France* 73 (1914): 23–140.

———. 'Saint Augustin et la competence de la jurisdiction ecclésiastique au 5e siècle.' *Mémoires de la Société Nationale des Antiquaires de France*, 7 ser., 10 (1911): 1–78.

Matthews, John F. *Laying Down the Law: A Study of the Theodosian Code*. New Haven, CT and London: Yale University Press, 2000.

Meer, Frederick van der. *Augustine the Bishop: Religion and Society at the Dawn of the Middle Ages*. Translated by Brian Battershaw and G.R. Lamb. New York: Harper and Row, 1965.

Monceaux, P. *Histoire littéraire de l'Afrique chrétienne depuis les origins jusqu'a l'invasion arabe*. 7 vols. Paris: Ernest Leroux, 1901–23.

Morris, John. 'Pelagian Literature.' *Journal of Theological Studies* 16 (1965): 26–60.

Munier, Charles. 'L'Influence de Saint Augustin sur la legislation de son temps.' In *Augustinus Afer: Saint Augustin. Africanité et Universalité. Actes du colloque international Alger-Annaba, 1–7 Avril 2001*, edited by Pierre-Yves Fux, Jean-Michel Roessli and Otto Wermelinger. Paradosis, Études De Littérature et de Théologie Anciennes, vol 45/1and 45/2. 119–24. Freiburg: Éditions Universitaires Fribourg, Suisse, 2003.

O'Donnell, James J. 'The Inspiration for Augustine's *De Civitate Dei*.' *Augustinian Studies* 10 (1979): 75–79.

Oort, Johannes van. *Jerusalem and Babylon: A Study into Augustine's 'City of God' and the Sources of His Doctrine of the Two Cities*. Leiden: Brill, 1991.

Optatus. *The Work of Saint Optatus against the Donatists*. Translated into English with notes critical, explanatory, theological and historical by the Rev. O.R. Vassall-Phillips. London: Longmans, Green, & Co., 1917.

Parker, Thomas M. 'St Augustine and the Conception of Unitary Sovereignty.' In *Augustinus magister: Actes du Congrès augustinien international Paris, 21–24 Sept. 1954*. 951–55. Paris: Études Augustiniennes, 1954.

Parson, Wilfred. 'The Influence of Romans XIII on Christian Political Thought, II: Augustine to Hincmar.' *Theological Studies* 2 (1941): 325–46.

Pope, Hugh. *Saint Augustine of Hippo: Essays Dealing with His Life and Times and Some Features of His Work*. London: Sand & Co., 1937. Reprint, London and Westminster, MD: Newman Press, 1949.

Rupprecht, A.A. 'Attitudes on Slavery among the Church Fathers.' In *New Dimensions in New Testament Study*, edited by R.N. Longenecker and M.C. Tenney. 261–77. Grand Rapids, MI: Zondervan, 1974.

Ryan, Edward A. 'The Rejection of Military Service by the Early Christians.' *Theological Studies* 13 (1952): 1–32.

Setton, Kenneth M. *Christian Attitude towards the Emperor in the Fourth Century*. New York: Columbia University Press, 1941.

Sparrow-Simpson, William J. *Saint Augustine and African Church Divisions*. London: Longmans, Green, 1910.

Swift, Louis J. *The Early Fathers on War and Military Service*. Wilmington, DE: Michael Glazier, 1983.

Testard, Maurice. *Saint Augustin et Cicéron*. 2 vols. Paris: Études Augustiniennes, 1958.

———. 'Saint Augustin et Cicéron: "A propos d'un ouvrage recent."' *Revue des Études Augustiniennes* 14 (1968): 47–67.

Treloar, John L. 'Cicero and Augustine: The Ideal Society.' *Augustinianum* 28, no. 3 (1988): 565–90.

Troeltsch, Ernst. *The Social Teaching of the Christian Churches*. Vol. 1. Translated by Olive Wyon; with an introduction by H. Richard Niebuhr. New York: Harper Torchbook, 1956.

Westermann, William Linn. *The Slave Systems of Greek and Roman Antiquity*. Philadelphia: American Philosophical Society, 1955.

Wild, John. Review of *A Companion to the Study of St Augustine*, by Roy W. Battenhouse. *Speculum* 31, no. 1 (1956): 131–34. http://www.jstor.org/stable/2850082.

Williams, George H. 'Christology and Church–State Relations in the Fourth Century.' Pts. 1 and 2. *Church History* 20, no. 3 (1951): 3–33; 20, no. 4 (1951): 3–26.

III TWO CITIES: EARTHLY AND DIVINE COMMUNITIES AND JUSTICE

Arquillière, Henri X. *L'Augustinisme politique: Essai sur la formation des théories politiques du Moyen Age*. Paris: Vrin, 1934. 2nd ed. Revised and augmented, 1972.

———. 'Réflexions sur l'essence de l'Augustinisme politique.' In *Augustinus Magister: Actes du Congrès Augustinien International Paris, 21–24 Sept. 1954*. 991–1001. Paris: Études Augustiniennes, 1954.

Augustine. Introduction to St Augustine, The City of God: *being selections from the De civitate Dei, including most of the XIXth book, with text.* Translation and running commentary by R.H. Barrow. London: Faber & Faber, 1950.

Bardy, Gustave. 'La formation du concept de "Cité de Dieu" dans l'oeuvre de Saint Augustin.' *L'année Theologique Augustinienne* 12 (1952): 5–19.

Barker, Ernest. 'St Augustine's Theory of Society.' In *Essays on Government*, 243–69. 2nd ed. Oxford: Clarendon Press, 1965.

Barr, Robert R. 'The Two Cities in Saint Augustine.' *Laval Théologique et Philosophique* 18 (1962): 211–29.

Bathory, Peter Dennis. *Political Theory as Public Confession: The Social and Political Thought of St Augustine of Hippo*. New Brunswick, NJ and London: Transaction Books, 1981.

Baynes, Norman H. *The Political Ideas of Saint Augustine's 'De Civitate Dei.'* In *Byzantine Studies and Other Essays*, 288–306. London: Athlone Press, 1955.

Beck, Randy. 'The *City of God* and the Cities of Men: A Response to Jason Carter.' *Georgia Law Review* 41(2006): 113–56.

Berman, Harold J. *Faith and Order: The Reconciliation of Law and Religion*. Grand Rapids, MI and Cambridge, UK: Eerdmans, 2000. First published 1993 by Scholars Press for Emory University.

Boler, John. 'Augustine and Political Theory.' *Mediaevalia* 4 (1978): 83–97.

Bourke, Vernon J. 'The Political Philosophy of St Augustine.' *Proceedings of the American Catholic Philosophical Association* 7 (1932): 45–55.

Burleigh, John H.S. *The City of God: A Study of St Augustine's Philosophy*. Based upon the Croall Lectures delivered in New College, Edinburgh. London: Nisbet, 1949.

Burnell, Peter. 'The Problem of Service to Unjust Regimes in Augustine's *City of God*.' *Journal of the History of Ideas* 54, no. 2 (April 1993): 177–88.

———. 'The Status of Politics in St Augustine's *City of God*.' *Journal of the History of Political Thought* 13, no. 1 (1992): 1313–29.

Burt, Donald X., 'Augustine on the State as a Natural Society.' *Collectanea Augustiniana* 40, no. 1 (1991): 155–66.

———. 'St Augustine's Evaluation of Civil Society.' *Augustinianum* 3 (1963): 87–94.

Caldwell, Gaylon L. 'Augustine's Critique of Human Justice.' *Journal of Church and State 2 (*1960): 7–25.

Carlson, Charles P. Jr. 'The Natural Order and Historical Explanation in St Augustine's *City of God*.' *Augustiniana* 21 (1971): 417–47.

Carlyle, A. J. 'St Augustine and the *City of God*.' In *The Social and Political Ideas of Some Great Mediaeval Thinkers*, edited by F.J.C. Hearnshaw. 42–52. London: G.G. Harrap, 1923.

Caton, Hiram. 'St Augustine's Critique of Politics.' *New Scholasticism* 47 (1973): 433–57.

Cavalcanti, Elena, ed. *Il 'De civitate Dei': l'opera, le interpretazioni, l'Influsso*. Papers presented at a meeting held in Rome, Nov. 7–9, 1994. Rome: Herder, 1996.

Clark, Mary T. 'Augustine on Justice.' *Revue des Études Augustiniennes* 9, no. 2 (1963): 87–94.

———. 'Platonic Justice in Aristotle and Augustine.' *Downside Review* 82 (1964): 25–35.

Combès, Gustave. *La Doctrine Politique de Saint Augustin.* Paris: Plon, 1927.

Congar, Yves M.-J. '*Civitas Dei* et *Ecclesia* chez S. Augustin: histoire de la recherché: son état présent.' *Revue des Études Augustiniennes* 3 (1957): 1–14.

Dodaro, Robert. 'Augustine of Hippo Between the Secular City and the City of God.' In *Augustinus Afer: Saint Augustin, africanité et universalité: actes du colloque international Alger-Annaba, 1–7 Avril 2001*, edited by Pierre-Yves Fux, Jean-Michel Roessli and Otto Wermelinger. Paradosis, Études de Littérature et de Théologie Anciennes, vol 45/1and 45/2. 287–306. Freiburg: Éditions Universitaires Fribourg, Suisse, 2003.

———. *Language and Justice: Political Anthropology in Augustine's De Civitate Dei*. PhD diss., Oxford University, 1992.

Doody, John, Kevin L. Hughes, and Kim Paffenroth, eds. *Augustine and Politics*. Lanham, MD: Lexington Books, 2005.

Dougherty, James. 'The Sacred City and the City of God.' *Augustinian Studies* 10 (1979): 81–90.

Dougherty, Richard J. 'Christian and Citizen: The Tension in St Augustine's *De Civitate Dei*.' In *Collecteana Augustiniana: Augustine, Second Founder of the Faith*, edited by Joseph C. Schnaubelt and Frederik Van Fleteren. 205–24. New York: Peter Lang, 1990.

Downey, Glanville. 'The Ethical City, the Secular City, and the City of God.' *Anglican Theological Review* 56 (1974): 34–41.

Dyson, R. W. *Natural Law and Political Realism in the History of Political Thought. Vol. 1, From the Sophists to Machiavelli*. Major Concepts in Politics and Political Theory 25. New York: Peter Lang, 2005.

———. *Normative Theories of Society and Government in Five Medieval Thinkers*: *St Augustine, John of Salisbury, Giles of Rome, St Thomas Aquinas, and Marsilius of Padua*. Lewiston, NY: Edwin Mellen, 2003.

East, John. 'The Political Relevance of St Augustine.' *Modern Age* 16 (Spring 1972): 167–81.

Ehler, Sidney Z., and John B. Morrall, eds. *Church and State Through the Centuries: A Collection of Historic Documents with Commentaries*. London: Burns and Oates, 1954.

Emmet, Dorothy. Review of *The Political and Social Ideas of St Augustine*, by Herbert A. Deane.' *Philosophical Quarterly* 16, no. 62 (1966): 72–73. http://www.jstor.org/stable/2217886.

Figgis, John Neville. *The Political Aspects of St Augustine's* City of God. London and New York: Longmans, Green, 1921.

Forhan, Kate L. Review of *Augustine and Politics as Longing in the World*, by John Von Heyking. *Journal of Politics* 65, no. 1 (2003): 295–97.

Fortin, Ernest L. *Collected Essays*. Edited by J. Brian Benestad. Vol. I, *Birth of a Philosophic Christianity: Studies In Early Christian And Medieval Thought*. Vol. II, *Classical Christianity and the Political Order: Reflections on the Theologico-Political Problem*. Vol. III, *Human Rights, Virtue, and the Common Good: Untimely Meditations on Religion and Politics*. Lanham, MD: Rowman & Littlefield, 1996.

———. *Christianisme et culture philosophique au cinquième siècle: la querelle de l'âme humaine en Occident*. Paris: Études Augustiniennes, 1959.

———. 'Justice as the Foundation of the Political Community: Augustine and his Pagan Models. (Book IV.4).' In *Augustinus: 'De civitate dei*,' edited by Christopher Horn. 41–62. Berlin: Akademie Verlag, 1997.

———. 'The Patristic Sense of Community.' Review of *The Populus of Augustine and Jerome: A Study in the Patristic Sense of Community* by Jeremy duQuesnoy Adams. *Augustinian Studies* 4 (1973): 179–97.

———. *Political Idealism and Christianity in the Thought of St Augustine*. The Saint Augustine lecture series, Saint Augustine and the Augustinian tradition. Villanova, PA: Augustinian Institute, Villanova University, 1971.

———. 'St Augustine.' In *History of Political Philosophy*. 3rd ed. Edited by Leo Strauss and Joseph Cropsey. 176–205. Chicago and London: University of Chicago Press, 1987.

Frazier, Thomas R. 'The Ethics of the City of God.' *Journal of Religious Thought* 26 (1969): 23–36.

Friberg, Hans Daniel. 'Love and Justice in Political Theory: A Study of Augustine's Definition of the Commonwealth.' PhD thesis, University of Chicago, 1944.

Garrett, Thomas M. 'St Augustine and the Nature of Society.' *New Scholasticism* 30 (1956): 16–36.

Gierke, Otto Friedrich von. *Political Theories of the Middle Ages*. Translated and with an introduction by Frederic W. Maitland. New York: Cambridge University Press, 1987. First published 1900, Cambridge University Press.

Gilson, Etienne. *Les métamorphoses de la cité de Dieu.* Cours inaugural de la chaire Cardinal Mercier, fait à l'Université de Louvain. Louvain: Publications Universitaires de Louvain, 1952.

———. 'St Augustine and the Problem of World Society.' Introduction to *City of God,* translated by Demetrius B. Zema and Gerald G. Walsh. xi–xcviii. Fathers of the Church 6. Washington, DC: Catholic University of America Press, 1960.

Goldsmith, Maurice M. Review of *The Political Ideas of St Augustine*, by Herbert A. Deane. *Journal of Philosophy* 61, no. 8 (April 1964), 260–63.

Haggerty, William P. 'Augustine, the "Mixed Life", and Classical Political Philosophy: Reflections on *Compositio* in Book 19 of the *City of God*.' *Augustinian Studies* 23 (1992): 149–63.

Hawkins, Peter S. 'Polemical Counterpoint in *De Civitate Dei*.' *Augustinian Studies* 6 (1975): 97–106.

Heyking, John von. *Augustine and Politics as Longing in the World.* Columbia, MO: University of Missouri Press, 2001.

Hodgson, Leonard. 'Christian Citizenship: Some Reflections on St Augustine, Ep.138.' *Church Quarterly Review* 145 (1947): 1–11.

Hundert, E.J. 'Augustine and the Sources of the Divided Self.' *Political Theory* 20 (1992): 87–104.

Jones, Norman. *Theology and Social Theory*. Oxford: Blackwell, 1990.

Kantorowicz, Ernst. *The King's Two Bodies: A Study in Medieval Political Theology*. Princeton, NJ: Princeton University Press, 1957.

Kilzer, Ernest. 'The Social Thought of St Augustine.' *American Benedictine Review* 3, no. 4 (1952): 293–305.

Lamotte, J. 'But et adversaries de Saint Augustin dans le *De Civitate Dei*.' *Augustiniana* 11 (1961): 434–69.

Lauras, Antoine. 'Deux Cités, Jérusalem et Babylone: Formation et évolution d'un thème central du *De Civitate Dei*.' In *La Ciudad de Dios*, t. CLXVII, numero extraord., *Estudios sobre la Ciudad de Dios*, vol 1, 117–52, El Escorial, 1954

——— and Henri Rondet, 'Le thème des deux cités dans l'oeuvre de saint Augustin.' In *Études Augustiniennes,* 28 (1953): 99–160.

Lavere, George J. 'The Political Realism of Saint Augustine.' *Augustinian Studies* 11 (1980): 135–44.

———. 'The Problem of the Common Good in Saint Augustine's *Civitas Terrena*.' *Augustinian Studies* 14 (1983): 1–10.

Lawler, Augustine Peter. Review of *Political Theory as Public Confession: The Social and Political Thought of St Augustine of Hippo*, by Peter Dennis Bathory. *American Political Science Review* 77 no. 3 (September 1983): 828–29.

Lewis, Ewart. Review of *The Political and Social Ideas of St Augustine*, by Herbert A. Deane. *Political Science Quarterly* 79, no. 3 (1964): 441–42. http://www.jstor.org/stable/2145911.

MacQueen, D.J. 'The Origin and Dynamics of Society and the State according to St Augustine.' *Augustinian Studies* 4 (1973): 73–102.

Marrou, Henri-Irenée. '*Civitas Dei*, civitas terrena: num tertium quid?' *Studia Patristica 2 – Texte und Untersuchungen* 64 (1957): 342–50.

Marshall, Robert T. *Studies in the Political and Socio-Religious Terminology of the 'De Civitate Dei.'* Patristic Studies 86. Washington, DC: Catholic University of America Press, 1952.

Martin, Jules. *La doctrine sociale de saint Augustin*. Paris: Tralin, 1912.

Martin, Rex. 'The Two Cities in Augustine's Political Philosophy.' *Journal of the History of Ideas* 33 (1972): 195–216.

Maxfield, John A. 'Divine Providence, History and Progress in Saint Augustine's *City of God*.' *Concordia Theological Quarterly* 66, no. 4 (2002): 339–60.

McIlwain, Charles H. *The Growth of Political Thought in the West: from the Greeks to the end of the Middle Ages*. New York: Macmillan, 1932.

———. Review of *The Political Aspects of St Augustine's City of God*, by John Neville Figgis. *American Political Science Review* 15, no. 3 (August 1921): 439–41. http://www.jstor.org/stable/1946707 (accessed August 2, 2010).

McKee, Donald K. 'Augustine's Political Thought.' *The Drew Gateway* 40, no. 2 (1980): 80–87.

Moorhouse, F. X. Millar. *The Significance of St Augustine's Criticism of Cicero's Definition of the State*. Regensburg: J. Hebbell, 1930.

Morino, Claudio. *Church and State in the Teaching of St Ambrose*. Washington: The Catholic University of America Press, 1969.

Morrison, Karl Frederick. 'Rome and the City of God: An Essay on the Constitutional Relationships of Empire and Church in the Fourth Century.' *Transactions of the American Philosophical Society*, n.s. 54, part 1 (1964): 3–52.

Niemeyer, Gerhart. 'Augustine's Political Philosophy.' In *Aftersight and Foresight: Selected Essays*, 267–88. Lanham, MD: University Press of America, 1988.

O'Connell, James. 'The Social Philosophy of St Augustine.' *Irish Ecclesiastical Record* 82 (1954): 297–309.

O'Daly, Gerard. *Augustine's City of God: A Reader's Guide*. Oxford: Oxford University Press, 1999.

O'Donovan, Oliver M.T. 'Augustine's City of God XIX and Western Political Thought.' In *The City of God: A Collection of Critical Essays*, edited with an introduction by Dorothy F. Donnelly. 135–50. New York: P. Lang, 1995.

———. *Common Objects of Love: Moral Reflections and the Shaping of Community*. Grand Rapids: Eerdmans, 2002.

———. *The Problem of Self-Love in St Augustine*. New Haven, CT: Yale University Press, 1980.

O'Meara, John J. *Charter of Christendom: The Significance of the 'City of God.'* New York: MacMillan, 1961.

Perry, Michael J. *Love and Power: The Role of Religion and Morality in American Politics*. New York and Oxford: Oxford University Press, 1991.

Powell, H. Jefferson. 'The Earthly Peace of the Liberal Republic.' In *Christian Perspectives on Legal Thought*, edited by Michael W. McConnell, Robert F Cochran and Angela C. Carmella. 73–92. New Haven, CT: Yale University Press, 2001.

Raeder, Linda C. 'Augustine and the Case for Limited Government.' *Humanitas* 16, no. 2 (2003): 94–106. http://www.nhumanities.org/raeder16-2.pdf (accessed August 2, 2010).

Ratzinger, Joseph. 'Herkunft und sinn der Civitas-Lehre Augustins.' *Augustinus Magister Communications, Paris, 21–24 septembre 1954*. 965–80. Paris: Études Augustiniennes, 1954.

Reuther, Rosemary Radford. 'Augustine and Christian Political Theology.' *Interpretation: A Journal of Bible and Theology* 29, no. 3 (1975): 252–65.

Rickaby, Joseph. *St Augustine's 'City of God:' A View of the Contents*. London: Burns, Oates, and Washbourne, 1925.

Rohr, John A. Review of *Moral Foundations of Constitutional Thought: Current Problems, Augustinian Prospects*, by Graham Walker. *American Political Science Review* 86, no. 2 (June 1992): 518.

Rosenblum, Nancy L., ed. *Obligations of Citizenship and Demands of Faith: Religious Accommodation in Pluralist Democracies*. Princeton, NJ: Princeton University Press, 2000.

Rougemont, Frédéric de. *Les Deux Cités: La philosophie de l'histoire aux different âges de l'humanité*. 2 vols. Paris: Sandoz et Fischbacher, 1874.

Shaffer, Thomas L. 'The Legal Ethics of the Two Kingdoms.' The Inaugural Seegers Lecture. *Valparaiso University Law Review* 17, no. 1 (1983): 1–40.

Strauss, Leo, and Joseph Cropsey, eds. *History of Political Philosophy*. Chicago: Rand McNally, 1963.

TeSelle, Eugene. 'The Civic Vision in Augustine's *City of God*.' *Thought: a Review of Culture and Idea, Fordham University Quarterly* 62 (1987): 268–80.

Vigna, Gerald S. *A Bibliography of St Augustine's De civitate Dei*. Garrett-Evangelical Bibliographical Lectures 13. Evanston, IL: Garrett-Evangelical Theological Seminary Library, 1978.

Walker, Graham. 'The Constitutional Good: Constitutionalism's Equivocal Moral Imperative.' *Polity* 26, no. 1 (1993): 91–111.

———. 'The Mixed Constitution after Liberalism.' *Cardozo Journal of International and Comparative Law* 4 (1996): 311–28.

———. *Moral Foundations of Constitutional Thought: Current Problems, Augustinian Prospects*. Princeton, NJ: Princeton University Press, 1990.

White, Michael J. 'Pluralism and Secularism in the Political Order: St Augustine and Theoretical Liberalism.' *University of Dayton Review* 22, no. 3 (Summer 1994): 137–53.

Wilhelmsen, Frederick D. *Christianity and Political Philosophy*. Athens, GA: University of Georgia Press, 1978.

Wilks, Michael J. 'Roman Empire and Christian State in the *De Civitate Dei*.' *Augustinus* 12 (1967): 489–510.

Williams, Rowan. 'Politics and the Soul: A Reading of the *City of God*.' *Milltown Studies* 19/20 (1987): 55–72

Worthington, Glenn. 'Michael Oakeshott and the *City of God*.' *Political Theory* 28, no. 3 (2000): 377–98. http://www.jstor.org/stable/192211.

IV AUGUSTINE'S JURISPRUDENCE: STATIC OR EVOLVING?

Chroust, Anton-Hermann. 'The Fundamental Ideas in St Augustine's Philosophy of Law.' *American Journal of Jurisprudence* 18 (1973): 57–79.

———. 'The Philosophy of Law from St Augustine to Thomas Aquinas.' *New Scholasticism* 20, no. 1 (1946): 26–71.

———. 'The Philosophy of Law of St Augustine.' *Philosophical Review* 53 (1944): 195–202. http://www.jstor.org/stable/2182025 (accessed August 2, 2010).

———. 'St Augustine's Philosophical Theory of Law.' *Notre Dame Lawyer* 25 (1949): 285–315.

Dougherty, Richard J. 'St Augustine on Law – Natural, Human, and Divine.' Paper presented, annual meeting of the Northeastern Political Science Association, Boston, MA, November 13, 2008.

Duval, Yves-Marie. 'L'Éloge de Théodose dans la "Cité de Dieu" (V, 26, 1): sa place, son sens et ses sources.' In *Histoire et Historiographie en Occident aux IVe et Ve siècles*. Chapter 1. Aldershot, UK and Brookfield, VT: Ashgate/Variorum, 1997.

Fortin, Ernest L. 'Augustine, Thomas Aquinas, and the Problem of Natural Law.' In *Classical Christianity and the Political Order: Reflections on the Theologi-Political Problem,* edited by J. Brian Benestad. 199–222. Lanham, MD: Rowan & Littlefield, 1996.

Gierke, Otto Friedrich von. *Natural Law and the Theory of Society, 1500 to 1800*. Cambridge: Cambridge University Press, 1934.

Gilson, Etienne, and Don Juan MacQueen. 'St Augustine's Concept of Property Ownership.' *Recherches Augustiniennes* 8 (1972): 187–229.

Hohensee, Heinrich. *The Augustinian Concept of Authority*. New York: Paulist Press, 1954.

Humbert, Michael. 'Enfants à Louer ou à Vendre: Augustin et l'Autorité Parentale (Epist, 10–24).' In *Les Lettres de Saint Augustin Découvertes par Johannes Divjak, Communications présentées au colloque des 20 et 21 Septembre 1982*. 189–204. Paris: Études augustiniennes, 1983.

Lardone, Francesco. 'Roman Law in the Works of St Augustine.' *Georgetown Law Journal* 21 (1933): 435–56.

MacQueen, D.J. 'St Augustine's Concept of Property Ownership.' *Recherches Augustiniennes* 8 (1972): 187–229.

Marcin, Raymond B. 'Tolstoy and the Christian Lawyer.' *Catholic University Law Review* 52 (Winter 2003): 327–49.

Margaret, Mary Sr. 'Slavery in the Writings of St Augustine.' *Classical Journal* 49 (1953–54): 363–69. http://www.jstor.org/stable/3292914 (accessed August 2, 2010).

Markus, Robert A. 'Two Conceptions of Political Authority: Augustine, *De Civitate Dei*, XIX, 14–15, and Some Thirteenth-Century Interpretations.' In *The City of God: A Collection of Critical Essays,* edited with an introduction by Dorothy F Donnelly. 93–118. New York: P. Lang, 1995.

McConnell, Michael W., Robert F. Cochran, Jr., and Angela C. Carmella, eds. *Christian Perspectives on Legal Thought*. Foreword by Harold J. Berman. New Haven, CT and London: Yale University Press, 2001.

Miller, Fred Dycus, and Carrie-Ann Biondi. *A History of the Philosophy of Law from the Ancient Greeks to the Scholastics*. Treatise of Legal Philosophy and General Jurisprudence 6. Dordrecht, The Netherlands: Springer, 2007.

Osgniach, Augustine J. *The Philosophical Roots of Law and Order: A Commentary on Christian Thought*. Jericho, NY: Exposition Press, 1970.

Stuntz, William J. 'Review of *Christian Perspectives on Legal Thought* by Michael W. McConnell, Robert F. Cochran, Jr., and Angela C. Carmella.' *Harvard Law Review* 116 (April 2003): 1707–49.

TeSelle, Eugene. *Living in Two Cities: Augustinian Trajectories in Political Thought*. Scranton, PA: University of Scranton Press, 1998.

———. 'The Story of an Encounter.' In *Augustine Today,* edited by Richard E. Neuhaus. 146–56. Grand Rapids, MI: Eerdmans, 1993.

——— 'Toward an Augustinian Politics.' *Journal of Religious Ethics* 16 (1988): 87–108.

Tinder, Glenn. Review of *Augustine and the Limits of Politics,* by Jean Bethke Elshtain. *American Political Science Review* 91, no. 2 (1997): 432–33.

Vance, Eugene. 'Augustine's *Confessions* and the Poetics of the Law.' *MLN*: *Modern Language Notes* 93, no. 4 (May 1978): 618–34. http://www.jstor.org/stable/2906597.

Witte, John, Jr., and Frank S. Alexander, eds. *Christianity and Law: An Introduction*. Cambridge, UK and New York: Cambridge University Press, 2008.

Wormser, René A. *The Law: The Story of Lawmakers, and the Law We Have Lived By, from the Earliest Times to the Present Day*. New York: Simon and Schuster, 1949.

Zuckert, Michael P. 'Bringing Philosophy Down from the Heavens: Natural Right in the Roman Law.' *The Review of Politics* 51, no. 1 (Winter 1989): 70–85.

V FUNDAMENTAL PRINCIPLES OF JURISPRUDENCE AND POLITICAL THEORY

A Augustine's Realism

Barnes, Jonathan. 'The Just War.' In *Cambridge History of Later Medieval Philosophy: From the Rediscovery of Aristotle to the Disintegration of Scholasticism, 1100–1600*, edited by Norman Kretzmann, Anthony Kenny, and Jan Pinborg. 771–84. Cambridge: Cambridge University Press, 1982.

Cadoux, Cecil J. *The Early Christian Attitude to War: A Contribution to the History of Christian Ethics.* London: Headley Brothers, 1919.

Dodaro, Robert. 'Eloquent Lies, Just Wars and the Politics of Persuasion: Reading Augustine's *City of God* in a "Postmodern" World.' *Augustinian Studies* 25 (1994): 77–137.

———. 'Pirates or Superpowers: Reading Augustine in a Hall of Mirrors.' *New Blackfriars* 72, no. 845 (January 1991): 9–19.

Elshtain, Jean Bethke. *Augustine and the Limits of Politics*. Frank M. Covey, Jr., Loyola Lectures in Political Analysis. Notre Dame: University of Notre Dame Press, 1995.

———. Review of *Augustine and the Limits of Virtue*, by James Wetzel. *Augustinian Studies* 24 (1993): 187.

Feehan, Thomas. 'The Morality of Lying in St Augustine.' *Augustinian Studies* 21 (1990): 67–81.

Niebuhr, Reinhold. 'Augustine's Political Realism.' In *Christian Realism and Political Problems*. 119–46. New York: Scribner, 1953.

———. *The Nature and Destiny of Man: A Christian Interpretation.* Vol. 1. *Human Nature*. New York: Scribner, 1945.

———. *Moral Man and Immoral Society: A Study in Politics and Ethics.* New York: Scribner, 1932.

Ramsey, Boniface. 'Two Traditions on Lying and Deception in the Ancient Church.' *Thomist* 49, no. 4 (1985): 437–50.

Ray, Roger D. 'Christian Conscience and Pagan Rhetoric: Augustine's Treatise on Lying.' *Studia Patristica* 22 (1989): 321–55.

Rist, John. 'Democracy and Religious Values: Augustine on Locke, Lying and Individualism.' *Augustinian Studies* 29, no.1 (1989): 7–25.

Russell, Frederick H. 'Only Something Good Can Be Evil: The Genesis of Augustine's Secular Ambivalence.' *Theological Studies* 51 (1990): 698–716.

Scott, Joanna Vecchiarelli. Review of *Augustine and Politics as Longing in the World*, by John von Heyking. *American Political Science Review* 96, no. 4 (2002): 816–18.

Springsted, Eric O. 'Will and Order: The Moral Self in Augustine's *De Libero Arbitrio*.' *Augustinian Studies* 29, no. 2 (1998): 77–96.

TeSelle, Eugene. 'Justice, Love, Peace.' In *Augustine Today*, edited by Richard E. Neuhaus. 88–110. Grand Rapids, MI: Eerdmans, 1993.

Villa, Dana. 'Beyond Good and Evil: Arendt, Nietzsche, and the Aestheticization of Political Action.' *Political Theory* 20 (May 1992): 274–308.

B Augustine's History

Armstrong, Arthur Hilary. *St Augustine and Christian Platonism* . The Saint Augustine Lecture, 1966. Villanova University. In *Augustine: A Collection of Essays*, edited by R.A. Markus. 3–37. New York: Anchor Books, 1972.

Arnhart, Larry. *Political Questions: Political Philosophy from Plato to Rawls*. New York: MacMillan, 1987. Reprint, Prospect Heights, IL: Waveland Press, 2003.

Auerbach, Jerold S. *Rabbis and Lawyers: The Journey from Torah to Constitution*. Bloomington and Indianapolis: Indiana University Press, 1990.

Bonner, Gerald . '*Quid imperatori cum ecclesia*? St Augustine on History and Society.' *Augustinian Studies* 2 (1987): 231–51.

Carlyle, A.J. *A History of Medieval Political Theory in the West*. Vol. 1, Edinburgh: William Blackwood and Sons, 1903.

Fortin, Ernest L. 'Augustine's City of God and the Modern Historical Consciousness.' In *Classical Christianity and the Political Order: Reflections on the Theologi-Political Problem,* edited by J. Brian Benestad. 117–36. Lanham, MD: Rowan & Littlefield, 1996.

Hoffman, Ernst. 'Platonism in Augustine's Philosophy of History.' In *Philosophy and History: Essays Presented to Ernst Cassirer,* edited by Raymond Klibansky and H.J. Paton. 173–90. New York: Oxford University Press, 1936.

Keyes, G.L. *Christian Faith and the Interpretation of History: A Study of St Augustine's Philosophy of History*. Lincoln, NE: University of Nebraska Press, 1966.

Marrou, Henri-Irénée. 'La Théologie de l'Histoire', In *Augustinus Magister: Actes du Congrès Augustinien International Paris, 21–24 Sept. 1954*, Vol. 3. 193–204. Paris: Études Augustiniennes, 1954.

———. 'Saint Augustin, Orose et l'Augustinisme Historique,' In *La Storiografia Altomedievale: 10–16 Aprile 1969. Centro Italiano di Studi Sull'Alto Medioevo*, 59–87. Settimane di studio 17. Spoleto: Presso la sede del Centro, 1970.

Marrou, Henri-Irenée. *St Augustine and His Influence through the Ages*. Translated by Patrick Hepburne-Scott with Edmund Hill. New York: Harper Torchbooks / London: Longmans, 1957.

Mommsen, Theodor E. 'St Augustine and the Christian Idea of Progress: The Background of the *City of God*.' In *Medieval and Renaissance Studies*, edited by Eugene F. Rice, Jr. 265–98. Ithaca: Cornell University Press, 1959.

Rist, John. 'Saint Augustine: Virginity and Marriage – 2.' *Canadian Catholic Review* 5 (1987): 57–64.

C Augustine on Interpretation and Rhetoric

Babcock, William S. 'Augustine's Interpretation of Romans, AD 394–396.' *Augustinian Studies* 10 (1979): 55–74.

Clinton, Robert Lowry. *God and Man in the Law: The Foundations of Anglo-American Constitutionalism*. Lawrence, KS: University Press of Kansas, 1997.

Douglass, Laurie. 'Voice Re-Cast: Augustine's Use of Conversation in *De Ordine* and the *Confessions*.' *Augustinian Studies* 27, no. 1 (1996): 39–54.

Eden, Kathy. *Hermeneutics and the Rhetorical Tradition: Chapters in the Ancient Legacy and Its Humanist Reception*. New Haven, CT and London: Yale University Press, 1997.

English, Edward, ed. *Reading and Wisdom: The 'De Doctrina Christiana' of Augustine in the Middle Ages*. Notre Dame, IN: University of Notre Dame Press, 1995.

Ortega Muñoz, Juan Fernando. 'Doctrina de San Augstín Sobre la Tolerancia en Material de Religion.' *La Ciudad de Dios* 179 (1966): 618–46.

Pollmann, Karla, and Mark Vessey, eds. *Augustine and the Disciplines: From Cassiciacum to Confessions*. Oxford: Oxford University Press, 2005.

Press, Gerald A. 'The Content and Argument of Augustine's *De Doctrina Christiana*.' *Augustiniana* 31 (1981): 165–82.

———. '*Doctrina* in Augustine's *De Doctrina Christiana*.' *Philosophy and Rhetoric* 17 (1984): 98–120.

———. 'The Subject and Structure of Augustine's *De Doctrina Christiana.*' *Augustinian Studies* 11 (1980): 99–124.

Van Fleteren, Frederick and Joseph C. Schnaubelt. *Augustine: Biblical Exegete*. New York: Peter Lang , 2001.

VI APPLICATIONS OF AUGUSTINE'S THOUGHT TO SELECTED TOPICS

A Law of War

Bainton, Roland H. *Christian Attitudes toward War and Peace: A Historical Survey and Critical Evaluation.* New York: Abingdon Press, 1960.

———. 'The Early Church and War.' *Harvard Theological Review* 39, no. 3 (July 1946): 189–212.

Elshtain, Jean Bethke, ed. *Just War Theory*. New York: New York University Press, 1992.

———. 'The Just War Tradition and Natural Law: A Discussion.' *Fordham International Law Journal* 28 (2004–2005): 742–55.

Hartigan, Richard Shelly. 'Saint Augustine on War and Killing: The Problem of the Innocent.' *Journal of the History of Ideas* 27, no 2 (1966): 195–204. http://www.jstor.org/stable/2708638 (accessed August 2, 2010).

Langan, John. 'The Elements of St Augustine's Just War Theory.' In *Ethics of St Augustine*, edited by W.S. Babcock. 169–89. Atlanta: Scholar's Press, 1991.

Lenihan, David A. 'The Just War Theory in the Works of Saint Augustine.' *Augustinian Studies* 19 (1988): 37–70.

McElwain, Hugh M. *St Augustine's Doctrine on War in Relation to Earlier Ecclesiastical Writers: A Comparative Analysis*. Doctoral thesis, Facoltà Teologica Marianum, Rome, 1959.

Regout, Robert. *La Doctrine de la Guerre Juste de Saint Augustin Á Nos Jours, D'après les Théologiens et les Canonistes Catholiques.* Paris: A. Pedone, 1935.

Russell, Frederick H. *The Just War in the Middle Ages*. Cambridge: Cambridge University Press, 1975.

Sheils, W.J., *The Church and War: Papers read at the Twenty-first Summer Meeting and the Twenty-second Winter Meeting of the Ecclesiastical History Society*. Studies in Church History 20. Oxford: Published for the Ecclesiastical History Society by Blackwell, 1983.

Stevenson, William R. *Christian Love and Just War: Moral Paradox and Political Life in St Augustine and His Modern Interpreters*. Atlanta, G A: Mercer University Press, 1987.

Swift, Louis J. 'Augustine on War and Killing: Another View.' *Harvard Theological Review* 66 (1973): 369–83.

Watt, Alan J. 'Which Approach? Late Twentieth-Century Interpretations of Augustine's Views of War.' *Journal of Church and State* 46 (2004): 115–30.

Windass, Stanley. *Christianity versus Violence: A Social and Historical Study of War and Christianity.* London: Sheed and Ward, 1964.

B Coercion of Heretics

Bouyer, Louis. 'Les Données de l'Enseignement Patristique sur le Problème de la Tolérance.' In *Tolérance et Communauté Humaine: Chrétiens dans un Monde Divisé,* by Roger Aubert and Louis Bouyer, *et al.*, Paris: Casterman, 1952.

Bowlin, John R. 'Augustine on Justifying Coercion.' *Annual of the Society of Christian Ethics* 17 (1997): 49–70.

Brown, Peter Robert Lamont. 'Religious Dissent in the Later Roman Empire: The Case of North Africa.' *History* 46 (1961): 83–101.

———. 'St Augustine's Attitude to Religious Coercion.' In *Religion and Society in the Age of St Augustine*. 262–78. New York: Harper and Row, 1972.

Burt, Donald X., 'Teoría Agustiniana Sobre la Tolerancia en Material de Religion.' *Augustinus* 5 (1960): 387–404.

Christenson, Ronald. 'The Political Theory of Persecution: Augustine and Hobbes.' *Midwest Journal of Political Science* 12, no. 3 (August 1968): 419–38.

Fortin, Ernest L. 'The Political Implications of St Augustine's Theory of Conscience.' *Augustinian Studies* 1 (1970): 133–52.

Joly, R. 'Saint Augustin et l'Intolérance Religieuse.' *Revue Belge de Philosophie et d'Histoire* 33 (1955): 263–94.

Markus, Robert A. 'Saint Augustine: Virginity and Marriage.' *Canadian Catholic Review* 5 (1987): 12–17.

O'Dowd, W.B. 'The Development of St Augustine's Opinions on Religious Toleration.' *Irish Theological Quarterly* 14 (1919): 337–49.

Ryan, John Paul. Review of *Obligations of Citizenship and Demands of Faith: Religious Accommodation in Pluralist Democracies*, by Nancy L. Rosenblum. Law and Politics Book Review http://h-net.msu.edu/cgi-bin/logbrowse.pl?trx=vx&list=APSA-CIVED&month=0010&week=b&msg=j6/X3qJCyg5G5Ab2akDqhw&user=&pw (accessed July 30, 2010).

Weithman, Paul J. 'Toward an Augustinian Liberalism.' *Faith and Philosophy* 8, no. 4 (1991): 461–80.

C *Marriage*

Fr. Coughlin, John, O.F.M. 'Marriage and Mulieris Dignitatem.' *Ave Maria Law Review* 8 (2010): 349–63.

Finnis, John Law 'Morality and "Sexual Orientation".' *Notre Dame Journal of Law, Ethics and Public Policy* 69, no. 5 (1995): 1049-76.

———. 'The Good of Marriage and the Morality of Secual Relations: Some Philosophical and Historical Observations.' *American Journal of Jurisprudence* 42 (1997): 97–134.

Hamilton, Vivian 'Principles of U.S. Family Law.' *Fordham Law Review* 75 (2006): 31–73.

Reid, Charles J., and John Witte Jr. 'In the Steps of Gratian: Writing the History of Canon Law in the 1990's.' *Emory Law Journal* 48 (1999): 647–88.

Reid, Charles J. 'The Augustinian Goods of Marriage: The Disappearing Cornerstone of the American Law of Marriage.' *BYU Journal of Public Law* 18 (2004): 449–78.

Witte, John Jr. 'The Goods and Goals of Marriage.' *Notre Dame Law Review* 76 (2001): 1019–59.

VII MISCELLANEOUS WORKS.

Arendt, Hannah. *Love and Saint Augustine*. Edited and with an interpretive essay by Joanna Vecchiarelli Scott and Judith Chelius Stark. Chicago and London: University of Chicago Press, 1996.

Babcock, William S. *The Ethics of St Augustine*. Atlanta, GA: Scholars Press, 1991.

Battenhouse, R.W., ed. *A Companion to the Study of St Augustine*. Grand Rapids, MI: Baker Book House, 1979.

Bonner, Gerald. *God's Decree on Man's Destiny: Studies on the Thought of Augustine of Hippo*. London: Variorum, 1987.

———. 'Review of *Augustine, Confessions, 1: Introduction and Text; 2: Commentary on Books 1–7; 3: Commentary on Books 8–13; Indexes*, by James J. O'Donnell.' *Speculum* 69, no. 3 (1994): 857–59.

Burt, Donald X. *Friendship and Society: An Introduction to Augustine's Practical Philosophy*. Grand Rapids, MI and Cambridge: Eerdmans, 1999.
———. 'Friendship and Subordination in Earthly Societies.' *Augustinian Studies* 22 (1991): 83–124.
d'Arcy, Martin Cyril, Maurice Blondel, Christopher Dawson, Etienne Gilson, Jacques Maritain, C.C. Martindale, Erich Przywara, John-Baptist Reeves, B. Roland-Gosselin, and E.J. Watkin. *A Monument to St Augustine: Essays on Some Aspects of His Thought Written in Commemoration of his 15th Centenary*. London and New York: L. Mac Veagh, 1930.
Deane, Herbert A. *The Political and Social Ideas of Saint Augustine*. New York and London: Columbia University Press, 1963.
d'Entrèves, A.P. *Natural Law: An Introduction to Legal Philosophy*. 2nd ed. London: Hutchinson, 1970. 1st ed, 1951.
de Lubac, Henri. 'The Problem of the Primitive state.' In *Augustinianism and Modern Theology*, chapter 8. New York: Herder and Herder/Crossroad Publishing, 1967.
de Veer, A.C. 'Rom. 14, 23 dans l'Oeuvre de Saint Augustin (Omne quod non est ex fide peccatum est).' *Recherches Augustiniennes* 8 (1972): 149–85.
de Vogel, C.J. 'Platonism and Christianity: A Mere Antagonism or a Profound Common Ground?' *Vigiliae Christianae* 39 (1985): 1–62.
Delhaye, Philippe. *The Christian Conscience*. New York: Desclee, 1968.
Grabowski, Stanislaus Justin. *The Church: An Introduction to the Theology of St Augustine*. St Louis and London: Herder Book Company, 1957.
Hannon, Patrick. 'Law and Virtue: Aquinas and Augustine.' *Ecclesiastical Law Journal* 3 (1994): 166–74.
Jaspers, Karl. *Plato and Augustine*. New York: Harvest, 1962.
Lavere, George J. 'The Influence of Saint Augustine on Early Medieval Political Theory.' *Augustinian Studies* 12 (1981): 1–9.
Macdonald, H. Malcolm. Review of *Trends in Medieval Political Thought*, edited by Beryl Smalley. *Journal of Politics* 28 (1966): 485–86.
Markus, Robert A. *Augustine: A Collection of Critical Essays*. Garden City, NY, Anchor Books, 1972.
McGrath, A.E. 'Justice and Justification: Semantic and Juristic Aspects of the Christian Doctrine of Justification.' *Scottish Journal of Theology* 35, no. 5 (October 1982): 403–18.
Mommsen, Theodor E. 'Orosius and Augustine.' In *Medieval and Renaissance Studies*, edited by Eugene F. Rice, Jr. 315–48. Ithaca: Cornell University Press, 1959.
Monachino, Vincenzo. 'El pensamiento de san Agustin sobre el empleo de la fuerza al servicio de religion.' In *Contribución Española a una Misionología Agustiniana: Colección de Trabajos Agustinianos Presentados a la VII Semana Intensiva de Orientación Misionera Celebrada en Burgos, del 8 al 14 de Agosto de 1954, Dedicada al Obispo de Hipona Con Motivo Del XVI Centenario de su Nacimiento*. Burgos: Instituto Español de San Francisco Javier para Misiones Extranjeras, 1955.
Neuhaus, Richard J., ed. *Augustine Today*. Encounter Series 16. Grand Rapids, MI: Eerdmans, 1993.
O'Donnell, James J. *Augustine*. Boston: Twayne , 1985.
O'Meara, John J. 'Augustine and Neo-Platonism.' *Recherches Augustiniennes* 1 (1958): 91–111.
Portalié, Eugène. *A Guide to the Thought of Saint Augustine*. Chicago: Regnery, 1960.
R., J H., Jr. Review of *St Aurelius Augustine, Bishop of Hippo, Concerning the Teacher (De Magistro) and on the Immortality of the Soul (De Immortalitate Animae)*, by George G. Leckie. *Journal of Philosophy* 35, no. 11 (May 1938): 302–3. http://www.jstor.org/stable/pdfplus/2017351.pdf.
Reid, Charles J. Jr. '*Marriage in Its Procreative Dimension*: The Meaning of the Institution of Marriage Throughout the Ages.' *University of St Thomas Law Journal* 6 (2009): 454– 85. http://www.stthomas.edu/law/programs/journal/Volume6num2/454–485.pdf (accessed July 30, 2010).

Ritschl, Dietrich. 'Some Comments on the Background and Influence of Augustine's *Lex aeterna* Doctrine.' In *Creation, Christ and Culture: Studies in Honour of T.F. Torrance,* edited by R.W.A. McKinney. 63–81. Edinburgh: T. & T. Clark, 1976.

Sabine, George H. *A History of Political Theory*. New York: Henry Holt, 1950.

Scanlon, Michael. 'The Augustinian Tradition: A Retrieval.' *Augustinian Studies* 20 (1989): 61–92.

Schall, James V. 'On the Place of Augustine in Political Philosophy.' *Political Science Reviewer* 23 (1994): 128–65.

———. *Reason, Revelation, and the Foundations of Political Philosophy*. Baton Rouge: Louisiana State University Press, 1987.

Schmidt, K.L. 'Royaume, église, *état* et peuple: relations et contrastes.' *Revue d'Histoire et de Philosophie Religieuse* 18 (1938): 145–73.

Smalley, Beryl, ed. *Trends in Medieval Political Thought*. Oxford: Blackwell, 1965.

Smolin, David M. 'The City of God Meets Anabaptist Monasticism: Reflections on the Twenty-Fifth Anniversary of Wisconsin v. Yoder.' *Capital University Law Review* 25 (1996): 841–85.

Ullmann, Walter. *Medieval Political Thought*. 1965. Reprint, with revisions, Harmondsworth: Penguin, 1979.

Voegelin, Eric. *The New Science of Politics: an Introduction.* Charles R. Walgreen Foundation Lectures. Chicago: University of Chicago Press, 1952.

Weithman, Paul J. 'Augustine and Aquinas on Original Sin and the Function of Political Authority.' *Journal of the History of Philosophy* 30 (1992): 353–76.

Wolin, Sheldon S. *Politics and Vision: Continuity and Innovation in Western Political Thought*. Boston: Little Brown, 1960.

Wood, Neal. 'Populares and Circumcelliones: The Vocabulary of "Fallen Man" in Cicero and St Augustine.' *History of Political Thought* 7 (1986): 33–51.

Part I
Augustine: His Life and His World

[1]

THE LIFE AND RELIGION OF SAINT AUGUSTINE

Whitney J. Oates

IMPLICIT in the immense variety of Saint Augustine's writings is an organic wholeness of attitude. This simultaneity of his thinking, or if you choose, the "all-togetherness," accounts for many of his strengths as well as his weaknesses. The first essential for one who embarks upon a study of this great man is an awareness of the total unity in the vast multiplicity of his works. It is no wonder that the critical interpreter, who must proceed from aspect to aspect, who must compartmentalize his analysis, finds himself face to face with a task of grave complexity. He cannot, for example, satisfactorily expound "the philosophy" of Saint Augustine, for if he does, he may be forced to accept a definition of philosophy as that which proceeds only from reason, and such a definition would be utterly unacceptable to Saint Augustine himself.[1] Philosophy, theology, religion, in his thought, are all deeply interfused, their functional relations so clearly felt, that for him it is futile to talk of any one of these apart from the context of the others. For him, data derived from reason are only half alive unless they are viewed in the perspective of faith and revelation, and the converse likewise is true.

This prime characteristic of Augustinian thought has exposed it to the attack of precise philosophical criticism which can point up with relative ease places where the rational defense may be weak. The same characteristic also makes the individual treatises difficult to read, for the main line of an argument may be blurred or obscured by the powerful associative memory of Saint Augustine. He may choose at any moment to develop a point tangential to the major question at issue, and can do so with complete justification and without irrelevance if, as he believes, all things are so closely interrelated. But as a consequence the effect of logical articulation is often lost. On the other hand, it would be the height of absurdity to deny logical power to Saint Augustine. It is revealed clearly in many individual passages, such as his proof for the existence of God in Book II of the treatise *On Free Will,* as well as in the over-arching logic of his great works, such as *The City of God.* A synoptic view of this masterwork discloses an architectonic skill which few can rival in the Western tradition.

Saint Augustine's thought cannot strictly be called a "system." It is rather a world view or a "universe view," one which comprehends God and all of reality from the highest order down to its most insignificant details in their manifold and complex inter-connections. In contrast, there have been many philosophers who have constructed "systems" from the time of the earliest Greeks on down through the nineteenth century, from the predecessors of Socrates through Hegel and his followers. Epicurus, for example, by blending the atomism of Democritus with an ethic of pleasure, forged an almost water-tight rationalistic materialism, which is systematic in the highest degree. In fact, so carefully wrought, so "closed" is his system, that his followers, and of course notably Lucretius, had only to invoke the *ipse dixit* of the master's authority to settle any debatable issue.

Aristotle also provides an illustration of the systematic thinker with whom Saint Augustine may be contrasted. The "master of them that know" had supreme confidence in reason plus a superb analytical insight into the nature of logical relations, as well as an insatiable eagerness to absorb, organize and understand all that the world of sense experience could offer. From these elements he erected a philosophical structure, logically coherent and so all-inclusive that, as everyone knows, it dominated the intellectual life of even more than the Western world for centuries. But Aristotelianism too, generally speaking, is a "closed" system, and, as such, it has tended to beget continuators and commentators. In a sense, Aristotle set for himself a task upon which he labored until it was completed. Similarly, Saint Thomas Aquinas undertook his enterprise of forging a Christian metaphysic, and to all intents and purposes, he finished his project in such a way that, in the opinion of many Catholic thinkers, it will never be necessary to attempt it again. It, too, can be called a "closed" system. For the most part the Thomist annotators have ramified and interpreted the thought of their master, since they have not felt the need to take their start from him and embark on new voyages of philosophical discovery.

In distinction to these creators of "closed" systems, there have been philosophers whose thought has been "open." Let it be understood, as a general definition, that an "open" system is one which comprehends within it all aspects of reality, one which recognizes the principle that "life runs beyond logic," and above all, admits the fact that human speculation on ultimate questions is always in process, and cannot in any final sense ever be completed. It is "germinal" and at the same time peculiarly vulnerable to strict rational attack. Plato perhaps is the most notable example of this second type. Any attentive reader of the *Dialogues* can observe that Plato wished more than anything else to prevent his thought from congealing. The very dialogue form or the principles underlying his dialectic convey his intense desire to keep his philosophical inquiry alive and not permit it to crystallize into a series of verbal formulae. This attitude is perhaps most clearly evident in the closing section of the *Phaedrus,* where Socrates insists that only the actual conversations of men, only the real contact of mind with mind, genuinely lives, while anything that is written partakes inevitably of a certain kind of death. Plato knows the terrible finality of words.

If it be fair to call Plato the creator of an "open system," it is interesting to observe the kind of influence he has tended to exert. Whereas the "closed system" stimulates the continuator and commentator, the "open system," with its wholeness of attitude or way of looking at things, tempts either those who undertake to complete the system—*i.e.*, to change it from an "open" to a "closed system"—or those who are inspired by the general attitude and hence are led on to creative philosophical speculation of their own. Plotinus and the Neo-Platonists were convinced that they were completing Platonism, and yet this so-called logical conclusion is a "closed system," marked by a dogmatism and an abandonment of radical dualism with which Plato himself would never have concurred. The other type of influence can be seen not only in philosophers from the Stoics on down through the centuries to such men as Alfred North Whitehead, but also in the poets and artists whose creative imaginations have been stirred by the Platonic vision.

Saint Augustine must be numbered among those whose thought is "open." Surely many an Augustinian has attempted the task of completion. Almost without exception the effort has only produced a strange variant of the original, and their labors bear the same relation to Saint Augustine as the Neo-Platonists do to Plato. In fact, since in the course of time many and often conflicting Augustinianisms have appeared, depending upon the particular aspect of the original view which has been selected for emphasis, Saint Augustine has now and again been partially "exiled" by some elements in the Catholic Church. Actually he has never been an "official" philosopher of the Church in the sense that Saint Thomas is. Indeed, it may be impossible that an "open system" can ever validly achieve such an official role. Yet the dynamic vitality of Saint Augustine's whole and "open" view, and its potential as a source of inspiration, has constituted one of the Church's greatest assets throughout its history. As for the conflicts which are possible outgrowths of any "open system," M. Etienne Gilson has succinctly suggested the solution: "The difficulties which at the present time beset Augustinianism are not an ill for which we need to find remedies, for Saint Augustine is not affected by any ill; all that is needed is to return from the Augustinianism of the Augustinians to that of Saint Augustine himself." [2]

The foregoing observations which contrast the "open" with the "closed system" are offered as generalizations to which exceptions may well be taken. Yet the basic distinction appears sound and should be particularly helpful in dealing with a figure like Saint Augustine. Furthermore, in contemplating the broad sweep of Western philosophy or the development of the Christian religion, it is not too difficult to observe how the "open" and the "closed system" complement each other. To designate a system as "closed" does not mean to derogate from its value or importance. Actually each has its distinctive philosophical and religious function; each fulfills a different need. In the Roman Catholic Church, no one can take the place of Saint Thomas, but as M. Gilson has remarked, "But to be Christian *qua* philosophy a philosophy must be Augustinian or nothing . . . [Saint Augustine is] at the very heart of Christian thought, side by side with Saint Thomas Aquinas, who may have differed from him, but has never left him." [3]

Christianity by its very nature has needed and needs now a spokesman of Saint Augustine's quality. What must be stressed in Christianity is its insistence that "all things are together." If reason runs riot, or if emotionalism gets out of hand, Christianity in its essence cries out—or at least should, to restore the balance. Early twentieth-century Protestantism illustrates a serious departure from the central insights of the religion envisioned by Saint Augustine. Somehow, under the influence of a naïve optimism and trapped in the contradiction that God could be removed from Christianity without undue loss, this deviation in the name of Protestantism propounded a Christian social ethics which liquidated its spiritual inheritance. Faced with the world cataclysm of our time it merely evaporated.

Reinhold Niebuhr, with a profound sense of the comprehensiveness of Christianity, has reacted vigorously against this modern version of Protestantism. His whole analysis sees both the human predicament and the Christian answers in terms of a series of closely interconnected paradoxes, and his development of these paradoxes reveals at every step that he recognizes fundamentally the "all-togetherness" of the Christian position. In fact, it would not be too much to say that his recognition of this basic quality of Christianity has given him his stature as a leading Protestant theologian. Yet another imbalance in its turn tends to vitiate Niebuhr's position. Planted squarely as he is in the prophetic tradition, he has concentrated too exclusively on the fallen state of man, or to put it somewhat facetiously, has been so busy rehabilitating sin as a fact of man's nature that other and equally important aspects of Christianity suffer from underemphasis.

Even these two illustrations, however random they may appear, should suffice to point out what Saint Augustine's balanced view can contribute to twentieth-century Christianity. But note, this is not to suggest a mere repetition or a slavish parroting of the Augustinian position. Rather, since it is an "open system," the suggestion is that Christian thinkers expose themselves to the stimulus of its balance, absorb the spirit of its comprehensiveness, and be encouraged thereby to reinterpret afresh the inclusive unity of Christianity. That our time is ready for such a revivification of the Augustinian attitude is indicated by the recent widespread and renewed interest in Augustinian studies. Why is it that now both Protestant and Catholic alike claim Saint Augustine as their own? Can it be too much to hope that somehow, via increasing familiarity with his insights into the nature of Christianity, men can come more fully to a sense of the abiding unity which underlies sectarian difference?

Saint Augustine's monumental figure appears at that point in history when finally all the diverse forces of the ancient world had come together into a cultural amalgam which was destined to disintegrate, or at least to be transmuted, almost at the moment of its formation. In the amalgam are to be found the elements of the Hebraic and Christian traditions deriving from the nearer East. Greek culture had developed independently of its neighbor to the west in Italy, and these two cultural strains began to be consolidated into their Graeco-Roman form in the first two centuries before the Christian era. The "world state" forged by the Emperor Augustus provided a period of relative peace and security which endured for approximately two hundred years and thus afforded an opportunity to the infant religion of Christianity to grow and develop with actually less opposition than is commonly supposed.

But in the third century the manifold forces of disintegration, which had been held in precarious check by the moribund splendor of the Antonines, broke loose with terrifying violence. Barbarian pressure existed on the frontiers. The economic stability under the early emperors proved to be specious. Imperial authority came more and more to rest upon military power, with "the consent of the governed" less and less a factor in the political structure. It is a miracle that out of this third-century chaos any kind of order was restored. By radically altering many of the traditional features of the Roman imperial organization, Diocletian was able to reintroduce a modicum of stability into the situation, though at the price of establishing a more or less oriental despotism. Many of the time-honored freedoms had forever disappeared, but still there remained a few important vestiges of the best that Rome had created, sufficient at least to permit the Empire to continue with some vitality.

Strangely enough, during the years of chaos and partial rehabilitation, Christianity had grown with astonishing speed. The new religion, whose members in small numbers puzzled and irritated the Roman administrators early in the second century, had become at the beginning of the fourth century a force of such proportions that the Emperor Constantine (whatever else may have been his motive) found it expedient to recognize Christianity as one of the official religions of the Roman state. Some years later Julian the Apostate made the last and futile effort to eradicate Christianity and re-establish the paganism of Greece and Rome. Thus actually it was not until midway in the fourth century after Christ that all the cultural elements of that world were fused, when at last appropriate recognition was given to the Hebraic and Christian constituents. But all was not well with the imperial central government. Its hold on the social, political and economic organism was at best tenuous. Nothing seemed able to stem the moral decadence and the collapse of morale in the body social. No doubt many a prophetic eye could see the inevitable end of Eternal Rome.

It was into this world of the mid-fourth century that Saint Augustine was born. No one of his contemporaries realized more fully the challenge of that age, nor did any one produce a more fundamental response to that challenge. For the matter of that, the challenge of our own time has not infrequently been compared with the epoch of Rome's decline. The combined concept of Challenge-and-Response, so brilliantly delineated by Arnold Toynbee in his *Study of History,* applies with peculiar pertinence to the life and work of Saint Augustine. As Toynbee discusses the different kinds of challenges, he distinguishes between those of a lower order, such as the external challenge of a geographic environment, and those of a higher order, which are inner and moral. These can only be met by a process of interiorization, which in turn will lead to the "etherialization" of man. This attainment of a spiritual dimension by man, Toynbee believes, constitutes the next major step in his evolution and can be accomplished by continually recognizing that challenges are inner, and must be met successively by inner responses. Such almost exactly was Saint Augustine's reading of the challenge of his time, and in a way all his writing is devoted to clarifying what the nature of man's inner response to that challenge should be. In fact, all his characteristic doctrines of God, human nature, the will, grace, time, the city of earth and the City of God, formulate what, according to Christianity, man's inner response to the challenge of the human predicament should *always* be.

Tagaste, a small town in North Africa, not far to the west of Carthage and some fifty miles south of the Mediterranean, witnessed the birth of Saint Augustine in 354 A.D.[4] The North Africa of this period preserved perhaps more than any other area of the Roman World the characteristic features of the earlier Empire, removed as it was from the storm centers of political and social unrest. Thus the boyhood of Saint Augustine was passed in the more or less normal environment of a family of modest circumstances in a small Roman provincial community. His mother, Monnica, had been reared in a Christian family and apparently exhibited early in life those virtues which marked her later career. She was married on her coming of age to Patricius, a local Roman official of good standing in the community. He was not a Christian, and owing to his somewhat uneven disposition, the relations between the two were not always as pleasant as they might have been. Shortly after Saint Augustine's birth, Monnica enrolled him as a catechumen in the Catholic Church, but decided to postpone the sacrament of baptism, which according to Christian practice in those times, took place upon the attainment of adulthood.

The biography of Saint Augustine can, and indeed should, only be sketched briefly here. The major sources for it consist of a contemporary life by Possidius and the great autobiography, the *Confessions,* wherein the whole man is recreated for us. In the present discussion it is only necessary to point to those aspects of his life which are most significant prior to his assumption of the Bishopric in 395-396 A.D. In his earliest boyhood (fortunately for his future career) he picked up enough of the native Punic language to enable him to be as much at home in it as he was in his own Latin. While Monnica was introducing him to the elements of Christianity, at school he was receiving a standard education. Unhappily, he conceived a hearty dislike for the Greek language, and, amazing as it may seem, never really mastered it. However, in spite of the early resistance to schooling as shown by any normal boy, he soon gave signs of becoming a brilliant student. His parents wisely determined, after he completed his elementary education in Tagaste, to send him to the advanced schools in Madaura, a center of pagan culture some miles south of Tagaste.

Saint Augustine departed for Madaura when he was about twelve and remained there for approximately four years. During this period he received his first broad grounding in Latin literature and thought, and at the same time was exposed thoroughly to the seamier side of life. At sixteen, he returned to Tagaste. Patricius and Monnica had developed further plans for his future education, since all indications reinforced their belief that a distinguished career, perhaps as a lawyer, lay ahead of him. However, a temporary lack of funds made it necessary to postpone his training, and the youth consequently spent a year of enforced idleness in his native village. An unoccupied sixteen-year-old lad is little if any comfort to his parents, and Saint Augustine proved no exception. In his *Confessions* he recalls with sorrow his abandoned life at that time, referring to it somewhat extravagantly in these words, "Behold with what companions I walked the streets of Babylon, in whose filth I was rolled, as if in cinnamon and precious ointments." [5]

One particular and seemingly insignificant episode left a lasting impression on his mind: the theft of some pears by a gang of youths of which he was an active member. Saint Augustine's references to the occasion in the *Confessions* perhaps appear out of proportion, yet in a way nothing could be more characteristic of his method of dealing with his own experience. The theft itself amounted to little more than a boyish prank of shaking down the fruit, stealing it, discovering that it was not particularly good, and giving what was left untasted to the pigs. This event, paralleled and forgotten in the life of practically every youth, fascinated and puzzled Saint Augustine. It presented a problem to him, and in the *Confessions* he gets it between his teeth, he worries it, and almost despite himself he cannot let it go. As he ponders it, he asks himself why he did it. Was it because the fruit was good? No. He had plenty of his own of far better quality. Was it because the companionship of his fellows was peculiarly pleasant?

No. Apparently he did not think well enough of them to explain the phenomenon on that ground. In the last analysis he could only conclude that there was an overpowering attraction in the evil deed itself. As a consequence this episode takes on a pervasive symbolic significance for Saint Augustine, since the problem "Whence evil," in one form or another, preoccupied his attention until the day of his death.

The following year, his seventeenth, saw Saint Augustine beginning the study of rhetoric in the city of Carthage. The immediately succeeding years followed the regular post-adolescent pattern of the time. One of his first acts was to take a mistress with whom he lived for the next thirteen years, and who bore him a son, Adeodatus. In his education he continued his brilliant record. Of all the works that he studied, the one which really captured his imagination was the *Hortensius* of Cicero, and Saint Augustine more than once acknowledges the debt he owed to its inspiration. At this time, too, he first came in contact with the Manichaean religion and enrolled as an "auditor," the technical name for anyone who wished to apprentice himself to that sect.

It is not difficult to see why the Manichaean religion would have appealed to Saint Augustine. With its very concrete tenet, expressed in a very concrete mythology, that the universe is a battleground between two opposing principles of Good and Evil, two co-eternal causes of Light and Darkness, Manicheism not only had the attraction of offering a simple answer to the problem of evil, but also one in terms of which individual men are relieved of all the inconveniences of moral responsibility. It was no doubt comforting for Saint Augustine at this time to be told that whatever evil he did was not his own responsibility, but that of an evil principle.

Beginning with the autumn of 373 A.D., Saint Augustine embarked upon a career as a teacher. First in Tagaste, then in Carthage, and next in Rome he forged ahead with great success. Before he left Carthage, he had become increasingly dissatisfied with Manicheism, especially because he was never able to discover among its devotees an individual who could answer the difficulties which inhered in the system. In Rome finally he abandoned the religion, and in turn more or less assumed the skeptical attitude of the Platonic New Academy. This shift in attitude, as students of Saint Augustine have frequently noted, was of major importance. Prior to this time and in particular under the influence of Manicheism, Saint Augustine's thought had been inveterately concrete. It was difficult for him to conceive of existence apart from material embodiments, or to move easily on a level of abstraction. But as he associated more closely with the Platonic tradition and its postulates concerning the existence and greater reality of that which is non-material, his habit of thought changed. During the Manichaean period, God to Saint Augustine could only exist in some kind of material terms. The Platonic tradition unquestionably prepared the way for him to accept and realize the meaning of Christianity's doctrine of God as Spirit.

Apparently the conditions for teaching rhetoric at Rome were not entirely satisfactory to Saint Augustine. Consequently when he heard that the city of Milan wanted to appoint a "professor" of rhetoric to be maintained at public expense, he applied for the position, was given a formal hearing, and received the appointment. In the autumn of 384 A.D. Saint Augustine moved his household to the North Italian city. With him went his mistress and son, a few close friends, and his mother, Monnica, who, long since a widow, had followed her brilliant son from North Africa to Rome. Monnica had only one firm aim in view and that was to see him embrace the Church. As Saint Augustine's autobiography records, her days were filled with tears and ceaseless prayers that he would abandon his life of unchastity and return to the faith into which he had been born. She believed that a legitimate marriage might provide the means to this end, but, so far as the record goes, never suggested that he formalize the union with his mistress.

Though deeply troubled in mind and heart, Saint Augustine went to Milan with the desire to win new glory in his profession, to gain wealth, and to marry a rich wife. He still was deeply entangled with the seductions of the material world and the pride which they inevitably engendered in him. But a new influence came into his life in the person of Saint Ambrose, the great Bishop of Milan, whose sermons and methods of interpreting the Scriptures had not a little to do with Saint Augustine's subsequent acceptance of Christianity. But the time was not yet ripe. Monnica busied herself in finding a suitable wife for her son, and finally discovered a fitting partner in a girl who would not reach the marriageable age for another two years. Saint Augustine acquiesced in this arrangement and, apparently without much ado, dismissed the woman whose name he never records and with whom he had lived for so many years. His reference to the separation in the *Confessions* is stark in its brevity: "My mistress being torn from my side as an impediment to my marriage, my heart which clave to her, was racked, and wounded, and bleeding. And she went back to Africa, making a vow unto Thee never to know another man, leaving with me my natural son by her."[6] It is difficult not to be shocked by this episode. Though there is no explicit evidence, it is natural to suppose that Saint Augustine reports the event to show clearly the extent of his own degradation at the time. In fact, he does not hesitate to add that, so great was his enslavement to the habit of sexual lust, immediately after the dismissal he took another mistress.

Saint Augustine's period of inner conflict continued for another two years. Intellectually he began to respond more and more to the preaching of Saint Ambrose and to further study of the Neo-Platonists. Finally in 386 he reached the decision, at least on intellectual grounds, to become a catechumen of the Catholic Church, and it was in the summer of that year when he had the decisive inner experience of his conversion, which is recorded in the famous Eighth Book of the *Confessions*. All doubt was now gone and his only desire was to prepare himself for baptism.

In order not to make an over-dramatic display of his new commitment to Christianity, Saint Augustine kept up his teaching obligations during the summer of 386, and withdrew quietly in the autumn with his few faithful friends to the famous retreat in Cassiciacum. It was there that he realized for the first time his idea of a community of scholars living together.[6a] From the conversations of this group of Christian scholars in Cassiciacum derive Saint Augustine's first great writings, the *Contra Academicos, De Vita Beata,* and *De Ordine*. In the spring of 387 Saint Ambrose administered to him the sacrament of baptism. Saint Augustine's life as a Christian began. The faithful Monnica, her life's dream finally realized, started the journey back to Africa with her son. On reaching Ostia, the two had their famous joint mystical experience recounted so beautifully in the Ninth Book of the *Confessions*. Shortly thereafter Monnica died in great peace of soul.

Saint Augustine and his friends stayed in Rome for about two years and then returned to Tagaste, where they established a monastery. It was not long before his unusual powers began to make themselves felt among the Christians of North Africa. In 391 he was ordained a priest in the community of Hippo Regius. Four years later he became auxiliary Bishop of the same community, and upon the death of the Bishop, Valerius, he succeeded to the charge of the diocese. Here begins his life of incredible activity. Not only was he fulfilling his duties as a diocesan administrator, but also he was an indefatigable preacher and writer of letters. He also became a leader in the general affairs of the Church and was its ardent advocate in the face of any heresy which he might deem dangerous. In addition, he saturated himself in minute study of the Holy Scriptures and became one of the most powerful exegetes in the history of the Church. And, as though this were not enough, he composed among other treatises the immortal masterpieces, *The Confessions, On the Trinity,* and *The City of God.*

In many ways, the activity of the thirty-five years until his death was dominated by Saint Augustine's desire to defeat heresy. Hence he devoted his boundless energy first against the proponents of the Manichaean religion. For this task he was singularly well fitted because of the many years when he himself had espoused the sect and made a genuine effort to commit himself whole-heartedly to it. Next he turned the fire of his polemic against the Donatists. This heretical group split from the Church largely over a dispute concerning the question whether a priest's sins as a fallible human being impaired the validity of his acts when he was functioning as a priest. The Donatists maintained that a priest must be sinless, while the Church held that, since all men are sinners, the priest shares the common lot of man, must accept it, but must be regarded as the valid, though imperfect, human instrument through which God does His work in the world. Actually, the doctrinal issue in the Donatist controversy soon became buried deep in a welter of political maneuvers, so that by and large Saint Augustine's anti-Donatist writings are perhaps more rewarding to those who are specialists in this aspect of the history of the Church, than to the modern general reader. It must be added, however, that Saint Augustine himself never lost sight of the basic theological issue at stake.

Saint Augustine's greatest efforts were turned against the most subtle and most dangerous heresy of them all, which was developed by his contemporary, the monk Pelagius. Beyond any question, the anti-Pelagian treatises of Saint Augustine deserve close attention not only because they contain a rounded statement of his mature position, but also because in them he develops specifically his argument concerning the crucial problem of the relation between sin, free will and the grace of God. Pelagius argued, and with a power which convinced many in the Christian community, that man can by the effort and initiative of his own free will bring about his own salvation. Furthermore, he maintained that God's grace was granted to men according to their merits. Pelagius thus raised one of the most difficult problems which the Church has ever had to face. Indeed, it is fair to say that in one guise or another it has faced Pelagianism throughout its entire history. In one way, the answer to Pelagianism is simple. If you accept its thesis, you turn man into God. You automatically arrogate to him that which is God's, in view of His omnipotence. You effectively invalidate the prime Christian virtue of humility, and, by the same token, seductively invite man to commit the deadliest of all the sins, the sin of spiritual pride. On the other hand, to deny the position of Pelagianism has profound implications for the concept of man's free will. If man's salvation comes from the grace of God, with the merits of man being at bottom irrelevant, what becomes of man's free will? In what sense is it valid, and what finally is the meaning of human freedom, which man values so highly, if his will is not genuinely free? These are the questions which Saint Augustine undertook to resolve when he accepted on behalf of the Church the challenge of Pelagius. He fought against the Pelagian heresy with a vigor equal to or greater than the zeal with which he opposed the Manichaeans and the Donatists.

Since the promulgation of the Darwinian hypothesis, it has been the fashion of the Western World to see evolution in everything. This pronounced trend has induced scholars very often to approach the masters of thought in the Western tradition with the purpose of demonstrating how their positions evolved. In certain cases this purpose cannot be realized without doing violence to the evidence. After all, there are some thinkers who arrive at a basic philosophy relatively early in life to which they adhere without any appreciable modification. Such men rather strive to work out ever more thoroughly the implications and ramifications of their initial views. Plato presents a good instance of this type of thinker. Despite the large amount of scholarly opinion to the contrary, the root philosophical view expressed in his early dialogues seems to be identical with that of the *Timaeus* and the *Laws,* the works of Plato's old age.

This point is particularly significant in the case of Saint Augustine. But the problem is not simplified by the fact of his enormous productivity, his seemingly incurable repetitiousness, and the prolixity of which he is aware and for which he often apologizes. A satisfactory interpretive point of departure appears to lie first in keeping distinct the two phases of his life and thought which are separated sharply from each other by the experience of his conversion. Prior to that event, Saint Augustine's thought "evolved" through several stages marked successively by Manicheism, skepticism, and Neo-Platonism. However, after the conversion, Saint Augustine reached a position which cannot in any genuine sense be said to evolve. At the moment of conversion, Christianity in its wholeness came to him in such a form as to preclude any "evolution." To be sure, there are considerable variations in emphasis in the vast Augustinian corpus which derives entirely from the post-conversion period. The influence of Neo-Platonism looms large at the outset. In the earlier works, likewise, not so much attention is devoted to the doctrine of grace. In fact, as time goes on, the shifts in emphasis are determined in general by the nature of the opposition which Saint Augustine might be attacking at any given moment. Thus, for example, under the pressure of the Pelagian heresy, he works out in its fullest detail the doctrine of grace.

M. Gilson in his excellent book, *Introduction à l'étude de saint Augustin,* has devoted his exclusive attention to the identification and interpretation of the major theses of the Augustinian position. In the conclusion, Gilson remarks that it has been his particular purpose throughout to discuss the "stable element" of Augustinianism. In this connection he recalls that in a review of Boyer, *L'Idée de vérité dans la philosophie de saint Augustin,* he took the author to task for not having approached the problem from an evolutionary point of view. Gilson here hastens to retract this criticism, and insists that even among the many variations in detail in the position of Saint Augustine, he has never been able to discover the slightest variation in its essential nature.[7] After all, if it is correct to contend that Saint Augustine's doctrine is an organic compound in the highest degree, and if it is correct to assert that this compound soundly reflects at once the inner coherence and the comprehensiveness of Christianity, Gilson's conclusion concerning the stable essence of Augustinianism must be accepted.

The origins out of which Saint Augustine developed his major theses have already been indicated in part. Among the pagan sources the most important is Plato. No one can fail to notice the affinity in temperament and attitude which obtains between the two. In view of the inherent compatibility of much of Plato's philosophy with Christianity, it is not surprising that Saint Augustine regarded him as the greatest of the Greek and Roman thinkers. It may be doubted that Saint Augustine knew Plato thoroughly at first hand, but it is absolutely clear that the essential nature of the Platonic philosophy had been mediated through to him not only by the Neo-Platonists but also by the Christian Platonists of Alexandria, who had done much to make explicit the kinship between Platonism and Christianity.

Saint Augustine apparently was not attracted to Aristotle. The evidence of his influence is rather to be felt implicitly in the tone of individual passages in the Augustinian corpus. From time to time Saint Augustine exhibits great sympathy for the Stoic position, as for example when, in *The City of God,* he devotes a chapter to the Stoic attitude toward the "perturbations" of the soul.[8] In addition to his Roman favorite Cicero, Saint Augustine quotes frequently from Virgil, Horace and others. Also, he uses the encyclopaedic information of M. Terentius Varro, who supplies him with a large amount of data on Roman antiquities and pagan theology.

Saint Augustine's detailed knowledge of the Holy Scriptures is overwhelming. Whether it be for the infusion of a devotional spirit into a passage, or for the advancement of an argument, or to cite a clinching authority for a hard-won point, or to unravel a knotty theological problem, Saint Augustine always has a scriptural reference ready to hand. *Genesis,* the *Psalms, Job,* and *Isaiah* of the *Old Testament* are perhaps the most frequently cited, and in the *New Testament* he turns most often to *Matthew, Luke, John,* and, of course, the Pauline Epistles, which shape more than any other influence the character of Saint Augustine's Christianity. And obviously, in addition, there are the long, specifically exegetical works such as the commentaries on *Genesis* and the *Psalms,* which bespeak a familiarity with the sacred writings both incredibly broad and deep.

The reader should never forget, when he is considering the major theses of Saint Augustine's Christianity, that his writing is all created in the light of his own intense mystical experience upon conversion. The inner conviction of its validity colors in one way or another everything he does and everything he says. In this respect he is to be found in the company of such men as Saint Paul, Saint Francis, Martin Luther, Pascal, and even, in a curious way, Descartes, all of whom enjoyed their greatest creative activity under the impulse of an extraordinary inner experience. With Saint Augustine, the primary result of *his* experience, which in turn produces the first and most important of the major strands in his thought, is his conviction that all things must be and are God-centered.

To illustrate this point, the very texture and attitude of the *Confessions* are more than sufficient. Take the opening words: first the quotation from the *Psalms,* "Great art Thou, O Lord, and greatly to be praised; great is Thy power, and of Thy wisdom there is no end"; and then a little later

Saint Augustine's own words, "Thou movest us to delight in praising Thee; for Thou hast formed us for Thyself, *and our hearts are restless till they find rest in Thee.*" [9] In a sense, the phrase which has been italicized provides the central clue to this first and all-important Augustinian theme. A recent critic, C. C. Martindale, S.J., in commenting on the fact that Saint Augustine feels no difficulty in exhibiting his emotions, remarks, ". . . the whole of the *Confessions* is an outpouring of his soul to God—God is the immediate audience; and only now and again does the author look aside (and down) towards his human hearers." [10]

Rarely if ever has a Christian thinker kept the focus of his attention so unwaveringly upon God. This is true not only in the obvious case of the *Confessions,* but also in works on rather specific subjects such as *Concerning the Teacher.* It makes no difference whether he is enunciating the principle, *pondus meum amor meus,* "My weight is my love," [11] as the fundamental condition of man's activity of will, or whether he expounds at length the very difficult Christian dogma of the Trinity as he does in *On the Trinity.* In each instance there is always the explicit orientation to God.

According to Saint Augustine, the gravest possible error arises when God is conceived as any other than omnipotent, omniscient and perfectly good. From this initial conviction, supported as it is by faith in the Biblical revelation as well as by reason, he develops his analysis of all created things. In the first place, he submits his doctrine of "natures." God is infinitely good and infinitely wise, and thus everything which He creates, by the very fact that He is the source of all existence, has a "nature" which is good. In other words, He cannot, since He is perfect good, create any "nature" that is not intrinsically good. These "natures" are not all on the same plane or level of existence. In fact, Saint Augustine consistently recognizes their hierarchic order. In the treatise *On Free Will,* for example, when he examines the universe of space and time, he distinguishes between three categories of things: first, that which *is, i.e.,* mere bodies in the physical universe; second, that which both *is* and *lives,* the class which comprises plants and animals; and third, that which *is, lives* and *knows,* in other words, man, who shares *existence* with mere physical bodies, *existence* and *life* with plants and animals, but who alone of created things, by virtue of his reason, is capable of *knowledge.* That there are different degrees of importance, Saint Augustine attributes to the infinite wisdom of God, who desired to create the universe in a majestic harmony in which things more valuable and important could not exist, if they cannot be compared with the less valuable. In the argument, harmony in this way depends upon the hierarchic ordering of things in creation. In other contexts, when Saint Augustine is not confining his analysis to the universe of space and time, but rather has total Reality within his purview, he recognizes three planes of being: body, soul and God. As soul controls body, so does God control the soul, to which He is in the closest proximity.[12]

Saint Augustine's doctrine of "natures," as can readily be seen, has important implications for the problem which modern philosophy sees in the "fact-value" relation. If a "nature" has its existence, *i.e.,* its "factuality," from a creative act of God, and if at the same time its goodness or "value" derives from the same source of creation, it becomes quite impossible to contemplate a "nature" without considering simultaneously its "existence-and-goodness." To put it in another way, a thinker does violence to the objective character of a "nature" if he attempts solely to analyze its being, as though its being could be abstracted validly from its goodness. This Augustinian attitude towards the relation of fact and value appears also when he considers the highest level of Reality, God. At one point in his treatise, *On the Trinity,* he writes, "But as He (*i.e.,* the Holy Spirit) is a substance together with the Father and the Son, so that substance is together with them great, and together with them good, and together with them holy, and whatsoever else is said in reference to substance; since it is not one thing to God to be, and another to be great or to be good, and the rest." [13]

Saint Augustine's theory of knowledge likewise is God-centered, as is his doctrine of "natures." Whereas Aristotle and, following him, Saint Thomas Aquinas, are empiricists in their theories of knowledge, always taking their start from the data provided to the knowing subject by the senses, and proceeding via a method of abstraction from them, Saint Augustine starts from within and from the illumination in man's soul which God has planted there. Hence his epistemology or theory of knowledge is regularly called one of Divine illumination. However, man's evidence for knowing that he himself exists functions in a way as a pre-condition for Saint Augustine's whole theory of knowledge. According to him, man can soundly affirm his own existence on the ground of the famous formula, repeated in one form or another in several of his works, *si fallor, sum,* "If I am deceived, I exist." Critics regularly cite this Augustinian principle as the forerunner of Descartes' *Cogito, ergo sum.* On the problem of the relation of these two formulae, Gilson has some very discerning remarks to make: "By placing the *cogito* at the beginning of his metaphysics as fundamental basis of the entire edifice, Descartes is committed beforehand, in the name of his mathematical method, to attributing to thought whatever is contained in his clear and distinct idea, and, correlatively, to attribute to it only what is thus contained in it.—The *cogito*—is but the first of that series of conceptual snippets which substitutes progressively a mosaic of abstractions for the continuity of reality. . . . Instead of being a method practiced upon ideas, Augustinianism is an enquiry concerning the concrete content of thought." [14]

As the statement of Gilson may perhaps suggest, the theory of Divine illumination rests ultimately upon Saint Augustine's adoption of an inner empiricism. What he experiences within his own mind, not what pours into it through the avenues of the senses, constitutes his point of departure. Always he gives the impression that this inner experience is a continuum, with no segment of it to be scrutinized apart from the context of the rest. The Augustinian procedure can be seen in his proof for the existence of God. In summary it runs as follows: Through the inner empirical method, man can realize that he possesses reason and that this possession makes him superior to inorganic beings, plants and animals. Also through inner empiricism man can recognize his own mutability, but can as well realize the existence of the immutable and unchanging, that which is superior to himself. Grounds for this latter realization appear when the mind in its inner experience grasps the immutability of mathematical relations, and in turn comes to grasp the concept of Truth itself. Having reached this point by the inner empirical method, Saint Augustine cannot see in this Truth anything other than God, who has granted men these inner powers, this Divine illumination, whereby God himself can be known, and all the complex relations of the creation can be understood. Thus the mind can know that God is the Creator of the "natures" which can be perceived in the world of sense experience, and they in turn can be dealt with in their true character, because inner experience with its guarantee of Divine illumination makes it possible for the mind to view them in their proper light.

The Augustinian metaphysics of knowledge then really begins with God and what God has planted in man's mind. Here perhaps lies the basic and irreconcilable difference between Saint Augustine and Saint Thomas, though the two views insofar as they are both genuine "philosophies" of Christianity are, as has been already indicated, ultimately complementary. Saint Thomas begins with outer experience and through a rational process reaches God. Saint Augustine begins with inner experience *and* God, and in these terms investigates and analyzes the content of thought. And it should be noted that the Augustinian approach to the problem is thoroughly in accord with the "fact-value" relation which is implicit in his doctrine of "natures." As Gilson has clearly pointed out, "The intelligibility of a concept resides less in the generality of its extension (*i.e.,* the Aristotelian and Thomistic attitude) than in the normative character which its necessity itself confers upon it." [15] The latter is of course the Augustinian attitude, which does not admit of isolating the capacity of forming concepts, but rather insists that the formation of a concept implicitly and inevitably involves the judgment of that which is conceived.

Gilson elsewhere has described Saint Augustine's theory of knowledge and its concomitant ground for his proof for the existence of God, as both the central and the vulnerable point of the Augustinian metaphysics. "The essential feature of such a position, whatever its ultimate interpretation, is a definition of the human intellect which leaves us nothing wherewith to account for the existence of truth. If Saint Augustine had simply held that man cannot know truth without an intellectual light given him by God, his analysis of the contingency and insufficiency of human thought would be lacking in a precise object; but if, as the consensus of the most important texts shows, this is the point on which his proof rests, it must necessarily follow that Divine illumination (to give it its traditional name) must reach thought directly. For either it reaches it directly, and in that case we grasp at the same time the sufficient reason of truth and God who is its foundation; or it reaches it indirectly, and in that case we are equally incapable of attaining to the existence of God and of accounting for truth." [16]

Obviously, no epistemology or theory of knowledge is totally without its dilemmas. But at the same time the reader should remember that Saint Augustine is not operating in a context bounded by limits within which reason alone can effectively operate. For him faith always precedes intelligence, but with the important proviso that faith and intelligence cannot be disjoined. Saint Augustine insists that man should begin with faith. "If you cannot understand, believe in order that you may understand." [17] Such is his spirit in the opening chapter of the treatise *On the Trinity,* "The following dissertation concerning the Trinity, as the reader ought to be informed, has been written in order to guard against the sophistries of those who disdain to begin with faith, and are deceived by a crude and perverse love of reason." [18] "Faith seeking understanding" is the hall-mark of Saint Augustine's view of the relation between faith and reason. Gilson well recognizes the profundity of this view when he says, "*Nisi crediteritis, non intelligetis* is and will always remain the charter of every Christian philosophy." [19] Saint Augustine's faith rests upon the revelation of the Holy Scriptures and the Incarnation of Christ, powerfully bulwarked by his own experience of conversion.

From his early manhood Saint Augustine had always been preoccupied with the problem of evil, and, as has already been suggested, probably was attracted to the Manichaean position because, whatever may have been its weaknesses, at least it presented a readily intelligible though not profound solution to the question. Hence it is not surprising that he turned his mature attention to the search for the nature of evil and grappled with it in terms of his Christian position. It is needless here to point out the stupendous difficulty of the problem. Suffice it to say that thinkers have speculated most fruitfully about it in the light of the distinction between cosmic evil and moral evil, a distinction to which Saint Augustine consistently adheres. So far as cosmic evil is concerned, he does not produce any unusual contribution, and it is fair to add that this aspect of evil did not capture his imagination. The theory which he adopts is Neo-Platonic in character, and is developed in accordance with his doctrine of "natures." As things are created by God, they are therefore good, and hence no intrinsic evil can be attributed to them. What we call evil in them is merely a want or failure or defect of goodness. On this ground, Saint Augustine can explain the superiority of certain things over others, and can account for the gradations in goodness as the result of the harmony which God chose to introduce into His creation. Whatever else which man may consider in the category of cosmic evil, Saint Augustine generally explains by assigning it to the infinite wisdom and goodness of God, who ordains all and whose ways are beyond human understanding.

In contrast, in connection with the problem of moral evil, Saint Augustine makes a creative contribution unrivaled in Christian thought. He did so by isolating the inner fact of the human will and seeing in it the ultimate source of moral evil. It is generally true that in the Greek philosophical tradition, the phenomenon of the will had never been explored with any great degree of systematic rigor. Plato, for example, to the extent to which he took seriously the Socratic paradox that knowledge is virtue, would not be expected to approach the moral problem through an analysis of the will. Indeed, in Plato, an awareness of the will is implicit rather than explicit. It appears in such places as the myth in the *Phaedrus* where the will is at least suggested when the inner struggle of the soul is prefigured in the image of the charioteer (reason) who endeavors to drive successfully an ill-matched team: the noble white horse which represents man's higher emotions, and the ugly mean black horse which represents man's baser desires. Or again, a notion of the will is not entirely absent, when in the *Republic* Socrates insists that a man can only achieve moral excellence by turning away from absorption in the material world and orienting himself towards the eternal and unchanging realm of Ideas, and the supreme Idea, the Good. And furthermore, the earlier Greek tradition as well as Plato himself cannot be said to be totally unaware of the will, when *sophrosyne,* self-control or temperance, is singled out as one of the four cardinal virtues.

Aristotle, particularly in the *Nicomachean Ethics,* made a considerable advance in studying the will more explicitly. Among the Stoics, the will plays a larger part than in any other system in Graeco-Roman culture. The Stoic would insist that, by combining a volitional act with the reason, man can discriminate between what is in his power and what is not, and thus fit himself into his proper position in the cosmic scheme. "Lead me, O Zeus, and Thou, O Destiny," the Stoic cries, and then concludes, "If with will recreant I falter, I will follow still."

The Ovidian phrase, "I know the right, and yet the wrong pursue," sums up the problem more succinctly than can be found elsewhere in the Graeco-Roman tradition. And yet the Hebrews knew it and threw much light upon it when, from the earliest days as a "stiff-necked folk," they refused to obey the commands of Yahweh. Saint Augustine, therefore, has this twofold background—the pregnant suggestions of the Greeks and Romans, plus the experience of the Hebrews down to Saint Paul—to bring to bear in his investigation of the will. But most important of all is his experience of conversion. The intensity of this event for Saint Augustine places beyond all doubt both the factuality and the ultimacy of the will. In the light of this spiritual climax, he looks back in his *Confessions* at many episodes in his earlier life and can understand them the better. He can now distinguish between acts of mere volition and acts undertaken with genuine liberty or freedom of will.

So he develops his famous analysis of the three states in which the will operates. The first exists when man through his will is only able to sin (*posse peccare*). This means that, though he has the illusion of freedom of will, the only alternatives available to him are those which involve sin. Such, according to Saint Augustine, is man's condition after Adam's fall before the grace of God has been visited upon him. All his acts prior to the advent of grace are merely volitional, since their purview is so severely limited. But in the second stage after grace has come, man is able not to sin (*posse non peccare*). This is the state of the first man Adam before the fall, and the one which Saint Augustine recognizes in himself after his conversion. Before that fateful event, he was totally absorbed in the things of this world. Possessed as he was of a brilliant mind, he advanced speedily to the heights in his profession. He knew and loved the adulation of the crowd. He knew and loved the pleasures of the flesh. He knew pride and was a victim of it. But at the same time he had an insatiable urge to get at the truth of things. When he followed along this path and became convinced intellectually that the Christian answer was correct, even then he only experienced a paralysis of the will. He wanted to become a Christian, but yet he could not, so deep was his entanglement in his worldly desires and passions. In his *Confessions* he records how he prayed to God, "Grant me chastity and continency, but not yet." [20] Then suddenly came the mysterious incident in the garden at Milan. Swept with overwhelming misery at his wretched state, he withdrew even from his faithful friend, Alypius, weeping in his sorrow and praying "How long, how long? Tomorrow and tomorrow? Why not now? Why is there not this hour an end to my uncleanness?" [21] Then he heard a child's voice, presumably chanting a refrain of some children's game, saying, "Take up and read, take up and read." He returned to the house, picked up the Holy Scriptures, opened the volume at random and read, "Not in rioting and drunkenness, not in chambering and wantonness, not in strife and envying; but put ye on the Lord Jesus Christ, and make not provision for the flesh, to fulfil the lusts thereof." [22] The miracle happened. Saint Augustine was now free to act righteously.

The third state of the will brings with it the inability to sin (*non posse peccare*). This is the final condition of beatitude, the ultimate happiness of those who have died their mortal death, and through the grace and salvation of God have attained to eternal life.

But in examining this profound analysis of the will with its three clearly identifiable states, it is impossible to dissociate from one another the Augustinian theories of the will itself, its freedom, the origin of moral evil, and of God's grace. In the treatise *On Free Will,* written not long after the conversion, Saint Augustine argues that the will is the source of moral evil. He can see no other more ultimate source, but the evidence for this conclusion lies mainly in Saint Augustine's immediate experience, and is of course completely in accord with his characteristic inner empirical method. But the next question naturally to arise is: Whence comes this will in man? If it comes from God, and if it is the source of moral evil, why then is God not ultimately the source of that evil? Is the will then to be considered a human good? Saint Augustine's answer is the Christian answer. The main tradition of the Christian Church has never deviated from it in any essential respect.

Simply stated, the will is a good which does come from God, for without it man would be unable to act rightly. Suppose man did not have a will. Under these conditions, he could not act rightly, for the concept of righteous action would have no meaning. But to be able to act rightly carries with it inevitably the possibility of acting wrongly. Presumably God could have created man without a will, but if He had done so, God would have taken from man the capacity for righteous action, a circumstance which is unthinkable. God therefore gave man a will, so that he could act rightly, but this involves also the capacity for wrong action. So, Saint Augustine contends, since God is supremely good, He cannot in any sense be considered as the source of evil or responsible for it. Therefore, man is the only other possible source, and through the operation of his will becomes responsible for moral evil.

Whatever may be the inadequacies of this theory of moral evil when it is subjected to rational analysis, it constitutes a powerful answer and one which is consistent with man's deepest inner experience of the fact that he possesses a will. Perhaps Dr. Johnson did say a final word on the problem of free will in his often repeated remark, "All theory is against the freedom of the will, all experience for it." But so far as the Augustinian doctrine of the will is concerned, it is important to keep in mind the distinction between the simple operation of the will as it exercises choice among alternative courses of action and genuine freedom of the will which can exist only if the individual has an alternative choice of both right action and wrong action. In this latter case, curiously enough, the choice is free, in the full sense of the word, only if right action is chosen. If wrong action is elected or if the will is in the state of *posse peccare* (*i.e.,* being able to sin), it can be called free only in a somewhat superficial sense. In other words, the concept of freedom in the full sense implies that the action chosen be good. If the action chosen is evil, then proper analysis shows that the will has not been really free, but rather has been enslaved by that which is not good.

In any discussion of freedom, two senses of the concept are present. One can be called "negative freedom," indicating freedom from restraint of any sort or order. All too frequently, thinking on this all-important human value has stopped at the negative level, and has failed to realize that there is always in freedom a positive aspect without which the concept itself loses a major portion of its meaning. The distinction between positive and negative freedom, *i.e.*, "freedom from" against "freedom for," is present in Saint Augustine's analysis of the will. Both in the case of mere volition as well as in the operation of a genuinely free will, negative freedom is assumed. Also neither type is dealt with without reference to the end result, but the designation of free will in the fullest sense is reserved for an operation of positive freedom, where the answer to the question "Freedom for what?" is unmistakably clear. It is freedom for the pursuit of God, God's Truth and God's Will. It is freedom that tears man away from slavery, from the seductions of worldly goods and desires, and leads him to the happiness which can only be found in God. Such, Saint Augustine insists, is the real meaning of Christ's words, "If ye continue in my word, then are ye my disciples indeed; and ye shall know the truth and the truth shall make you free." [23]

This, in substance, is Saint Augustine's account of the origin and character of moral evil. Sin comes from a perverted will, man's will that has lost touch with God. But how does man's will become rightly oriented towards God? Saint Augustine repeats the Pauline reply: by the grace of God, which is the grace revealed in Jesus Christ. The Pelagians charged that Saint Augustine, notably in his treatise *On Free Will,* had in effect expressed a position no different from their own. Unquestionably, at that moment in his career he was absorbed in the problem of the will, and consequently did not emphasize grace. Yet however much he concentrates upon the will, the presence of grace is never absent from his thought. Saint Augustine unwaveringly maintains that man is saved by grace and only by grace. The first man, Adam, was created with a will which was able not to sin. But Adam sinned and the taint of his sin was transmitted to his progeny so that all men since Adam have wills which are only able to sin. But God in his infinite mercy has seen fit to save men from this bondage to sin, and has done so by the free gift of grace. In order that man should know precisely the nature of grace, God sent His Son to become man. In the life and teaching of the Son, this knowledge becomes available to man. The wills of those to whom God elects to give grace are changed from the state of being only able to sin to the state of being able not to sin.

But to whom does God elect to grant His grace? Saint Augustine is lost in mystery in the face of this question. If grace is only given to those who by virtue of their right actions deserve it, then it cannot be given to any of Adam's descendants, as Saint Augustine sees it, for they are only able to sin, and therefore do not deserve it. Hence sinners are the only possible recipients. But why does God select one and not another? In God's infinite wisdom lies the answer, which human wisdom cannot penetrate. However,

Saint Augustine is certain that the great majority of men are not chosen, and hence are to endure everlasting punishment in eternal death. This "pitiless theology," as Bishop Welldon has pointed out, "rests upon no sure Scriptural base,"[24] but the fact remains that it is Saint Augustine's position, and one, as will be seen, which served to make the whole problem more difficult for him. In any event, in the Augustinian doctrine of grace, man's good works do not, and indeed cannot, precede its gift. Good works are possible after the gift of grace, for then man's will has been transformed to the state of being able not to sin. To look at it in another way, grace is given so that good works may be performed.

The theological dilemma inherent in this position perhaps can never be solved by the human intellect. Obviously, the Christian Church must reject the Pelagian thesis that man can work out without God's help his own salvation. Man, in Christian doctrine, cannot have this power without overstepping the limits marked out for him by the fact that God created him. Yet if this is the case, what can man's will actually accomplish when he is in a state of sin? Perhaps he can try to prepare himself by acts of faith to receive God's grace, but even in this situation, may not the very will to prepare himself by faith be the first indication that God has actually given him grace? After grace has in fact been granted, then the problem is less difficult, for man now knows that he is capable of right action, and by the same token knows that it is still possible for him to sin. In this state the virtue of humility becomes of crucial importance, because if a man believes that he has received the gift of grace and therefore will not sin, he actually sins in the highest degree, for he has become a victim of the sin of spiritual pride. But if he always remembers that every action he undertakes may be a wrong action, or may carry in it the taint of imperfection which is his because he is a man, then his humility will be preserved.

Even though the doctrine of grace appears on rational grounds to diminish the significance of the will and the validity of man's initiative, even though grace and free will appear to be in certain respects mutually exclusive, still it is true that Saint Augustine espoused both doctrines with equal fervor. And as the struggle against the Pelagians grew more intense, the more vigorously he asserted their simultaneous validity. Yet whatever may have been the rational consequences for the doctrine of the will, any conclusion other than that man is saved only by God's grace was unthinkable to Saint Augustine. If man can save himself, then God can no longer be conceived as omnipotent. Moreover, God's goodness and mercy are really not possible without the doctrine of grace in its Augustinian and substantially Pauline form. For if grace comes, as the Pelagians would have it, after the performance of good works, there is no room for God's mercy, which by its very nature must go to the sinner.

A real remaining difficulty concerns God's justice. In the Pelagian view, God, though not finally omnipotent, is just in that He rewards the righteous and punishes the sinner. In the Augustinian view, God's justice can be seen in the case of those to whom He has granted grace, but who though able not to sin, still are able to sin. But the puzzle lies in discerning God's justice in the selection of those to whom He will grant grace. In this connection, Saint Augustine can only remind man that his understanding is desperately limited and that it is no little thing for him to impugn in any way God's justice. Perhaps Saint Augustine's problem would have been less difficult had he not assumed that the great majority of men were doomed to eternal damnation. Certainly the New Testament notion that God's love, grace and redemption are somehow available to all sinners implies that the category of those who are able not to sin should be comparably conceived.

In order to understand why Saint Augustine saw no incompatibility between his doctrine of the will and the doctrine of grace, it is best, as M. Gilson has suggested,[25] to approach the problem not by attempting to establish a rational harmony between the two, but rather to try to see them as they were co-present in Saint Augustine's own inner life. Following his own method of inner empiricism, he could no more deny the existence of his will than he could the very existence of himself. Nor, by using the same method, could he deny the existence of grace. His conversion at bottom supplied him with the decisive evidence in the case of both doctrines. Prior to the conversion, he could see his will at work, but only within a limited sphere. Just before the event, he "wanted to will" a certain action, *viz.*, the acceptance of Christianity, but he could not. His will was powerless. Then, suddenly, the powerless will was transmuted into a powerful will. There could be for Saint Augustine only one explanation for this phenomenon: God's grace had come to him. Something had been done for him which he could not do for himself. So through God's grace, the will which he always possessed became a free will. Viewed in the perspective of this experience, the compatibility of the will and grace is established in the mind of Saint Augustine beyond any question.

But where in this tangled theological enigma can a place be found for God's foreknowledge? Saint Augustine was thoroughly aware of this problem as well, and again the God-centered nature of his thought is apparent. God must be omniscient, as well as omnipotent and perfect Good. If He is omniscient, it follows that He knows all that has been, is, and will be. Therefore He knows who will be saved, and who will be damned. But if He foreknows these things, why then does not this situation reduce man to a complete condition of automatism, by removing every vestige of free initiative from him? Saint Augustine by no means attempts to evade the difficulty of the problem. One characteristic solution which he offers maintains that man is not coerced to perform a certain act just because God accurately foreknows the act which will ensue. God foreknows it, yet man does it through an act of volition on his own part. Saint Augustine introduces a human illustration to clarify the nature of his argument. If, for example, one individual accurately predicts that another man will cross a road, this does not mean that the accurate prediction compelled the following action.

Though this argument is not without its value, Saint Augustine's more profound thought on the question involves a consideration of his views on the nature of time. His thought concerning time is always marked by excessive humility, but at the same time he faces the problem squarely. He will not offer a facetious solution, he remarks in the *Confessions,* as a certain person did, when asked what God was doing before the creation, by replying, "He was preparing hell for those who pry into mysteries." [26] Rather, Saint Augustine's attitude is typified by the frequently quoted remark, "What, then, is time? If no one ask of me, I know; if I wish to explain to him who asks, I know not." [27] Or again, in *The City of God,* when he is discussing the problem of the creation of the angels and their temporal relation, if any, to God, after offering a tentative theory, he says, "If I make this reply . . . I fear I may be accused of recklessly affirming what I know not, instead of teaching what I know." [28] Yet despite his modesty, Saint Augustine's speculation concerning time is one of his outstanding contributions to Western thought.

In the discussion of time, his indebtedness to Plato is particularly evident. In the myth of creation contained in the *Timaeus,* Plato distinguishes between time and eternity.[29] He asserts that time came into being with the creation, and consequently it is only accurate to speak of past, present and future in connection with things found in the physical universe. It is incorrect to say that God, or the Demiurge, the Master Craftsman, as He is called in the *Timaeus,* has been or will be. The only proper assertion which can be made is that God *is*. He, like a Platonic Idea, *is,* immutable, unchanging, outside of space and time. Saint Augustine adopts this Platonic analysis in its essence.[30] He asserts that for God there is no such thing as temporal sequence. Temporal sequence is a distinguishing feature of the created universe, whereas in God's mind, since He eternally *is,* with no past or future, all things are present simultaneously. If, for example, man says that God will be, he really is speaking metaphorically, and in effect is transferring and applying to God his own spatial and temporal condition.

The application of Saint Augustine's philosophy of time to the problem of God's foreknowledge should be clear. If God is in an eternal present, then all knowledge is present to Him. From God's point of view, it would not be precise to say that He foreknows, for actually, by virtue of His eternal nature, He simply *knows*. Foreknowledge, since it itself is a temporal concept, is therefore a concept which is produced by the human mind, which is itself a temporal entity. Man, to be sure, uses the term God's foreknowledge, but this tends to confuse him, since the term implies that God, like man, is a Being in whom knowledge is characterized by temporal sequence. Though perhaps this type of thinking on time and eternity may fall far short of solving the problem of the relation of the will to God's "foreknowledge," at least it suggests that the two fall into separate categories, and that no investigation of the problem can be fruitful if this notion is neglected. The will is in the category of time. God's knowledge, or "foreknowledge," is in the category of eternity. The real question then becomes: Does an all-inclusive eternally present knowledge in God necessarily mean that that knowledge exercises absolute coercive control over the human will which is in time? Saint Augustine would reply in the negative, because he will never deny the reality of the will. If we are puzzled by the dilemma, he would admit freely that to understand the nature of God's knowledge lies infinitely beyond human power.[31]

Saint Augustine's thinking on the question of time and eternity is absolutely fundamental for his philosophy of history contained in his greatest work, *The City of God*.[32] This masterpiece, composed over a period of about fourteen years from 413-426 A.D., elaborates certainly the first Christian philosophy of history, if not, as many would maintain, the first genuine philosophy of history ever to appear. The initial stimulus for the composition of *The City of God* arose from the shattering event of the sack of Rome by Alaric and the Goths in 410 A.D. It is impossible to imagine the impact of this catastrophe upon the minds of the Empire's citizens at the time. That the Eternal City was at the mercy of barbarians was inconceivable. As the significance of the event penetrated more deeply into the mind of Saint Augustine, he saw new meaning in human history, and therefore undertook to explain the phenomenon in the light of the Christian interpretation of Reality.

The vast work which resulted falls into two main sections. The first, comprising Books One to Ten, begins with an attack upon those pagans who assigned the Christian religion as the cause for the calamities of the times, and in particular the sack of Rome. They vigorously maintained that the gods, deserted by men under the persuasion of Christianity, were wreaking their vengeance on the Empire. By passing in review the events of Roman history, pagan theology and philosophy, Saint Augustine delineates what men normally would call an "earthly city," indeed the greatest earthly city the world had ever known. In the second part of the work, Books Eleven to Twenty-two, he introduces at the outset the concept of the City of God with which the earthly city may be contrasted. He then proceeds to outline the creation of the universe, of the angels and the first man Adam, his sin and the penalty of death. Next he describes the evidences of the earthly and the heavenly cities and their histories as they are to be found in sacred writings, followed by a more detailed analysis of the City of God through the times of Noah, the kings of Israel and the prophets, on down to the time of Christ. The earthly and the heavenly cities are then viewed in their respective courses to the end of the world. The closing portion is apocalyptic in character and looks at all of history in the perspective of the last judgment, the punishment of the wicked and the eternal blessedness of the saints.

Apparently the dualism of the "two cities" was suggested to Saint Augustine by a rather obscure African writer of the fourth century, named Tyconius, who used the notion symbolically in a commentary on the Apocalypse.[33] Saint Augustine, however, sees in the "two cities" a principle in terms of which time and human history can be understood in relation to eternity. But who are the members or the citizens of these two cities? Saint Augustine makes this beautifully clear in one short statement: "Accordingly, two cities have been formed by two loves: the earthly by the love of self, even to the contempt of God; the heavenly by the love of God, even to the contempt of self. The former, in a word, glories in itself, the latter in the Lord. For the one seeks glory from men; but the greatest glory of the other is God, the witness of conscience. The one lifts up its head in its own glory; the other says to its God, 'Thou art my glory, and the lifter up of mine head.' "[34] One city is self-oriented, the other is God-oriented. If this is the distinction between the two, then it is apparent that no specifically human or historical institution can be cited as a precise illustration. For example, Saint Augustine would deny that the Church in its external and physical manifestations is coextensive with the City of God, since there are many individuals within the Church who are obviously devoted to self. Nor, on the other hand, can Rome absolutely be equated with the earthly city, for among the citizens of Rome are to be found those whose glory is God. The true citizens of the City of God are those in this life who have received the gift of God's grace, plus those who have gone and will go to eternal glory with the saints. The remainder, who have never deviated in their love of self and the goods of this world, make up the citizenry of the earthly city. Their destiny in turn will be everlasting punishment.

Saint Augustine's estimate of the Roman state is in accord with his analysis of the two cities. In the famous nineteenth book of *The City of God,* he offers his illuminating definition of a people and a republic: "But if . . . we say that a people is an assemblage of reasonable beings bound together by a common agreement as to the objects of their love, then, in order to discover the character of any people, we have only to observe what they love . . . and it will be a superior people in proportion as it is bound together by higher interests, inferior as it is bound together by lower. According to this definition of ours, the Roman people is a people, and its weal is without doubt a commonwealth or republic. But what its tastes were in its early and subsequent days, and how it declined into sanguinary seditions and then to social and civil wars, and so burst asunder and rotted off the bond of concord in which the health of a people consists, history shows. And yet I would not on this account say either that it was not a people, or that its administration was not a republic, so long as there remains an assemblage of reasonable beings bound together by a common agreement as to the objects of love. But what I say of this people and of this republic I must be understood to think and say of the Athenians or any Greek state, of the Egyptians, of the early Assyrian Babylon, and of every other nation, great or small, which had a public government. For, in general, the city of the ungodly, which did not obey the command of God that it should offer no sacrifice save to Him alone, and which, therefore, could not give to the soul its proper command over the body, nor to the reason its just authority over the vices, is void of true justice." [35]

With this definition before him, Saint Augustine goes on to argue that without true religion there can be no true virtues, along with the implication that no society or state can be truly just without a proper orientation towards God. Yet the Roman state, particularly in the earlier stages of its development, remains most impressive to Saint Augustine. He sees that its success arose from its devotion to a certain kind of justice, and that the peace which it produced from time to time was indeed a peace of a certain sort. Because a degree of justice and virtue did exist, he can explain why the Roman state endured for so long a time, but also he can understand why with all its strength it began to disintegrate. The entire attitude is summed up in the well-known Augustinian observation that the Roman virtues were but "splendid vices." So long as Roman justice, for example, was motivated by national pride, or a desire for imperial power or glory, it could only be a spurious virtue, majestic, powerful, "splendid" indeed, but it inevitably falls short of being a true virtue, and becomes "vicious" because it has not been inspired by the love of God. At bottom, Saint Augustine in his analysis of society and history is applying again in these fields the principle already mentioned, *pondus meum, amor meus.*

Critics have frequently noted that the Greeks and the Greek philosophers were prevented from developing any thoroughgoing philosophy of history because their thought was dominated by a cyclical conception of time. Greek mythology, for example, repeats again and again the theme of the deterioration from the Golden Age on down through the various stages to the Age of Iron, followed by a return to the Golden Age and repetition of the cycle. The Stoic theory, that the universe goes through an everlastingly repeated process of mechanical involution and evolution to and from the primordial element of fire, is likewise a case in point. In terms of Christianity it is impossible to find meaning in history, if time is cyclical. But the Hebraic and Christian tradition had always proclaimed that time is linear. It begins with the creation and pursues its straight-line course on through till the millennium, the day of the last judgment and the end of the world.

Saint Augustine realized the full implications of this view of time for the philosophy of history. He sees in history the profound evidence that man is and must be God-centered, that his virtues, if they are to be really such, must derive from the love of God, and that his will must be oriented accordingly. All these ideas are finally sanctioned by the belief that man has an ultimate destiny, the destiny of an immortal life. As the desire for happiness is seen to be that which dominates the wills of men in this mortal life, so is the eternal happiness of an immortal life with God man's final purpose or goal. The nature of this supreme and final value therefore determines and orders the values which man seeks in this life. In other words, that which comes at the end of time provides the ultimate criterion by which all that happens in time must be judged. Saint Augustine further contends that these principles which are valid in the life of the individual human being are equally valid for society. In this perspective of time, eternity and ultimate destiny, he can understand, first, why the Roman state was as strong as it was, and why, in turn, it could never endure without end. *The City of God* presents the full-length argument for this conclusion.

The task of selecting a series of basic writings from the vast works of Saint Augustine is, to say the least, overwhelming. The nature of the problem itself carries with it the inevitable result that no selection will please everyone. Furthermore, the simultaneous presence of all his complex thought in the mind of Saint Augustine surely does not make the question of choice any the less difficult, for many of the most concise expressions of his central views are to be found in widely scattered individual places, in his sermons, or letters, or in the extended exegetical commentaries. On the other hand, the Augustinian compresence of thought can be viewed legitimately as an asset for one who seeks to bring together a collection of writings which will portray fully the entire position. As a consequence it is perhaps more than a pious hope that the present group of treatises will not have omitted anything of importance.

In making a selection from the Augustinian corpus, the first essential works are clearly *The Confessions, The City of God* and *On the Trinity. The Confessions* has been included in its entirety, but certain portions of the other two have been omitted. Because of the limited available space, the alternatives were either to print the three works complete and virtually eliminate the minor treatises, or, on the other hand, to eliminate the less essential parts of *The City of God* and *On the Trinity,* and consequently be able to include a far more extensive and representative collection from the minor writings. The second alternative, for good or ill, has been adopted. Certain books and chapters from the first ten books of *The City of God* have therefore not been included. The omitted sections contain much that is less significant and which most bear the marks of Saint Augustine's tendency to be repetitious and over-wordy. The second half of the work appears complete, since it contains the pulling together and interpretation of the evidence which has been amassed in the earlier books. The architecture of the whole should be readily discernible, and in order that no important detail be wanting, synopses of the omitted sections have been prepared. The books of the treatise *On the Trinity* which are included have been selected in accordance with the same general principles, with those omitted likewise covered in outline. For an edition of "basic writings," the presentation of these two great masterpieces in a somewhat abbreviated form has certain signal advantages. Everything possible has been done to prepare a text which will be easily apprehendable without, because of the repetitious elements, damaging in any significant particular the nature of the whole. Saint Augustine's habits of composition being what they are, it is even possible to argue that the shortened forms are superior for all but the most specialized student.

In choosing the block of minor treatises or selections from the remainder of the works of Saint Augustine, certain writings almost automatically suggested their exclusion. The commentaries, such as those on *Genesis, Job* and *The Psalms,* as well as the homilies on the *Gospel According to Saint John,* fall into this category. The sermons have also not been included, though there are a number whose absence may be keenly felt. This is also true of the letters, particularly the famous correspondence with Saint Jerome. In view of this genuinely embarrassing embarrassment of riches,[36] the decision was reached to include as many *complete* shorter treatises as the limitations of space would permit which would contain a fully rounded expression of Saint Augustine's mature thought. For this reason, the anti-Donatist writings, with their particular air of doctrinal dispute against the background of ecclesiastical politics, have not found their way into the collection. Instead, it seemed better to present with reasonable thoroughness the period immediately following the conversion (when the influence of Greek thought was strong), the attack upon the Manichaeans, and most important of all, the great writings directed against the Pelagians. If this objective has in some measure been achieved, this edition will have fulfilled its legitimate function.

In addition to the treatise *On Free Will,* a detailed analysis of which, but not the full text, is included, twelve essays comprise the group of selections. The first of these, *The Soliloquies* and *On the Immortality of the Soul,* reflect the times when Saint Augustine was moving from his Platonism into his more completely Christian mode of thought. The essay *On the Morals of the Catholic Church* (to which he wrote a sequel *On the Morals of the Manichaeans,* not here included) is typical of the anti-Manichaean writing. *On the Teacher* throws important light on Saint Augustine's theory of knowledge, while *On the Profit of Believing* continues the attack upon the Manichaeans, as does the short essay *On the Nature of the Good. On the Spirit and the Letter* illustrates well the Augustinian method of dealing with the Holy Scriptures. *On Nature and Grace, On the Grace of Christ and Original Sin,* and *On Grace and Free Will* contain the best of Saint Augustine's arguments against the Pelagians. The *Enchiridion,* written nine years before his death, is the most complete short statement of Augustinian Christianity, an expository essay unrivaled in its depth and clarity in Christian literature. *On the Predestination of the Saints,* composed within two years of Saint Augustine's death, rounds out the picture of his version of Christianity, which ranges from the simplicity of the deepest spiritual insights to the complexity of the most profound and baffling theological dilemmas.[37]

Not infrequently public lecturers have found it effective to close a speech or a series of addresses with the final words of *The City of God,* "Let those who think I have said too little, or those who think I have said too much, forgive me; and let those who think I have said just enough join me in giving thanks to God." In one way these words let us know the spirit of the man. But Saint Augustine's God-centered soul is revealed in all its illumination in the great prayer with which he concludes his work *On the Trinity:* "O Lord our God, we believe in Thee, the Father and the Son and the Holy Spirit. . . . Directing my purpose by this rule of faith, so far as I have been able, so far as Thou hast made me to be able, I have sought Thee, and have desired to see with my understanding what I believed; and I have argued and labored much. O Lord, my God, my one hope, hearken to me, lest through weariness I be unwilling to seek Thee, 'but that I may always seek Thy face.' [38] Do Thou give strength to seek, who has made me find Thee, and hast given the hope of finding Thee more and more. My strength and infirmity are in Thy sight: preserve the one and heal the other. My knowledge and my ignorance are in Thy sight; where Thou hast opened to me, receive me as I enter; where Thou hast closed, open to me as I knock. May I remember Thee, understand Thee, love Thee. . . . Set me free, O God, from that multitude of speech which I suffer inwardly in my soul, wretched as it is in Thy sight, and flying for refuge to Thy mercy; for I am not silent in thoughts, even when silent in words. And if, indeed, I thought of nothing save what pleased Thee, certainly I would not ask Thee to set me free from such multitude of speech. But many are my thoughts, such as Thou knowest, 'thoughts of man, since they are vain.' [39] Grant to me not to consent to them; and if ever they delight me, nevertheless to condemn them, and not to dwell in them, as though I slumbered. Nor let them so prevail in me, as that anything in my acts should proceed from them. . . . When, therefore, we shall have come to Thee, these very many things that we speak, and yet come short, will cease; and Thou, as One, will remain 'all in all.' [40] And we shall say one thing without end, in praising Thee in One, ourselves also made one in Thee. O Lord, the one God, God the Trinity, whatever I have said in these books that is of Thine, may they acknowledge who are Thine; if anything of my own, may it be pardoned both by Thee and by those who are Thine. Amen."

Whitney J. Oates

NOTES FOR INTRODUCTION

[1] Cf. the excellent discussion of this point by E. Gilson, "The Future of Augustinian Metaphysics," in *A Monument to Saint Augustine* (London, Sheed and Ward, 1930) pp. 289 ff.

[2] *Ibid.*, p. 300. In his essay, E. Gilson delineates clearly what I have called the "openness" of Saint Augustine's position. He also gives a splendid statement of the relation between Saint Augustine and Saint Thomas from the Roman Catholic point of view.

[3] *Ibid.*, p. 308

[4] For convenient reference and general information concerning the life and writings of Saint Augustine, cf. V. J. Bourke, *Augustine's Quest of Wisdom* (Milwaukee, The Bruce Publishing Co., 1945)

[5] *Conf.*, Bk. II, chap. 3

[6] *Conf.*, Bk. VI, chap. 15

[6a] Saint Augustine, with his conversion, decided upon a life of celibacy, and the formation of the group at Cassiciacum contributed greatly to the influence which he exerted later in the development of monasticism.

[7] *Introduction à l'étude de saint Augustin* (Paris, Librairie Philosophique, J. Vrin, 1929) p. 293, note 1

[8] *City of God,* Bk. XIV, chap. 8

[9] *Conf.*, Bk. 1, chap. 1

[10] C. C. Martindale, S.J., "A Sketch of the Life and Character of Saint Augustine," in *A Monument to Saint Augustine,* p. 84

[11] *Conf.*, Bk. XIII, chap. 9

[12] Cf. Bourke, *Augustine's Quest of Wisdom,* p. 112, and the references there cited.

[13] *On the Trinity,* Bk. VI, chap. 5

[14] "The Future of Augustinian Metaphysics," in *A Monument to Saint Augustine,* pp. 301-302

[15] *Introduction à l'étude de saint Augustin,* p. 124. The translation from the French is mine.

[16] "The Future of Augustinian Metaphysics," in *A Monument to Saint Augustine,* pp. 298-299

[17] Cf. M. C. D'Arcy, S.J., "The Philosophy of Saint Augustine," in *A Monument to Saint Augustine,* pp. 159 ff.

[18] *On the Trinity,* Bk. I, chap. 1

[19] "The Future of Augustinian Metaphysics," in *A Monument to Saint Augustine,* p. 290

[20] *Conf.*, Bk. VIII, chap. 7

[21] *Conf.*, Bk. VIII, chap. 12

[22] Rom. xiii. 13, 14

[23] John viii. 31, 32

[24] *De Civitate Dei,* edited by J. E. C. Welldon (London, Society for Promoting Christian Knowledge, 1924) Bk. XIII, chap. 23, vol. II, p. 74, note 20

[25] *Introduction à l'étude de saint Augustin,* Deuxième Partie, chap. III

[26] *Conf.*, Bk. XI, chap. 12

[27] *Conf.*, Bk. XI, chap. 14

[28] *City of God,* Bk. XII, chap. 15

[29] Cf. *Timaeus,* 37 c 6 ff.

[30] Cf. *Conf.*, Bk. XI, chaps. 10-21, where Saint Augustine discusses at length the nature of time.

[31] Cf. the interesting treatment of this problem in Boethius, *The Consolation of Philosophy,* Bk. V

[32] For the best Latin text and commentary in English on *The City of God,* see the edition of Welldon, referred to in note 24 above.

[33] Cf. the excellent discussion of the question by Christopher Dawson, "Saint Augustine and His Age," in *A Monument to Saint Augustine,* pp. 58 ff.

[34] *City of God,* Bk. XIV, chap. 28. The scriptural reference is to *Psalms,* iii. 3.

[35] *City of God,* Bk. XIX, Chap. 24

[36] Apart from letters and sermons, Saint Augustine composed 232 books.

[37] For the reader who wishes to explore the minor treatises further, the following are suggested: *Contra Academicos, De Vita Beata, De Musica, De Quantitate Animae, De Vera Religione,* and *De Doctrina Christiana.* For Saint Augustine's views of the creation of the world, cf. *De Genesi ad Litteram.* Also of great interest is the *Retractationes,* written late in his life, in which he goes over carefully and modifies the detail of many passages in his preceding works.

[38] *Ps.* cv. 4

[39] *Ps.* xciv. 11

[40] *I Cor.* xv. 28

[2]

Life, Culture, and Controversies of Augustine

Robert Markus

Life

Augustine was born in the North African town of Thagaste in 354, in the province of Numidia. His father, Patricius, was a town councillor of modest means. His mother, Monnica, and the entire household except for his father were Christians; his father was baptized on his deathbed. Augustine had a brother and a sister, and perhaps other siblings. At some financial sacrifice he was sent to school at Madauros, to learn grammar and rhetoric. At the age of sixteen he was recalled home, where he spent a year, on which he later looked back as depraved (*conf.* 2.3.5–2.9.17). He was helped by friends and relatives to find the means to go to Carthage to continue his studies. There he carried on what he later came to see as a life of dissipation, captivated by theatrical shows, until at the age of eighteen he read a now-lost work of Cicero's, the *Hortensius*. This won him over to an arduous quest for "the immortality of wisdom" but, lacking the name of Christ, as he later wrote, failed to grip him entirely (3.4.7-8). Turning his attention to the Christian Scriptures, he found these wanting in style in comparison with Cicero and gave his allegiance to the teaching of the Manichees, who seemed to him intellectually more sophisticated. He adhered to their sect while teaching the liberal arts at Carthage and became a "Hearer"; but gradually he became disillusioned with the sect's teaching (4.1.1–4.11.21 and 5.3.3–5.7.13). Meanwhile he had moved to Rome, enjoying the hospitality of Manichean patrons. This move, in furtherance of his career, later appeared to him as God's secret guidance (5.8.15). His expectation that his students would be better behaved than they had been in Carthage met another disappointment: their failure to pay. With the support of the new prefect of the city, Q. A. Symmachus, Augustine was appointed to teach rhetoric in Milan, now the imperial residence in the West. In Milan he frequented the preaching of the bishop Ambrose, and gradually found himself becoming interested in the content as well as the polished rhetorical technique of his sermons (5.8.14–5.14.24).

This was to be another turning point in his career. Ambrose's sermons turned him away from the Manichees, but Augustine, in line with the teaching of the Academics, remained skeptical about the possibility of finding any truth he could trust as certain. He became a catechumen (5.14.25). His mother, who had followed him to Milan, found him a suitable girl to marry; the concubine with whom he had lived faithfully for over thirteen years was sent home to Africa. Their much-loved son, Adeodatus, who was to die young, remained with Augustine in Milan. Augustine took a mistress to be his temporary partner until the girl reached a marriageable age. Under the influence of Ambrose's preaching, Augustine began to be able to conceive of a nonmaterial being and to turn his back on Manichean dualism and determinism as well as on astrology (7.1.1–7.8.12). At the same time he was introduced to "books of the Platonists," some Neoplatonic literature translated into Latin. In the circle of learned clergy around Ambrose, as in Ambrose's sermons, Augustine discovered a form of Christianity interpreted in Neoplatonic terms. When he came to reread the Gospels, he found Christian doctrine (especially the prologue of the Fourth Gospel), though not the historical facts of Christ's incarnation nor the summons to humility, foreshadowed in these texts (7.9.13–7.21.27). Held back, as he later saw the matter, by the bonds of lust, Augustine still deferred a decision about committing himself to Christian baptism. His decision was finally inspired by a discovery of the appeal of the ascetic life and by a chance alighting suggested by the chant of neighboring children, which he saw as divinely inspired, on an apposite Pauline text (Rom. 13:13-14). His state of indecision was finally at an end. He brought himself to embrace a life of chastity and resigned his post to retire with his mother, his son, his close friend Alypius, and other friends to a country estate near Milan lent them by a friend, at Cassiciacum. Here they spent the months until the following Easter meditating on and debating the questions over which they were exercised. That Easter (387) Augustine was baptized in Milan. His philosophical dialogues were written during this period and the years immediately following. He also began a project to write a series of books on the liberal arts, of which he completed only the work *On Grammar*, which had been lost from Augustine's own library before he listed its contents, and the surviving *On Music* (*retr.* 1.60). Resolved to return to Africa, Augustine, while waiting for a passage in Ostia, shared a vision with his mother, who died very soon afterward. After a further delay in Rome he returned to Thagaste.

There he founded a small community with some friends. His aim appears to have been to lead a form of shared ascetic life and to continue his studies and meditation in the company of like-minded friends. On a visit to Hippo, a coastal town some 150 miles from Thagaste, probably in 391, he was ordained as a priest under pressure from the local populace to act as assistant to the aged, Greek-speaking bishop, Valerius. Augustine's first request was to be given study leave to enable him to acquire a knowledge of the Scriptures such as would equip him for the task of ministering to the people (*ep.* 21). At Hippo he again organized a monastic community, and later, as bishop, another for the clergy attached to the episcopal residence, and lived a communal life with them until his death. On Valerius's death, and on his nomination (not quite in conformity with ecclesiastical norms), Augustine succeeded him as bishop of Hippo (395/96).

The bishop's primary duties arose directly from the nature of his office. Augustine saw the bundle of his responsibilities as a burden *(sarcina)* which he sometimes felt weighing heavily upon him (for one of his most heartfelt expressions of its weight, arising from a particularly disastrous decision, see *ep.* 209.10). As head of the local Christian community, he was the chief minister in the regular celebration of the Eucharist and the administration of baptism; he preached to his congregation and took pastoral care of its members; he was in charge of his clergy, the ecclesiastical property, the financial and legal business of his church (much of which he apparently delegated to business-like clergy), and the administration of the system of alms distribution. He was expected to take care of orphans, widows, and the poor and to defend the downtrodden, and to be hospitable. He also had oversight of monks and nuns in his diocese and took charge of Christianizing the countryside around his see. To such ecclesiastical functions the power given him by legislation and the prestige of his position in local society brought added responsibilities. The bishop had to arbitrate in legal disputes, and to use his good offices to reconcile the parties in family disagreements (most often concerned with testamentary disputes) or in cases of civic friction. He was also expected to intercede with the civil authorities on behalf of members of his flock. Local officials still played an important part in African towns and were a force, often in opposition to the bishop, with which he had to reckon, and he frequently found himself frustrated by them. In the conditions of the African church in Augustine's time, a learned bishop would also be in demand to undertake public debating with dissidents and to act as visiting preacher in other churches. Augustine preached in Carthage frequently, on his many visits to the city, and in smaller towns on the way there or back; he also undertook a number of journeys for the purpose of settling various matters of ecclesiastical administration, to intervene personally in urgent affairs, or to take part in doctrinal debate. All these functions can be amply documented from Augustine's correspondence and the biography by Possidius. A very large part of Augustine's time and effort was taken up with writing: the extensive correspondence and a corpus of works (including contributions to major controversies: see below) and sermons (taken down by shorthand writers) amount to the largest to survive from any ancient author. Augustine catalogued these toward the end of his life, taking the opportunity to correct some errors he detected, and stated the occasion for the writing of each work. His biographer, Possidius, was to compile a more complete list after Augustine's death, using the resources of the episcopal library in Hippo, which contained an almost complete set of Augustine's works.

Augustine remained in the episcopal office until his death in 430, while Hippo was under siege from the Vandal invaders. Possidius recounts that he comforted himself amid these calamities with a sentence enjoining detachment from the fate of earthly goods, recalled from "a certain wise man" (Possidius, *v. Aug.* 28), in fact the Neoplatonist philosopher Plotinus; and that he died reading the penitential psalms (*v. Aug.* 31).

Culture

Christians never developed their own system of education as an alternative to the existing Roman schools. Augustine received the same education his pagan fellows would have; they shared the same language, the same secular culture, the same horizons of knowledge. In the late Roman world this culture, especially at its higher levels, was predominantly literary in content and rhetorically orientated. A high value was placed on the ability to write and speak in

LIFE OF AUGUSTINE		LIFE OF AUGUSTINE
Born at Thagaste, November 13	354	Birth of John Chrysostom
	355	Death of Donatus of Casa Nigrae
	356	Conversion of Marius Victorinus in Rome; death of Antony of Egypt.
In school at Thagaste; serious illness	361	Emperor Julian decrees equality of cults; issues laws for schools
	362	Council at Alexandria with Athanasius and Egyptian bishops
	364	Rogatist schism in Africa
In school in Madaura	366/69	Election of Damasus as bishop of Rome; social unrest in Rome
Interrupts his studies; returns to Thagaste	369/70	Beginnings of Priscillianism in Spain near 370
Goes to Carthage to study (late fall). Takes a mistress	370	Basil became bishop of Caesarea
His father, Patricius, dies; Adeodatus is born	370/71	Gregory becomes bishop of Nyssa; Martin becomes bishop of Tours
Reads Cicero's *Hortensius*. Becomes a Manichee	372/73	Gregory becomes bishop of Nazianzen; revolt of the Berber chief Firmus
Teaches rhetoric in Thagaste.	373	Athanasius of Alexandria dies; rebaptism prohibited (*CT* 16.6.1)
Death of a friend (375/376)	374	Ambrose baptized (November 7) and consecrated bishop of Milan (December 7)
Teaches rhetoric in Carthage	376	
	379	Death of Basil of Caesarea
Writes *De pulchro et apto* (*conf.* 4.15.27)	380/81	Theodosius issues the Edict of Thessalonica (*CT* 16.1.2)
Reads the *Categories* of Aristotle	381	Council of Constantinople; Theodosius forbids pagan cults
	382	Council of Rome
Meets Faustus of Milevis in Carthage. Teaches in Rome	383/84	Symmachus, Prefect of Rome; death of Pope Damasus (384)
Appointed official Orator in Milan (fall)	384	Symmachus petitions Milan for the Altar of Victory; Ambrose responds
Panegyric of Bautone	385	Jerome goes to Palestine. Priscillian executed in Trier
Monnica arrives in Milan. Panegyric of Valentinian II	385	
Reads some Platonic books	386	Finding of relics of Saints Gervasius and Protasius (July 17)
Studies Paul's letters. Visited by Ponticianus	386	Siege of the basilicas in Milan; purge of Manichees at Carthage
Converts to Christianity; retires to Cassiciacum	386	Struggle of Ambrose against the Empress Justina
Returns to Milan. Baptized by Ambrose, April 24. Death of Monnica	387	
Returns to Rome with Alypius; some anti-Manichean writings	387/88	
Sails to North Africa and goes to Thagaste	388	Maximus invades Italy (autumn)
	389	Baptism of Paulinus of Nola
Deaths of Adeodatus and Nebridius (388-90)	390	Thessalonica massacre by Theodosius; penance imposed by Ambrose
Ordained a priest in Hippo	391	Aurelius made bishop of Carthage, imperial edict against paganism

LIFE OF AUGUSTINE		LIFE OF AUGUSTINE
Debate with Fortunatus in Hippo (August 28-29)	392	
Speaks at the Council of Hippo (October)	393	Maximian separates from the Donatists
Suppression of *Laetitia* at Hippo	394	Theodosius conquers Eugenius; Paulinus of Nola ordained a priest
	394	Donatist Council at Bagaï suppresses Maximianist schism
Succeeds Valerius as bishop of Hippo; studies Paul anew	395/97	Revolt of Maurus Gildo, Count of Africa
Participates at Councils of Carthage (June and August)	397	Death of Ambrose (April 4); succeeded by Simplicianus
Preaches at Carthage during the summer	397	*Breviarium Hipponense* approved at Council of Carthage
	398	Defeat of Gildo; execution of Optatus, Donatist bishop of Timgad
	399	Consulship of Manlius Theodorus; Honorius initiates laws against paganism
	401	Donatist Bishop of Calama held responsible for attack on Possidius
In Milevis for Council on August 7	402	Alaric invades Italy; defeated by Stilicho; death of Symmachus
	403	Bishop of Bagaï attacked by Donatists and badly wounded
	405	Edict of unity against the Donatists on February 12 (*CT* 16.5.8)
	408	Riot in Calama when Possidius breaks up a pagan procession
In Carthage at times between May 19 and September 11	410	Alaric enters Rome; many refugees flee to North Africa
Participates in the *Collatio* (June 1-8)	411	*Collatio* of Donatists called at Carthage; Donatists condemned
Begins the *City of God*; Synod at Cirta, June 14	412	Edict against the Donatists
September to December: preaches regularly in Carthage	412	Condemnation of Celestius
In Carthage: intercedes against the execution of Flavius Marcellinus	413	Marcellinus executed (September 13)
	414	Orosius goes to Jerusalem for two years
	415	Synod at Diospolis examines Pelagius
At a council at Milevis that condemns Pelagius and Caelestius	416	Orosius comes to Council of Carthage; brings relics of Stephen
Receives Orosius's History	417	Innocent I condemns Pelagius and Celestius
At Caesarea in Mauretania, September 20	418	Zosimus condemns Pelagius and Celestius
Beginning of the long confrontation with Julian of Eclanum	419	First work of Julian of Eclanum appears
Affair of Antonius of Fussala	423	Eraclius builds a memorial to S. Stephen at Hippo
Scandal at Hippo (Sermons 355 [December 18] and 356 [after Epiphany])	425	
Visits Milevis to regulate succession of Severus	426	Eraclius nominated as Augustine's successor
Leaves Hippo in the winter for his health; begins *Retractationes*	426	
	429	Vandals enter Africa
Death and burial of Augustine (August 28)	430	Vandals lay siege to Hippo

the manner of the approved "classics." The classical writers, especially Cicero and Vergil, Sallust and Terence, were known, often almost by heart, and venerated by many; their works provided the models for fine expression. In pagan circles they were also treated as fountains of religious truth, often revealed by means of allegorical exposition. Philosophical knowledge was for the most part obtained at second hand. The high literary culture of Augustine's age was essentially derivative and parasitic on its classical origins. Augustine was evidently widely read and very much at home within the Latin literary heritage of his age; although he could read Greek, and improved his knowledge of it late in life, his knowledge of the language was insufficient for him ever to feel at ease in it; Greek authors were not easily accessible to him except at second hand or in translations.

The relationship between Christianity and secular culture had long been problematic, but by the middle of the fourth century an easy coexistence had come into being. The old question, "What has Athens to do with Jerusalem?" (Tertullian, *apol.* 46), had lost its relevance in a world in which Christianity had become respectable, patronized by emperors, a passport to advancement. Christians had no qualms about sending their children to the public schools. Even the emperor, Constantius II, took an interest in education and the liberal arts. Distinguished men of letters were now to be found in growing numbers among the Christians. There was little sense of an opposition between Christianity and "pagan" culture. This easy symbiosis, however, was disturbed in the 360s, and almost exclusively in the Eastern Empire, by the pagan revival initiated by the emperor Julian (361-63). It was his propaganda that opposed the traditional civilized and civilizing *paideia* of what he called "Hellenism" with the folly and barbarity of the "Galilean superstition"; his decree prohibiting Christians from teaching in the public schools gave practical effect to this opposition. Christians were not the only ones who strongly opposed the decree, but Julian's early death ended the confrontation. A conflict on similar lines, however, broke out in the West in Augustine's time. The old senatorial aristocracy saw themselves as the guardians of traditional Roman values, upholding the traditional pagan religion and the high literary culture of their class against Christianity, which they feared as a threat to their prestige and the prestige of the culture they sought to foster. The conflict reached its climax in the 390s. The reserve shown toward secular culture by many leading Christians, including Augustine, Jerome, and others, had its roots in these tensions. They could not conceal their sense of being ill at ease in a culture they loved but saw as identified with the "pagan" cause. Augustine makes no secret of his youthful love of Vergil and Cicero, but he took care later in life to distance himself from them even though he continued to be heavily in debt to pagan philosophers such as Plotinus, Porphyry, and most of all, perhaps, Cicero.

During the years around his conversion, in the 380s and the early 390s, Augustine's writings are heavily indebted to a fundamentally Platonic view of the universe, of human nature and human destiny. In Ambrose's Milan he had encountered Christianity in a form deeply colored by conceptual structures of Platonist origin, and he had no sense of a conflict between his newly embraced Christian beliefs and the views of the world, of the soul, of good and evil rooted in Neoplatonism. A tension opened only in the middle 390s, when a deeper rereading of the Pauline corpus called into question the harmonious coexistence of Pauline and Platonic conceptual structures in Augustine's mind. Although his intellectual and spiritual perspectives underwent a huge shift, philosophical ideas of Platonic (and also of Stoic) origin continued to play an important part in his writings.

Augustine was too conscious of the indispensability of much of secular learning. In his *De doctrina Christiana*, begun in 395 but only completed thirty years later, he faced the problem head-on: Of what use are the liberal arts, which composed the round of secular studies, to a Christian? His answer was in line with one old strand in the Christian evaluation of secular studies, that represented by Clement and, especially, Origen in Alexandria: Christians must "spoil the Egyptians," take their valuable possessions, and make use of them in the service of the true God. For Augustine this meant making use of the liberal arts in the study of the Scriptures. These scholarly disciplines were necessary for the full understanding of the Scriptures. In principle this provided a means for integrating them within a Christian, Scripture-based education, though it also gave them a narrow and wholly instrumental function within a Christian culture.

Controversies

From the time he became bishop of Hippo, Augustine never ceased to be involved in controversy. Of his major works, only the *Confessions*, *De doctrina Christiana*, the *Literal Commentary on Genesis* (on

Gen. 1-3), *On the Trinity*, and the *Enchiridion* are not primarily controversial in intent, though even these touch on some of the controversies he was engaged in. Although there are frequent references in his sermons and other works to the error of the Jews, there was in effect no real controversy between Christians and Jews at this time. The existence of the Jews was accepted and even seen as part of the divine plan, in which they had a clearly allocated place. Rather different is another steady undercurrent which surfaces frequently in Augustine's writing and preaching: the pagans. Although the Christianization of the empire had gone a long way by Augustine's time, there were still many non-Christians, pagans mingled with the predominantly Christian populations of the towns; and the more backward countrysides in some provinces of the empire had been little touched by Christianity (hence by Augustine's time the epithet "pagan" had acquired the extra, pejorative connotation of "backward"). Although much of Augustine's antipagan polemic is antiquarian in nature, being aimed at the literary and intellectual traditions which gave contemporary educated paganism its somewhat antiquarian flavor, he also often addresses the beliefs and practices of living pagans. Pagans were sometimes present in Augustine's congregations, and his preaching is sometimes aimed directly at them (e.g., *s.* Dolbeau 25 [Mainz 61]). His great work, *De civitate Dei*, was self-avowedly written against the pagans (even though much of its actual argument is aimed at Christians who were perplexed over the way they should react to the disasters of their times). The pagans Augustine had in mind here were the vociferous objectors to the "Christian times," who blamed the sacking of Rome by the Visigoths in August 410, and the other disasters of the early years of the century, on the Roman state's rejection of its ancient gods. A fair body of letters in Augustine's correspondence consists of exchanges with pagans, mostly educated upper-class men with a genuine interest in the questions on which they sought Augustine's views.

In his anti-Manichean works Augustine was conducting a sustained dialogue with something in his own personal history (see above, p. 500) as well as debating with some actual representatives of the movement. Manicheism, although repeatedly legislated against since the time of Diocletian, was widely propagated and flourished in African and other cities of the empire. Its itinerant preachers were debating with Christians in public, and their adherents formed a far-flung network with links often useful to members of the sect such as Augustine (see above, p. 500). Their teaching derived from Mani, a Mesopotamian sage of the third century. The movement's central tenets are known from the works of its opponents, as well as at first hand from fairly recently discovered Manichean literature. Behind its fantastic mythology was a radically dualistic cosmology and revulsion from the material world. The origin of the material world was ascribed to an evil creator, whose power was perpetually at war with that of a good creator who was not responsible for the evil in the world. Human beings were seen as caught up in this intercosmic conflict between the good and the evil powers, the light and the darkness. Manichees identified human salvation as the liberation of the particle of light trapped within their material bodies. The dietary provisions and sexual discipline of their code for the "Elect" among their adherents were designed to promote this end. The "Hearers," of whom Augustine was one, had a somewhat freer lifestyle and were expected to support the Elect. Augustine gradually came to find their teaching incoherent. The solution it offered to the problem of evil held him longest in its grip: it was not until he had heard Ambrose's preaching that he came to discard the view that a person is not responsible for the evil he perpetrates, that being the work of the evil nature which forms one part of the person. In his later thought the unity of the person and his responsibility for his actions often appear as the nub of Augustine's confrontation with Manicheism and the decisive point over which he rejected its teaching.

The fate of Arianism had been sealed at the Council of Constantinople (380), having been outlawed by the council and the new emperor, Theodosius I. It had, however, a long future among the Germanic tribes who had received Christianity in an Arian form and remained Arians in the areas in which they settled within the Roman imperial frontiers. It also continued well into the fifth century in isolated pockets among the Roman population, and had its leaders and preachers. It was against this last remnant of Arianism and its representatives that Augustine's anti-Arian works were directed.

Augustine was confronted with Donatism not long after his ordination to the priesthood in 391. The schism was by this time some eighty years old. The division had its origins in the conditions which prevailed in the African church during the last persecutions, in the early years of the fourth century and, especially, at the time of their cessation. Early in 305 or soon after, the persecution initiated by

Diocletian's decree two years before was called off. The conditions of effective toleration that now prevailed revealed tensions within Christian communities which had been brought about during the time of persecution. Christian laypeople and their pastors had reacted to the measures taken against them by the civil authorities with differing degrees of determination. There were more and less rigoristic factions, fanatics and prudent compromisers, in many churches. The surrender of copies of the Scriptures to the authorities (*traditio*, "handing over") by the clergy was generally regarded as apostasy; but there was a wide range of attitudes toward "collaborators," or those who had failed to make a sufficiently determined stand in the resistance. A disputed election to the see of Carthage between 308 and 311 established the formal schism between the two factions. Neither imperial intervention nor the decisions of church councils in Europe could heal the schism.

Donatism was dominant in the province of Numidia; Hippo was within an area in which Donatists were in the majority and Catholics in a position of weakness. From the time of the council which met in Carthage in 393, Augustine was in a key position. He had already called for conciliar action to deal with the African church's troubles (*ep.* 22.1.2). At the council he had been asked to expound the creed to the assembled bishops; henceforth, he was the trusted collaborator of Aurelius, the bishop of Carthage and the leader of the African episcopate. Augustine took a leading part on the Catholic side in the conference called by the government in the hope of healing the division between Catholics and Donatists in 411, held at Carthage. Augustine issued a summary of its proceedings and went on expounding and defending the Catholic case.

After 411, however, Pelagianism came to occupy more of Augustine's attention, and the controversy with its representatives, more of his energies. He died while composing the last of his works against the Pelagian bishop Julian of Eclanum (*c. Jul. imp.* 6.41 and *ep.* 224). The British monk Pelagius aroused Augustine's suspicion by his teaching. At first, however, Augustine regarded Pelagius as an ally in his championing of the responsibility of the human will against the determinism of Manichean doctrine. Augustine could sympathize with a movement which preached "authentic Christianity" to Christians who bore the name "Christian" without living up to the moral demands imposed by the "name." Pelagius and his disciples called for perfection not only from ascetics dedicated to its pursuit, but from all. Gradually, however, Augustine became conscious of a theological gulf opening between him and the Pelagians. In the course of his struggle to vindicate the supremacy of God's grace, with the full backing of the North African church, positions hardened, especially in the depressing dialogue of the deaf between Julian of Eclanum and Augustine. The doctrine upheld by the African episcopate was endorsed by the imperial government and the bishops of Rome, and was identified with "Catholic" teaching. It became the orthodoxy of the African theological tradition and was widely accepted, except in Gaul. Augustine's views were little known in the Eastern Church, but they still played an important part after the Council of Orange (529) watered them down and restated them in a less uncompromising formulation.

→ Alypius; Arius, Arianism; Church and State; *Confessiones;* Donatus, Donatism; Heresy, Schism; Hippo Regius; Mani, Manicheism; Monnica; Pelagius, Pelagianism; Possidius; *Retractationes;* Rhetoric

Bibliography

G. Bonner, *St. Augustine of Hippo: Life and Controversies* (London, 1963); Brown, 1967; P. Brown, *Religion and Society in the Age of Saint Augustine* (London, 1972); H. Chadwick, *Augustine,* Past Masters (Oxford, 1986); Hagendahl, 1967; R. A. Markus, *Conversion and Disenchantment in Augustine's Intellectual Development,* The Saint Augustine Lecture 1984 (Villanova, 1989), reprinted in *Sacred and Secular: Studies on Augustine and Latin Christianity* (London: Variorum, 1994, XVIII); R. A. Markus, *The End of Ancient Christianity* (Cambridge, 1990); H.-I. Marrou, *Saint Augustin et la fin de la culture antique* (Paris, 1938), with *Retractatio* (1949); J. J. O'Donnell, *Augustine,* Twayne's World Authors (Boston, 1985); Van der Meer, 1961.

Robert A. Markus

Part II
Two Cities: Justice in the Early and Divine Community

[3]

THE TWO CITIES IN AUGUSTINE'S POLITICAL PHILOSOPHY

By Rex Martin

There has been a surprisingly wide divergence of interpretations of Augustine's conception of the state, especially with respect to the political bearing of his concept of the Two Cities and to his position on the nature and role of justice in the governance of states. In this essay I wish to develop a single, coherent reading of Augustine's theory out of the themes and passages that are generally regarded as the matrix of his conception of the state and, then, to confirm and extend this reading by directing it against some of the major alternative interpretations of his theory.

What are these themes and passages which provide the agreed upon field of interpretation and reinterpretation? There is, first, the concept of the Two Cities and the political interpretation given it. Then, second, there is the well-known passage in the *City of God* (IV. 4, pp. 112–13) where Augustine draws an analogy between a kingdom (*regnum*) and a robber band. Finally, we have Augustine's reflections on, and apparent reworking of, Cicero's definition of a commonwealth (*res publica*).[1] These themes and passages are all of a piece. The political interpretation placed on the idea of the Two Cities will affect the reading one gives to the "robber band" and "commonwealth" passages. The conception that one develops of the state in these passages will be a feature of the way that the idea of the Two Cities is construed. Most commentators appear to regard Augustine's basic position as a consistent one. Differences have come, however, in determining exactly what this position is.

I think the simplest approach to Augustine's position is by way of the Two Cities. According to Augustine, the twofold division of the universe into the "City of God" and the "City of Earth" originated in the prideful revolt of the (now fallen) angels in heaven. As it had been in heaven so it was on earth. Men had primevally lived on earth in peace and comity (joined with one another in natural, familial affection) until the Fall, which brought sin into the world. The two cities

[1]References to and citations of the text of Augustine's *City of God* will generally occur in the body of the paper and will follow a single style—e.g., IV.4, pp.112–13, where the numbers denote, respectively, the book (IV), the chapter (4), and the page numbers of the passage in question. The page references are to the Modern Library edition of the *City of God*, trans. by Marcus Dods and others (New York, 1950). For Augustine's discussion of Cicero's definition see, in particular, II.21, pp.60–63 and XIX.21, 23, 24, pp. 699–701, 706.

on earth had their germ in Cain and Abel. Cain, the fratricide, built the first earthly city, "but Abel, being a sojourner, built none" (XV.1, p. 479). Thus, Augustine can say,

> Accordingly, two cities have been formed by two loves: the earthly by the love of self, even to the contempt of God; the heavenly by the love of God, even to the contempt of self. . . . In the one, the princes and the nations it subdues are ruled by the love of ruling. . . . But in the other city there is no human wisdom, but only godliness, which offers due worship to the true God, and looks for its reward in the society of the saints, of holy angels as well as holy men, "that God may be all in all" (XIV.28, p. 477).

One model for interpreting Augustine's Two Cities is to *identify* the Earthly City with the state and the City of God with the institutional church. Assuming for the sake of argument that this model is fundamentally sound, we can ask what consequences for the evaluation of political life would follow from the model. As regards the state as such, when taken on its own terms, the consequence would appear to be a radical devaluation of the political side of things and a considerable measure of pessimism respecting the means and ends of man's political condition. On the other hand, the institutional church—at least in the Christian dispensation—would literally be the City of God on earth.

What political implication this would have, however, is not altogether clear. It would seem, though, that if the state could be Christianized through some special relationship with the institutional church, then a fundamentally different evaluation of such a state would be warranted. The basic point here would be to distinguish the state *per se*, on its own principles, from the state as Christianized through some organic relationship with the institutional church.[2] The function of the identification model would be to validate this distinction, to justify this way of looking at politics, and to legitimate the notion of a Christianized state.

The twofold identification which I have described, of the state with the City of Earth and of the church militant with the City of God, could lead to a "clericalist" doctrine of the state. This seems to have happened in the Middle Ages, when there was a strong current of

[2]A variety of possible arrangements could be suggested as suitably satisfying the "organic relationship" in question. Among the alternatives are: (a) some sort of theocracy, (b) Caesaro-papism of the Byzantine sort, (c) a cooperative relationship between church and state within a single polity, as in Charlemagne's conception of the Holy Roman Empire, or (d) a cooperative relationship between two types of authority within a single Christian society, as in the "formula" of Pope Gelasius. It has even been said that the mere establishment of the Christian church or simply the official toleration of Christianity would be sufficient. See J. N. Figgis, *The Political Aspects of St. Augustine's "City of God"* (Gloucester, 1963; originally published in 1921), 60–61.

"clericalist" rhetoric in which the identification model was asserted, or at least presupposed.[3] That we should accept this tradition of political rhetoric as an interpretation of Augustine is doubtful. For it may well be that the medieval analysis was about medieval politics rather than about Augustine and, hence, not fundamentally an interpretation of the political doctrine of the *City of God.* In modern times, however, scholarly interpretations have been advanced which lend weight to taking the clericalist doctrine, and the identification model, as a substantially correct account of Augustine's own position. As Figgis says, "Their views are stronger evidence of what Augustine meant, than is the constant use that was made of him by medieval thinkers. The medieval habit of taking tags as text-proofs, apart from the general purpose of the writer, discounts their value as evidence. Besides this there was an immediate polemical interest at stake."[4]

Although the identification model would appear to have a certain validity, or at least great historical interest, its acceptability as a substantially correct account of Augustine's position would require the support of Augustine's text, as it bears on the notion of the Two Cities and his analysis of the state. It is my own opinion that the identification model is altogether too simple to fit the salient details of Augustine's own rendering of the Two Cities, as I shall try to make clear in what follows.

Let me begin by elaborating the contention that Augustine had an essentially tripartite conception of the city of God. The first conception is that the city of God is an "eternal city"; as such it is composed of the Trinity, the unfallen or loyal angels, and the eternally predestined-to-grace portion of the human race. The eternal citizenship of the human portion, which is *potentially* eternal "in time" and *actually* eternal "at the end of time" (i.e., in the Heaven of Book XXII), is referred to by Augustine in phrases such as "the eternal life of the saints" (XII.19, p. 402) and "a future eternal priesthood" (XVII.6, p. 583).

The second conception of the city of God is that it is an associa-

[3]The term "clericalist" is Figgis's (64). A number of medieval thinkers can plausibly be cited as holding the clericalist doctrine on grounds of the identification model: Hildebrand (see Figgis 88–89 for discussion and citation); Engelbert of Admont (Figgis, 85, 97–98); James of Viterbo (C. H. McIlwain, *The Growth of Political Thought in the West* [New York, 1932], 159; McIlwain also cited Hildebrand, 160); the anonymous source cited in the anti-papalist tract *Rex pacificus* (H. A. Deane, *The Political and Social Ideas of St. Augustine* [New York, 1963], 232–33); and Giles of Rome (Deane, 232, 332, n. 25; Giles is also cited by McIlwain, 159n).

[4]Figgis, 77. Ritschl, for example, appears to identify the state with the City of Earth (Figgis, 55, 128, n.6 for discussion and citation). Gierke holds a theocratic interpretation of the state based, again, on identifying the City of God with the church (Figgis, 77, 131, n.9). Similar views are held by Dorner and Ritschl (Figgis, 131, nn.8, 10).

tion (a collective only "in concept" but taken distributively in fact) of individual persons who love God, as distinct from those who love themselves and the things of this earth. By this rubric of "two loves" Augustine divided *all* mankind into two groups, those who live after "the flesh" and those who live after "the Spirit" (XIV.1, p. 441). Members within each group have nothing in common except the peculiar characters of the "love" (or "will") which motivates them. These individuals are not corporately embodied as such in any single institution or set of institutions on earth; yet they are spoken of as forming two "cities." Accordingly, I shall refer to this as the "individualistic" conception of the city of God, for it denotes only individuals and their love.

The third conception of the city of God is that it is a visible and institutional entity. Before Christ, this entity was the Hebrew nation (not state). Christ "took away the kingdom" from Israel, because Israel had become his "enemy" (XVII.7, p. 585), and put it under his own headship in his church, the catholic church. It is especially noteworthy that Augustine used this terminology to describe what he believed to have been an *historical* occurrence, the transfer of God's institutional "kingdom" on earth from the Hebrew nation to the Christian church.

Too many roadblocks stand in the way of any literal and complete identification of the city of God with the church. The term "church" should properly refer only to the New Testament "Kingdom" of Christ. Thus, all the individual persons who lived *before* Christ can never be included within the church. Furthermore, the Godhead and the angels who compose part of the "eternal" city can in no sense be called part of the church (although Christ *is* called "head" of the church). These two exceptions will hold true no matter how broadly one chooses to interpret the term "church" (providing, of course, that the term is strictly confined to the New Testament or Christian dispensation).

If one prefers to limit "church" to the "institutional" or "visible" church, then one must be prepared to admit that the "individualistic" church can never be fully comprehended in it. There will always be some predestined individuals (i.e., members of the "eternal" city) who at any given time are not members of the "visible" church and even individuals who love God but, for one reason or another, have not affiliated themselves with the "visible" church (e.g., martyrs who die for Christ but outside the church and who are admitted to his kingdom by the "baptism of blood" rather than to his church by the "baptism of water"). Finally, there are always members of the "visible" church who do not belong to the "eternal" or "individualistic" cities; their presence within the "institutional" city or church thus makes it impossible to "identify" that city with either of the other two cities.

Sometimes texts in the book which explicitly identify the city of God with the church are seized upon as proving some kind of complete identification. (See, for examples, VIII.24, pp. 273–74; XIII.16, p. 424; XVII.4, p. 573; XVIII.29, p. 634.) However, such grasping at textual straws is futile, if it is admitted (as it must be) that neither "city of God" nor "church" is used unequivocally. We are merely pushed back to examining the specifics, and such examination will invariably show that no wholesale identification is possible. But to say this is not to dismiss the claim that there is an "institutional" sense of the term "city of God." And it is clearly true that the institutional church, for Augustine, is to be regarded as exemplifying this sense in the Christian era.[5] His point was that the city of God on earth should not be identified exclusively with either of the two Christian "societies"; rather, it was that the institutional view of the church must be set over against and integrated with that of the "individualistic" church of the true saints.

The individuals who compose the "individualistic" church are members of that city of God by virtue of their love; they are also—for the most part—members of the institutional church. The institutional

[5]The problem here is to establish unmistakably that Augustine did refer with one sense of the term "city of God on earth" to the institutional church. Our *locus classicus* is Augustine's exegetical discussion of Noah's ark (XV.26, 27, pp. 516–20). He said about the ark: "This is certainly a figure of the city of God sojourning in this world; that is to say, of the church, which is rescued by the wood on which hung the Mediator of God and men, the man Christ Jesus" (516). The condition of the church's "sojourning" is the condition of the animals in the ark (i.e., "the clean and unclean together," 519). This inclusion of both "clean" and "unclean" in the ark (i.e., saved and unsaved in the church) is an image appropriate to the visible or institutional church but hardly to the church conceived as an association of individuals bound together solely by their love of God. Hence, the image of the ark provides not only the looked-for proof text but also the principle of differentiating the individualistic from the institutional sense of the term "city of God on earth." Augustine's clearest statement of his twofold conception of the church under the single heading of "Kingdom of heaven" (or City of God) is found in XX.9, which deals with the millennial reign of Christ; see esp. pp. 725–27. This chapter provides another discussion of the church/city of God along the same lines as in the Noah's ark sections. On the theme of the institutional church as itself a mixed community, see Augustine's discussion of heretics in the church (XVIII.49, p. 660 and, esp. 51, pp. 661–63). The notion of the city of God as a sacramental body seems, also, to point to the institutional church. At two points this is unmistakable, where Augustine conjoins the themes of the church as a mixed community and as a sacramental body. (See the Noah's ark chapters, especially the analogy of the door of the ark with the wounded side of Christ [p. 516], and I.35, p. 38.) Finally, there is his idea that the city of God in the Christian era is prefigured by the Hebrew nation. Augustine several times treated of this foreshadowing with special reference to public, corporate worship. (See especially X.1, p. 305; VII.32, p. 238; X.32, p. 343.) The presence of the concept of public worship here definitely points to an institutional church.

church conceived as a divine and providentially directed institution can be said to act for and in the interest of the individualistic church. It is the historical "deputy" of God and, as divine, "stands for" God and his people (the "individualistic" church); the institutional church has the mission of carrying the religion of Christ throughout the Christian era and of guaranteeing the truth of this religion, with respect to both cult and doctrine.

As long as the institutional church is divinely directed to do God's work it *is* the city of God on earth in a most important and indispensable way. Regardless of the general character of its membership and because it always contains the greater portion of the saints on earth, the catholic church (in Augustine's opinion) goes on its pilgrimage, inheritor of the "kingdom" of God from the Hebrews, house of worship, dispenser of the sacraments, and teacher of scripture. It is the peculiar medium through which God's will is worked and is a sharer in God's grace as truly as is the "individualistic" church. Each church, admittedly in its own way and in a nonexclusive and limited sense, is an aspect of the city of God on earth. The conclusion I draw is that Augustine did not treat "City of God on earth" and "institutional church" as identical in meaning. But I have argued that there is a unique relationship here, between the City of God and the visible church, which requires some term to describe it.

Figgis has suggested the notion of a "symbol."[6] While Noah's Ark may be a symbol of the church (by way of analogy), the institutional church is not in that sense a "symbol" of the City of God. For some features of the church are not simply analogous to traits of the City of God but are, rather, actual historical functions of the City of God on earth. Perhaps the word to describe the relationship is a stronger one: the institutional church *represents* or is the *agent* of the divine City in certain of the functions the church actually performs, i.e., in worship, sacraments, scripture, and authoritative discipline. Rather than a simple identity there is an identification at certain points and for certain purposes. It is this claim which I would urge against both Figgis and Deane.[7] Although I endorse their contention that Augustine does not identify the City of God on earth with the institutional church, I claim that this fact alone does not require us to withdraw the notion of a Christianized state, since there is still the relationship of special representation.

[6]Figgis, 51, 68. Bluhm refers to the "identification," of the city of God with the institutional church, as "only figurative": *Theories of the Political System* (Englewood Cliffs, 1965), 163.

[7]Both Figgis (51–52, 121) and Deane (24, 34, 121) do, of course, deny the simple identification model. Figgis does it with the qualification "*sans phrase*"; Deane's denial is unqualified: it is "absolutely impossible to identify the City of God . . . with the visible Christian Church in this world" (24).

Deane, however, wants to deny the Christianized state interpretation altogether. To accomplish this, he wants to deny not only the simple identification model but also any notion of special representation. His claim here is quite uncompromising: "No earthly state, city, or association can ever claim to be a part or a representative of the City of God. . . . Even the visible Church, which contains many of the reprobate along with the elect, is not an earthly division of the City of God, although . . . it is more closely related to that City than any earthly state or society can ever be."[8]

One might well agree with Deane, as I do, that the Christianized state is not an Augustinian notion. But I do not think that one can give as his reason that there is *no* basic relationship, either of identity or of representation, between the City of God and the institutional church in Augustine's eyes. It seems to me to run against the grain of Augustine's text to say that the institutional church is "not an earthly division of the City of God" and to suggest that it differs from (other) earthly states or societies only in degree. Rather, I contend that there is a special relationship—representation—and this might provide warrant, although an attenuated one, for retaining the notion of a Christianized state as a possible interpretation of Augustine. Indeed, Sabine has managed to squeeze the whole Christianized state doctrine through the needle's eye of the relationship of representation. He has alleged, though noting that the City of God could not be "identified precisely" with "existing human institutions," including the church, that the Kingdom of Christ was "embodied" in "the church and Christianized empire." This "conception of a Christian commonwealth" is, Sabine says, Augustine's "most characteristic idea" and is based on "a philosophy of history [i.e., the idea of the Two Cities] which presents such a commonwealth as the culmination of man's spiritual development."[9] I would agree with Sabine to this extent: the Christianized state idea must at least be left open as a possibility,

[8]Deane, 29 (see also 28). It is difficult to say here whether Deane is expounding Jesus' opinion or Augustine's. But he is clearly expounding Augustine later, when he says that the City of God "has no earthly representative" (120). If this remark is taken to refer exclusively to *states* I would agree, but if it is meant to include the church militant as well (as it does on 121), I cannot agree.

[9]The passages cited are from G. H. Sabine, *History of Political Theory* (3d ed.; New York, 1961), 190–91. It is interesting to note that Sabine presses the Christianized State notion on Augustine, by reference to the Two Cities concept, while specifically asserting that the church "represents" the City of God "even though the latter cannot be identified with the ecclesiastical organization" (190). It is difficult to say exactly what Sabine was referring to with the phrase "Christian commonwealth." I presume that it referred, at least in part, to the "Christianized empire" of the next page. In any case, we do find Sabine endorsing the claim of James Bryce that "the theory of the Holy Roman Empire was built upon Augustine's City of God" and we do find him talking about Augustine's espousal of the notion of "a Christian state" (191–92).

given the idea of a partial identification—i.e., in the relationship of agent representation—of the city of God with the Church.

But what about the other basic member of the Two Cities, the City of Earth? Do we have any textual license to *identify* the state *qua* state and the City of Earth? In dealing with this question, I think an *a priori* move might prove helpful: I would suggest that we try to develop a parallel between the institutional church in its relation to the City of God and the state in its relation to the City of Earth. On these *a priori* grounds, we could rule out the relationship of simple identification. Moreover, Figgis' notion of a symbolic relationship would appear warranted—as the text, at a number of points, would confirm. (For example, Cain, who is the first man to be a citizen of the City of Earth, also founded the first city. He was a fratricide, as was Romulus, who founded Rome. [See XV.1, p. 479; XV.8, pp. 488–89; XV.5, pp. 482–83.].) Finally, the idea of some sort of agent representation would, on *a priori* grounds, appear appropriate.[10]

The question is, How would this representation take shape? At what point(s) would the identity hold? For an answer I think we can revert to the passage where Augustine spoke of Two Cities formed by two loves, "the earthly by love of self." There are many forms of self-love, of concern for the things of this life, that could be cited but the one Augustine specifically mentions is the "love of ruling." Obviously, this is a notion relevant to politics. But does it imply that the state as such, through the love of ruling, specifically represents the City of Earth? I do not think it was the state *per se* that Augustine had in mind, for he says, "In the one, the princes and the nations it subdues are ruled by the love of ruling" (XIV.28, p. 477).

It is not the state as such, i.e., any particular state taken at random or all of them taken together, but the *imperial state* that peculiarly represents the City of Earth. The imperial state (e.g., Assyria, Egypt, Rome) plays a role toward the City of Earth analogous to that played by the institutional church towards the City of God. This basic parallelism descends even to details. The translation of empire theme, which we have already noted in relation to the church, is found also in the succession of the great earthly empires (for example, XVIII.21, p.627).

It has been observed by Figgis (p.53) and Deane (p.171), in particular, that Augustine was personally an anti-imperialist. (See, for

[10]It is interesting to note that Figgis will allow only a "symbolic" representation of the City of God by the church, and Deane not even this; but the relationship between the City of Earth and the State is treated, in each case, in a non-parallel fashion. Deane, for example, suggests that "states of this world are in some sense regarded as *parts* of the earthly city" (31, italics added; see also Deane, 30, and Figgis, 51, and 58).

example, IV.15, p.123.)[11] However, the connection of this attitude to the notion that the imperial state "represents" the City of Earth has not been sufficiently noted. At several points Augustine asserts the essential similarity of all imperial states in their motivation by love of domination and their imposition of rule by war and force, and asserts the connection of this feature of imperial states with what he called the City of Earth, a connection such that we could call these great imperial states the exemplars and institutional representatives of the City of Earth. The earthly city is the city of earthly "loves" or lusts and the master lust is the lust of domination. This lust is a form of pride; it is the pride which apes God himself. This, then, is the principle of the imperial state in its role as the agent representative of the City of Earth: "The earthly city, . . . though it be mistress of the nations, is itself ruled by its lust of rule" (I. preface, p.3; also V.19).

The notion of a basic parallelism within the Two Cities concept is, I think, substantially sound. Sabine puts the institutional aspect of the parallelism well: "Augustine did think of the Kingdom of evil as at least *represented* by the pagan empires, though not exactly identified with them. He also thought of the church as *representing* the City of God, even though the latter cannot be identified with the ecclesiastical organization" (p.190; italics added).

My analysis of Augustine's political philosophy is based on the claim that he does not *identify* either of the Two Cities with institutions on earth. The two cities have a simple corporate character and identity only beyond the Final Judgment, in Heaven and Hell. With respect to this world, the concept of the Two Cities refers primarily to two types or classifications of men. However, I have argued that there are earthly institutions that "represent" and do the work of the two cities in human history: the imperial states are special embodiments of the City of Earth and, after the advent of Christ, the institutional church is the unique and indispensable representative of the City of God.

[11]Augustine had an ambivalent attitude toward the Romans' acquisition of empire. He does not trace it simply to the love of ruling but, also, includes the provocations of Rome's neighbors among the causes of empire. The empire accrued to Rome in part as the result of fighting "just wars" (IV.15, p. 123; Augustine makes this same point at III.10, p. 81). He also provides a special reason (or cause) for Rome's empire: God "helped forward the Romans, who were good according to a certain standard of an earthly state" (V.19, p. 173). At another point he says that by Rome "God was pleased to conquer the whole world, and subdue it far and wide by bringing it into one fellowship of government and laws" (XVIII.22, p. 628; also XIX.7, p. 683). It is, in the light of this, understandable that Augustine would be reluctant to accept the "fall" of Rome (see IV.7, p. 115). The hold of the Roman myth was powerful on its loyal subjects, Christian and pagan.

This conception of the institutional church as the special representative of the City of God allows us neither to dismiss nor to validate the notion of a Christianized state. For it is possible that the church might appropriate some sort of political apparatus for its own purposes just as the Hebrew nation had generated a state, the Hebrew Kingdom. The issue remains open. On the other hand, it is the *imperial* state, and not the state as such, that represents the City of Earth. This fact will allow us to dispense with any identification, whole or partial, of the state *per se* with the "earthly City."[12] In short, the concept of the Two Cities on its own, although it provides the superstructure of Augustine's political doctrines, does not give us all the essential details of Augustine's political philosophy. In particular, the concept does not provide us with sufficient information to determine Augustine's notion of the nature and role of justice in the state, or to establish whether Augustine was advocating the notion of a Christianized state. It does not, in fact, provide us even with Augustine's conception of the state, since any essential link between the state as such and the City of Earth has been broken.

Exception could well be taken to my claim. It has been pointed out, for example, that Cain, the germ of the City of Earth, founded the first town. But even if we allow that this first city is the first state, I would ask what we might conclude about the *nature* of the state. For the crucial question is, What is the nature of the state in Augustine's opinion? The connoisseur of the *City of God* might here invite attention to one of Augustine's most famous political passages, the one that begins: "Justice being taken away, then [*Remota itaque iustitia*], what are kingdoms but great robberies? For what are robberies themselves, but little kingdoms?" and ends: "Indeed that was an apt and true reply which was given to Alexander the Great by a pirate who had been seized. For when that king had asked the man what he meant by keeping hostile possession of the sea, he answered with bold pride, 'What thou meanest by seizing the whole earth; but because I do it with a petty ship, I am called a robber, whilst thou who dost it with a great fleet art styled emperor' " (IV.4, pp.112–13).

I would suggest, however, the importance of considering this pas-

[12]Insofar as Augustine can be said to be concerned with the political state as such, I think we can say that he saw the state *qua* state as belonging to the things of this world, as distinct from the things of heaven. Certainly this much can be read into Augustine's oft repeated observation that Cain founded the first city (XV.1, p. 479). This, together with the fact that Augustine pointed Abel out as a shepherd, not as a ruler of men, indicates that Augustine did not regard the rule of man over men as part of the economy of Eden.

sage in its context, as many commentators have failed to do (e.g., Carlyle, McIlwain, d'Entrèves). Its context is precisely that discussion of imperial states and their imaging forth of the City of Earth in their "lust for domination" which I have been discussing. (Indeed, the most extended treatment of the theme of the imperial state is found in Book IV of the *City of God.*) I suggest that the context of this passage is crucial, that the systematic import of the passage is overlooked if the context is ignored, and that we obtain a very different reading of it if we keep these points in mind. Let us read the passage as being, not about justice in Kingdoms, but about the nature of imperial states. Augustine can be taken as saying: set the issue of justice aside, for imperial states are not particularly just. They are really nothing but big robber bands. While robber bands and empires do have certain features in common with the conventionally more acceptable political arrangements (all have princes, pacts of confederation, binding rules), the crucial point they have in common is how they do their business: by imposition. In principle there is no difference: if a robber band could take possession of cities and subdue people, it would be an imperial state. What makes an imperial state is not that the gang is rid of the robber instinct but, rather, that they have gotten too big to be called to account.

The force of this reading of IV.4, as being about the nature of the *imperial* state, is brought out not just from the general context but also from the explicit reference to empire on which the passage concludes and, finally, from a passage which comes in another chapter shortly after. Here we find Augustine explicitly linking Rome to Assyria and ultimately tying in both, as imperial states, with the City of Earth; he concludes the chapter, speaking of the Assyrians, on this note: "But to make war on your neighbors and thence to proceed to others, and through mere lust of dominion to crush and subdue people who do you no harm, what else is this to be called than great robbery?" (IV.6, p.114). It would seem that this passage clearly refers back (in the phrase "great robbery") to IV.4. But, more important, the passage connects IV.4 with the theme of the imperial state (Assyria and Rome) and the essential tie-in of the imperial state, through the "lust of dominion," to the City of Earth. (See also, for examples of this complex linkage, IV.7, p.114; XVI.17, pp.541–42, XVII.2, pp. 610–11.)

In saying all this I am not meaning to suggest that Augustine's discussion of the "Kingdom" and the "removal of justice" has no political bearing beyond the imperial state theme at all. If we make a distinction between an imperial state and a "domestic" state, I think it would be true to say that Augustine's discussion does have a bearing on the latter as well. But what that is exactly can be brought out more clearly by relating it to Augustine's discussion of Cicero's definition of the "commonwealth" (*res publica*).[13] At the same time, in turning to this discussion of "commonwealth," we shall be able to remedy certain defects mentioned earlier in our discussion of Augustine's political philosophy by rounding out the political meaning of his Two Cities.

Cicero's famous "definition" of the ideal political community is given in his *Republic* through his spokesman Scipio.

> Well, then, a commonwealth is the property of a people (*res publica res populi*). But a people is not any collection of human beings brought together in any sort of way, but an assemblage of people in large numbers associated in an agreement with respect to justice (*iuris consensu*) and a partnership for the common good.

This definition can be effectively divided into two basic political ideals: (1) law and justice and (2) the common good. [14] Augustine takes up this definition at two points in the *City of God*, in Book II and Book XIX.

In II.21, pp.60–63, he begins by claiming that Cicero himself had said that "even in his time [the Roman republic] had become entirely extinct, and that there remained extant no Roman republic at all" (p.60). Now, the natural question is why Cicero would say this, and Augustine leads up to answering this question. Scipio is cited as saying that the concord (i.e., "concord of the upper, lower, and middle classes") which is required in a republic "by no ingenuity can be retained where justice has become extinct" (p.61). Indeed, according to Augustine, Scipio asserts that a republic "cannot be governed without the most absolute justice [*summa iustitia*]" (p.61). Here Augustine, who is following Cicero's own text closely (*De Republica*, pp.67, 183,

[13]The term *res publica* is normally translated either as "republic" (which is etymologically related to it) or as "commonwealth." Since "republic" has misleading connotations and since "commonwealth" conveys more in the way of content, this latter term seems preferable. See A. P. d'Entrèves, *The Notion of the State* (Oxford, 1967), 28–35, esp. 33, and, 75, n. 2.

[14]Cicero, *De Republica*, trans. by C. W. Keyes (Cambridge, Mass., 1928), 65. Cicero emphasizes the primacy of justice in his definition: "For what is a state except a partnership in justice" (77). D'Entrèves has raised the interesting question whether Cicero's *iuris consensu* should be translated "agreement with respect to justice," as many translators (including Keyes) have it, or, alternatively, as "consent to law" (d'Entrèves, 24, n.2). I have seen one translation that renders the phrase "agreement about rights." In English the difference in sense is striking and the whole meaning of the passage would appear to change, depending on which of these renderings was used. However, the Latin *iuris*, whether it is translated justice or law, conveys the basic notion of moral right or rightness. Hence, even if we translate the term as "law," it has the connotative force of "just law" or "law according to justice." (See d'Entrèves, 75–77.) This same point could be derived, philosophically, by noting that Cicero grounds civil law in justice and ultimately in "right reason" or "natural law": *De Legibus* (Keyes translation), 317, 345, 381, 385, and *De Republica*, 211. Augustine, to all appearances, takes *iuris* as meaning *iustitia* (justice); although his argument would go through if it were put in terms of "rights" as well.

and 219), points out that Scipio later "repeats with commendation his own brief definition of a republic" and that Scipio goes on to argue that a "republic, or 'weal of the people,' then exists only when it is well and justly governed, whether by a monarch, or an aristocracy, or by the whole people" (p.61). Augustine, then, paraphrases the conclusion of Scipio (Cicero): a republic given over to injustice is "not only blemished . . . but by legitimate deduction from those definitions, it altogether ceases to be" (pp.61–62).

Augustine's point is ultimately a *moral* one. His claim is simply that Cicero (through his spokesman Scipio) regarded the "morality of the community" as essential to a republic (by making justice and the common good part of its "definition"), and that the Rome of Cicero's day had lost this morality to the degree that Cicero himself regarded it as no longer a republic. But at this point Augustine strikes a new note. He suggests that, perhaps, Cicero and other admirers of the antique Roman republic have failed to inquire "whether, even in the days of primitive men and morals, true justice flourished in it; or was it not perhaps even then, to use the casual expression of Cicero, rather a colored painting than the living reality" (pp.62–63). But Augustine immediately adds that he will "consider this elsewhere," and then briefly indicates what he will take up later on.

He wants, first, to show that by Cicero's own definition Rome was *never* a republic "because true justice had never a place in it." But, second, Augustine says that a "more feasible" (*probabiliores*) definition than Cicero's would allow us to say, as Cicero had wanted to say, that "there was a republic of a certain kind, and certainly much better administered by the more ancient Romans than by their modern representatives." Finally, Augustine wishes to show that "true justice has no existence save in that republic whose founder and ruler is Christ, if at least any choose to call this a republic; and indeed we cannot deny that it is the people's weal. But if perchance this name [republic], which has become familiar in other connections, be considered alien to our common parlance, we may at all events say that in this city is true justice; the city of which Holy Scripture says, 'Glorious things are said of thee, O city of God' " (all passages:II.21, p.63).

Augustine's new points, which he promised to develop later on, are taken up again in Book XIX. Before I turn to his remarks there, I think it would be helpful to note certain things that can serve as guidelines in working our way into Augustine's own position. First, I think it clear that Augustine in II.21 has not been talking about *the* state as such but rather about a more specialized notion, that of the republic, with particular reference to the Roman republic. Again, it is clear that "republic" is not a descriptive term but primarily an evaluative term denoting a principle, that of the "weal of the people." Second, the evaluative point that Augustine wanted to make is put in terms of "true justice," as differentiated, presumably, from Cicero's idea of justice. What historic Rome lacked is "true justice" but the "republic whose founder and ruler is Christ" has it. But, third, this true republic—and Augustine is reluctant to call it a republic at all—is better called, he tells us, the City of God. This might be taken as the looked for textual evidence which would proclaim a politicized church in some sort of Christianized State. But I think the context ought to govern our judgment here. We have already been told that the state, the Roman or any other, is not going to be Christianized: rather "the people of Christ . . . are enjoined to endure [not take over] this earthly republic, wicked and dissolute as it is" so they can "win for themselves" a place among the "assembly of angels" in that "republic of heaven" where "God's will is law" (see II.19, p.59). The "true republic" is clearly this "republic of heaven" or heavenly City of God, which Augustine is reluctant to call by a political name at all (like "republic") since it is not even of this earth, let alone a political state.

There is, I think, an obvious but implicit dichotomy introduced here: between the "earthly republic" and the heavenly, between the political and the celestial city, between the temporal-historical and the eternal-divine, between philosophical and theological categories, as it were.

Finally, I think we can take Augustine as endorsing Cicero's distinction between the antique republic (existing before Christ and the Roman emperors and coming to an end in Cicero's own day) and Rome's "modern representatives," which include the Romans of the imperial state, under the emperor, of Augustine's own day. Rather than contrasting the Christianized State with the pagan state, Augustine was indicating that he favored the antique Roman State, which was pagan, over the "modern" Roman empire in which Christianity was established! But we have no paradox here, if we allow that Augustine's basic distinction was between the "republic of heaven" and the "earthly republic."

It is important, in this context, to note that Augustine nowhere makes an explicit distinction between heathen and Christian states (see Deane, 123). This fact in itself and his obvious preference for the antique Roman republic, which is repeated at XIX.24, p.706, make it difficult to see how the Christianized State interpretation has come to have the credibility that it has in recent scholarship.[15] That Augustine should prefer the earlier republic of Rome over the later empire is, unlike the basic distinction between the "earthly republic" and the

[15]Augustine's basic attitude towards politics, following the Pauline tradition, is passive, negative, almost indifferent. It would seem that one could hardly advocate the Christianized State on the one hand and say, on the other, "What does it matter under

heavenly, not grounded on theological considerations. It is a political preference, and a regard for the grounds of this preference is crucial where we are concerned with his political philosophy.

It is important in analyzing Augustine's reformulation, in Book XIX, of Cicero's definition of a commonwealth to separate the theological from the political motif. Theologically, Augustine seems to have two motives in undertaking his reformulation: (1) to show that *true* justice depends on the correct apprehension and worship of God, and (2) to suggest that no secular or political state could claim to be a true commonwealth because it could not institutionalize true justice and ultimately would not serve the true common weal of men.[16]

The key to his political point is provided in Augustine's proposed alternative definition of the commonwealth:

> A people is an assemblage of reasonable beings bound together by a common agreement as to the objects of their love; then, in order to discover the character of any people, we have only to observe what they love. Yet whatever it loves, if only it is an assemblage of reasonable beings and not of beasts, and is bound together by an agreement as to the objects of love, it is reasonably called a people; and it will be a superior people in proportion as it is bound together by higher interests, inferior in proportion as it is bound together by lower. According to this definition of ours, the Roman people is a people, and its weal is without doubt a commonwealth or republic (XIX.24, p.706).

This new definition is, presumably, the "more feasible" definition which Augustine had promised in II.21 and it is a definition which

---

whose government a dying man lives [and we are all dying men], if those who govern do not force him to impiety and iniquity?" (V.17, p. 166). This observation would appear to be doubly telling against those who assert that Augustine wanted to turn the whole body of true saints (the "individualistic" city of God) into a *political state*. See, for example, Otto Butz, *Of Man and Politics* (New York, 1964), 60–62 and G. Combès, quoted in Deane, 303, n.67. Indeed, to attempt to institutionalize the "individualistic" city in any way on earth is what Gilbert Ryle would call a category mistake.

[16]Augustine's *primary* reasons for challenging Cicero's definition are theological, not political. This interpretation can be confirmed by the text of Augustine's argument.

(a) As to justice he says: "There is no republic where there is no justice. Further, justice is that virtue which gives every one his due. Where, then, is the justice of man, when he deserts the true God and yields himself to impure demons? Is this to give every one his due? Or is he who keeps back a piece of ground from the purchaser, and gives it to a man who has no right to it unjust, while he who keeps back himself from the God who made him, and serves wicked spirits, is just?" (XIX.21, p. 699).

(b) Augustine repeats his charge at a later point: "For in general, the city of the ungodly, which did not obey the command of God that it should offer no sacrifice save to Him alone . . . is void of true justice" (XIX.24, p. 706).

(c) As to the common good Augustine says: "And why need I speak of the advantageousness, the common participation in which, according to the definition [of Cicero] makes a people? . . . If you choose to regard the matter attentively, you will see that there is nothing advantageous to those who live godlessly, as every one lives who does not serve God but demons" (XIX.21, p. 700).

Augustine acknowledges as his own.[17] But why is Augustine's own definition so radically different from Cicero's? Why didn't he stick, basically, to Cicero's definition? He could, for example, have amended Cicero's definition easily enough. He could have said that "true justice" and the "true weal" of men are not political goods at all; they are appropriate only to the church as a community of the righteous. In the final analysis, the only "true republic" that, by strict Ciceronian definition, could ever exist is the Kingdom of Heaven, the celestial city of God; and this is not in human history at all. However, he could have added that certain *moral* qualities, like justice and concern for common well-being, qualities that are radically imperfect over against "true justice" might still serve to *define* a political "commonwealth."[18] Why did Augustine not retain Cicero's definition and footnote it, as it were, to draw the basic differentiation between a correct theological and a correct political usage of the terms "republic," "justice," and "well-being"?

In answering this question I shall argue that Augustine's departure from Cicero is more apparent than real. Cicero had wanted to distinguish a republic from a tyranny, the crux of the differentiation being *justice*. Why justice? Because Cicero thought that justice is the cement that binds a state, made up of different classes, into a harmonious whole (see *De Republica*, 75, 183). In other words justice belongs to the *definition* of a "republic" because what a republic is, a *res populi*, i.e., partnership of classes, requires justice in order to exist. In short, without justice the orders (classes) would clash, and there would be no social harmony and no "commonwealth." Cicero's evaluation is that a concord of the classes, a *res populi* or republic, is the highest political good and he claims that justice, since it is *factually*

[17]This definition is consistent with what Augustine had said earlier and in a less litigious context: "A civic community . . . is nothing else than a multitude of men bound together by some associating tie" (XV.8, p. 489; also I.15, p. 21). Similar statements can be found in Augustine's letters and other works. Although Augustine developed his new "definition" in response to Cicero and with respect to historic Rome, he intended it to be applied generally: to every society "which had a public government" insofar as the basic sense of the definition ("reasonable beings bound together by a common agreement as to the objects of love") could be satisfied (XIX.24, p. 706).

[18]One of the most important features of Deane's analysis is to show that Augustine made an explicit distinction between "true justice" (*vera iustitia*) and an "image" (*imago*) of justice: Deane, 96–103, esp. 98, 125. If Augustine were to make the point that "true justice" is not a political category, it would *not* follow that justice (i.e., the "image of justice") did not belong in the "definition" of the republic. So far as I can tell, Deane is the first one to insist on the importance for Augustine's political theory of this distinction. The failure of Carlyle, Figgis, McIlwain, and Sabine to draw the distinction introduces a serious distortion into their analysis; in addition, Carlyle and McIlwain did not seem sufficiently alert to the fact that Augustine was concerned with a *definition*.

necessary to social peace and harmony, belongs to the basic agenda of any republic.

This is the way that justice gets into Cicero's definition of the republic. But here we are using "definition" in an extended sense. It includes a definition in the strict sense: the statement "republic = df. *res populi* or social partnership." And it includes a non-definitional element as well; the factual claim that the practice of justice is necessary for the existence of a harmony of the classes. Further, I think it worth noting that the content of this extended definition can be looked at either descriptively (we can describe and, presumably, verify a harmony of the classes) or evaluatively (a harmony of the orders is the highest political good).[19]

Augustine's new "definition" follows this pattern of analysis quite closely. Augustine's basic distinction is drawn between a republic and a "kingdom" of the robber band variety. Now these terms do not denote constitutional entities but, rather, principles of political and social organization. A republic is a matter of "common agreement" (which recalls Cicero's harmony of social classes) but a kingdom or regime (*regnum*) is not organized on the principle of agreement but, rather, on the principle of imposition from above. And this recalls Cicero's notion of tyranny where social harmony was replaced by the dictatorship of one man over all or of one class over the others. The only difference of any apparent importance, and it is really incidental at this point, is that Cicero's notion of popular concurrence referred to a harmony of social classes whereas that same notion in Augustine referred to a harmony of individual persons, without reference to class.

Regimes or kingdoms are structured on the principle of the lust of domination. They are in essence exactly like imperial states, and this is why the word "kingdom" (*regnum*) can be indifferently applied either to imperial states or to "domestic" regimes. The only difference is that imperial states lord it over subject peoples who were once independently organized politically while "domestic" *regna* are juntas that rule over other men in a single state. In either case a *regnum*, be it an imperial state or a regime ruling in a state, is not the property of

[19]Cicero apparently thought that a harmony of the classes (i.e., the ideal of a *res publica*) could best be achieved in a "mixed constitution," one which combines a monarchial element with a consultative senate and a popular assembly: *De Republica*, 71, 83, 105, 125, 151, 179. His analysis is somewhat hard to follow since he sometimes uses terms designative of political institutions (like "kingship" or "senate") and sometimes class terms (like "leading citizens" or "the masses"). Indeed, much of the vocabulary of classical political philosophy is ambiguous on this score: for example, "aristocracy" and "democracy" have both an institutional and a class reference. In any case, Cicero's intent seems clear enough, despite the ambiguity; and his precise position on this question of the constitution is not an issue in this paper, since it has no exact correlate in Augustine's political philosophy.

the people but of their masters. I think Augustine's political philosophy rests on two fundamental distinctions: the one between the heavenly city of God and the "earthly republic"; the other, within the "earthly republic," between a *res publica* and a *regnum*. But the nature of this latter distinction requires further mapping.

The distinction of *regnum/res publica* is drawn by McIlwain (see p.156 where he puts *civitates* and *regna* on one side, over against *res publicae* on the other). McIlwain's point is, I think, fundamental but his way of drawing it is defective. First, he treats it as a terminological distinction which Augustine explicitly drew, whereas I suggest that Augustine's distinction was not drawn at the terminological level at all. Second, he treats the distinction as having to do with *kinds* of states, not so much constitutional kinds as religious kinds (pagan/Christian).[20] But I would assert that Augustine is not contrasting kinds of states but rather, polar political styles, principles of political organization. His distinction is drawn by preference and reflects the grounds on which the preference is based.

If anything is clear, it is that Augustine regards a state organized on the principle of "common agreement" as preferable to one organized on the principle of subjection. This is clear for the simple reason that Augustine endorses the first principle (for it is the principle of organization in Augustine's own definition), and the principle of subjection he condemned (in IV.4) as nothing better than a "grand robbery." I regard the crucial point of difference between these principles, i.e., the difference between agreement and imposition, as the ground of his basic evaluation. And it is a *political* evaluation (for there is here no contrast intended between the divine and the political but, rather, only between the political good and the political bad).[21]

It is also clear from other passages that Augustine took a negative

[20]Deane rejects McIlwain's distinction of *regnum/res publica* because he does not see that Augustine uses his terms in the way McIlwain has indicated: Deane, 297, n.28. Even more objectionable is the interpretation McIlwain puts on the distinction once he has drawn it terminologically. He says that all pagan states are *regna*, since they are, as pagan, deprived of justice but that republics would have the quality of justice; and he suggests, but does not say, that a Christianized State would be a republic. Even so, I think the distinction of *regnum/res publica*, if interpreted along the lines I am suggesting, can be used to point to a genuine principle of distinction in Augustine's political thought.

[21]D'Entrèves construes Augustine as offering a value-neutral definition of the *state* (23–27). This view is, I think, mistaken. The whole notion of a "republic" was introduced and discussed in an evaluative way. In contrast to d'Entrèves I would say that Augustine was "defining" a "republic," where that term referred to a political value which could be exemplified or not in any state. The very notion of a republic, as we find it in XIX.21, for example, is itself an entirely favorably evaluated notion. (For additional discussion, see d'Entrèves' chapter, "The State—A Neologism," 28–36.)

view, morally, of the whole principle of imposition and subjection. He speaks of robbers who "invade the peace of other men" and ultimately would have a city or nation "submit itself" to their brigand's peace in a passage (XIX.12, p.687), recalling his earlier robber band passage (in IV.4). He also speaks of "wicked men [who] wage war to maintain the peace of their own circle, and wish that, if possible, all men belonged to them, that all men and things might serve but one head, and might, either through love or fear, yield themselves to peace with [them]! It is thus that pride in its perversity apes God. It abhors equality with other men under [God]; but, instead of His rule, it seeks to impose a rule of its own upon its equals" (XIX.12, p.689).

We have then, in Augustine's theory, two basic kinds of political values in the organization of states: the community principle, defined by basic social agreement, and the regime principle, defined by an imposed order. However, Augustine's evaluations do not end here, for he recognizes that human freedom (in its political form, i.e., common agreement as to desired political ends) can have a variety of objects. And these objects will themselves vary in moral quality, "higher interests" as opposed to "lower." What Augustine called "true justice" can never be an interest or object of the state (at least, Augustine never allowed that it could). Even strict Ciceronian justice might be unattainable, for Augustine appears to believe that human justice, with or without a proper relationship to God, would always be imperfect, even when judged by internal or human standards, like those of Cicero (XIX.23–27, pp. 705–08). But if a state were to dedicate itself to some attainable "image of justice" (but not to the impossible goal of "true justice") then presumably it would have chosen a "higher interest." Or we might infer that, if a state were to undertake certain tasks in the interest of the church, as, for example, the use of its coercive power in the maintenance of the doctrines and discipline of the church, then that would be a "higher interest." If we interpret the Christianized State notion as meaning, not that a republic can only be a Christian state or that political justice is ultimately a theological and ecclesiastical category, but simply that service to the church is a political good (a "higher interest"), then Augustine might be said to hold this notion.[22]

Whether the highest attainable political goal is service to the church or an image of justice, I will not venture to say. But if a commonwealth can have "lower" interests and still remain a commonwealth, then it

[22]Augustine came, rather reluctantly and rather late, to advocate state coercion of heretics and the suppression of schism by political means. See his *Correction of the Donatists*, in *Works* (trans. J. R. King; Edinburgh, 1872), III, esp. 485; also the very excellent chapter 6 on heresy by Deane, 172–220.

is clear that virtues like justice (i.e., an "image of justice") or service to the church are not essential to its being a commonwealth, although such virtues may be essential to its merit as a commonwealth. The "image of justice," although it is a high aspiration, is not—perhaps for that very reason—necessary to maintain the conditions for the *existence* of the commonwealth. Justice belongs then (in Reinhold Niebuhr's phrase) "not to the *esse* but to the *bene esse* of the commonwealth."

There may be, however, something other than justice that is essential to the very existence of a commonwealth as defined, and, hence, that belongs of necessity on its agenda. This is, of course, a question of fact. Put in this way, it would seem that Augustine's conclusion is not difficult to fathom. What does belong to its basic agenda, according to him, is peace.

> The earthly city, which does not live by faith, seeks an earthly peace, and the end it proposes, in the well-ordered concord of civil obedience and rule, is the combination of men's wills to attain the things which are helpful to this life. The heavenly city [on earth] makes use of this peace only because it must, until this mortal condition which necessitates it shall pass away. . . . [The heavenly city] makes no scruple to obey the laws of the earthly city, whereby the things necessary for the maintenance of this mortal life are administered; and thus, as this life is common to both cities, so there is a harmony between them in regard to what belongs to [this mortal life] (XIX. 17, pp.695–96).

Augustine's notion of peace is complex, but if we take it just in reference to the theme of commonwealth, I think it is clear that he meant it to be more than simply "law and order," the policemen's peace. It does, however, include the suppression of civil commotion and riot; but if this were all, there would be no ultimate distinction between a commonwealth and a regime. Rather what he points to is a "well-ordered concord" in which obedience follows from a rational conception of permanent and mutual interests and not from fear and repression. Augustine says, "The peace of all things is the tranquillity of order. Order is the distribution which allots things equal and unequal, each to its own place" (XIX.13, p.690). At the basis of the Augustinian commonwealth is "order," which requires a rough, pragmatic, but effective "distribution." The Augustinian minimum political agenda is *Pax, ordo, lex, societas*.[23] Under his new definition of commonwealth, the necessary condition for one to exist is "the tranquillity of order."

How different, really, is this "tranquillity of order" from Ciceronian justice? Not very. What ultimately divides the two men,

[23]Ernest Barker, "Introduction" to J. Healey's translation of the *City of God* (London, Everyman, 1947) I, xxvii.

after we make the true justice/image of justice distinction, is a fine line. Augustine's "tranquillity of order" can be achieved with a rough and ready justice (i.e., imperfect even by human standards). It does not require an "absolute justice," in Cicero's phrase. If Ciceronian justice (strict fair dealing between men and between classes, giving to each his own) is an "image" of the "true justice," then Augustinian justice (the "order" requisite to tranquillity) is an image of this image. The degree to which Augustine has moved from Cicero is marked in this proposition: the true test of any state is an appropriate tranquillity.

This marks a difference, a relative devaluation of strict justice in favor of a lesser but more comprehensive good, civil peace. But it is not a rejection of justice as a political category, as Carlyle seemed to think, or of the need for some sort of rough justice; rather, it is a prudential appeal to the strictly necessary conditions for the continuing existence of the "republican" political style.[24]

Augustine's point here is simply a factual one, as was Cicero's, but they differ as to the facts. Cicero thought that a strict justice was required for the existence of a people's state (*res populi*). Augustine believed that a less than strict or perfect justice, i.e., by human standards, was required as a matter of fact. The "tranquillity of order" replaces "absolute" justice on the basic agenda for the commonwealth and this shift is reflected in the difference between Cicero's "definition" of a republic and Augustine's own "more feasible" one.[25]

Augustine's real break with Cicero came, not on the "definition" of the commonwealth (for they agree that it is a matter of popular concurrence in *res populi*) nor on the empirical determination of its necessary conditions (for the difference here is only one of degree and

[24]Carlyle seemed to hold the view that Augustine, in effect, simply got rid of the notion of justice as a political category: A. J. Carlyle, *A History of Medieval Political Theory in the West* (New York, originally published in 1903) I, 170, 174. Carlyle regarded this as quite momentous, out of line with literally centuries of earlier and subsequent political thought (see 169, 221). At the same time Carlyle is bemused that "Augustine seems to take the matter lightly" (166). And he was even led to conclude in another place that Augustine may not have "realized the enormous significance of what he was saying," in F. J. C. Hearnshaw, ed., *Social and Political Ideas of Some Great Medieval Thinkers* (London, 1923), 50. But I would suggest that all this represents too simplistic a reading of Augustine's text.

[25]Figgis, of course, recognizes the important role peace plays in Augustine's political thought but he does not see that what Augustine meant by peace (the "tranquillity of order") is essentially continuous with Ciceronian justice (62–64). Deane, on the other hand, tends to *equate* Augustinian peace with what Augustine called the "image" of justice (125, 136). I do not think there is adequate textual warrant for Deane's treatment; moreover, it makes the difference between Augustine's definition and that of Cicero, admittedly more apparent than real, wholly inexplicable. I would suggest that Augustine's "peace" and Cicero's "justice" do differ in name but that they point to the same kind of thing; the only difference between them is one of degree.

of vocabulary), but on the question of the moral status of politics. Cicero, like the great classical political philosophers Plato and Aristotle, had idealized politics. Politics had as its end the highest human good; the state was, in principle, morally adequate to men. Men could realize their true end in political association: in Aristotle's famous phrase, man is a "political animal." Cicero's emphasis on strict or absolute justice was symptomatic of this basic evaluation just as Augustine's devaluation of justice as a political necessity was symptomatic of a different evaluation.

The point is that Augustine rejected the classical idealization of the state; this is far more central than how he stood on Cicero's definition. There is a gulf of radical discontinuity between Augustine and classical politics. In this sense, Augustine can be said to have written an anti-politics. His program was to put the things of this world, even the best of states, under the things of the next, to commit oneself wholly only to what is absolute, to idealize nothing. Christian political philosophy, like the Christian himself, is a stranger here below; it can be in the world but not of it. The good state, the "republic" with meritorious common interests, can be pointed out, but the state is not a church and the church should not become a state. The church must look beyond, to the heavenly republic. This is the basic truth of the Christian religion, as it must be the constant theme of Christian political philosophy. This is, I think, the political theme of the *City of God*. It is the political meaning of the concept of the Two Cities.

University of Kansas.

[4]

THE ORIGIN AND DYNAMICS OF SOCIETY AND THE STATE ACCORDING TO ST. AUGUSTINE

PART I

D.J. MacQueen

Status Quaestionis

THERE HAS long been an urgent need for a monograph dealing with St. Augustine's doctrine of the state, its origins and its structure. Our opening remark may come as a surprise—or even, indeed, as something of a shock—to those nurtured on G. Combès' *La Doctrine politique de saint Augustin*, a study which until comparatively recent times, has dominated the field without any serious rival. But this work, perhaps in part because of its scope, is flawed—*inter alia*—by an inexcusably large number of incorrect references and interpretations. Among the latter one might instance the unequivocal assertion (*op. cit.* pp. 192-95): Augustine *condemned* torture. What a pity that Combes' dictum, so attractively convincing in its agreement with the evidence given, turns out—when all the texts are sifted—to be no more than a painful half-truth![1] In the event, *he* is the authority in whose name Etienne Gilson repeatedly declares that "Augustine was *always* a foe of . . . torture" (italics added: see *The Christian Philosophy of Saint Augustine*, p. 332, fn. 58, *ad fin.*).[1a] In 1952 R. T. Marshall published his dissertation entitled: *Studies in the Political and Socio-Religious Terminology of the de Civitate Dei*, thus breaking the ground for a preliminary analysis of this topic in English. Two years later appeared H. X. Arquilliere's *L'Augustinisme politique. Essai sur la Formation des Théories politiques au moyen Age*—a treatise which (as its title indicates) is mainly concerned with the repercussions of Augustine's political teaching upon medieval Europe.

---

[1] It is quite clear that Augustine does NOT condemn the use of torture in secular legal procedures. His reasons for this attitude are explained at length in *de civitate Dei* XIX, 6; PL 41, 632-33. It is no less clear that he abhors such physical coercion in ecclesiastical tribunals or inquiries connected with Donatist outrages (*epist.* 104, 4, 17). For the Roman judicial background involved, consult J. A. Crook, *Law and Life of Rome*, pp. 274-75; also the *Oxford Classical Dictionary*, Torture [1081-82].

[1a] Cf. Gilson's *Introduction à l'Étude de saint Augustin*, p. 231, fn. 4 (*ad fin.*).

By far the most important recent analysis, in any language, of the Bishop's notions about society and politics, Herbert Deane's *The Political and Social Ideas of St. Augustine* continues to enjoy a deservedly high reputation: to its author accordingly, every student must acknowledge his debt and express due admiration. At the same time there are some points at which (to quote Deane himself), "we shall have to indicate reservations or objections to (Dean's) interpretations of Augustine's political doctrines" (*op. cit.* p. 302). In a slightly different framework of reference, several "reservations" or "objections" on our part to these political doctrines (as interpreted by Deane), have already seen the light of day.[1b] With regard to the inquiry now before us, it may suffice (at this stage of the argument), to voice a suspicion that Deane has not correctly understood how Augustine is able to reconcile, within the unity of a single, coherent concept, what seem to be two mutually exclusive propositions. Of these the first is: the riches of the whole world belong to the faithful man, while the infidel has not even a farthing. The second proposition reads (and we again translate): God has distributed (the rights of ownership and possession) to mankind through the emperors and kings of this world.[2] It is surely obvious that the very nature, function and administrative powers of the secular state are involved in this crux, however it be resolved. A further important problem, connected with the above, and to which Deane (so far as we can see) has likewise devoted no attention), might be formulated thus: in what sense, if any, is the state—for Augustine—an institution of the "natural order", like, e.g. marriage? This question of course implicates the various nuances of meaning distinguished by him in his use of the respective key-words *natura*, *ordo* and *lex* (*ius*). It is perfectly true that Professor Deane does treat each of these four vocabulary items carefully and in detail. Yet he nowhere seems to come to grips with the vital issues raised, for example, so explicitly and clearly by R. A. Markus in his new thought-provoking study, *Saeculum*, as regards varying senses of these same terms.[3] Can it be that Deane is not even aware of the problem?

Introduction.

For better or worse, St. Augustine produced neither a *de regimine principum* nor any related treatise about, say, "law" or "justice", as

[1b] *St. Augustine's Concept of Property Ownership*, in *Recherches augustiniennes*, vol. 8—1972, especially pp. 211-12; 216; 224; 228.

[2] *Epist.* 153, 6, 26; *in Ioan. evang. tract.* 6, 25.

[3] See e.g. his Appendix B, De Civitate Dei XIX, 14-15, and the Origins of Political Authority, pp. 192-210; also pp. 211 ff.

he himself received and understood such ideas from Sacred Scripture, the Church Fathers, and Graeco-Roman antiquity. But in some of his works—notably the *de Civitate Dei* and the *Contra Iulianum*—he did dwell at length upon various topics associated with his doctrine about authority in the state, and the origins of both.[4] Despite his classical inheritance, our author was—owing to the circumstances of the times in which he lived—a pioneer and a trail-blazer. In these circumstances, he stands greatly to gain by a comparison with Thomas Aquinas, who apart from the advantage of teachers and contemporaries of great eminence, inherited several hundred years of continuous Christian tradition and reflexion. In Aristotle, also, Aquinas could find to hand (albeit in translation) a thinker of many gifts who had reasoned long and systematically about socio-political life in its possible forms and structures. Plotinus, on the contrary, although interested in social problems and in contact with men of the world, was (and remains) an exceptionally difficult Greek author to understand and to translate, as those who have attempted either can testify![5] Augustine did however possess, as a foundation for future achievements and insights in the domain of politics, one providential asset denied (alike because of personal temperament and other, adventitious factors) to his illustrious commentator- and critic-to-be: the fecundating alluvial soil accumulated by thirty-three years of pre-conversion experiences as a *homo terrenus*.

I. *Society, Order and the Common Good*

St. Augustine's doctrine of the state can be understood and expounded only within the wider framework of his particular vision of "society". Elucidation of this cardinal concept will appear below at the appropriate point. Suffice it here to say that for him, the structure of "society" is hierarchical,—i.e. it comprises an ascending and progressively more diversified series of units which, at least on a preliminary basis, we may tabulate as follows:

a) the rational creature
b) the family
c) the state, or body civic
d) the human race
e) the Society of God (*civitas Dei*)

---

[4] *De civitate Dei* XIX, 14-16; PL 41, 642-45: *Contr. Iul.* IV, 12, 61; PL 44, 767-68.

[5] *The Oxford Classical Dictionary*, Plotinus [847-48].

f) the Catholic Church
g) the Devil's Society (*civitas diaboli*).

According to Augustine, universal history commences at the moment when the world was created from nothingness. This event might be properly said to mark the beginning of time, as distinct from eternity.[6] In the case of (a) above, the creative process involves a "conversion" from self to Creator[7] and a "formation" in harmony with the "order" of each.[8] It is now appropriate that we examine more closely the meaning of the latter term, as an obvious key-word in the Bishop's technical vocabulary.

A study of the texts would indicate that *ordo* seems to bear at times an objective, "dynamic" or active sense, and sometimes a subjective, "static" or passive sense. In fact, of course, the two uses are strictly co-relative, the first always implying the second. Let us illustrate from Augustine himself who writes: *(Deus) . . . naturas essentiarum gradibus ordinavit.*[9] This passage stresses the role of God as the *Agent* and *Giver* in the operation, and is hence an example of the "dynamic" use.[10] The second, or passive, meaning, lays emphasis upon the *recipient* in the transaction, and what is received: *iustum est ut omnia sint ordinatissima.*[11] Meanwhile, both senses appear to be simultaneously present in our author's phrase: *ordo rerum* (universal order), that is, a cosmic structure which rising from the inanimate through life to intelligence, finds its apex in God the Creator: First (and highest) Essence, Life, and Wisdom.[12] We may here further remark that the notions of "order" and "disorder" as mutually opposed "tendencies" in respect of being, clearly indicate that for Augustine, these key-words designate "dynamisms", i.e. forces in motion.[13] Rather than an aggregation of relatively stable metaphysical essences, he therefore views the created world as the theatre of a perpetual clash, an unending tension between contrary and irreconcilable principles. Of these the most important in our author's thought include being and non-being, the eternal and the temporal, the spiritual and the physical, immutability and the mutable, unity and plurality. For him, then, the fact of

[6] *De civitate Dei* XI, 6; cf. *de Gen. ad litt. imperf.* 3, 8.
[7] *De duab. anim.* 8, 10.
[8] *De lib. arbitr.* I, 17, 45.
[9] *De civitate Dei* XII, 2; PL 41, 350.
[10] *De ord.* I, 5, 14; *ibid.* I, 7, 17; *ibid.* I, 10, 28 (*ad fin.*).
[11] *De lib. arbitr.* I, 6, 15 (*ad fin.*).
[12] *De vera relig.* 31, 57.
[13] *De civitate Dei* XI, 28; PL 41, 342: "Ita enim corpus pondere, sicut animus amore, fertur quocumque fertur." *De mus.* VI, 11, 29, and *enarr. in ps.* 31, 2, 5.

creation itself argues the existence of an omnipresent hierarchy comprising creatures (as also the products of rational and moral activity in culture and socio-political life) so variously disposed that even human reason can recognize them as "superior" or "inferior", etc. according to their individual "modes". But God is not merely the Summit of order; for the latter actually originates within the Godhead Itself, inasmuch as the Holy Ghost unites the Father and the Son in a self-subsistent Love that is both the Model and the Source of all creaturely order and love.[14] Thus to the concept of "governance",[15] which dominates the structure of *ordo* (and is no less deeply rooted in the permanent tradition of pagan classical philosophy), Augustine adds a new —and decisively other—dimension of meaning, whose far-reaching effects will become increasingly apparent as our exposition proceeds.

Augustine is a "many-splendoured" genius. One of his more remarkable talents (despite some few admitted ἁμαρτήματα) reveals itself as a felicitous ability to adapt typical Graeco-Roman notions to distinctively Christian insights. (As we write these lines, there comes to mind a shoddy generalization of W. H. C. Frend: "a great man . . . whose attempt to reconcile the three determining influences in his life, Manichaeism [sic !], Neo-Platonism and Christianity, ultimately failed").[16] The example to which we refer in the present discussion is—as might be expected—"the common good". The word and concept of *bonum commune* are Roman and occur repeatedly in classical Latin literature, e.g. in Vergil and in Seneca.[17] Roman political theorists constantly taught that every occupant of public office must protect the citizens' common good before his own private interests.[18] Little by little this principle became a general ethical norm, explaining the essentially social nature of man and exploiting it in the interests of the common good.[19]

---

[14] *De Trin.* VI, 10, 12.

[15] The following are some basic refs: Plato, *Phaed.* 80[a]; Aristotle, *Polit.* I, 1254[b]; Plotinus, *Enn.* I, 1, 4; Cicero, *de offic.* I, XXIII, 79; Seneca, the Philosopher, *epist. moral.* 114, 23-24. St. Augustine's own understanding and adaptation of this concept are summarized in his *Enarratio in psalmum* 145, 5; PL 37, 1887: "rationalis anima . . . legem accepit, haerere superiori, regere inferiorem." Cf. *de act. cum Fel. Man.* II, 4; PL 42, 538: ". . . animam habentem liberum arbitrium, sub se ipso et super caetera collocavit; ut si serviret superiori, dominaretur inferiori . . ."

[16] P. 210, *The Early Church*: we shall discuss his views later.

[17] *Aen.* XI, 435; *dialog.* VIII, *de otio* I, 1, 4.

[18] Cic. *de Republ.* 342E; 420B; *de offic.* I, 25, 85.

[19] *De offic.* III, 5, 24.

St. Augustine, inheriting this notion of the priority or preeminence of the *bonum commune*, adapts and realigns or rearranges it under a new heading; in his thought, charity has replaced, or at any rate, transcended the classical virtues of *humanitas* and *magnitudo*: "communia propriis, non propria communibus anteponit (charitas).[20] The preference for a common good is not however a limited rule for a special perfection: it is rather a general precept of Christian perfection as such: "Tanto magis itaque inhaeretur Deo, quanto minus diligitur proprium".[21] Augustine's cosmology also exemplifies the same principle. For him, as for all Graeco-Roman philosophers—and especially for the Stoics—the whole of the universe is better than its parts.[22] His doctrine concerning the priority of the common good in the state and in society proceeds naturally from his theology of charity and from his cosmology. In the Society of God, this priority is teleological, since its human component is wholly composed of individual families which nevertheless constitute a unity wherein the metaphysical principle of the whole and the parts is assured, for all the parts are ordained to the whole. But among the Greeks and Romans, there had been a progressive divinization of the *cosmos* and of its concrete political manifestations.[23] Against this our author affirms that over and above the realm of human affairs—in which the state and the common good are the better and the best—stands the Heavenly Society and above this in turn God himself, the only true ultimate Common Good.[23a]

II. *CIVITAS, SOCIETAS: Terms of Reference, Meaning, Relationship*

For Augustine the beginnings of the *civitas*, as an organised expression of man's political and social life, antedate the earliest records of secular history. Nevertheless this institution stems from a unity itself

[20] *Epist.* 211, 12; PL 33, 963.

[21] *De Trin.* XII, 11, 16; PL 42, 1006.

[22] *De ord.* II, 19, 51.

[23] Cf. Marc. Aurel. *M. Antoninus, Imperator ad se ipsum*, IV, 23; I, 60, 11. 14-18. For the apotheosis of the emperors see C. Kaerst, *Geschichte des Hellenismus*, II, 376 ff.

[23a] *De civitate Dei* XIX, 16; PL 41, 644-45: *epist.* 137, 5, 17. My recent article, *St. Augustine's Concept of Property Ownership* (*Recherches augustiniennes*, Vol. 8, 1972), discusses *inter alia*, much of the background of this footnote insofar as it influenced Augustine: see especially Appendix B: "Communiter Possidere" and the Christian Ideal of Ownership (pp. 228-29). For a study of the principle of the priority of the common good in Latin classical literature and in St. Augustine, see I. T. ESCHMANN: *A Thomistic Glossary on the Principle of the Pre-eminence of a Common Good*, in *Mediaeval Studies*, V (Toronto, 1943), pp. 124-36.

prior to even the most ancient forms of communal existence. The unity here in question is actually one of "racial stock" (*genus*) or origin; and the fellowship to which it has given rise precedes and in a sense transcends the entire domain of the social and of secular politics. Now the source and nature of this fellowship depend upon the fact that al men without exception, and irrespective of nationality, language, or physical appearance, are descended from Adam—the first representative of the human race and its patriarch. It is this life that mankind ever repeats and so to speak recapitulates, thus achieving a unity at once generic and moral. We say "generic" precisely because all men are related through descent from a common progenitor; and "moral", inasmuch as they are united, not merely by the possession of a common nature, but also an awareness of the obligations implied by membership in one and the same family.[24]

Nevertheless in Adam's children, the opening chapters of human history already reveal not one, but two sorts of men. For although these were brothers, born of the same parents and sharing the same nature, they were yet characterized by two radically dissimilar wills: as proto-types, they foreshadow and prefigure two radically distinct collectivities.[25] The first of these, the *civitas Dei*, consists of those who, acknowledging Christ as their Leader, are predestined to reign with Him forever. The title of the second is *civitas diaboli* or *civitas terrena*, and describes the hosts of the wicked who, since they follow Satan as their chief, are predestined with him to eternal separation from God in hell. Between them, these two communities universally embrace the angelic creation, and the whole human race from its beginnings to the end of the world.[26]

We have stated that Augustine's use of *civitas* reflects a broadening of its standard classical connotation: in saying this, we must also emphasize the elements of the original meaning retained by him. In one context of reference—perhaps its commonest—*civitas* signifies a body of citizens considered collectively as members of a political organization.[27] Apart from having introduced differing criteria of organization, Augustine retains this force of the word. Secondly, *civitas* means a "state" or "community", i.e., a unit of political association organized in accordance with some distinctive principles of

---

[24] *De vera relig.* 27, 50; cf. *de civitate Dei* XII, 22.

[25] *Ibid.* XV, 1.

[26] *Ibid.* XV, 1; cf. also XIV, 1.

[27] Cic. *de republ.* VI, 13, 13. Cf. *de civitate Dei* XV, 1, 1; see also *ibid.* XV, 8; *epist.* 138, 2, 10.

authority and order.[28] This notion is also present in St. Augustine's usage of the term, except that again the principles of authority and order operative here are not political. Finally, *civitas* connotes "citizenship", that is to say, the exclusive status of being a citizen. Within the Roman Empire, this privilege had been based upon circumstances of birth or upon a grant made by the Roman people:[29] in the *Civitas Dei*, however, as also in its opposition, citizenship depends upon a deliberate act of free will involving the acceptance or rejection of Divine grace.[30]

In normal Roman usage, *respublica* was the technical word employed to designate the state, including the "ideal" or "theoretic" state; hence this term always translates the Platonic "*πολίτεια*". *De republica* as a title, would then suggest an account of the organization of its human and material resources. St. Augustine's use of *civitas* in this connexion seems already to imply that with such ideas he is not primarily concerned.[31] Rather than a treatise upon either Utopia or the Rome of his day, the *de Civitate Dei* must therefore be considered as a description of and a judgement upon persons and things partly contained and involved within history, partly "mystical". Here it is important to note that in so qualifying persons and things, Augustine does not by any means intend us to suppose that they are "unhistorical" —as he understands history—unreal, or otherwise external to the

---

[28] Caes. *bell. gall.* I, 12; cf. *de civitate Dei* XIX, 21. In AD 212, by enacting the *Constitutio Antoniniana*, Caracalla extended Roman citizenship to all the *peregrini* in the Roman Empire, the *dediticii* being alone excepted. For *dediticii*, consult Pauly-Wissowa, *Real-Encyclopaedie der Classischen Altertumswissenschaft*, achter Halbband pp. 2359-63; for *peregrinus* see *ibid.* siebenunddreissigster Halbband, pp. 639-55.

[29] *The Cambridge Ancient History*, VII, 415: "The *caput* of a Roman citizen was the sum of the rights which he enjoyed in virtue of his birth. These . . . (were) defined as 'citizenship' . . . (*civitas*), etc." See also S. Katz, *The Decline of Rome*, pp. 29-30, 141.

[30] *De catech. rud.* 19, 31, PL 40, 333: " . . . duae . . . civitates . . . nunc permixtae corporibus, sed voluntatibus separatae . . ."

[31] When Cicero wrote his treatise about the state in imitation of Plato's work on the *πολίτεια*, he entitled it not *de civitate* but *de republica*, because in classical Latin the former never refers to an "ideal" state, or the "constitution of a commonwealth"—the precise sense that Cicero here required. By including in the title of his masterpiece the term *civitas*, Augustine on the other hand would appear to suggest that the society described thereby is no less historically (and metaphysically) "real" than the states of secular history. Indeed he believed (as we shall attempt to establish), that the *Civitas Dei* was a much more "real" entity—i.e. had a greater measure of being (and therefore, goodness)—than any purely secular state or commonwealth.

realm of truth and fact. There is no reason to doubt that *mysticus*[32] and its various derivatives meant to him what the ordinary English equivalent of this word signifies, i.e., something possessed of "a certain spiritual character or import by virtue of a connexion or union with God transcending human comprehension" . . . .[33]

Now it is to this feature of his approach and method of treatment that Augustine particularly averts in his title: *de Civitate Dei*. For there, by adding the word *Dei* (of God), he in effect applies a criterion or selective principle that isolates for consideration one distinctive *civitas* from among the many which have existed in the past and will appear in the future. But according to Augustine, it is in the ultimate analysis the plans and purposes of God for mankind, as revealed in the Scriptures, that alone give significance and direction to the flux of human history. Thus it is perhaps exact to describe Augustine as a "theologian" of history rather than a "philosopher"—or the author of a "philosophy"—of history.[34]

---

[32] It seems clear that the original meaning of *μυστικός* (*μυέω, μύω,*) was "closed", "shut", whence the transition to "hidden", "secret" (of religious rites and doctrines). See H. G. Liddell and R. Scott, *A Greek-English Lexicon: μύστης, μυέω, μύω,* (vol. II, 1156-57). With this word is associated *μυστήριον*, meaning originally "a secret rite" and then "a hidden truth" or "secret revealed by God". The word *μυστικός* (*mysticus*) does not occur in the New Testament, but makes its first appearance in Christian literature in the third century. Two common uses of it may be distinguished. The first of those applies to the "typical" or allegorical interpretation of Scripture so frequent in the Alexandrine School (see *Revue pratique d'Apolog.* XVIII; 1919, pp. 547-56). The second use is exemplified by Origen (*In Ioan.* I, 30: XIII, 24; GCS, Or. IV, 37, 29; 248, 27). Here the sense approximates to that of *μυστήριον* (*mysterium*) so frequently used by St. Paul, i.q., a hidden salvific truth (*Rom.* XVI, 23) or the hidden nature of an institution (*Eph.* V, 32: see F. Prat, *La Théologie de St. Paul*, II, pp. 467-68). It is, perhaps, this connotation that Augustine reproduces in the instance under present discussion. See further J. De Ghellinck, *Pour l'Histoire du Mot Sacramentum*, I; J. M. Le Blond, *op. cit.* pp. 144 (and fn. 20); 291-307: H. De Lubac, *Corpus Mysticum*, Introduction and pp. 45 ff.; C. Couturier, *Sacramentum et Mysterium dans l'Œuvre de Saint Augustin*, and H. Rondet, M. Le Landais, A. Lauras, C. Couturier, *Études Augustiniennes*, Paris, 1953, pp. 163-274.

[33] *The Oxford English Dictionary, mystical* (vol. VI, 817).

[34] It is the fashion among many modern commentators of St. Augustine to see in the *de civitate Dei* the expression of a "philosophy" or a "philosophical criticism" of history (see for example E. Hoffman, *Platonism in Augustine's Philosophy of History*, in *Philosophy and History*, pp. 173-90; J. T. Shotwell, *The History of History*, I, p. 369; and R. H. Barrow, *op. cit.* p. 22; cf. however, E. K. Rand, *The Building of eternal Rome*, pp. 203-04). Now the phrase "philosophy of history" was derived originally from Voltaire (*Œuvres complètes de Voltaire*, Paris, Delangle Frères, 1827, vol. XIX, p. 338 and fn. 1; see, further,

In his account of the *Civitas Dei*, Augustine virtually equates it on several occasions with what he calls a *societas*.[35] Now in classical Latin this word (the parallel substantival form *socius* means "ally" or "partner") denotes a number of allies or partners regarded as a collective unit. Alternatively, it may suggest the abstract idea of the relationship existing among such persons. By an extended usage this word can therefore signify any group of human beings united for a common aim or cause. Hence it may be applied with equal propriety to the association of allies in war and of partners in commerce, the unified life of a city or state, and indeed the human race itself viewed as a collectivity.[36] The basic and prevailing notion found in all these

A. G. Widgery, *Interpretations of History*, p. 158), who coined it to describe his ideal of a connected history of the human mind as opposed to a mass of merely incidental and unrelated historical detail. The formula has however since suffered varying modifications of meaning at the hands of Hegel and the nineteenth century positivists. By applying it to the *de civitate Dei*, the writers named above presumably express their belief that this work represents either an exclusively "rational" interpretation, on its author's part, or historical events and other data, or the result of approaching these data from one particular "philosophical viewpoint" or selective principle. Now since Augustine has left on record no opinion regarding the desirability or even possibility of the former procedure, we cannot presume to invent one of his behalf. What does however clearly emerge from a study of the relevant texts is the fact that he himself invariably evaluates and interprets the significance of historical events in accordance with certain presuppositions forming part of a body of theological beliefs whose ultimate literary source is the Bible. He expounds, and where necessary amplifies the content of history (as he envisages it) in the light of what Revelation teaches concerning the origin, nature, and final destiny of man. It would then appear evident that in positing, for example, such notions as Divine Providence and the existence of angels, Augustine has entered a domain accessible and subject to the criteria of neither "philosophy" nor even "history" itself—at least as commonly understood. Certainly reason alone is powerless to make a judgement regarding the historical character of the notions just mentioned. This doubtless explains why E. Gilson (*op. cit.* p. 175), and K. Loewith, (*Meaning in History*, p. 166), qualify by the phrase "theology of history" the perspective and methodology of an historian to whom the subject-matter of his inquiry becomes intelligible only when ordered from the particular viewpoint of Holy Scripture (for a modern "philosophy of history" see R. G. Collingwood, *The Idea of History*, especially pp. 14-52, and consult Loewith, *op. cit.* pp. 160-73, for a full discussion of Augustine's interpretation of history).

[35] *De civitate Dei* XV, I, 1; *ibid.* XII, 1; *ibid.* XI, 53. Cf. Cic. *de republ.* I, 32, 49.

[36] Cic. *pro Q. Rosc. Com.* VI, 16; *de fin.* IV, 2, 4; Sall. *Bell. Iug.* 77, 3. With the second text compare Augustine's constant use of *societas humana*: e.g. *de civitate Dei* XIX, 7 (*ad init.*). See R. T. Marshall: *Studies in the political and socio-religious Terminology of the de Civitate Dei* (dissert., CUA, Washington, D.C., 1952), especially pp, 8-48, 79-80. There is now a more recent and extensive analysis by H. Deane: *The Political and Social Ideas of St. Augustine.*

contexts is clearly that of "fellowship"—an expression which in most instances satisfactorily reproduces the essence of what St. Augustine himself seems to have understood by *societas.*

The "equation" mentioned at the beginning of the last paragraph would further indicate "society" as the only appropriate term to translate *civitas* in the two titles *civitas Dei* and *civitas terrena* (*civitas diaboli*). From our standpoint this rendering conveys more adequately than any other the joint implications of *civitas* and *societas.* For in English the word "society" readily evokes the concept of a group of persons united by some common interest, discipline, and purpose transcending all limitations of race, time or political allegiance and organisation. And this—so we believe—is the precise meaning and framework of reference that St. Augstine himself intends.[37]

III. *St. Augustine's Critique of the Role of Justice in Graeco-Roman Political Theory*

We have seen that any attempt to grasp in its essence and explain the "Society of God" by recourse to criteria or standards of comparison derived exclusively from secular historical patterns would involve a formal contradiction of Augustine's own teaching. Yet more than one thousand years' heritage of continuous and accumulated Graeco-Roman speculation stands behind the word which he himself habitually uses to describe those two Societies comprising the subject-matter of the *de civitate Dei.* St. Augustine's behaviour here exemplifies but a single phase of his overall indebtedness and conformity to classical theories regarding politics and society.[38] In connexion with the particular problem of the mutual relationships between city-state and individual citizen—relationships that any systematic expose of political (and moral) doctrine must meet and resolve—his conscious conformity,

[37] There are two principal arguments which in the opinion of the present writer tell convincingly against the almost unanimous preference for "city". In the first place, this word suggests a purely or primarily politico-social microcosm, a mere unit of civic administration invariably associated with a particular geographical site and confined by definite territorial boundaries. Secondly, "city" does not, in normal usage, even remotely evoke the idea (integral to the Augustinian notion) of a continuity of existence co-terminous with universal history itself. Yet to support his own use of this expression to translate *Civitas Dei,* one of Augustine's recent commentators has produced no more by way of argument than the debatable remark that ". . . any other rendering is open to . . . objection . . . ("city") is a convenient BLANK which the reader will fill up as he reads . . ." (R. H. Barrow, *op. cit.* p. 21). In this connexion consult L. S. Mazzolani, *The Idea of the City in Roman Thought,* transl. by S. O'Donnell.

however partial will, we trust, become increasingly apparent with the progress of the present section. In adopting *civitas*, then (as well as its correlatives *respublica, populus*), our author acknowledges—initially, at least—the classical tradition incorporated in those terms as an ancient and readily accessible body of principles prerequisite to any serious analysis of the nature of a true society.

Augustine's search for that single quality or mark characteristic of and essential to a genuine society (*civitas*) was clearly motivated in the first place by the conviction—inseparable from his own specific purpose—that such an undertaking must both frankly face and account for the available historical evidence. Now what could be more proper, in pursuit of such evidence, than to choose as one's test case the Roman Empire itself,[39] some of whose most eminent writers and historians had themselves already examined this identical problem? Among the former, Cicero had composed a dialogue dealing with the nature of a "state", from which Augustine derived material amply illustrative of orthodox classical opinion on the matter. In order fully to appreciate his analysis and criticism of the Ciceronian doctrine, we will however be obliged, at this point, to integrate such criticism within the general context of St. Augustine's own account of the historical origin and nature of society.

Here we may well begin our task by recalling Augustine's conviction that every human being is both an individual and a person, naturally equal with (and independent of) his fellows because created in the image of God. From this posulate it follows that no one can legitimately claim any intrinsic right to exercise political authority over others. Without original sin, that is, man's power would be confined to the animal world and the lower creation in general which he dominates because of the gift of reason.[40] The question now arises as to how, in the light of the above principles, one is to account for—much less justify—the fact of "society" and the organized political hierarchies that have resulted therefrom. At this point Augustine appeals to

[38] Here we may mention in particular Cicero's *de legibus, de officiis*, and the *de republica*, which together with his *de inventione* and *de divinatione*, constitute Augustine's chief sources. For a general account of the above works within this context see G. Combès, *La Doctrine politique de Saint Augustin*, pp. 34-8.

[39] A statement as to St. Augustine's "patriotism" and his general estimate of the Roman achievement might perhaps be expected at this point. But since this appraisal is based in the last resort upon his opinion regarding classical morality—which we cannot here discuss—see the *de civitate Dei* I, 15, 1; III, 21; V, 12, 5; V, 18, 2.

[40] *De lib. arbitr.* II, 17, 46; *de Gen. contr. Man.* II, 11, 16. Cf. *de civitate Dei* XIX, 15.

the laws of human nature itself as an explanation of why men have tended from the beginning of history to enter into association and fellowship with each other.[41] He states the first of those laws in terms of an innate creaturely desire to secure and maintain peace. And here, he says, experience is available to show that the pursuit of peace, however questionable its immediate motive, strengthens the bond of communal life, thereby providing added protection against danger and distress.[42] Secondly, awareness of a common natural endowment and a sense of generic kinship induced Adam's issue to seek the union and mutual agreement which not only define the purpose but underpin the basic structure of all human society as well as of lesser communities.[43] But this first step once taken, there gradually began to appear a complex of duties, rights and responsibilities whose very existence amply demonstrated the need of an hierarchical principle. Men now urgently required a theory or pattern of authority in compliance with which some would rule and others obey. As regards the choice of an appropriate criterion for determining and measuring the qualifications of those who covet or who already hold the reins of power within a given society, Augustine will be content to accept on a purely provisional basis the time-honoured Roman virtue of justice. The operation of this standard—thus located—is best viewed and its *rationale* most readily vindicated by reference to the lowest and least complex element in the communal unity of a *societas* (or *civitas*). Our author has been quoted above to show that order characteristically produces a "fitting arrangement" or congruity of parts, whereby what is inferior in the scale of being and perfection tends to obey the superior. So, too, within the family—the *seminarium civitatis*[44]—it is the father, as reason and precedent both enjoin, who rules the members of his household.[45]

---

[41] *Ibid.* XIX, 12, 1, 2.

[42] The belief that the rise of human society and the enactment of social and civil legislation must be attributed solely to motives of mutual security and of protection against enemies and other external dangers is characteristic of the Epicurean School: Diog. Laert. *de vit. phil.* X (Epicurus), 154; also *ibid.* 150.

[43] See above, fn. 24 (second ref.).

[44] *De civitate Dei* XV, 16, 3; PL 41, 459.

[45] *Ibid.* XIX, 16. This, says Augustine, exemplifies the fact that rule must be exercised not by the richest or most powerful individual in the state, but by the best, as determined by the order of nature itself. Now the simplest and lowest organization of social and political life is the family, where the authority of the father is so ancient and renowned that even unjust princes love to hear the title of *paterfamilias* applied to them (*ibid.* XIX, 16). What obtains in the family is also illustrated—on the one hand—in the individual human being,

St. Augustine's scattered, incidental comments upon the origin of the state and its "power-structure" reflect an apologetic purpose undoubtedly dictated in part, at least, by his polemical reaction to Cicero's treatise entitled *de republica.* This work—still incompletely recovered—was popular in the Africa of Augustine's day and doubtless familiar to all his readers.[46] In it Scipio Africanus the Younger, who is the chief speaker, uses a figure of speech—borrowed from the vocabulary of music—to describe the social bond which he asserts can alone guarantee the security of any commonwealth. Every society, says Scipio, should resemble an agreeable "harmony" (*harmonia*)[47] through modulation of the diverse elements composing the totality of its structure. In the case of the state, the "harmony" thus obtained is what Roman political theorists would call a "concord" (*concordia*);[48] but this quality without which no republic can exist, is itself unattainable unless accompanied by justice. Scipio further develops his argument through an appeal to the definition of a "commonwealth" (*respublica*) as the "weal" of the "people" (*populus*).[49] Now the latter word is to be understood here not as equivalent to any nondescript mob (*qualiscumque multitudo*) but rather a multitude united in fellowship by agreement upon what is just, and by its members' pursuit of the common good. This definition once admitted, the conclusion necessarily follows that should the sovereign power of a particular commonwealth become unjust, we cannot in fact rightly consider such a community to be a "commonwealth" at all. For there is no "wealth of the people" if there be no "people"; and there can be no "people" without mutual recognition of "rights" (*iura*), and no "rights" in turn without "justice" (*iustitia*).[50]

---

where the soul (as the higher principle) rules the body, and God the soul and —on the other—in the state, where kings, generals, and magistrates govern the body politic just as soul rules body and reason rules the passions. Augustine found this conception of authority—*optimo cuique dominatum ab ipsa natura datum*—elaborated by Cicero in his *de republica* III, 25, 37: cf. *Contr. Iul.* IV, 12, 61; PL 44, 767-68.

[46] Cic. *epist. ad fam.* VIII, 1, 5 (*ad fin.*); *opera* (BT), (written to him by M. Caelius Rufus): "Tui πολιτικοὶ libri omnibus vigent."

[47] *De civitate Dei* II, 21, 1. Cic. *de republ.* II, 42, 69. In early Greek ἁρμονία had no special musical connotation, being used typically of a joiner's task (cf. *Od.* V, 248). Later because of its general sense of "fitting", "arranging" (ἁρμόζω), it began to be used with particular reference to the stringing and tuning of musical instruments.

[48] *De civitate Dei* II, 21, 1.

[49] *Ibid.* XIX, 21, 1. Cic. *de republ.* I, 25-39.

[50] *De civitate Dei* XIX, 21, 1.

The above line of thought, valid as far as it goes, does not however resolve the main argument or principle at stake between St. Augustine and the classical tradition as represented by Cicero. For while both have so far agreed that justice is the social bond of a state, and both define it as essentially a virtue which renders to each his due,[51] Augustine further insists that any true concept of justice must involve recognition of God as final and supreme End. Now from this position it follows in the first place that within the individual human being, body must necessarily be subject to soul and the latter to the Creator of both.[52] In the world external to himself, man must further ordinate and refer to God his use of every other creature (person and thing). In its widest sense, then, justice is seen to include not only man's due ordering of himself as a composite being to the Divine, but also his ordered employment of all things as so many means to their one common End. From Augustine's viewpoint, violation of justice is thus virtually equivalent to the violation of order itself, with all the disastrous results consequent thereupon. The distinction between "true" and "false" justice (*uera, falsa iustitia*) accordingly reduces to this: the first recognizes and serves God as Creator, while the second rejects Him, making ends-in-themselves of lesser creatures. Now in pagan

---

[51] *Ibid.* XIX, 21, 2. Cic. *de invent.* II, 53, 160.

[52] *De civitate Dei* XIX, 4. This text introduces the problem of the body-soul relationship in Augustine's thought. Here it should in the first place be remarked that while always retaining traces of neo-Platonic influence, he rejects from the beginning the viewpoint that would make matter a tomb or prison-house of spirit: *de anim. et eius orig.* IV, 2, 3. Cf. Plot. *Enn.* IV, 8, 1, the references here being to *Gorg.* 493a and *Crat.* 400bc. Plotinus later makes this opinion his own: *ibid.* IV, 8, 3-5. Augustine also condemns by implication the belief that the soul's entry into matter is a "fall" and its greatest source of evil: *de civitate Dei* X, 24, (see also now R. J. O'Connell, *Pre-existence in Augustine's Seventh Letter*, in *Revue des Études augustiniennes* 1969; XV, 1-2, pp. 67-73). One example of his earlier pronounced neo-Platonic bias; *de quant. anim.* 13, 22 (*ad fin.*). Cf. Plato, *Alcib.* 129e; Plot. *enn.* I, 1, 7: I, 1, 4. But in the *de Trinitate*, a masterpiece of theological analysis, written when he was in full possession of his own thought, Augustine produced a definition that represents his last word upon this problem: (XV, 7, 11). We may observe that the transcendent superiority of spirit to matter here emphasized follows logically from a doctrine wherein it is man's rational component that alone mirrors the Divine and where nothing intervenes between the soul and God: *de immort. anim.* 15, 24 (and fn. 15, above). Cf. Plot. *enn.* V, 1, 3. See *epist.* 238, 2, 12, where Augustine grapples with the difficulty of explaining the unity of being and nature in man according to a metaphysical system wherein he is thought to consist of two distinct substances. For further discussion of this topic, consult A. C. Pegis, *In Defense of St. Augustine* (*Essays in Modern Scholasticism*, pp. 111-14).

Rome, or in any other state in which demons, deceased citizens or even animals are worshipped,[53] "true" justice by definition cannot exist. This once conceded, it becomes impossible to resist the conclusion that the particular states—or commonwealths—and peoples thus affected have not true being as such, i.e. they *are not*.[54]

Why was St. Augustine led to abandon the concept of justice as the social bond uniting every genuine society and to seek a fresh definition? One might be tempted in the light of the above, to reply that the absence of "true justice" in all so-called "societies" (save that whose Head is Christ) deprives them forthwith of their right to this title. Such an assumption, perfectly accurate as far as it goes, does not however disclose Augustine's real problem. We may perhaps best appreciate the central and indeed crucial difficulty he had to resolve by once more restating his paramount concern. This was to devise a formula applicable not merely to the Society of God, but to the Devil's Society as well, since this—and the pagan empires that represent it in human history—also have a certain mode of being. If, however, the social bond were "true", and therefore Divine justice, how could one avoid the contradiction implicit in a doctrine teaching that the Society of God, founded on this Divine justice, alone truly *is*, and yet affirming that two societies undeniably exist? The only possible escape from the above dilemma lay in doing exactly what Augustine did. This was, as we shall see, to produce an entirely new concept of the state, with a *differentia* quite other than justice—at least as understood by classical moralists.[55]

IV. *Love as the Social Bond of a Society: Being, Order and the Two Loves in Augustine's Thought*

Having applied Scipio's formula to the Rome of Roman history,[56] St. Augustine concludes that in point of historical fact it does not fit.

---

[53] See R. H. Barrow, *op. cit.* pp. 212-18, for a useful summary of the history of belief in demons in Greek and early Christian religious thought.

[54] *De civitate Dei* XIX, 21.

[55] The relation of justice to love or charity and to the other virtues is mentioned in fn. 78, below.

[56] St. Augustine's two chief historical sources were Livy and Sallust. He nowhere mentions Tacitus nor can any quotations from or even references to that author be verified beyond doubt in his writings. Tacitus' criticism of Roman morals and institutions belong in the main to the period following the birth of Christ, so that his work was not well adapted to St. Augustine's purpose. Livy is only twice mentioned by name (*de civitate Dei* II, 24: III, 7), although Augustine uses him more extensively than Sallust (cf. S. Angus, *The Sources of the first*

Rejecting justice as the bond of union, he therefore proposes an entirely different and original definition of a people: an association of rational beings united by the agreement of all its members upon a common object of love.[57] Several features of importance and interest arising from this definition require notice here. In the first place, by making the activity of "love" (*diligere*) the specificatory principle of a "people" (*populus*), and hence of a "commonwealth" (*res publica*), "state" (*civitas*) or "society" (*societas*),[58] Augustine implies a particular relationship—both ontological and moral—between the notions of "order" and "love". Secondly, his emphasis upon the necessity of "a group of rational creatures" (*multitudo rationalis*) assumes special significance when we pause to compare the Augustinian doctrine of society with the results of Stoic philosophical speculation in the same field. Indeed, because of the influences contributing to Augustine's doctrine, a brief survey of the historical development that this speculative process itself underwent may help further to clarify his general notion of society.

The exponents of the old *Stoa* characteristically depicted the entire physical universe—rather than humanity alone—as the habitat and true native land of the sage.[59] To them this embodied a single order and law—itself the expression of universal reason, in which all men participate. Their significant use of the word *κόσμος* to designate this order in contrast with human disorder was, to be sure, no novelty within Stoicism, being old even in Plato's day.[60] The absolute ethical

---

ten Books of Augustine's de Civitate Dei, dissert., Princeton, 1906, pp. 38, 52-7), the reason probably being that his writings were too large and cumbrous for ready consultation. On the other hand, Sallust is nearly always referred to by name and frequently quoted *verbatim* . This need cause no surprise, considering that in the first place he was *the* standard historian taught in the schools of Augustine's (*de civitate Dei* I, 5). Augustine's flattering opinion here had been previously affirmed by Quintilian, *Inst. orat.* X, 1, 101; Martial, *epigram* XIV, 191; and Tacitus himself, who spoke of Sallust as *rerum Romanarum florentissimus auctor*: *Ann.* III, 30. Moreover, his gloomy description of persons and events in general, as also his scathing condemnation of the corrupt morals of Rome prior to the appearance of Christianity, made Sallust an excellent witness for St. Augustine to arraign against his own countrymen. Augustine's use of Sallust's *Catiline* and *Histories* is tabulated in H. Kuhlmann, *De veterum Historicorum in Augustini de Civitate Dei Libro primo altero tertio Vestigiis*, p. 2: see also B. Maurenbrecher, *Sallusti Crispi Historiarum Reliquiae.*

[57] *De civitate Dei* XIX, 24.

[58] See above, fns. 27, 35, 49, 50 and 57.

[59] Plut. *de commun. notit.* XXXIV, 1076F. For the *motif* of self-preservation cf. *de doctr. christ.* I, 25, 26-7.

[60] *Gorg.* 508 A; *opera* (SCBO), III, 508a.

rigorism of the earlier Stoics, with its unqualified refusal to admit the possibility of any progress (προκοπή)[61] in virtue and wisdom gradually yielded, in middle and later Stoicism, to a fresh viewpoint. Formerly, this School had classified mankind at large in two exclusive categories —the wise and the foolish. But conceding at last that few, if any, in fact attain the unearthly heights of a *sapiens*, the Stoic professor no longer automatically graded "the man in the street" as a fool. For perhaps, after all, he might be a *proficiens*, i.e. a disciple or neophyte following the path of progress in true philosophy. This re-defined attitude led in turn to one further important result. Because human beings are innately social, obedience to the promptings of reason demands that men should live in community: here the unifying bond and architectonic principle remains, as always, Logos. But Logos also counsels the development of the primary instinct of self-preservation implanted by nature in every animal. Little more, in the first stages, than an unenlightened egoism, this crude sentiment was expected, according to the ethics of the School, to enlarge its scope and radiate outwards in ever-widening circles to embrace all within the kingdom of reason. And from the latter—we may note—not even enemies and slaves were debarred, since were not all equally subject to the same immutable law?[62] Thus even in its new or at any rate modified form, the κόσμος of Stoic thought retains its original unity. For the professors of Stoicism, there could be only one real "city" or "state" (πόλις) since all men must live according to this same rule of universal reason— that is: ὁμολογουμένως ζῆν,[63] or as Seneca expressed it: *vita sibi concors* ("a life at harmony within itself").[64] Whatever be their precise meaning, these phrases envisage at any rate only one way of life for all men, rather than as many ways as there exist individual city-states. And the life here meant is in essence a social one, to the extent that the wise man's duties as a citizen would remain even if he belonged to no city. With this conception of the sage as an integral member of "society"—however variously the latter term be understood—St. Augustine finds himself in complete agreement. For according to him, the life of the state is social by its very nature.[65]

---

[61] Von Arnim, *Stoicorum Veterum Fragmenta*, IV, προκοπή, προκόπτω, 122.

[62] Cic. *de leg.* I, 7, 23; cf. also *de nat. deor.* II, 154; Sen. *de otio* XXXI; M. Aurel. *medit.* II, 16; III, 11; IV, 4, etc.

[63] Stob. *Ecl.* II, 132.

[64] *Epist.* LXXXIX, 15; *L. Ann. Sen. ad Luc. epist.* (BT), p. 379, l. 25.

[65] Sen. *epist.* LXVIII, 2; Cic. *Tusc. disput.* IV, 23, 51. Cf. *de civitate Dei* XIX, 5; 17: cf. *ibid.* XII, 28. For a convenient summary of Stoic doctrine generally, see G. Rodier, *Études de Philosophie grecque*, pp. 219-308. The reason why the life of every state *must* be social is explained in fns. 52, 53 and 54, below.

It can be seen even from the above brief analysis that the influence of Stoic notions of society upon Augustine is far from negligible. To begin with, he acknowledges the rule of order, law, and reason as the sovereign manifestation of Divine governance in the universe. Again, he unhesitatingly affirms the metaphysical and moral unity of the *cosmos*—a unity constituted precisely by recognition and acceptance on the part of rational beings of the order and law binding upon all. Within this *cosmos* he furthermore admits the traditional distinction of three levels of social life and organization: the individual, the state, and finally the world.[66] There are also other aspects of classical and Stoic doctrine concerning society to which St. Augustine seems especially receptive and sympathetic. Prominent among these is the Graeco-Roman attitude to the institution of friendship. A typical child of his age in this regard, he had himself more than once known the ardours of such an attachment. No one, on the other hand, was more acutely aware—from personal experience—both of the dangers and of the disappointments inherent in associations of this kind.[67]

Having indicated their areas of agreement, we must now stress the fundamental differences that separate Augustine from Stoicism in the matter of social theory. These differences, however, need no lengthy discussion since in essence they all reduce to one: the Christian notion of Deity. For as we have seen, it is the Divine nature and attributes themselves upon which St. Augustine's doctrine concerning reason, law, and order ultimately depends.[68] Now, central and supreme among such attributes, as he understands them, is love or charity.[69] Here we may recall that the Roman pantheon did indeed contain Amor—the god of love.[70] It is perhaps unnecessary to observe that the disposition represented by this divinity and his Greek prototypes bears little likeness to Augustine's conception of *amor* as a Christian virtue.[71] And in any case, the notion of a personal and theocentric love has no significant part to play either in the ethical theory of the Stoics or in

[66] Cf. E. Zeller, *Stoics, Epicureans and Sceptics*, pp. 320-23 and refs.

[67] *Conf.* II, 9, 17 (referring to his evil companions in the theft of the pears; *ibid.* III, 4, 7; IV, 7, 12). Here the ref. is to a fellow-youth with whom Augustine formed a friendship while teaching in Tagaste (*ibid.* IV, 4, 7).

[68] See *Contr. Faust. Man.* XXII, 27: *Enarr. in ps.* 148, 10-12; PL 37, 1943-46: *de ord.* I, 7, 17.

[69] *De Trin.* VI, 10, 12.

[70] Sen. *Hippol.* 194 ff; *trag.* (BT) II, 305. *Contr. Faust. Man.* XX, 9.

[71] Cf. M. C. D'Arcy, *The Mind and Heart of Love*, p. 87: "In the Greek idea of love the ultimate Eros, which stirs and draws all hearts, is in itself indifferent and uncaring of all save itself. But the God who is . . . revealed in the Gospels is a living and loving God . . ."

their teaching about the state. But—as has been shown above—St. Augustine's theory of love lies at the very heart of his thought relative to society. Thus once again, we perforce conclude that despite many secondary though important similarities of outlook and emphasis, his doctrine—by its insistence upon a definitively Christian interpretation of reason, law, and order—marks a radical departure from accepted classical speculation in the corresponding field.

It is a characteristic feature of Augustine's social theory that he refuses to dissociate the individual person from the larger unity of the state or society. For him this solidarity is nowhere more strikingly apparent than in the nature and activity of love as it attracts and unites man to his fellows. Here St. Augustine cites in evidence the phenomenon of a public assembly, which as a professional teacher of rhetoric he would have assuredly had many opportunities to study. At the beginning of such an assembly—a dramatic spectacle, for example—the spectators are completely unknown to each other, with no contact except that provided by their place of meeting, and no common interest save their appreciation of the theatre. If however, some particular actor happens to display unusual talent in his performance, those who admire it are not content to focus their sentiments on the actor alone. Rather, their enthusiasm tends to overflow individual limits and embrace all those similarly affected. In this manner, the common love of a group, with one person as its centre, spontaneously though unconsciously creates a society.[72] Augustine also insists upon a secondary but to him none the less significant result of such a process: mutual love of the sort here in question not merely makes a society one, but furthermore provides a criterion by means of which it can be distinguished from all others. From this, two important conclusions follow: first, there exist as many societies as there are collective loves, and second, to know the object of a people's love is know that people itself.[73] For a man's personal qualities are most fully revealed by the nature of the things that he loves: *talis est quisque, qualis eius dilectio est.*[74] But in fact there are, as there always have been, only two loves in men[75]—those two, precisely, that have founded the two So-

[72] *De doct. christ.* I, 29, 30.

[73] *De civitate Dei* XIX, 24.

[74] Thus if a man wishes to discover of which of the two great Societies he is a member, he needs only to ask himself what the object of his love is: *Enarr. in ps.* 64, 2.

[75] These two loves, reduced to their simplest form, can be defined as the love of what is good and—ad its contrary—the love of evil. And because each individual represents all mankind as a homogeneous element thereof (de civitate Dei IV, 3), and so, in a sense the two Societies comprising it, the two basic

cieties. One of these, the Society of God, is characterized by a love of Him. The other, the Earthly Society, loves itself to the exclusion of God.[76]

Thus, according to Augustine, there imposes itself upon every creature endowed with reason the observance of a hierarchy of loves corresponding to the orders of being and goodness—of which God is also the source and end. But even at the lower levels of creation, it is possible to find behaviour comparable with human love, and in particular with that most basic, innate, and universal of all loves—love of one's own existence. Brute beasts, for example, may be said in a sense to "love" the carnal life of their senses, in that they conform to it as to their common good, and see nothing further. Even trees, which do not love by any conscious tendency nevertheless strive, as it were, to become more abundant in their fruitfulness.[77]

The right use of material objects necessarily involves reference to an external standard of moral values ultimately rooted in a fundamental distinction between 'means' and 'ends'—God being the absolutely Final End. Now according to St. Augustine, there does in fact exist a sort of 'calculus' (*aestimatio*) which can be employed to determine the comparative 'weights' of a given miscellany of things in the scales of ordered love. Because an object selected at random may attract varying degrees of desire in varying contingencies, it follows that, depending upon particular circumstances and individual tastes, any and all *desiderata* are liable to receive alternately an excess or a deficiency of due love. He who is intent upon living the good life will therefore use this calculus to subordinate his appetite of the moment as a means (*uti*) to his love of an object more honourable in itself (*frui*)—i.e. something that will make him better. One of Augustine's preferred definitions of 'order' is precisely a virtue which enables its recipient to discern and use means as means and ends as ends. To this obviously all-important moral excellence he also applies the name of *prudentia*—

---

loves may even occur in one and the same person: *ibid.* XI, 28; PL 41, 341-42: ". . . possunt enim ambo esse in uno homine . . ." (See 1st ref. in 80[a], below). For the homogeneity of the human race cf. *de civitate Dei* XII, 9, 2; PL 41, 357: "ex uno quippe homine, quem primum Deus condidit, genus humanum sumpsit exordium . . ." The classical concept of two basic, mutually exclusive loves is found in Plato (*Phaedr.* 246[b]; 256[b-c]), and Plotinus: *Enn.* III, 5, 1; 2-3.

[76] *De civitate Dei* XIV, 28; PL 41, 436: "Fecerunt itaque civitates duas amores duo; terrenam scilicet amor sui usque ad contemptum sui." Man's *contemptus sui* is based upon true self-knowledge: of himself, he *is* and *has* nothing, except his sins. His being and all other blessings come from God: *Enarr. in ps.* 70, *serm.* 1, 1; *serm.* 137, 4, 4.

[77] *De civitate Dei* XI, 28. Cf. Plot. *Enn.* I, 4, 1.

a disposition enabling the possessor to distinguish between things good, bad and indifferent. 'Disorder'—the corruption of 'order'—occurs when the hierarchy of ordinated loves is reversed or inverted: witness the miser who so lusts after gold as to forget (or ignore) the claims of justice and the God to Whom all treasures belong by right. Let us observe in this text, as elsewhere, St. Augustine's concern to stress the role of charity as the originative and dynamic principle of justice. God loves man, and seeks his love in return: charity expressed as justice gives first to Him, and then to all others, what is their due.[78]

Next in the scale of secondary goods and ends occur the inevitable problems created by the day-to-day contacts and dealings of human beings with each other. Here the golden rule of charity enjoins: love all men equally. But since it is quite impossible to show benevolence to everyone in material affairs, there intervenes an appropriate 'order' based primarily (though not exclusively) upon the demands of kinship and affinity. Any who are bound to us by intimate ties have the first call upon our loving care, followed in turn by others in accordance with individual needs and our own ability to serve them.[79] These and all other licit human relationships derive their ultimate sanction and *raison d'être* from two Divine commands: *Thou shalt love the Lord thy God with thy whole heart and thy whole soul and thy whole mind and thou shalt love thy neighbour as thyself.* How does St. Augustine interpret these "categorical imperatives", so solemnly (and forcefully) reaffirmed by Christ as the foundation of "all the Law and the Prophets"? The wording of the second Dominical precept just reproduced itself suggests two initial problems, the first of which may be stated as follows: the commandment to love my neighbour as myself does not indicate how or by what means I ought to set about doing this. Yet—and here is the second difficulty—the former type of love is assumed to depend on the latter, which thus becomes in effect a yard-stick for appraising the quality of neighbourly love. From this it would appear

[78] *De doctr. christ.* I, 27, 28. *Ibid.* I, 3, 3-4, 4; *ibid.* I, 22, 20; PL 34, 20-21; 26. For further discussion of *frui-uti* in St. Augustine's thought, see Fruitio Dei in DS, Vol. V, 1964, cols. 1547-52, and the two following texts: *contr. Faust. Man.* XXII, 78; *de diver. quaest.* 30. The four cardinal virtues are all forms of love: *de mor.* I, 15, 25 (for *avaritia*, see e.g. *de civitate Dei* XII, 8). But justice, like charity, constitutes a "general" virtue in its own right (*de Gen. contr. Man.* II, 10, 14; PL 34, 204): "... iustitia ... ad omnes partes animae pertinet, quia ipsa ordo et aequitas animae est, qua sibi ista tria concorditer copulantur; prima, prudentia; secunda, fortitudo; tertia, temperantia; et in ista tota copulatione atque ordinatione iustitia". It follows that *perfect* justice is *diligere potius potiora, et minus minora* (*de vera relig.* 48, 93; PL 34, 164).

[79] *De doct. christ.* I, 28, 29. Cf. Cic. *de offic.* I, 45, 160.

in turn that self-love is, from at least one viewpoint, of prior importance in the scale of affections postulated by the commandment. Why then —we might enquire—has it been made a mere referent instead of the object of a direct and specific injunction? In answer to the latter query (which it is more convenient to consider first), St. Augustine has a traditional explanation ready to hand. The human mind and will—he says—do not require a special precept prescribing love of self, for the good and sufficient reason that man is naturally so constituted as to be incapable of refraining or abstaining from such an attachment. And what is more, from the moment that he begins to love himself, his affection spontaneously though unconsciously overflows and reaches out to embrace God in its superabundance. Let us here further observe that St. Augustine no less firmly holds as true the converse proposition: a man who aims at loving God (even to the exclusion of self) is nevertheless impelled—through some intrinsic necessity of his nature—to associate the subject of that love with its object in and by one and the same act of delectation.[80] The result of this process is twofold, involving as it does a unique reciprocity between creature and Creator. For in the first place, the very activity of loving God conduces to union with Him. *Deum diligis? Deus eris.* Again, the soul simultaneously becomes so identified with its own appetition (*talis est quisque, qualis ejus dilectio est*) that these two henceforth constitute an inseparable moral unity. In such a situation, love of God is once more seen to equate with self-love as St. Augustine consistently represents it throughout the texts thus far examined.

No student of the DCD needs to be reminded of its author's celebrated aphorism that two loves founded two societies: *amor Dei usque ad contemptum sui; amor sui usque ad contemptum Dei.*[80a] Compared with the material studied in the last paragraph, a profound and far-reaching transposition of meanings and terms has clearly occurred within the framework of these dicta and the numerous other passages in which Augustine elucidates their basic content. It would be otiose to anticipate our study of the contrasted notions of pride (*amor sui*) and humility (*amor Dei*) as Augustine develops and illustrates them from the DCD (and other works). Let us here make just this initial point: the two groups of texts which we are considering are not merely

[80] *De Trin.* XIV, 14, 18; PL 42, 1049-50; *de mor.* I, 26, 48. Though twofold in outreach when expressed and practised as a precept, charity itself remains in essence one and undivided: *serm.* 265, 8, 9. Why twofold? see *epist.* 155(b) 4, 15; PL 33, 672-3; *de mor.* I, 26, 49; PL 32, 1331-2.

[80a] The first two texts quoted on p. 126: *in epist. Ioan. ad Parth.* 2, 2, 14; PL 35, 1997: the third occurs in *de civitate Dri* XIV, 28; PL 41, 436.

adversative, but mutually exclusive. What gives to each its individual significance (and validity); what factors in particular, ultimately explain the two radically divergent concepts of self-love there presented can not be fully understood without recalling what it means, for Augustine, to be a rational creature endowed with free will. Human nature, for example, is neither self-made nor self-sufficient. If it were, man (as the source of his own wisdom) would require no other teacher. His love, flowing out in tranquillity from himself would return, undeflected to him, its sole centre of reference and terminus, thus at once assuring both indefectible personal happiness and access to the plenitude of self-realisation. But what are the facts? God, the Author of human nature, is both external and superior to what He has made. Man therefore not merely owes his being to the Creator, but also needs Him to attain wisdom, and—above all—beatitude . . .[80b]

Confronted by these basic ontological and moral realities, how is man to love his neighbour as himself? Without the first sin, our problem could never have arisen. The collective circumstances assumed in the first series of texts would continue to prevail. But Adam's fall has widened the natural gap between creature and Creator to the proportions of a humanly impassable gulf; man's appetition is irrevocably flawed, as the very existence of the Devil's Society suffices to prove. Thus every son of Adam stands at a cross-roads; for either charity (love of God and neighbour) or cupidity (love of the world) must ultimately determine his major options; there is no third choice.[80c] In terms of the two great Commandments which Christ has promulgated, he can only practise true self-love (and so obtain happiness, the universal *desideratum*) by referring each action to Him from Whom men receive all that is theirs to give. When, accordingly, one who knows how to love God in the sense just described is bidden: love your neighbour, the precept simply enjoins that so far as in a man lies, he must—by benevolence, counsel, reproof—commend such love of God to his neighbour as to a second self. Expressed in a differing idiom, St. Augustine's doctrine affirms that ordered self-love relates its prior, no less than remoter objects of concern to God as so many means (*uti*) to the sole End, Who is loved in and for Himself alone (*frui*). And this desire (*charitas*) is one which embraces the entire gamut of human life and nature, thus excluding any vacuum, as it were, wherein less worthy forms of appetite (*cupiditas*) might gain

---

[80b] *Ibid.* XI, 25.

[80c] *Enarr. in ps.* 31, 2, 5; PL 36, 260: "Amor Dei, amor proximi, charitas dicitur: amor mundi, amor huius saeculi, cupiditas dicitur."

a foothold in opposition and in detriment to the total outreach of God-centred love.[81]

Just as material goods may be abused or misused by men, so also Augustine attributes various forms of disordered love to human beings in their relationships with each other. Among those singled out for special mention, two—"lust" (*luxuria*) and "boastfulness" (*iactantia*)—had long been besetting sins of his. According to Augustine, the first argues no vice in the beautiful body desired but rather an inordinate appetite in the one who loves corporeal pleasures at the expense of temperance—a virtue which teaches men to give prior place to the incorruptible beauties of the spiritual order. Rather than a taint inherent in every work of praise as such, boastfulness should properly be considered the fault characteristic of a man so in love with others' approval that he despises the voice of his own conscience.[82]

Thus it is God alone for whom we may cherish love in which no excess is possible.[83] In all other loves, due moderation must be observed—so Augustine insists—if one wishes to preserve virtue, without which in turn no man can live a perfectly ordered life.[84] This is the force of Augustine's briefest and most succinct definition of virtue: "the order of love" (*ordo amoris*)[85]—an order itself determined by the hierarchy of ends mentioned above.

Thus far our analysis of St. Augustine's notion of order in society has suggested three conclusions of major importance for the present discussion. In the first place, it is the will, or love—enlightened by reason—that ordinates a man's moral and intellectual life towards God, his final End; to material things; and to his fellow creatures considered as persons. Secondly, we have shown that while order in the widest sense includes the totality of possible relationships as between creatures and Creator, these relationships themselves arise among and primarily concern the ingredients of being because being

81 *De civitate Dei* X, 3, 2; PL 41, 280-281. *De doct. christ.* I, 22, 21; PL 34, 26-27.

82 *De civitate Dei* XII, 8.

83 *Epist.* 109, 2 (written to Augustine by his friend Severinus).

84 *De civitate Dei* XV, 22.

85 *Ibid.* XV, 22. Augustine's most probable source for his conception of virtue as an ordered love would seem to be the Bible . . . ordinavit in me caritatem (*Canticle of Cancticles* II, 4). Another possible parallel source is the Latin translations made by St. Jerome and Rufinus of *Canticles* I and II (CGS, *Origenes Werke*, VIII, 26-241), where a complete theory of order appears in the commentaries. See H. Pétré, *Ordinata Caritas. Un Enseignement d'Origène sur la Charité*, *Recherches de Science Religieuse* XLII, 1, (janvier-mars, Paris: 1954), 40-57.

is the substrate of all reality. Lastly it was established that in Augustine's view a state or society exists as such only to the extent that it is united by a love in which all its members participate. Now we have already seeen that both of the great mystical Societies possess a characteristic form of love. Since, however, their loves differ—the one being in fact diametrically opposed to the other—the unity and hence the being and order of each[86] must reveal a correspondingly radical difference. The further development of our present line of inquiry—order and disorder in universal society—therefore demands a more precise study of these two loves, as Augustine understands them, and the manner in which they make things "one". In this connexion it should be recalled that individual beings—whether of physical or of spiritual nature[87]—are able to achieve a merely relative degree of unity, and this by the fitting arrangement or congruity of their parts as well as by an imitation of God which represents the only way wherein they can mirror the Divine attributes.[88] Situated within this framework of reference, our problem will then be to discover in what sense and to what extent the two mystical Societies repectively imitate, or approximate to, the properties of true being.

Now it is important at this point to note that the specificatory character of order within the society is defined by Augustine as love for no other reason than that love is the unifying principle of every true society. Moreover, just as in the case of the individual, so here also the ground or basis of the relative unity—and, therefore, being—of any society is the likeness of its constituent elements. And this likeness consists in "concord"[89] or "harmony",[90] which may be said to imitate unity either in the resemblance of equal parts or the proportion of unequal parts. One example of harmony—a commonplace of Graeco-Roman political philosophy—is found by Augustine within the whole pattern and structure of authority characteristic of the secular state, which reproduces the organization of subordinate entities like the individual, the family and the institution of friendship.[91] To consider

---

86 *De mor.* II, 6, 8; cf. Plot. *Enn.* V, 3, 15.

87 *De mus.* VI, 17, 58.

88 *De divers. quaest.* 46, 2; *de Gen. ad litt. imperf.* 16, 59; *de Trin.* VI, 10, 11.

89 To Augustine "concord" in the life of the state is, as it were, a meeting or juxtaposition of wills (loves) in all that pertains to the necessities of human existence. Within this area the Society of God—save in what concerns religious faith and practice—does not dissociate its aims and purposes from those of the Early Society: *de civitate Dei* XIX, 17.

90 Cf. fn. 47, above; also *de vera relig.* 30, 55.

91 Like the state, friendship derives its existence from similarity of character and habits among those participating therein; cf. *de mus.* VI, 17, 58.

the first case mentioned, for instance, every human being is composed of two parts or elements, one of which must perforce govern and control the other. Of these the soul represents the higher principle, as the seat of the intellect and of wisdom, while the body, because of its passions and appetites, represents the lower. Similarly within the family there is a basic problem of authority involving the father and his children, the master and his slaves. Here again, the father's right to rule his household is confirmed by both reasons and tradition, so that the existence of the family as such may be said to depend upon maintenance of the proper relationship between its two chief constituent parts. Finally, within the state itself some officials of major rank and authority (emperors, kings, generals, magistrates) are required to exercise supreme delegated command while the citizen body at large must render respect and obedience to them. Thus there may be predicated a very real relation of subordinate similitude as between passion and reason, flesh and spirit, man and God, slaves and masters, children and parents, citizens and the totality of the body politic, and in general, the ruled and their rulers.[92]

Now Augustine is not concerned to deny or challenge the desirability of this relationship, as far as it goes. Nor indeed does he oppose the accepted Roman thesis requiring officers of state to esteem and enforce the dictates of justice, in accordance with whose laws the higher principle governs the lower, as the soul rules the body. He does, however, as we have said, change the entire perspective of "likeness" and "imitation" as previously understood by substituting mutual love and the common love of a personal God for the supreme pagan criterion of abstract justice and a Stoicized notion of deity.[93]

As, then, within the secular state—itself no different in this respect from any other complex entity—so too in the case of the Heavenly Society Augustine assumes an ontological similitude of component parts. This similitude is "harmony" or "concord", i.e. a meeting or union of wills.[94] But in addition thereto, he posits a likeness in the order of morality. This, according to him, stems from the fact that the members of the Heavenly Society share and practise a virtue —love—which is identical in each case. For just as the individual soul tends to become more stable and self-consistent insofar as it maintains the same virtuous habits and dispositions,[95] so also by reason of its collective love for God the Society of God achieves the ontological

[92] Fn. 25, above.
[93] Fns. 48-51.
[94] Fn. 69.
[95] *De mus.* VI, 17, 58.

and moral unity, stability, and permanence inseparable from true being. And such love, be it noted, is both the instrument and the measure of any ordered imitation of the Divine. For—so Augustine insists—to love God is the only way to become like Him and to share His attributes.[96]

According to Augustine, the Earthly Society also possesses a distinctive form of imitation, love, and therefore unity. But this imitation is perverse, since its ultimate model and pattern is Satan rather than Christ, i.e. creature in place of Creator. The love of self that characterizes the Devil's Society is similarly perverse, being both "privative" and "separative". It is "privative" precisely because, depriving this Society's members of their common Good, it induces them to seek their good within themselves.[97] Such self-love is also "separative", inasmuch as it alienates and divides each member both from God and his neighbour.[98] Love of this sort by its very nature evidently lacks all power of "intercommunication": it therefore is not and cannot possibly be a "social bond" or unificatory principle. This, of course, is not to say that St. Augustine fails to recognise within the Earthly Society the existence of a congruity or similarity of component parts, i.e. a meeting of wills, and therefore a certain measure of unity. Thus some of its members, for example—as in the case of the Roman Empire—happen to profess a common notion of justice. But as we have seen, Augustine does not admit pagan justice to be a "bond of union" in any ontological or moral sense.[99] His reasons for this attitude surely gain added significance in the light of our earlier analysis of self-love. For the essence of the classical definition of justice is "to each his own".[100] As interpreted by the standard Greek or Roman commentators, this formula—with its accent upon the separative, the purely individualistic and the negative aspects of ethical obligation—may well have appeared to St. Augustine to be nothing but a juridical expression of the self-love pervading the Earthly Society. Again, one might argue that the members of this Society are also united by the fact of a common allegiance to their leader, Satan. Now according to Augustine, the pride which they imitate in Satan does indeed create a kind of social and moral

[96] *De civitate Dei* VIII, 1; *de divers. quaest.* 35, 2; *in epist. Ioan. ad Parth.* 2, 2, 14.

[97] According to St. Augustine, this pernicious self-love (*damnosus sui amor*) is called "privative" (*privatus*) because ". . . potius a detrimento quam ab incremento dictum elucet. Omnis enim privatio minuit . . . ex communi ad proprium . . . redigitur" (*de Gen. ad litt.* XI, 15, 19; PL 34, 436-37).

[98] *Ibid.* XI, 15, 19.

[99] See fns. 32-34, above.

[100] Cf. fn. 31.

solidarity whose corporate manifestation is found precisely in the Satanic Society itself (*corpus diaboli*).[101] But the Devil revolted against God—the only source of true and enduring unity—and hence was condemned to an eternity of separation from Him.[102]

If, then, a society as such is constituted in unity—and therefore being—solely by a common love, it follows that the Earthly Society is not a true Society, for while its members each possess a certain—indeed an identical—sort of love, this latter is quite evidently not a love shared by all in the sense that it is directed toward a common object. Hence the Earthly Society *is not*, i.e. it has neither unity nor the goodness of being. In a word, it is disordered. That this conclusion follows logically from an overall survey of Augustine's doctrine concerning love and order—as applied to the "state"—could not easily be denied. That it appears to contradict the position previously attributed to him is open to even less doubt. How can we reconcile this seeming discrepancy in St. Augustine's thought? The answer here lies in a reconsideration of how he himself understands the problem of being. It will be recalled from our earlier discussion of this question that Augustine says of creatures that they both *are* and *are not*.[103] They *are* insofar as each owes its existence to a nature constituted by mode, species, and order.[104] They *are not* because having been created from nothing, each is mutable and therefore liable to a ceaseless fluctuation between being and non-being.[105] Now the Earthly Society, wherein disorder rules supreme, constantly "tends" or "moves" toward non-being—without, to be sure, ever reaching its term. We may also note that, according to St. Augstine, the same Society's separation or "aversion" from God while on earth—a separation which results precisely in the disorder or non-being (and hence of evil) just noted—is also to persist throughout eternity.[106]

(To be continued.)

D. J. MacQueen
University of Ghana
Legon, Accra

[101] *De Gen. ad litt.* XI, 24, 31.
[102] *De civitate Dei* XIV, 11, 2.
[103] *Enarr. in ps.* 70, *serm.* 2, 6-7; PL 36, 895-96. Cf. *de mor.* I, 12, 20.
[104] *De nat. bon.* 3, 5, 8, 9, 13, 22, 23.
[105] *Ibid.* 10.
[106] Above, fn. 26.

[5]

AUGUSTINE'S CRITIQUE OF HUMAN JUSTICE*

GAYLON L. CALDWELL

"What shall I say of these judgments which men pronounce on men? . . . . Melancholy and lamentable judgments they are . . . . " This was the conclusion of a fifth-century theologian who probed the practice of human justice.[1] And, with the possible exception of the occasional individual who has succumbed to the occupational hazard described by the Advisory Council of Judges as risking "the danger of becoming convinced that both as a man and as an official he is omniscient and omnipotent,"[2] it is a conclusion that is probably mirrored by any judge as he surveys his decisions. The experience is not limited to professional judges, since everyone frequently finds himself in a situation in which he must pass judgment on his fellows, if not from the bench, then from the jury box, as arbitrator in neighborhood disputes or in domestic squabbles. When he is obliged to judge there are many times that, with St. Augustine and the Psalmist, he would cry to God: "From my necessities deliver Thou me!"

Although it is significant that the verdict of a Christian bishop of a third-rate city in Roman Africa should retain its validity across a millennium and a half of human history, Reinhold Niebuhr provides a short explanation of why it should not be surprising: "Augustine was, by general consent, the first great 'realist' in western history."[3] Not that Augustine's description of legal judgments as "lamentable" made him a "realist" in the sense that cynics claim that appellation for, on the contrary, he recognized that "melancholy and lamentable" judicial decisions need not be the norm for human justice—that they are "lamentable" precisely because they might be other than they are. Rather, he is a "realist" because he gave an adequate account of the tensions within men, between man and man, and between man and his institutions, purged of the optimistic expectancy of the classical

---

*The author acknowledges with gratitude the financial assistance of the Lilly Endowment Research Program in Christianity and Politics which made this study possible, and appreciation to his colleagues at the seminar held at Duke University in 1958.

[1]Augustine, *The City of God,* bk. XIX, c. 6. Emphasis added.

[2]*Advisory Council of Judges of the National Probation ad Parole Association, Guides for Sentencing* 7 (1957).

[3]Reinhold Niebuhr, *Christian Realism and Political Problems* (New York: Scribners, 1953), p. 120.

philosophers who had taught that reason, by itself, was capable of bringing all sub-rational forces under control. For unlike the Greeks, Augustine had an understanding of *sin,* and located its seat in the will rather than in a carnal body that might be subdued by a virtuous mind. If the Hellenistic philosophies had intrigued him with the potentiality of human reason, the Hebrew scriptures had convinced him that sin was the consequence of human pride. From his encounters with Hebrew, Greek, and Roman thought, he had confronted the ideal of justice: from his Christian heritage he discovered why that ideal of justice is never completely realized by human beings. He forged his ideas in the heat of disputations with infidels, schismatics, and heretics, but he tested them, too, in concrete situations that arose from his multifarious concerns as a pastor at a time in history when civil power was tottering. The poor conditions of provincial courts during the fifth century led non-Christians as well as Christians to the houses of distinguished bishops, for, although purely voluntary tribunals, episcopal courts received jurisdiction over disputes brought before them and their decrees were given legal effect by the Roman state. Augustine spent most of his time in court.[4]

To an age that has little relish for theology but a great deal of admiration for "realism," Augustine's critique of human justice is an attractive object of study because it affords a standard by which lay and professional judges may analyze their own decisions as well as criticize those of others. It is a standard informed by Biblical and classical insights and tempered by vast social experience. Before one dismisses its premises as unsuited to the present age regardless of their validity for the religious situation obtaining in the collapsing Roman Empire, he should consider that ancient Romans and contemporary Americans share the same humanity and their cultures share the same premises. Nor are the differences between the Roman and Anglo-American legal systems sufficient to restrict Augustine's thought to antiquarian interest. He never concerned himself with a critique of his own legal system, but addressed himself to its executors *qua* men. His ideas have meaning and value for the twentieth century because one recognizes himself in Augustine's description of man and has experienced with him the appalling responsibility of passing judgment on his fellows.

[4]Joseph McCabe, *St. Augustine and His Age* (New York: G. P. Putnam's Sons, 1903). According to McCabe, Augustine "soon won a reputation throughout Africa as an arbitrator and mediator, and petitions came to him from all quarters." *Id.*, p. 265.

For these reasons he does have something to contribute to the internal dialogue of a modern judge although he does not provide a convenient code that converts jurisprudence into mechanics.

The project here undertaken is to determine the principles suggested by St. Augustine whereby one might judge his fellows more justly, and then apply these to the analysis of a recent case in American law. The first requires a consideration of the nature of man, his communities, his wrong-doing, and its punishment— always, the Bishop of Hippo would insist, in their context with God. The second will reaccount the fact situation of a leading case, its unlike interpretations, and a reconsideration of the decisions from an Augustinian position.

I

Fundamental to Augustine's theory of justice is his conception of the pattern of creation, sin, judgment, and restoration that he held to emerge invariably from the dialectical relationship of God and His creatures. This relationship may be indicated briefly: God, in His goodness, creates and sustains man; man, in his pride, sins; God, in His righteousness, pronounces judgment; but in His love, restores. This sequence of events, which follows the divine pattern of justice, may not proceed at the same pace in any two circumstances. Rather, it may move at a different rate and with varied observable effects in the experiences of individuals, communities, and civilizations. It culminates beyond history in a last judgment and a final salvation. Through faith one can discern the rhythm of this pattern and know that it is inexorable, just and beneficent. This is the archetype of human justice.

According to Augustine, in His creation of the cosmos, God effected an hierarchical order in which equality obtains among members of the same class and where the higher orders have dominion, in love, over the lower. This hierarchy was conceived to have been made up of broad general classes, i.e., among things that have life: sentient creatures rank above those with no sensation; intelligent agents rank above creations with no intelligence; and immortals are placed above mortals. The end is peace within and among orders with the two categories of rational creatures, angels and men, enjoying the eternal peace of God. In his acceptance of Genesis as the valid version of creation, Augustine repeatedly stresses the words: "And God saw everything that he had made, and behold, it was very good." In the beginning there was no corruption, no unjust domination, no vice. God desired men to live together in harmony and peace and to underscore this, derived them all from Adam so that the bonds of relationship would supplement the implanted tendency for fellowship. "He did not intend," Augustine wrote, "that His rational creature, who was made in His image, should have dominion over anything but the irrational creation—not man over man, but man over beasts."[5] Yet everywhere is experienced man's dominion over man: master over slave, father over children, king over subjects, judge over the prisoner at bar. To understand why this appears to be the natural order and why God permits such domination to exist, a consideration of Augustine's conception of sin is necessary.

Peace between man and God, the "well-ordered obedience of faith to eternal law," was disrupted by the unwillingness of Adam and Eve to accept their positions as creatures. In their pride, they presumed to be like God. Pride had led man to live only for himself. "It was this that made him listen with pleasure to the words, 'Ye shall be as gods,' " the Bishop of Hippo held. "By craving to be more, man becomes less; and by aspiring to be self-sufficing, he fell away from Him who truly suffices him."[6] This sin could not be attributed to the desires of the flesh, as Platonists avowed, because this creation was "very good." It is not the body, but the corruptibility of the body which burdens the soul.[7] Therefore, the original sin must be attributed to will, which although created "good," nevertheless was free. Since the will cannot become evil without desiring to do so, Augustine held that its failings are justly punished.

Adam's legacy to posterity included a proud and disobedient will and a corrupted society into which men are born and live as slaves of their appetites—men who "run to such enormities in sin, that even the beasts devoid of rational will . . . would live more securely and peaceably with their own kind than man."[8] Yet God's original good creation was not completely vitiated, and "though there is sin, all things are not therefore full of sin."[9] Thus, although the human mind is tainted by sin, nevertheless, it is "capable of knowledge and of receiving instruction, fit to understand what is true and

[5]Augustine, *The City of God*, bk. XIX, c. 15.

[6]*Id.*, bk. XIV, c. 13.

[7]*Id.*, bk. XIII, c. 16.

[8]"For not even lions or dragons have ever waged with their kind such wars as men have waged with one another." *Id.*, bk. XII, c. 22.

[9]*Id.*, bk. XI, c. 23.

to love what is good."[10] Virtue, then, is possible to attain and it is achieved by learning, but Augustine insisted it have a theocentric reference.[11] The primary concern of the virtuous person is "to wage perpetual war with vices—not those that are outside of us, but within; not other men's but our own."[12] The virtuous man submits himself to God, his body to his soul, and his vices, even when they rebel, to his reason, "which either defeats or at least resists them . . . " In doing these things he becomes a pilgrim in the City of God.[13]

Since the fall from the perfect harmony ordained by God, men have perpetually struggled to establish a universal harmony ordained by themselves. Because "there is no vice so clean contrary to nature that it obliterates even the faintest traces of nature,"[14] the artificial orderings of man more or less reflect the just arrangement of God. Although human laws are diverse, they all tend to the same end: earthly peace, i.e., "well-ordered concord." Similarly, just as God decrees judgment for sin which violates divine peace, human rulers, although not particularly concerned with *sin,* punish the disturbance of civil peace as *crime,* and heads of families discipline the wrong-doing that disturbs domestic peace. Were it not for their vitiated condition, all men would recognize that, except in perverted communities, both crime and wrong-doing are identical with sin and are traceable to pride. The City of God, whether in the international, national or family community, knows no *malum prohibitum* but only *malum in se.*

However, the pattern of divine justice is not always discernible in the Earthly City. Whenever a pilgrim of the City of God is called to govern his fellows (and Augustine insisted that he must serve), he remembers the divine pattern and not only recognizes himself as a sinner judging sinners, but also recognizes himself as an agent for the redemption of the sinners. However, human

---

[10]*Id.*, bk. XXII, c. 24.

[11]Otherwise it becomes "inflated with pride" and so actually is vice.

[12]*Id.*, bk. XIX, c. 4. "For however well one maintains the conflict, and however thoroughly he has subdued these enemies, there steals in some evil thing which, if it do not find ready expression in act, slips out by the lips, or insinuates itself in the thought; and therefore his peace is not full so long as he is at war with his vices. For it is a doubtful conflict he wages with those that resist, and his victory over those that are defeated is not secure, but full of anxiety and effort." *Id.*, c. 27.

[13]Persons who, by the grace of God and their own free will, commit themselves to the "love of God, even to the contempt of self" form the City of God; those who indulge "the love of self, even to the contempt of God" belong to the Earthly City. *Id.* at bk. XIV, c. 28. This simple division exhausts all possibilities since "no man can serve two masters."

[14]*Id.*, bk. XIX, c. 12.

judges often do not recognize that redemption is the concomitant of judgment. Augustine does not doubt that the human judge may know this, for he writes of a "spiritual light with which our mind is somehow irradiated," and insists that "our power to judge is proportioned to our acceptance of this light."[15] The quality of justice will vary directly with the quantity of pride in the public officers, since pride makes judgments punitive; but when pride does not obscure this illumination, any man will realize that "evil is removed, not by removing any nature, or part of nature, which has been introduced by evil, but by healing and correcting that which had been vitiated and depraved."[16] Judges who indicate the latter disposition may properly be called "true fathers of their households." St. Augustine affords an example of the application of justice in the primordial unit of society in these words:

> And if any member of the family interrupts the domestic peace by disobedience, he is corrected by word or blow, or some kind of just and legitimate punishment, such as society permits, that he may himself be the better for it, and be re-adjusted to the family harmony from which he had dislocated himself.[17]

In a letter to Marcellinus, whom Emperor Honorius had appointed as tribune and special legate to preside over and judge the joint conference of Catholic and Donatist bishops at Carthage in 411, Augustine advised how civil justice should be applied by a governmental official:

> As a Christian judge, you must play the part of a loving father, you must show anger for wrong-doing, but remember to make allowance for human weakness; do not indulge your inclination to seek vengeance for the vile acts of sinners, but direct your effort to the cure of the sinner's wounds.[18]

Although Augustine's criticism of human justice centers on the

[15] *Id.*, bk. XI, c. 27.

[16] *Id.*, bk. XIV c. 11.

[17] *Id.*, bk. XIX, c. 16.

[18] Augustine, *Epistles,* No. 133. Concerning the curious circumstances that an interested party had been named to judge the dispute, McCabe wrote: "Marcellinus was a zealous Catholic, and was much influenced by Augustine; and of the imperial inclination there could be no doubt. It is true that Marcellinus offered to retire if the Donatists desired another judge; but the tone of their reply, declining the offer, shows that they had no hope of securing an impartial judge. The debate was a farce, and the verdict a foregone conclusion." McCabe, *op. cit., supra* note 4, p. 317.

failure of its practitioners to recognize that they are sinners judging sinners and their consequent inability to make their judgments restorative rather than retributive, this does not exhaust his suggestions as to the principles that should be applied in promoting and protecting the peace of the Earthly City. Due to his lack of system, these specific principles must be gleaned from his voluminous writings. However, they are capable of being stated simply: (1) It is possible for people to live without crime and they should do so from love of righteousness, although fear has proved to be an effective deterrent.[19] (2) The magistrates should be more concerned with establishing the responsibility for crime than punishing the criminal.[20] (3) When apprehending and detaining suspected persons, the public officials must respect the law.[21] (4) In order to obtain evidence, the least savage of allowable techniques of torture should be employed.[22] (5) There is value in a frank and full confession of guilt.[23] (6) Whenever practicable, restitution must be made.[24] (7) If a guilty person should not prove amenable to correction, he should not be permitted to glory in his wrong-

---

19Presumably this would not apply to the *malum prohibitum* offense that was inimicable to the faith. Otherwise, the pilgrim should respect the authorities of the various communities. "At present it is enough that we live without crime;" he wrote, "and he who thinks he lives without sin puts aside not sin, but pardon." Augustine, *The City of God*, bk. XIV, c. 9. To Macedonius he wrote: "However, men are not to be called good because they refrain from wrong-doing through their fear of such things, (i.e., 'the powers of kings, the death penalty of judges, the barbed hooks of the executioner, the weapons of the soldier, the right of punishment of the overlord, even the severity of the good father')—no one is good through dread of punishment but through love of righteousness—even so, it is not without advantage that human recklessness should be confined by fear of the law so that innocence may be safe among evil-doers, and the evil-doers themselves may be cured by calling on God when their freedom of action is held in check by fear of punishment." Augustine, *Epistles*, No. 153.

20"It is more important to find out than punish . . . . " *Id.*, at No. 133.

21Cf. his action in the illegal detention of Faventius, *supra* at 9-10.

22Augustine praised Marcellinus for not "stretching the defendants on the rack, nor by tearing him with hooks, nor by burning them with fire, nor by beating them with rods—a form of discipline used by schoolmasters, by parents themselves, and often even by bishops in their courts." Augustine, *Epistles*, No. 133. His best known attack on the insufficiency of torture as a method of disclosing truth is found in his *City of God*, bk. XIX, c. 6.

23He especially castigated Adam and Eve for casting about for an excuse for their disobedience to God and found the pride which dictated such behavior to be "worse and more damnable" than the sin they had committed. He did not allow that persuasion made the transgression less. What he especially appears to lament is the fact that: "Here there is no word of begging pardon, no word of entreaty for healing." *Id.*, bk. XIV, c. 14.

24Cf. his letter to Macedonius discussed *supra* at 14.

doing.[25] And, finally, (8) It is the obligation of authorities to lead offenders to God by example and teaching.[26] In his intercessions with secular authorities on behalf of alleged and actual malefactors, Augustine convincingly documented the fact that he practiced the ideas he advocated.

An interesting example is Augustine's efforts on behalf of Faventius, a tenant farmer who took sanctuary in his church. Faventius had some reason to fear the lord of the estate, "and waited there, as refugees generally do, to see if his difficulty could be settled by our intervention."[27] As time passed he grew careless, left the safety of sanctuary to dine with a friend, and was abducted. The Bishop immediately alerted the tribune of the coast guards, but the latter failed to find Faventius. Augustine then conducted his own search and finally located the house in which the tenant was confined. Florentinus, the detaining officer, refused to permit Augustine's priest to see his prisoner although the priest had brought Florentinus a copy of the law stipulating the rights of an accused. The Bishop wrote at least four letters in the attempt to secure for Faventius his privilege under the law of having an examination in the municipal court to discover whether or not he wished thirty days under light guard to set his affairs in order. Epistle 113, apparently the second Augustine had written to the tribune of the coast guards regarding the matter, requested that the letter be forwarded to the arresting officer and suggested that an agreement might be reached "by friendly discussion." If not, Augustine pledged himself to trust the verdict of the trial court. Epistle 114, to Florentinus, began tersely:

> By whose authority and command you carried off Faventius is something for you to look to for yourself, but this I know, that all authority set up under the power of the emperor is subject to law . . . . I sent a copy of the law by my brother and

[25]"For he who sins is still worse if he rejoices in his loss of righteousness . . . . certainly it is more suitable for a wicked man to grieve in his punishment than to rejoice in his fault." Augustine, *City of God*, bk. XIX, c. 13. In a letter to Macedonius, he observed: "Just as it is sometimes mercy to punish, so it may be cruelty to pardon." Augustine, *Epistles*, No. 153.

[26]Augustine was not at all reluctant to insist on the obligation of magistrates to set a good example. In 413 he chided Caecilian, Prefect of the Province of Africa, for remaining a catechumen. Augustine, *Epistles*, No. 151. In *Epistle* No. 112 he had urged the Roman Proconsul into communion; and to Macedonium, Vicar of Africa, he recommended that "you rouse the men subject to your authority. (i.e., in his secular position) and lead them to worship God, both by the example of your own devout life and by your zeal for their welfare . . . . " *Id.*, No. 155.

[27]*Id.*, No. 115.

> fellow priest, Caelestinus, which you certainly ought to have known about, even before I sent it. . . . However, I'm sending it again in this letter . . .

He urged that Florentinus "kindly grant this favor to your own reputation and to my request" and concluded by reminding the detaining officer of his obligation to do "what the law of the emperor commands, since you are a public official in his service." Epistle 115, to Fortunatus, bishop of Cirta, hinted that Faventius' place of confinement had been changed and "there is reason to fear that he may suffer some kind of harm if he is brought before the governor's tribunal." Augustine suspected this because "although the judge has the highest reputation for honesty, he has to deal with a very rich man;" so "to prevent his money from influencing the court," Augustine requested Fortunatus to take the letter to the governor and read it to him. "Ask him to put off the hearing of the case," Augustine pleaded, "since I do not know whether he is guilty or innocent." Significantly, he urged the governor "not to make light of the fact that the laws were not observed in regard to the man." Although it is not known what became of the unfortunate Faventius, the letters preserve Augustine's righteous indignation over the lack of what contemporary Americans know as "due process of law."

The Donatist controversy, an interesting chapter in the history of Christianity, is particularly fascinating for a student of Augustinian legal ideas. In it the Bishop is seen as occupying a prominent role, first as the public challenger of the Donatist theological position, then as the instrument in securing the imperial edicts which outlawed the schismatic faction, and finally, as intercessor on behalf of Donatist prisoners.[28] His consistent attitude was that disturbers of the civil peace should be apprehended, instructed in their error, and then shown mercy by the courts and administrators. To this end he was prepared to cooperate with the administrators, plea to the judges, threaten both administrators and judges, and suggest suitable remedies to everyone concerned.

[28]In a letter to an Italian priest, who apparently had described the horrors of the barbarian invasions, Augustine mentioned the criminal activities of members of the outlawed sect: "Donatist clerics and Circumcillions, i.e., roving bands of lay toughs have so ravaged our churches that the deeds of barbarians might be less destructive. What barbarian could have thought up the idea of throwing lime and vinegar, as they do, into the eyes of clerics, after inflicting horrible blows and wounds on other parts of their bodies? They plunder and burn houses; they carry off the stored crops and trample down the growing ones; by threatening to do the same to others, they force many to be rebaptized." *Id.*, No. 111.

After the Council of Carthage, unreconstructed Donatists were branded criminals and were apprehended both by civil and ecclesiastical authorities. In 412 the public officers arrested several Donatists who confessed to the murder of one of two delegates sent to the imperial court following the Council of Carthage four years earlier. They also admitted to having beaten a Catholic priest after cutting off his finger and putting out his eye. Augustine immediately wrote the following to Marcellinus regarding these prisoners:

> I have been a prey to the deepest anxiety for fear your Highness might perhaps decree that they be sentenced to the utmost penalty of the law. . . I beg you by the faith which you have in Christ, and by the mercy of the same Lord Christ, not to do this, nor to let it be done under any circumstances . . . . However, we do not object to wicked men being deprived of their freedom to do wrong, but we wish it to go just that far, so that, without losing their life or being maimed in any part of their body, they may be restrained by the law from their mad frenzy, guided into the way of peace and sanity, and assigned to some useful work to replace their criminal activities.

Then, in the event that his plea was not sufficiently effective, he concluded with these words:

> If you will not hear the request of a friend, hear the considered opinion of a bishop; in fact, since I am speaking to a Christian, I may say without conceit, in a matter of such importance, that it is your duty to listen when a bishop commands.[29]

In order to insure that the judgment on the prisoners be inspired by a desire to restore rather than to seek retribution, Augustine enclosed a letter which he requested Marcellinus to deliver to the Proconsul of Africa. Augustine saluted this official with the words: "I know, of course that you are steeped in the Christian faith, and this gives me greater confidence in addressing your Excellency not only with a request," and he continued, "but even with a warning . . . . " Augustine admitted that "ruling a province is different from ruling a church" since "the former must be governed by instilling fear, the latter is to be made lovable by the use of mildness" and frankly stated that if he were making the plea to a non-Christian judge he would employ a less direct approach,

[29] *Id.*, No. 133.

"but even so I should not fail to present the case of the Church." He then suggested a suitable judgment:

> By a monstrous crime they tore limbs from a living body; do you by a work of mercy make them apply to some useful work the wholly intact limbs which they exercised in their unspeakable deeds . . . . They cut short the lifespan of a minister of the Church by killing him; do you lengthen the span of years for the living enemies of the Church so that they might repent?

His summation contained a veiled threat:

> Men are wont to appeal from a too light sentence when their convicted enemies are treated too leniently, but we so love our enemies that we would appeal from your severe sentence if we did not rely on your Christian obedience.[30]

Four years previously he had written Donatus, then Proconsul of Africa, concerning the death penalty that had been decreed for convicted Donatists and threatened that the Church would not bring such cases to the court in the future if capital punishment were not abandoned. In this letter he more fully explained his position:

> But, there is one thing only about which I have grave misgivings, when you administer justice; namely, that you decide to apply the penalty with more regard for the gravity of their crimes than for the exercise of Christian clemency. . . . We beg you by Christ himself not to act thus rigidly. We are not looking for vengeance on earth over our enemies . . . Hence, in applying the deterring effects of judges and laws, we wish them to be restrained, but not to be put to death; otherwise they might incur the punishment of everlasting judgment . . . Act against their offenses so that some of them may repent of having sinned.[31]

In the year 414 Macedonius, Vicar of Africa, sent to enforce imperial decrees against the Donatists, inaugurated a series of letters with the Bishop of Hippo that not only permitted the latter to expound his ideas of justice, but also hinted of a tension between the secular authorities and the ecclesiastical intercessors. In his first letter, Macedonius raised three issues: (1) He doubted if priestly intercession is a part of religion and asked: "How can we

[30]*Id.*, No. 134.
[31]*Id.*, No. 100.

argue that any crime, of whatever sort, should be forgiven us, and how can we approve it by wishing it to go unpunished?" (2) He opined that "human behavior has now come to this pass that men wish to have the punishment of their crime remitted and at the same time to keep the profit which they have gained by their evil deeds." And, "your priestly office thinks that intercession should be made for these, also . . . . " Finally, (3) he feared that relaxation of discipline would encourage others to commit crime.[32]

Augustine responded with alacrity and at great length. Briefly stated, his argument to answer the first point raised, was as follows: The clerics pitied the man while detesting the crime, and the greater the vice the less they wanted the culprit to die unrepentant since there is no other place to correct morals except in this life. "Consequently," he wrote, "we are forced by our love for humankind to intercede for the guilty lest they end this life by punishment, only to find that punishment does not end with this life." In the event that intercession was successful, the Church was prepared to deal with its members. For example, in the case of public sins "we keep them from participation in the Sacrament of the altar" so that by repentance and punishing themselves they atone to "Him whom they have flouted by their sin." Thus, the ones who sincerely repent do not let their wrong-doing go unpunished and as for those who do not repent, Augustine is sure that "no one who despises His high and holy judgment escapes it." But if God shows patience to them in this life, he argued, how much more should His creatures do so! "You see, then," he concluded, "that it is a matter of religion and does not involve us in a share of evil doing when we intercede, if not as criminals for criminals, at least as sinners for sinners, and, I think, with sinners—please take this as spoken sincerely and without offense."

Concerning the second complaint, the Bishop readily admitted that if restitution of goods is possible but is not made, this is *pretense* rather than *repentance*. Now it may be, he continued, that repentance without restitution of goods is possible since the culprit may have dissipated his ill-got gains. However, he insisted, if a criminal has suffered physical punishment at the hands of the offended party he has already paid. If intercession is made to the creditor, he has been afforded an opportunity for showing mercy. Probably stung by the implication of the tendency of the clergy to

---

[32] *Id.*, No. 152.

show too much mercy to the villain and too little concern for the victim, Augustine stated flatly:

> This, indeed, I would say with complete assurance, that the one who intercedes for a man to save him from restoring his ill-gotten goods and who fails, when someone has fled to him for refuge, to force him to make restitution as far as he honestly can, is a party to the theft and the guilt.[33]

However, as a trained rhetorician with wide experience, Augustine declined to leave the argument while on the defensive. Instead, he suggested other circumstances to Macedonius that are not unfamiliar:

> If there is to be a more sincere regard for justice, it would be more honest to say to the advocate: 'Pay back what you received when you stood against truth, supported evil-doing, deceived the judge, won your case by lying,' as you see that many of the most honorably and eloquent men seem to allow themselves to do, not only with safety but even with renown.

Who is more cruel, the Bishop of Hippo asked the Vicar of Africa, the one who steals from or cheats a rich man or the one who destroys the poor man by usury?

The third point posed more difficulty for St. Augustine because he accepted it in principle. He did not meet it directly. He acknowledged that "when we intercede for an offender who deserves condemnation, there sometimes are consequences which we do not intend." He indicated that such consequences might take either of two forms: (1) That the unrepentant "goes on rioting about more extravagantly" and his escape from death "may be the cause of many other deaths," or, (2) that he does repent but others seeing he has escaped punishment commit the same crime. Augustine was particularly concerned about the unrepentant and disclosed that the bishops "threaten them, sometimes with human, but especially and always with divine, judgment." Further, they might be rebuked and reproached, "some in private, some publicly, according as the diversity of character shows the possibility of reforming them." And finally, "we even cut them off from Communion at the holy altar." In spite of all this, his case seems to rest finally on this ground:

> Yet, I think these evil consequences are not to be laid to our

[33] *Id.*, No. 153.

> charge when we intercede with you, but, rather, the good aims which we have in view and which we intend when we act thus . . . .[34]

In his final communication, Macedonius capitulated, but not without a few barbs for the African clergy:

> For you do not insist, as most men in your circle do, on extorting from me whatever any anxious client happens to want, but you suggest what you think can properly be asked of a judge weighed down by many cares . . . Therefore, I have granted to those you have recommended the fulfillment of their desires, having previously opened the way to hope.

He concluded the letter:

> I have written this in the midst of my preoccupation with other cares, which may be vain when we think of the end of the world, but are still pressing enough, being part of the consequences of our being born.[35]

Augustine replied with a homily on the insufficiency of philosophy as a guide to happiness and a plea that Macedonius lead the men subject to his authority to God.[36]

II

Morissette v. United States,[37] now a leading case in criminal law, provides an excellent opportunity for an Augustinian criticism because it is primarily concerned with an aspect he found to be crucial, and that most judges find most difficult—intent.

"This would have remained a profoundly insignificant case to all except its immediate parties," Justice Jackson began in his opinion for a unanimous Court, "had it not been so tried and submitted to the jury as to raise questions both fundamental and far reaching in federal criminal law . . . . "[38] The fact situation was simple and essentially undisputed: Joseph Morisette, a 27-year old junk dealer with a small family, went deer hunting with his brother-in-law in a large wooded tract leased by the federal government from the State of Michigan for use as a target bombing range.

[34] *Ibid.*
[35] *Id.*, No. 154.
[36] *Id.*, No. 155.
[37] 342 U.S. 246 (1951).
[38] *Id.*, 247.

Signs stating "Danger—Keep Out—Bombing Range" were posted about the site but were ignored by the local hunters who knew the woods as good deer country. Morissette failed to get a deer and thought to defray the expenses of the trip by taking a load of simi-lated bomb casings and selling them as scrap. These casings had been dumped into piles "to get them out of the way" and some had accumulated for as long as four years and were rusting out. He loaded the casings into his truck in broad daylight, took them to a farm and flattened them with a tractor, in full view of passersby, reloaded the scrap and hauled it 180 miles to Flint where it sold for $28 a ton. He realized $84 for his effort. When apprehended some weeks later he voluntarily and candidly confessed, but alleged that he thought the casings had been abandoned. He was indicted for "knowingly" converting government property to his use, tried in district court, and sentenced to a fine of $200 and two months in prison.[39]

In appealing the conviction, two questions were raised: (1) whether criminal intent had to be proved, and, (2) whether the trial jury had been improperly instructed.[40] The district court had instructed the jury: "The question of intent is whether or not he intended to take the property. He says he did. Therefore, if you believe either side, he is guilty."[41] In affirming the decision, the court of appeals said, *inter alia*:

> The appellant contends that, in order to constitute a crime, there must have been a felonious intent in his mind at the time he converted to his use property of the United States on premises leased by it. This argument was rejected, the district judge taking the practical and correct view that the statute means what it says and is violated when a person 'knowingly converts to his use' government property. . . . Manifestly, the purpose of Congress in enacting section 741 was to afford added protection against the taking of government property. As we have interpreted the statute, appellant was guilty of its violation beyond a shadow of a doubt, as evidenced even by

[39]18 U.S.C. § 641, so far as pertinent, recites: "Whoever embezzles, steals, purloins, or knowingly converts to his use or the use of another, or without authority sells, conveys or disposes of any record, voucher, money or thing of value of the United States or of any department or agency thereof, or any property made or being made under contract for the United States or any department or agency thereof . . . . Shall be fined not more than $10,000 or imprisoned not more than ten years, or both; but if the value of such property does not exceed the sum of $100, he shall be fined not more than $1,000 or imprisoned not more than one year or both." 62 *Stat.* 725 (1948), 18 U.S.C.A. § 641 (1950).

[40]*Morissette v. United States*, 187 F.2d 427 (1951).

[41]*Morissette v. United States,* 342 U.S. 246, 249 (1951).

> his own admissions. . . . The lenient sentence imposed evinced a sound exercise of judicial discretion vested in the district courts in empowering them to make the punishment fit the crime within the limits of the statute violated.[42]

In a dissenting opinion, Judge McAllister insisted that Morissette's act was certainly a trespass against the right of the owner to its property, but he urged that the crime of larceny requires proof of felonious intent. His view of the case may be summed up in these words: "The intent of appellant was the crucial point in the case. Whether his intent was innocent or wrongful was a question for the determination of the jury."[43]

The Supreme Court adopted the interpretation of the dissenter, and one passage of its opinion, squarely in the Augustinian tradition, is as follows:

> The contention that an injury can amount to a crime only when inflicted by intention is no provincial or transient notion. It is as universal and persistent in mature systems of law as belief in freedom of the human will and a consequent ability and duty of the normal individual to choose between good and evil.[44]

The legal problem is aggravated by the increasing number of "public welfare" offenses, i.e., when public health and morals are threatened. In such instance, felonious intent is not required to be proved because such requirement would unduly hamper the enforcement of regulatory statutes. Also, in these cases, "penalties commonly are relatively small," Justice Jackson observed, "and conviction does no grave danger to an offender's reputation."[45] Felonies, however, are also statutory crimes and the common law heritage has required that knowledge is a part of the definition of such crimes. Courts have not attempted to draw a line for distinguishing between acts that require a mental element and those that do not, but have been content to decide which rule to apply in

---

[42]*Morissette v. United States,* 187 F.2d 427, 428, 429, 431 (1951).

[43]*Id.,* 440-41.

[44]*Morissette v. United States,* 342 U.S. 246, 250 (1951).

[45]*Id.,* 256.

each case when the legislature has not specifically provided for it.[46]

In the instant case, the Court decided: "We think presumptive intent has no place . . . . "[47] and Justice Jackson concluded:

> Whether that intent existed, the jury must determine, not only from the act of taking, but from that together with defendant's testimony and all the surrounding circumstances. . . . Had the jury convicted on proper instructions it would be the end of the matter. But juries are not bound by what seem inescapable logic to justices . . . . They might have refused to brand Morissette as a thief. Had they done so, that, too, would have been the end of the matter.
>
> Reversed.[48]

III

In this particular case Augustine's ideas about human justice based upon the divine pattern of creation, sin, judgment and redemption, could have informed the defendant, prosecutor, jurors, and judges. It is undeniable that Joe Morissette breached the civil accord by carrying away things of value from another's property and converting them to his own use. The peace of the Earthly City is not maintained by such irresponsible conduct. As a responsible adult he properly can be expected to know that his assumption that the bomb-casings were abandoned was not an acceptable substitute for permission to take them. Nor would it be difficult for an Augustinian to recognize the type of pride by which Morissette justified his act. It is the conviction that "all the rules do not apply to me" and it is a conviction as pervasive in human society as it is destructive of community harmony. It is this attitude which required correction, regardless of the technical problem of "felonious intent."

Apparently the grand jury recognized this need when it re-

[46]See 5 *Vanderbilt Law Review* 828 (1952), but compare 66 *Harvard Law Review* 130 (1952) which states: "In previous cases the Court had interpreted the absence of 'international' in a criminal statute as a deliberate omission of the wrongful intent requirement." (Citing United States v. Blaint, 258 U.S. 250, and United States v. Behrman, 258 U.S. 280 (1922), "The statute in these cases contained no language that might be construed as requiring intent." Justice Jackson's discussion affirms this observation, but adds: "This has not, however, been without expressions of misgiving." *Morissette v. United States,* 342 U.S. 246, 256 (1951).

[47]*Id.*, 275.

[48]*Id.*, 276.

turned the indictment; the trial judge sensed the same truth when he determined the sentence; and the circuit judges considered that substantial justice had been realized when they commended the district court for having made the "punishment fit the crime." However, there is strong doubt that an Augustinian would acquiesce in the punishment meted out and agree that justice had been realized. It is undeniable that Morissette, due to pride, had been guilty of wrong-doing defined by the secular law as a "crime." His responsibility for this wrongful act was established by the apprehending authorities apparently without the guarantees of the law having been disregarded. The defendant had made a frank although less than the "full" confession which the Court's opinion implied,[49] but any introspective human judge, recognizing the psychological difficulty—if not the sheer impossibility—involved in stripping himself totally of defenses in a confession, would have been satisfied with the result. Augustine would have considered Morissette's cooperation as "repentance," and would have argued that since the defendant evidently was amenable to correction, he should be required to make restitution and be released. Had this been done, the celestial pattern of following sin with judgment and judgment with healing would have been practiced. Such gentle correction might have resulted in the leading of the offender to God. Instead, the offender was branded with the odious appellation of "criminal" and was led to prison. It is difficult to perceive the redemptive properties of this sentence in the case of Joe Morissette.

The crucial problem for every human judge is to determine the nature of punishment to be pronounced on the defendant. The chief criterion proposed by Augustine of Hippo is unequivocal and his supporting principles are easily applied in determining a judgment. Had Augustine been a party to the internal conversation of the prosecutor as he considered whether to begin suit against Morissette for trespass or to seek to convict him as a criminal, the Bishop would have inquired which of the alternatives promised to be more redemptive for the defendant. But, further, did the public require restitution, or retribution as well? And, finally, was the prosecutor concerned with leading the offender to God or was he rather concerned with sacrificing Morissette to a false god known as "Success"? Had these questions not altered the nature of the

[49]The record reports: ". . . after considerable hedging, he finally admitted under questioning by the judge that he knew the bomb casings were on government property when he took them." *Morissette v. United States,* 187 F. 2d 427, 428-29 (1951).

prosecution, the theologian would be expected to remind the sentencing judge that there was no obligation to impose a prison term, nor was there a minimum fine—it could have been set at $85. Had simple restitution been demanded, few would have complained that justice had not been served.

The petit jurors obviously had little opportunity to extend mercy and it is beyond knowing whether or not they would have branded Morissette as a thief. To them Augustine's counsel would be to take account of human weakness and to remember that they are sinners judging a sinner. However, this does not imply that a sentimental refusal to return a guilty verdict is praiseworthy. Augustine believed that although no man can live without sin, he insisted that all men can live without crime, and he recognized a crime-ridden community as a perversion of the ordained secular order. He realized that although a criminal is to be apprehended primarily for his own sake, sometimes a criminal must be restrained for the sake of the community. Did the Supreme Court err, then, by reversing the conviction of Morissette? The defendant had offended society, had been apprehended, had evidenced repentance, had been judged, and then had been released on a legal technicality. One can only conclude that Augustine would have applauded the Court for its redirected emphasis on intent while he would have mourned the "lamentable" decisions that had brought Joe Morissette before the highest court of the land.

Just as St. Augustine of Hippo seemed always to wrap his counsel in a threat, the unsolicited advice he sent a Roman officer fifteen centuries ago provides a suitable conclusion to this inquiry into his insights concerning human judging:

> In exercising the power which God has given you, a man over men, I am sure you call to mind the divine judgment at which judges, too, will have to give account of their judgments.[50]

[50] Augustine, *Epistles,* No. 134.

[6]

Justice as the Foundation of the Political Community: Augustine and his Pagan Models

Ernest L. Fortin

Remota iustitia, quid sunt regna nisi magna latrocinia? (civ. IV 4)

Like Plato's *Republic* and Cicero's *De re publica*, Augustine's *City of God* is in the main a book about justice. More specifically, it is a book about justice as it came to be understood in the Christian West, thanks in large measure to Augustine himself. From it we learn how, against all odds, Christianity, the religion of love, became the official religion of the Roman Empire, the epitome of the ancient world's most spectacular military achievements, and how the Empire, acquired through conquest, became in the minds of later generations a symbol of just rule. The purpose of the book may be said to be twofold: to encourage the practice of justice among human beings, and, by stressing the limitations of human justice, to caution against excessive zeal in its pursuit. It accomplishes this purpose by laying out a moral ideal whose demands are more stringent than even the most stringent demands of the philosophers, and by showing how this lofty ideal may be accommodated to the realities of the political life.

The theme of justice is first introduced as part of Augustine's response to the pagans who worshipped the gods of Roman mythology for the sake of the "enlargement and well-being" of the Empire[1] and blamed Christianity for its recent political setbacks

1 See the frequent allusions to this question throughout the rest of Book IV, esp. chapters 3, 13, 15, 20, 28; also III 14. Rome's appetite for aggrandizement had

(civ. IV 2; retr. II 43,1). The latest of these was the sack of Rome by Alaric and his Goths in 410, a dramatic if largely symbolic event popularly interpreted as an act of revenge on the part of Rome's gods, whose cult had been outlawed (by Theodosius in 380) and replaced by the cult of the Christian God (cf. civ. IV 2).

Formulated in these crudely polytheistic terms, the pagan argument was not likely to carry much weight with the social elite, whose sole aim in propagating it was to discredit the new religion and inflame the populace against it (II 5; IV 1). The real concern was not with the wrath of the gods but with the impact that the spread of Christian morality was bound to have on Roman public life. Rome, the nation "dedicated to Mars" and the pursuit of the manly virtues (II 5; IV 29), owed its greatness, not to the protection of Jupiter or any of its other gods, whose existence had long ceased to be taken literally by educated Romans (III 3–4) but to its military prowess. By enlisting human beings in the service of a "higher and nobler" country, Christianity sundered the unity of the city and weakened the unconditional claim that it makes on the allegiance of its citizens (ep. XCI 1). Its doctrine of the universal brotherhood of human beings and their equality before God, its precept enjoining the love of one's enemies, and its demand that evil be requited with good were all fundamentally at odds with the single most important fact of Roman political life, its imperialism and the desire to maintain its hegemony over the conquered nations (ep. CXXXVI 2, and CXXXVIII 3, 9–17). The situation was all the more precarious as the country's security was being threatened by the presence of hordes of marauding barbarians on its borders.

Implied in the pagan argument that Christianity was hostile to Roman expansionism is the notion that large political entities are preferable to smaller ones and worth defending for that reason. Such was the position taken by the rulers of the great ecumenical empires of antiquity, including the Roman emperors, whose eyes were set on the ultimate goal of all conquest, world domination. It was emphatically not the position taken by the leading thinkers of Greece and Rome, for whom the political association most

caused it to become an object of "universal dread" among the nations of the ancient world (IV 5). Unless otherwise noted, all references either in the text or in the footnotes are to *City of God*.

favorable to the attainment of human perfection is the one that is large enough to satisfy all of one's natural needs, but not so large as to exceed one's capacity to know and love. Only under conditions such as these can citizens enjoy the freedom, friendly relations, and mutual trust required for their active engagement in public life.[2] Human beings are by nature "political," that is to say, members of a *polis*, and not a megapolis like Babylon, a city reputed to have been so large that when one part fell to the enemy, the rest of the city did not hear about it until three days later.[3] A universal and despotic empire is not the most suitable locus of moral education or the best soil in which to plant the seeds of justice. Quite the contrary. The larger the city, the more likely it is to abound in injustices, bloody insurrections, and civil strife (XIX 5).

It is important to note in this connection that Augustine himself never drew from Christianity's unique character as a "universal religion" (X 32) the conclusion that all human beings should be united politically so as to form a single world society. The *City of God* depicts the happiest condition of humankind as one in which small cities and kingdoms exist side by side in neighborly concord (IV 15). Desirable as it may be, such a condition will never be fully and permanently realized. Whether we like it or not, war is inevitable. The wicked wage war on the just because they want to, and the just wage war on the wicked because they have to. In either case, independent cities and kingdoms eventually give way to large kingdoms established by the conquest of the weaker by the stronger. The most that can be hoped for in practice is that the just cause will triumph over the unjust one; for nothing is more injurious to everybody, including evildoers themselves, than that the latter should prosper and use their prosperity to oppress the good. The very size of the Empire, its customary belligerency, and the wealth pouring into it from different parts of the world had become major obstacles to the inculcation of the virtuous habits that make for a healthy political life. Rome was vulnerable, not because of the growing power

2 See on this subject the remarks by L. Strauss 1953, 130–31.

3 Cf. Arist., Pol. III, 1276a28. On the long controverted issue of the naturalness of civil society for Augustine, see among more recent studies G. Post 1964, C. Nederman 1988.

of Christianity, as was alleged by its detractors, but because of its inability to live up to its own standards of justice and morality.

Much of the framework for Augustine's lengthy discussion of this subject was provided by Cicero's *De re publica.* Instead of founding a new city in speech, as Socrates does in Plato's *Republic*, Cicero took as his model an actual city, Rome (cf. *De re publica* II, 21–22.), whose virtues he purposely magnified in an effort to rekindle a measure of civic-mindedness in the hearts of his fellow countrymen. Augustine, who writes primarily in defense of Christianity, sets out to unmask Rome's vices, which he traces back to the very origins of the city. Book II of the *City of God* deals with Rome's spiritual and moral evils, epitomized by the lewdness of the city's theatrical spectacles. Book III concentrates on the external disasters that had befallen Rome over the centuries. The analysis follows closely (although not exclusively) Book II of the *De re publica,* bringing out into the open a number of unpleasant truths that are only hinted at by Cicero and using Rome as a witness against itself to bolster Augustine's case. A few examples will illustrate the point.

3.1 Rome and its Injustices

In order to demonstrate Rome's superiority to all other cities, Scipio, Cicero's spokesman in the dialogue, begins by recalling the memorable events of earlier Roman history. It has been granted on all hands that justice is the soul of politics and that its choicest fruits are nowhere more conspicuously displayed than in Rome itself. One soon discovers, however, that the lavish praise bestowed upon Rome is accompanied by an undercurrent of criticism that extends to the whole of its history.

The catalogue of thinly disguised injustices begins with Romulus, the founder of the city, who gained sole control of it by doing away with his brother Remus and later consolidated that control by treacherously "murdering" the Sabine king, Titus Tatius, whom he had been forced to accept as a partner on the throne after the infamous incident of the abduction of the Sabine women.[4] The changes introduced into the Roman regime at this

4 civ. III 15. The *De re publica* II 14, speaks first of the "demise" (*interitus*) of

time can be seen as a series of concessions aimed at placating the senatorial faction, whose ambitions may have been thwarted by Romulus's ruthless behavior. A fate similar to that of Titus Tatius was reserved for Romulus himself, whose assassins sought to conceal their crime by inventing the implausible story of his deification and translation to the realm of the gods. The event, said to have taken place during a sudden eclipse of the sun, had as its sole witness a rustic named Proculus Julius, who was suborned by the senators to give his testimony (*De re publica* II 10; cf. civ. III 15).

Nor does the situation improve with the passing of time. Another king, Ancus Martius, is identified in the Roman Annals as "the son of Numa's daughter," an odd statement that causes one of the interlocutors, the distinguished jurist Laelius, to complain that the Annals are "obscure" on this point, for "they know the mother of this king but not his father" *(De re publica* II 33). The natural son, for such he must have been, had connections in high places indeed! The same pattern of injustices is repeated in a variety of ways under the reigns of later rulers, among them Tarquinius Superbus, admittedly a wicked king, whose excesses were responsible for the downfall of the monarchy and the hatred which the Romans harbored toward it from that moment on (civ. III 15; *De re publica* II 48). Lucretia has to commit suicide in order to vindicate her honor. Her husband Collatinus, although innocent, is forced into exile (civ. II 16; III 16; cf. *De re publica* II 53). Clearly, all was not well in the state of Rome's affairs.

As the story unfolds, we find Rome embarking upon a series of military ventures that would eventually make of her the mistress of the civilized world. These wars were called "just" for no other reason than that they had been "declared" (*De re publica* II 31) and were allegedly waged for the defense of Rome's allies. Still, it did not take many centuries for Romulus's village to grow into a world empire. Whatever its motives may have been, Rome was not eager to restore its allies to independent status once they had been successfully defended. Behind its relentless conquests lay an insatiable *libido dominandi* or desire to dominate that was

Tatius, and shortly afterwards of his having been "murdered," *eo interfecto*, presumably by Romulus.

stoked by the constant need to appease or distract an unruly populace and its ambitious leaders, the tribunes. We had been given to understand that all these events were the result of careful planning on the part of not just one lawgiver, as in the case of Athens and Sparta, but of the long succession of sagacious rulers with whom the city had been blessed (II 2). Yet everyone is finally obliged to admit that most of what took place was due to accident or necessity much more than to design. Scipio sums the matter up nicely, if somewhat wistfully, when he confesses that "the nature of public affairs often defeats reason" (II 57). The alternative to Plato's perfect city in speech, it turns out, is not Rome, the perfect city in deed, as was claimed earlier, but the "dung of Romulus", *Romuli faex* (Cicero, *Ad Atticum* II 1,8).

Little wonder that, by the end of Book II, the participants in the dialogue are prepared to return to the question of justice and its relation to civil society with a renewed sense of urgency. Their patriotism remains unshaken, but, now that they have been properly "edified," it has become easier to persuade them to look to nature itself rather than to Rome for an exemplar of the most perfect city (II 39, 66). What the reader has been treated to is a whitewash of sorts, a vastly "embellished" panorama *(picta coloribus:* II 21) of the Roman republic in what was supposed to be its heyday. For all his pains to invest Roman history with an aura of unimpeachable dignity, Cicero was as radical in his approach to the problem of civil society as was Plato. He too seems to have despaired of ever finding in Rome, or for that matter anywhere else on earth, anything that even comes close to simple justice on the level of politics.

3.2 Augustine's Moral Ideal. Augustinian Extremism

The standard that informs Augustine's diagnosis of Roman life is encapsulated in the biblical command of the love of God and neighbor, coupled with the Ciceronian notion of an eternal or natural law, defined as "that law which enjoins the preservation of the natural order and forbids its disturbance" (XIX 15), and, elsewhere, as the law requiring that all things be "most properly ordered" *(ordinatissima)* at all times (lib.arb. I 15). This perfect order entails the total subordination of the lower to the higher both within the individual and in the whole of society. Individual human beings are rightly ordered when what is most noble in them, reason, rules the spirited part of the soul, when both reason and spiritedness combine to rule the desiring part, and when reason itself is ruled by God. A similar order exists in society at large when virtuous subjects obey wise rulers who govern in accordance with the divine will. Thus understood, the natural law represents the optimal rather than the minimal requirements of the moral life. What it imposes as a duty on everyone is the possession and exercise of all the virtues, including theoretical wisdom, despite the fact that the latter is the preserve of a small number of naturally gifted and well educated individuals. This uncommonly high standard underlies some of Augustine's most extreme, one is almost tempted to say "outrageous", pronouncements regarding morality.

Take, to begin with, the discussion of the early Roman republic and its heroes, for whom Augustine professes sincere admiration but whose moral qualities, he says, should be "reckoned vices rather than virtues."[5] Moral virtue is that by which one is ordered to the proper end of human existence, which is God himself. In order to be effectively pursued, this end must be known. It follows that the pagans, who lacked this knowledge and worshipped false gods, were not truly virtuous. Even when sought on their own account and not for the sake of some external good, the virtues they claimed to possess were marred by the pride that inflated them. For Augustine, as for Plato, there is no such thing as moral virtue properly so called, by which I mean moral virtue unaccompanied by the dianoetic or intellectual virtues. Among the writers of classical antiquity, Aristotle and his followers are the only ones to speak of the nonphilosophic virtues as genuine virtues apart from their connection with theoretical wisdom, which is inaccessible to most people.[6] Au-

5 civ. XIX 25: "It is for this reason that the virtues which the mind seems to itself to possess and by which it restrains the body and the vices ... are vices rather than virtues so long as there is no reference to God in the matter." Ibid., V 19: „No one without true piety, that is, true worship of the true God, can have true virtue."

6 It is in this precise sense that Aristotle has been called the "discoverer of moral virtue." Cf. L. Strauss 1964, 27.

gustine's blanket condemnation of pagan virtue would thus seem to be grossly unfair to its practitioners insofar as, by his own admission, it makes impossibly high demands on them. Moreover, it was on the face of it highly impolitic since by berating pagan virtue Augustine was casting discredit on the very qualities on which Rome's ability to defend itself depended.

A second notable case in point is Augustine's statement that "Rome was never a republic because true justice never had a place in it" (II 21, 4). Cicero had rightly defined the republic or commonwealth as a "group of rational beings held together by a common acknowledgment of right and a community of interests." Upon examination, however, Augustine finds himself compelled to amend that definition by striking from it any reference to the key notion of right or justice, the "bond of human beings in cities",[7] on the ground that it is not to be found in any of them. Civil society, he says, is a group of rational beings held together, not by an acknowledgment of right, but by "a common agreement as to the objects of their love," regardless of the quality of that love or the moral goodness or badness of its objects (XIX 24). Only in this truncated form can Rome be said to have been a republic. Cities are mere compacts of wickedness entered into, not for the sake of virtue or the truly good life, but for the sole purpose of preserving a modicum of peace among people who would otherwise be constantly at one another's throats. Augustine's reformulation of Cicero's definition has frequently been taken to mean that he regarded the state as an amoral entity with no stake whatever in the character of its citizens, that politics has nothing to do with ethics, and that Augustine is best read as a Machiavellian before the letter, a champion of "value-neutrality," or a precursor of modern social science positivism.[8] To say this, however, is gravely to misconstrue Augustine's thought. Augustine does not disagree with Cicero's definition. The philosophers are right in pointing to justice as the healthy condition of cities, but they are unable to secure its performance. The argument may be summarized as follows: by asserting the

7 Aristotle, Pol. I 1253a37; cf. civ. II 21,1, where Augustine explains that concord is the strictest bond of any city and that it cannot be preserved where justice has become extinct.

8 See the discussion of this point in H. A. Deane 1963, 117–18.

desirability of justice and at the same time its practical impossibility, philosophy discloses its own inherent limitations; it thus implicitly proclaims the need to supplement human justice with a higher and more effective form of justice.

The same grim judgment regarding the possibility of human justice is expressed in a picturesque way by means of the story of Alexander and the pirate, which challenges us with the assertion that kingdoms are nothing but robber bands or "gigantic larcenies" *(magna latrocinia)* and larcenies nothing but "small kingdoms" *(parva regna)*, that, save for the magnitude of the crimes involved and the impunity with which they are committed, what Alexander does on a grand scale and with a huge fleet is not essentially different from what a pirate does on his own and with a single ship (IV 4). The passage of Cicero's *De re publica* from which Augustine borrows this story (III 24) has unfortunately come down to us in a mutilated state, but we at least know that it belonged to a section of the dialogue in which for the sake of argument Philus defends the view that justice is the right of the stronger and hence a matter of convention rather than of nature.[9] People abide by it not because it is desirable for its own sake but for reasons of necessity or self-interest. Down deep, the brightest among them know that it is only a pretense. Even though no ruler will admit it publicly, every society is organized for the benefit of those who run it. This is manifestly true of all corrupt regimes, but it is also true in a more subtle way of the just regimes, be they monarchies, aristocracies, democracies, or some judicious mixture of the three; for even the best of cities is governed by laws that cannot but favor the interests of its dominant class and thus benefit some of its members at the expense of others.

This is as much as to say that the perfectly just regime has never existed in practice and never will. The choice of one regime over another always entails a trade-off of some sort in which the gains registered on one front are offset by the losses incurred on another. There is no such thing as a truly common good. Even the most decent citizen is willy-nilly implicated in the systemic inequities of the society whose life he shares and to whose perpetuation he contributes by working in it, paying taxes

9 See Augustine's discussion of the conventionalist view of justice in II 21, 1.

to it, and possibly holding office in it. Viewed in this light, the difference between the conqueror and the pirate is indeed negligible. Both are in it for themselves and neither one can claim any moral superiority over the other.[10] What one does by sea the other does by land; the thievery is the same on both sides. Since, for the pirate, justice is a mere cover lending a kind of spurious dignity to one's selfish pursuits, the conqueror cannot appeal to it to defend his way of life. To anyone who accepts the conventionalist premise that "right" is just a polite name for the will of the stronger, that is to say, of the *de facto* ruler, no qualitative difference separates the two.

The question is whether the pirate can dismiss as irrelevant the distinction between the private enterprise in which he is engaged and the public character of the ruler's activities. As a "soldier of the sea," as he has sometimes been called, the pirate is literally a man without a country. Having renounced all allegiance to a common cause, he lives for himself and himself alone. His pretext is that the common cause with which the ruler has identified himself is unworthy of that kind of dedication; and he is convinced that in his heart of hearts the ruler knows this too. In the eyes of the pirate, the ruler's "justice" is a mere show, a form of hypocrisy with which he himself can dispense. If the pirate can speak this way, however, it is only because he abstracts from the crucial consideration that pirates, who bear no public responsibilities, are condemned to living inglorious lives, whereas conquerors, who are in a position to establish the conditions

10 The best commentary on the story of Alexander and the pirate that I know of is the following exchange between the pirate Menas and Antony's lieutenant Enobarbus in Shakespeare's *Antony and Cleopatra*, II,vi,83–95:
Menas. You and I have known, sir.
Enobarbus. At sea, I think.
Menas. We have, sir.
Enobarbus. You have done well by water.
Menas. And you by land.
Enobarbus. I will praise any man that will praise me:
though it cannot be denied what I have done by land.
Menas. Nor what I have done by water.
Enobarbus. Yes, something you can deny for your own safety:
you have been a great thief by sea.
Menas. And you by land.
Enobarbus. There I deny my land service.

of relative safety and prosperity from which countless others will profit for a long time to come, are often glorious, even if the glory they seek is first and foremost their own. Their conquests are never or only very rarely just, but this does not prevent their later being used for nobler purposes, as appears to have happened in Rome under some of its better emperors.

Despite its verging on cynicism, the pirate's argument nevertheless contains an element of unpleasant truth, which is that in the end a man is only as good as the cause to which he has committed himself. This alone is enough to establish between political rule and piracy a deeper kinship than the legitimate ruler is willing to acknowledge. In the contest between the two antagonists no clear winner has emerged. But the debate has not been in vain. Its very inconclusiveness forces us to ask whether *any* political cause is worthy of the sacrifices that it demands of its devotees, and, if not, whether one should not look for a third possibility wherein the nagging tensions and contrarieties of human existence might find a more satisfactory solution. Surveying the problem from this higher vantage point, Cicero had philosophy to turn to as an alternative to the political life and a "consolation" for its disappointments. Augustine tells the same story to remind his readers that only by embracing the Christian faith will one ever be able to transcend the distinctions that dominate the political life and satisfy one's longing for wholeness.

Strange as it may seem to us, Augustine's habit of equating "justice" with supreme justice, *summa iustitia* (II 21,1) and "city" with the perfectly just city has nothing unusual about it. It merely conforms to the general principle that the unqualified noun designates the perfected object. A thing is called good to the extent that it has all that belongs to it by reason of its nature. As the old Scholastic adage had it, *bonum ex integra causa, malum ex quocumque defectu.*[11] To speak of a chair *tout court* is the same

11 See, in a similar vein, Aristotle, EN II, 1106b28–35: "It is possible to fail in many ways, ... while to succeed is possible only in one way (for which reason also one is easy and the other difficult): to miss the mark easy, to hit it difficult; for these reasons also, then, excess and defect are characteristic of vice, and the mean of virtue. For men are good in but one way, but bad in many." Cf. Thomas Aquinas, *S.T.*, I–II,19,6, ad 1: *Bonum causatur ex integra causa, malum autem ex singularibus defectibus*. Thomas's formulation is derived from the *De Divinis Nominibus* of the Pseudo-Dionysius.

thing as to speak of a good chair, inasmuch a defective chair is not a chair in the full sense of the word. If I walk into a furniture store and ask for a chair, I do not have to specify that I want a good chair and would sound ridiculous if I did, for "good" in this instance adds nothing to what I mean when I use the word "chair" without qualification.

The same principle applies to the notions of virtue and the city, which in the final analysis can only mean perfect virtue and the best city. As its etymology implies, the term "perfection," from the Latin *perficere*, "to bring to completion," is synonymous with wholeness. To the extent to which it lacks any of the things that belong to it by nature, the virtue or the city in question is less than what its name indicates and thus falls short of its definition. Aristotle intimated as much when he stated that "what a thing is when fully developed," whether it be a human being, a horse, or a city, "we call its nature" (*Politics*, 1252b33). That is why, toward the end of Shakespeare's *Julius Caesar*, Antony cannot praise the slain Brutus more highly than by calling him simply "a man":

This was the noblest Roman of them all.
All the conspirators save only he
Did that they did in envy of great Caesar;
He only, in a general honest thought
and common good to all, made one of them.
His life was gentle, and the elements
So mix'd in him, that Nature might stand up
And say to all the world: "This was a man!" (V,v, 68–75)

What renders Augustine's approach to these matters problematic at first sight is that it overlooks the fact that some cities are better than others, or that there are degrees of goodness or badness.[12] A

12 This is the issue that is often dealt with in a roundabout way under the heading of "fuzzy logic" by modern philosophers. The example often used for purposes of illustration is that of a chariot that is falling apart and will eventually be reduced to a heap of broken wheels, shafts, and panels in a corner of the yard. The question is, At what point did the chariot cease to be a chariot? To which the answer can only be: when it first began to disintegrate, however slightly. No matter how one looks at it, a chariot with a missing spoke, let alone a missing wheel, is less of a chariot than one that is whole. If my chariot is not too badly

more commonsensical approach to the problems of ethics and politics will generally shun sweeping statements of the kind that Augustine relishes but that are of little use to statesmen, whose first task is not to speculate about the nature of civil society but to improve the lives of the imperfect societies they are called upon to govern. This is not to suggest that Augustine was incapable of offering sound practical advice when asked to do so, but only to say that his more extreme statements serve a different purpose, that of casting in the sharpest possible light the intrinsic limitations of the political life. As he himself admits, there are other, "more plausible" *(probabiliores)* definitions of the city, according to which "Rome was indeed a republic, albeit one that was much better administered by the ancient Romans than by their descendants" (II 21, 4). What accounts for his predilection for the more uncompromising formulations of the same issues is a question to which we shall return in due course.

3.3 The Adaptation to the Needs of the Political Life

The problem at hand is ultimately rooted in the fact that Christianity, unlike Judaism, has no political program of its own and neither imposes nor recommends any particular form of government or social organization. The pious Jew, who had been given a divine and hence perfect law by which to live, knew that by obeying that law he was doing what was pleasing to God. Christians, who were no longer under the Law, had no such assurance. They were simply told to obey their temporal rulers (Rom. 13: 1–7), whoever these might be (probably Nero, when Romans was written). At the same time they were urged to follow Christ, a notoriously vague injunction that can be taken to mean almost anything from going out into the wilderness and leading the life of an anchorite (like Antony of the desert), to preaching a Crusade (like St. Bernard), conquering a new world for Christ (like the *reyes cristianos* of Spain's "golden age"), or running soup

damaged, I may continue to call it by that name, but only to indicate that the time has not yet come to discard it, either because it is still serviceable or because it can be repaired.

kitchens to feed the hungry (like Mother Teresa). To its credit, the Christian Church learned early on, in the struggle against Gnosticism, the first great internal threat to its existence, that unless it was able to demonstrate the compatibility of its teachings with life in society, it would suffer the fate of the fanatical sects of late antiquity and be suppressed.

In this process of accommodation, Christians could appeal to a noble precedent, the Book of Genesis, which, in its account of the devolution from the state of innocence to the post-lapsarian state and thence to the post-diluvian state, provided some indication as to how human beings could adapt to less than perfect conditions of humanity without losing sight of the ideal of perfection to which they are called. To cite only one example, the precepts of the Noachide convenant accorded to human beings the right to put capital offenders to death (Gen. 9:5), a harsh practice justified only by the spread of evil in the world.

The problem was not unfamiliar to the classical philosophers, who had to face it like everyone else and invented their own way or ways of dealing with it. For Plato, who has a tendency to study all things in the light of their highest metaphysical principles or the "ideas," the only form of justice worthy of the name is absolute justice. But such principles are not directly applicable to actual cities and must be "diluted" in order to become operative. In all but the rarest instances, obstacles stemming from their bodily nature prevent human beings from becoming perfect lovers of justice.[13] Few of them allow the love of the true and the beautiful to rule their lives and take precedence over the love of their own, a situation that rulers are obliged to tolerate, if only because any attempt to eradicate its causes would entail the use of a disproportionate amount of force and inflict even greater harm on people. Accordingly, the justice that we find in society at large, when we do find it, is at best a shadow or a pale image of true justice. It is what Plato terms "vulgâr" or "so-called" virtue (cf. *Phaedo* 61a; *Republic* 518d).

In keeping with his more down to earth outlook, Aristotle opted for a different approach, defending the existence of natu-

13 In *On Free Choice of the Will*, III 18–22, Augustine traces these obstacles to two causes, "ignorance" and the "difficulty" involved in the effort to overcome one's lower self.

ral right while simultaneously maintaining that the whole of it is variable (EN V, 1134b18 f.). His solution consists in holding firm to the view that certain actions are intrinsically good and should be performed, whereas others are intrinsically evil and should be avoided. Yet, extraordinary circumstances, of the kind that tend to arise in times of war or national emergency, may occasionally render just an act that under normal circumstances would be unjust and vice versa. A classic example is the sacrifice of an innocent person for the sake of the common good when the latter cannot be preserved by any other means. In extreme cases such as these, what is chosen is not, as is often said, a lesser evil – a moral person never chooses evil, great or small – but the greater good that is secured by momentarily laying aside the ordinary rules of justice.

A third formulation was offered by Cicero, who spoke of something called the "right of nations," *ius gentium*,[14] by which he meant that part of natural right which is harmonizable with the social life and mediates between natural right in the strict sense and civil right.[15] Included in this right of nations are such matters as private property and slavery, both of which represent a departure from strict natural right: private property, because material goods do not necessarily belong by nature to their *de facto* owners, who may or may not know how to use them well or be inclined to do so; and slavery, because the people who have the misfortune of being reduced to that state (usually prisoners of war) do not necessarily deserve their fate.

Cicero's solution is the one that prevailed for many centuries in the West through its incorporation into Roman Law and its absorption into the Christian tradition *via* Isidore of Seville's widely disseminated encyclopedia, the *Etymologies* (V,iv). It was later modified slightly and systematized by the great Scholastics of the Middle Ages. In response to Aristotle's teaching regarding

14 The expression, which may have been coined by Cicero himself (cf. *De re publica* I 2; *De officiis* III 69), is apparently modeled on Aristotle's *koinos nomos*, Rhet. I, 1372a and 1375a.

15 Such is the meaning attributed to the expression by Thomas Aquinas, according to whom *ius gentium* belongs in part to natural right and in part to positive right. Cf. I–II,95,5; II–II,57,3. The best account that I have seen of the use of *ius gentium* in Cicero is that of M. P. Zuckert 1989.

the variability of natural right, Thomas Aquinas introduced a distinction, not found as such in Aristotle, between the primary and immutable precepts of the natural law and its secondary precepts, which are subject to change (I-II,94,5). Thomas's distinction was not without its problems, however, for there were passages in the Bible that seemed to call into question the immutability of even the primary precepts. If these precepts are truly immutable, how could God command the sacrifice of Isaac (Gen., 22:1f.), the theft perpetrated by the Israelites at the time of the Exodus (Exod., 12:35–36), and Hosea's extramarital relations with a prostitute (Hosea, 1:2)? Aquinas's answer is that in each of these cases the *matter* of the deed has undergone a change. For example, the killing of Isaac, had it occurred, would not have been an act of murder because God, who is the author of life, is free to take it or order it to be taken whenever he sees fit. Nor was anything "stolen" from the Egyptians. God, the universal landlord and ultimate proprietor of all things, merely transferred the ownership of the goods in question from one nation to another (I–II,94,5, ad 2).

Finally, in their quest for ever greater precision, some late-medieval thinkers distinguished between two forms of natural right: absolute natural right, whose principles brook no exceptions and are binding on everyone at all times, and conditional, relative, or secondary natural right, which presupposes the Fall and sanctions such institutions as private property, slavery, and coercive political rule, all of which were absent from the state of original justice and are necessitated – hence "justified" – only by the human being's present inability to live fully in accordance with the dictates of reason.[16]

None of these approaches corresponds exactly to the one adopted by Augustine, who, as far as I can tell, avoids the expression *ius gentium* (with which he was undoubtedly familiar from Cicero), never speaks of primary and secondary natural law precepts, and is silent on the distinction between absolute and relative natural right, lest by invoking any of these theories he should confer upon

16 See, for example, Ockham, *Dialogus*, Part III, Treatise ii, Book 3, chap. 6. R. Hooker, *Laws of Ecclesiastical Polity*, I,10,13. A theory of relative natural right is attributed, misleadingly in my opinion, to the early Christian writers by E. Troeltsch 1960, Vol. I, 100, 153f, 201, et passim.

such necessary but imperfect practices as private property, slavery, and coercive government a greater degree of sanctity or inviolability than their inherent imperfection warrants. His own guiding principle is more directly biblical: the precept of the universal love of God and neighbor, in which, as he constantly reminds us, the entire message of the New Testament is summed up.[17] It is not necessary to add that this lofty ideal is beyond the reach of ordinary human beings, for "there is no one, however laudably he may live, who does not yield in some points to the lust of the flesh" (I 9,1). The weakness of a human nature wounded by sin and the frequent intractability of human affairs are such as to require that the principles of Christian morality be diluted or softened if they are to retain their effectiveness. What we end up with in most cases is a kind of "lesser justice," better suited to the conditions of this life: *iustitia minor huic uitae competens (De spiritu et littera*, XXXVI 65).

Nowhere is this more apparent than in matters pertaining to warfare, the area in which the ordinary principles of justice have always been put to their severest test, to such an extent that Plato relegated these matters to the realm of practical wisdom rather than justice. According to the just war theory, to the elaboration of which Augustine is perhaps the most important early contributor, a war is just when it is waged to repel an unjust aggressor, defend an ally, secure a legitimate right of passage, rescue victims of oppression in countries other than one's own whenever feasible, and the like. The theory stipulates that all other means of redress shall first have been exhausted, that the war shall be undertaken only out of necessity and for the sake of peace, and that it shall be carried out without undue harshness or violence. In all these cases, the assumption is that a war can be just on one side only, for "when we wage a just war, our enemies must be sinning" (XIX 15). If justice was on the side of Rome, the invading barbarians were guilty of injustice.

But were the barbarians wholly unjust in their behavior toward Rome? The picture is far from clear. There is plenty of evidence to show that in many instances they were themselves acting out of necessity and under pressure from powerful hordes

17 In the *De doctrina christiana*, Augustine goes so far as to say that anyone who has understood that principle can dispense with Scripture altogether.

to the east before whom they had little choice but to flee. Besides, in the course of the negotiations, Rome had few scruples about breaking faith with them, to the point of engaging in unspeakable treacheries. Thousands of barbarians serving in the Roman army were butchered once the reaction against them set in, and others, after having been promised asylum, were reduced to the most abject slavery upon their arrival (cf. Bainton 1960, 99–100). Rome, too, bore its share of responsibility for the troublesome situation in which it found itself. Augustine all but says it was only getting what it deserved.

Beyond that was the nasty question of the justice of Rome's own borders, often hinted at but rarely broached explicitly in the literature of the period. It was no secret that for the most part these borders been had acquired by force or unjust aggression. But how can a war undertaken for the defense of unjust borders be considered just? The problem is not unlike the one that arose more than a thousand years later in the wake of the Spanish conquest of the New World. Even if one grants the legitimacy of wars of civilization and agrees that according to natural justice the European invaders had some right to vast tracts of land that were not being put to good use,[18] one can hardly hold it against the native Americans for taking up arms in their own defense. To this must be added the fact that it is rarely possible to engage in warfare without directly or indirectly inflicting harm on noncombatants and innocent bystanders.

All in all, Augustine's just war theory left many things unsaid, although not unnoticed. If anything can be thought to have motivated it, it is the conviction, not that a war is ever completely just, but that one cause may be "more just" *(iustior)* than another (XV 4). There are limits to how far one can go in establishing a nation's right to the territory over which it rules or in laying down rules for the defense of that territory. For Augustine, the choice was between civilization and barbarism, and it was in the light of this choice that the decision to support one side or the

18 In classical political theory, property belongs in the strictest sense to the one who knows best how to use it and is disposed to act in accordance with that knowledge. Everyone nevertheless recognized that this was not a principle that cities could adopt as a matter of course, for any attempt to do so would result in chaos.

other had to be made. No one had fewer illusions than he did about the justice of the Roman Empire. If his heart was still with it, it is because he thought that the prospects for justice, slim as they always are, were greater within it than outside of it.

3.4 The Rejection of the Notion of a Christian Polity

Augustine's remarks on the problem of justice as it poses itself on the level of the political life often appear to be directed less against his pagan adversaries than against his coreligionists and, in some cases, his own disciples. Many prominent Christian writers of that period – Eusebius, Ambrose, Prudentius, and Orosius among them – had interpreted in a literal or temporal sense certain Old Testament prophecies relating to the blessings of the messianic age and had predicted an era of unprecedented material well-being under the auspices of Christianity and as a direct outcome of its emergence as a world religion uniting all human beings in the cult of the one true God. The signs of this momentous transformation, it was claimed, were already abroad. Swords were being turned into plowshares, justice and peace were on the verge of forging a permanent alliance, and the kingdom of God was about to be inaugurated, not in heaven, as some less worldly-minded apologists of the Christian faith were predicting, but here on earth. To the Christian was promised the best of both worlds. Not only did Christianity hold out the prospect of eternal bliss in heaven, it offered the answer to our most pressing problem here on earth.

Augustine dismisses all such speculations as ingenious but unfounded in Scripture and contrary to its teaching (XVIII 52). He does not deny that human art and industry have made "stupefying advances" in the course of the centuries, but he is quick to add that this material and intellectual progress is not necessarily accompanied by a corresponding increase in moral goodness; for if these inventions have benefited man, they can also be used to destroy him (XXII 24). He further rejects outright the notion that evils will disappear or even diminish as time goes on. No doubt, God, being all-powerful, could do away with evil altogether, but not without the loss of a greater good for humankind.

In their own way, the evils that he permits contribute to the human being's spiritual advancement. They serve as a test for the just and a punishment for the wicked. They likewise insure that God will be loved for himself and not just for the material advantages accruing to us as a consequence of our good deeds; and by imposing on us the necessity of overcoming these evils both within and outside of ourselves, they enable us to reach an ever higher level of virtue and moral perfection.[19]

The unresolved issue is why, preferring as he so often does an all-or-nothing approach to moral matters, Augustine was so intent on painting the bleakest possible picture of the political life. The answer to that question is unfortunately not one that we, as products of a liberal democratic tradition that is unaware of or unsympathetic to the classical notion of the regime as a *total* way of life, are in a good position to appreciate. We may recall that in the *City of God* and the writings related to it Augustine set two goals for himself. The first was to counter the charge that Christianity was to blame for the Empire's weakness in the face of the threat posed to its existence by the massing of barbarians on its borders. The second was to entice the pagan elite of his time to embrace the new faith, something that a number of them were reluctant to do on the ground that it taught people to be more concerned with the good of their souls than with that of the fatherland. The problem was brought home to Augustine in a poignant way by one of his friends, the aged Nectarius of Calama, a pagan whose heart still burned with patriotic fire, who had imbibed from Cicero's *De re publica* the loyal citizen's sentiment that there is no limit in either time or measure to the claim that their country has upon the care and service of right-hearted men, and who could not countenance a religion that was liable to dampen that sentiment (Augustine, Letter XCI,1).

The difficulty is that the means by which these two goals might be met were in obvious tension with each other. One consisted in moderating the patriotic zeal of Augustine's pagan friends so as to win them over to the Christian faith; the other, in reinforcing the patriotic zeal of his fellow Christians so as to attach them more firmly to the service of their earthly country.

19 Cf. I 29; XXII 22 and 23. On this whole subject, see to begin with T. E. Mommsen 1951, 346–74.

The critique of Roman political life and Roman religion that permeates so much of the *City of God* was specifically designed to make the pagan nobility aware of the problematic character of their devotion to Rome, admirable as it may have been in other respects. Its manifest one-sidedness – Rome was never a republic, the pagan virtues are nothing but vices, all rulers are pirates in disguise and all cities robber bands – brings home to us the relevance of the episode of Alexander and the pirate that we discussed earlier. Only by downplaying the merits of Roman political life and focusing on its defects could Augustine hope to persuade the pagan "holdouts" of his day that the time had come to embrace the new faith.

What the discussion of justice in the *City of God* has finally made clear is that there is no such thing as a Christian polity. Christian wisdom and political power may occasionally coexist in a single subject, the person of the Christian ruler, but even in that case they remain distinct, cooperating with each other whenever possible but never merging one into the other. It is no accident that in the *City of God* Constantine and Theodosius, the two most famous early Christian emperors, are praised more for their defense of the Church or their humility than for their civic virtues.[20] Christianity as Augustine understands it does indeed provide a solution to the problem of human society, but the solution is not one that is attainable in and through human society. Like that of the classical philosophers, albeit in a different way, it remains essentially transpolitical; for "only in heaven has been promised that which on earth we seek."[21]

Bibliography

Bainton, R. 1960: Christian Attitudes Toward War and Peace, New York.
Deane, H. A. 1963: The Political and Social Ideas of St. Augustine, New York.
Duval, Y. M. 1966: L'élogie de Théodose dans la Cité de Dieu (V,26,1), in: Recherches augustiniennes 4, 135–178.

20 civ. V 25 and 26. Cf. Y. M. Duval 1966. Of Theodosius, Augustine says that "he rejoiced more to be a member of the Church than he did to be a king on earth."
21 en.Ps. XLVIII 6.

Mommsen, Th. E. 1951: St. Augustine and the Christian Idea of Progress. The Background of the City of God, in: Journal of the History of Ideas 12, 346–374 (repr. in: Medieval and Renaissance Studies, 265–298).
Nederman, C. 1988: Nature, Sin and the Origins of Society: The Ciceronian Tradition in Medieval Thought, in: Journal of the History of Ideas 49, 13–26.
Post, G. 1964: Studies in Medieval Legal Thought: Public Law and the State, 1100–1322, Princeton.
Strauss, L. 1953: Natural Right and History, Chicago.
– 1964: The City and Man, Chicago.
Troeltsch, E. 1960: The Social Teachings of the Christian Churches, New York.
Zuckert, M. P. 1989: Bringing Philosophy Down from the Heavens: Natural Right in the Roman Law, Review of Politics 51, 70–85.

[7]

The Problem of Service to Unjust Regimes in Augustine's *City of God*

Peter Burnell

The ethical principles of civil life were matters of great concern to Augustine, but his opinions (actual or supposed) in this area, and two in particular, have tended to be unattractive to the contemporary mind: his undoubted support of religious persecution and his apparent willingness to regard as a duty acquiescence in the civil injustices perpetrated by established authorities.[1]

These are distinct issues, the latter being the subject of this article, but they cannot be treated quite separately. They originated near the opposite extremes of Christian civil experience—the doctrine of compliance to unjust regimes (at least from St. Peter on) in the martyred church[2]; support for religious persecution in the later, privileged church of Augustine's own time (indeed, in Augustine's own writings)—and yet it was especially in justifying religious coercion (of the Donatists) that Augustine elaborated his views on the main ethical principles of civil life.[3] Since those views must be basic to any discussion of politics in his thought, an outline of them will be necessary as a preliminary here.

Augustine's general notion of justice—which applies to any society, indeed any human enterprise—is that it consists in devotion to reunion with God and ultimately in nothing else. Injustice, therefore, consists in disordered love, and

[1] For criticism of the first see Peter Brown, *Augustine of Hippo. A Biography* (London, 1969), 235, 239-40, and Robert Markus, *Saeculum: History and Society in the Theology of St. Augustine* (Cambridge, 1970), 142, 150. For criticism of the second see Peter Brown, "Saint Augustine," Beryl Smalley (ed.), *Trends in Medieval Political Thought* (Oxford, 1965), 14, and Oliver O'Donovan, "Augustine's *City of God XIX* and Western Political Thought," *Dionysius*, 11 (1987), 105.

[2] 1 *Pet.* 2.12-17 and 3.13-17. Cf. Augustine, *City of God* (cited as *CD*—Teubner edition [Stuttgart, 1981], 2.19).

[3] See Peter Brown, "St. Augustine's Attitude to Religious Coercion," *Journal of Roman Studies*, 54 (1964), 107-16.

Augustine describes it as a form of lust.[4] Thus he argues the general dependence of other morality on the larger morality that is religion,[5] for in the end there is no distinction between religion and morals, religion subsuming all.[6] This is the somewhat abstract notion implied by a number of passages in the *City of God.* The idea was, however, already established in his thought in a more concrete form, as specifically civil justice; for a few years earlier, in 408, in the middle of the long struggle against the Donatists, he had applied it politically in a letter which in effect builds a full-scale defense of the suppression of that sect, on the grounds that enforcing communion in the Catholic faith is the most important part of civil justice.[7] Many former Donatists, he says, are now grateful for having been coerced into the Catholic church. To have tried to stop that persecution would have been to interrupt a rescue operation.[8] Similarly, he argues, more good would be done by taking food from a hungry man than by leaving it in his reach, if by satiety he would grow oblivious to morals. This concerns priorities in governmental morality. It assumes that, other things being equal, distributive justice would lead one, for example, to let a hungry man have his food; but distributive justice is not in its own sealed compartment; so spiritual salvation can and, where threatened, does outweigh it (moral matters here again being subsumed under spiritual). Religion, provided it be true religion, thus has complete priority for him in civil affairs.[9]

Also, though in a more limited way, civil affairs have a bearing on religion. Although Augustine makes clear in the *City of God* that salvation does not necessarily depend on our living under any particular kind of government, he also makes clear that civilizations can be immoral and that their moral condition is of spiritual importance.[10] He describes the decline in the mores of antediluvian man as a decline in civilization: the first *civitas* was itself tainted, having been founded by Cain after he had killed Abel. It then went from bad to worse morally and by a process of social involvement (*concretio*) infected the originally wholesome line that stemmed from Seth.[11] As a result, most human beings were rejected by God and destroyed in the Flood.[12] That, one is led to conclude, is what comes from allowing oneself to be involved in the injustice of one's own society: one's relationship with God is jeopardized.

[4] *CD* 5.19, 5.24, 15.4, 15.7. Cf. Y. M. Duval, "L'éloge de Théodose dans la *Cité de Dieu* (V, 26.1)," *Recherches Augustiniennes*, 4 (1966), 139-43.

[5] *CD* 2.25-28. Cf. Alasdair Macintyre, *Whose Justice? Whose Rationality?* (Notre Dame, 1988), 153-55.

[6] *CD* 2.19.

[7] *Epistle* 93.2.4 (J. P. Migne, *Patrologia Latina* [cited as *PL*], 33, 323). On the dates of Augustine's writings see the chronological tables in Brown, *Augustine*.

[8] Cf. *Epistle* 173.4 (*PL* 33, 755).

[9] For Augustine's emphasis, in this context, on the exclusive validity of the Catholic church, see W. H. C. Frend, *The Donatist Church* (Oxford, 1971), 242.

[10] For the limited bearing of politics on religion see *CD* 5.17.

[11] *CD* 15.8, 15.22.

[12] *CD* 15.24.

So the unity of religion and morality (here morality in a civil form) cuts the other way, too: the immorality of civilization can pollute people in their religion. Some human beings survived the Flood. What had been destroyed was Cain's rotten civilization and those who had rotted in it or from its effects. Thus in the *City of God* Augustine interprets human moral life (again in a continuum with religion) in partly civil terms. For rhetorical reasons his concern in this passage is only with the negative side of the connection. When reaffirming his support for coercion of the Donatists during the same period, however, he uncovers the positive side of the connection: in the letter he wrote in 417 to the Roman commander Boniface he says that kings of the earth should serve God not only as men but as kings (*in quantum sunt reges*) and that their proper way to do that is by institutionalizing religious truth at the civil level.[13] Sometimes, then, religious duty must be done by civil means.

On Augustine's thinking after about 400 the view taken here is an unconventional one. R. A. Markus has argued that in Augustine's later writings the state is secular, having no proper part in either of the two spiritually constituted "cities."[14] But though, as Markus says, the middle-aged Augustine spoke increasingly of kings rather than kingdoms, verbally down-playing the institution of the state in such contexts, the passage just mentioned says that kings in so far as they are kings have the unique duty of enforcing Christian orthodoxy, which is to say they have that duty in virtue of their kingdoms. Hence, while not denying that there is considerable further complexity in this area, one may conclude that even as late as 417 he was thinking of the state as properly an instrument of the church.[15]

While retaining this opinion, Augustine was no political perfectionist as he grew older. As Markus points out, by the time he came to favor religious persecution (that is, by 408), he had left behind his quasi-messianic, "Eusebian" idealism about Christian emperors.[16] Its place was taken, however, not only by pessimism but also by a more serviceable kind of optimism based on experience. The successful suppression of the Circumcellion terrorists and the spectacle of genuine conversions resulting from persecution had convinced him to reverse his political position and support religious coercion.[17] He came to favor a certain

[13] *Epistle* 185 (*De Correctione Donatistarum*). 5.19 (*PL* 33, 801).

[14] Markus, *Saeculum*, 144. On Augustine's emphasis on the morals of individual rulers rather than of societies see Duval 1966, 175.

[15] For an extended treatment see Peter Burnell, "The Status of Politics in St. Augustine's *City of God*," *History of Political Thought* (forthcoming).

[16] Markus, *Saeculum*, 147. Cf. Frend, *The Donatist Church*, 231. For a succinct account of Augustine's earlier, "Eusebian" views, see Alfred Schindler, "Querverbindungen zwischen Augustins theologischer und kirchenpolitischer Entwicklung, 390-400," *Theologischer Zeitschrift*, 29 (1973), 100-101. Cf. F. Edward Crantz, "The Development of Augustine's Ideas, on Society before the Donatist Controversy," *Harvard Theological Review*, 47 (1954), 305.

[17] Cf. *Retractationes* 2.5 (*PL* 32, 632). On the Circumcellions see Brown, *Augustine*, 335, and Neal Wood, "*Populares* and *Circumcelliones*: The Vocabulary of 'Fallen Man' in Cicero and St. Augustine," *History of Political Thought*, 7 (1986), 41-47.

bluff governmental pragmatism in dealing with heretics and saw this as precedented in the methods God himself had followed with the recalcitrant children of Israel, buffeting the chosen people with privations and testings: the Roman state was doing the same for the Donatists.[18]

Yet that pragmatism raises our main question. A civil regime might provide some sort of wholesome moral and religious structure but still leave much to be desired in that respect. Given some possibility of political influence, what, if anything, should be done about the ways in which such a state falls short in this most important function (to help its citizens towards salvation)? Would Augustine's pragmatism extend only to swallowing one's moral distaste and allow no political opposition aimed at further improvement for that vital purpose?

The question is problematic, not immediately and straightforwardly answerable, as it is widely thought to be. Two of Augustine's disquisitions in the *City of God*, on the nature and origins of civil society, are especially important here.[19] These passages not only crystallize in a developed form some of the general notions outlined above but reveal three convictions of Augustine's which, taken together, make the nature of the problem clear.

The first is that injustice is unavoidably part of civil life: for Augustine the consequences of original sin are always the underlying human problem, and affect civil affairs as they do all areas of experience. Because of our inherited moral enfeeblement, all civil societies will be unjust in some degree. He did not think that the establishment of a Christian empire by Constantine and Theodosius had fundamentally changed that: the label "Catholic" is not a guarantee of perfect civil justice. All civil life is lived in the middle ground between perfection, stopping well short of perfection, and utter chaos.[20]

The second conviction is that we human beings, though morally crippled and in any case having as our deepest need a beauty and order beyond this world, still have civil duties. One must officiate in a law court, for instance, when called upon. The fact that such duties must be performed in the midst of an iniquitous system—for horrible things, he points out, happen in a law court—does not mean that we may run away from them. "Human society constrains him [the wise man] and sets him plainly to this duty. To desert human society he considers unspeakable wickedness [*nefas*]."[21]

The third conviction is that despite the effects of original sin, civilization is susceptible of moral improvement. Augustine points out, for instance, that it can respond sensitively to natural law, as when innate human decency impelled later communities to put a legal ban on marriage between cousins, which earlier

[18] *Epistle* 93.2.4-5 (*PL* 33, 323).

[19] *CD* 19.6 and 15.16.

[20] *CD* 19.6.

[21] *CD* 19.6. All translations are, unless otherwise attributed, those of the author.

communities had had to allow.[22] It can also be improved by specifically Christian influence.[23] (The entire work is, of course, a defence of the wholesomeness of Christianity's influence on the Roman empire.) Thus, despite the Fall, civilizations can make some moral progress at both natural and supernatural prompting. The middle ground of imperfect order that they occupy is still fertile with moral potentiality.

In the light of his general views these three convictions of Augustine's bring to the fore the dilemma of ethical principle that concerns us here: although it is spiritually disastrous to cooperate with the working of civil injustice (witness the fate of antediluvian man), one is supposed to cooperate in civil affairs, which even at the best of times entail the working of injustice. The problem is how, or whether, to avoid complicity. Should one oppose injustice by changing the system where one can? Or should one accept the complicity after all? One must do one or the other, for of the three logical possibilities—cooperating, opposing, or abstaining—abstaining is not an option: while not necessarily refusing all excuses, Augustine has refused the permanent ubiquity of social injustice as an excuse for permanent retreat from public life. Thus we are morally doomed, as we do our civil duties, to help injustice along unless opposition can be one of those duties.

Failure to face this consequence has meant that the solutions offered by the commentators who have discussed the problem do not actually work as solutions. For example, the distinction between absolute and relative natural law which according to E. L. Fortin is Augustine's own solution, has some relevance but does not quite touch the point at issue.[24] Painful and loathsome deeds are not necessarily immoral ones. To say that in an imperfect world one should sometimes resort to actions that in an ideal world one would always avoid addresses the general fact that we have melancholy duties, not the particular danger that some of them might also involve immorality. That still, therefore, leaves us with the dilemma. E. Teselle's conclusion, that Augustine sees the church as having a duty of reforming the state, is correct, but on the particular point it begs the question.[25] What norms would govern the means of reform? If, for instance, the only admissible means were preaching and example, the dilemma facing people as they do their civil duties would still be untouched. Given Augustine's presuppositions, the only resolution, short of capitulation, that would not avoid the issue would be to give general moral permission to intend reform or possibly to attempt revolution, depending on what might be necessary or feasible: that is, permission not to give perfect acceptance to the *status quo*.

[22] *CD* 15.16.

[23] *CD* 15.16.

[24] Ernest L. Fortin, "Idéalisme politique et foi chrétienne dans la pensée de saint Augustin," *Revue des études Augustiniennes*, 8 (1972), 255.

[25] Eugene Teselle, *Augustine the Theologian* (London, 1970), 278.

It is precisely this that Augustine is commonly described as flatly refusing to countenance. "All men must give absolute obedience to God's ministers, the kings and rulers of this earth, no matter how impious or wicked they may be." That is H. A. Deane's account of Augustine's position.[26] P. R. L. Brown, in an essentially similar account, politely points out the deficiency: that such a "very static view of political society" is "the weakness of Augustine's position," which, he says, "takes an ordered political life for granted."[27] Though mildly phrased, this is a serious criticism. In the context of Augustine's thought, it involves the suggestion that for him it is acceptable to get one's hands morally dirty in certain kinds of human relationship, as long as one keeps one's heart religiously pure. There would be a form of cynical dualism here. The prevailing consensus is that, nevertheless, that is what Augustine thought. Henry Chadwick succinctly summarizes this accepted view: "The follower of Christ would render to Caesar the obedience of his body, and to God that of his mind and soul."[28]

On other grounds, however, it would be surprising if Augustine took quite this position. It violates the principle of the unity of religion and morality. In his *Expositio* on *Romans* (written at about the time he became a bishop) the interpretation of the Pauline "be subject to the powers that be"—we must obey civil powers because we must not discard responsibilities originating in our having bodies—is part of an anti-dualistic argument.[29] Furthermore, in his ninety-third letter the case for religious coercion by the state rests partly on the notion that spiritually weak people, when assailed by an unjust regime, are vulnerable to its mischievous spiritual effect.[30] The coercion was thus an urgent need. Neither passage suggests a rigidly doctrinaire limitation on what is politically allowable, given grave importance of the cause.

The scholarly consensus must therefore be looked at more closely, to see whether it has adequate grounds and gives a complete account of Augustine's position. First, it presumably addresses only the works of Augustine's middle age and old age. As E. Portalié once pointed out, the younger, preepiscopal Augustine had, by means of a clear hypothetical example, defended the propriety of using revolution to correct civil injustice.[31] Secondly, it is true that Augustine the bishop on occasion forbids opposition, let alone revolution, against civil injustice; but does he do so categorically? The debatable word in Deane's "absolute obedience to kings and rulers" is "absolute." The passage

[26] Herbert A. Deane, *The Political and Social Ideas of St. Augustine* (New York and London, 1963), 145.

[27] Brown 1965, 14.

[28] Henry Chadwick, *Augustine* (Oxford, 1986), 103.

[29] *Expositio Quarundam Propositionum ex Epistula ad Romanos* 72 (Paula Fredriksen Landes, *Augustine on Romans* [Chico, Ca., 1982], 40-41).

[30] *Epistle* 93.6.20 (*PL* 33, 331). Cf. *Epistle* 185.1.2 (*PL* 33.793).

[31] Eugene Portalié, S.J., *A Guide to the Thought of Saint Augustine*, tr. Ralph J. Bastian, S.J. (London, 1960), 282: *De Libero Arbitrio* 1.6.14 (*PL* 32, 1229).

he quotes from *De Catechizandis Rudibus* (written when Augustine had been a bishop for about five years) asserts indeed that one has a duty of obedience even to a wicked tyrant but does not add or imply that the injunction is absolute.[32] This is a *secundum quid* matter, for the passage does not deal with questions such as what deeper operative principle might be revealed in a time of *stasis*, where an opportunity arose for just improvement in return for bold action. Brown's argument is that for Augustine the state exists to control certain evils of social life, thus liberating human beings for higher concerns. Once it is fulfilling that necessary but minimal role, it should be left to itself and may be taken for granted. Since it is not an instrument of justice in any greater or deeper sense, one has no right to disturb it by demanding more of it. Reason has already been given here for a different view of Augustine's thinking on this matter.[33]

However, even assuming for argument's sake that this is an accurate account of his thinking, should it be taken as held without qualification? Even if one should passively accept civil mediocrity in return for continued stability, the continued stability cannot be taken for granted: it can always break down, as Augustine was aware. He might, of course, have discounted such occasions (opportunities for radical intervention, disobedience) as unimportant. Brown argues that he did. "Occasions for disobedience," he says, "do not worry Augustine."[34] They do not always worry him. Brown cites a sermon in which Augustine condemns the lynching of a tyrannical garrison-commander in Hippo.[35] This illustrates Brown's point clearly, for it recommends martyrdom in place of such blatant law-breaking. Only duly appointed people may execute. But it is not an argument against either reform or revolution, for stopping short of addressing such possibilities is not the same as precluding them; nor does he always stop short of addressing them.

Intended audience is the important factor here. When haranguing his flock Augustine is prepared to assume the existence of settled and constant government. Hence he talks in extremes: official executions (*publica supplicia*), as opposed to open banditry (*aperta latrocinia*). In the *City of God* it is a different matter. That work was written with a far more sophisticated audience in mind, and is historically and philosophically panoramic. His discussion of civil society there is correspondingly more subtle and comprehensive. In particular, as Y.-M. Duval points out, the fall of Rome to the Goths had given Augustine's cultured pagan opponents some polemical ammunition.[36] When replying to them he must face the doctrinal implications of partial breakdown in the governmental order; now there can be no taking an ordered political life for granted. Hence, many passages in that work refer to times of political instability, radical civil change,

[32] Deane, *The Political and Social Ideas*, 144: *De Catechizandis Rudibus* 21.37.

[33] Again, for a more extended argument see Burnell (forthcoming).

[34] Brown, *Augustine*, 6.

[35] *Sermon* 302.11.10-19.17 (*PL* 38, 1389-92).

[36] See Duval, "L'éloge de Théodose," 173.

and revolution.[37] Some are of particular interest because they also touch on the principles, not merely the practices, of civil life.[38] It is in those passages, if anywhere, that Augustine may be expected to give an adequate picture of his opinions, or at least his assumptions, on the question at issue.

The first of these passages, written around 415, when he was about sixty, is part of a long survey of Roman history (Book III, chapters 15-16) demonstrating the absence of any help or supervision by the pagan gods.[39] The passage concerned is about the expulsion of the Tarquins. On one level it takes an anti-revolutionary position: Junius Brutus and his companions were imprudent to expel Tarquin and establish a republic without waiting to see how the king would respond to his citizens' grievance. But a fundamental distinction applies here between a person's own political views—a prudential matter, concerned with how ethical principles are to be applied to specific circumstances—and the ethical principles themselves (with their general grounds of application).

Our problem concerns the latter. Augustine's change of mind in favor of persecuting the Donatists illustrates the distinction. (He had long before accepted the principle, that rough measures are justified as means to bring about true conversions. Only on prudential grounds had he opposed the practice: he had not thought that it would actually work, and on prudential grounds he changed his mind.[40]) In this passage Augustine's own political view is that the Romans were indecent in their haste for revolution. Yet in taking that view he makes the general assumption that civil revolution is a permissible kind of action in itself. Arguing that the Romans should have waited to see involves supposing that if Tarquin had then proved callous and intransigent, revolution might then have been appropriate. This is not a logical implication but a matter of practical congruency in argumentation. If, for example, one were an outright pacifist, one would be unlikely to suggest that Chamberlain should have waited longer before declaring war, to see what Hitler's plans were after Poland.

In another passage Augustine discusses the gladiators' revolt led by Spartacus in 73 B.C.—an event demonstrating that merely having got hold of some imperial power, as Spartacus had, is not a sign of virtue.[41] In a celebrated passage in the preceding chapter Augustine has conceded that one can treat societies without reference to justice, simply as organized frameworks for people to lead their lives in, but that if one does, there will logically no longer be any essential difference between kingdoms and gangs; for with such a simple and general definition, the gap between Alexander the Great and a pirate will be

[37] *CD* 1.1-7, 1.10-19, 1.22-30, 1.33-35, 2.3, 2.17, 2.22, 3.15, 4.5, 4.15, 5.12, 18.20, 18.45-46, 19.7, 19.12.

[38] *CD* 3.15-16, 4.5, 19.7, 19.12.

[39] *CD* 3.1-31.

[40] *Epistle* 185.7.25-31 (*PL* 33, 804-7). Cf. Markus, *Saeculum*, 139.

[41] *CD* 4.5.

a matter only of degree, as a pirate once pointed out.[42] The case of Spartacus illustrates this particularly well because by a disconcerting success he briefly filled that gap. When the empire was still new and firm, his gang of gladiators got control of a large segment of Rome's power. Thus the significant event here is not Spartacus's partial overturning of Roman rule but his partial achievement of a new one.

The wider context clarifies Augustine's purpose. A main component of his argument here (Book IV, chs. 2, 3, 5) is that God inscrutably involves His providence in the history even of unjust empires. While they last, they are the "powers that be." That even applies to Spartacus's gladiators. Were they a scurvy crew? That makes no difference, argues Augustine: look what the Romans were when they started. Did the gladiators wield great power only for a little while? Well, both Augustine and his opponents agree that an individual emperor or king is divinely helped to his exalted position; yet no individual lives very long. This argumentation makes clear that for a while Spartacus and his gladiators were, for the people they controlled, the powers that be.

Establishing that a given government is the powers that be establishes also, for anyone who takes St. Paul seriously, a presumptive duty of obedience to that government. Yet it hardly needs to be added that Augustine still thought it perfectly proper to do what one could to oppose and undermine the rule of such patent riff-raff as Spartacus's gladiators while they exercised their control. Indeed the discomfited Romans and those who supported their cause did just this with eventual success. That this is so and the principle that makes it so are clear from Augustine's assertion a few chapters later that imperial interference by Rome, invasion, destruction of other political systems, and annexation are justified as occasional moral necessities.[43] One should not desire such things for themselves, but they are justified when they prevent a greater evil, the unjust, lording it over the just. This would certainly allow for fighting and unseating Spartacus. His gladiators "indulged in whatever pleasures they wished; they did whatever lust suggested" (*usi voluptatibus quibus voluerunt, quod suggessit libido fecerunt*). Even pagan Rome, by contrast, had rightly put some limit on public depravity, as Augustine concedes later in the work.[44] We may conclude that for him Roman law, albeit built into an empire itself originally built on a lust (the *libido dominandi*), was at least committed to putting some restraint on that Protean moral disease.

Thus Roman rule was better, less incompatible with devotion to God as an end, than the regime of that licentious mob. One can speculate that Augustine might have thought the conditions decisively different if the gladiators had established stable government, but then the historical events would not have provided such an instructive middle case. The inchoate government of Spartacus is an exception (for Augustine a rare one) to the rule of obedience to the powers

[42] *CD* 4.4.

[43] *CD* 4.15.

[44] *CD* 12.13.

that be. It was too powerful to be denied the title of government, too chaotic to be taken seriously as such. Exceptions to rules show the supersession of one principle by another that more rarely applies. The principle usually applying is obedience to the powers that be; the superseding one, the duty of trying to ensure that civil power is in the hands of the least unjust persons or groups possible; and as we have seen, Augustine proceeds to point out that this may involve overturning a regime. The passage as a whole establishes an important principle, that civil justice, or rather some approximation to it, is basic to a governmental system's right to be left alone. It follows that governmental systems as such are for him not sacrosanct.

Augustine returned to the same issues in a theoretical way ten years later in two passages (Book XIX) which considerably deepen our understanding of his thinking on the matter. In the first (chapter 7) the subject of just war comes up again. In the course of ridiculing the ideal of philosophical bliss in this world, he lists the grotesque and inexorable miseries of the human condition, prominent in which is war. Foreign wars are past history, he says, but civil war within the empire is not. He now reaffirms the principle established in book IV: invasion, annexation, etc. are nothing to rejoice in, but injustice in one's adversary (*iniquitas ... partis adversae*) justifies them. As before, there would be other preconditions, such as the practical usefulness of violent action (for wars are fought to attain or reestablish peace); but those are matters of prudence, of where and when. What primarily justifies such action is the enemy's injustice no matter whether the war is civil or foreign.

The importance of this principle depends on how generally one may understand it. Augustine no doubt envisages such wars mainly within the range of his experience: that is, as waged by the Roman authorities to reimpose order. But as we have seen, such circumstantial considerations are not universally determinative for him. His arguments have been quite clear: Rome had not always been big, and anyway mere size is not the crucial point. In this passage, too, he has already mentioned other kinds of wars, events of the distant past. For both those reasons we may understand his statements on just war to be general ones which are not tied to a contemporary range of manifestations. All war that is justified by Augustine's specification—war that changes a society in the direction of justice—has an obvious revolutionary dimension. Thus his point about the limits to a state's right not to be subverted is a general point.

The other passage (chapter 12) takes a theoretical position on the subject of civil unrest. In the course of a disquisition on Cacus, the monster in Virgil's *Aeneid*, Augustine compares that creature's turbulent inward condition with a civil community in *stasis*.[45] The passage illustrates the doctrine that peace is the universal motive in creatures. All that the monster, that prodigy of ferocity, ever really wanted was peace (stability and well-being). This leads to the analogy with civil life: in Cacus's internal political structure mortality has risen up and

[45] *CD* 19.12; Virgil, *Aeneid* 8.190-305.

tried to force his soul out of his body. That has caused an inward civil emergency, and reason has had to intervene and bring about a radical alteration in internal policy. That in turn has led to disconcerting changes in the outward actions of this microcosmic state. The crucial point is that mortality's original rebellion arose "out of need" (*ex indigentia*):[46] the mortality is an unavoidable and universal fact; the need, its inevitable result in the circumstances. The consequent revolutionary intervention of reason is on mortality's behalf. Mortality in this analogy constitutes a number of legitimate needs. So the whole sequence of events, culminating in Cacus's savage acts, originates in necessities involved in staying alive (*vivendi necessitate*). The analogy provides us with a clear and simple hypothetical case. There is no suggestion that alternative ways were open either to Cacus's mortality or to the frantic citizens of the analogy. Thus the comparison is with legitimate revolution and makes no sense unless there can be a necessity that leads a downtrodden and desperate citizenry into sedition and legitimately causes a revolution.

In principle Augustine's view of civil life is not, therefore, static. It does not make endless cooperation with wickedness a necessary concomitant of a Christian's civil duties. Though a long way from the sort of "liberation theology" that regards the Gospel as predominantly political, Augustine's position implicitly allows for considerable development in radically reformative or even revolutionary political directions. Such development would of course be quite foreign to his "politics" but not to his principles. His support for religious coercion was authoritarian. But the arguments with which he supported that coercion are quite concordant with his openness in principle (in both the early and late books of the *City of God*) to changing the structure of civil society by political intervention. Indeed, thinking that civil society should above all be an efficient instrument for changing potential "citizens of this world" into "citizens of God" practically requires thinking that it legitimately might be shaped to such purposes when it could be. That this ultimately is Augustine's position shows that his thinking in this area has more openness, more internal consistency, and also rather more constancy on essentials than has been conventionally thought.

It is important to add that by reciprocal signification the Cacus analogy also indicates the tendency of revolutions to have regrettable moral consequences. Cacus's internal revolution has resulted in acts of horror. Thus even as our original dilemma is in essence resolved a second one immediately replaces it because of the injustice that plagues radical change in society. This second dilemma is, however, of a different nature. There is now no implication that we are morally bound to cooperate in wrong; merely that we are circumstantially bound to it; for it is not that we have the duty to act out moral failure deliberately but that, as we take what few chances for enhanced moral success civil life might

[46] Augustine, *The City of God*, tr. Henry Bettenson (Harmondsworth, 1972), 868, misleadingly rendered "because of its insatiable desires" in the Penguin translation.

occasionally offer, we are in practice almost always going to fail. Presumably that consideration would in potentially revolutionary circumstances give one serious pause; but however difficult or depressing such a dilemma might be, it is still only a prudential dilemma, not one of moral principle.

As we have seen, this distinction applies to Augustine's thought precisely because he was able to consider societies and historical periods profoundly different from his own. In an article on Augustine's political pessimism O. O'Donovan attributes that rather bleak view of politics to "Augustine's foreshortened historical perspective," which "prevented him from seeing what kinds of revolution are possible in political structures."[47] Yet the passages discussed here show both that Augustine had a clear notion of the moral terms on which political life is lived and that he knew that very different conditions could pertain (conditions foreign to his experience), where the same moral terms would demand very different kinds of action. The cause of his pessimism about politics was not foreshortened historical perspective but a steady awareness that the frustrating and demoralizing effects of original sin would persist as long as the world lasted. Not much can be done about the frustration. As for the demoralization, his picture of civil man is like that of the rower in Virgil's *Georgics*, who if he slackens for an instant will be tumbled headlong downstream.[48] One is either going to achieve little practical progress, or none. Yet it is necessary to try because resignation to the perpetuation of civil wrong is an impossible ethical luxury.

University of Saskatchewan.

[47] O'Donovan, "Augustine's *City of God XIX*," 105.
[48] Virgil, *Georgics* 1.201-3.

[8]

PLURALISM AND SECULARISM IN THE POLITICAL ORDER: ST. AUGUSTINE AND THEORETICAL LIBERALISM*

Michael J. White

Hanc [pacem populus alienatus Deo] autem ut interim habeat in hac vita, etiam nostri interest; quoniam, quamdiu permixtae sunt ambae civitates, utimur et nos pace Babylonis; ex qua ita per fidem populus Dei liberatur, ut apud hanc interim peregrinetur. (It is also in our interest that [the people alienated from God] meanwhile possess this peace in this life; for so long as both cities are intermixed, we also make use of the peace of Babylon; from Babylon the people of God is so liberated through its faith that it may for a while sojourn in its midst.) Augustine, *De civ. Dei*, 19.26

With respect to Augustine's mature political thought, R. A. Markus writes as follows:

> The main lines of his thinking about history, society and human institutions in general (the *saeculum*) point towards a political order to which we may not unreasonably apply the anachronistic epithet 'pluralist', in that it is neutral in respect of ultimate beliefs and values.[1]

However, Augustine's political thought during the time period with which this conference is especially concerned, the 390s, is represented by Markus as something of a passing aberration. During this period Augustine was attracted to (but never wholeheartedly embraced) a tenet associated with 'Theodosian Christianity': the state, in particular, the Christianized Roman Empire, has a special role in salvation history; the consequent politicization of Christianity's evangelical mission has, in fact, ushered in *tempora Christiana*.[2] Augustine soon—even before the sack of Rome in 410—repudiated such a view and began to work out the conception of the 'neutrality' of the political order alluded to by Markus in the preceding quotation. But he did not repudiate at least one practice that seems a natural corollary of the Theodosian viewpoint, political coercion with respect to religious matters. Indeed, his famous justification of coercion, which includes his interpretation of the injunction of the master to the servant found in the parable of Luke 14, '*compelle intrare*' ('compel them to come in'), occurs in *Ep.* 93, which was written in 408. Although Markus discusses some reasons for the survival of Augustine's support for the practice of religious coercion beyond the demise of the theoretical support for it (in the form of what I am calling the Theodosian viewpoint), he sees unresolved tension between Augustine's continuing support for at least some forms of religious coercion and his mature, secularist conception of the political order. Markus' view depends on his interpreting the empirical 'pluralism' and 'secularism' of Augustine's mature conception of the state as anticipating the neutrality that is often a key feature of modern theoretical political liberalism. My aim in this paper is to argue that there is no legitimate inference to be made from the empirical pluralism and secularism of Augustine's mature political thought to even a budding commitment, on his part, to theoretical neutrality of the sort characteristic of modern liberalism. I shall also maintain, as a corollary, that Augustine's support for at least some forms of religious coercion is quite consistent with his mature, pragmatic conception of political authority. Indeed, his pragmatic conception of political power seems to accord quite well with one modern Catholic point of view in favor until the Second Vatican Council, a point of view that was, in fact, urged by Pope Leo XIII in several social encyclicals of the 1880s.

The pluralism and secularism characteristic of most modern liberal conceptions of the political order are, in fact, manifestations of another more fundamental characteristic of the liberal conception, i.e., the *neutrality* of the political order. I first discuss the nature and place of this feature of modern theoretical liberalism. Then I turn to Augustine, arguing that it has no place in his mature political thought.

The neutrality associated with modern theoretical liberalism amounts to more than what I shall term *formal* neutrality. Formal neutrality, as I understand it, is simply a matter of the state's being concerned with the welfare of all its citizens, with its not institutionally 'writing off' the welfare of some of its citizens as being of no concern to it. The principle of equality under the law is a good illustration of this conception of formal neutrality. Formal neutrality does not, of course, preclude the state's treating different classes or sorts of person in different ways. It also seems to be quite compatible with various policies, e.g., regulation of 'private morality,' to which the paradigmatic theoretical political liberal will object.

The other sort of neutrality, with which I am more concerned, is neutrality 'amongst competing conceptions of the good'[3] or neutrality with respect to 'what might be called the question of the good life.'[4] Some contemporary theorists have *defined* theoretical political liberalism in terms of this sort of neutrality. Ronald Dworkin, for example, defines liberalism in terms of its interpretation of the requirement that a government 'treat its citizens as equals' (which, he claims, is identical to the requirement that the government 'treat all its citizens as free, or as independent, or with equal dignity').[5] Thus, according to Dworkin, 'the liberal theory of equality rules out. . . appeal to the inherent value of one theory of what is good in life'[6] in the political realm.

Several features of the place of neutrality within theoretical liberalism seem to be especially important. The first is that most forms of liberalism are committed to neutrality as an instrumental rather than a fundamental value.[7] A commitment to neutrality with respect to conceptions of the good as an ultimate value, something to be valued for its own sake, is not very plausible—except, perhaps, in the context of 'skepticism about theories of the good.' But most liberals do not explicitly wish to embrace such skepticism.[8] The obvious question, then, is the following; if theoretical political liberalism regards neutrality as having basic but instrumental value, what ultimate value or final end is neutrality of instrumental value in achieving? Although I am certain other answers are possible, there seem to be three distinct sorts of answer that theoretical liberals have given to this question. (i) The political stance of neutrality is necessary for recognizing and promoting the autonomy of persons, conceived as a (or, perhaps, *the*) essential characteristic of persons. (ii) The political stance of neutrality is necessary for reasons of epistemic utility: that is, it allows the 'free competition' among conceptions of the good that is the necessary (or, at least, most efficient) means toward the true, 'most true,' or 'most adequate' conception's coming to be recognized as such by the greatest number of persons. (iii) In social contexts of empirical pluralism, or widespread disagreement about the proper conception of the good, the political stance of neutrality is expedient—i.e., the necessary (or, at least most efficient) means for forming political organization and maintaining its stability and, hence, for obtaining whatever essential benefits (e.g., absence of a state of *bellum omnium contra omnes*) that such political organization confers.

This is not the place for detailed consideration of these three answers. However, for my present purposes, it is worth remarking on a few features of each answer. (i) is perhaps most attractive to those who would like to tie theoretical political liberalism to the 'natural rights' tradition. It obviously assumes that there are certain essential features of persons which, as a matter of fundamental morality, must be respected and furthered. It is sometimes claimed—as by Dworkin—that the 'equal dignity' or 'equal respect' due persons *qua* persons enjoins the political stance of neutrality by means of which each is given maximal leeway to form his own conception of the good and work out his own fate in terms of that conception.[9] Or it is sometimes claimed that the essential rationality of persons, in particular the exercise of some form of practical reason, requires this same leeway with respect to each person's forming his own conception of the good and working out a 'rational life plan' in terms of that conception. John Rawls, for example, sometimes argues in this fashion, remarking in his most recent book that 'to see reasonable pluralism as a disaster is to see the exercise of reason under the conditions of freedom itself as a disaster.'[10]

With respect to such accounts of the instrumental value of neutrality, it seems that *autonomy* is the essential feature that must, so to speak, do the work. There are certainly historical (and respectable) accounts of 'human dignity, the sacredness of persons, inherent human worth, and fundamental respect that is owed to all persons simply because they are persons'[11] that do not entail the autonomy of persons in the sense of the necessity of the unfettered self-determination of their conception of the good.[12] And there are certainly historical (and respectable) accounts of reason, including 'practical reason' that do not entail autonomy in this same sense. In other words, if the demands either of inherent human dignity, respect, or worth or of the untrammeled exercise of human reason are to be invoked here, the more essential notion of autonomy must somehow be built into these metaphysical or religious notions.

To consider an example of what I have in mind, John Locke is especially successful in providing the sort of conceptual framework in which a cogent story can be told concerning the need to respect human autonomy. The source of human autonomy, for Locke, is theological. In particular, the form of Protestantism embraced by Locke makes the notion of a person's divine vocation a private matter, tailor-made, as it were, by God for the particular person, and only the business of God and the person in question. We are, individually, 'the workmanship of one omnipotent and infinitely wise Maker', and we are, individually, 'sent into the world by his order, and about his business.'[13] With such a privatized conception of vocation, it is surely plausible to favor a political order that guarantees maximal autonomy to the individual person, consistent with a similar guarantee for other persons. Later attempts to derive the neutrality of liberalism from some notion of autonomy often give the impression of a 'moral doctrine [that] is cut off from it traditional roots,' which 'simply hangs in midair.'[14]

Source (ii) of liberalism's commitment to neutrality as an instrumental value, its derivation from considerations of epistemic utility, also has traditional roots, I suspect.[15] Like many claims of utility, the claim that a context of neutrality is most conducive to 'truth (with respect to the conception of the good) winning out' is a factual claim that would be terribly difficult to sustain (or reject) in empirical terms. Metaphors from the economics of capitalism—e.g., the 'free exchange of ideas,' 'competition in the marketplace of ideas'—are often employed in this context. Such metaphors perhaps have most force in situtations where some factual matter is to be decided or a theory that best explains some factual data is being sought. In such cases, it makes some sense to suppose that the truth or most satisfactory explanation of some data 'will out' (in the long run). Justification of the political stance of neutrality with respect to conceptions of the good in terms of epistemic utility requires the extension of this perspective to issues of value and morality (at least, 'private' morality). It is arguable that the extension of this perspective to issues of value and morality is suspect. For it is surely true that, with respect to value and morality, training and formation have at least as important rôles to play as does 'discovery of facts' or selection of the best theoretical explanation of such facts. At any rate, the justification of the stance of neutrality in terms of epistemic utility has, I suspect, a fairly recent pedigree that is tied to the rise of the ideology of free-market economics. Plato, among many others, thought differently about the matter:

> The tolerance in such a [democratic] city! It certainly does not show any petty concern for trifles. Indeed it despises those things we solemnly spoke of when we were founding our city, as that, unless a man had an exceedingly fine nature, he would never become a good man unless from early childhood he played fine games and followed fine pursuits. How magnificently this city tramples all this underfoot and does not give a thought to what a man was doing before he enters public life.[16]

Finally, there is (iii), the derivation of liberalism's commitment to neutrality from considerations of political expediency in contexts of widespread disagreement about conceptions of the good. One suspects that empirical pluralism was a key feature in the development of the stance of neutrality in actual liberal states. In social contexts of fairly great empirical pluralism, i.e., in contexts in which there is, as a matter of fact, wide divergence with respect to conceptions of the good, it may be prudent, as a *pragmatic* political matter, to adopt a policy of *laissez-faire* or neutrality, to such a degree as this seems necessary and feasible, with respect to conceptions of the good. What theoretical political liberalism does is to transform this practical necessity (or, at least, matter of practical prudence) into the theoretical virtue of neutrality.

In his seminal *A Theory of Justice* John Rawls represents this transformation of empirical pluralism into theoretical neutrality by means of his contractarian device of the 'original position.' Individuals having diverse and competing interests, conceptions of the good, and 'rational plans of life' are to derive 'principles of justice' that are to be applied to any political organization. In order for there to be any point to political organization (and any possibility of forming and sustaining it), it is also assumed that there is a certain commonality of interests of individuals in the original position:

> Now the assumption is that though men's rational plans do have different final ends, they nevertheless all require for their execution certain primary goods, natural and social. Plans differ since individual abilities, circumstances, and wants differ; rational plans are adjusted to these contingencies. But whatever one's system of ends, primary goods are necessary means.[17]

A shared interest in the acquisition of primary goods provides the commonality that is the *raison d'être* of the political order, and the just distribution of these primary goods is the 'foundational task' of that order. Rawls' characterization of primary goods as 'things which it is supposed a rational man wants whatever else he wants'[18] may be misleading. I do not think that the question of what should count as primary goods is, for Rawls, *primarily* an empirical question about the uniformity of human nature, i.e., a question about the consilience of human wants and needs. Particularly with respect to what Rawls calls the 'primary social goods,' their function is that of means: ' with more of these goods men can generally be assured of greater success in carrying out their intentions and in advancing their ends, *whatever these ends may be*.'[19]

Since Rawls allows for the possibility of widely differing *final* ends and 'full' conceptions of the good, a reasonable question is whether it is likely that there would be much consilience about what should be considered primary goods, considered as means to these ends. After all, one would expect that rather different means, particularly *social* means, would be appropriate for achieving different final ends or furthering different conceptions of the good. According to the liberal conception, it is the primary *métier* of political organization to serve as an unbiased umpire, balancing the competing interests of individuals in conformity with the principles of justice. In other words, the *political* stance toward these varied ends and conceptions of the good must, perhaps within certain limits, be one of neutrality. This fundamental feature of the liberal conception of polity is represented by Rawls' game-theoretic version of the contractarian account of the legitimacy of the political order. Rational, self-interested individuals in an 'original position' are to decide on general principles (the 'principles of justice') for assessing political organization. In effect, this amounts to adopting general principles concerning the equitable distribution of primary goods. The problem about different final ends and conceptions of the good leading to different conceptions of primary goods, considered as means to furthering those ends—as well as different conceptions of what constitutes their 'just' distribution—is circumvented by emptying these final ends and conceptions of the good of their substantive content. Individuals in the original position are placed behind Rawls' famous 'veil of ignorance': not only are they to be made ignorant of their particular assets, abilities, and socio-economic and political rôles; they also are to be denied knowledge of their particular conception of the good and 'rational life plan' with its individual final ends. Rawls argues that, since an individual in the original position (a) will have strong commitments to his ends and his full conception of the good but (b) does not know what those ends or the content of that conception is, it is rational for such an individual to adopt a *laissez-faire* political attitude toward such ends/ conceptions of the good. In practice, this amounts to coming to an agreement about primary social goods such that these goods will allow an 'arbitrarily selected' individual maximal leeway for pursuing his own ends and furthering his own conception of the good (compatible, of course, with a similar leeway for other individuals). Consequently, we find Rawls specifying, in 'broad categories,' primary social goods as 'rights and liberties, opportunities and powers, income and wealth.'[20]

In his recent *Political Liberalism* Rawls again notes the role of political expedience in his theory:

> we are to recognize the practical impossibility of reaching reasonable and workable political agreement in judgment on the truth of comprehensive doctrines [of the good], especially an agreement that might serve the political purpose, say, of achieving peace and concord in a society characterized by religious and political differences.[21]

However, Rawls—as well as most liberal theorists, I believe—are reluctant to base their theoretical commitment to neutrality solely on considerations of political expediency in contexts of empirical pluralism of values/conceptions of the good. For example, most such theorists would insist on the rightness of the stance of political neutrality, and the so-called freedoms that are derived from it, even in social contexts of great cultural homogeneity and agreement concerning the 'comprehensive doctrine' of the good. Consequently, Rawls insists that his representational device of the original position, with its individuals constrained, behind the veil of ignorance, to select general principles, represents the norms of 'public reason' or (practical) rationality and reasonableness:

> the guidelines and procedures of public reason are seen as selected in the original position and belong to the public conception of justice. As I remarked earlier (§1.4), the reasonable, in contrast with the rational, addresses the public world of others. The original position as a device of representation helps to show how it does so.[22]

It is important to point out that, in fact, not *all* possible 'rational plans of life' or conceptions of the good are accorded non-preferential tolerance. Such plans/ conceptions must be consistent with Rawls' principles of justice; otherwise they are to be judged socially immoral. As Rawls puts it, 'since in the full theory rational plans must be consistent with the principles of justice, the human goods are similarly constrained.'[23] Rawls' 'first principle of justice' is a typical *laissez-faire* principle of liberalism: 'each person is to have an equal right to the most extensive basic liberty compatible with a similar liberty for others.'[24] So, any 'life plan' or conception of the good that might have the effect of constraining the 'independent choices' of *other* individuals with respect to their life plans and the development of their conception of the good is ruled out *ab initio*. In *Political Liberalism*, such conceptions of the good, or rather, the attempt to further such conceptions in the political sphere, are ruled out as 'being unreasonable.'[25] It is true that Rawls is more concerned in his recent work with the relation between 'reasonable pluralism' with respect to comprehensive doctrines of the good and support for his own version of the 'core of liberalism' (i.e., his particular principles of justice). But his theoretical device for representing practical rationality and reasonableness (derivation of principles by those in the original position, curtained behind the veil of ignorance) still has the effect of favoring comprehensive doctrines of the good that are (or can be rendered) sufficiently private and individualistic—or, in other words, those doctrines compatible with theoretical political liberalism. The use of such a device to represent 'public rationality' does not seem especially plausible if comprehensive doctrines—and the obligations that they impose—of a more communitarian or paternalistic sort are included in the grab bag.

The effect of theoretical liberalism's commitment to neutrality is to privatize conceptions of the good. And the effect of this privatization is a final characteristic of theoretical political liberalism to which I wish briefly to allude: 'a neutralist theory,' to quote Peter Jones, 'has to make a sharp distinction between the right and the good; that is, between the rules of right (or principles of justice) within which conceptions of the good are to be pursued, and the conceptions of good themselves.'[26] In other words, principles of right or morality (at least the *public* ones about which we should all care) are to be somehow separated (at least in the political sphere) from 'comprehensive doctrines' or conceptions of the good and, indeed, are to constrain (morally) the permissible range of conceptions of the good (again, at least, as far as the political sphere is concerned). The right, to be agreed upon by liberal consensus, is to have a moral 'clout' and obligatory character that no conception of the good is to have—at least within the political order. For example, Dworkin rules out what he terms 'external preferences' ('preferences people have about what others shall do or have')[27] as constituents of conceptions of the good of which the political order should take any account. Of course, one might maintain that such a separation of right from good and the constraint of the latter by the former is simply a matter of political expediency in contexts of diverse and irreconcilable conceptions of the good. But most liberal theorists want to ground this key feature of theoretical liberalism in something more than political expediency.

We have now seen the sense in which theoretical political liberalism embraces pluralism in the form of a stance of political neutrality with respect to (many but by no means all) rational plans of life and conceptions of the good. It is an almost immediate corollary that liberalism will be committed to a secularist conception of the political order. Rawls, appealing to his game-theoretic version of the contractarian model, quickly establishes the corollary. Individuals 'in the original position,' it is to be supposed, *may* have 'moral, religious, or philosophical interests which they cannot put in jeopardy unless there is no alternative.'[28] However,

> they do not know, of course, what their religious or moral convictions are, or what is the particular content of their moral and religious convictions as they interpret them.

> Indeed, they do not know that they think of themselves as having such obligations. The possibility that they do suffices for the argument, although I shall make the stronger assumption. Further, the parties do not know how their religious or moral view fares in their society, whether, for example, it is in the majority or the minority. . . The question they are to decide is which principle they should adopt to regulate the liberties of citizens in regard to their fundamental religious, moral, and philosophical interests.[29]

The answer to this question, Rawls immediately informs us, is a principle of (maximal) 'equal liberty of conscience.' The point of Rawls' mechanism is to represent the commitment of liberalism to the political stance of neutrality or impartiality with respect to moral, religious, and philosophical convictions. (Of course, the 'morality' in question is 'private morality'—which is to say, just those issues that are generally agreed to be 'moral' but toward which it is deemed proper for the state to adopt this stance of neutrality; note that, unlike the case of morality, liberalism generally leaves no room for the private/public distinction with respect to religion.)[30] To use the language of the early Marx, the liberal state declares itself irreligious (and, with respect to many issues of morality, amoral) 'in a political way' and thus commits itself to attempting to eliminate the influence of religion and 'private' morality/philosophy with respect to political/legal matters. [31]

I turn now to the 'neutrality' and 'pluralism' that Markus finds in Augustine's mature conception of the political order, which turns out to be very different from the neutrality and pluralism characteristic of theoretical political liberalism. I shall argue that the neutrality and pluralism discerned by Markus is simply a consequence of the fact that Augustine's mature conception of political order is so 'minimalist' that there is an important sense in which he cannot be said to *have* a political theory.

Once Augustine has relinquished any attachment to a Theodosian (or Eusebian, or Constantinian) conception of the state (in particular, the Roman empire) as having any particular rôle in salvation history, what conception of the political order is he left with? As a number of commentators have pointed out, the significance of the 'two cities' of *De civitate Dei* is essentially eschatological: only at the end of the *saeculum* will there be a winnowing by which the citizens of the two cities, the sacred Jerusalem and the profane Babylon, are separated out. In this age, all institutions, perhaps especially the political, are characterized by a thoroughly mixed membership. To use the terminology of Rawls, the 'rational plans of life,' with their particular final ends, and the 'conceptions of the good' of these two types of person are radically different. The citizens of the earthly city seek their 'enjoyment' (*fructus*), the ultimate 'ends of good and evil,' in this life,

> locating the *summum bonum* in the body or in the soul or in both—that is, to speak more explicitly, in pleasure or in virtue or in both, in quietude or in virtue or in both, in pleasure along with quietude or in virtue or in both, in the first things of nature or in virtue or in both. These the Truth has laughed to scorn, saying through the prophet: *The Lord knows the thoughts of men*, or, as the apostle Paul has cited the testimony: *The Lord knows the thoughts of the wise, that they are vain.*[32]

For the citizens of the heavenly city, the political order cannot effect anything that is a proper *final* end or object of enjoyment, *fructus*; like all that pertains the *saeculum*, that is, all that is secular, the political order is merely an object of *usus* or practical employment as a means. That to which the political order is principally a means is peace. Although the intermixed citizens of both cities can benefit from this peace, citizens of the heavenly city, who are the principal object of Augustine's concern both as bishop and Christian man of letters, benefit from it only indirectly and in a limited fashion. Unlike, for example, St. Thomas, Augustine does not possess a clear, positive conception of the natural good that is enjoyable, in principle, by all persons irrespective of their supernatural destiny. In the words of J. van Oort, 'Augustine did not see temporal goods separately as neutral goods, but according to the use man makes of them. That use is either good or evil, and in this way temporal goods belong to one of the two cities, either that of God or that of the devil.'[33] The upshot is that, for Augustine, there is very little room for the commonality of interests that is the *raison d'être* of the political order. It is in this sense that Augustine does not have much by way of political *theory*: he does not have a 'thick' conception of legitimate temporal good or goods of human beings, irrespective of their final destiny, which it is the particular function of the political order to advance.

As we shall see, Augustine does frequently speak of political authority as 'restraining the wicked' and 'restraining evil desires.' This may suggest a very comprehensive (and, perhaps, 'illiberal') rôle for the political order. I shall argue that there is nothing *in principle* in Augustine's mature political thought that rules out such a comprehensive political program. But political organization always involves, as a matter of fact, limitations imposed by its thoroughly mixed membership of persons, with their radically differing 'comprehensive doctrines of the good.' This empirical pluralism leaves the 'thin' function of promoting peace. What Markus terms 'the institutions of political and judicial authority, with their coercive machinery'[34] exist for securing peace. And, as Augustine puts it in a letter to the Christian official of the Empire Macedonius (in which Augustine is counseling mercy and justifying his episcopal practice of pleading for leniency on behalf of the condemned):

> Surely, therefore, not without purpose have there been ordained the king's power, the judge's right of the sword [*jus gladii*, i.e., right of capital sentence], the executioner's hooks, the ruler's discipline, and even the good father's severity. All these have their own methods, causes, reasons, and usefulness. When these are feared, the wicked are restrained, and the good live more quietly among the wicked.[35]

In a similar vein Augustine uses, in a well known passage from Book XIII of the *Confessions*, the figure of the sea to represent the gathering together (*congregatio*) of the '"embittered" (*amaricantes*, i.e., the reprobate) into one society.' This *congregatio* has the effect of 'restrain[ing] the evil desires of souls and set[ting] limits to how far the waters are to be permitted to proceed so that their waves may be broken on one another.'[36]

However, Augustine sees even the 'thin' function of preventing a *bellum omnium contra omnes* primarily in 'personal' terms, as the exercise of power by individual officials. This attitude is certainly consistent with much that is in the New Testament, e.g., Our Lord's comment to Pontius Pilate[37] as well as St. Paul's elaboration of this comment in the *Epistle to the Romans*.[38] The exercise of *potestas*, by whoever exercises it and whatever form it is exercised, is a part of God's general providential concern to set limits to wickedness, especially the wickedness of the *amaricantes* or reprobate. In the words of Markus,

> In Augustine's mature thought there is no trace of a theory of the state as concerned with man's self-fulfillment, perfection, the good life, felicity, or with "educating" man towards such purposes. Its function is more restricted: it is to cancel out at least some of the effects of sin.[39]

What 'theory' of the state remains? My answer is 'practically none;' what remains is not a theory of political order but rather an empirical and pragmatic attitude toward the exercise of power.[40] Exercise of power within the *civitas terrena* has, as Augustine puts it in *Ep.* 153 quoted above, 'its own methods, causes, reasons, and usefulness' as part of God's general providential care for the world. It is no doubt desirable, Augustine holds, that political power be exercised in non-capricious, legal, just, and moderate ways by righteous men. But, to consider political institutions empirically, such benevolent exercise of power is the exception rather than the rule. By its very nature, political authority is 'repressive;' and, in view of the corrupted nature of the humans exercising such authority, it will frequently be harsh as well—even cruel. Yet, even when political authority is harshly or unjustly exercised, it still fills the general providential function of preventing the anarchical wickedness of the *bellum omnium contra omnes*. With respect to its fulfilling a more 'positive' function, however, there is abundant evidence that it would be foolish of citizens of the heavenly *civitas peregrina* to put much trust or confidence in any form of earthly polity.

Even when political power is exercised in the best way possible (and by those capable of best exercising it), Augustine's attitude is hardly enthusiastic. A single example must suffice. In the same letter to Macedonius quoted above, Augustine argues that possessions that are used badly are 'possessed badly' and do not, therefore, properly belong to the person who uses them badly: 'you see, therefore, that many ought to restore things that do not belong to them (*multi debeant reddere aliena*), even if few are to be found to whom restitution is due.' This line of thought leads Augustine to a singular conclusion concerning civil law: 'But in these times the iniquity of those who possess badly is tolerated, and certain laws are established among them [viz., those that possess badly], which are called civil, not because it may transpire that they become good users on this account, but that bad users may be less troublesome.'[41] The concept of civil law, in other words, is not understood by Augustine as embodying (or as the basis for establishing) some distinction between *good* or *virtuous* use/possession, on the one hand, and *right* or *legitimate* use/possession, on the other. Rather, it simply limits some of the more anarchic and 'troublesome' consequences of bad use/possession. We see here the antithesis of a salient feature of theoretical liberalism to which I alluded earlier: insistence upon a sharp distinction between the right and the good, with private comprehensive doctrines of the good to be constrained by a public conception of the right.

Augustine is fully cognizant of the *empirical* fact of diversity of human conceptions of the good and of 'plans of life' with their varying final ends. Indeed, he begins Book XIX of *De civitate Dei* by considering (and rejecting) 288 conceptions of the human good! He also has a quite realistic—some would doubtless say cynical—view of the rôle of political power in adjudicating conflict as well as of the empirical limitations of political power in effecting even this limited end in a humane and just manner. So, without a conception of the political order as having a specific rôle in salvation history and with a full realization of the diversity and vacillation of humans' conception of their own interests and of the good (which diverse conceptions represent, in fact, the multifarious expressions of ignorance and evil of fallen human nature), Augustine surely has a clear grasp of the empirical 'pluralism' of ends characterizing the political order. He would no doubt agree that, in some social contexts, it is politically expedient to deal with such diversity in much the way that the modern liberal state does. However, he does not make the move of the theoretical political liberal: that is, he does not transform empirical, political expediency or necessity into the theoretical 'virtue' of a *laissez-faire* principle of political neutrality with respect to conceptions of the good. Furthermore, as we have seen, Augustine possesses a very 'thin' conception of the rôle of political organization. A consequence of human nature's being what it is is that—again as an empirical fact—'commonality' or consilience of interests of human beings in the social realm does not extend much further that the common desire for peace. And political authority is more or less effectively and more or less harshly exercised primarily for this end. But, again, Augustine does not anticipate modern libertarianism is attempting to infer from this empirical fact the theoretical conclusion that a general virtue of the exercise of political authority is the rigorous limitation of the scope of its concerns.

The consequence is that Augustine is left with a radically pragmatic attitude toward the exercise of political authority rather than an elaborated 'theory' of ideal or correct political functioning. Like all the institutions of the *saeculum*, political authority is to be *used* (*utendum*) by citizens of the *civitas peregrina*, as circumstances permit, to further the ends of the heavenly city, which of course are their own proper ends. But the details of such use can, it seems, greatly depend upon various contingencies; what is an appropriate particular use in one set of circumstances may not be appropriate in other circumstances. Consequently, there is nothing in principle in Augustine's political thought to rule out the use of political coercion, such as he came to advocate with respect to the Donatist schismatics. Of course, there is also nothing in his mature thought that, as a matter of general political principle, *enjoins* such a use of political authority. Consequently, it is not surprising to find Augustine discussing the advisability of coercion in pastoral, theological, scriptural, psychological, and practical terms. Strictly *political* considerations, considerations phrased in terms of 'human' or political rights, liberties, etc., of the sort that would invariably be raised in modern discussions simply do not occur.[42]

Markus, in his study *Saeculum*, recognizes (and, indeed, discusses in detail) these aspects of Augustine's treatment of the political coercion of the Donatists. He points out, for example, that Augustine thought of political coercion of the schismatics not in terms of any distinctive, proper function of the existing polity but as an exercise of political authority by the Church exercised through her sons who happened to possess political authority:

> Neither in his dealings with imperial nor in his writings in defence of religious coercion did he ever consider Christian rulers and civil servants as parts of a governmental machinery, of the 'state'. He thought of them as members of the Church. Through them, it is the Church that 'uses power'. Once he even spoke of coercion *by* the Church. The concept of 'state' is conspicuous by its absence from all Augustine's discussions of this theme.[43]

It is then surprising—to me at least—to find Markus writing some pages later as follows:

> Augustine's attack on the 'sacral' conception of the Empire liberated the Roman state, and by implication, all politics, from the direct hegemony of the sacred. Society became intrinsically 'secular' in the sense that is it not as such committed to any particular ultimate loyalty. . . . His 'secularization' of the realm of politics implies a pluralistic, religiously neutral civil community. Historically, of course, such a society lay entirely beyond the horizons of Augustine's world. After centuries of development it has begun to grow from the soil of what has been Western Christendom; but it is still far from securely established in the modern world. It is assailed from many sides. Even Christians have not generally learned to welcome the disintegration of a 'Christian society' as a profound liberation for the Gospel. Augustinian theology should at least undermine Christian opposition to an open, pluralist, secular society.[44]

Surely, there is something fundamentally wrong with this train of thought. In repudiating the Theodosian (Constantinian, Eusebian) theory, according to which political organization has a central, perhaps even definitory, rôle to play in furthering the ultimate ends relating to salvation history, Augustine *is*, in an important sense, saying that the political order 'is not *as such* committed to any particular ultimate loyalty' (emphasis added). But lack of such commitment, which is essentially an empirical fact, is also characteristic of all other institutions of this age (the *saeculum*) in which the citizens of the two cities, with their radically different loyalties, are thoroughly mixed. It hardly follows that this recognition of what Augustine takes to be empirical facts about human nature and the secular order 'implies a pluralistic, religiously neutral civil community,' in the sense that Markus suggests.

To draw such a conclusion is, in effect, to follow theoretical political liberalism in attempting to transform what may, in certain circumstances, constitute prudential political *practice*, derived from empirical facts about human diversity, into the supposed theoretical virtues of an 'open, pluralist, secular society.' As we saw earlier in this paper, in order to make such an inference plausible, most theorists of political liberalism have felt the need to rely on more premises than the simple empirical fact of diversity of conceptions of the good and of 'rational plans of life' with their differing final ends and ultimate loyalties. As we have also seen, two historical candidates are (i) the 'derivation' of the stance of political neutrality from a conception of the autonomy or practical rationality/reasonableness of human beings and (ii) the derivation of such a stance from considerations of epistemic utility. Although I do not have the space to argue the case, I do not believe that there is any indication of a commitment to such additional premises on Augustine's part.[45] Indeed, his doctrine of freedom in terms of the radical dependency of will and intellect on God and the consequent (Pauline) explication of freedom as liberation from sin points in an entirely different direction.

As an alternative to the liberal inference from empirical fact to theoretical virtue (supplemented, usually, by the sorts of premise we have discussed), there is Augustine's pragmatic attitude toward the use of political authority. One uses political authority to as little or as great an extent as one can in furthering the ends of the celestial city—always with the recognition of the limited and transitory effectiveness of this attempt and with sensitivity to balancing positive and negative aspects of the employment of 'political means.' Does such a pragmatic attitude toward the use of political authority impose some theoretical or moral Kantian 'principle of universalization'—i.e., acceptance of the claim that each person has an equal 'right' or 'liberty' to pursue, within the political context, his own agenda in the same pragmatic fashion? Not so far as I can see. Of course, it is realistic to expect that the agenda of the citizens of the *civitas peregrina* may, likely as not, suffer at the hands of the citizens of the *civitas terrena*. From Augustine's perspective, the persecutions were fairly recent history and the sack of Rome a current event. So he is well aware of this possibility. However, he is also aware of the tendency of Christianity to thrive in circumstances of social and political adversity. In view of this awareness, as well as his general eschatological orientation, the possibility of 'getting the short end of the stick,' so to speak, holds no terror for Augustine. Thus it surely could not, for Augustine, be made to serve the sort of theoretical function that it serves in Rawls' account of 'rationality/reasonableness' in terms of the judgments of persons in the original position.

In conclusion, I should like to point out that one feature of what I have termed St. Augustine's 'pragmatic attitude' toward the political order survived into modern Catholic social thought. In 'social encyclicals' such as *Immortale Dei* and *Libertas praestantissimum*, Pope Leo XIII repudiates such 'liberties' (as understood by theoretical political liberalism) as those of worship, speech, teaching, and conscience. This is not the place to rehearse Leo's arguments nor to explore the subtleties of his theoretical anti-liberalism. Suffice it to say, he denies the liberal *laissez-faire* principle that advocates a position of political neutrality with respect to religious matters and issues of so-called 'private' morality. However, he also recognizes the empirical fact of the development of the liberal state and allows for a pragmatic stance of accommodation (within limits) toward such states:

> Yet, with the discernment of a true mother, the Church weighs the great burden of human weakness, and well knows the course down which the minds and actions of men are in this our age being borne. For this reason, while

> not conceding any right to anything save what is true and honest, she does not forbid public authority to tolerate what is at variance with truth and justice, for the sake of avoiding some greater evil, or of obtaining or preserving some greater good. God Himself, in His providence though infinitely good and powerful permits evil to exist in the world, partly that greater good may not be impeded, and partly that greater evil may not ensue. In the government of States, it is not forbidden to imitate the Ruler of the world; and, as the authority of man is powerless to prevent every evil, it has (as St. Augustine says) *to overlook and leave unpunished many things which are punished, and rightly, by divine Providence*. But if, in such circumstances, for the sake of the common good (and this in the only legitimate reason), human law may or even should tolerate evil, it may not and should not approve or desire evil for its own sake;
>
> . . .
>
> But, to judge aright, we must acknowledge that the more a State is driven to tolerate evil the further it is from perfection.[46]

Although grounded in a 'thicker' (primarily Thomistic) conception of political order than that of St. Augustine, Leo's opposition to theoretical political liberalism is certainly consistent with the views of St. Augustine, and some of his arguments are found in Augustine—e.g., the argument that the state that represses or fails to support authentic Christian *cultus* is essentially deficient with respect to the political virtue of justice (in this case, justice towards God).[47] But also in conformity with Augustine's political pragmatism is Leo's advocacy, in certain contexts, of practical acquiescence and participation in the liberal state. This advocacy is, of course, entirely consistent with the active support, in more favorable circumstances, of the just Catholic state, founded on principles inimical to theoretical political liberalism. Indeed, such a form of polity is, in absolute terms, certainly preferable to the pluralist and secular liberal state.

There is a popular perception that the Second Vatican Council's *Dignitatis humanae* (*Declaration on Religious Freedom*) represents the ultimate departure of the Church from the mature thought of St. Augustine with respect to religious 'toleration.' There is much truth in this perception. A rather deeper issue is the extent to which this document also represents a departure from the thought of Leo XIII: does it represent not only acceptance of the empirical fact of the modern liberal state but also fundamental concessions, in matters of principle, to theoretical political liberalism? The answer to this question is not, I think, as obvious as it is sometimes assumed to be. But, of course, a different forum would be the appropriate place for the further discussion of this matter.

Department of Philosophy
Arizona State University

NOTES

*This paper has benefitted, I hope, from the thoughtful and constructive comments of various colleagues and friends, as well as my fellow participants at the 1993 Richard R. Baker Philosophy Colloquium, 'Augustine on Human Goodness.' I should like to thank all of these persons, including Sarah Broadie, George Carver, Phillip Cary, Peter DeMarneffe, Charles Dresser, Jeffrie G. Murphy, Sean O'Connor, Patrick Powers, and Steven Reynolds.

1 R. A. Markus, *Saeculum: History and Society in the Theology of St Augustine* (Cambridge,1970), p. 151.

2 For more on the thought of the earlier Church in Africa, as well as that of the Donatists, on the relation between the Church and the world, particularly its political structure, see Marcus, *Saeculum*, Ch. 5, '*Afer scribens Afris*: The Church in Augustine and the African Tradition', pp. 105-132; also the classical work by W. H. C. Frend, *The Donatist Church* (Oxford, 1952).

3 Peter Jones, 'The Ideal of the Neutral State,' in *Liberal Neutrality*, ed. Robert. F. Goodin and Andrew Reeve (London and New York, 1989), p. 12.

4 Ronald Dworkin, 'Liberalism', in *A Matter of Principle* (Cambridge, Massachusetts, 1985), p. 191.

5 Dworkin, p. 191.

6 Ibid., p. 195.

7 See Robert E. Goodin and Andrew Reeve, 'Liberalism and Neutrality,' in *Liberal Neutrality*, pp. 1-8.

8 See Dworkin, p. 203: 'Liberalism cannot be based on skepticism. Its constitutive morality provides that human beings must be treated as equals by their government, not because there is no right or wrong in political morality, but because that is what is right.' The phrases used by Dworkin here, 'constitutive morality' and 'political morality', are telling. There is an important, perhaps even necessary, tendency (to be further discussed in the text of this paper) of political liberalism to separate the 'right' from the 'good' and to make the former into something common and public, the latter into something individual and private. Having made such a move, the liberal can then *afford*, if he or she so likes, to regard the latter (unlike the former) from a relativistic or skeptical perspective.

9 Dworkin, pp. 191 ff.

10 John Rawls, *Political Liberalism* (New York, 1993), pp. xxiv-xxv.

11 The phrase is that of Jeffrie G. Murphy, 'Afterword: Constitutionalism, Moral Skepticism, and Religious Belief,' in *Constitutionalism: The Philosophical Dimension*, ed. Alan S. Rosenbaum (New York, 1988), p. 242.

12 It is perhaps a bit misleading, for at least some versions of liberalism tying the stance of neutrality to the autonomy of persons (such as that of Dworkin), to characterize neutrality as 'instrumental' with respect to the end of respecting the automony of persons. Rather, neutrality is *constitutive*, at least in part, of this end. (My thanks are extended to Jeff Murphy for making this point to me.)

13 John Locke, *The Second Treatise of Government*, 2.6.

14 Murphy, p. 247.

15 John Stuart Mill's *On Liberty* supplies one historical precedent for such a conception of the value of neutrality. Mill's view, however, is rather more subtle than the view sketched in the

text. Consider, for example, the following remark: 'But, indeed, the dictum that truth always triumphs over persecution, is one of those pleasant falsehoods which men repeat after one another till they pass into commonplaces, but which all experience refutes' (J. S. Mill, *On Liberty*, ed. Alburey Castell [Arlington Heights, Illinois, 1947], Ch. II, p. 27). A page later, however, he writes that 'The real advantage which truth has, consists in this, that when an opinion is true, it may be extinguished once, twice, or many times, but in the course of ages there will generally be found persons to rediscover it, until some one of its reappearances falls on a time when from favorable circumstances it escapes persecution until it has made such head as to withstand all subsequent attempts to suppress it' (ibid., p. 28).

[16] *Rep.* 8.558b, trans. G. M. A. Grube, *Plato's Republic* (Indianapolis, 1974), p. 207.

[17] John Rawls, *A Theory of Justice* (Cambridge, Massachusetts, 1971), p. 93.

[18] Ibid., p. 92.

[19] Ibid. (emphasis added)

[20] Ibid.

[21] Rawls, *Political Liberalism*, p. 63.

[22] Ibid., p. 62.

[23] Ibid., p. 425.

[24] Ibid., p. 60.

[25] See, e.g., *Political Liberalism*, pp. 60-61, 64-65, 138.

[26] Peter Jones, 'The Ideal of the Neutral State,' p. 13.

[27] See 'Liberalism,' pp. 196-197.

[28] Rawls, *A Theory of Justice*, p. 206.

[29] Ibid.

[30] The idea of a private/public distinction with respect to religion, with an 'overlapping consensus' of religious opinions forming the latter has, in fact, previously found its way into the practice of liberal states. Some—although, I think, increasingly few—liberals might want to defend such a distinction, perhaps especially those who would like to derive theoretical liberalism's liberties from a natural rights source.

[31] See Marx's 1844 essay on Bruno Bauer's *Die Judenfrage*, translated as 'On the Jewish Question,' in *Karl Marx: Early Writings*, trans. and ed. T. B. Bottomore (New York, 1963), pp. 3-31. This obviously is not the place to consider whether Marx is correct is seeing this fundamental commitment of the liberal state as fraught with contradiction and as, ultimately, impossible to fulfill.

[32] *De civ. Dei*, 13.4.

[33] Johannes van Oort, *Jerusalem and Babylon: A Study into Augustine's 'City of God' and the Sources of His Doctrine of the Two Cities* (Leiden, 1991), p. 151.

[34] Markus, p. 95.

[35] *Ep.* 153.6.16.

[36] *Conf.* 13.17.20.

[37] Non haberes potestatem adversum me ullam, nisi tibi datum desuper. (You would not have any power over me unless it had been give to you from above.) *Ioan.* 19.11.

[38] Omnis anima potestatibus sublimioribus subdita sit: non est enim potestas nisi a Deo. . . (Every soul is to be subject to the higher powers: for there is not any power except from God. . .) *Rom.* 13.1.

[39] Markus, p. 94.

[40] By 'pragmatic' I do not, of course, mean 'unprincipled.' We are always constrained by the principles, 'moral' and otherwise, taught by the Christian faith. As my fellow colloquist Patrick Powers points out, the virtue that is always particularly pertinent to political matters is prudence. Sarah Broadie suggests that a 'theory of the state' might be taken as either (a) a 'scientific' theory explaining the existence and forms of a common social phenomenon or (b) an attempt to 'ground' or justify some form(s) of political organization. Augustine, as I interpret him, is not particularly interested in either enterprise.

However, as my colleague George Carver points out, it is important to note that Augustine *does* have a developed doctrine of the distinction between 'grace' and 'nature', a doctrine that proved to be historically important. Particularly, in his anti-Manichaean polemics, he emphasizes the point that nature is *not* intrinsically evil; and this point certainly applies to political organization as part of the natural order. Yet, it seems to me unwarranted to infer that Augustine's doctrine of the grace/nature distinction supplies him with a political theory or, indeed, a 'thick' conception of the political order. For an attempt to provide Augustine with a 'thicker' and more 'positive' conception of the political order, see especially Charles Journet, 'Les trois cités: celle de Dieu, celle de l'homme, celle du diable,' *Nova et Vetera*, vol. 33 (1958), pp. 25-48. Van Oort, who considers Journet to have been overly influenced by 'Thomistic premises,' discusses the critical responses to this attempt in his *Jerusalem and Babylon*, pp. 151 ff.

[41] *Ep.* 153.6.26.

[42] For more on this matter, see especially P. R. L. Brown, 'St. Augustine's Attitude to Religious Coercion,' *Journal of Roman Studies*, vol. 54 (1964), pp. 107-116.

[43] Markus, p. 148.

[44] Ibid., p. 173.

[45] It is, however, interesting to consider a passage in an early letter (*Ep.* 23, 392 A.D.) by Augustine, pointed out to me by Phillip Cary. Augustine (as Catholic priest, not yet bishop), in writing to a Donatist bishop Maximinus, eschews the use of force to settle their theological and ecclesial differences. He remarks that it is not his purpose 'that unwilling men should be forced into any communion, but that the truth should become known to those seeking it in utmost quiet' (*Ep.* 23.7). This comment may be read as expressing Augustine's commitment, eventually abandoned, to a particular expression of the stance of neutrality, viz., religious 'toleration,' on the basis of something like what I earlier termed grounds of epistemic utility: the truth will out in the open and unconstrained marketplace of ideas. Of course, what he is explicitly suggesting is something more limited: the gift of faith, in a concrete and particular set of circumstances, is most apt to be effectively received in circumstances of mental serenity. It is not, I think, clear that Augustine believes that from this claim can be extrapolated something like a general justification of religious toleration (let alone an even more general justification of the stance of political neutrality with respect to conceptions of the good) in terms of epistemic utility.

[46] Pope Leo XIII, *Libertas praestantissimum* (On Human Liberty), in *Papal Thought on the State: Excerpts from the Encyclicals and Other Writings of Recent Popes*, ed. Gerald F. Yates, S.J. (New York, 1958), pp. 49-50.

[47] Cf. ibid., p. 43, and *De civ. Dei*, 19.21.

Part III
Augustine's Philosophy of Political Authority and Law

[9]

THE FUNDAMENTAL IDEAS IN ST. AUGUSTINE'S PHILOSOPHY OF LAW

Anton-Hermann Chroust

St. Augustine's philosophy of law constitutes the decisive (and happy) transition from ancient classical (Plato, Stoics, Neo-Platonism) legal and political thought to Christian legal and political philosophy. With some modifications he preserved for ages to come what undoubtedly was best in ancient intellectual tradition. At the same time, he gave this noble tradition a novel foundation. In this he became the ultimate authority for all future legal and political theories not only throughout the Middle Ages, but also for certain aspects of modern jurisprudence. Strictly speaking, he founded what might be called a "theological jurisprudence" which harmoniously integrated his views about law or legal philosophy and his basic theological teachings, insisting that theological-Christian considerations not only permeate the whole of law and legal theory, but in fact constitute the only sound foundation of true law and true jurisprudence.

St. Augustine's philosophic and jurisprudential thought may indeed be called the crossroads of ancient and medieval intellectual history and possibly the decisive instance in the transition from pagan to Christian intellectualism. His remarkable learning, his astounding acquaintance with many aspects of ancient philosophy, as well as his discriminating insights and judgments, played a decisive role in channelling the philosophic erudition of classical antiquity, Hellenic and Hellenistic, into the newly arising Christian world. Unlike the ancient classical traditions, however, St. Augustine's particular philosophic wisdom is not one of abstract speculation, discursive analysis or purely theoretical contemplation (*theoria*) of abiding truths. His was, and this cannot be stressed often enough, a wisdom born of a comprehensive understanding of charity and love; that is, the sort of wisdom which King Solomon extolled[1] and of which St. James speaks in his *Epistle*: "Every good gift and every perfect gift is from above, and cometh down from the Father of light."[2] This gift enlightens the heart of man and influences his mind and will, in and through a profounder understanding of the grandeur and glory, the perfection and beauty of all things created, ordered, and ordained through and within the divine love. St. Augustine was convinced that the ultimate foundation (as well as the order of thought manifest in his own philosophy) was infused rather than speculative or analytical wisdom, in other words, was

[1] *Proverbs, passim.*
[2] *Epistle of St. James* I. 17.

the highest of all gifts that God may bestow upon man.

St. Augustine's decisive influence on the major trends of jurisprudential thought can be discerned for almost a millennium.[3] It was still strongly felt not only during the period of "high scholasticism"—in a certain way and with some modifications, the "Platonist" Augustine held his own against the revival of presumably Aristotelian teachings—but also during the late Middle Ages and, as a matter of fact, during the Renaissance, Reformation, the seventeenth and eighteenth centuries, and indeed in modern times. This is not the place, however, to discuss in detail the extent to which his own philosophic outlook was shaped by the basic teachings of Plato, by the Stoics, by "Middle Platonism," and by the Neo-Platonists.

It might be permissible to assert that, philosophically speaking, St. Augustine's most important and most far-reaching contribution to early Christian philosophic thought and, incidentally, to legal philosophy or the "metaphysics of law," is his interpretation of Plato's concept of the Ideas (*ousiai*). As is commonly known, Plato's Ideas are "autonomous absolutes" and "absolute entities" domiciled in the purely intelligible but ultimately undefinable realm of pure and perfect intellect and existence. St. Augustine, probably influenced by "Middle Platonism" (Albinus, Gaius and Atticus), by the "Neo-Pythagoreans" (Nicomachus of Gerasa), and by Neo-Platonism (Plotinus, Ammonius, Iamblichus, Porphyry, and others), on the other hand, regards the Platonic Ideas as "thoughts in the Divine Mind." In other words, he "transfers" them from the impersonal and absolutely intellectual cosmos (*kosmos noetikos*) to the Divine Intellect without, however, identifying them with this Divine Intellect. This becomes evident in his *De Diversis Quaestionibus* 83, *quaestio* 46: *De Ideis,*[4] where we are informed that "the Ideas constitute the basic forms or principles and as such are both enduring and immutable. They themselves are not created, and for this very reason they are enduring and immutable. And for this reason they are contained in the Divine Intellect or Mind. Since they are neither generated nor subject to corruption, it is maintained that all that might possibly exist or perish is formed after these Ideas [which are thoughts in the Divine Intellect]."[5] And in *Retractiones* I, 3.2,[6] St. Augustine insists that "Plato did not err when he stated that there exists a purely intellectual world, although as regards this particular issue he [*scil.,* Plato] did not employ the terminology customarily used in the tradition of

[3] A.-H. Chroust, "The Philosophy of Law from St. Augustine to St. Thomas Aquinas," *The New Scholasticism,* vol. XX, no. 1 (1956), pp. 26-71.

[4] J. P. Migne, *Patrologia Latina,* vol. 40, col. 30, subsequently cited as PL 40, 30.

[5] M. Grabmann, "Des Heiligen Augustinus *Quaestio de Ideis* (*De Diversis Quaestionibus* 83, qu. 46) in Ihrer Inhaltlichen und Geschichtlichen Bedeutung," *Philosophisches Jahrbuch der Görresgesellschaft,* vol. 43 (1930), pp. 297 ff.

[6] PL 32, 588.

the Church. . . . He called this purely intellectual world the eternal and immutable reason itself through which God created the [visible] world."[7] This interpretation of the nature and "domicile" of the (Platonic) Ideas—of the constant and immutable forms or principles of all things created also decisively determined St. Augustine's fundamental attitude towards law and legal philosophy in general, in that among other matters it influenced his concept of the *lex aeterna.*

While some Greek philosophers advocated the absolute transcendence of the *logos,*[8] the Stoics in particular insisted that the *logos* as such is immanent in the physical universe and, as a matter of fact, is this universe. Hence, the physical universe is but the manifestation as well as the ontological reality of this *logos*—a doctrine which amounts to a sophisticated form of materialistic and pantheistic naturalism where the joyous submission to the cosmic *logos* (which is the divine itself), the living "according to nature" and, hence, according to the "law of nature," constitutes the supreme moral norm. It was thus that the Stoics identified the impersonal cosmic *logos* (and the cosmos itself) with the *lex aeterna,* the *lex aeterna* with nature (and perfect orderliness), and nature with God. The Stoic *lex aeterna* or cosmic *logos,* however, is a wholly "impersonal force," a sort of "universal vital energy" or "natural rationality" which permeates the universe and, at the same time, is co-extensive with this universe both in its general and particular aspects and functions.[9]

St. Augustine, who was quite familiar with Stoic teachings (mostly through the writings of Cicero), was fully aware not only of the far-reaching advantages inherent in the notion of a *lex naturalis* or *lex aeterna,* but also of the distinct disadvantages of the specifically Stoic views about the *lex aeterna.* Thus, while rejecting the essentially pantheistic and materialistic-naturalistic implications of the Stoic concept of the *lex naturalis* or *lex aeterna* (or cosmic *logos*), which in fact identified God with the *lex aeterna,* he outright adopted the Stoic notion of a sublime rational orderliness which is the most characteristic aspect of the universe. Perhaps St. Augustine's most far-reaching and most significant contribution to the issue of the *lex aeterna* is his awareness of the grave dangers inherent in any effort to equate the cosmic orderliness or *lex aeterna* with God Himself, as the Stoics had done. To avoid this equation, he declared

7 A similar notion can be found in St. Augustine, *De Civitate Dei* X. 3, 1 (PL 41, 280).

8 See, for instance, Heraclitus of Ephesus, frag. 114 (Diels-Kranz), who insists that all human laws derive their ultimate meaning from the divine law. The Pythagoreans (frag. 10, Diels-Kranz) believed that the cosmic harmony is the ultimate principle of all order and, hence, the eternal or divine law. The absolute transcendency of the *logos* (the Ideas, the "One," etc.) constitutes the foundation of Plato's whole philosophy.

9 See, for instance, H. von Arnim, *Stoicorum Veterum Fragmenta,* vol. III (1903), frag. 527; frag. 1022; frag. 1046, *et passim.* See also Diogenes Laertius, *The Lives and the Opinions of the Philosophers,* book VII, *passim.*

the cosmic *logos* or *lex aeterna* a "deliberate act" of God—without doubt a most radical alteration of the Stoic tradition—which presupposes a personalist and theistic conception of God, insisting that "the Divine Wisdom is the universal law."[10]

In order to comprehend the ultimate meaning of St. Augustine's concept of the "universal law," it must be realized that for him "law" and "order" are two closely related or correlated and frequently synonymous terms. By "order" St. Augustine means primarily the fundamental norm or standard in accordance with which the whole creation acts and exists.[11] "Order," however, also signifies an "internal harmony," the sort of mutual "peace" that exists, and must exist, among all creatures irrespective of their relative rank or disparity, assigning to each its proper place.[12] This "peace," in the final analysis, is the "tranquillity of orderliness." Orderliness, then, is also the harmonious co-existence as well as interaction of every part in its relation both to the whole and to all other parts, where each creature assumes and holds its proper, that is, divinely ordained, place. St. Augustine refers here to the "internal *natural* order" characteristic of the universe, which, due to divine providence, encompasses all things.[13] The term "order," however, also has a moral significance. This follows from St. Augustine's statement that "this is not the proper order, nay, cannot at all be called order, when that which is superior should be sub-ordinate to that which is inferior";[14] or when he insists that "the rational soul acts morally only when it observes the universal order—when in all of its distinctions, choices and evaluations it subordinates the lesser to the greater, the corporeal to the spiritual, the inferior to the superior, and the temporal to the eternal."[15] It is the observance of this universal, divinely ordained order which also constitutes the road to God.[16] "Orderly deportment," according to St. Augustine, is a conduct which wholly

[10] *De Diversis Quaestionibus* XCIII, quaest. 79, 1 (PL 40, 90).

[11] *De Ordine* I. 10, 28 (PL 32, 901). Similar notions were stated by Cicero, *De Natura Deorum* II. 38, 97, and *ibid.*, II, 40, 101; Cicero, *De Divinatione* I. 57, 127; Cicero, *Acad. Prior.* I. 7, 29; Cicero, *De Officiis* I. 4, 14, and *ibid.*, I. 40, 142-144. St. Augustine was well acquainted with some of Cicero's writings, especially with Cicero's philosophic works. He admits that Cicero's *Hortensius* (which had been influenced by Aristotle's *Protrepticus*) aroused in him an abiding interest in philosophy. See St. Augustine, *Confessiones* III. 4, 7. See also PL 46, 165 (*sub titulo* "Cicero"), where the many citations from Cicero's writings by St. Augustine are listed.

[12] *De Civitate Dei* XIX. 13, 1 (PL 41, 640). This "internal harmony" also applies to individual man. Only an "orderly person," that is, a person who lives, thinks, and acts in conformity with the divinely ordained orderliness enjoys true "peace of mind" in that he is at peace with God. See also note 16, *infra.*

[13] St. Augustine frequently relates the concept of order to that of beauty. See *De Vera Religione* XXX. 56 (PL 34, 146-147); *ibid.*, XLIII. 76 (PL 34, 156); *De Civitate Dei* XIX. 13, 1 (PL 41, 640).

[14] *De Libero Arbitrio* I. 8, 18 (PL 32, 1231).

[15] *Epistola CXL* 2, 4 (PL 33, 539).

[16] *De Ordine* I. 9, 27 (PL 32, 990). See also note 12, *supra.*

conforms to a fundamental norm. This fundamental norm, in turn, applies both to the physical and moral universe. And the moral universe encompasses the basic moral norms, precepts, and dictates which define and determine man's practical relations to God, to the universe, and to his fellow men, that is, to the Creator and His creations.

In keeping with certain fundamental aspects of ancient philosophic tradition, St. Augustine frequently treats "law" and "order" as two essentially synonymous concepts. It may be noted that he infers the meaning of the term "law" (*lex*) from *"legere"* (to read) or *"elegere"* (to select). In his opinion, *lex* also signifies the "selection of what is just."[17] Although St. Augustine clearly distinguishes between the temporal or human law and the eternal law, whenever he refers to the *lex* in general, he has usually in mind the *lex aeterna*—the eternal law. This follows from his query to his friend, Evodius: "What law is it that is called the supreme reason (*summa ratio*), which must always be obeyed; through which evil men merit the miserable and just men the beatific life; and by virtue of which that law which we have defined as the temporal [or human] law (*lex temporalis*) may properly be issued as well as properly modified. . . ?" And Evodius replies: "Obviously, this is the *lex aeterna*."[18] Then St. Augustine proceeds defining further the *lex aeterna*: it is that law or norm which justifies and constitutes the very foundation of the most perfect orderliness.[19] As such it is also the most concise and most sublime manifestation of the divine wisdom[20] and of the divine intellect.[21] In other words, the *lex aeterna* is the incontestable justification and ultimate expression of the perfect order or orderliness that encompasses

[17] *Quaestiones in Heptateuchum* III. 20 (PL 34, 681). This statement might be under the influence of Cicero, *De Legibus* III. 5. St. Thomas Aquinas, *Summa Theologiae* I-II, *quaest.* 90, art. 1, on the other hand, maintains that the term "*lex*" is derived from *ligare* (to bind), because "it binds one to act." St. Thomas, *ibid.*, art. 4, ad 3, however, also admits that the term "*lex*" is derived from *legere*. This is probably the correct derivation. See also Isidore of Seville, *Etymologiae* III. 2, 3; (anonymous) *Cod. Borgh.* 139 (saec. XIII), Vatican Library, fol. 97, *et passim*. This anonymous treatise, which is definitely under the influence of St. Augustine, discusses the nature of the *lex aeterna* and that of the *lex naturalis*. It also maintains that the term "*lex*" is not derived from either *legere* or *ligare*, but is actually a "combination" of both *legere* and *ligare*. A.-H. Chroust, *op. cit. supra*, note 3, p. 50.—When St. Augustine derives the term "*lex*" from *legere* (to read), he probably wishes to convey the following: Rational and pious man, who believes that God's orderly resolve or *lex aeterna* is "spelled out" in the orderly observable universe and written on the hearts of men, can "read" this indelible "writ" in his heart or in the visible universe.

[18] *De Libero Arbitrio* I. 6, 14-15 (PL 32, 1228). See also *ibid.*, I. 15, 31-32 (PL 32, 1237 ff.). In *De Legibus* II. 5, 11, Cicero insists that we must distinguish between the temporal laws which are prescribed for the people and the "divine reason (*divina* mens) which is the supreme law"—definitely a Stoic notion.

[19] *De Libero Arbitrio* I. 6, 15 (PL 32, 1229). See also Cicero, *Acad. Prior.* I. 7, 29; Cicero, *De Officiis* I. 4, 14; Cicero, *De Natura Deorum* II, 38, 97.

[20] See note 10, *supra*.

[21] *Ibid.* See also *Ennaratio in Psalmum XXXVI*, sermo 3 (PL 36, 383-385).

everything created. Hence St. Augustine calls the *lex aeterna* "the Divine Intellect (*ratio divina*) and the Will of God which commands us to comply with the natural order and forbids us to disturb it."[22] In this sense the *lex aeterna* is also the most perfect expression of a most sublime reason governing the universe.[23] The wisdom (or intellect) and the will of a personal God constitute the ultimate wellspring and the unchallengeable justification, nay, the final necessity of that orderliness and harmony which is characteristic of everything that exists or acts. It is the divine mind and the divine resolve which not only created but also maintain both the natural order and the moral order.[24] This natural (physical) and moral order, which in its sublime rationality is eternal and immutable, possesses all the aspects or characteristics of a law which likewise must be eternal and immutable. This law is the manifestation of the Divine Intellect and the Divine Will and as such is declaratory of the eternal and immutable truths.[25] This, then, is the Augustinian *lex aeterna* "which is called the supreme reason or principle . . . and through which everything we may justifiably call temporal law is done and altered in the proper manner."[26] In other words, the *lex aeterna* is also the ultimate norm or standard for the positive or human law. By way of a brief summary it may be said that the *lex aeterna* of St. Augustine is declaratory of the expression of an absolute universality, objectivity, rationality, and necessity.

By defining the *lex aeterna* as "the divine intellect and the will of God," St. Augustine touched upon the dual—ontological and voluntarist—aspects of the *lex aeterna*. On the one hand, he calls it the supreme reason, the divine intellect and the wisdom of God. In so doing he also alludes to the fact that this *lex aeterna* is "in" the divine mind or intellect as the foremost "exemplar" of order, harmony, normativity, and rationality. It is, in other words, God's understanding as to how everything must be ordered—how His creation must

[22] *Contra Faustum Manichaeum* XXII. 27 (PL 42, 418). See also *ibid.*, XXII. 30 (PL 42, 420); *ibid.*, XXII. 61 (PL 42, 438); *ibid.*, XXII, 73 (PL 42, 446). Similar notions were stated by Cicero, *Philippica* X. 12, 18, Cicero, *De Legibus* II. 4, 8, and *ibid.*, II. 4, 10; I. 6, 18: "Law is the supreme reason, inherent in nature, which commands that which must be done and forbids the opposite." Cicero, *De Republica* III. 22.

[23] *De Libero Arbitrio* I. 5, 15 (PL 32, 1229). See also Cicero, *De Legibus, loc. cit. supra,* note 22, and *ibid.*, II. 5, where we are told that "the Divine Mind is the highest law."

[24] Unlike the Stoics, St. Augustine does not hold that God Himself is this order. He is merely the absolute justification for and the absolute originator of this order. It is the intellect and the will of God which constitute the cause as well as the foundation of all orderliness, both physical and moral. Hence, the natural and the moral order itself is something sublime, eternal, immutable and absolutely rational—in brief, perfect. St. Augustine, however, never identifies God Himself with the *lex aeterna,* barring one curious exception, namely *De Vera Religione* XXXI. 57 (PL 34, 147), where he states that "God Himself is this highest law."

[25] *De Vera Religione* XXXI. 57 (PL 34, 147).

[26] *De Libero Arbitrio* I. 6, 14 (PL 32, 1229). See also note 18, *supra.*

be "arranged" if it is to achieve its proper or ordained end in and through this order. On the other hand, St. Augustine designates the *lex aeterna* as being declaratory of the divine resolve to bind forever any and all of His creation to this constant, immutable, and perfect order devised by the divine intellect and promulgated by the will of God. In this latter sense it is also a divine command and indeed the most universal and most absolute divine command declaratory of the will of God. It may be maintained, therefore, that the *lex aeterna* of St. Augustine constitutes both the "ideal" and the "idealized" resolve of God as regards His creation.

It may be remarked here that St. Augustine's theistic definition of the *lex aeterna* was destined to become the basic concept and the authoritative pronouncement for the whole medieval (scholastic) jurisprudence or natural law theories.[27] It was fully adopted and further elaborated by a number of medieval scholars and theologians, especially by St. Thomas Aquinas,[28] whose *Treatise on Law* (*Summa Theologiae* I. II. quaest. 90-97) constitutes the first systematic and comprehensive treatment of the fundamental problems of legal philosophy undertaken by the High Middle Ages.[29] It should not be over-

---

[27] See, in general A.-H. Chroust, *op. cit. supra,* note 3, pp. 26 ff.

[28] St. Thomas Aquinas cites St. Augustine's definition of the *lex aeterna* in *Summa Theologiae* I - II, quaest. 91, art. 1 (referring to *De Libero Arbitrio* I. 6, 15): "On the contrary, Augustine states that that law which is the supreme reason cannot be understood otherwise than unchangeable and eternal." *Summa Theologiae* I-II, quaest. 91, art. 2 (referring to *De Libero Arbitrio, loc. cit.*): "The eternal law is that law by which it is right that all things should be most orderly." See also *Summa Theologiae* I-II, quaest. 91, art. 3, object. 1; *ibid.,* quaest. 93, art. 3, object. 3 (in his reply St. Thomas also refers to *De Libero Arbitrio* I. 5. 15). *Summa Theologiae* I-II, quaest. 93, art. 4, ad 2, refers to *De Vera Religione* 31. 57, while *Summa Theologiae* I-II, quaest. 93, art. 6, object. 3, refers to *De Libero Arbitrio* I. 5. 15, and to *De Civitate Dei* XIX. 12. See also *Summa Theologiae* I-II, quaest. 106, art. 2, ad 3; *ibid.,* quaest. 102, art. 1, object. 2.

[29] The high esteem in which the philosophy of law of St. Thomas Aquinas has been held by modern non-Catholic scholars might be gathered from the following remarks: R. Jhering, *Der Zweck im Recht,* vol. II (1902), pp. 161 ff., states that "[t]his great mind [*scil.,* St. Thomas] correctly understood the realistic, practical and historical facts of moral life. . . . In amazement I ask myself how it is possible that such truths, once they are uttered, could have been forgotten so completely by our Protestant scholars? What false roads could have been avoided had they taken these truths to heart. For my part, I would probably never have written my book [*scil., Der Zweck im Recht*] had I known these truths. For the fundamental ideas which have preoccupied my mind can be found in this gigantic thinker in perfect clarity and most concise formulation." J. Kohler, likewise a Protestant German scholar, in his *Lehrbuch der Rechtsphilosophie* (1923), p. 38, remarks that "it is the deathless accomplishment of St. Thomas Aquinas . . . to have formulated the problem of natural law in a manner which is closest to truth." After having referred to the secular natural law tradition which followed in the wake of H. Grotius, Kohler exclaims (*ibid.,* p. 43): "How much wiser and profounder were the ideas advanced by St. Thomas!" The same Kohler, in Holtzendorf-Kohler, *Enzyklopädie der Rechtswissenschaft* (1906), I. 3, points out that "scholastic thought, particularly St. Thomas . . . constitutes the acme of jurisprudential discussion. . . ." J. Frank, in the Foreword to the sixth edition of his *Law and the Modern Mind,* states on p. XVII: "I do not understand how any decent man today can refuse to adopt, as the basis of modern civilization, the fundamental principles of Natural Law, relative to human conduct, as stated by Thomas Aquinas."

looked, however, that St. Augustine's notions of the *lex aeterna* are influenced by certain fundamental views advanced by ancient philosophers about absolute justice and absolute or objective moral truth—views which he integrated into Christian teachings or doctrine.

After having defined and discussed the *lex aeterna,* St. Augustine proceeds to deal with some of its "attributes" or characteristics. First of all, the *lex aeterna* is and must be eternal. In the further pursuit of this topic, St. Augustine asks his friend Evodius "whether or not this law [*scil.,* the *lex aeterna*] must be considered by any intelligent person as something eternal and immutable." And Evodius unhesitantly replies: "I consider this law to be both eternal and immutable."[30] In his *De Ordine,* St. Augustine likewise refers to an eternal and uneradicable law—the *lex aeterna*—which applies to all men, including sinners, evil men, and ignorant people.[31] Aside from being eternal, the *lex aeterna* is also immutable: "It [*scil.,* the *lex aeterna*] remains unchangeable and as such guides all that is changeable by a most beautiful (sublime) governance."[32] In the *De Vera Religione,* St. Augustine also points out that "the norm of all order [*scil.,* the *lex aeterna*] rests in the eternal truth. It cannot be disturbed by the vulgar masses nor by the course of secular events. As a power it rises above all spatial limitations, and as to its timelessness and eternity it remains immovable and unchangeable above all times."[33]

Aside from being eternal and immutable, the *lex aeterna,* in the words of St. Augustine, is also "all-encompassing." Without exception, it controls and governs the whole of creation, and every creature is subject to its "commands." Nothing can possibly escape it or remain "outside" the *lex aeterna* or the universal and eternal order of which it is declaratory:[34] "Since the All-Highest God governs everything He Himself has created in a most excellent manner, there cannot be anything disorderly or lawless in the universe, whether or not we are aware of this fact."[35] Essentially the same notion is stated in the *De Civitate Dei,* where we are told that "in no manner can anything remain outside the laws imposed by this All-Highest Creator and Administrator (or Orderer) by Whom the peace and order of the universe is administrated."[36] And finally, in the *Contra Faustum Manichaeum,* St. Augustine once more

[30] *De Libero Arbitrio* I. 6, 15 (PL 32, 1229).

[31] *De Ordine* II. 14, 11 (PL 32, 1000). See also St. Augustine, *Contra Faustum Manichaeum* XXII. 27 (PL 42, 419). Similar views can be found in Cicero, *De Republica* III. 22; Cicero, *De Natura Deorum* I. 15; Cicero, *De Legibus* II. 4, 8, and *ibid.,* II. 4, 10.

[32] *De Diversis Quaestionibus* LXXXIII, *quaest.* 27 (PL 40, 18). See also *De Libero Arbitrio* I. 6, 15 (P, 32, 1229), quoted in text to note 30, *supra;* Cicero, *De Republica* III. 22.

[33] *De Vera Religione* XLIII. 81 (PL 34, 159).

[34] *De Ordine* II. 7, 21 (PL 32, 1004).

[35] *De Diversis Quaestionibus* LXXXIII, *quaest.* 27 (PL 40, 18).

[36] *De Civitate Dei* XIX. 12, 3 (PL 41, 640).

emphasizes that everything created is also controlled by the *lex aeterna*: "The beastly nature (or creature) does not sin, because it does not act against the *lex aeterna* to which it is subjected in a manner which makes it impossible for this beastly nature (spiritually) to participate in the *lex aeterna.* Likewise, the angelic sublime nature does not sin, because it participates in the *lex aeterna* in such a manner that God alone becomes its pleasure by submitting to the will of God without experiencing any temptation whatever. Man, however, . . . must subject to rational control whatever he has in common with the beasts, and submit to God what he has in common with the angels, until after having achieved moral perfection and immortality, he rises above the beasts and reaches the level of the angels."[37] It is thus that the *lex aeterna* ultimately determines everything and every creature. The non-rational or beastly creatures, like the rational or angelic creatures, are subjected to it, however with this one difference: unlike the rational or angelic creature, the irrational or beastly creature is not aware of this subjection.

Evil, too, St. Augustine avers, is subjected to the *lex aeterna*: "I do not believe that anything might happen outside the order imposed by God (the *lex aeterna*). Evil originated somehow, but it does not originate by God's ordination. Justice, however, cannot admit that evil should remain outside the universal order of things and, hence, relegated it by force to its proper place."[38] Evil and sin are conscious and deliberate defections from the *lex aeterna*—they are a perversion of the *lex aeterna*[39] and of the universal moral order which is based on the *lex aeterna*: "Sin is, therefore, any deed or word or desire which is contrary to the *lex aeterna* . . . ,[40] and illicit is whatever this *lex aeterna* prohibits. . . ."[41] St. Augustine puts particular emphasis on the fact that God detests evil and sin, because they disturb the divinely ordained universal order, that is, violate the *lex aeterna* "which commands us to observe the natural [*scil.*, the divinely ordained] order, and forbids us to disturb this order."[42] For God loves this order which is declaratory of His intellect and of His will. But this universal order comprises both good and evil: "For who would dare to deny, my Great Lord, that Thou governest everything in a most orderly manner."[43]

[37] *Contra Faustum Manichaeum* XXII. 28 (PL 42, 419). See also Cicero, *De Officiis* I. 4, 14.

[38] *De Ordine* II. 7, 23 (PL 32, 1005).

[39] *Contra Mendacium* VII. 18 (PL 42, 529).

[40] *Contra Faustum Manichaeum* XXII. 27 (PL 42, 418).

[41] *Ibid.*, XXII. 28 (PL 42, 419). See also St. Augustine, *De Musica* VI. 11. 30 (PL 32, 1180); St. Augustine, *Epistola CXC* I. 4 (PL 33, 59).

[42] *Contra Faustum Manichaeum* XXII. 27, cited *supra*, note 22.

[43] *De Ordine* I. 5, 14 (PL 32, 984). Here St. Augustine might be influenced by *St. Matthew* 5:45: "For He [*scil.*, God] maketh His sun rise on the evil and on the good, and sendeth rain on the just and the unjust."

The *lex aeterna,* which is the universal and divinely ordained order and governance, also is the *ratio aeterna* of all that has been created.[44] It "resides" in every creature in a germinating manner[45] as the *ratio seminalis* or *ratio seminaria* and as such becomes manifest—or realizes itself—in all things created. In other words, it manifests itself in the form of laws which constitute and determine the specific "inner nature" of each particular creature. This *ratio aeterna* or *lex aeterna* so to speak reveals itself in every and all creatures, and it does so in the form of the *lex naturalis.* St. Augustine explains the relationship of the universal order (*lex aeterna* or *ratio aeterna*) to the "inner order" (*lex naturalis*) which is characteristic of each individual creature or thing, in the following manner: the *lex aeterna* becomes manifest and concretely meaningful in and through laws that are in complete harmony with, and declaratory of, the most miraculous universal administration and governance, to wit, the *lex aeterna* and the *ratio aeterna.* Through these laws God "manages" the particular creatures.[46] Within an all-encompassing order, the *lex aeterna* or the *ratio aeterna,* which are "domiciled" in the divine mind, direct everything to its proper end through the proper means or intermediaries.[47] The total and all-encompassing order or orderliness of the universe, that is, the *lex aeterna* or *ratio aeterna,* becomes manifest as well as effective in and through the *rationes seminales* (or *rationes seminaria*) which are so to speak "implanted" in each and every individual thing, including man. These *rationes seminales* or "germinating principles" constitute the particular natural order and the particular nature of each and every individual creature.[48] They are an essential part or aspect of the eternal and perfect plan by which God governs the universe: "The *Verbum Dei* contains the *rationes aeternae* of everything that has been created through the *Verbum Dei.*"[49] Hence, the *Verbum Dei,* which in this instance is synonymous with the *lex aeterna* or the *ratio aeterna,* is the ultimate and eternal cause not only for the universal order, but also for each and every "individual" or specific order appropriate to every particular species and every individual thing, including the *lex naturalis.*

---

[44] *De Ordine* I. 10, 28 (PL 32, 991). See also Cicero, *De Natura Deorum* II. 38, 97, and *ibid.,* II. 40, 101.

[45] St. Augustine combines here the Platonic doctrine of the absolute transcendence of the Ideas and the Stoic notion of the "immanent *logos*" as well as the Stoic concept of the "germinating *logoi.*"

[46] *De Chatechizandis Rudibus* XVIII. 30 (PL 40, 333).

[47] *De Libero Arbitrio* I. 5, 11-I. 7, 17 (PL 32, 1227-1231).

[48] *Quaestiones in Heptateuchum* II. 21 (PL 34, 602). See also *De Genesi ad Litteram* X. 20, 35-36 (PL 34, 424), and *ibid.,* X. 21, 37 (PL 34, 425); IV. 33, 51 (PL 34, 318); *De Trinitate* III. 8, 13 (PL 42, 875).

[49] *De Genesi ad Litteram* IV. 24, 41 (PL 34, 313). See also *De Civitate Dei* V. 11, 41 (PL 41, 153).

Aside from the *lex aeterna, ratio aeterna* or universal and divinely ordained order and orderliness, St. Augustine also speaks of the *summum bonum,* the *ipse bonum* and the *incommutabile bonum* through which everything created, including man, becomes good.[50] It appears that with St. Augustine the ultimate and fullest realization or attainment of this *summum bonum* is the absolutely necessary prerequisite for a rational-intelligent understanding of the ultimate meaning of the good. The *lex aeterna* or the *ratio aeterna,* we know, constitutes the absolute order characteristic of the divine creation. Everything that is orderly in terms of the *lex aeterna,* that is, everything that complies or is in complete accord with the *lex aeterna* and the absolute and universal order for which the *lex aeterna* stands, is good or "a good" and, hence, in complete accord with the *ratio aeterna, ratio divina* and the *summum bonum.* The highest concept or principle of the most perfect orderliness, namely, the *lex aeterna,* is therefore also declaratory of the *summum bonum,* that is, of God. The *summum bonum,* therefore, constitutes not only the ultimate and absolute source or justification of all that is good and true, but is also the *bonum omnis boni* and the *veritas omnis veritatis.* Hence, only because of the *summum bonum* can anything created ever be called good;[51] and only in God are the *summum bonum,* the *lex aeterna* and the *ratio aeterna* one and the same thing.[52] It will be noted that by introducing the notion of a *summum bonum,* St. Augustine deviates from an imperativist ethics based on a divine command in that with the *summum bonum* he proclaims the *perseitas boni,* that is, a *bonum* which transcends and, at the same time, is immanent in this world of ours.

With St. Augustine the ultimate moral significance of man's actions and volitions is not anchored in his individual freedom, but in the determination of his deportment or will by the *lex aeterna* and by the realization of the *summum bonum*—in man's submission to the *lex aeterna* and to the eternal and divinely ordained universal order which is declaratory of the *summum bonum.* In other words, the moral significance of man's deportment is determined by the degree to which he approximates the *summum bonum* and by the degree to which he deliberately and joyously submits to the *lex aeterna.* It might be noted that St. Augustine's definition of the *summum bonum* as well as that of the *lex aeterna* advocates what subsequent medieval theologians

50 *De Trinitate* VIII. 5, 8 (PL 42, 953). See also *ibid.,* XIII. 9. 12 (PL 42, 1023); XIV. 18, 24 (PL 42, 1055); *Confessiones* I. 1 (PL 32, 661); *De Quantitate Animae* XXXIII. 70 ff. (PL 32, 1075-1077). It might be maintained that with St. Augustine ethics is in fact a doctrine of the *summum bonum,* a view which he inherited from ancient philosophy.

51 *De Trinitate* VIII. 304 (PL 42, 949-952).

52 *De Vera Religione* XI. 21 (PL 34, 131); *De Libero Arbitrio* II. 9, 26 (PL 32, 1254); *De Trinitate* XIV. 15, 21 (PL 42, 1051-1052).

and philosophers have called the *perseitas boni,* namely, the absolute and objective nature of the good and of all basic moral or legal norms and standards[53]—a thoroughly Platonic standpoint.

The *lex naturalis,* according to St. Augustine, is the conscious participation of rational man in the *lex aeterna.* By *lex naturalis* he understands above all the *lex rationis* or the "law of reason."[54] This *lex rationis,* however, is but one aspect of the "general law of nature" which, as regards rational and moral man, signifies the *lex naturalis moralis* addressed to rational moral man. The *lex naturalis moralis* or simply the *lex naturalis* is imprinted or impressed upon the soul or heart or mind of man and hence is actually the imprint of the *lex aeterna* on the rational soul.[55] Or to state this issue differently: the *lex aeterna* is the universal and absolute "norm" or standard of and for everything, including man, while the *lex naturalis* (*moralis*) signifies the particular form in which the moral aspects of the *lex aeterna* can be apprehended by rational though finite man. "The *lex naturalis* is . . . transcribed or inscribed on the rational soul of man,"[56] and this *lex naturalis* "is also in the intellect or reason of man . . . and it is inscribed into his heart in a most natural manner."[57] For this reason the *lex naturalis* is also called the *lex intima,* because it is implanted in the innermost recesses of man's mind and heart. Hence, the *lex naturalis* may also be called the "subjective" or "personalized" manifestation of the *lex aeterna.* This manifestation of the *lex aeterna* is engraved on the soul or mind or heart of man. It is thus within ourselves that we may discover the principle of all moral norms, including the notion of justice, the *lex naturalis moralis.* The realization that these truths and norms are actually "in" us, that is, in our soul or mind or heart, becomes for St. Augustine the basis of an important moral imperative, namely, to know and understand ourselves. This being so, we must seek God (and the *lex aeterna* and the *lex naturalis*) not in the heavens, but in ourselves.

The fundamental precepts of the *lex naturalis* are known, or can be known, by all men capable of right reasoning, no matter how morally depraved these men may be. This is so because God, Who inscribed the *lex naturalis* on the

[53] See, for instance, *Contra Mendacium* VII. 18 (PL 40, 529), quoted in note 39, *supra.*

[54] *Epistola CLVII* 3. 18 (PL 33, 683).

[55] This is a thoroughly Platonic notion. In Plato, rational man remembers the objective truths (the Ideas) once visualized (*anamnesis*) in a pre-mundane existence. These objective truths are imprinted on the memory of man. It is these "imprints," Plato maintains, which make true knowledge possible.

[56] *De Diversis Quaestionibus* LXXXIII, quaest. 53. 2 (PL 40, 36). See also *De Libero Arbitrio* I. 6, 18 (PL 32, 1229); Cicero, *De Legibus* I. 10, 30; Cicero, *De Finibus Bonorum et Malorum* V. 21, 50; Cicero, *De Republica* III. 20. This statement about the *lex naturalis* being transcribed on the hearts, minds or souls of men is also quoted in St. Thomas Aquinas, *Summa Theologiae* I. II, quaest. 93, art. 2.

[57] *Epistola CLVII* (PL 33, 681). See also *De Spiritu et Littera* XXI. 36 (PL 44, 222), and *ibid.,* XVII. 30 (PL 44, 219); XXVI. 44 (PL 44, 227); XXVI. 46 (PL 44, 229).

hearts or souls or minds of all men, speaks to every man through the *lex naturalis*. Hence, no one, not even the heathens, unbelievers or the most depraved people, may plead ignorance of the *lex naturalis*. Man's moral conscience, which can never be silenced, is the *lex naturalis* of these heathens.[58] Everyone, believer or unbeliever, is called upon by his moral conscience to acknowledge the existence of the *lex naturalis*. This fact also explains, according to St. Augustine, why even heathens and unbelievers and morally depraved men have devised a number of most useful moral precepts. These precepts, in turn, are the result of the workings of Divine Providence (or of the *lex aeterna*) which permeates everything and everyone, including the unbeliever and the morally depraved.[59] Through His commandments God calls men back to the *lex naturalis* which as often as not these men try to escape.[60] The rational soul, illuminated by the Divine Light and assisted by the proper use of natural reason, counsels itself in all moral matters. For the soul can read within itself that which it ought to do and that which it ought not to do.[61] This is also the reason why even totally godless people do think of eternity, and why they frequently and correctly praise or denounce certain human habits or *mores*.[62] In no man, no matter how morally depraved he may be, has the image of God been blurred by vice to such an extent as to deprive this man of the faculty of distinguishing at least the most general outlines of the *lex naturalis*.[63] But in the hearts of the pious, just, and pure, the voice of the *lex aeterna*, that is, the *lex naturalis*, always remains most articulate and most audible.[64] But it is not permissible for mortal man to judge the *lex aeterna* and, concomitantly, the *lex naturalis*, for he may only listen to its dictates[65] and thus know what he may do and what he may not do.[66]

It is within ourselves that we find the basic norms and precepts of the *lex naturalis*, and together with them, the fundamental principles of true justice. The basic principle of natural justice, according to St. Augustine, "is that habit of the rational soul which . . . renders to everyone and everything his proper dignity, and which, in doing so, always considers the principle of

[58] *De Sermone Dei in Monte* II. 9, 32 (PL 34, 1283). St. Augustine refers here to St. Paul, *Epistle to the Romans* 2:14-15.

[59] *De Doctrina Christiana* II. 40, 60 (PL 34, 63).

[60] *Ennaratio in Psalmum* LVII. 1 (PL 36, 673).

[61] *Ennaratio in Psalmum* CXLV. 5 (PL 37, 1887-1888).

[62] *De Trinitate* XIV. 15, 21 (PL 42, 1052).

[63] *De Spiritu et Littera* XXVIII. 48 (PL 44, 230). See also *Epistola CLVII* 3, 15-21 (PL 33, 681-685), where St. Augustine insists that the *lex naturalis* is a *lex rationis* which no iniquity can possibly delete from the mind or heart of man.

[64] *Sermo in Scripturis* LXXI. 58 (PL 38, 500).

[65] *De Vera Religione* XXXI. 58 (PL 34, 148).

[66] See also *Quaestiones in Heptateuchum* II. 67 (PL 34, 618).

common usefulness."[67] In its ultimate and truest nature, justice and, for that matter, law (*ius*) as such "cannot be the product or invention of mere personal opinion, but must be something that is implanted in man by a certain innate power."[68] Hence, as regards the rational soul, justice, or the principle of natural justice is as self-evident as the *lex aeterna* or the *lex naturalis*. Not even the greatest of malefactors can ever lose completely this "sense of justice."[69] Through the light of natural reason, man becomes aware of this principle of justice as well as of the *lex naturalis*, while man's moral conscience always reminds him of the *lex aeterna* which is the foundation both of the *lex naturalis* and of the basic principles of natural justice.[70] Natural justice, above everything else, is declaratory of man's realization of the universal and absolute order, moral and cosmic, decreed by God Himself. At the same time it is man's rational and deliberate compliance with this universal and absolute order. Injustice, therefore, is the absence of the right conception (or the deliberate defiance) of this universal order—the *lex aeterna* and its manifestation, the *lex naturalis*. Like every other evil, injustice is, in the final analysis, the absence of the proper concord in the many-faceted and manifold relations among the different creatures, and the absence of the proper attitude of these creatures towards God. It is man's willful disturbance or defiance of the universe and divinely ordained order or orderliness—that is, man's defiance of God—something which the *lex aeterna* and *lex naturalis* expressly forbid.[71] Justice or the principle of justice, then, is a *habitus animi*. The rational soul is "spontaneously" aware of this principle of justice, an awareness which no depravity can possibly obliterate or eradicate. Like the natural awareness of the *lex aeterna* or of the *lex naturalis*, man's spontaneous awareness of the principle of justice comes to him through the light of reason

[67] *De Diversis Quaestionibus* LXXXIII, quaest. 31, 1 (PL 40, 20). It might be noted that "justice" is defined in the *Digest* of Justinian I, 1, *De Iustitia et Iure* 10 (Ulpian, *Liber* 1 *Regularum*) and in the *Institutes* of Justinian I. 1, as follows: "Justice is the constant and perpetual intent to render unto everyone what is his by right." See also Cicero, *De Inventione* II. 160: "Justice is the habit of the soul which . . . renders unto everyone his dignity." Cicero, *De Finibus Bonorum et Malorum* V. 23; Cicero, *Ad Herennium* III. 3. The Roman jurists (see, for instance, Ulpian, *Regularum Libri* VII I. 10) "translated" the essentially Stoic nomenclature of Cicero into Roman legal terminology. Thus the Ciceronean "*habitus animi*" (*De Inventione* II. 160) becomes with Ulpian the "*constans et perpetua voluntas*," and the Ciceronean "dignitas" (*De Inventione* II. 160; *Ad Herennium* III. 3) becomes plain "ius."

[68] *De Diversis Quaestionibus* LXXXIII, quaest. 31, 1 (PL 40, 20). See also Cicero, *De Legibus* II. 4. 8.

[69] *De Trinitate* XIV. 15, 21 (PL 42, 1051-1052), and *ibid.*, XII. 15, 24-25 (PL 42, 1011-1012). Like the *lex naturalis*, justice, which is a *habitus animi*, is imprinted on the heart or mind of man, an "imprint" which not even the worst of iniquities or depravity can ever erase. See *Confessiones* II. 4. 9 (PL 39, 678); *Epistola* CLVII *passim* (PL 33, 674-693).

[70] *De Trinitate* XIV. 15, 21 (PL 42, 1051-1052).

[71] *Contra Faustum Manichaeum* XXII. 27 (PL 42, 418 ff).

properly employed. Justice or an "*a priori* sense of justice," it might be claimed, is firmly and perennially embedded in man's moral conscience. It might also be important to note that St. Augustine calls justice a *habitus animi,* rather than a "divine inspiration" or "divine command." This is fully in keeping with his efforts to combine an imperativist ethics with an "ontological," that is, Platonic, ethics.

What, then, in the opinion of St. Augustine, is the specific content of the *lex naturalis*? It has already been shown that natural justice consists in rendering unto everyone his due—the *suum cuique tribuere*—and that natural justice always must be related to the common (or universal) good or common utility. For reasons of common utility, certain aspects or principles of natural justice and, hence, the *lex naturalis,* in the course of history turn into custom, social tradition or plain laws, until these aspects or principles, that is, natural justice or the *lex naturalis,* are sanctioned (and enforced) by religion as well as by the fear of painful retaliatory legal sanctions.[72] What then, according to St. Augustine's formula of natural justice, constitutes "everyone's own or due (*suum*),"[73] a notion which occupies a central position in his theory of natural justice? In order to define and explain the nature of this "*suum*" more precisely, St. Augustine refers to the natural or ontological (divinely ordained) order to which everyone and everything is subjected. Natural justice, then, is whatever contributes to the greatest possible orderliness, that is, to the maintenance of the most perfect order as it is ordained by God Himself and as it finds its most perfect expression in the *lex aeterna* and in the *lex naturalis.*[74] The *suum,* then, is the ultimate role or "place" assigned to everything and everyone within the universal order, a role which everything and everyone has to play in accordance with the role or place it or he holds in this universal order. In other words, this *suum* signifies that everything and everyone must see to it that it or he is "most orderly." The observation and actualization of this universal order, which is the most perfect order, constitute the ultimate meaning of St. Augustine's concept of natural justice: "God ordained and created everything . . . and He ordered and arranged the whole of creation after the manner of distinct degrees or steps, proceeding from the earth to the heavens, from the visible to the invisible, from the mortal to the immortal. This harmonious inter-relation and inter-action of the whole of creation, this most orderly beauty, ascends from the most lowly to the most high. Nowhere

[72] *De Diversis Quaestionibus* LXXXIII, quaest. 31, 1 (PL 40, 20). See also note 67, *supra.*

[73] *De Diversis Quaestionibus* LXXXIII, quaest. 31, 1 (PL 40, 20). See also note 68, *supra.*

[74] *De Libero Arbitrio* I. 6, 15 (PL 32, 1229). See also *Ennaratio in Psalmum CXLV* 5 (PL 37, 1887-1888), and note 61, *supra.*

is this harmonious inter-relation and inter-action disrupted, for despite all dissimilitudes it always remains perfectly balanced and integrated. And this sublime orderliness and beauty in its entirety praises God."[75] In the light of this statement, the *summum bonum,* the *suum* and the true natural justice are that ultimate perfection which, within the ontological and moral order ordained by God and expressed by the *lex aeterna,* is assigned to and hence attainable for everyone. He who fully achieves his unique individuality and does so in conformity with his being a "link" in the infinite "chain of being" or "chain of meaning" is just and good in that he is truly himself.

In compliance with the notion that natural justice is essentially the observance of or reverence for the divinely ordained order by rendering unto everyone, including God, his due, St. Augustine insists that the rule, "do nothing unto another what you would not do unto yourself," constitutes the second principle which sheds some light on the concrete meaning or content of the *lex naturalis* and of natural justice in particular: "The *lex naturalis* . . . instructs man that he should do nothing unto another he would not have done unto himself."[76] In all our dealings with our fellow men we must always observe the Golden Rule which, according to St. Augustine, constitutes the "practical" or "applied" aspect of the basic principle or precept of the *lex naturalis* and of natural justice in general.[77] These two moral precepts, namely, to "render unto everyone his due," and to "do nothing unto another you would not have done unto yourself," therefore, are for St. Augustine what St. Thomas Aquinas later called the primary principles of natural law.[78] Every other precept of natural law, in the final analysis, is but a conclusion from or application of these two basic "guidelines."

The *lex aeterna,* according to St. Augustine, is also the immutable and absolute norm or standard for all human, temporal, or positive laws. Nothing may rightfully be called lawful or just except what is derived from the *lex aeterna,* the ultimate source of all lawfulness and justice.[79] The wise and good lawgiver will always shape his laws or commands after the *lex aeterna* which suggests to him what in the light of local or temporal circumstances he

[75] *Ennaratio in Psalmum CXLIV* 13 (PL 37, 1878). See also *De Civitate Dei* XIX. 12, 3 (PL 41, 460): "In no way, therefore, may anything be detracted from the laws originating with this Highest Creator and Maintainer, by Whom the universal peace and order are administrated."

[76] *Epistola CLVII* 3. 15 (PL 33, 681). See also *De Ordine* II. 8, 25 (PL 32, 1006); *Ennaratio in Psalmum CXVIII, sermo* 25, 4 (PL 37, 1574); *De Doctrina Christiana* III. 14, 22 (PL 34, 74).

[77] *De Ordine* III. 8, 25 (PL 42, 1006).

[78] St. Thomas Aquinas, *Summa Theologiae* I-II, quaest. 94, art. 2, and art. 4.

[79] *De Libero Arbitrio* I. 6, 15 (PL 32, 1229). See also *De Civitate Dei* XIX. 21, 1 (PL 41, 649).

may command and what he may prohibit.[80] Human laws which are not ultimately derived from, and sanctioned by, the *lex aeterna* (or by the *lex naturalis*) are unjust or "lawless" laws. As such they should not be obeyed.[81]

Temporal or human laws, at least just human laws, are also "images" of the *lex aeterna*—a distinctly Platonic notion. Although these temporal laws, which are devised to govern people, are many, varied, and frequently in a state of change, the one single law or norm from which they are ultimately derived and from which they derive their ultimate authority, namely, the *lex aeterna,* is wholly immutable.[82] Here the question arises, why should man stand in need of temporal laws, particularly since all men, as rational creatures, not only have the natural law (that is, the "moral manifestation" of the *lex aeterna*) imprinted on their hearts, minds, or souls, but also are, through their *naturalis ratio,* capable of drawing the proper inferences from the first principles or precepts of the *lex naturalis*? St. Augustine's answer to this query is this: Originally the law—the natural law—was not written down. Since it was infused into man's nature by God Himself and hence known to all men, there was no need for a written law, a *lex formata in literis,* that is, a human, temporal, or positive law. But at some later time, because of man's evil and sinful inclinations and vices, the *lex aeterna* and the *lex naturalis* gradually came to be "obscured" in the minds of men, and its knowledge or understanding became rather vague. It was thus that the *lex aeterna* and the *lex naturalis* lost their hold on the heart and mind of man. In other words, with the fall of man and with man's subsequent wickedness, human or temporal laws became a necessity. They had to be promulgated by men for men in order that there might be once more legal and moral authority. With the promulgation of just temporal laws which had been fashioned after the *lex naturalis,* the *lex naturalis* (which progressively had been obscured if not discarded through sin and evil deeds) once more became manifest and authoritative, at least indirectly.[83]

Since man is what he is, especially after his fall, neither the *lex aeterna* nor the *lex naturalis* makes human or temporal laws superfluous. On the contrary, St. Augustine insists, the *lex naturalis,* in order to realize and actualize itself more fully in history, actually stands in need of human or temporal

[80] *De Vera Religione* XXI. 58 (PL 34, 148).

[81] *Epistola CV* II. 7 (PL 33, 398) St. Augustine might be here under the influence of *St. Matthew* 22:21: "Render . . . unto Caesar the things that are Caesar's, and unto God the things that are God's." See also St. Paul, *Epistle to the Romans* 13:7.

[82] *De Libero Arbitrio* I. 6, 15 (PL 32, 1229). See also Cicero, *De Legibus* I. 6, and *ibid.,* II. 4, 25.

[83] *Epistola CLVII* III. 15 (PL 33, 681); *De Vera Religione* XXXI. 58 (PL 34, 148); *Sermo CXXV* 2 (PL 38, 689); *Sermo CLIV* 1 (PL 38, 833); *Sermo CLV* 3, 3 (PL 38, 842); *Sermo CLVI* 2, 2 (PL 38, 850-851); *Sermo* CLXX 1, 1 (PL 38, 927); *Contra Faustum Manichaeum* XIX. 7 (PL 42, 351).

laws.[84] The plurality and diversity of the different positive legal systems which we encounter in the course of history as well as the many historical changes within one and the same legal system, however, are no valid proof against the unity, validity, and immutability of the *lex aeterna* and the *lex naturalis*.[85] Neither do they disprove the thesis that all human or positive laws—the just or equitable human laws—in the final analysis are ultimately derived from the single *lex aeterna* or from the *lex naturalis*. Human laws, to be sure, frequently ignore, tolerate, and even create or encourage many situations which are definitely contrary to the dictates of the *lex aeterna* and those of the *lex naturalis*.[86] St. Augustine concedes that all this is a most regrettable fact which may be observed in all places and at all times. In a spirit of frank realism he points out, however, that human or temporal laws are concerned primarily not with the promotion of moral virtue or of the moral life as such, but rather with the preservation of peace and order among men by preventing, deterring and punishing the worst abuses and the crudest social maladjustments that might endanger and even destroy this peace and order.[87] For it is of the essence of the temporal or secular law and legal order to preserve a minimum of civil peace and through this civil peace to secure the successful survival of secular society.[88]

According to St. Augustine, the state or body politic is "a multitude of human (rational) beings bound together by a certain social tie," that is, by the bond of concord, and subject to the same laws.[89] He defines the idea of social order under the rule of human laws as "that disposition which assigns to equal as well as unequal things (or persons) their proper place."[90] For a rational and harmonious order of all things and all men, including the secular state or the rule of temporal laws, presupposes not only a diversity among

[84] *De Vera Religione* XXXIII. 58 (PL 34, 148).

[85] *De Doctrina Christiana* III. 14, 22 (PL 34, 74). See also *De Libero Arbitrio* I. 6, 15 (PL 32, 1229); *De Civitate Dei* XIX. 17 (PL 41, 646).

[86] *De Civitate Dei* XV. 6, 2 (PL 41, 459); *De Libero Arbitrio* I. 5, 13 (PL 32, 1228); and *ibid.*, I. 5, 14 (PL 32, 1228-1229).

[87] *De Libero Arbitrio* I. 5, 13 (PL 32, 1228). See also *Epistola CLIII* VI. 26 (PL 33, 665).

[88] *De Libero Arbitrio* I. 5, 31 ff. (PL 32, 1257-1258); *De Civitate Dei* XIX. 14 (PL 41, 642), and *ibid.*, XIX. 17 (PL 41, 645).

[89] *De Civitate Dei* XV. 8, 2 (PL 41, 447). See also *ibid.*, XIX. 21, 2 (PL 41, 645); *Quaestiones X Evangeliae* II. 46 (PL 35, 1360); *Epistola CXXXVIII* II, 10 (PL 33, 655); *Epistola CLV* III. 9 (PL 33, 670). All these definitions of the secular state reflect the influence of Cicero on St. Augustine. See, for instance, Cicero, *De Republica* III. 25, 20.

[90] *De Civitate Dei* XIX. 13, 1 (PL 41, 640). This definition of St. Augustine is actually one of the important intellectual legacies of the ancient world. Through the authority of St. Augustine it was to become one of the fundamental tenets of social, legal, and political thought during the Middle Ages. See, for instance, A.-H. Chroust, "The Function of Law and Justice in the Ancient World and the Middle Ages," *Journal of the History of Ideas*, vol. II (1946), pp. 298 ff.; A.-H. Chroust, "The Corporate Idea and the Body Politic in the Middle Ages," *Review of Politics*, vol. IX (1947), pp. 437 ff.

different men (and the concomitant "tensions" that arise from this diversity), but also a disparity in the treatment of different things and different men or "unlike people," "because thus did God make man."[91] A well-adjusted and properly ordered society is a peaceful society and consists in the concord of all citizens. It is a "structure" where the right to rule and the duty to obey are perfectly balanced.[92] For it should be obvious that "it is good for some people to serve and to obey in particular, while it is good for all people to serve God in general."[93] In this world of ours, the *civitas Dei* and the secular or political state both exist side by side and, hence, must collaborate in many ways.[94] Both are confronted by essentially the same or similar problems; both have to combat similar evils.[95] The universal peace and order introduced, maintained, and secured by the secular state, therefore, are also of the greatest importance to the true *civitas Dei* and to the ultimate realization of the latter on this earth.

The laws of the secular state, like all human or temporal laws, have their ultimate justification in the *lex aeterna* or in the *lex naturalis,* provided they do not "antagonize" the *lex aeterna* or the *lex naturalis.* The ultimate purpose and the ultimate function of the secular state is to unify a (disorganized) multitude into one single and uniform lego-political order so that peace may reign among men. Insofar as the secular state or legal and political order does not defy the express commands of God, that is, insofar as it is in conformity with the *lex aeterna* and the *lex naturalis* (*moralis*), this secular state is founded upon divine ordination.[96] As such it serves not only the maintenance of peace and social order, but it is itself part of the universal and divinely ordained order expressed in the *lex aeterna.* But "there is nothing in the temporal or secular law that could be called 'just' or 'lawful,' unless the citizens had derived this secular law from the *lex aeterna.*"[97] Hence, we should reject or ignore all those human, temporal, or positive laws which do not flow directly from the *lex aeterna,* that is, from the eternal "fountain head of all justice and lawfulness." This being so, the true legislator must always promote human or temporal laws "according to immutable norms; and according to these immutable norms [*scil.,* the *lex aeterna*] he must also deter-

[91] *De Civitate Dei* XIX. 15 (PL 41, 643). See also *ibid.,* XIX. 14-16 (PL 642-645).
[92] *Ibid.,* XIX. 13, 1 (PL 41, 640). See also *ibid.,* XIX. 16 (PL 41, 645); XVIII. 2, 1 (PL 41, 559).
[93] *Ibid.,* XIX. 21, 2 (PL 41, 649). See also *ibid.,* XIX. 16 (PL 41, 644).
[94] *Ibid.,* XIX. 17 (PL 41, 645-646). See also *ibid.,* XIX. 4 (PL 41, 642).
[95] *Ibid.,* XV. 2 (PL 41, 439). See also *ibid.,* XVIII. 54, 2 (PL 41, 620); XVIII. 2, 1 (PL 41, 559).
[96] *Ibid.,* XIX. 14 (PL 41, 642-643).
[97] *De Libero Arbitrio* I. 6, 15 (PL 32, 1229). See also note 79, *supra.*

mine what for the time being should be commanded and what should be prohibited."[98]

The divinely ordained and instituted universal order which encompasses everything constitutes the foundation of every legal and political order. Within this universal order God endowed man both with intellect and a "social nature." It is this intelligent (and rational) as well as social nature of man—the rational mind of man on which the moral dictates of the *lex aeterna* or the *lex naturalis* have been imprinted—that compels him to form and enter into unions with other humans, such as the family and the secular state.[99] Hence the intelligent and social nature of man is at the basis of all social institutions or structures. It is for this reason that the individual as such always is and always remains the fundamental and essential element as well as the seed of any secular state or organized society.[100] "In the same manner as the single letter is the basic element of a phrase, so the individual is the fundamental constituent of the secular state or secular realm."[101] The natural "social disposition" of rational man (in other words, the law of nature or *lex naturalis* itself) induces or compels man to enter into associations with other men in order to bring about and maintain peace and order and thus promote and realize on earth the universal harmony exemplified in the *lex aeterna*.[102] According to St. Augustine, nothing is more "socially minded" than the human race which because of sin and evil inclinations finds itself torn asunder by strife and mutual hatred.[103] Thus because of the corruptness of their depraved natures men have a natural disposition or urge to live within legally and politically organized societies.[104]

The institution of the family is the first manifestation or the first fruit of the "social nature" or natural social urge of intelligent and rational man. The family constitutes the germ cell of the secular state: it is the smallest unit within the larger unit called the secular state. And as every beginning already points to the ultimate goal, so the domestic peace and harmony presages the peace and harmony which the secular state provides and secures. By the same token, the authority as well as the obligations of the parents and the duty of the children to this authority presage the legal and political authority of the secular state over its subjects, and the duty of the citizens to respect and submit

[98] *Quaestiones in Heptateuchum* II. 67 (PL 34, 618). See also *De Vera Religione* XXXI. 58 (PL 34, 148), and note 66, *supra*.

[99] *De Civitate Dei* XIX. 12, 2 (PL 41, 639). See also Cicero, *De Republica* I. 25, 39; Cicero, *De Finibus Bonorum et Malorum* V. 23; Cicero, *De Officiis* II. 21.

[100] *Ennaratio in Psalmum* IX 8 (PL 36, 121). See also Cicero, *De Finibus Bonorum et Malorum* V. 23, 65; Cicero, *De Officiis* I. 17, 54.

[101] *De Civitate Dei* IV. 3 (PL 41, 114). See also Cicero, *De Officiis* I. 17, 54.

[102] *De Civitate Dei* XIX. 12, 2 (PL 41, 634). See also note 99, *supra*.

[103] *De Civitate Dei* XII. 27 (PL 41, 376).

[104] *Opus Imperfectum Contra Iulianum* VI. 12 (PL 45, 1522).

to this authority.[105] In other words, the secular state, and the legal order or social structure promulgated by it, essentially is nothing other than the further or progressive "evolution" of the same principles which constitute the foundation of the family and of the domestic order. Children must obey the commands of their parents, unless these commands run contrary to the laws of the state or the *lex naturalis* (*moralis*); and the citizens or "subjects" of a state must abide by the laws of this state unless they run contrary to the commands of God (and to the dictates of the *lex naturalis*).[106] This, according to St. Augustine, is the natural order of all things as it had been ordained and commanded by God Himself. Only within and through this order can man ever establish and secure that peace, order, and harmony which God has intended for all people. In brief, the secular state and the legal as well as political or social order are intended to meet the universal human yearning after peace and, at the same time, to accomplish the will of God Who wants us to live in peace and harmony with one another. The secular state, therefore, above all must prevent any disturbance of the natural (i.e., divinely ordained) order of things,[107] without attempting, however, to remedy every evil, every wrong, and every injustice that may exist.[108] For it is of the essence of human or temporal law and, hence, of the secular state, to prevent only the worst excesses and to restrain the worst of evildoers. To accomplish this, the secular state enacts temporal laws. It does so not in order to make its citizens virtuous or pious men, but solely in order to deter and restrain the worst of evildoers.[109] Human laws, St. Augustine reminds us, are made by fallible human beings, although they are, or ought to be, made in close imitation of the *lex aeterna* and the *lex naturalis*. As such they are primarily an instrument for the more efficient control of certain affairs or actions of man.[110] It is through the efficacy of human laws that the secular state attempts (and sometimes succeeds) to guarantee the maintenance of human society and of the social institutions of man.[111]

The peace, harmony, and order which the secular state secures or guarantees are vital parts or aspects of the universal peace and harmonious orderliness decreed by God Himself. The true peace of every individual human being ultimately consists in his submission to the universal order or *lex aeterna*, that is, to the will of God: "The peace of mortal man with immortal God is disci-

---

105 *De Civitate Dei* XIX. 16 (PL 41, 644-645).
106 *Sermo LXII* V. 8 (PL 38, 418).
107 *De Doctrina Christiana* II. 25, 40 (PL 34, 55). See also *ibid.*, II. 39, 58 (PL 34, 62); *De Civitate Dei* XIX. 21, 2 (PL 41, 649); *Epistola CLIII* VI. 6, 16 (PL 33, 660).
108 *Epistola CLIII* VI. 6, 26 (PL 33, 665). See also note 87, *supra*.
109 *Ibid.*
110 *De Civitate Dei* XV. 16, 2 (PL 41, 459).
111 *De Libero Arbitrio* I. 15, 32 (PL 32, 1238). See also *ibid.*, I. 15, 33 (PL 32, 1239).

plined obedience to His *lex aeterna* performed in a spirit of true faith. The peace of men among themselves is harmonious and orderly concord. Peace of the family or household is the orderly rule and subjection of all those who live in this close association. Peace of the secular state consists in the proper and orderly arrangement of ruler and ruled among all citizens . . . Peace of all things is a well-disposed order."[112] All this, St. Augustine avers, has been ordained by God Himself, the wisest and most just creator, legislator, and orderer of all things.[113] It is thus that St. Augustine ultimately relates to God also the temporal laws and the secular state, two institutions which, at least on the surface, seem to have been devised by humans for the purpose of protecting and securing all men and all human institutions. St. Augustine also derives directly from the will of God not only the right to command or rule as well as the duty to obey or submit, but also the fair distribution of these rights and duties. For, according to St. Augustine, "there is no power but that granted by God."[114] In another place St. Augustine states that the Eternal Truth proclaims its commands and commandments through the mouths of righteous rulers. If these righteous rulers "command what is good—right and just—then no one else speaks through them than Christ Himself."[115] Even the power of the tyrant is from God, because God gives power both to good and evil rulers, according to His will.[116] The many kingdoms and empires have actually been founded by Divine Providence,[117] for we cannot presume that God, the creator of the universal order, intended to exempt the secular kingdoms, no matter how corrupt they may be, from His providential order.[118] As a matter of fact, it is He who legislates to the whole of mankind through the mouths of emperors and kings.[119]

In conclusion it may briefly be noted that St. Augustine's "philosophy of law" is, strictly speaking, not a "jurisprudential theory of law," but rather what might appropriately be called a "theological jurisprudence," something eminently befitting a theologian who makes no pretense at being a lawyer, an expert in the history of Roman Law, or perhaps a "political scientist." This should also explain why he did not compose a distinctly technical or juristic treatise on law or on legal theory. His remarks about law and legal philosophy and about the state, which are dispersed throughout many of his religious writ-

[112] *De Civitate Dei* XIX. 13, 1 (PL 41, 640).
[113] *Ibid.*, XIX. 13, 2 (PL 41, 641).
[114] *Epistola XCIII* VI. 20 (PL 33, 331).
[115] *Epistola CV* III. 11 (PL 33, 400). See also *ibid.*, III. 7 (PL 33, 398).
[116] *De Civitate Dei* V. 21 (PL 41, 167). See also *ibid., XIX.* 15 (PL 41, 644); *De Bono Coniugale* XIV. 10 (PL 40, 384-385).
[117] *De Civitate Dei* V. 1 (PL 41, 141).
[118] *Ibid.*, V. 21 (PL 41, 167). See also *ibid.*, V. 1 (PL 41, 141); and note 117, *supra;* Cicero, *De Republica* III. 22.
[119] *Tractatus in Ioannis Evangelium* VI. 25 (PL 35, 1437).

ings, are closely interwoven with his theological views and religious teachings. Hence, whenever he touches upon problems or issues connected with certain aspects of law, legal theory, and political order, he does so primarily with a view of demonstrating that theological considerations and religious truths not only permeate the law, but in fact constitute the sole true foundation of the law.

[10]

TWO CONCEPTIONS OF POLITICAL AUTHORITY: AUGUSTINE, *DE CIVITATE DEI*, XIX. 14–15, AND SOME THIRTEENTH-CENTURY INTERPRETATIONS

R.A. Markus

THIRTEENTH-CENTURY scholastics were addicted to quoting statements of Saint Augustine's, as of other *sancti*, as *auctoritates* in support of their opinions. The conventions of the scholastic employment of *auctoritates* are now tolerably well known. A modern scholar will not be surprised by frequent divergences between the meaning of such statements in their original setting and the meaning given them by one or other thirteenth-century theologian. Thirteenth-century theologians would have been even less worried by such divergences. Their analysis can, nevertheless, be illuminating. In this paper I shall examine the use made by a number of thirteenth-century writers of Saint Augustine's statements about the origins and nature of political authority and subjection, mainly in the *De civitate Dei*, book xix, chapters 14 and 15. This is one of the points at which we should expect the impact of Aristotelian ideas to show itself most clearly on political thought. It is here that we may best test the validity of the rival claims that the impact of these ideas revolutionized medieval political thought or, alternatively, that they stood in direct continuity with traditional, patristic and especially Augustinian thought-forms.[1]

[1] The most distinguished of the scholars who have made this claim is Otto Schilling, particularly in his *Die Staats- und Soziallehre des heiligen Thomas von Aquin*, 2nd ed., Munich, 1930 [henceforth: *SSLThom*]. Out of innumerable statements in the book, to some of which we shall have to return, we may quote from his own summary: 'The influence of Aristotelianism is unmistakable in Saint Thomas's theory of the state, whether one examines his views on the purpose and origin of the state, on the forms of the state, or on its functions or on many other topics. But both in general and in detail he succeeded in giving his own theory a unique stamp, mainly through giving, with the aid of tradition and especially of Augustinian ideas, the christian element its proper significance.' *SSLThom*, p. 238. Schilling's interpretation of Augustine's political theory is elaborated more fully in his *Die Staats- und Soziallehre des heiligen Augustinus* (Freiburg-im-Breisgau, 1910) [henceforth: *SSLAug*]. Of the more generally held view we may take A. J. Carlyle's as representative: 'To the Stoics and the Fathers the coercive control of man by man is not an institution of nature. By nature men, being free and equal, were under no system of coercive control. Like slavery, the introduction of this was the result of the loss of man's original innocence, and represented the need for some power which might control and limit the unreasonable passions and appetites of human nature. . . . It was not till Aristotle's *Politics* were rediscovered in the thirteenth century that Saint Thomas Aquinas under their influence recognized that the

The purpose of this paper is not directly to adjudicate on this large problem raised by the confrontation of two opposed interpretations of the history of medieval political thought. It is a much more modest one, which nevertheless lies at the centre of the larger problem. In the first part of the paper I examine the meaning of Augustine's statements concerning the origins of political authority, obligation, and subordination in these two chapters of his *De civitate Dei*, in the light of other relevant passages. In the second part I shall turn to some thirteenth-century interpretations of the same chapters by a number of writers of both the Aristotelian and what is traditionally referred to as the 'Augustinian' schools. Anything like a full study of their theories of political authority is beyond my scope. An examination of their various attempts to come to grips with the Augustinian view of the origins of this authority will, however, enable us to watch at close quarters what Augustine meant as seen through thirteenth-century preoccupations, and how far this meaning was modified by Aristotelian preoccupations.

1. *De civitate Dei*, xix. 14–15

Augustine never discusses the question of the state's origin both directly and in detail. The fullest remarks on this theme occur in these two chapters of his *De civitate Dei*, and, as we shall see, even these are not wholly centred on the problem with which we are concerned. Allusions and quotations by medieval writers, when debating our problem, are most frequently to these two chapters. They make a suitable starting-point to our inquiry.

Chapter 14 begins with a statement about the ends which the two 'cities' pursue, the main theme under discussion in book xix. 'In the earthly city the use of temporal things is referred to the enjoyment of earthly peace; whereas in the heavenly city it is referred to the enjoyment of eternal peace.' Augustine now goes on to expound what the peace is which is desired by all men. As he describes it, it is identical with what he has called 'eternal peace'; this alone ultimately satisfies all human longings. He continues with an account of how man is to conduct himself so as to attain this eternal peace. He is to obey the two chief commandments of God: to love God and to love his neighbour as himself. The latter must include having consideration for one's fellow men,

State was not merely an institution devised to correct men's vices, but rather the necessary form of a real and full human life.' R. W. and A. J. Carlyle, *A History of Medieval Political Theory in the West*, iii (1915), p. 5. Among more recent discussions, cf. W. Ullmann, *Principles of Politics and Government in the Middle Ages* (1962), p. 231 f.; I gratefully acknowledge the help I have had from Dr. Ullmann, by no means confined to his book. I have also profited from some criticisms by Dr. M. J. Wilks.

encouraging them to love God,[1] and being prepared to be thus encouraged by others. In this way only can men achieve 'peace' with their fellows; first with those close to them 'either by the order of nature, or by the bonds of society', their families and household, then with others more remote in so far as life brings them into contact with them. The chapter ends with a picture of the 'domestic peace', defined as the 'ordered harmony of authority and obedience of the household'.[2] This is the point in the chapter at which 'authority' (*imperare*, *imperium*) is brought into the discussion. Hitherto Augustine had been speaking of the duties of the head towards his household in terms of 'care for' and 'guidance' (*consulere*). This duty is now defined in terms of authority: 'to guide is to exercise authority (*imperant enim qui consulunt*) . . . and to be guided is to obey (*obediunt autem quibus consulitur*) . . .'. Authority and obedience (*imperare–obedire*) are a wider notion, to which giving and receiving guidance (*consulere–consuli*) are assimilated, a little arbitrarily, as a special case of the wider pair of concepts. Authority and obedience may present a very different face from the idyllic harmony sketched here; but in the household of the just man who lives by faith, those who rule in reality serve the subjects whom they appear to be ruling; and they rule 'not through a craving for power but in virtue of their obligation of caring for and guiding [their subjects] (*neque enim dominandi cupiditate imperant, sed officio consulendi*); nor with pride in lordship, but with merciful concern'.

The burden of the chapter is an exhortation to men in a place of authority and particularly a place of authority in household and family, how to conduct themselves in relation to their subjects. In the heavenly city the exercise of authority must be conceived as service. Augustine does not discuss the origin of social institutions at all in this chapter. He is concerned solely with how a man is to live within social institutions, particularly of family and household, as a citizen of the heavenly city. To this extent the chapter is concerned with two ways of exercising power within any social grouping.

The following chapter shows that the fact that in any institution power can be exercised on the model of a *paterfamilias* or otherwise has no implications for Augustine concerning the origins of institutions. The opening sentence of this chapter refers back to the previous chapter: 'this is what the order of nature prescribes, this is how God

[1] The range of meanings and overtones brought into play by Augustine's use of *consulere* can only rarely be rendered adequately without more than one equivalent in English. I use 'have consideration', 'care for', 'guide', 'encourage'.

[2] *ordinata imperandi obediendique concordia cohabitantium*; cf. also *De civ. Dei*, xix. 13.

created man'; and referring to Gen. i. 26, Augustine explains that God did not wish man, whom he made rational and in his own image, to rule over any but irrational creatures. Man was given dominion or authority not over other men, but over beasts. Thus the first just men of old were shepherds rather than kings. The condition of servitude is rightly imposed on sinners. The origin of the servitude in which man is subjected to another in virtue of the bondage of his condition, is sin. Only in this chapter does Augustine begin to speak about the origin of any social institution, and the institution he discusses, that of slavery, is unambiguously traced to sin as its origin. Augustine stresses that it is nevertheless a just enactment of God; for although 'nobody is the slave either of man or of sin by nature, as God first created man, nevertheless penal servitude is ordained by the same law as the one which enjoins the order of nature to be kept and forbids its transgression: for if nothing had been done against that law in the first place, there would be no need for the coercion of penal servitude'. The chapter concludes with an exhortation to slaves, to behave so as to achieve freedom, after a manner, in their servitude, by serving their masters with loving fidelity 'until iniquity shall pass away and all domination and human power shall be emptied and God shall be all in all'.

It is generally not noticed that Augustine is insisting on two things in these chapters: that, on the one hand, servitude is a condition or institution whose origin is not to be found in man's nature as created; and, on the other hand, that there is a way of exercising authority—and subjection—either in accordance with the order of nature or otherwise. Augustine explicitly includes the relation between master and slave among those in which he asserts that 'this [way of conducting oneself in it] is prescribed by the order of nature'.[1] Although, then, the

[1] Schilling, *SSLAug*, p. 46, n. 1, gratuitously altering the text in his footnote, takes *hoc* to refer to *officium consulendi ac providendi*. This clearly cannot be the case; *hoc* must refer to the whole of the last sentence of ch. 14, or to the argument as a whole of which it serves as the conclusion. It is noteworthy, however, that despite this, Schilling did not interpret the passage as asserting that political authority was an institution derived from the *ordo naturae*. Although he thought that this was in fact Augustine's view, his arguments for this are based on other passages, to be considered in due course. Schilling interpreted the two chapters under discussion as making a distinction between two ways of exercising power: either despotically, or as 'sympathetic guidance' (*teilnehmende Fürsorge*), ibid., p. 55. What he failed to notice is the shift in chapter 15 to a discussion of institutions, that of slavery. Gustave Combès, in his *La Doctrine politique de Saint Augustin* (Paris, 1927), pp. 76 f., also appears to be clear that these passages exclude political authority from the state of man's innocence. He bases his opinion that political authority is nevertheless a natural institution for Augustine on 'the intervention of a second law of nature', which impels men to associate with each other. Their original freedom, in his

institution itself originates in sin, the exercise of authority in it need not be and ought not to be sinful but in accordance with the order of nature. We must conclude that these chapters give no ground for the opinion that for Augustine the state and political authority are, or can be, an institution of nature. Chapter 14 asserts nothing about institutions, and speaks only about the exercise of authority, and chapter 15 indicates that he thought that the natural order could be observed within an institution belonging to the order of fallen, sinful nature.

Apart from this general principle, our two chapters assert nothing explicitly about the nature of political authority. There is a phrase in chapter 14 which suggests that Augustine would have distinguished it from the kind of authority enjoyed by a father over his family; for he distinguishes within the household over which the *paterfamilias* presides those who are close to him 'by the order of nature' (i.e. his family) and those who are close 'by the order of society' (i.e. his household slaves, &c.). The impression given—it is no more—is that the 'order of nature' is thought of as coextensive here with the family. There is nothing specific in the text to show whether political authority is to be taken, with slavery, as originating in sin, or, with the family, as arising from the order of nature. None the less, in the absence of positive grounds for excepting political authority, the most natural way of reading what Augustine says about the subjection of man to man is to take it quite generally, including within its scope the subjection of men to their rulers. The verse quoted from Genesis (i. 26), 'Let them have dominion over the fish of the sea and over the birds of the air and over every creeping thing that creeps upon the earth', and Augustine's comment that God did not wish man to rule over other men, taken in their most immediately natural sense, would exclude any kind of dominion of men over other men; and the observation in the following sentence that for this reason just men were at first shepherds rather than kings clinches the appositeness of interpreting Augustine as wishing to include political dominion within his meaning. Finally, the conclusion of the chapter also suggests that Augustine thought of all institutions of human domination and power as on a level with slavery, at least in respect of their final destiny. It is at least striking that he does not dissociate political from other forms of authority, as one might expect him to have done if he had thought of it as different in origin and kind. A long

view, is cancelled out by this law, and characterized men only in *une vie errante et solitaire*, in which men were alone with their consciences before God. His arguments are rarely more than assertions based on quotations torn from their context and linked by innuendo. An attempt to refute them would contribute little to an understanding of Augustine's views.

passage,[1] which recalls *De civitate Dei*, xix. 15 at a number of points, gives a similar impression. Here Augustine discusses the dominion exercised by the bad over the good. What is interesting for our purpose about this passage is not Augustine's defence of such a state of affairs, which rests on his view that it is God's dispensation *ad tempus*, and will be done away with at the end; it is the equivalence between slavery and all political authority, secular power, and dignity on which some stress is laid. Though the origins of the institutions are, again, not under discussion, the effect of the passage is to reinforce the impression that slavery and other institutions of human subjection are not fundamentally distinguished in Augustine's mind.

Augustine clarifies his position to some extent when he explains[2] that a harmonious social existence is natural to man, and a desire for such an existence implanted in man by nature. His account of such a state implies that in it men are equal before God, until perverse imitation of God disrupts the social harmony. Rejecting equality with his fellows, man wishes to impose dominion on them. Three assertions are clearly made here: that man's nature is social, not solitary; that by their original nature men are equal and subject to God, not to one another; and that subjection to one another is the consequence of sinful pride. The last assertion, we may note, is made without particular reference to slavery; and a similar argument[3] involving political subordination suggests that this should be taken as included among the results of sin. Augustine sometimes refers to man's dominion over lower creatures as *potestas naturalis*, and traces this to man's superiority to other creatures in virtue of being made to God's image and likeness.[4] Gen. i. 26, invoked here as in *De civitate Dei*, xix. 15, gives no grounds for including any form of subordination of man to man within the range of this *potestas naturalis*.

None of this, however, would suffice for a conclusive refutation of the view that for Augustine the state is natural. The case for this view rests almost entirely on the twin assertions[5] that Augustine admitted a natural subordination of men to men, notably in the family, and that the state is in this respect homogeneous with the family and therefore belongs to the order of nature. It is important, therefore, to examine more closely the manner in which Augustine distinguished natural from non-natural forms of subjection between man and man, and whether

[1] *Enarr. in Ps.* 124. 7–8. [2] *De civ. Dei*, xix. 12. 2.

[3] Ibid. xviii. 2. 2: *hinc factum est ut non sine Dei providentia . . . quidam essent regnis praediti, quidam regnantibus subditi. . . .*

[4] *In Ep. Joann. Tr.* 8. 6–8.

[5] Cf. Schilling, *SSLAug*, pp. 57–60; Combès, op. cit. (above, p. 71, n. 1), pp. 79–80.

political institutions really do belong with those of the family, or, rather, with slavery.

That Augustine did not exclude all forms of subjection from the order of nature in the state of primitive innocence there can be no doubt. He asserts this quite explicitly in commenting on Gen. i. 26 in a work of 419.[1] It gives us to understand, he argues, that reason is to have dominion over irrational life; this subjection is just, whereas iniquity or adversity subject men to the service of others. But, Augustine goes on to observe, the verse does not exclude 'a natural order [of subjection] in mankind, too, such that in virtue of it women should be subject to men and sons to their fathers; for in these cases, too, it is right that the weaker in reason should be subject to the stronger'. How little inclined Augustine was to extend this 'natural order of subjection' to include political subjection we may gauge from the opening remark, which began this train of reflections. There Augustine commends the patriarchs, apropos of Gen. xlvi. 32, for being shepherds—and one recalls the comparison of shepherds and kings in *De civitate Dei*, xix. 15 —for 'this sort of dominion and subjection, whereby beasts are subjected to men and men in charge of beasts, is undoubtedly right'. It is clear that the oft-invoked text cannot serve to justify the opinion that political authority is based on a natural order of subjection among men. An analysis of the antecedents of this text, however, reveals the structure of ideas in Augustine's mind of which this theme forms a part. The view that there is a natural subordination among men is, of course, not by any means expressed here for the first time in his work. It is clearly asserted in his great commentary on Genesis, written *c.* 401–14. Commenting in this work[2] on the verse 'To the woman [God] said "I will greatly multiply thy pain in childbearing . . . and thou shalt be under thy husband's power and he shall have dominion over thee",[3] Augustine observes that the text clearly speaks of what woman's condition is to be as a punishment for her sin. All the same, he insists, we are not to doubt that even before sin woman was so made that she should be under man's dominion. The punishment should therefore be understood as consisting in that kind of subjection (*servitutem*) 'which belongs to a certain condition rather than to love (*quae cuiusdam conditionis est potius quam dilectionis*); so that we should understand that this kind of servitude, too, whereby men afterwards began to be servants of each other, has its origin in the punishment of sin'. The servitude which Augustine identifies with loving subordination belongs to the nature

[1] *Quaest. in Hept.* i. 153.

[2] *De Gen. ad litt.* xi. 37. 50.

[3] *ad virum tuum conversio tua et ipse tui dominabitur*—Gen. iii. 16, in Augustine's text.

in which man and woman were originally created. In their fallen state, however, this mutual service in charity is over-laid by the kind of subjection by which one person owes service and obedience to another in virtue of his condition or status. And this kind of subjection is a result of sin. Within it, service and dominion can be exercised as an office of charity; but the partnership may fall short of this and be a case of one being dominated by the other. The Apostle, Augustine says, exhorts married partners to the former (Gal. v. 13), and absolutely forbids woman to dominate over man (1 Tim. ii. 12). The distinction between service as required by the natural order of subordination and service as owed in virtue of status and condition is identical with the distinction alluded to in *De civitate Dei*, xix. 15.[1]

This extensive commentary on the book of Genesis contains the first germs of many of the ideas which we meet later in the *De civitate Dei*. It is important therefore to note that it gives no countenance to the suggestion that Augustine linked the institutions of marriage and the state as belonging to the natural order as created. On the contrary: it is clear that the service and subjection which a man owes another in virtue of being subject to him as to his legitimate ruler is an instance of subjection in virtue of status only; it has nothing to do with any possible moral or intellectual superiority of the ruler over his subject. This emerges with all clarity from the theory of divine providence which Augustine elaborates in book viii of the commentary, which stands, like so many of these seminal ideas, behind the applications they find in the *De civitate Dei*.

His theory of divine providence led Augustine to dissociate the authority of man over woman, and other forms of natural subordination, from purely institutional forms of subjection to authority, such as exist in the state. With the insertion of man (and angels) into the universe, an element of freedom and rational agency is introduced: as Augustine expresses it in a fine and untranslatable image, with man 'the bud (*oculus*) of reason is grafted on to the world, as on to a great tree of things'.[2] With this grafting, the divine gardener's operation becomes two-fold. His providence operates in two channels, through the processes of nature and through the acts of wills. In his grand catalogue of the works of man which fall under the operation of providence, Augustine mentions 'the administration of societies' specifically as under God's *providentia voluntaria*. A few paragraphs later[3] he returns to the same duality

[1] Cf. above, p. 71: *rationalem . . . noluit nisi irrationalibus dominari* and the consequent duty (ch. 14) of the just man to serve those whom he rules; and the subjection of man to man *conditionis vinculo*, rooted in sin.

[2] *De Gen. ad litt.* viii. 9. 17.

[3] Ibid. viii. 23. 44.

of God's providence, and enumerates examples of natural subordination which God's providence secures among natures thus: 'he first subjected all things to himself, then he subjected corporeal to spiritual creatures, irrational to rational, earthly to heavenly, female to male, those of lower value to those of higher, the more restricted to the more comprehensive'. Neither slavery nor political subjection is mentioned here. From the two passages taken together we may infer that the subjection of woman to man, as of those inferior in some relevant respect to those superior, derives from the order of nature; whereas the subjection of men to political authority (and slavery) does not.

It is in this great commentary on Genesis that Augustine first came to grips with the idea of nature. The distinction here developed, under the impulse of that reflection, between the twin channels of providential order lies behind the later discussions of the *De civitate Dei*. It underlies, for instance, the fine chapter[1] devoted to providence in which Augustine describes, in a passage of sweeping rhetoric, the all-embracing range of God's providence in nature, and then adds that 'the kingdoms of men, their dominations and their subjections (*regna hominum eorumque dominationes et servitutes*)' are in no way to be thought remote from 'the laws of his providence'. These laws are obviously identical with the law Augustine refers to in *De civitate Dei*, xix. 15, the law which ordains penal servitude on the one hand, and enjoins the order of nature to be observed and forbids its transgression on the other.[2] There is a clear reference embedded here to the dual operation of divine providence elaborated in the *De Genesi ad litteram*. Augustine's view that the institutional subjection of man to man is rooted in human sin and is part of a divine dispensation for sin, has deep roots in his thought about the operation of divine providence in the world. The subjection of wives to their husbands and of children to their parents is not, in the relevant sense, institutional; it is clear and generally agreed that Augustine held these to be ordinances of nature. Nor, it is also clear, is society itself institutional in this sense. For as we have seen,[3] a social existence was in Augustine's view natural to man. God had created man with a view to social existence,[4] and the saints shall live in sociable union.[5] Men are driven 'by the laws of their nature' to enter a social existence;

[1] *De civ. Dei*, v. 11.

[2] Cf. above, p. 71: *poenalis servitus ea lege ordinatur quae naturalem ordinem conservari jubet, perturbari vetat* . . .; Augustine is not speaking of a natural law, as some commentators suggest, but of a law (that of divine providence) which enjoins the observance and forbids the disturbing of the order of nature.

[3] Cf. above, p. 73, n. 2.

[4] *De civ. Dei*, xii. 21 (22, Dombart and Kalb); and 27 (28, Dombart and Kalb).

[5] Ibid. xix. 3. 2; 5.

but Augustine conceives this 'natural' society as a society of equals living in concord and subject only to God.[1] That he envisaged a wide variety of grades of intelligence and ability among men we need not deny. But he was certainly not so naïve as to assume that political authority and subjection were in fact often based on such a hierarchy of ability, and he certainly did not seek to justify the claims of political authority on grounds of any alleged natural superiority of ruler to subject, such as he attributes to the husband or the father over his family. He did think that the superior abilities of the wise man should find expression in concern for and guidance of the less wise. This is in accordance with the order of nature, displayed by the *paterfamilias*,[2] and it should be the pattern for the conduct of anyone in a position of authority. But the institutions of government, coercion, and punishment are brought into human society by sin. They are God's just punishment for man's transgression, and they are also his providential dispensation for coping with its consequences, disorder, strife, and lack of concord. Like society, the family, too, can be disordered by sin; here, too, disobedience may require coercion and punishment.[3] The parallel between society and the family is, indeed, important to Augustine. But it does not imply that political authority is grounded in the order of nature, as is paternal. A ruler or magistrate should behave like a *paterfamilias*; but the analogy between the two men holds only in respect of family life in the fallen state of man. For the coercive power which is part of the very substance and meaning of political authority also exists in the family; it enters the family, as it enters society, through sin and disorder. But a family is a family without it—we may conceive, even in a sinful world, of a family in which paternal authority is an exercise of care and guidance without coercion. But coercive power is part of the essence of political authority. Without it the state is not a state, though we may imagine lesser societies without it. Political authority, coercive power and its apparatus are what transform society

[1] *De civ. Dei*, xix. 12. 2. This section is in fact only indirectly concerned with this question. Harald Fuchs's fine analysis of the chapter in *Augustin und der antike Friedensgedanke* (*Neue philologische Untersuchungen*, 3, Berlin, 1926), pp. 17–36, shows that Augustine is here primarily interested in the universal drive towards *pax* operative throughout nature, human and non-human. The sociable nature of man is only an illustration of this general principle. The final sentences of section 2 of the chapter, on the *perversa imitatio Dei* which seeks to subject others naturally and originally equal with oneself under God to one's own rule, is a further illustration of the natural drive towards peace operative even in this disordered state.

[2] Ibid. xix. 14, 16. This commonplace is frequent in Augustine's correspondence, e.g. in *Epp.* 104. 2. 7; 130. 12; 133. 2; 138. 2. 14, &c.

[3] *De civ. Dei*, xix. 16; 12. 1.

into a state. Society, so we may summarize Augustine's view, has its origins in the order of nature; the state is a dispensation rooted in sin.

It remains to consider the analogy between the authority enjoyed by the soul over its body and that enjoyed by the ruler over his subjects. The application of this analogy would clearly point away from the view I have ascribed to Augustine. It would suggest that the relations of political authority are based on a natural order of command and obedience such as Augustine undoubtedly thought obtained between soul and body. Gustave Combès, indeed, saw the force of the analogy, and quoted[1] a passage from Augustine's *Contra Julianum* to clinch his interpretation of Augustine's theory of the state as natural. As this work is likely to be not very much earlier in composition than the later books of the *De civitate Dei*, it is worth examining its use of this analogy with some care. In the passage adduced by Combès[2] Augustine is quoting Cicero's *De republica*:

> Is it not clear that nature always gives authority (*dominatum*) to the better, for the great profit of the weaker? Why else should God rule over men, the mind over the body, reason over lust and anger and the other vicious parts of the soul? . . . But we must advert to the different forms of rule and subjection. The mind is said to rule both its body and its lusts; but it rules its body as a king rules his subjects or a parent his children, whereas it rules its lusts as a master rules his slave, with coercion and repression. Kings, emperors (*imperatores*),[3] magistrates, fathers and victorious nations have authority over their subjects in the way that the mind has authority over its body. . . .

Undoubtedly, Cicero here links political authority with paternal and likens them both to the natural authority of superior over inferior, such as the mind has in relation to its body; and Augustine quotes the passage with approval. Nevertheless, Cicero's view is not Augustine's. We may begin by noting the evident reserve with which Augustine quotes Cicero against his Pelagian opponent. Secular letters are no ground—Julian had himself appealed to Cicero—on which to refute bishops charged with expounding the holy scriptures; rather should such literature be deemed to be mad ravings if such a conflict appears.[4] All the same, since worldly literature sometimes contains 'traces of the truth' (*vestigia veritatis*), Julian's arguments can be answered from the very source of his own[5] —this is how Augustine introduces his appeal to Cicero. We need not lay too much weight on the views expressed in it; Augustine makes it only too clear that the passage is introduced as a polemical device. He

[1] Op. cit. (above, p. 71, n. 1), p. 80.

[2] *C. Iul.* iv. 12. 61.

[3] Whatever Augustine's historical knowledge, *imperatores* here could scarcely have made him think of anything but emperors.

[4] *C. Iul.* iv. 12. 61.

[5] Ibid. iv. 12. 60.

wishes to confute Julian on his own ground, rather than by theological argument from the scriptures. Augustine's use of this Ciceronian analogy is, however, of considerable interest and repays elucidation.

Cicero is concerned with distinguishing two kinds of authority among men, one which is in accordance with nature, and one which is despotic. The analogy with the two ways in which the mind rules its body and its passions is intended to throw light on the two ways of ruling men. Augustine reverses the application of the analogy: he is concerned with the soul and bodily passions, especially in their disorganized state in man's fallen condition. It is to illuminate this relation of mind to body that he uses the analogy with political authority. Cicero's analogy would have been just as useful to him for this purpose had it contrasted only paternal authority with despotic, omitting royal authority.[1] But since Augustine was not directly concerned with discussing the nature of political and despotic authority, as Cicero had been, he saw no harm in quoting the whole passage as it stood.

The origin of royal authority was in fact one of the issues over which Augustine sharply disagreed with Cicero.[2] For Cicero, ancient kingship was wielded, in accordance with the order of nature, by the justest and wisest of men; whereas one of the themes which appears in the *De civitate Dei* with almost monotonous frequency is the theme of the origin of kingship in conquest, domination, and lust for power. And repeatedly Augustine dwells on the significance of the fact that the Old Testament patriarchs were shepherds rather than kings.[3] There can, therefore, be no justification for inferring from Augustine's use of the passage from Cicero's *De republica* that he grouped kingship—and other non-despotic forms of political authority—with paternal and other natural forms of authority. Once in the *De civitate Dei*[4] Augustine refers to Cicero's argument, using it, on this occasion, in its original sense, that is to say, as an argument justifying political authority on the

[1] In *De civ. Dei*, xiv. 23. 2 Augustine, in the course of a similar argument, merely refers to this passage of Cicero's *De republica* without quoting it in full. It is significant that in his summary he omits mentioning royal authority, and reduces the dichotomy between the two types of authority to the basic form in which it was acceptable to him. Cicero, he writes, 'when discussing the varieties of authority (*de imperiorum differentia*), took an analogy from human nature: the limbs of the body are ruled like sons, on account of their readiness to obey, whereas the vicious parts of the soul are coerced, like slaves, by a harsher kind of rule'. Nothing could give a clearer indication of the sense in which he understood the analogy, and what really mattered to him in its application.

[2] This is noted by Schilling, *SSLAug*, pp. 53–54. Schilling refers to Cicero, *De leg.* 3. 2; *De off.* 2. 12 and, by way of pointing the contrast, to *De civ. Dei*, xvi. 4. 17; xviii. 2; v. 12, &c.

[3] *De civ. Dei*, xix. 15; *Quaest. in Hept.* i. 153.

[4] xix. 21. 2.

analogy of the natural rule of the mind over its body, rather than in the reverse direction. But in doing so, Augustine takes every care to evacuate the argument of all its force. In earlier parts of his *De republica*, as Augustine summarizes Cicero, he had argued the case for injustice, and suggested that a commonwealth could not exist without it, for the rule of one man over others is unjust, and yet, there can be no dominion over nations without it. Now, Augustine says, Cicero changes his standpoint, and meets this argument by asserting that this subjection is justified by the fact that 'it is good for such men to be subjected, for subjection is to their benefit', in that by removing from the wicked the power to hurt, they will be better off when tamed than they had been untamed. Augustine passes over this classical piece of imperialist dogma without comment—he had plenty to say about it earlier in his work—and goes on to note Cicero's further justification of such rule by invoking the analogy of nature: 'Why else should God rule over men, the mind over the body, reason over lust and the other vices?' But his answer to the rhetorical question drastically deflates its Ciceronian implications, and turns its significance in another direction. Cicero's examples show, he says modestly, that for some people subjection is good,[1] and that subjection to God is good for all. For the mind which is justly subject to God rules justly over its body; and with the Ciceronian claim for political authority and subjection quietly by-passed, Augustine returns to the point with which the present excursus had begun: the meaning of justice and the need for it in the *res publica*, defined as Cicero had defined it. His handling of Cicero's argument shows profound reserve about Cicero's aligning of political authority and subjection on the side of natural authority and subordination.

The views on the origin of political authority which I have traced in Augustine's works appear to be his settled views from about 401 onwards. Before this time he does not appear to have devoted much thought to this question. From remarks scattered through his earlier works a somewhat different view of the nature of political authority can be pieced

[1] This view, too, is anticipated in *De Genesi ad litteram*, where Augustine notes the value to be set upon the *ordo reipublicae in cujusdam pacis terrenae vinculum coercens etiam peccatores* (ix. 9. 14); cf. also *De doctr. christ.* ii. 25. 39–40; 39. 58. This is, of course, a commonplace of patristic literature, and finds its classical expression in Irenaeus, *Adv. haer.* v. 24. 2. There are good grounds for thinking that Augustine was acquainted with Irenaeus's work; cf. B. Altaner, 'Augustin und Irenäus', *Theol. Quartalschr.* cxxix (1949), pp. 162–72. Schilling quotes (*SSLAug*, pp. 46 f.) several passages from other writers containing similar views on the origins of political authority; but he does not admit that the apparent similarity entitles us to infer that Augustine derives 'the whole political order from sinfulness as its source' (ibid., p. 51).

together.[1] The strand in Augustine's reflection on society which we have been studying is only one among several which shaped his views on the state and its functions; views which sometimes gave rise to tensions in his mind, some of which he never fully resolved. In so far as our present theme can be isolated as a coherent theme in his thought, it seems very likely that his deepened study of St. Paul in the mid 390's helped to give it shape. This is the source of his consciousness of the power of sin over human nature. The shift from an early optimism is nowhere more marked than in his reflection on society. The whole complex cluster of themes which go into the making of this reflection is too wide for study here. From a wider point of view, the revolutionary effect of thirteenth-century Aristotelianism could be summed up quite simply as lying in the assertion of the innate value of the natural order as a positive force for good, as against Augustine's refusal to assign value to the things of nature, *per se*, in a sinful world. But here I shall be concerned with a narrower question: just how, precisely, did Augustine and his thirteenth-century interpreters respectively think of political society in relation to the natural order? Stating the question in these terms one does, of course, run the risk of giving Augustine's own treatment of the theme an air of spurious terminological precision. The looseness of his conception of 'nature' is too notorious to require comment; and the extent to which one should speak of his conception of 'political' authority, and still more of the 'state', is open to debate. But we may, at any rate, summarize the result of the inquiry of this first section by saying that the terms in which Augustine came to formulate his views on politically organized society (that is to say, on society articulated within the framework of government and its agencies, law, enforcement and the machinery of their administration: roughly what we should nowadays call the 'state') were those which he thought appropriate to the treatment of the institution of slavery, rather than those which he applied to the human family.

The crucial point at stake in the theological discussions of the origins of political authority is the question as to whether it is to be treated on the model of the authority of a master over his slave, or on that of a husband and father over his wife and family. These are the paradigm cases which give us a clue to the senses in which the concept of 'nature' is applied to social groupings. What is meant by asserting—or by denying—that political authority belongs to the natural order depends on the meaning attached to 'natural': it will clearly be something very

[1] Cf. the penetrating study by F. E. Cranz, 'The Development of Augustine's Ideas on Society before the Donatist Controversy', *Harvard Theol. Rev.* xlvii (1954), pp. 255–316.

different according as to whether, and in what sense, the 'natural order' is held to include or to exclude the institution of slavery. If there is a sense in which political society was, for Augustine, 'natural'—and we shall see that some of his medieval interpreters thought that there was such a sense—it is a sense very different from that in which he thought the family to be 'natural'. We may, therefore, conclude, without fear of distorting his view though in a language slightly more formalized than his own, that after *c.* 400 Augustine continued to think, with Cicero,[1] that man was a social animal by nature, but that he came to reject the view that he was also naturally a political animal.[2] Of this latter view there is no trace in the two chapters of the *De civitate Dei* which we have examined; and interpreted in the context of the ideas with which they belong in Augustine's thought, and particularly in the light of his *Auseinandersetzung* with Cicero's views, they clearly assert the contrary.

2. *Some thirteenth-century interpretations*

Although our two chapters of the *De civitate Dei* find no place in the exposition of Gen. i. 26–27 in the *Glossa ordinaria*, or in the discussion of political authority in the *Sentences* of Peter Lombard,[3] they were nevertheless common property to medieval theologians and were often invoked in debates about the origins of authority and subjection. The purpose of this second section of my paper is to shed some light on the interpretation of Augustine's views primarily by St. Thomas Aquinas. St. Thomas's first work, his commentary on the *Sentences*, though written before Aristotle had made his full impact on Aquinas's political thought with the Latin version of the *Politics*, was already marked by strong Aristotelian influence, especially of the *Ethics*. In his *Scriptum super Sententiis* we can observe Thomas in dialogue with the tradition of the schools on the one hand, and with his contemporaries, notably St. Albert the Great and St. Bonaventure, on the other.[4] To throw Thomas's views into sharper relief, I shall begin by comparing them with Bonaventure's and Albert's, referring, incidentally, to one or two other writers. The comparison with Bonaventure serves to assess St. Thomas's views in relation to a theologian less intoxicated with the new learning and more reserved about its results than was Albert, Thomas's teacher and one of the leaders of the Christian Aristotelian revival of the century.

[1] *duce natura congregabantur homines*—*De off.* ii. 21. 73.

[2] Ibid., and *De fin.* v. 23. 66: human nature has *quiddam ingenitum quasi civile atque populare quod Graeci πολιτικόν vocant* . . . .

[3] Lib. ii, dist. 44.

[4] Cf. M. D. Chenu, *Introduction à l'étude de Saint Thomas d'Aquin*, 2nd ed. (Paris, 1954), p. 235.

Of the three writers it is Bonaventure whom we should expect to follow Augustine's teaching most closely. We may begin with his comments on Distinction 44 of the second book of the *Sentences*. Bonaventure makes an important distinction here[1] between two ways in which we can speak of something being against the *jus naturae*: either absolutely (*simpliciter*) or within the limits of nature in a particular condition (*secundum aliquem statum*). The statement that authority (*potestas dominandi*) is against natural right, Bonaventure says, is true only if understood in the second sense; that is to say, it is not true of nature as such, in all its states, only of nature in its state of original integrity 'in which there was no place for servile subjection (*subjectio servitutis*) or authority (*praelatio potestatis*)'. The conclusion is Augustine's, and a commonplace of medieval theology; but there is a refinement introduced in the distinction between 'nature' taken *simpliciter* and 'nature' taken *secundum aliquem statum*, a distinction which tends to be notoriously blurred in Augustine's language. The distinction is of some importance in Bonaventure's discussion of our problem in the next *quaestio*.[2] Here he distinguishes three ways in which we may take *potestas dominandi vel praesidendi*: first, we may take it, *largissime*, to include a man's power to use something as his possession. Secondly, we may take it to mean, *communiter*, a man's power to command someone else who is capable of reason and obedience. Finally, we may take it, *proprie*, to mean the power to coerce subordinates. Authority taken in its first sense obtains in nature in all its states. The second kind exists in nature *in via*, both in its original integrity and in its fallen state. Bonaventure illustrates this second type of authority by that which a man has over his wife or a father over his child, both of which, in his view, exist in nature, whether in its original or its fallen state. Authority in its third sense, however, understood as coercive power, exists in fallen nature only; *servitus* is to be reckoned as *poena peccati*, or, as he puts it in his reply[3] to an objection, men possess dominion over other men *quodammodo praeternaturaliter*, *in punitionem peccati*, whereas their dominion over lower creatures belongs to them by nature. Bonaventure concludes his analysis with the remark that it is authority in its third sense, as coercive power, that is under discussion now; and this concluding remark indicates how completely he is in agreement with Augustine. For what is under discussion is political authority; and, like Augustine, Bonaventure cannot divorce this from coercive power, and, like Augustine, too, he refuses to assimilate it to the sort of authority

[1] *In Sent.* ii, D. 44, a. 2, q. 1, ad 4m.

[2] Ibid., q. 2. The treatment and phraseology of Richard of Middleton (*Comm. in Sent.* ii, D. 44, a. 2, q. 2) are very closely parallel.

[3] Ibid., ad 3 m.

enjoyed by a husband over his wife or a father over his child. Bonaventure's refinement of the vocabulary of 'nature' and his care in applying it here has enabled him to define a sense in which political authority can be said to be 'natural'. But it is a sense in which its status is 'natural' in the way that slavery is 'natural', not in the way that the human family is. Bonaventure's profound fidelity to Augustine's thought is scarcely concealed by the greater precision of his terminology.

One phrase, however, of Augustine's chapter which Bonaventure adduces in support of his view gave him some trouble. This is the statement[1] that dominion and subjection are ordained by the same law as that which bids the observance of nature and forbids its transgression. Like many more careless readers, Bonaventure misunderstood Augustine's statement. He took it to mean that dominion and subjection were ordained by the order of nature, whereas Augustine had asserted the quite different position that the same eternal providence stands behind human subjection as operates in the natural order. Even in its misunderstanding of Augustine's text Bonaventure's argument is revealing. The statement, he says, applies only to fallen nature, 'so that the wicked might be restrained and the good protected': for otherwise man's corrupt nature would make social life impossible. In the state of innocence, however, there would have been no need for such dominion and subjection, for here all would have remained equably *in gradu et statu suo.*[2] Bonaventure was anxious not to allow Augustine's statement—erroneously understood—to call into doubt his view of authority. The distinction between nature *simpliciter* and nature *secundum aliquem statum* enabled him to avoid this neatly: it was only necessary to identify the 'order of nature' in Augustine's statement with that of nature in its fallen state. Thus notwithstanding his misunderstanding of Augustine at this point, Bonaventure succeeded in bringing the statement into line with the theory of political authority which he had learnt from Augustine. Like Augustine, he saw human subjection to rulers—even to non-Christian rulers—as a human institution sanctioned by a dispensation of divine providence,[3] but not as an ordinance of nature.

Bonaventure's treatment of our theme is clearly a great advance on the cursory remarks given it by Alexander of Hales.[4] If one considers it

[1] Cf. above, pp. 71 and 76, n. 2.

[2] Loc. cit., ad 4 m.

[3] Loc. cit., a. 3, q. 1.

[4] His comments on *Sent.* ii, D. 44 in his *Glossa* take a different direction and do not discuss *dominium*. He touches on the theme of *dominium* in the *Summa*, P. iii, q. 48, m. 1 (the passage may well be from his pen). Here he is content to affirm (ad 3 m) the commonplace taken from Gregory's *Moralia* xxi. 15. 22, cited here, that men are equal and not made to dominate each other by nature but have fallen into this state through their perversity.

together with St. Thomas's comments in his *Scriptum super sententiis*,[1] and another text of the mid or late 1250's, from the *Summa* attributed to Alexander of Hales,[2] it is not easy to escape the impression that the new approach to this question owed something to perplexities aroused by quite recent intellectual movements. Perhaps it was such perplexities that prompted the author of the article in the *Summa fratris Alexandri* to a meticulous re-reading of Augustine's key texts. In his article he is concerned with the question whether Adam had dominion over other men before his fall. The authorities cited against an affirmative answer are, significantly, identical with those used by Bonaventure in the article I have discussed. They are: (1) the statement that freedom is part of man's original condition (here fastened on to Isidore, *Etym.* v. 4. 1); (2) Augustine, *De civitate Dei*, xix. 15; and (3) the famous passage of distinctly Augustinian inspiration from Gregory the Great, *Moralia* xxi. 15. 22–23. The argument begins by distinguishing two forms of *dominium*, that of superiority by reason of higher excellence on account either of origin or of priority in time, or by reason of superior knowledge or virtue; and *dominium* as *auctoritas praesidendi, immo potius possidendi.* In language very similar to Bonaventure's, the former is referred to as *dominium* understood *communiter, sive nomine extenso*, the latter as *dominium* taken *proprie*. Corresponding to the two kinds of *dominium* there are two kinds of subjection (*servitus*): *obsequium reverentiae et libertatis*, the freely given service and respect of the naturally inferior to his acknowledged superior, and the servile subjection owed in virtue of condition and necessity (*necessitatis, conditionis, scilicet servilis*). The passage from Augustine's *De Genesi ad litteram*[3] which we have considered above is invoked, and interpreted, rightly, as distinguishing 'the service of generosity or love (*servitus liberalitatis sive dilectionis*) from that of enforced, unwilling service owed in virtue of condition (*servitus contradictionis sive violentiae*); and in conclusion the author asserts, with a reference to Augustine's *De civitate Dei*, xix. 15, that only the first kind of authority could have existed in nature before the fall.

This is entirely within Augustinian horizons. The only thing that the author fails to make clear, in contrast with Bonaventure, is whether he considers political authority as an instance of the authority of natural superiority, or as to be classified with the *auctoritas praesidendi, immo*

[1] Cf. below, p. 89.

[2] P. ii, q. 93, m. 1. V. Doucet, in the *Prolegomena* appended to the Quaracchi edition of the *Summa* (vol. 4, p. ccclvi), assigns the block of which it forms a part to the years 1255–7, and is inclined to attribute it to William of Milton or to somebody working under his supervision. The possibility that it may be the work of a pupil of St. Bonaventure's is not proven, but cannot be discounted.

[3] xi. 37. 50; cf. above, p. 74.

potius possidendi, along with authority over slaves. The author can scarcely have failed to realize that it was in fact political authority that his inquiry was about; for Bonaventure makes this clear, and the two discussions have so much in common—the authorities used, the framework of thought, the whole *Problemstellung*—that we may suspect either a direct relation between them, or, at least, a fairly well crystallized approach to debating the theme in the schools. In these circumstances it is difficult to envisage the possibility that two Franciscan theologians could have given as radically opposed answers to the question as would be implied by interpreting the present article as asserting a natural origin for political authority.

Be this as it may, the author of the article shows an exact and penetrating understanding of Augustinian passages often misunderstood, not only by his contemporaries. We have already noted his very relevant comments on Augustine's distinction between the service of 'generosity or love' and the enforced 'subjection of condition'.[1] His remarks[2] on the final sentences of *De civitate Dei*, xix. 14 and the first of chapter 15, though they take some liberty in interpreting the text, are equally penetrating. Augustine's words do not imply, he says, that men are by nature made to dominate other men, but that men in a position of authority have the twofold duty of instructing their subjects (*officium consulendi*) and of caring for them (*providendi misericordia*). He appreciated that Augustine was here speaking not of the origins of authority but of conduct in authority. Further, he shows quite remarkable insight into Augustine's conception[3] of a twofold providential order, working through nature on the one hand and through human actions on the other. It is with a perceptive paraphrase of this doctrine and a reference to *De civitate Dei*, xix. 15 that he answers[4] the objection that if men were not naturally subordinated to each other, this would constitute a breach of the principle seen operating throughout nature. In conclusion, he denies the force of the argument that things are made by nature to form a hierarchy in which some are subordinated to others: for inanimate things are, so to speak, made to be 'pushed around' by each other, whereas man, being made in God's image, is directly related to him without intermediaries. Wherefore, his argument continues, God had made man in such a condition of freedom that he was not bound to serve anybody in order to attain his own good, which he was to pursue freely and unhindered. So long as he remained subject to God, he was subject to no one else, as are other creatures which are not themselves responsible for their actions but act on impulse. The writer

[1] Cf. p. 85, n. 3.
[2] Loc. cit., ad 1 m.
[3] Cf. above, pp. 75–76.
[4] Loc. cit., ad 3 m.

shows little originality; but his understanding of Augustine's texts is impressive. His way of facing the perplexities raised by current debate was the scholar's way, by returning to the authentic source of the tradition he was representing.

The most striking contrast between these Franciscan writers and St. Albert the Great is that his ideas in political authority are not worked out in the context of a theory of *dominium* at all, and that his theory of *dominium* is elaborated without reference to the standard choice of texts, from Augustine and Gregory. Thus in his early commentary on the *Sentences*, he shares the simple, untheoretical approach which marks Alexander of Hales's treatment of the corresponding themes. There is no attempt here[1] to relate what is said about the duty of obeying ecclesiastical or secular authorities to any theoretical framework; there is no talk whatever of *dominium* or *servitus*, of nature and sin. When he returns, perhaps some twenty-five years later, to the same theme in his *Summa*,[2] the theoretical framework of the discussion is provided by Aristotle's *Politics*. By the time he came to write his *Summa*, Albert had come to see the institutions of human society in Aristotelian terms. And although he does devote an article[3] to the theme of *dominium*, it has no application to political authority. Even the very definition of what constitutes *dominium* excludes in advance the possibility of treating political authority as a case of *dominium*. For one of the factors essential to 'perfect *dominium*' (the only kind discussed) is the supremacy of someone worse than or inferior to the subject. Such subjection to somebody (or something) inferior in rank or value will constitute a restriction of a rational being's freedom. Of the ways enumerated by Albert, in which such servitude occurs, only one is of interest to us, the *servitus conditionalis* 'whereby a man is subjected to another in such a way that all his actions and possessions are referred to that person, and that whatever he does or possesses he does and possesses in the other's name. . . . This subjection originates in sin, for it is just that he who has sinned against his superior by nature, against the Father, should be subjected to his equal by nature. . . .' Although the argument follows the Augustinian lines, there is no reference to any of the Augustinian passages which Albert might have invoked to confirm his view. The similarity with Augustine's view is, however, deceptive—and it may be that it was an awareness of this that kept Albert from appealing to Augustine. Albert may be in full agreement with Augustine on the origins of slavery; but he holds a very different view of subjection to political authority. His precise, almost legal

[1] *In Sent.* ii, D. 44, a. 6.

[2] P. II, q. 141, m. 3.

[3] P. II, q. 39, m. 2, a. 1, p. 1, q. 1.

description of *servitus conditionalis* indicates that his remarks on it refer to slavery only, and are not intended to embrace other forms of subjection of man to man. Nothing is said here about political authority, for the very good reason that *dominium*, defined in the unusual way as it is by Albert, excluded political authority by definition.[1] He saw the state through Aristotle's eyes[2] and appears to have felt no need to relate this vision to traditional patterns of debating the nature of authority.

The only reference I have discovered to any of the relevant passages from Augustine is one to *De civitate Dei*, xix. 15. This occurs, however, in a context only remotely and indirectly related to the problem of authority, in the course of an objection in a question concerned with the providential order in the universe.[3] Here Albert quotes the opening sentences of the chapter, and concludes from them that 'if a man rules over a man or a sinner over a just man, which frequently happens in the world, then there is confusion, not order'. He answers[4] by saying that 'the rule of man over man or of sinners over just men confounds the *ordo particularis*; but the order of universal justice is thereby made the greater and the more beautiful'. We may well doubt if Albert would have allowed that political authority as such amounted to a disturbance of the *ordo particularis*. Augustine's distinction between the two modes of providence is, likewise, identified[5] with his own distinction between the two senses of 'order'. Albert's interests lay elsewhere, and he felt no need to be more than perfunctory here. He relied on traditional, Augustinian, ideas for his views on slavery, on Aristotelian ideas for his views on politics; and the pressure to clarify their relations by-passed him.

His pupil, St. Thomas Aquinas, appears from the start to have been much more anxious to relate his Aristotelian ideas on society to the Augustinian views on subjection generally current in the schools in the 1250's. Although he had not yet a complete translation of Aristotle's *Politics* at his disposal, he could learn Aristotle's view of man as *animal politicum* from the *Ethics*,[6] a work already well known to him when he

[1] There is an extended discussion in *Sum. theol.* p. II, q. 26, m. 1, again on quite traditional lines, of two forms of subjection, the servitude which has its origin in sin, and subjection to those wiser or better, in accordance with the order of nature and reason. The latter has nothing in common with servitude, for one is freely subject to the other. Albert calls this form of subjection *subjectio providentiae et regiminis*. Although he is speaking of the angelic hierarchy of subordination, he clearly wishes to assimilate political authority to this form.

[2] Cf. . . . *de numero eorum quae sunt natura homini, id est quae sunt naturalia homini, civitas est, et communicatio civilis sive politica. Comm. in lib. Pol. Arist.* L. I, c. 1. [3] *Sum. theol.*, p. II, q. 63, m. 1, ob. 3. [4] Ibid., ad 3 m.

[5] Ibid., ad ult. qu. 1, referring to *De Gen. ad litt.* viii. 23. 44, discussed above, p. 75. [6] e.g. 1097^b11, 1162^a18, 1169^b18.

composed his *Scriptum super Sententiis*. In this, his earliest work, he already shows a concern to relate the two sets of ideas within a single framework.[1] That his way of dealing with the problem owes something to the current debates we may guess from his very selection of texts: they include the texts from Augustine and from Gregory which we have seen being repeatedly invoked. In his answer to the question whether there would have been authority (*praelatio seu dominium*) in the state of innocence, Thomas begins with distinguishing two 'modes' of authority: one is for the sake of government (*ad regimen ordinatus*), the other for the sake of domination (*ad dominandum*). With a reference to Aristotle's *Ethics* (apparently $1161^a30–^b10$), he remarks that the second mode is analogous to a tyrant's authority over his subjects, the first to a king's: for the former dominates over his subjects for his own benefit, the latter rules them for their good. The authority of domination could therefore exist in the state of innocence only over creatures made to subserve human purposes, not over other men; for men are not made to serve human ends. This subjection comes about only in so far as their condition is assimilated, as a consequence of sin, to that of irrational creatures. Only the authority of ruling men in their own interests could have belonged to man in his creational integrity.

The distinction between two 'modes' of authority is quite at home within a fundamentally Augustinian context. In *De civitate Dei*, xix. 14 Augustine had been speaking of two ways of exercising power; what Aquinas says about two 'modes' of *dominium* can be translated into Augustine's less formal speech without difficulty. He uses traditional material to state the distinction between tyrannical rule (assimilated naturally to the rule of a master over his slaves) and non-tyrannical. It is essentially the same distinction as Augustine had made between the ruler who rules *dominandi cupiditate* and the ruler who rules *officio consulendi*. On the matter of the exercise of power, and its harmony or lack of harmony with the order of nature, there is no disagreement between Aquinas and Augustine. A strain begins to show as soon as Aquinas turns to answering objections based on the Augustinian view of the institutions of human subjection. To reconcile them with his views, Thomas has to confine their significance by interpreting them as referring to the exercise of authority. Thus one objection[2] is based on Augustine's *dictum* that since man was made in the image of God, he was placed only above other creatures, not above his fellow men, over whom he would have no dominion but for sin; another,[3] based on the same chapter of *De civitate Dei*, asserts that since *dominium* implies

[1] *In Sent.* ii, D. 44, q. 1, a. 3. [2] Ibid., ob. 2. [3] Ibid., ob. 3.

servitus as its correlative and since the latter, as all the fathers agree, was introduced on account of sin, there could have been no *dominium* or *praelatio* in the absence of sin. Aquinas answers both together,[1] remarking that these statements refer to the second mode of authority, that of domination. This, of course, had been far from Augustine's intention; but it was a means that lay ready to hand to effect a reconciliation. But Aquinas was not content with as perfunctory and superficial a reconciliation as satisfied Albert. In the article we are considering, he goes on to examine political authority explicitly; and his procedure shows a real attempt to clarify in his own mind how far the Augustinian assessment of political authority is acceptable.

Having distinguished the two modes of *dominium*, of which only the one 'ordained for the sake of government' could have belonged to nature in its original integrity, he further considers this mode of authority in respect of three functions (*usus*) enumerated as follows: first, the direction of subjects in 'what is to be done'; second, the providing for needs such as common defence of the people against enemies; third, the correction of morals, 'so that the wicked may be coerced to perform the actions of virtue' by punishments. Of these functions, Aquinas says, only the first would have had a place in the absence of sin, for there would have been no need for the others. Thus, to secure agreement with Aristotle, Aquinas has driven a wedge into the substance of political authority. For Aristotle, as, indeed, for Augustine, political authority was not conceivable without coercive power. This belonged to its very essence, and this was one of the reasons why Augustine thought that all earthly kingdoms were, as institutions, rooted somehow in the dispensation of sin. Aquinas wished to concede this, and he also wanted to speak, with Aristotle, of the political order as an ordinance of nature. In his attempt to reconcile the two ways of thought, he left what Augustine would have regarded as the distinctive features of political authority in the world of fallen man; but he dissociated them as in some way adventitious to the essence of political authority, which could have existed without such features. He did not notice that in doing this he was in effect rejecting Augustine's protest against assimilating political to paternal authority. What Aquinas left on the side of nature, Augustine would not have recognized as 'political'. For Augustine the institutional life of the Roman Empire was still a daily reality. That he thought more readily of governmental institutions in concrete terms than Aquinas need cause no surprise. Even with the great acceleration in the growth of governmental institutions in his own

[1] Ibid., ad 2 m and *similiter* ad 3 m.

century, Aquinas could readily break down their institutional character into a series of 'functions' which could be isolated in this way.

If Thomas purchased agreement with Augustine by almost evacuating 'political authority' of meaning, his agreement with Aristotle was purchased at the same price. This appears from his manner of dealing with the objection that according to Aristotle[1] kings and other rulers had to be instituted in order to make laws with coercive power, a power lacking to mere exhortation by wise men; and that there would have been no need for this if men had remained in their original state of justice. Aquinas answers this[2] argument with the simple assertion that in respect of 'that function' (he refers to the coercive function) there would have been no authority in man's original state; whereas there would have been in respect of the other governmental functions.[3] It would have been just as unreal to Aristotle as to Augustine to drive a wedge into the substance of government in this way. He would no more have recognized political authority in the guise of a citizens' advice bureau than would Augustine.

There are many signs that Aquinas was dissatisfied with this manner of solving his problem. With his deepening appreciation of Aristotle, he came to see the full force of Aristotle's view that man is by nature *animal politicum*.[4] The view that man was by nature *animal sociale* was,

[1] *Eth.* 1179ᵃ33 f.

[2] Loc. cit., ad 4 m.

[3] Aquinas speaks of these in the plural. This must be a slip, as the article only allows one *usus* in the original state of innocence.

[4] St. Thomas's terminology and its development could be investigated with profit. I can see no grounds for the suggestion by W. Ullmann, op. cit. (p. 69 n.), p. 245, n. 2, that Aquinas's addition of *sociale* to Aristotle's *politicum* may have come from Macrobius. There is no evidence adduced for this in M. Schedler, *Die Philosophie des Macrobius und ihr Einfluss auf die Wissenschaft des christlichen Mittelalters* (*Beitr. z. Gesch. d. Phil. d. MA.*, 12 (1), 1916), referred to on this point by Dr. Ullmann, op. cit., p. 247, n. 2. Doubtless Macrobius was the source for much of the treatment of the political virtues, but the addition of *sociale* to *politicum* seems to me to have had no significance to Aquinas. The suggestion (made to me by Dr. M. J. Wilks) that the distinction between the two adjectives was forced on Aquinas by the discovery that Augustine could speak of a primitive order of society in which there was no coercion, whereas coercion is inseparable from Aristotle's conception of *politicum*, is attractive; but it requires testing against a survey of Aquinas's usage and its development. A cursory and far from exhaustive study of his language suggests to me that it is on the whole more likely that he began with an appreciation of Augustine's view of man as social by nature, and then came to see that Aristotle meant more than this by asserting that man was naturally *animal politicum* (or *civile*); and that as he came to see man in more thoroughly Aristotelian terms, he tended to expand the meaning of *sociale* so as to make it effectively synonymous with *politicum* (or *civile*). He uses the terms *civile*, e.g. *In Pol.* i, lect. 1, or *politicum*, e.g. *Sum. theol.* i–ii. 61. 5; *In Eth.* i, lect. 9; ix, lect. 10; but he speaks more often of man as *animal sociale*: e.g. *Sum. theol.* i. 96. 4; i–ii. 95. 4; ii–ii. 109. 3, ad 1; *Sum. c.*

by itself, entirely traditional, and could be found—on occasion in almost the very words—in Augustine.[1] With growing understanding of Aristotle, Thomas came to see that Aristotle's views on man as *animal politicum* were more far-reaching than the traditional view of him as *sociale*;[2] and he was clear that from the Aristotelian point of view there could be no distinction between *politicum* and *sociale*, as if the former were no more than a particular form or species of the latter. Social existence, in Aristotle's perspective, was identical with political existence. The *polis* was not society plus political structure, and a 'society' without political structure would have been even less than chimerical in his eyes: for at least a chimera could be imaginatively constructed from elements experienced separately. If for Aristotle a society which[3] was not political was meaningless, it was not so for Augustine and the Christian fathers. For Aristotle the archetypal society was the *polis*; for them it was the family of the saints in heaven. For them there could be a real distinction between that kind of society and the politically organized society which they knew in the Empire. From their point of view 'social' and 'political' were by no means synonymous concepts, as they had to be for Aristotle. As St. Thomas came to regard society increasingly from an Aristotelian standpoint, it is not surprising that in his vocabulary, too, *sociale* and *politicum* should have tended to lose their distinctive features. The profound significance of St. Thomas's Aristotelian view of society is entirely beyond the scope of this paper, though its growth in his mind could still profitably be mapped with more precision than it has yet received. We must return to his understanding of Augustine's view, and consider how he interpreted it later

Gent., iii. 117, 128, 129, 147; *In Eth.* i, lect. 1. Sometimes he uses *sociale et* (or *vel*) *politicum*, e.g. *Sum. theol.* i–ii. 72. 4; *Sum. c. Gent.* iii. 85; *De reg. princ.* i. 1. Schilling asserts (*SSLThom.*, pp. 80–81) that Aquinas distinguished the two concepts and only used them as synonymous where this did not affect his argument. I can find no support for this view in the references he gives. I am inclined to agree with I. T. Eschmann's judgement: 'unless special reasons suggested to Aquinas the exact textual reproduction of the Aristotelian principle [that man is a *political* animal] he prefers to say that man is a *social* animal'. (*St. Thomas on Kingship*, translated by G. B. Phelan, with introduction and notes by I. T. Eschmann (Toronto, 1949), p. 4, n. 2). Generally speaking, the terms appear to be used interchangeably.

[1] Cf. above, pp. 73, n. 2; 76, 82.

[2] One of the many indications of his increasing appreciation of the far-reaching implications of Aristotle's view has been noted by Fr. Eschmann, loc. cit., p. 4, n. 3, who draws attention to the fact that St. Thomas gradually came to the view that Avicenna's arguments for man's being naturally a social animal ceased to satisfy Aquinas because they were 'incapable of demonstrating the conclusion that man is a *political animal*' (italics in text).

[3] I am, of course, excluding, for this purpose, lesser groupings such as the household or small community.

in his career, after the Aristotelian vision of society had established itself more deeply in his mind.

The one occasion when Aquinas returns to consider our two chapters of Augustine's *De civitate Dei* is in connexion with his restatement of his views on the origins of authority in his *Summa theologiae*. The framework within which he places his article[1] on man's dominion over man in the state of innocence is entirely traditional. It follows articles devoted to man's authority over the lower creation, original equality of men, and so forth. His answer to the question about dominion over men is also, at first sight, impeccably traditional. It begins with a distinction between two kinds of *dominium* reminiscent, but not identical with, the early distinction we have considered. Where the early work contrasted two mutually exclusive modes of authority, one exercised for the benefit of the master, the other for that of the subject, we now find the distinction drawn between authority as a general concept (*secundum quod communiter refertur ad subjectum qualitercumque*), related to any form of subjection, and authority in a special sense, understood as the correlative of servitude. This latter could not have existed in the state of innocence; the former could. This way of stating the distinction between two sorts of *dominium* may be logically equivalent to the earlier manner of speaking; but it creates a much firmer impression that Thomas wishes to affirm, in the first place, that *dominium* does belong to the state of nature before the fall. Instead of asserting that in one mode it did and another it did not exist in the state of innocence, he now says that *dominium* belongs to this state, except for one form of it, the form found in slavery. Another difference between this and the earlier treatment is noteworthy: whereas the two 'modes' of authority distinguished had been two ways of exercising authority, the contrast is here drawn in institutional terms: it is between authority as existing in slavery and authority as existing, among other institutions, in the 'office of governing free men'.

The crucial difference, however, between this and the earlier treatment of the same theme is the greater simplicity and assurance with which Thomas now speaks. The hesitations and qualifications which he had found necessary are now gone; most significantly, the further enumeration of the three 'functions' of authority is omitted. The purpose of that enumeration had been to discuss the extent to which authority *ad regimen ordinatus* could be found in the institutions of political authority. Aquinas was, at the time, still too much of a traditionalist to be prepared to throw to the winds Augustine's insistence

[1] i. 96. 4.

that these institutions, with their necessarily coercive character, were infected with the dispensation of sin. He had sought to reconcile Augustine and Aristotle by dividing political authority into three functions and allocating one of these to nature, the others to sin. Now he treats political authority as all of a piece; and it belongs to the institutions grounded in nature. What Aquinas had come to discern in the course of the ten years or so between the two works was that coercive power belonged indivisibly to the stuff of political existence. There can be no doubt that this insight came to him with his growing understanding of Aristotle's political theory.[1] The insight excluded the possibility of compromise on the lines that he had experimented with in his youth.

In his explanation for the reason of his opinion Aquinas remarks that a subject is ruled in servile fashion in so far as he is ruled for his master's benefit; and this conflicts with the primitive order of nature. A subject is governed, however, as a free man, in so far as he is directed to his own good or the common good; and this sort of dominion must have existed before the fall, for man is by nature a social animal, and social life, according to Aristotle, would be impossible without a directive authority. The appeal to Aristotle underlines what is in any case clear: Aquinas is thinking in terms of genuine political authority with the full apparatus of governmental machinery and the power of enforcement. This is what is now traced, unambiguously, to an origin in nature. The break with the Augustinian theory of the origins of political authority appears to be complete. But Aquinas invokes *De civitate Dei*, xix. 14–15 in the course of a second argument added to prove that authority over free men would have existed in the state of innocence. It would have been inconvenient, he says, if those with a superabundance of wisdom and justice could not have devoted their superior gifts to the service of others less well endowed. 'Wherefore Augustine says that "the just rule

[1] The extent to which the unitary conception of political authority is derived from Aristotle appears strikingly in *Sum. theol.* i. 92. 1 ad 2 m, where *subjectio civilis* is coupled with *subjectio oeconomica* and contrasted with *subjectio servilis*. References to passages in which Aquinas can be seen to assume that the power of coercing refractory subjects belongs to the essence of political authority could be multiplied. The following must suffice here: *Sum. theol.* i–ii. 95. 1; *In Eth.* x, lect. 14; *In Pol.* i, lect. 1. It is most explicitly argued in *In Pol.* iii, lect. 5. Most revealing, perhaps, is the surprising presence of the idea in as unhospitable a context as that provided by the pseudo-Dionysius's speculations on the angelic hierarchy; cf. *In div. nom.*, ch. 12. Schilling (*SSLThom.* p. 48) recognized that coercive power was for St. Thomas included in political authority; he refers to *Sum. theol.* i–ii. 105. 2 and *In Pol.* iii, lect. 9 to substantiate the view that judicial and penal systems belong to the essence of the state as conceived by St. Thomas. It is Schilling's attempt to father on Augustine the view that all this belongs to the order of nature (ibid., p. 101) which must be rejected.

not through a desire for power but through an obligation to give guidance; this is what the order of nature prescribes, this is how God created man".'[1] Augustine's admonition to people occupying a position of authority has been finally turned on its head: the obligation to act as a *paterfamilias* rather than as a tyrant is turned into a justification of precisely the thing Augustine wished to deny: that political society is, like a family, a natural institution. Augustine's wholesale exclusion of all human dominion of man over man from the state of innocence is quoted as an objection;[2] Aquinas's imperious reply to all the objections, that they are valid only against the first mode of authority—authority over a servile subject—conceals a radical change of attitude to political authority. It is scarcely surprising to find St. Thomas using, among his favourite models for political authority, the analogies rejected by Augustine. Without misgiving he returns, time and again, to the image of political authority as modelled on the relation of soul and body, or of God and the world.[3]

Augustine and the tradition which he helped to inspire may not have been always wholly clear about the meaning of 'nature'.[4] But both Augustine, and some, at least, of his followers were clear enough about a radical difference they detected between the kind of authority and subjection to be found in the family and the kind found in slavery. In its essentials, this basic dichotomy was retained by Aquinas. The real problem lay in answering the question as to which side of the dividing line political authority was to be placed. Aquinas's first answer to this question had been, in effect, to evade its force. He had tried to split political authority by drawing the line across its very substance. Later, with increasing insight into the meaning of 'political authority', acquired through Aristotle, he came to discern the unsatisfactory character of his compromise. He now opted unambiguously for what, from the

[1] *Sum. theol.* i. 96. 4, quoting *De civ. Dei*, xix. 14–15; cf. above, pp. 70 f.

[2] Loc. cit., ob. 1.

[3] e.g. *De reg. princ.* i. 1, 9; ii. 1 (= i. 12); *Sum. c. Gent.* iii. 78. The analogy between political authority and the two ways in which the mind rules its body: *Sum. theol.* i. 81. 3 ad 2 m; i–ii. 58. 2; 9. 2 ad 3 m; 17. 7, &c. *In Pol.* i, lect. 3 reveals its source. Interestingly, Aristotle's application of the analogy differs slightly from Cicero's version found in and rejected by Augustine.

[4] This consideration has been given more weight, I believe, than it deserves in this context by Dr. W. Ullmann, op. cit. (p. 69 n.), pp. 238 f. Whether Augustine had an adequately clear conception of 'nature' or not, he was as clear as he was emphatic that subjection was of two kinds, typified by servile subjection and by subjection to parental authority respectively. Aquinas certainly drew the line more carefully in giving the concept of 'nature' greater precision (as Bonaventure had also done); but the crucial break with Augustine's theory lay in transferring political authority from one side of the line to the other (as Bonaventure had refused to do).

Augustinian standpoint, was a revolutionary view. He was too clear-sighted to be unaware of this revolution in political thinking. He had understood the Augustinian theology of society clearly enough, and loyalty to its tradition made him wish to fit his Aristotelian views into its framework. His understanding of Augustine's views Thomas shared with Bonaventure; with Albert he shared the fascination of the new Aristotelian vision of human society. Without a very much fuller study of contemporary debates, his originality in the way he accomplished the revolutionary transition from the one to the other tradition cannot be assessed. It is clear, however, that of the writers here considered, at any rate, he alone combined an appreciation of the real significance of Augustine's views with a growing, and in the end triumphant, commitment to Aristotle's ideas on man as *animal civile*. As the new ideas took a deeper hold in his mind and served to crystallize his fundamental thought about man in society, the tensions proved insurmountable. He knew he had in effect broken with the old tradition, that the whole perspective of his thought had altered. It was no longer a matter of interpreting Aristotle within a traditional framework, but of fitting Augustine—by manhandling him, if need be—into the Aristotelian scheme.

The new preoccupations of political thinkers of the age of Boniface VIII, and the fourteenth-century controversies about dominion by grace,[1] were soon to eclipse the problem with which we have watched Aquinas grapple. New calls were made on Augustine's theology of authority, which are not our concern here.[2] We may, however, catch a last glimpse of Augustine's two chapters in a writer who stands on the confines of the intellectual worlds of Aquinas and of the world of the papalist theologians of the fourteenth century, Ptolemy of Lucca, his disciple and the continuator of his work on kingship, which has come down to us, completed by Ptolemy, as *De regimine principum*. Both in his continuation of Thomas's work[3] and in his *Determinatio compendiosa de jurisdictione imperii*[4] Ptolemy refers to *De civitate Dei*, xix. 14–15. It would be out of place to consider his arguments—such as they are—in this paper. The transition from Augustine's words to Aristotle's *Politics*, effected in both passages without the slightest misgiving, is part of his inheritance from St. Thomas and was only made possible for him by his master's work. There is no trace here of any

[1] An early appearance of our theme within the new context of debate can be seen in James of Viterbo, *De reg. Christ.* ii. 3.

[2] The most stimulating discussion of these known to me is the recent work of M. J. Wilks, *The Problem of Sovereignty in the Later Middle Ages* (Cambridge, 1963).

[3] *De reg. princ.* iii. 9.

[4] ch. 17.

sense of tensions of thought, no trace of an inward struggle to reconcile a cherished tradition with new insight. Without scrutiny, all roads can now be assumed to lead in the same direction. Ptolemy of Lucca was the herald of a comfortable obliviousness to a profound cleavage in the tradition of Christian political thought.[1]

That the cleavage between Augustine's theology of political existence and the teaching of Christian Aristotelians is a matter of political thought perhaps requires some defence. Speculations about the kind of authority which might have existed in the Garden of Eden are not obviously and immediately relevant to an assessment of political life and institutions as experienced by actual human beings. Even such fine scholars as R. W. and A. J. Carlyle could altogether by-pass the political significance of the patristic and Augustinian denial that the state is a natural institution with a contemptuous reference[2] to 'these curiously unhistorical and infelicitous interpretations of human institutions', and their replacement by 'the sane and penetrating conceptions of Aristotle'. In a general way, of course, the assertion that political authority belongs to nature obviously serves to heighten its importance and dignity.[3] But to be content with this observation is to fail to appreciate the fundamental divergence between the two conceptions of political authority. What is involved is a radical disagreement, expressed in perhaps quasi-mythological terms, about the purpose of political authority and the meaning of freedom in society.

The older tradition which Augustine took up had perhaps been clearer in its insistence than was Augustine himself that to regard the Roman state as a divine dispensation for sinful men was at once an

[1] The same assumption can be seen at work in the treatment of this theme by Giles of Rome. Political authority is essentially bound up with man's social existence, as Giles insists, in entirely Aristotelian language, equating *vita politica* with *vita socialis*. This being, in his view, natural to man, he interprets the opening statements of Augustine's *De civitate Dei*, xix. 15 as referring only to slavery. See his *in Sent.* ii, D. 44, q. 1, a. 2–3. The assumption that Aquinas and Augustine were asserting the same view of the origins of political authority and subjection had a long future. Its history in Christian political thought of Aristotelian inspiration and its effects on some of the social attitudes encouraged by it would make a fascinating study.

[2] Op. cit. (p. 69, n.), v (1928), p. 6.

[3] Thus E. Lewis, for instance, rightly remarks that 'the Aquinist view of the state obviously implies a more positive view of the functions of government within the state' (*Medieval Political Ideas*, i (London, 1954), p. 151). Even Otto Schilling, notwithstanding his resolve to effect a far-reaching *rapprochement* between Augustine and Aquinas, notes that the Augustinian approach lays greater stress on the limitations of state-power than does the Aristotelian (Cf. *SSLThom*, pp. 60–61).

endorsement of its legitimate authority and a reminder of the restricted sphere of its competence. That state, like all others, originated in sin, and its purpose was both punitive and remedial. Political authority and its coercive agencies exist for the purpose of coping with the consequences of man's sin, with the disorganization and conflict endemic in the human condition; to prevent men from devouring each other like fish, in Irenaeus's graphic image.[1] The sphere of the state is social order, security, material needs; the state is not a means of salvation. Augustine shared the basic insights of this way of thinking. In his *De civitate Dei* he restated them powerfully against the views to which the christianization of the Empire during the fourth century had given rise. In his day it was almost the current orthodoxy to think of the Roman Empire as a divinely appointed vehicle of human salvation; and at least one of the central strands in his work on the Two Cities is the rejection of this view of the Empire and, with it, of any human society whatsoever.[2] The sphere of the state, as it emerges from book xix of his great work, is the region of overlap between the two eschatologically distinct societies, the earthly and the heavenly cities. Political authority, so we may paraphrase its seventeenth chapter, exists to secure those purposes in the pursuit of which all its subjects are united, whether their ultimate allegiance is to God or to their own selfish ends. Whichever of the two 'cities' men belong to by their ultimate allegiance, they have a common interest in 'earthly peace', though the quality of their concern for it will differ according to where their ultimate loyalties lie. This 'earthly peace' comprises the sphere of economic necessity and public order and defence.[3] This is the state's concern.

The particular strand of Augustine's political reflection which we have considered here is one which allies him with Christian thinkers of a period before the official recognition granted to Christianity by the Empire, and with Donatist and other schismatic writers opposed to the imperial state-Church.[4] There is, of course, much in Augustine's political thought that dissociates him sharply from this tradition of thought. It is enough to refer to his tragic, if not wholly unprepared, conversion to the policy of *coge intrare*. With his endorsement of the

[1] *Adv. haer.* v. 24. 2.

[2] Cf. my paper 'The Roman Empire in early Christian Historiography', *Downside Rev.* lxxxi (1963), pp. 340–54, with a note on the relevant literature.

[3] This is suggested by what Augustine says in *De civ. Dei*, xix. 13. 2 when he observes that God endowed man with 'the goods appropriate to this life that is the temporal peace required for the sustenance and safety of this earthly life, and whatever is necessary for the defence and recovery of this peace . . .'.

[4] On these, cf. W. H. C. Frend, 'The Roman Empire in the eyes of Western Schismatics during the Fourth Century A.D.', *Misc. hist. eccles.* (Stockholm, 1960), pp. 9–22.

policy of imperial coercion of heretics at least one of the main lines of his intellectual development was given a new twist. Only when the development of the whole relevant range of his thought is taken into account[1] shall we be in a position to see how far the Donatist controversy and its exigencies obscured the central core of Augustine's political thought. In any case, the complexity of its development and the variety of its themes assured Augustine of the possibility of finding a place for the state enforcement of orthodoxy and morality within a body of thought which was not, fundamentally, hospitable to ideas of this kind. His famous letter[2] to Vincent, Rogatist bishop of Cartenna, was in some ways an expression of those very views which he attacked in the *De civitate Dei*. But traces of views like those expressed in the letter to Vincent survive even in this very differently orientated work; and they find clear expression in other writings. There are elements in Augustine's mature political thought which tend to undermine his attack on any conception of human institutions, of the Roman Empire in particular, as the vehicle of salvation for men.

If Augustine was compromised on the subject of the range of legitimate political authority, on the scope to be allowed it in enforcing morality and orthodoxy, Aquinas saw the issues at stake with greater clarity. It is neither necessary nor possible to sketch here the systematic coherence between his views on its functions as an agency of enforcing Christian morality and orthodoxy, and his views on the state as a natural institution. It will scarcely be questioned that these views form, by and large, part of a single systematic exploration of the implications of his Aristotelian theory of political authority. He perceived the radical divergence between his own views on these subjects, and the views implied by Augustine's theology of authority and subjection. Nothing illustrates this divergence better than the two different conceptions of freedom involved.

Augustinian and Aristotelian theologians were agreed that any subjection which restricts the subject's liberty cannot have belonged to nature in its original state. The Augustinian tradition, in excluding political authority from this state, implied that any interference with a subject's activities constitutes a restriction of his freedom. It may be a salutary and necessary restriction; but for all that, a man is unfree

[1] Despite the full and fair treatment by H. A. Deane, *The Political and Social Ideas of St. Augustine* (New York and London, 1963), we are still far from possessing such an account. On the problem of religious coercion and Augustine's attitude to it the most penetrating study is the paper read at the Fourth International Conference on Patristic Studies, Oxford, 1963, by P. R. L. Brown, *Journal of Roman Studies*, liv (1964), pp. 107–16.

[2] *Ep.* 93.

to the extent that he is coerced against his will. Political authority conceived as grounded in human nature implies a totally different conception of liberty. It becomes an agent of men's true interests, which only their shortcomings conceal from them. In securing the true goal of man, authority may override his actual wishes without thereby restricting his freedom, for it will express the 'free' choice of what Sir Isaiah Berlin has called[1] 'his "true", albeit submerged and inarticulate self'. St. Thomas had, of course, no difficulty in agreeing that slavery was incompatible with freedom;[2] but the grounds on which he establishes this are not that this kind of subjection is a curtailment of the range in which men can act as they wish unhindered by other men, but that it curtails it without regard to their own good. The subjection of free men to their ruler implies no diminution of their freedom, so long as they are ruled for their own or for the common good. In exercising this kind of dominion over his subjects, a ruler 'rules over another *ut libero*',[3] and such a ruler 'is appropriately called the servant of his subjects'.[4] Augustine had exhorted rulers to act thus; but he had no illusions about political authority, even when exercised in accordance with the order of nature, amounting to a restriction of men's freedom. His account of the origins of political authority brings into play what Sir Isaiah Berlin has called the 'negative concept of freedom': the sense according to which any coercion implies a diminution of liberty. St. Thomas's conception relies on the 'positive sense', according to which the purpose for which a man is coerced determines whether his freedom is being restricted or not. What is at stake between the two conceptions of political authority, in the end, is the meaning of freedom.

R. A. Markus

[1] *Two Concepts of Liberty* (Oxford, 1958), p. 18.

[2] The argument of *Sum. theol.* i. 96. 4 on slavery is anticipated in *in Sent.* ii, D. 44, q. 1, a. 3, ad 1 m, in reply to the famous passage of Gregory's *Moralia* (xxi. 15. 22), which asserts man's original freedom.

[3] *Sum. theol.* i. 96. 4. The phrase by itself does not, of course, imply that a man is free even though coerced. It can be taken to mean that he is free in no more than a legal sense, i.e. that he is not a slave. But St. Thomas's argument does in fact presuppose that a man remains free in being coerced, provided that it is for his own or the common good.

[4] *In Sent.* ii, D. 44, q. 1, a. 3, ad 1 m.

[11]

ROMAN LAW IN THE WORKS OF ST. AUGUSTINE*

REVEREND FRANCESCO LARDONE†

ONE may inquire whether the study of the writings of the early Fathers from a legal point of view is only a matter of culture or if it has any practical importance. It is the aim of this paper to show that such a study has a practical importance not only in the field of law, but even in that of theology. Here we are concerned only with the writings of St. Augustine. The writings of this Father present many phases, because he was a theologian, a philosopher, a moralist, an historian, a writer, an orator, a jurist.[1]

The juridical culture of Augustine is very extensive. In his writings he covers the entire field of law; public and private law; constitutional and penal law; and in private law, the law of persons, the substantive law and the adjective law. Really he did not intend to put down legal writings; above all he was a Father, so he cannot be called a jurist in a strict sense, although we can be sure that he knew the law.

It is a mystery how Augustine acquired his legal culture. Perhaps he engaged in the study of law in his youth, during his training as a rhetorician and orator. Perhaps he continued this study for the sake of culture with his companion and pupil Alipius, who was a lawyer. It seems that he had the ambition to secure a "Praesidatus," *i. e.*, of becoming an officer of the Roman administrative and judiciary machine.[2] If so, we can take for

* List of abbreviations: C. = Code of Justinian; C. Th. = Theodosian Code; D. = Digest; G. = Institutes of Gaius; I. = Institutes of Justinian; M. = Migne (Patrology); XII T. = 12 Tables.

† Professor of Roman Law, Catholic University of America; author of *Imperial Constitutions of Theodosius II and the Council of Ephesus* (1932) 20 GEORGETOWN LAW JOURNAL 456.

1 In 1930 the Catholic University of Milan, Italy, on the occasion of the fifteenth centenary of St. Augustine's death (Aug. 28, 430, A. D.), commemorated his multifarious activities in a volume: ST. AGOSTINO; Milano, *Societa Editrice*, VITA E PENSIERO.

2 Conf. 6, 11.

granted he would have also a juridical qualification for such an office. But anyhow we are sure he had a large amount of legal culture, and this is evidenced by his writings.

The writings of St. Augustine are very numerous, and it is not our purpose even to name them. The most complete collection of his works numbers 15 volumes in quarto of about 1000 pages each; it was edited by Migne in his Patrology. This is the edition quoted in this article.[3] Evidently the huge quantity of Augustine's writings renders the enterprise of a research more difficult. Perhaps this furnishes an explanation of the lack of existing studies on St. Augustine as a jurist. In this kind of work it is customary to look into all the writings of a Father. This difficulty of research explains also why this paper is incomplete, in the sense that the research has not been exhaustive; I confess I did not read the fifteen volumes. From this point of view this paper aims to be only an essay, a sample, of the legal culture of St. Augustine.[4]

The number of Augustinian passages of legal flavor is tremendous. Moreover, as I have said, they cover the entire field of law. A selection was therefore imperative. The passages registered here refer to the branch of private law and specifically to some institutions of substantive law. An explanation for this is necessary. The search for legal fragments in early patristic literature concerns, of course, the system of law in force at those times, *i. e.*, Roman Law. In such a research one of the most important points is to see whether the Fathers were fostering Roman Law conceptions, accepted Roman Law viewpoints, or they opposed it, trying to reform it. In a word, through the Fathers one sees the possible influence of Christian Doctrine in Roman Law. In this big question, nowadays, the Romanists admit the influence of Christianity in Roman Law in various fields. One point, however, is still under discussion; whether Christian conceptions had any bearing in the field of substantive law. Dr. Riccobono favors

[3] It was necessary to quote Augustinian passages in their original Latin here, because even an ideal translation cannot render the precision of the legal Latin terms.

[4] Here I submit only a few passages of those I have found.

this view.[5] Starting the research on St. Augustine I had this question in mind; that explains therefore the reason why the Augustinian passages registered here refer to substantive law.

ON OWNERSHIP

On the Nature of Ownership.	In *Joann. Evangel. Tract.* 6, 25;	M. 3, 1437
	Enarr. in Ps. 49, 17;	M. 4, 576
On the Use of Riches.	*Sermo.* 50, 4;	M. 5, 327
	Epist. III cl., *epist.* 153, 26;	M. 2, 665
On the Superfluous.	*Sermo.* 206, 2;	M. 5, 1041
	Enarr. in Ps. 147, 12;	M. 4, 1922
On Heredity.	*De diver. quaest.* 83, 75, 1;	M. 6, 86
	Enarr. in Ps. 49, 2;	M. 4, 565
	Enarr. in Ps. 36, 18;	M. 4, 393

In substantive law ownership is a fundamental institution. St. Augustine dealing with this matter shows his technical knowledge of the Roman Law conception of the right of property, but he patronizes the more liberal Christian conception.

These two paragraphs[6] evidence a fundamental dis-

[5] RICCOBONO, *Influenza del Cristianesimo sulla Codificazione di Guistiniano* (1900, Bologna) *Riv. Scientia.*

[6] In *Joann. Evang. Tract.* 6, 25; Migne 3, 1437: "*. . . jure divino, Domini est terra et plenitudo ejus: pauperes et divites una terra supportat. Jure tamen humano . . . haec villa mea est, haec domus mea, hic servus meus. Jure ergo humano, jure imperatorum. Vultis legamus leges imperatorum, et secundum ipsas agamus de villis? Si jure humano vultis possidere, recitemus leges imperatorum. Sed quid mihi est imperator? Secundum jus ipsius possides terram. Aut tolle jura imperatorum, et quis audet dicere: mea est illa villa, aut meus est ille servus, aut domus haec mea est? . . .*"

Enarr. in Ps. 49, 17; M. 4, 576: "*. . . mea sunt illa (bestiae ferae) quae non possides, mea sunt ista (pecora) quae possides (dicit Dominus). Si enim servus es tu, totum peculium tuum meum est. Neque enim est peculium domini quod sibi servus comparavit, et non erit peculium Domini quod ipse Dominus servo creavit? Ergo meae sunt bestiae silvae quas tu non cepisti: mea sunt et pecora in montibus quae tua sunt, et boves qui sunt ad praesepe tuum: omnia mea sunt, quia ego creavi ea.*"

tinction made by Augustine in matter of ownership. According to the law of man, the law of the Emperors, the property of the world is fractioned, divided, and we speak of this house of mine, of your slave, etc. But according to the law of God, the whole property, the earth, belongs to God. How, therefore, can one say "This house is mine, that is yours, that is your slave?" (In *Joann. Evangel. Tract.* 6, 25.)

In *Enarr. in Ps.* 49, 17, he passes to analyze more closely what is property for man.

Note here his accurate terminology. "Only God owns," and Augustine uses the *"meum esse,"* the classical legal expression for ownership, the Roman dominium. For property of man he uses *"possessio,"* which renders the meaning of possession versus *"dominium,"* of holding a thing vs. that of owning it. He illustrates this expression further with the example of slaves. A slave cannot own, he simply possesses. The possession of a slave is legally called *"peculium."* The *peculium* is owned by the master of the slave, the slave simply possesses it, whether it has been given him by his master, or it has been acquired by the slave himself. God is the Master, man compared with God, is like a slave, he is God's creature.

From this Christian conception of ownership, that is, that man has not the real ownership of his property, but is only a possessor of it, a user, Augustine draws practical conclusions: one must use his possessions fairly; one must give the superfluous to the poor.

On the Use of Riches.[7] St. Augustine here speaks of the

[7] *Sermo* 50, 4; M. 5, 327: *Illius est ergo aurum et argentum qui novit uti auro et argento. Nam etiam inter ipsos homines tunc quisque habere aliquid dicendus est, quando bene utitur. Nam quod juste non tractat, jure non tenet. Quod autem jure non tenet, si suum esse dixerit, non erit vox justi possessoris, sed impudentis incubatoris improbitas."*

Epist. Cl. III, *epist.* 153, 26; M. 2, 665: ". . . *nonne omnes qui sibi videntur gaudere licite conquisitis, eisque uti nesciunt, aliena possidere convincimus? Hoc enim certum alienum non est, quod jure possidetur: hoc autem jure quod juste, et hoc juste quod bene. Omne igitur quod male possidetur alienum est; male autem possidet qui male utitur. . . Sed inter haec tolleratur iniquitas male habentium, et quaedam inter eos jura constituuntur, quae appellantur civilia: non quod hinc ut bene utentes sint, sed ut male utentes minus molesti sint. . ."*

fair use of worldy possessions. In his dialectical ability he forms a kind of sorites here; it is according to the right what is right, it is right what is good, therefore what is not good, it is not according to the right, *"jure quod juste, juste quod bene . . . igitur quod male possidetur alienum est."* This in scholastic terminology could be rendered thus: "Mine and right are reversible, therefore what is right is mine, and what is not right cannot be mine."

This Augustinian conception, so striking as it is rendered here, was not entirely foreign to Roman Law before the time of Augustine, if we remember the fragment of Gaius "One ought not to misuse his right"[8] *(Male . . . nostro iure uti non debemus),* but such a doctrine was not developed until later, particularly in the codification of Justinian. Then it took deeper root, a more definite form in the doctrine that prohibits the unfair use of one's right. So the Augustinian expressions seem to be a kind of anticipation in this legal development of property conception. Augustine himself points here to some provisions of civil law in this matter, but of course they are faint, they aim not to the "better use" of possessions, but only to the "less noxious" use.

On the Superfluous. To give the superfluous to the poor, is therefore but a consequence of the stated doctrine, and Augustine says that the superfluous is not in our ownership and we must give it away.[9]

On Heredity. In matter of acquisition of property there are some Augustinan fragments which deal about hereditary succession, and precisely about the title of succession. St. Augustine talks about this matter in a figurative way, explaining theological conceptions and using for that purpose Roman Law terminology.

St. Paul says that Christians are "the heirs of God, and

[8] G. 1, 53.

[9] *Sermo,* 206, 2; M. 5, 1041:". . . *Intelligit animus christianus, quantum remotus esse debit a fraude alienae rei; quando sentet simile esse fraudi, si superflua sua non tribuerit indigenti."*

Enarr. in Ps. 147, 12; M. 4, 1922:*Caetera quae superflua jacent, aliorum sunt necessaria. Superflua divitum, necessaria sunt pauperum. Res alienae possidentur cum superflua possidentur."*

joint heirs of Christ,"[10] and Augustine explains how that happens.[11]

Note here how he stresses the title of succession to God, the filiation from God; and the brotherhood with Christ. These are the strongest titles also in Roman Law.

He stresses the point of the joint heredity of Christ and Christians.[12]

An important matter in case of succession was not only to have a title but to have a good judge at hand who would assess the patrimony of the heredity to the title-holder, because it happened also in the days of Roman Law that quarrels, counter-claims, were frequent in such instances. And Augustine comes in to assure the Christians they will find a good judge in God Himself who is at one time the Testator and the Judge.[13]

---

[10] Ad. Rom. VIII, 17.

[11] *De diversis quaest.* 83, 75, 1; M. 6, 86: "*Sicut Apostolus ad Hebraeos dicit 'testamentum testatoris morte firmatur'; propterea mortuo pro nobis Christo, Novum Testamentum firmatum esse asserit. . . Si ergo queramus quomodo simus, secundum ejusdem Apostoli verba 'cohaeredes Christi, et filii atque haeredes Dei': cum etiam hereditas morte decessoris firma teneatur, nec ullo alio modo possit hereditas intelligi; respondetur, ipso quidem mortuo factos nos esse haeredes, quoniam et filii ejus etiam dicti sumus. . . Haeredes ergo ejus dicimur, quia reliquit nobis pacis ecclesiasticae possessionem. . . Cohaeredes autem ejus efficiemur, cum in fine saeculi mors absorbetur in victoriam. Tunc enim similes Ei erimus, quanto videbimus eum sicuti est. . .*"

[12] *Enarr. in Ps.* 49, 2; M. 4, 565: "*Tanta enim charitas est in illo haerede (Christo), ut voluerit habere cohaeredes. Quis hoc avarus homo velit habere cohaeredes? Sed et qui invenitur velle dividit cum eis haereditatem, minus habens ipse dividens quam si solus possideret: haereditas autem in qua cohaeredes Christi sumus, non minuitur copia possessorum, nec fit angustior numerositate cohaeredum; sed tanta est multis quanta paucis, tanta singulis quanta omnibus.*"

[13] *Enarr. in Ps.* 36, 18; M. 4, 393: "*Fratres . . . custodite hereditatem nostram de qua securi sumus nos in testamento Patris nostri esse: non in aliqua charta frivola alicujus hominis, sed in testamento Patris nostri. Inde securi sumus: quia qui fecit testamentum haeredi suo ipse judicabit de testamento suo. In rebus humanis alius est testator, alius judex: et tamen qui tenet testamentum, vincit apud judicem alterum, non apud alterum judicem mortuum. Quam ergo secura est nostra victoria, cum ille judicabit qui testatus est, etsi enim mortuus est Christus ad tempus, sed jam vivit in aeternum.*"

ON OBLIGATIONS

On *Mutuum. commodatum.* *De Ser., Dom. in monte.* lib. 1, c. 20, 68. M. 3, 1263.
On *Usura, fenus.* *Epist.* cl. II, *epist.* 43, 25. M. 2, 665.
Serm. ad popul., Serm. 39, 6. Migne, 5, 239.
Serm. 358, 5. Migne, 5, 1586.
Enarr. in Ps. 36, 26. M. 4, 1386.
Ps. 54, 12. M. 4, 638.
On *Depositum.* *Enarr. in Ps.* 52, 9. M. 4, 618.
Ps. 57, 2. M. 4, 674.
De Spiritu et Littera, 31, 54. M. 10, 235.
On *Emptio, Venditio.* *Serm.* 177, 3. M. 5, 910.
Serm. 177, 10. M. 5, 959.
Enarr. in Ps. 70, *Serm.* 1, 17. M. 4, 886.
Serm. 329, 1. M. 5, 1454.
Serm. 336, 4. M. 5, 1473.
On *Locatio Operarum.* *Enarr. in Ps.* 93, 12. M. 4, 1201.
Serm. 223, 1. M. 5, 1112.
On *Furtum.* *Quest. in Heuptath.* 284. M. 3, 627.
On *Injuria.* *Enarr. in Ps.* 145, 15. M. 4, 1894.
De Serm. Dom. in monte lib. 1, 62 and 66. M. 3, 1263.
On *Restitution.* *Serm.* 178, 8. M. 5, 963.
Epist. cl. III, ep. 153. M. 2, 663.
On *Dolus.* *In Joann. Evangel. Tract.* 7, 1, 18. M. 3, 1446.
Enarr. in Ps. 14, 3. M. 4, 143.
Ps. 5, 8. M. 11, 86
On *Plus Petitio.* *Enarr. in Ps.* 118, *Serm.* 11, 6. M, 4, 1531.

This section deals with personal rights. Roman Law sources classify this matter in two items: obligations arising from agreement or contracts *(obligationes ex contractu);* and obligations arising not from agreement but from the contingency of certain facts, *e. g.,* torts (*obligationes ex delicto, etc*). Here we contemplate examples of contracts; *mutuum, commodatum, depositum,* sale, the contract of labor, and examples of delicts: theft, and insults.

On Mutuum, Commodatum, Donatio.[14] *Mutuum* is a loan of money or of things which are consumed by using them, *e. g.*, wine, oil, etc., with the agreement that the borrower has the obligation to return the same amount of the same quality he has received. *Commodatum,* on the contrary, consists of a loan of things not consumable by use, *e. g.*, a barrel, a carriage, etc. The essential element of *mutuum* and *commodatum* consists in the obligation of returning what has been borrowed.

Donatio, a promise to make a gratuity, creates also an obligation, but of course, here it is essential that the thing given must not be returned.

St. Augustine shows a thorough knowledge of these three Roman obligations, and puts two questions thereof. First, when a Christian makes a gratuity to his brother for the sake of charity, this donation could even be considered as a loan, because although his brother does not make any return, God Himself makes restitution for that, and therefore there is a kind of *mutuum.* The second question is: according to the legal conception that *mutuum* and *commodatum* require the return of the thing borrowed, can a Christian have any merit before God if he lends to his brother and expects a return from him? St. Augustine says that even *mutuum* and *commodatum* are meritorious, because the Gospel says "From him that would borrow of thee turn not away." [15]

The whole Augustinian terminology of this fragment is

---

[14] *De sermone Domini in monte,* lib. 1, 20, 68; M. 3, 1263: ". . . *'Qui voluerit a te mutuari ne aversatus fueris. . .' Mutuatur autem omnis qui accipit, etiam si non ipse soluturus est: cum enim misericors Deus plura restituat, omnis qui beneficium praestat, feneratur. Aut si non placet accipere mutuantem nisi eum qui accipit redditurus, intelligendum est Dominum duo ipsa genera praestandi esse complexum. Namque aut donamus quod damus benevole, aut redituro commodamus. Et plerumque homines, qui proposito divino praemio donare parati sunt, ad dandum quod mutuum petitur pigri fiunt, quasi nihil recepturi a Deo, cum rem quae datur, ille qui accipit exsolvat. Recte itaque ad hoc beneficii tribuendi genus nos divina hortatur auctoritas dicens, 'et qui voluerit a te mutuare, ne aversatus fueris': id est ne propterea voluntatem alienes ab eo qui petit, quia et pecunia tua vacabit, et Deus tibi non redditurus est, cum homo reddiderit: sed cum ex praecepto Dei facis, apud illum quae haec jubet, infructuosum esse non potest. .*"

[15] MATTH. V, 42.

legal, *mutuum, commodatum, fenarari, donatio, dare, praestare, solutio.* Note particularly the technical use of "*dare*" for passing ownership and not mere possession, in "*ad dandum quod mutuum petitur,*" and in "*donamus quod damus.*"

On Usura, Fenus.[16] *Usura* and *fenus* mean interest on loans. In Roman Law *mutuum* and *commodatum,* loans are gratuitous contracts, *i. e.,* they do not admit as such any payment of interest. The borrower must return only the same amount of the same quality he has received and not a cent more. This is essential to such contracts, because they are gratuitous obligations. But this simply means that interest was not included in the *mutuum* and *commodatum* themselves, that is, in the contract itself; not that interest was prohibited. Romans met this difficulty by adding to the contract of loan another agreement for the interest, so interest was due not by loans *(ex mutuuo),* but by another distinct agreement only motivated by the loan. In conclusion, in case of loans with interest we have two contracts, the loan, and the stipulation for the interest.

The rate of interest varied according to different periods. In the times of St. Augustine, 6 per cent was the ordinary maximum lawful interest.[17] Interest above this rate was considered usurious and was punished by the penalty of quadruple, *i. e.,* the victim could recover 4 times the amount of interest paid.[18]

St. Augustine in this matter disagrees with Roman Law. We took note in his above mentioned fragments on *mutuum* and *commodatum,* that he accepts the Roman Law conception that the return of the thing borrowed is essential to these contracts. Here once more he implicitly agrees with Roman Law, admitting another essential character of this contract, *i. e.,* that they are gratuitous. But he stands

16 *Epist.* cl. 2, *epist.* 43, 25; M. 2, 665: "*. . . quid dicam de usuris, quas etiam ipsae leges et judices reddi jubent? An crudelior est qui subtrahit aliquid vel eripit diviti, quam qui trucidat pauperem fenore? Haec atque hujusmodi male utique possidentur, et vellem restituerentur: sed non est quo judice repetantur.*"

17 C. Th. 2, 33, 4.

18 C. Th. 2, 33, 2.

strongly against agreements of interest,[19] denouncing them as an unjust appropriation "*male . . . possidentur.*" Evidently he does not admit any interest at all, because he does not talk about excessive interest, but only about interest which is protected by law and courts, and says that it must be returned, although, he adds, no court enforces this view.

It is admitted that the Church in the past forbade any interest on loans; here we have an evidence of the matter.

This fragment is also important because it gives an example of how Christianity tried to correct Roman Law, although this very instance did not influence the codification of Justinian.

In the following passages St. Augustine discusses the matter of *usura* once more, but from another point of view.[20] He repeats that *usura*, that is, interest on loans is forbidden, but only between man and man, but not between man and God. God invites men to make such bargains with Him directly by works of mercy. The Scripture says "He that hath mercy on the poor, lendeth to the Lord; and He will repay him." The Latin text of St. Jerome, contemporary of Augustine, renders the legal terminology better "*fenaratur Domino qui miseretur pau-*

19 *Epist.* 43, 25.

20 *Sermo* 39, 6; M. 5, 239. *Sermo* 358, 5; M. 5, 1586. *Enarr. in Ps.* 36, 26; M. 4, 1386: "*Non sitis feneratores, et ideo nolo quia Deus non vult. . . Deus noster qui te prohibet esse feneratorem, jubet te esse feneratorem: et dicitur tibi, fenera Deo. Si feneras homini, habes spem: si feneras Deo, spem non habebis? Si feneraveris homini, idest, mutuam pecuniam tuam dederis, a quo aliquid plus quam dedisti expectes accipere: non pecuniam solam, sed aliquis plus quam dedisti, sive illum triticum sit, sive vinum, sive oleum, sive quolibet aliud; plus quam dedisti expectas accipere, fenerator es, et in hoc improbandus, non laudandus. Quid ergo, inquis facio ut sim utiliter fenerator? Attende quid facit fenerator. Minus vult dare certe, et plus accipere: hoc fac et tu, da modica accipe magna. Vide quam late crescat fenus tuum; da temporalia accipe aeterna: da terram, accipe coelum. Et cui dabo forte dicis? Ipse Dominus procedit quem feneres, qui te jubedat ne fenerares. Audi Scripturam quomodo feneres Domino: 'feneratur Domino qui miseretur pauperis' (Prov. 19, 17). . . Cum autem pauper orat pro te tamquam Deo dicit: Domine mutuum accepi, fidedic me. Proinde et si non tenes pauperem redditorem, sed idomeum tenes fideiussorem. . . Quomodo solent dicere fidejussores? quid dicunt? Ego reddo, ego accipio, mihi das. Putasne et hoc dicit Deus?*"

peris: et vicissitudinem suam reddet ei."[21] The Latin "*feneratur*" means here to make a loan with interest.

Augustine brings this legal fiction of lending to God further. What place is given to God in this bargain? What is God's connection with lender and borrower? The loan does not go to God Himself, but to the poor. Well, Roman Law is at hand once more. In matter of loan, the responsibility of restitution can rest not only on the borrower, but also on a third person as surety. In such a case when the borrower cannot meet his duty the surety is liable for the fulfillment of the obligation. This is the institution called "*fideijussio.*" St. Augustine applies such a conception in this case and says; "When the poor prays for thee, he says, as it were, to God, 'Lord I have borrowed this, be Thou surety for me'; then, though you have no bond on the poor man to compel his repayment, you shall have a responsible security (in God)."

It is worthy of notice that St. Augustine uses the technical terminology of "*fideijussio.*" Moreover he uses quite a peculiar expression that is rarely found in the Roman Law sources, the word "*fidedicere*" (saying the surety). Commonly the sources say "*fidem dare*" (to give surety), or "*fidem promittere*" (to promise a surety), but seldom use "*fidem dicere*" as Scaevola.[22]

In this set of fragments, specifically in his commentary on *Ps.* 54, St. Augustine, in dealing about *usura,* makes a figurative application of its meaning which is not in any way borrowed from Roman Law, but shows his strong sympathy for legal terminology, and in a broad sense conveys the meaning of the *usura, i. e.,* of asking more than what has been given.[23]

On Depositum.[24] In these passages there is question of

[21] PROV. 19, 17.

[22] In D. 17, 1, 62, 1.

[23] *Enarr. in Ps.* 54, 12; M. 4, 638: "*Est et alia usura pejor, quando non dimittis quod tibi debetur. . . Verbum contumeliosum audisti, vis exigere damnationis supplicium. Vel tantum exige quantum dedisti, fenerator injuriarum. Pugno percussus es, interfectionem quaeris. Usura mala.*"

[24] *Enarr. in Ps.* 52, 9; M. 4, 618: "*. . . commendatur nescio cui sacellus: non vult reddere, pro suo computat, non putat non posse repeti, jam pro suo habebit, reddere detrectat. Videat quid timeat amittere,*

depositum, because all the elements of such a contract are present. There is the *depositum, i. e.,* a bag of money, or a quantity of gold, given to somebody, entrusted; as Augustine says *"Commendavit"*; this is just the word the Roman Law sources use, in case of a *depositum. "Quid est enim aliud commendare quam deponere?"* (What else does it mean, the word entrusting, but to deposit).[25] There is the obligation of the depository to return the thing received. There is no compensation for the custody of the thing entrusted. And moreover Augustine stresses the great part that good faith plays in it and this is the typical element that places the *depositum* among the obligation *ex bona fide* or *bonae fidei.*

We can be sure that St. Augustine in the use of the word "faith" meant the legal element required in matter of obligations and not the religious Christian faith. He knows of the distinction of these two meanings of the word faith; he stresses it in the following passage: *"de spiritu et littera."* [26]

On Emptio-Venditio.[27] This passage is very plain. St.

---

et quid nolit habere: in dubium veniunt pecunia et fides: quae pretiosior est, ibi gravius damnum timendum. Tu autem ut aurum teneas fidem perdis. . ."

Enarr. in Ps. 57, 2; M. 4, 674:*"Ecce nescio unde amicus venit, et nullo teste aurum commendavit; solus hoc novit, et tu, quantum ad homines attinet. . . Commendavit ille atque discessit, nulli suorum notum fecit, redditurum se sperans, et ab amico quod dederat recepturum; ut humana sunt, mortuus est, habet heredem, veliquit filium: ignorat filius quid pater habuerit, quid tibi commendaverit. . . Ecce cogitas aurum negare, ecce cogitas heredi amici tui prorsus abscondere. Interrogaveram paulo ante quid sit melius, aurum an fides. . . Ecce locutus es mihi meliorem esse fidem, et in judicio tuo melius duxisti aurum. . ."*

25 PAPIN, in D. 16, 3, 24.

26 *De Spiritu et Littera,* 31, 54; M. 10, 225: ". . . *(fides) quam adhibemus cum aliquid credimus, non quam damus cum aliquid pollicemur; nam et ipsa dicitur fides. Sed aliter dicimus, non mihi habuit fidem: aliter, non mihi servavi fidem. Nam illud est, non credidit quod dixi: illud, non fecit quod dixit. Secundum hanc fidem qua credimus, fideles sumus Deo: secundum illam vero qua fit quod promittitur, etiam Deus ipse fidelis est nobis."*

27 *Sermo* 177, 3; M. 5. 910: *"Certe quando pro tuis necessitatibus procedis ad publicum, das nummos, et emis tibi panem, aut vinum, aut oleum, aut lignum, aut aliquam supellectilem: das et accipis, aliquid*

Augustine here deals with the contract of sale. A point he stresses is that here we are in the presence of an onerous obligation. In Roman Law not every obligation is onerous, the *mutuum* (loan), the *depositum* (deposit), for instance, are gratuitous obligations in the sense that only one party has a duty, while the other contracting party has no duty. So it happens in other judicial bargains, that one acquires something gratuitously, and Augustine here mentions the case of *inventio* (finding), of donations, of heredity; but sale exists only when for acquiring something one must part with something.

Another element of the Roman sale is touched by Augustine, the price or the payment in money. The buyer must pay for the thing bought, the price is money *"pretium, nummos"*; if he pays not with money, but in kind, there is an "exchange," which is another contract. This point that is touched here only indirectly by Augustine is very clear in the following fragment:

On Permutatio (Exchange).[28] The exchange in Roman Law differs from a sale particularly in the point that the return for the thing given must be another "thing" and not money. St. Augustine shows his clear perception of the difference of sale and exchange; of giving money for "bread, wine, oil, firewood, furniture" in the sale, and giving "gold (not money) for oil" in the exchange; and mentions the utility of exchange to avoid transportation of goods, *e. g.*, between Africa and other places.

In the fragment on exchange he shows, of course, his legal wit by applying the conception of exchange to theology. "In a certain sense, he says, our Lord and God wishes us to be merchants. He makes an exchange with

amittis, aliquid acquiris: hoc est emere. Nam si nihil amittas, et habeas quod non habebas: aut invenisti, aut donatum accepisti, aut hereditate acquisisti. Quando autem aliquid amittis ut aliquid habeas, tunc emis: quod habes emptum est, quod amittis pretium est. . . "

28 *Sermo* 177, 10; M. 5,959: "*. . . quodam modo Dominus Deus noster mercatores nos vult esse, mutationem nobiscum facit; quod hic abundat damus, quod ibi abundat accipimus: quemadmodum plerique trajecticias merces faciunt. aliud dant alibi, et quo veniunt aliud accipiunt. Verbi gratia dicit amico suo, accipe hic a me aurum et da mihi in Africa oleum: et migrat et non migrat; jam quod desiderat accepit.*"

us: we give (in charity), what here abounds, we receive what there (in heaven) abounds."

On Trading.[29] Here Augustine comments on prices of resale, and admits that a merchant can sell at a price higher than the real cost of the goods, provided he does not conceal with lies or false swearings the real cost.

In the following passage with a verve of a jurist he applies the terminology of the *emptio-venditio* to the theological conception of the Christ's Redemption of the World.[30] Note the technical words of "*commercium, solutus, sacculus* (bag) *pretii, empti, impensum, reddiderunt.*"

And, he discusses the deal of the Cross from the point of view of the dealers and of those who are concerned with it. The persecutor opens the bag, the redeemer pays. Judas is the vendor, the Jew is the buyer. The parties had a bad bargain. The vendor does not get the price and the buyer does not have the "thing" (Christ). The Christian gets the benefit.[31]

---

[29] *Enarr. in Ps.* 70; *Sermo* 1, 17; M. 4. 886: "*. . . inquit (Psalmista), 'tota die salutem tuam quia non cognovi negotiationes.' Quae sunt istae negotiationes? Audiant negotiatores et mutant vitam . . . si peccatum est negotiatio. Hinc enim, o negotiator . . . quando . . . pro pretiis rerum quam vendis, non solum mentiris, verum etiam falsum juras: quomodo in ore tuo tota die laus Dei? . . . Ergo . . . corrigant se Christiani; non negotientur. Sed ait mihi negotiator: ecce ego affero quidem ex longiquo merces ad ea loca in quibus non sunt ea quae attulero, unde vivam, tampquam mercedem laboris mei peto, ut carius vendam quam emerim. Ubde enim vivam? . . . Sed agitur de mendacio, de perjurio. Hoc vitium meum est non negotiationis. . . Non ergo meam culpam actum ad negotium transfero: sed si mentior ego mentior, non negotium. Possem enim dicere: tanto emi sed tanto vendam; si placet, eme. Non enim istam veritatem audiens emptor repelleretur, et non potius omnes accurrerent: quia plus fidem quam mercedeum diligerent. .*"

[30] *Serm.* 329, 1; M. 5, 1454: "*Egit enim (Dominus) in cruce grande commercium: ibi solutus est sacculus pretii nostri: quando latus ejus apertum est lancea percussoris, emanavit inde pretium totius orbis. Empti sunt fideles et martyres: sed martyrum fides probata est testis est sanguis. Quod illis impensum est, reddiderunt. .*"

[31] *Sermo* 336, 4; M. 5, 1473: "*Conscidit saccum lancea persecutor, et fudit pretium nostrum Redemptor. Cantet Christus Redemptor, gemat Judas venditor, erubescat Judeus emptor. Ecce Judas vendidit, Judaeus emit malum negotium egerunt, ambo damnificati sunt, se ipsos perdiderunt, venditor et emptor. Emptores esse voluistis quanto melius*

On Locatio Operorum.[32] In these passages St. Augustine shows his legal acquaintance with the *locatio operarum,* the contract of labor. The example of the worker in the vineyard is very technical, because Roman Law in this contract for labor, means only manual labor. So is the word *"mercedem,"* the hire, the pay for the work.

The doctor contemplates the case of the worker who does not fulfill his obligation: he has no right to the pay: this is also the view of Roman Law because *locatio operarum* is a bilateral contract.

The instance of the dishonest worker in Roman Law would find the sanction of a penalty in a general sense as it is viewed by St. Augustine. Even the expression of the *"paterfamilias"* is Roman, in the sense used here, because he is the only one of the Roman family who can directly be sued for the pay.

On Furtum. St. Augustine commenting on Exodus 22, 2, talked on the permission of killing a thief.[33]

The first part of this fragment refers to the enactment contained in the Exodus and the second part refers to Roman Law. The *"Antiquae Leges Saeculares"* quoted by Augustine are the Twelve Tables. *"Si nox furtum faxsit, si im occisis, jure caesus esto* (If a theft be committed at night and thief be killed, let his death be deemed lawful);

redempti essetis? Ille vendidit, iste emit: infelix commercium: nec iste habet pretium, nec iste habet Christum. Huic dico ubi est quod emisti? Huic dico, ubi vendidisti, te deceptisti. Exulta, o Christiane, in commercio inimicorum tuorum tu vicisti. Quod iste vendidit et ille emit, tu acquisisti."

32 *Enarr. in Ps.* 93, 12; M. 4, 1201: *"In vinea operaris, fac opus tuum accipies mercedem tuam. A patrefamilias non exigeres antequam operareris, et a Deo exigs antequam opereris? . . . Quad si dolosus es, vide ne non solum non accipias mercedem, sed et poenam invenias: quia voluisti esse operarius dolosus. . ."*

Sermo 233, 1; M. 5, 1112: *". . . in praesenti vita laboremus: in futura speremus. Modo tempus est operis: tunc mercedis. Qui piger est in exhibendo opere, impudens est in exigenda mercede. . ."*

33 *Quaest. in Heptateuch. lib.* 2, 84; M. 3, 627: *"Intelligitur . . . tunc non pertinere ad homicidium, si fur nocturnus occiditur: si autem diurnus, pertinere. . . Poterat quippe discerni quod ad furandum non ad occidendum venisset, et ideo non deberet occidi. Hoc est in legibus antiquis saecularibus, quibus tamen ista est antiquior, invenitur, impune occidi nocturnum furem quoquo modo, diurnum autem si se telo defenderit: jam enim plus est quam fur."*

luci . . . si se telo defendit. . . ." (If in the daytime, only if he defends himself with a weapon).[34] The version of Roman Law given here by St. Augustine corresponds literally to a passage of Cicero:[35] "*nocturnum furem quoquo modo, diurnum autem, si se telo defenderit.*"

This Augustinian fragment has another similarity with another Roman Law source. The "*Mosaicarum et Romanarum legum collatio.*[36] This Roman Law collection which aims to show the parallels between the Bible and the Roman Law registers at title 7 the same passage of the Exodus, and compares it, in 7, 2, with the "*Sententiae Pauli*" 5, 23, 1 and 9. St. Augustine and the unknown author (somebody says that he is a father, Jerome, Ambrose, etc.) of the *Collatio* work in the same line, with the same matter, and are substantially the same. Mommsen in his edition of the *Collatio* has discovered other similarities between St. Augustine and the *Collatio.*

On Injuria. Injuria in Roman Law has several meanings. Sometimes it is used as in D. 9, 2, for a wrong in a general sense, *e. g.*, a damage caused by negligence (an unintentional fault, *damnum injuria datum*Q. Sometimes *injuria* has a more specific meaning as in D. 47, 10 for an intentional wrong, *e. g.*, an insult. St. Augustine here deals only with *injuria* in its specific meaning of insult.

In his commentary on *Ps.* 145, 15, the doctor gives the etymology of *injuria*, pointing out to the contrast of "*jus*" (the right) and "*injuria*" (the wrong), what is un-right, because he says "right and wrong are contrary; *jus et injuria contraria sunt.*" [37]

---

[34] T. 8, 12 and 13.

[35] In his *Pro Milone*, 3, 9.

[36] In Fontes Juris Romani Antejustiniani of Riccobono, etc., p. 485: *Mosaicarum et Romanarum legum collatio*, 7, 1: "*Quod si duodecim tabularum nocturnum furem, quoquo modo, diurnum autem si se audeat telo defendere, interfici jubent, scitote, juris consulti, quia Moyses prius hoc statuit, sicut lectio manifestat. MOYSES dicit: Si perfodiens nocte parietem inventus fuerit fur et percusserit eum alius et mortuus fuerit hic, non est homicida is qui percusserit eum. Si autem sol ortus fuerit super eum, reus est mortis percussor: et ipse morietur.*"

[37] *Enarr. in Ps.* 145, 15; M. 4, 1894: "*. . . non enim omnis molestia injuria est. Quidquid enim jure pateris non est injuria. . . Latrones multa patiuntur, sed non injuriam. . . Jus et injuria contraria sunt. . . Vide quid feceris, non quid patiaris. Si jus fecisti, injuriam pateris: si injuriam fecisti, jus pateris.*"

It seems here as though St. Augustine knew the writings of Ulpian. Ulpian[38] says "It is called *injuria* what is not done lawfully, and it is said that what is not done according to the law is *injuria (injuria ex eo dicta est, quod non jure fit; omne enim quod non jure fit, injuria fieri dicitur.")*.

Even the case of the robbers seems to have a parallel in other fragments of the classical jurists.[39]

In his commentary on the Sermon of Mount,[40] Augustine enters into a more lengthy discussion of *injuria* as a delict. Two points are particularly important here, the Augustinian legal commentary of the gospel and the opposition of the Christian doctrine to the teaching of the law.[41]

---

38 In D. 47, 1, pr.

39 As one of Gaius in D. 9, 2, 4, pr., and another of Ulpian in D. 9, 2, 5, pr.

40 Lib. 1, 62, 66.

41 *De sermone Domini in Monte*, lib. 1, 62 and 66; M. 3, 1263, 62: "*In hisce sane generibus trium exemplorum nullum genus injuriae pretermissum esse video. Namque omnia in quibus improbitatem aliquam patimur, in duo genera dividumtur: quorum alterum est quod restitui non potest: alterum quod potest. Sed in illo quod restitui non potest, vindictae solatium quaeri solet. . .*"

66: . . . *tenebitur ergo in hoc injuriarum genere, quod per vindictam luitur, iste christianus modus, ut accepta injuria non surgat in odium, sed infirmitatis misericordia paratus sit animus plura perpeti. . .*

Aliud injuriarum genus est, quod in integrum restitui potest: cujus duae species. una ad pecuniam, alteram ad operam pertinet. Quapropter illius de tunica et vestimento, hujus de angaria mille passuum et duum millium exempla subjecta sunt: quia et reddi vestimentum potest: et quem adjuveris opera potest te etiam ipse, si opus fuerit adjuvare. Nisi forte ita potius distinguendum est, ut prus quod positum est de percussa maxilla, omnia significet quae sic ingeruntur ab improbis, ut restitui non possint nisi vindicta; secundum quod positum est de vestimento omnia significet quae possunt restitui sine vindicta. . .; tertium vero ex utroque confectum sit, ut et sine vindicta et cum vindicta possit restitui. Nam qui operam indebitam violenter exigit sine ullo judicio, sicut facit qui angariat hominem improbe, et cogit se illicite adjuvari ab invito, et poenam improbitatis potest luere, et operam reddere, si hanc ille repetat, qui improbum pertulit. In his ergo omnibus generibus injuriarum Dominus docet patientissimum et misericordissimum, et ad plura perferenda paratissimum animum Christiani esse oportere."

According to St. Augustine, who also renders the point of view of Roman Law, *injuriae* (insults) can be classified as follows: Insults, which in their redress imply a restitution of property, *e. g.*, return of a coat that has been taken away; and insults which do not demand a restoration of property, but are repaired only by a penalty, *e. g.*, a fine inflicted on the wrongdoer; and insults which imply compensation and penalty. Our Father applies this juridical cast commenting on Matth. V, 39-41: "If one strike thee on the right cheek, turn him also the other: and if a man will contend with thee in judgment, and take away thy coat, let go the cloak also to him; and whosoever will force thee one mile, go with him other two." The case of the taking away of the coat, which is an insult, enters into the category of those *injuriae* whose redress implies a restoration of property. The slapping in the face is a case of *injuria* which is punished only by a penalty, no restoration of property being possible. The case of "*Angariatio*," the one who is forced to walk with another, *e. g.*, when one is forced to do something for another, enters into the last category of injuries which can be redressed by a penalty and a compensation, in the way that the wrongdoer may be ordered either to pay or to do some work for the victim who was forced to do some work for him. This evidences how Augustine with much ability picks up evangelical expressions of a legal flavor and comments on them from a legal viewpoint. Note in particular the technical terminology of "*injuria, vindicta, vindictam luere, poenam luere, pecunia, operi.*"

In regard to the moral question, after his legal analysis of the gospel, St. Augustine comes out and does not urge his Christians to conform with the teaching of Roman Law, but with that of the gospel. "In all these classes of *injuriae* . . . the Lord says that a Christian must be patient and compassionate and thoroughly prepared to endure many things." This is a practical example of the way in which many Roman legal conceptions have been attacked by Christian Doctrine.

More General Elements of Obligations

Besides these passages on specific Roman Law obligations there exists in St. Augustine's works other fragments which refer to more general elements of obligations, *e. g.*, duty of restitution, matter of deceit, etc. Let us have a few examples.

On Restitution (of things which belong to others).[42] The first passage shows some legal peculiarities. From it we learn: of the duty the privates had to return to the owner things lost and found *(memor legis)*: of the method of advertisement, *i. e.*, by the privates themselves with public notice *(proponere pittacium publice)*: of the wording of one of these notices: and of the percentage given to the founder (10 per cent, *solidi viginti* on the *ducenti* found).

This fragment (and the next, too), shows also the interest taken by Christianity in the support of the law. Augustine narrates the related story to his audience trying to set a good example to be imitated by his Christians. This is a kind of real influence of Christianity in Roman

[42] *Sermo* 178, 8; M. 5, 963: "*. . . dicam quod fecerit pauperrimus homo, nobis apud Mediolanum constututis; tam pauper ut proscholus esset grammatici: sed plane christianus, quamvis ille esset paganus grammaticus; melior ad velum, quam in cathedra. Invenit sacculum, nisi forte me numerus fallit, cum solidis ferme ducentis; memor legis proposuit pittacium publice. Reddendum sciebat: sed cui redderet ignorabat. Proposuit pittacium publice: 'Qui solidos perdidit, veniat ad locum illum, et quaerat hominem illum.' Ille qui plangens circumquaque vagabatur, invento et lecto pittacio, venit ad hominem. Et ne forte quaereret alienum, quaesivit signa, interrogavit sacculi qualitatem, sigillum, solidorum etiam numerum. Et cum omnia illa fideliter respondisset, reddidit quod invenerat. Ille autem repletus gaudio, et quaerens vicem rependere, tamquam decimas obtulit illi solidos viginti: qui noluit accipere. Obtulit vel decem: noluit accipere. Saltem rogavit vel quinque acciperet: noluit ille. Stomachabundus homo projecit sacculum: nihil perdidi, ait: si non vis aliquid a me accipere, nec ego aliquid perdidi. Quale certamen, fratres mei, quale certamen? qualis pugna, qualis conflictus? Theatrum mundus, spectator Deus. victus tandem ille quod offerebatur accepit: continuo totum pauperibus rogavit, unum solidum in domo sua non dimisit.*"

Epist. cl. 3, *epsit.* 153; M. 2, 663: "*Nolentes . . . reddere, quos novimus et male abstulisse et unde reddere habeant, arguimus, increpamus . . . aliquando . . . sancti altaris communione privamus.*"

Law, and it has been known even in earlier periods. We have an example of this in the letter of Pliny to the Emperor Trajan, in which the Roman Governor points out that the law among Christians was enforced by sake of religion.[43]

The second passage shows how the Church enforced the obligation of restitution even by inflicting ecclesiastical penalties.

On Dolus (Deceit).[44] In these passages St. Augustine shows his acquaintance with the Roman legal conception of deceit. *Dolus* in the Roman legal conception implies some kind of fraud and not only a deceiving purpose that sometimes may be permissible. Note that the last passage corresponds almost verbatim with the definition of *dolus* given by Servius:[45] *"Dolum . . . Servius . . . definit cum aliud simulatur et aliud agitur."*

On Plus Petitio (excessive claims).[46] This is an interesting passage: from a Roman point of view this is the most interesting argument of the entire list. Outside the application of the *"Plus petitio"* to the theological case this fragment is important for the history of Roman Law. *"Plus petitio"* consists in claiming more than what is actually due; and it has been punished in different ways

---

[43] *Plinius ad Trajanum* 1096: *"Adfirmabant autem hanc fuisse summam vel culpae suae vel erroris, quod essent soliti stato die ante lucem convenire carmenque Christo quasi deo dicere secum invicem sacramento non in scelus aliquod obstringere, sed ne furta, ne latrocinia, ne adulteria committerent, ne fidem fallerent, ne depositum appellati abnegarent."*

[44] *In Joann. Evang. Trac.* 7, c. 1, 18; M. 3, 1446: *"Dolus fraus est, simulatio est. Quando aliquis aliquid in corde tegit, et aliud loquitur, dolus est. . ."*

Enarr. in Ps. 14, 3; M. 4, 143: *". . . lingua agitur dolus, cum aliud ore profertur, aliud pectore tegitur. . ."*

Enarr. in Ps. 5, 8; M. 11, 86: *". . . dolus . . . est. cum aliud agitur, aliud simulatur. . ."*

[45] In D. 4, 3, 1, 2.

[46] *Enarr. in Ps.* 118; *sermo* 11, 6; M. 4, 1531: *". . . Ipsi primi homines per serpemtem decepti . . . non fuissent . . . nisi plusquam facti fuerant esse voluissent. . . Plus enim volentes habere quam acceperant, et quod acceperant amiserunt. Cujus vestigium veritatis quae ubique dispersa est, quo institutum est, et in forensi jure deprehensum est, quo institutum est ut plus petendo causa cadat: id est ut qui plus petierit quam ei debetur, et quod ei debebatur amittat. . ."*

according to the different period of Roman Law. At the time of Cicero it was punished by losing the claim.[47] So it was in the second century after Christ in the time of Gaius.[48] It was still so in the Hermogenian Code 5, at the end of the third century after Christ (294-304 A. D.). This rigor finally was corrected by a constitution of the Emperor Zeno in 486 A. D.,[49] and the same provision is taken by Justinian.[50] St. Augustine's testimony that "*Plus Petitio*" existed at his time, is quite important because it refers to a period in which exists a gap in the Roman Law sources, the period between the Hermogenian Code and the Constitution of Zeno, *i. e.*, between 304 to 486 A. D. The Th. Code of 439 A. D. is silent in this matter.

CONCLUSIONS

From a reading of these passages of St. Augustine some conclusions naturally follow, and with these I finish.

1. St. Augustine knew Roman Law. Remember the countless number of legal terms he uses with precision; his ability in applying them in figurative sense; his art of parallelism comparing theology with law; his agility, promptitude, effectiveness of managing legal expressions; his wit. These qualities can hardly be found even in a professional jurist.

2. On the question of interference of Christianity and Roman Law, Augustine's writings show how the Church sometimes adopted and supported Roman Law conceptions even enforcing them, and sometimes took an antagonistic attitude, as evidenced in the Augustinian conception of the nature of ownership, in the prohibition of loans with interest, on the Christian reaction in matter of injuries, and so on. This evidences the effective pressure of Christianity towards the reformation of Roman Law.

3. Augustine's works furnish a sample of the rich harvest that is promised to those who engage in this comparative study of patrology and Roman Law.

---

[47] *Cic. De Orat.* 1.

[48] G. 4, 58.

[49] C. 3, 10, 1.

[50] I. 4, 6, 24 and 32.

4. Reading Augustine's writings we realize how Roman Law acquaintance is very useful to understand the Fathers who make free use of legal expressions and conceptions.

5. Augustine's works demonstrate how the writings of the Fathers are very useful to the study of Roman Law; sometimes in the field of the history of the Roman Law sources and institutions; sometimes in the field of criticism of the sources, *e. g.*, for the research of Christian interpolations, and consequently many times in matter of exegesis or interpretation of Roman Law sources.

Part IV
Selected Fundamental Principles of Jurisprudence and Political Theory

[12]

Will and Order: The Moral Self in Augustine's *De Libero Arbitrio*

Eric O. Springsted
The Center of Theological Inquiry
Princeton, New Jersey

It was Santayana who said, "We don't know who it was that discovered water, but we can be sure that it wasn't the fish." A similar lack of awareness of deep context can often affect philosophical discussions. Believing, because of a similarity in the way a problem is stated in two or more philosophers, that those philosophers are talking about the same thing, we are often unaware that the problems they each find most pressing may be quite different.

The "problem of evil" is one such example. The logical form of the problem is consistent from Epicurus to Augustine to Hume and beyond: the triad of propositions "God is perfectly good," "God is omnipotent," and "evil exists," is logically inconsistent. Similarly, discussions of the "free will defense" seem to have consistent premises and arguments, and the issues are timeless; if humans are not free, God does not justly punish them for erring. Free will is also vital to the positive freedom that makes human life valuable. Yet, ultimately what a thinker such as Augustine is trying to think about when talking about free will in the context of the problem of evil may be very different than what Hume and much of the modern world is talking about. Hume and many moderns, for example, are usually trying to decide whether belief is a reasonable option, whether they should assent, whether they should will to believe. Augustine, however, is trying to figure out how to bring his will into line with the order of a world in which there is evil. What lies behind this difference in approach are two very different views of what it means to be a moral self, and of what it means even to have a will.

In order to uncover what that role of the will may be, and thus Augustine's understanding of the moral self, I shall in this essay examine Augustine's *De Libero Arbitrio.*[1] While it is, indeed, a philosophical defense of God's justice, it has another, equally important emphasis, a theological emphasis, called by Gilson "the search for God through the will."[2] It is this theological interest that is central to his discussion, an interest that is of more than historical interest. For in the end, Augustine also represents an alternative to the modern sense of the self, that is, that the self can be a distant spectator to questions of God, good and evil, and decide on the basis of unengaged, unparticipated reason. The alternative Augustine provides is that such questions are questions to the self and demand its engagement. This is an alternative that may be a far more helpful way of discussing and understanding problems of Christian belief in the face of evil and also of the relation between faith and reason than is often seen in much contemporary philosophy.

I

In his thorough treatment of free will in Augustine, Christopher Kirwan offers a highly sophisticated discussion of Augustine's "free will defense" that is a helpful place to begin. For, despite its thoroughness, it does not engage the problem of the moral self; rather it overlooks at a crucial point the theological issue of what a will is for and the question of the moral self. As such, helpful as it may be otherwise, it construes Augustine's argument within the context of a much more modern sense of the moral self and misses the overall goal of Augustine's argument. But for that it is helpful in raising the issue of what that goal might be.

In the course of examining Augustine's defense of free will Kirwan notes that the range of what Augustine must defend is rather obvious: humans must be able to sin. However, he adds, the degree of that free will is rather problematic and therefore in the interest of saying something about how Augustine can

1. Cited herein as *lib.arb.* and by book and chapter. Translation by A. S. and L. H. Hackstaff as *On Free Choice of the Will*, Indianapolis: Bobbs-Merrill, 1964.

2. Etienne Gilson, *The Christian Philosophy of St. Augustine* (New York: Random House, 1960) Part Two.

defend God as a just punisher and a benevolent Creator, Kirwan distinguishes between three degrees of freedom.[3]

The first is what he calls "freedom of spontaneity," or acquiescence. Simply put, this degree of freedom allows that we have a will, that it is ours and not the result of compulsion. In the Stoic examples he gives, the will is the internal ability to accept our destiny as ours, even when the external result is the same whether or not we acquiesce.

The second degree of freedom he notes is the freedom treated by Hume, when in the *Enquiry concerning Human Understanding* he defines freedom as: "By liberty, then, we can only mean *a* power of acting or not acting, according to the determinations of the will."[4] This sort of freedom, Kirwan explains, is a "two-way power"; that is, a single power to choose to do something or not to do something; "for which half of it the free man exercises depends on the determinations of his will."[5] (NB: Apparently Kirwan understands this as a power to *act*. However,—and this will be an important point below—this seems to ignore the intermediate possibility where a certain kind of "two-way power" can also exist in the first sense of freedom, i.e., where we have the power not only of acquiescing in our fate, but also defying it. The difference is subtle; it is, nevertheless, important for, as we will see below, this intermediate possibility may signal a different *kind* of freedom and not just a different degree of freedom.)

The third degree of freedom, which arises when the alternatives presented to the second degree of freedom are not desirable, is when "acting and not acting are not only alike possible but also alike eligible."[6] As this degree of freedom is not discussed by Augustine, it shall be ignored.

Now Kirwan certainly is on firm ground by attributing both of the first two degrees of freedom to Augustine, as least as they have been summarized here. The second is particularly crucial to anybody's case of defending God as a just punisher, especially as a punisher of postlapsarian humans. Without the freedom to defy the divine will and the responsibility for bringing about a state of affairs contrary to God's own plan, it is difficult to see how anyone can be justly punished. Augustine himself says: "The will is moved to action by what can be seen. And while people have no power over what they see or touch,

3. Kirwan, *Augustine* (London: Routledge, 1989) pp.83–88

4. 8.73

5. Kirwan, p.85

6. Kirwan, p.88

they do have it in their power either to accept or reject . . . Hence it is that the rational substance selects from both classes what it wills, and by virtue of its selection achieves misery or blessedness."[7]

If, however, Kirwan is right in attributing both of the first two *degrees* of freedom to Augustine, and this brings us closer to our point, he has also glossed over two very different *kinds* of freedom in discussing the two degrees. While there is, indeed, a difference between degree #1 where we can choose to acquiesce, and degree #2 where we have a "double power" of choosing to act or of choosing not to act, that is not entirely the difference between the two freedoms. There is also an important contextual difference between the two freedoms, for the first has far more to do with what we might call "subjective intentions," with issues of belief and even character, and the second has more to do with "objective intentions," with what we enact in the world. What is at stake can be seen by looking at the classical sources Kirwan himself uses to illustrate the two degrees. If we look closely, Hume does not simply add a *degree* of freedom that the Stoics miss; he, in fact, has a very different sense of the person and the will which causes him, and others who subscribe to the same sense of the self, to see the problem as they do. Here is where the "intermediate" possibility of acquiescing or not acquiescing plays a role and constitutes, in fact, an alternative possibility.

The difference can be seen this way. For the Stoics what is at stake in the freedom of the will is a question of one's very rationality, and hence humanity. To acquiesce to fate—to will it for one's own—is nothing more or less than choosing to accept one's own providential role in the world as a whole. To choose one's providential role and honor God by doing so is to be one's true self. For example, Epictetus says: "If, indeed, I were a nightingale, I should be singing as a nightingale; if a swan, as a swan. But as it is, I am a rational being, therefore I must be singing hymns of praise to God. This is my task; I do it, and will not desert this post, as long as it may be given me to fill it . . ."[8] This, of course, explains why Stoic conceptions of free will traditionally did not involve a double power; defiance made little sense. For to will to defy the divine order with respect to one's role may well be to cease having that role at all, and to

7. *lib.arb.* III.XXV.255. "Sed quia voluntatem non allicit ad faciendum quodlibet, nisi aliquod visum; quid autem quisque vel sumat vel respuat, est in potestate, sed quo viso tangatur, nulla potestas est: fatendum est et ex superioribus et ex inferioribus visis animum tangi ut rationalis substantia ex utroque sumat quod voluerit, et ex merito sumendi vel miseria vel beatitas subsequatur."

8. Arrian's Discourses of Epictetus, Bk. I, chapter XVI.

play another, one belonging to a less than rational nature. It would be seen as becoming something else. This is undoubtedly why Epictetus also warns: "Only consider at what price you sell your freedom of will (*prohairesis*)."[9]

What is crucial for us to note here is that here the issue of the will is fundamentally a moral one and that moral issue is one that is linked to who one is as a person. Questions of the will for the Stoics are not simply questions about choosing from a range of options, nor is one's freedom simply the ability to choose. Rather, to choose is to be some person within some larger moral context; or, even more exactly, to will is not so much choosing to *become* some sort of person or other, but a matter of *being* some sort of person in one's choosing. Willing is therefore not always of external possibilities or of exercising agency over some public possibility; it is also self-referential.

It is therefore also important to understand that discussions of the will in this sort of context are far more concerned with a moral evaluation of what we might call the "inner person" than with any specific acts he or she may perform. That this is not so with a Humean conception of liberty is obvious from the very context and content of Hume's own definition of liberty as the freedom to act or not act according to determinations of the will. Anyone who is at all familiar with the *Enquiry* of course knows Hume's intent. He is seeking to undo the Gordian knot of the metaphysical questions of the will and its causality that one all too quickly encounters in discussions of free will. He cuts the knot by pointing out that the question of freedom is not one of metaphysics, but simply a question of the ability to do or not do something. It has nothing to do with the metaphysical status of the will or with moral valuation. This is an impressive move. But at the same time we are impressed we do need to be aware that cutting the Gordian knot that way also does away with the picture of the person that the Stoics relied on. For Hume, or at least his followers, the person is, and only is, his or her public acts. There is nothing else to be.

It is already agreed that Kirwan is correct to suggest that Augustine has an operative conception of both the first two degrees of freedom, and there is an obvious text which we have cited to prove it. But what now seems not to be clear in Kirwan's discussion is that in which those degrees lie. For example, Kirwan establishes that the second degree of freedom is understood by Augustine through a discussion of power (*potestas*) in his works. But this still does not answer the question of, power for what? A great deal depends upon how

9. Ibid. Bk.I, chapter II.

we answer this question for it provides a clue to the very nature of the will in Augustine and its purposes.

For the question of "power for what?" is a question about whether we take the power of the will to be most importantly an internal power, as the Stoics seemed to take it, or an external power, a power to act as Hume took it. The difference lies in whether we put emphasis on the power to accept or reject, say, an argument, or, more importantly, a world view, or on the power to do or not to do something. Or, put otherwise, it is a difference between understanding the will as an internal activity that lies at the center of our concept of a person or understanding it as the structure of uncoerced, publicly identifiable activity, which gives us a very different sense of the person.

Once we put it this way, though, we must recognize that the different kinds of freedoms are not, of course, mutually exclusive. In fact, they can be complementary, at least as long as we assume that a prior internal activity of willing somehow lays behind public activity. But if that is a picture that looms large in the popular mind, it also begs a question that many modern philosophers want to challenge. Following Hume's argument and an updated version of it given by Gilbert Ryle,[10] it has been largely assumed that such an account involves a redundancy and an infinite regression, as it involves a (supposedly) quasi-causal account of the will to explain actions. Ryle's argument suggests that to be consistent this account must needs require a cause for the will and a cause for that cause *ad infinitum*.

This is an important argument and will require a response later on. But what is important to consider first is that if Augustine sees the will as a matter of deciding between possibilities, the most important choice is accepting or rejecting a certain view of the self and its relation to the world and God. Whether one consents to the world and its creator does matter. What makes that choice crucial for Augustine is that it is this consent that determines the moral quality of the will and person. Its exercise determines who we are, just as, at the opposite end, nietzchean *ressentiment* determines a certain kind of character. The interest in who we are morally is a primary interest of Augustine when discussing the question of evil. The question of evil on this account is not just a question of an unhappy state of affairs that can be evaluated neutrally from the outside and for which the will, not God, should be blamed. The question of evil and the role of the will is a matter about willing itself, about our choices and selves

10. Gilbert Ryle, *The Concept of Mind* (London: Hutchinson, 1949), Chapter III, "The Will".

within the world. It is a question of how and who we shall be in the world. It is thus to a great degree a matter of our subjective intentions within a state of affairs. We can now turn to a closer examination of *De Libero Arbitrio* to see how.

II

In the opening sentence of *De Libero Arbitrio* Evodius asks simply "Is God the cause of evil?" A seemingly straightforward question, it is actually open ended in a way that Augustine exploits extensively. On the one hand, it is straightforwardly a question about God's justice. That there is evil in the world, no one denies; therefore, we ask, is God the cause of it? There is no doubt that a chief intent of *De Libero Arbitrio* is to answer this question by arguing that God is in no way to blame for evil, except the sort that one experiences in being punished justly. On the other hand, though, there is another way of taking this question and answering it. That way is to treat it more broadly, more scientifically. In this case asking whether God is the cause of evil or not is not so much asking a question of theodicy *per se*, as it is, ingenuously and non-rhetorically, asking the question of "just where *does* evil come from?" That this sort of "scientific" question was also in Augustine's mind is clear from his own description of *De Libero Arbitrio* in the *Retractationes*. There he notes that this book was begun in Rome at a time when "we wanted to explore and discuss the origin of evil." The conclusion of that discussion, he adds, was "that we concluded that the sole cause of evil lay in the free choice of the will,"[11] which was why he titled the book "On Free Choice of the Will."

Finding that the origin of evil lies in the free choice of the rational creature exculpates God, a not unimportant conclusion in itself. However, we miss a good deal of Augustine's point in this treatise if we do not take seriously that the book also has another sort of conclusion, namely, a broader one about evil and the will. This other conclusion in turn affects how we understand the exculpation of God with respect to evil.

What this other sort of conclusion is and its importance can be seen by bearing in mind two things. One, Augustine did at an earlier time have another answer to the origin of evil that also vindicated God, i.e. Manichaeanism, and two, the reasons why he abandoned that answer. Those reasons were, as he himself makes clear, a newfound ability to think of God as immaterial, but just

11. *Retractationes* I.IX.1. "Cum adhuc Romae demoraremur, voluimus disputando quaerere, unde sit malum...Et quoniam constitit inter nos, diligenter ratione discussa, malum non exortum nisi ex libero voluntatis arbitrio . . ."

as important, a realization that evil is not an external thing—an obstacle in one's path, as it were—but a deformation, a privation of some good.

The point here is that if simply providing an argument that would exonerate God for bringing about a state of affairs were the whole problem, Manichaeanism is not a bad argument. Most people even have a certain psychological predisposition to it. The problem, though, as Augustine came to see it, is that that argument ultimately is no good because it misrepresents both God and evil. For evil is not simply an unfortunate state of affairs that can be recognized by just anybody; it is not simply external to the thinker as the Manichaeans assumed (i.e., somebody else's fault, as it were.) It also has something to do with the person who sees that state of affairs as a problem.

This is then to say that Augustine has an entirely new way (at least for him) of thinking about where evil comes from, and that, in turn, forces him to think about what we call "the problem of evil" in a very different light. This new light above all causes him to locate the site of evil within beings, that which is deformed, and it causes him to locate it at the point of their deficiencies. More existentially, what this must have forced Augustine to realize was that whatever else evil was, it was at least somehow a part of him, and that it was *his* own deficiencies and not some external obstacle that was the problem. Nothing could be farther from Manichaeanism, ancient or modern, which, in effect, denies one's essential moral responsibility for who one is, which blames it on external factors. That he was concerned about this problem can be seen in the *Confessions* he explicitly contrasts the Christian doctrine of recognizing one's own fault with what the astrologers teach: "It is good to make confession to you, Lord and to say, 'Have mercy on me; heal my soul, for I have sinned against you' . . . Astrologers try to destroy this entire saving doctrine when they say: 'The reason for your sinning is determined by heaven,' and 'Venus and Saturn or Mars was responsible for this act.'"[12]

There is little need or time to go over ground that has already been well covered by others[13] as to where Augustine even got his notion of the will. What is crucial to note, though, is that for Augustine the will, together with memory and intelligence, is not simply something we have; it *is* us. As he has Evodius

12. *Confessions* IV.iii. (4). trans. H. Chadwick. (Oxford: Oxford, 1991). ("Bonum est enim confiteri tibi, Domine, et dicere: 'Misere mei: cura animam meam, quoniam peccavi tibi' . . . Quam totam illi salubritatem interficere conantur, cum dicunt: 'De caelo tibi est inevitabilis causa peccandi' et 'Venus hoc fecit aut Saturnus aut Mars' . . . ")

13. cf. Albrecht Dihle, *The Theory of the Will in Classical Antiquity* (Berkeley: The University of California Press, 1982).

say: "I find nothing which I can call my own if the will by which I accept or reject objects of choice is not my own will."[14] So, once he is in possession of a concept of the will and recognizes it as being integrally tied to who we are as persons, we may observe that it is no difficult step to conclude that moral evil has its root in the will. Moral evil, the evil done by conscious, willing agents, is thus not simply a matter of evidence against God's goodness or power; it is a problem for the thinking and willing agent.

But let us be careful to understand exactly how evil is rooted in the will, for it is two different, although not entirely unrelated, things to say that the deficiency is in the act willed or to say the deficiency is in the willing will itself. And for Augustine it is clearly the latter that he is worried about. As he says in discussing the evil of adultery: "Perhaps then lust (*libido*) is the evil element in adultery. As long as you look for evil in the overt act itself, which can be seen, you are in difficulty."[15] Similarly he argues that Adam's sin was something present in him even before he ate the apple.[16] It is also clear why Augustine is worried about the willing will itself for, not only does it color the external act, but, also, if evil is a privation of form, it is the will itself that is deficient. Thus the problem of evil for Augustine is not simply whether evil is logically compatible with God's existence, goodness and creativity, it is also an existential problem of our own selves. The problem of evil reflects back on the questioner as the possible source of the deficiency. Evil may not simply be a matter of choosing bad things; it may also be a reason to question the choosers.

To recognize that it is the will itself and its motions that Augustine is most concerned about goes a long way toward explaining certain features that many moderns find unsettling in reading *De Libero Arbitrio*. Chief among these is a certain lack of concern Augustine seems to demonstrate toward the problem of suffering.[17] To be sure he does not ignore it entirely. However, such a thorny problem as that of the suffering of innocent children, which we find terrifically important, is not even brought up until the closing chapters of the final

14. *lib.arb.* III.I.12. "Video, et quodammodo tango, et teneo vera esse quae dicis: non enim quidquam tam firme atque intime sentio, quam me habere voluntatem, eaque me moveri ad aliquid fuendum; quid autem meum dicam, prosus non invenio, si voluntas qua volo et nolo non est mea . . ."

15. *lib.arb.* I.III.20. "Fortassis ergo libido in adulterio malum est: sed dum tu foris in ipso facto quod jam videri potest, malum quaeris, pateris angustias."

16. Cf. *lib.arb.* III.XXIV. See also *De Genesis ad Litteram* Bk.11.5..

17. As Bonner notes. (G. Bonner, *St. Augustine of Hippo: Life and Controversies* [1963, reissued Norwich: The Canterbury Press 1986] p.211.

book.[18] Even then the problem is answered only within the larger context of an argument that Augustine has been developing about the just order of the world. (This question of order will be taken up below.) Now, I do not think that Augustine was an insensitive man; indeed, far from it. Rather it is that the problem of suffering which seems to us to be *the* moral problem of evil is not the one with which Augustine is dealing. His problem is with the will itself.

But why this emphasis on the will itself ? Whereas we as moderns tend to take a "God's-eye view," a stance of complete objectivity, toward knowledge, for Augustine one's moral knowledge is not simply something one has; it is, as assented to, what we are. Thus the questions of "whence evil?" and the compatibility of evil with God's goodness are also questions that involve self-knowledge. Reflection for Augustine is morally reflexive. And as such questions of the moral order of the universe are also, at their root, questions of one's own identity.[19] Therefore Augustine is not only concerned with exculpating God in a work such as the *De Libero Arbitrio*, but is also concerned, and perhaps most concerned, to clarify his sense of the moral person and its responsibilities. His emphasis on what we are calling the internal motions of the will, rather than its outward powers, is crucial to his case. Or perhaps better put, God is exculpated precisely when we understand ourselves morally.[20]

18. *lib.arb.* III.XXIII

19. Charles Taylor in his groundbreaking work on the western concept of the self observes how Augustine, by introducing the notion of the will into moral philosophy, differs from his classical Greek predecessors—and from us. He writes: "What is morally crucial about us is not the universal nature or rational principle which we share with others, as with Plato and Aristotle, but now also this power of assent, which is essentially in each case mine . . . From this, the idea can grow that moral perfection requires a personal adhesion to the good, a full commitment of the will. (*Sources of the Self: The Making of the Modern Identity* [Cambridge: Harvard University Press, 1989] p.137.)

20. In this vein it should be observed that Augustine in the *Retractationes* fully recognizes that a number of philosophical issues were not resolved in *De Libero Arbitrio*. Nevertheless, he adds, "our reasoning led to the conclusion that we may believe or even know that God ought to be praised, whatever the truth about the unresolved questions to which there appeared no true solution from any point of view—or rather from all points of view on the same questions." (*Retractationes*, I.IX.2) ("In his libris ita multa disserta sunt, ut incidentes nonnulae quastiones, quas vel enodare non poteram, vel longam sermocinationem in praesenti requirebant, ita differrentur, ut ex utraque parte, vel ex omnibus earundem quaetionum partibus, in quibus non apparebat quid potius congrueret veritati, ad hoc tamen ratiocinatio nostra concluderetur, ut quodlibet corum verum esset, luadndus crederetur, vel etiam ostenderetur Deus.")

III

The important issue in Augustine's eyes thus becomes one about the will itself, about the way it wills and not simply what it wills to do. That is the problem of the moral self. And to the extent that *this* is his problem, it is not just a theoretical problem. It is a spiritual one as well. Or, better put, all theoretical questions for Augustine are moral and spiritual questions. For it is a problem not only of explaining, say, to a neutral observer, how the will can be deficient in its willing and leaving it at that. This question also has existential interest for the inquirer. As such, it is a problem of redirecting the will of the inquirer through the course of argument so that it may will properly. Augustine claims: "In our journey of devotion, our goal is God. If therefore we think of him otherwise than as He is, our thinking compels us to walk in vanity, not blessedness . . ."[21] But not only is the goal that one should ultimately will properly, by so willing one should understand better as well. The goal of right thinking is knowledge of God in the deepest sense. By willing to see things as they are, and not just as we would like them to be, is the important moral dimension of knowledge.[22] That surely is a cornerstone of the Augustinian "*credo ut intelligam.*"

Thus the deep purpose behind the *De Libero Arbitrio* is to get the soul to understand itself morally and to understand that it cannot understand itself morally unless it understands itself in relation to God. In this sense, Augustine's argument is a sort of *itinerarium mentis ad Deum*. (Indeed, it corresponds at numerous points to Bonaventure's later meditation of that name, and may have served as a model for it.) While space does not permit a detailed analysis of Augustine's entire argument to demonstrate this as fully as might be desired, four observations about the course of the argument can be made that would lead one to read Augustine's argument in just such a way.

1. Much of the opening chapter of the book is about education. At first this seems somewhat beside the main point of the book as a whole. But that chapter

21. *lib.arb.* III.XXI.201. "Ad illum enim tendimus itinere pietatis. Si ergo aliud de illo senserimus quam est, intentio nostra non in beatitatem, sed in vanitatem nore ire compellet. De creatura vero si quid aliter quam sese habet senserimus, dummodo non id pro cognito perceptoque teneamus, nullum periculum est."

22. While Augustine's view is often sharply different than the modern one, it is not unknown in contemporary philosophy; it has been argued that this was also Wittgenstein's view and what drove his view of philosophy. Cf. Phillip Shields, *Logic and Sin in the Writings of Ludwig Wittgenstein* (Chicago: University of Chicago Press, 1992).

concludes with this observation: "If every kind of understanding is good and no one learns who does not understand, then everyone who learns is doing good."[23] This needs to be taken not simply as a general point about education and the relation of the understanding to good and evil, but also as a reminder about how to take the discussion that is about to unfold. To try to understand these things about God, good and evil is itself an education, and an initial willing of the good. Augustine and Evodius and the reader are about to educate themselves and bring their minds and wills into line with the truth.

2. Book I defines evil as "love of those things which a man can lose against his will,"[24] i.e., an improper love of things. "Improper love" is to be understood here as loving something in such a way that it is misused, i.e., being made to serve a purpose for which it is not intended in the eternal order. This question of use and misuse Augustine thinks is a problem of the will, for while we have a mind that can understand what is proper and what is not, clearly the mind does not always direct us; in evil men it is not the mind that is in control.[25] (Here Augustine's notion of the will most clearly diverges from much prior ancient philosophy, such as in the Socratic dialogues, which tended to discuss moral problems largely as a matter of knowledge.) The good will, on the other hand, is that "by which we seek to live rightly and to come to the highest wisdom."[26] It comes to the highest wisdom by willing as its own the eternal law by which "everything is ordered in the highest degree."[27] Thus the moral problem of the will for Augustine is not only the object of choice but also the order to which we assent. In this case, an option is being presented to the will. This is underlined as he also points out that the evil of punishment that God visits upon the evil will is that it gets pretty much what it wills, i.e., an ordering that is not eternal and which flies in the face of things as God has ordered them.[28] The punishment for injustice is being unjust, of living a life that can never find harmony.

---

23. *lib.arb.* I.I.9. "Si ergo omnis intelligentia bona est, nec quisquam qui non intelligit, discit; omnis qui discit, bene facit.."

24. *lib.arb.* I.IV.31. "Quam esse jam apparet earum rerum amorem, quas potest quissque invitus amittere."

25. E.g *lib.arb.* I.IX.70.

26. *lib.arb.* I.XII.83. "Voluntas qua appetimus recte honestamque vivere, et ad summam sapientam pervenire."

27. *lib.arb.* I.VI.51. " Ut igitur breviter aeternae legis notionem, quae impressa nobis est, quantum valeo verbis explicem, ea est qua justum est ut omnia sint ordinatissima."

28. Cf. *lib.arb.* I.XI.

3. While Book II opens with the question of whether or not God gave a good gift in giving rational beings free will since they so obviously misuse it to their own detriment, little time is spent actually discussing this question. What does get discussed at length in this book is the question of whether God exists. But let us pay careful attention to the sort of argument Augustine uses here. It is the so-called "ideological argument," for it seeks to prove the existence of God from the reality of ideas. It does so by establishing a hierarchical order in the soul—sense depends upon the inner sense which depends upon the reason—to show that the reason itself which is the essential person itself relies on the immutable truth which is God. Now Augustine's point is not simply that God exists, another item among others. Rather, the point is also existential for it grounds my own existence in God's—and that is what convinces me of God's existence.[29]

But there is more, too. Keeping in mind the conclusions of Book I, i.e., that one comes to the highest wisdom by willing the eternal as one's own, the further conclusion that can be drawn now is that not only is one dependent on God but that to be dependent on God means to recognize and will the order God has established between the faculties of the soul and between the soul and God. The argument of Book II thus presents an example of order in the universe that consists of at least two items: the soul and God. Wisdom—the goal of inquiry—is willing, is assenting to the order wherein the soul depends on God. One is less of a person for failing to assent to this order. But note also that this is not an external order, but rather an internal one. Thus when the ostensible problem of Book II is solved—that free will is the good gift of God because God gives only good gifts—what the truly free will is, is also established.

4. Much of the argument of Book III deals with the question of how the will ever turns from God, concluding that that movement is *sui generis*. This book also does seek to establish the consistency of the freedom of the will with God's foreknowledge and justice. But an equally important argument is also given that continues the lines drawn in the earlier two books. That is an argument that depends upon what John Hick has called "the principle of plentitude" and the "aesthetic theme."[30] Simply put, this is an argument that suggests that good is within the totality of the universe, and within that totality any seeming

29. As Taylor explains: "So I recognize that this activity which is mine is grounded on and presupposes something higher than I, something which I should look up to and revere. By going inward, I am drawn upward." Taylor, ibid., p.134.

30. John Hick, *Evil and the God of Love* (London: Macmillan, 1966), chapter 4.

evils are not only counterbalanced but even contribute to an overall goodness, as seeming imperfections in a painting when viewed too closely contribute to its beauty when viewed from a proper distance. This is not the place to debate whether this argument contributes to an effective theodicy or not. In fact, it may not be an argument within a theodicy for Augustine at all. It may rather be a primary religious intuition, a characteristic and defining belief inherent in Christian faith that no evil is outside God's good providence. What does need pointing out is what its function within Augustine's argument as a whole is. That function is to now introduce the inquiring soul, who, after Book II, sees itself as part of a moral order dependent on God, to an even larger world order. By doing so the will is given the opportunity now to assent to that larger order as ordained by the Creator.

Taken this way, the argument may be less about God's morality in creating a universe where certain evils occur and more a question directly posed to the will about its own moral stance toward the creation. It is thus at least an invitation to disabuse our minds of what Leibniz was later to call our "anthropocentric conceit," the view that our desires are the basis on which the world order is formed. As Augustine himself put it in response to those who cavil about suffering: "They cannot see the highest good—what it is and how great it is—yet they wish everything to be the same as their idea of the highest good."[31] Now while it certainly may be argued that Augustine himself tailored the highest good in this book to his own vision, his point remains intact: the goodness of the will is integrally tied to its assent, its willingness to play its role within the order of the whole.

Thus the point that ultimately needs to be raised about Augustine's *De Libero Arbitrio* is this: that the moral self is determined not so much by its public action or even potentiality for action as it is by the vision of the good to which it assents and to which it is thereby bound. Whether we assent to another as the center and orderer of the world or whether we make ourselves its moral center, that is what determines our moral self. But that further means that what is morally important about us is our inner willing. It is the attempt to affect and purify that willing that is the ultimate goal and cornerstone of Augustine's own arguments in *De Libero Arbitrio*.

31. *lib.arb.* III.XXIII.233. "Sed haec dicunt vel sentiunt, quia iniquissime de rebus existimant, qui cum summum bonum quod et quantum sit aspicere nequeant, talia volunt esse omnia, quale putant esse summum bonum."

IV

If this is Augustine's position, there are obvious difficulties for the modern philosopher in taking it seriously. First, as we noted earlier, there is Hume's anti-metaphysical counter account of the will to contend with and Ryle's "ghost-in-the-machine" caricature of inner willing. Second, insofar as what is being willed, what is being assented to for Augustine is an order of the universe, we are also led to ask whether all of Hume's objections in the *Dialogues concerning Natural Religion* about the fancifulness of most accounts of the order of the universe—that they lack proper epistemological justification—don't, in fact, apply here quite well.

Hume's and Ryle's arguments need to be taken seriously. But they also need to be taken in context. The "ghost-in-the-machine" criticism *is* an apt caricature of a certain position that understands the will as an inner activity needed to explain outer activity or to characterize it as free or moral. But, as Stephen Clark has argued, we do not necessarily have to understand the will as an *explanation* for voluntary activity.[32] Moreover, as Iris Murdoch has suggested, while this argument is "perfectly sound over a certain range,"[33] it does not mean that an act of the will is not "an introspectible movement . . . (whose only structure) *is* its outer structure."[34]

So what is crucial to ask is whether or not Augustine's position is hopelessly metaphysical in the bad sense of the word, an unwarranted explanation for a perfectly normal phenomenon. The course of the argument here has been to suggest that it is not metaphysical in that sense at all; rather Augustine is most fundamentally seeking to bring to light certain crucial root concerns of human moral identity and the relation of human identity to philosophical positions

32. "Who said that volitions were acts? Or anything but another name for the agent herself, her will? But suppose they are such mental acts: why is it assumed that they are only 'voluntary' if preceded by another act? One might as well suggest that the presence of water could not be the cause of something's being wet on the grounds that there must then be an infinite array of meta-waters to explain why water itself was wet. Water is present in itself, and so is wet; a volition is essentially voluntary, and transmits its voluntariness to what it causes. By assenting, or 'putting one's will in it,' one accepts responsibility for what occurs, and is the cause of it, within a universe that has allowed the opportunity. Mere physical motions are not essentially voluntary, and there is even a class of sort-of-acts that are not; the act of assenting is axiomatically an act of assent, whether to an intellectual argument or to a practical option." Stephen R. L. Clark, *A Parliament of Souls* (Oxford: Oxford University Press, 1990), p.64.

33. Iris Murdoch, *The Sovereignty of Good* (New York: Schocken Books, 1971), p.15.

34. Murdoch, ibid. p.13.

in general. What is "metaphysical"—and there are certainly metaphysical elements present in Augustine's thinking—in this case becomes something more like a matter of articulating this moral insight about human beings. It is a later generation that has forgotten the original impetus for the thought that comes to see it as something other than what it meant to be.

What, therefore, is Augustine's insight that needs to be preserved? First, it is that questions about the will are moral and spiritual questions, and that moral and spiritual questions insofar as they are linked to our sense of self are not always secondary to questions of so-called "objective" knowledge. Indeed, in many instances these moral and spiritual questions often shape and configure questions of fact.[35] The question of who we are *is* a moral question and bespeaks a fundamental moral struggle of the human being. As such we struggle with ourselves to know about the order of the world in which we live and struggle to put ourselves in some kind of larger order. The order we assent to is crucial to our self-understanding, and hence to a best account of the moral person.

In order to show how it may be an example can be taken from Simone Weil's discussion of what she calls "the love of the order of the world."[36] This is a love she claims is an "implicit love of God," for in it God is really, though secretly, present, i.e., in it God has secretly wed the soul to himself. Weil gives us an analogy to help show the difference between having this sort of love and not having it. Morally we are subject to an illusion, she suggests, that is analogous to the one we experience whenever we look up into the sky on a cloudless day and it appears that the sky is a bowl inverted above us, thus making it appear as if we were at the center of a spherical world. In the moral case the illusion is that it appears to us as if we were at the center of the world. We thus appear as terrifically important, and what else is of value can be ranked by its proximity to us. Now there is no problem with this illusion; it is entirely natural. The moral problem, Weil says, is when we assent to this illusion and believe ourselves *actually* to be the center. However, if and when we consent to not being the center this love of God is born. Weil writes:

> To empty ourselves of our false divinity, to deny ourselves, to give up being the center of the world in imagination, to discern that all points in the world are equally centers and that the true center is outside the world, this is to consent to the rule of mechanical necessity in matter and of free choice at

35. As Hilary Putnam has also suggested. Cf. his *Reason, Truth and History* (Cambridge: Cambridge University Press, 1981).

36. Simone Weil, *Waiting for God* (New York: Harper & Row, 1973), pp.158–181.

> the center of each soul. Such consent is love. The face of this love, which is turned toward thinking persons, is love of our neighbor; the face turned toward matter is love of the order of the world, or love of the beauty of the world which is the same thing.[37]

For Weil this love of, this assent to the order of the world is clearly something that makes a difference to our moral personhood. But how? Why is it not simply an entertaining image which deserves no special consideration when making moral evaluations? In the first place Weil thinks it is because there are real consequences that come from our deepest assents. She notes that, based on the sort of beauty that we love, we form an image of order that we seek to emulate in our projects; for beauty, or fittingness, is a sort of finality to which we aspire in all our projects. For example, she says: "The love of power amounts to a desire to establish order among the men and things around oneself, either on a large or small scale, and this desire for order is the result of a sense of beauty. In this case . . . the question is one of forcing a certain circle into a pattern suggestive of universal beauty." The result in the case of the love of power, though, is that "it is not the universe and it hides it."[38] Thus the order to which we assent and which we seek to emulate affects several, if not all, of our projects. It affects what we take to be beauty in another human being, it affects our political institutions and associations, and it above all, Weil thinks, affects the sort of science we have.

But here the modern philosopher may well ask: "Why not just worry about these consequences and evaluate them on their own merits, instead of on the basis of what amounts to a private vision?" Or he may ask: "Why this vision and not another, if either can produce the same result?" Or even: "Is not this concern with the internal motions of the will simply an unholy fascination with one's self ?" No, Weil would argue to all these questions, precisely because our assent not only has consequences in act, *but also produces the very quality of our evaluations, and affects what we take to be valuable.* A prime example of how this is so can be seen in why Weil even describes the renunciation of the perspective of the autonomous self in the "love of the order of the world" as a love of God. For, as she makes clear, the value of this renunciation itself rests in an assent to and certain understanding of God as one who gives himself so that others may live.

37. Weil, ibid. p.160.

38. Weil, ibid. p.168.

To assent to that as one's moral vision is to evaluate life in a very different way, and to bind one's will to a very definite vision. It is in this way that the internal motions of the will are not otiose, but rather are of primary importance to our standing as moral persons. For what is at stake ultimately in the assent of the will is the moral vision of ourselves in relation to the world and God, whether we see ourselves as self-sufficient or dependent upon another. If there is anything morally substantial to us, what we will to think of ourselves is crucial to that substance. This is not self-obsession, as it is not a matter of being closed in on oneself. It is a sense of oneself in relation to others. It is, in fact, an openness.

The second of Augustine's insights to be highlighted—and this responds to Hume's criticisms about the fancifulness of claims about the order of the world—is that this assent and the moral and spiritual struggle it implies is at the heart of what faith is. Conversely, faith is itself a fundamental human question for Augustine. Just what is at stake here can be seen by looking at Hume again.

In the *Dialogues* there are two conversants who might be said to have faith: Demea, who appears to believe gleefully a whole set of things about the universe without evidence, and Philo, who believes fewer things, but believes them on bad or weak evidence. In the essay on "Miracles" in the *Enquiry concerning Human Understanding*, faith itself is ironically taken as the greatest example of a miracle because good epistemological sense dictates against the probability of what is believed. In both the *Dialogues* and the *Enquiry* faith is then taken pretty much as blindly willing, blindly assenting to what reason shies away from affirming.

Now, there is a sense in which Augustine does take faith to be belief in something one cannot prove. As late as the *Homilies on the Gospel of John* he talks about faith as believing what God says simply because God says it—among other things that it is.[39] There is also a sense, particularly at the time that he wrote *De Libero Arbitrio*, in which he is seeking to assent to an order of the universe which we would regard as highly fanciful, and without sound

39. Cf. *Tr. in Io.* 29.6: "Audiat consilium, qui dicit: Nondum intellexi. Magna quippe res et profunda cum fuisset dicta, vidit utique ipse Dominus Christus hoc tam profundam non omnes intellecturos, et in consequenti dedit consilium. Intelligere vis? Crede. Deus enim per prophetam dixit: 'Nisi credideritis, non intellegetis . . .'" But he adds: "Sed si creditis in eum, creditis ei; non autem continuo qui credit ei, credit in eum. Nam et daemones credebant ei, et non credebant in eum." Also cf. *Sermo* 144.2.2: "Sed multum interest, utrum quisque credat ipsum Christum, et utrum credat in Christum . . . Nam si fidem habet sine spe ac sine dilectione, Christum esse credit, non in Christum credit."

available evidence to prove this. At Cassiciacum shortly after his conversion he began a project, of which *De Libero Arbitrio* was a part, of showing how all the liberal arts led to the knowledge of God. Thus he does have a sense of what faith is that overlaps with Hume's understanding. But that is not all that Augustine is doing; it is not, at the deepest levels, even what he is primarily doing. For he is not primarily seeking evidence for the order of the universe; not only is he trying to provide an alternative to Manichaean determinism and to see the goodness of the creation, he is ultimately trying to bring his identity into conformity with whatever that order is as being God's will. The heart of the ideological argument is precisely this, for in it the particulars of the universe are not at question; it is a question of how one relates oneself to that on which all else depends. That relation for Augustine is the real heart of faith; faith is not simply belief without evidence.

It is important to understand *that* relation as being at the heart of Augustine's project because it is his relation to God that Augustine continues to ponder and struggle with for the rest of his life. The intellectualistic liberal arts project was soon given up; the struggle to conform with God's will was not. There is, of course, a sense in which Augustine did not change many of his views on cosmology, nor given the expectations of his age should he have done so. But he did refocus the terms of that struggle with the will of God. After writing *De Libero Arbitrio* he wrote about assent in the *Confessions* in explicit terms of moral and spiritual struggle. His great final work, *The City of God*, is a moral vision born of coming to understand himself and his world in the moral and spiritual terms of the Bible—and thus the Bible itself in the terms of a historical human struggle with questions of who and whose we are.

Thus faith for him was not simply belief in what mind could not or did not know, as it appears to be for Hume and much of philosophy of religion after Hume. It was the moral and spiritual struggle of the will, in conjunction with the memory and intellect, to bring himself into conformity with God. Taken in conjunction with Augustine's first insight—that this moral struggle of the will is at the heart of our very identity—we thus come to see what is at the heart of Augustine's philosophical enterprise. It is a very different vision than the modern one. But it is also very different from what it is often characterized as being by modern philosophy, for it is not a case of bad metaphysics, but has an underlying moral seriousness—a sense that philosophy contributes to who we are—that a good deal of modern philosophy lacks. For the moral order to which we assent makes us who we are, and that may be a far more important question about the freedom of the will than any other.

To be sure there is also something mysterious about this inner quest, at least insofar as it is something to which public reason and method have no direct access. But it is not, for all that, incomprehensible or unheard of, as Augustine knew quite well. Indeed, it may very well be at the root of the very common enterprise of understanding who we are. For as Augustine writes in the *Homilies on the Gospel of John*:

> Give me a lover, and he feels what I say. Give me one that longs, one that hungers, one that is travelling in this wilderness, and thirsting and panting after the fountain of his eternal home; give such, and he knows what I say.[40]

40. *Homilies on the Gospel of John*, 26.4. Translated J. Gibb. Vol. VII, *The Nicene and Post-Nicene Fathers*, ed. Philip Schaff. [reprinted Grand Rapids: Wm. B. Eerdmans, 1974].

[13]

Augustine's Political Realism

Reinhold Niebuhr

The terms 'idealism' and 'realism' are not analogous in political and in metaphysical theory; and they are certainly not as precise in political, as in metaphysical, theory. In political and moral theory 'realism' denotes the disposition to take all factors in a social and political situation which offer resistance to established norms into account, particularly the factors of self-interest and power. In the words of a notorious 'realist', Machiavelli, the purpose of the realist is 'to follow the truth of the matter rather than the imagination of it; for many have pictures of republics and principalities which have never been seen'. This definition of realism implies that idealists are subject to illusions about social realities, which indeed they are. 'Idealism' is, in the esteem of its proponents, characterized by loyalty to moral norms and ideals, rather than to self-interest, whether individual or collective. It is, in the opinion of its critics, characterized by a disposition to ignore or be indifferent to the forces in human life which offer resistance to universally valid ideals and norms. This disposition, to which Machiavelli refers, is general whenever men are inclined to take the moral pretensions of themselves or their fellow-men at face value;

for the disposition to hide self-interest behind the façade of pretended devotion to values, transcending self-interest, is wellnigh universal. It is, moreover, an interesting human characteristic, proving that the concept of 'total depravity', as it is advanced by some Christian realists, is erroneous. Man is a curious creature with so strong a sense of obligation to his fellows that he cannot pursue his own interests without pretending to serve his fellow-men. The definitions of 'realists' and 'idealists' emphasize disposition, rather than doctrines; and they are therefore bound to be inexact. It must remain a matter of opinion whether or not a man takes adequate account of all the various factors and forces in a social situation. Was Plato a realist, for instance, because he tried to guard against the self-interest of the 'guardians' of his ideal state by divesting them of property and reducing their family responsibilities to a minimum? Does this bit of 'realism' cancel out the essential unrealism, inherent in ascribing to the 'lusts of the body' the force of recalcitrance against the moral norm; or in attributing pure virtue to pure mind?

Augustine was, by general consent, the first great 'realist' in western history. He deserves this distinction because his picture of social reality in his *De Civitate Dei* gives an adequate account of the social factions, tensions, and competitions which we know to be wellnigh universal on every level of community; while the classical age conceived the order and justice of its *polis* to be a comparatively simple achievement, which would be accomplished when reason had brought all sub-rational forces under its dominion.

This difference in the viewpoint of Augustine and the

classical philosophers lies in Augustine's biblical, rather than rationalistic, conception of human selfhood with the ancillary conception of the seat of evil being in the self. Augustine broke with classical rationalism in his conception of the human self, according to which the self is composed of mind and body, the mind being the seat of virtue because it has the capacity to bring all impulses into order; and the body, from which come the 'lusts and ambitions', being the cause of evil. According to Augustine the self is an integral unity of mind and body. It is something more than mind and is able to use mind for its purposes. The self has, in fact, a mysterious identity and integrity transcending its functions of mind, memory, and will. 'These three things, memory, understanding, and love, are mine and not their own,' he declares, 'for they do what they do not for themselves but for me; or rather I do it by them. For it is I who remember by memory and understand by understanding and love by love.'[1] It must be observed that the transcendent freedom of this self, including its capacity to defy any rational or natural system into which someone may seek to co-ordinate it (its capacity for evil), makes it difficult for any philosophy, whether ancient or modern, to comprehend its true dimension. That is why the classical wise men obscured it by fitting its mind into a system of universal mind and the body into the system of nature; and that is also why the modern wise men, for all their rhetoric about the 'dignity' of the individual, try to cut down the dimension of human selfhood so that it will seem to fit into a system of nature. This conception of selfhood is drawn from the Bible, rather than from philosophy, because the transcendent

[1] *De Trin.*, 15, 22.

self which is present in, though it transcends, all of the functions and effects, is comprehensible only in the dramatic-historical mode of apprehension which characterizes biblical faith. Augustine draws on the insights of neo-Platonism to illustrate the self's power of self-transcendence; but he rejects Plotinus' mystic doctrine, in which the particular self, both human and divine, is lost in a vast realm of undifferentiated being.

Augustine's conception of the evil which threatens the human community on every level is a corollary of his doctrine of selfhood. 'Self-love' is the source of evil rather than some residual natural impulse which mind has not yet completely mastered. This excessive love of self, sometimes also defined as pride or *superbia*, is explained as the consequence of the self's abandonment of God as its true end and of making itself 'a kind of end'. It is this powerful self-love or, in a modern term, 'egocentricity', this tendency of the self to make itself its own end or even to make itself the false centre of whatever community it inhabits, which sows confusion into every human community. The power of self-love is more spiritual than the 'lusts of the body' of which Plato speaks; and it corrupts the processes of the mind more than Plato or Aristotle knew. That is why Augustine could refute the classical theory with the affirmation that 'it is not the bad body which causes the good soul to sin but the bad soul which causes the good body to sin'. At other times Augustine defines the evil in man as the 'evil will'; but with the understanding that it is the self which is evil in the manifestation of its will. 'For he who extols the whole nature of the soul as the chief good and condemns the nature of the flesh as if it were evil, assuredly is fleshly both in the love of the soul and in the hatred of the flesh.'[1] This concise statement of the Christian position surely refutes the absurd charge of moderns that the Christian faith is 'dualistic' and generates contempt for the body. It also established the only real basis for a realistic estimate of the forces of recalcitrance which we must face on all levels of the human community, particularly for a realistic estimate of the spiritual dimension of these forces and of the comparative impotence of 'pure reason' against them. Compared with a Christian realism, which is based on Augustine's interpretation of biblical faith, a great many modern social and psychological theories, which fancy themselves anti-Platonic or even anti-Aristotelian and which make much of their pretended 'realism', are in fact no more realistic than the classical philosophers. Thus modern social and psychological scientists are for ever seeking to isolate some natural impulse such as 'aggressiveness' and to manage it; with equal vanity they are trying to find a surrogate for Plato's and Aristotle's disinterested 'reason' in a so-called 'scientific method'. Their inability to discover the corruption of self-interest in reason or in man's rational pursuits; and to measure the spiritual dimension of man's inhumanity and cruelty, gives an air of sentimentality to the learning of our whole liberal culture. Thus we have no guidance amid the intricacies of modern power politics except as the older disciplines, less enamoured of the 'methods of natural science', and the common sense of the man in the street supply the necessary insights.

[1] *De Civ. Dei*, 15, 5.

AUGUSTINE'S POLITICAL REALISM

II

Augustine's description of the social effects of human egocentricity or self-love is contained in his definition of the life of the 'city of this world', the *civitas terrena*, which he sees as commingled with the *civitas dei*. The 'city of this world' is dominated by self-love to the point of contempt of God; and is distinguished from the *civitas dei* which is actuated by the 'love of God' to the point of contempt of self. This 'city' is not some little city-state, as it is conceived in classical thought. It is the whole human community on its three levels of the family, the commonwealth, and the world. A potential world community is therefore envisaged in Augustine's thought. But, unlike the stoic and modern 'idealists', he does not believe that a common humanity or a common reason gives promise of an easy actualization of community on the global level. The world community, declares Augustine 'is fuller of dangers as the greater sea is more dangerous'.[1] Augustine is a consistent realist in calling attention to the fact that the potential world community may have a common human reason but it speaks in different languages and 'Two men, each ignorant of each other's language' will find that 'dumb animals, though of a different species, could more easily hold intercourse than they, human being though they be'.[2] This realistic reminder that common linguistic and ethnic cultural forces, which bind the community together on one level, are divisive on the ultimate level, is a lesson which our modern proponents of world government have not yet learned.

Augustine's description of the *civitas terrena* includes

[1] *De Civ. Dei*, 19, 7. [2] *Ibid.*, 19, 21.

an emphasis on the tensions, frictions, competitions of interest, and overt conflicts to which every human community is exposed. Even in the family one cannot rely on friendship 'seeing that secret treachery has often broken it up'.[1] This bit of realism will seem excessive until we remember that our own generation has as much difficulty in preserving the peace and integrity in the smallest and most primordial community, the family, as in integrating community on the highest global level.

The *civitas terrena* is described as constantly subject to an uneasy armistice between contending forces, with the danger that factional disputes may result in 'bloody insurrection' at any time. Augustine's realism prompts him to challenge Cicero's conception of a commonwealth as rooted in a 'compact of justice'. Not so, declares Augustine. Commonwealths are bound together by a common love, or collective interest, rather than by a sense of justice; and they could not maintain themselves without the imposition of power. 'Without injustice the republic would neither increase nor subsist. The imperial city to which the republic belongs could not rule over provinces without recourse to injustice. For it is unjust for some men to rule over others.'[2]

This realism has the merit of describing the power realities which underlie all large-scale social integrations whether in Egypt or Babylon or Rome, where a dominant city-state furnished the organizing power for the Empire. It also describes the power realities of national states, even democratic ones, in which a group, holding the dominant form of social power, achieves oligarchic rule, no matter how much modern democracy may bring such

[1] *De Civ. Dei*, 19, 5. [2] *Ibid.*, 19, 21.

power under social control. This realism in regard to the facts which underlie the organizing or governing power refutes the charge of modern liberals that a realistic analysis of social forces makes for state absolutism; so that a mild illusion in regard to human virtue is necessary to validate democracy. Realistic pessimism did indeed prompt both Hobbes and Luther to an unqualified endorsement of state power; but that is only because they were not realistic enough. They saw the dangers of anarchy in the egotism of the citizens but failed to perceive the dangers of tyranny in the selfishness of the ruler. Therefore they obscured the consequent necessity of placing checks upon the ruler's self-will. Augustine's realism was indeed excessive. On the basis of his principles he could not distinguish between government and slavery, both of which were supposedly the rule over man by man and were both a consequence of, and remedy for, sin; nor could he distinguish between a commonwealth and a robber band, for both were bound together by collective interest; 'For even thieves must hold together or they cannot effect what they intend.' The realism fails to do justice to the sense of justice in the constitution of the Roman Empire; or for that matter to the sense of justice in a robber band. For even thieves will fall out if they cannot trust each other to divide the loot, which is their common aim, equitably. But the excessive emphasis upon the factors of power and interest, a wholesome corrective to Cicero's and modern Ciceronian moralistic illusions, is not fatal to the establishment of justice so long as the dangers of tyranny are weighed as realistically as the dangers of anarchy.

Augustine's realistic attitude towards government rests

partly upon the shrewd observation that social peace and order are established by a dominant group within some level of community; and that this group is not exempt from the corruption of self-interest merely because the peace of society has been entrusted to it. (One thinks incidentally how accurately the Augustinian analysis fits both the creative and the ambiguous character of the American hegemony in the social cohesion of the free world.) The realism is partly determined by his conception of a 'natural order' which he inherited from the early Christian fathers, who in turn took it from that part of the Stoic theory which emphasized the primordial or primitive as the natural. This Stoic and Christian primitivism has the merit of escaping the errors of those natural law theories which claim to find a normative moral order amid the wide variety of historic forms or even among the most universal of these forms. The freedom of man makes these Stoic conceptions of the 'natural' impossible. But it has the weakness which characterizes all primitivism, whether Stoic, Christian, or Romantic, for it makes primitive social forms normative. A primitive norm, whether of communal property relations or unorganized social cohesion, may serve provisionally as an occasion for the criticism of the institutions of an advancing civilization, more particularly the institutions of property and government; but it has the disadvantage of prompting indiscriminate criticism. This lack of discrimination is obvious in primitivistic Stoicism, in early Christianity, in seventeenth-century Cromwellian sectarianism, in Romanticism, and in Marxism and anarchism.

Augustine expressed this idea of a primitive social norm as follows: 'This is the prescribed order of nature. It is thus that God created man. For "let them", He says, "have dominion over the fish of the sea and the fowl of the air and over every creeping thing, which creepeth on the earth". He did not intend that His rational creature, made in his image, should have dominion over anything but irrational creation—not man over man but man over beasts. And hence the righteous men of primitive times were made shepherds of cattle rather than kings of men.'[1] This primitivism avoids the later error of the absolute sanctification of government. But its indiscriminate character is apparent by his failure to recognize the difference between legitimate and illegitimate, between ordinate and inordinate subordination of man to man. Without some form of such subordination the institutions of civilization could not exist.

III

If Augustine's realism is contained in his analysis of the *civitas terrena,* his refutation of the idea that realism must lead to cynicism or relativism is contained in his definition of the *civitas dei,* which he declares to be 'commingled' with the 'city of this word' and which has the 'love of God' rather than the 'love of self' as its guiding principle. The tension between the two cities is occasioned by the fact that, while egotism is 'natural' in the sense that it is universal, it is not natural in the sense that it does not conform to man's nature who transcends himself indeterminately and can only have God rather than self for his end. A realism becomes morally cynical or nihilistic when it assumes that the universal characteristic

[1] *De Civ. Dei,* 19, 15.

in human behaviour must also be regarded as normative. The biblical account of human behaviour, upon which Augustine bases his thought, can escape both illusion and cynicism because it recognizes that the corruption of human freedom may make a behaviour pattern universal without making it normative. Good and evil are not determined by some fixed structure of human existence. Man, according to the biblical view, may use his freedom to make himself falsely the centre of existence; but this does not change the fact that love rather than self-love is the law of his existence in the sense that man can only be healthy and his communities at peace if man is drawn out of himself and saved from the self-defeating consequences of self-love. There are several grave errors in Augustine's account of love and the relation of love to self-love; but before considering them we might well first pay tribute to his approach to political problems. The virtue of making love, rather than justice, into the norm for the community may seem, at first blush, to be dubious. The idea of justice seems much more relevant than the idea of love, particularly for the collective relationships of men. The medieval tradition which makes the justice of a rational 'natural law' normative even for Christians when they consider the necessities of a sinful world, seems much more realistic than modern forms of sentimental Protestantism which regards love as a simple alternative to self-love, which could be achieved if only we could preach the idea persuasively enough to beguile men from the one to the other. Augustine's doctrine of love as the final norm must be distinguished from modern sentimental versions of Christianity which regard love as a simple possibility and which think it significant to assert the obvious proposition that all conflicts in the community would be avoided if only people and nations would love one another. Augustine's approach differs from modern forms of sentimental perfectionism in the fact that he takes account of the power and persistence of egotism, both individual and collective, and seeks to establish the most tolerable form of peace and justice under conditions set by human sin. He inherited the tradition of monastic perfection; and he allows it as a vent for the Christian impulse towards individual perfection, without however changing the emphasis upon the duty of the Christian to perfect the peace of the city of this world. Furthermore, he raises questions about monastic perfection which, when driven home by the Reformation, were to undermine the whole system. 'I venture to say', he writes, 'that it is good for those who observe continence and are proud of it, to fall that they may be humbled. For what benefit is it to anyone in whom is the virtue of continence, if pride holds sway? He is but despising that by which man is born in striving after that which led to satan's fall . . . holy virginity is better than conjugal chastity . . . but if we add two other things, pride and humility . . . which is better, pride or humility? . . . I have no doubt that a humble married woman is to be preferred to a proud virgin . . . a mother holds a lesser place in the Kingdom of God because she has been married, than the daughter, seeing that she is a virgin. . . . But if thy mother has been humble and thou proud, she will have some sort of place and thou none.'[1]

While Augustine's doctrine of love is thus not to be confused with modern sentimentalities which do not take

[1] Sermon CCCIIV, ix, 9.

the power of self-love seriously, one may well wonder whether an approach to politics which does not avail itself of the calculations of justice, may be deemed realistic. We have already noted that Augustine avails himself of the theory of the 'natural law' only in the primordial version of the theory. If primordial conditions of a 'natural order' are not to be defined as normative, the only alternative is to assume a 'rational order' to which the whole of historical life conforms. Aquinas, in fact, constructed his theory of the natural law upon classical, and primarily Aristotelian, foundations. It was the weakness of both classical and medieval theories that they assumed an order in history conforming to the uniformities of nature. Aristotle was aware of deviations in history greater than those in nature; but he believed that there was nevertheless one form 'which was marked by nature as the best'. There is, in other words, no place in this theory of natural law for the endlessly unique social configurations which human beings, in their freedom over natural necessity, construct. The proponents of 'natural law' therefore invariably introduce some historically contingent norm or social structure into what they regard as God's inflexible norm. That was the weakness of both classical and medieval social theory; and for that matter of the natural law theories of the bourgeois parties of the eighteenth century, who had found what they regarded as a more empirically perceived 'natural law'; but the modern empirical intelligence was no more capable than the deductive rational processes of classical and medieval times to construct a social norm, not coloured by the interests of the constructor, thus introducing the taint of ideology into the supposed sanctities of law. We must conclude therefore that Augustine was wise in avoiding the alleged solution of a natural law theory, which was the basis of so much lack of realism in both the classical and the medieval period, and which can persist today long after the Aristotelian idea of fixed form for historical events has been overcome, as the dogma of a religious system which makes its supposed sanctities into an article of faith. His conception of the radical freedom of man, derived from the biblical view, made it impossible to accept the idea of fixed forms of human behaviour and of social organization, analogous to those of nature, even as he opposed the classical theory of historical cycles. Furthermore, his conception of human selfhood and of the transcendence of the self over its mind, made it impossible to assume the identity of the individual reason with a universal reason, which lies at the foundation of the classical and medieval natural law theories. It is in fact something of a mystery how the Christian insights into human nature and history, expressed by Augustine, could have been subordinated to classical thought with so little sense of the conflict between them in the formulations of Thomas Aquinas; and how they should have become so authoritative in Roman Catholicism without more debate between Augustinian and Thomistic emphases.

Augustine's formula for leavening the city of this world with the love of the city of God is more adequate than classical and medieval thought, both in doing justice to the endless varieties of historical occasions and configurations and in drawing upon the resources of love rather than law in modifying human behaviour.

Every 'earthly peace', declares Augustine, is good as far as it goes. 'But they will not have it long for they used it not well while they had it.' That is, unless some larger love or loyalty qualifies the self-interest of the various groups, this collective self-interest will expose the community to either an overt conflict of competing groups or to the injustice of a dominant group which 'when it is victorious it will become vice's slave'. Let us use some examples from current national and international problems to illustrate the Augustinian thesis. There is, or was, a marked social tension between the middle classes of industrial owners and the industrial workers in all modern industrial nations. In some of them, for instance in Germany and France, this tension led to overt forms of the class conflict. In others such as Britain, the smaller European nations and America, this tension was progressively resolved by various accommodations of interest. Wherein lay the difference? It did not lie in the possession of more adequate formulas of justice in some nations than in others. The difference lay in the fact that in some nations the various interest groups had, in addition to their collective interest, a 'sense of justice', a disposition to 'give each man his due' and a loyalty to the national community which qualified the interest struggle. Now, that spirit of justice is identical with the spirit of love, except at the highest level of the spirit of love, where it becomes purely sacrificial and engages in no calculation of what the due of each man may be. Two forms of love, the love of the other and the love of the community, were potent in short in modifying the acerbities and injustices of the class struggle. The two forms of love availed themselves of various calculations of justice in arriving at and defining their *ad hoc* agreements. But the factors in each nation and in each particular issue were too variable to allow for the application of any general rules or formulas of justice. Agreements were easier in fact if too much was not claimed for these formulas. Certain 'principles' of justice, as distinguished from formulas or prescriptions, were indeed operative, such as liberty, equality, and loyalty to covenants; but these principles will be recognized as no more than the law of love in its various facets.

In the same manner the international community is exposed to exactly the tensions and competitions of interest which Augustine describes. There are no formulas of justice or laws which will prevent these tensions from reaching overt conflict, if the collective interest of each nation is not modified by its loyalty to a higher value such as the common civilization of the free nations. Where this common loyalty is lacking, as in our relation with Russia, no formula can save us from the uneasy peace in which we live. The character of this peace is just as tentative as Augustine described it. Whenever common loves or loyalties, or even common fears, lay the foundation for community, it must of course be our business to perfect it by calculations of justice which define our mutual responsibilities as exactly as possible.

It must be noted that the Augustinian formula for the leavening influence of a higher upon a lower loyalty or love, is effective in preventing the lower loyalty from involving itself in self-defeat. It corrects the 'realism' of those who are myopically realistic by seeing only their own interests and failing thereby to do justice to their interests where they are involved with the interests of others. There are modern realists, for instance, who, in their reaction to abstract and vague forms of international idealism, counsel the nation to consult only its own interests. In a sense collective self-interest is so consistent that it is superfluous to advise it. But a consistent self-interest on the part of a nation will work against its interests because it will fail to do justice to the broader and longer interests, which are involved with the interests of other nations. A narrow national loyalty on our part, for instance, will obscure our long-range interests where they are involved with those of a whole alliance of free nations. Thus the loyalty of a leavening portion of a nation's citizens to a value transcending national interest will save a 'realistic' nation from defining its interests in such narrow and short-range terms as to defeat the real interests of the nation.

IV

We have acknowledged some weaknesses in the Augustinian approach to the political order which we must now define and examine more carefully. Non-Catholics commonly criticize Augustine's alleged identification of the *civitas dei* with the visible Church. But we must absolve him of this charge or insist on a qualification of the criticism. He does indeed accept the Catholic doctrine, which had grown up before his day; and he defines the visible Church as the only perfect society. There are passages in which he seems to assume that it is possible to claim for the members of the Church that they are solely actuated by the *amor dei*. But he introduces so many reservations to this assertion that he may well be defined in this, as in other instances, as the father of both Catholicism and the Reformation. Of the Church, Augustine declared, 'by faith she is a virgin. In the flesh she has few holy virgins';[1]

[1] Sermon CCXIII, vii, 7.

or again: 'God will judge the wicked and the good. The evil cannot now be separated from the good but must be suffered for a season. The wicked may be with us on the threshing floor . . . in the barn they cannot be.'[1] The reservations which he made upon the identification of the Church and the kingdom laid the foundations for the later Reformation position. But these reservations about the sinners who might be present in the visible Church cannot obscure a graver error in his thought. This error is probably related to his conception of grace which does not allow for the phenomenon, emphasized by the Reformation, that men may be redeemed in the sense that they consciously turn from self to Christ as their end, and yet they are not redeemed from the corruption of egotism, which expresses itself even in the lives of the saints. This insight is most succinctly expressed in Luther's phrase '*justus et peccator simul*' (righteous and sinners at once). When Augustine distinguished between the 'two loves' which characterize the 'two cities', the love of God and the love of self, and when he pictured the world as a commingling of the two cities, he does not recognize that the commingling is due not to the fact that two types of people dwell together but because the conflict between love and self-love is in every soul. It is particularly important to recognize this fact in political analyses; for nothing is more obvious than that personal dedication is no guarantee against the involvement of the dedicated individual in some form of collective egotism.

We have frequently referred to Augustine's definition of the 'two loves' which inform the 'two cities' of which 'the one is selfish and the other social', the one loving self

[1] *Comm. on Ps.* CXI, 9.

to the point of the contempt of God and the other loving God to the point of contempt of self. The question is whether Bishop Nygren[1] is right in defining the Augustinian conception of *amor dei* as rooted in a classical rather than a biblical concept.

In defence of Augustine it must be said that he is not insensible to the two facets of the love commandment and therefore does not define the *amor dei* in purely mystical terms as a flight from this world. He insists on the contrary that the *amor dei* is 'social' and he offers the concord among brethren as a proof of the love of God. But nevertheless Nygren is right in suggesting that the thought of Plotinus has coloured Augustine's conceptions sufficiently so that the *agape* of the New Testament is misinterpreted by Augustine's conception of *charitas* and *amor dei*. The *agape* form of love in the New Testament fails to be appreciated particularly in two of its facets: (*a*) the equality of the 'two loves', the love of the neighbour and the love of God (enforced in the Scripture by the words 'the Second is like unto it') is violated by Augustine under the influence of Plotinus even as a later medieval Catholic mystic, Saint John of the Cross, violates it when he regarded the love of the creature as a ladder which might lead us to the love of God, but must be subordinated to the latter. Augustine wants us to love the neighbour for the sake of God, which may be a correct formulation; but he wants us to prove the genuineness of our love of God in the love of the neighbour, or by leading him to God. Thus the meeting of the neighbour's need without regard to any ultimate religious intention is emptied of meaning. The love of the neighbour is for him not

[1] Anders Nygren, in *Agape and Eros*.

part of a double love commandment but merely the instrument of a single love commandment which bids us flee all mortality including the neighbour in favour of the immutable good. (*b*) The second facet of the *agape* concept of the New Testament which tends to be obscured is the notion of sacrificial love, the absurd principle of the Cross, the insistence that the self must sacrifice itself for the other. It is not fair to Augustine to say that he neglects this facet of meaning for he seems to emphasize it so constantly. He comes closest to its meaning when he deals with the relation of humility to love. Yet it seems fair to say that he was sufficiently imbued by classical mystical thought forms so that the emphasis lies always upon the worthiness or unworthiness of the object of our love; the insistence is that only God and not some mutable 'good' or person is worthy of our love. This is a safeguard against all forms of idolatry. But it does not answer another important question: when I love a person or a community do I love myself in them or do I truly love them? Is my love a form of alter-egoism? The Augustinian *amor dei* assumes that the self in its smallness cannot contain itself within itself and therefore it is challenged to go out from itself to the most ultimate end. But it hardly reveals the full paradox of self-realization through self-giving which is a scandal in the field of rational ethics as the Cross is a scandal in the field of rational religion. Yet it is the source of ultimate wisdom. For the kind of self-giving which has self-realization as its result must not have self-realization as its conscious end; otherwise the self by calculating its enlargement will not escape from itself completely enough to be enlarged. The weakness of Augustine in obscuring these facets of the *agape* principle may be illustrated, without unfairness I hope, by referring to his treatment of family love. He questions the love of mate or children as the final form of love, but not for New Testament reasons. He does not say: 'When you love your wife and children are you maybe really loving yourself in them and using them as the instruments of your self-aggrandizements?' He declares instead, in effect, you must not love your family too unreservedly because your wife and children are mortal. They also belong to the 'rivers of Babylon', and, if you give them absolute devotion, the hour of bereavement will leave you desolate. Of course Augustine is too much the Christian to engage in a consistent mystic depreciation of the responsibilities and joys of this earthly life. After all, his whole strategy for the 'commingling' of the two cities revolves around the acceptance of the ordinary responsibilities of home and state but in performing these tasks for the ultimate, rather than the immediate end. 'What then?' he asks. 'Shall all perish who marry and are given in marriage, who till the fields and build houses? No, but those who put their trust in these things, who prefer them to God, who for the sake of these things are quick to offend God, these will perish. But those who either do not use these things or who use them as though they used them not, trusting more in Him who gave them than in the things given, understanding in them His consolation and mercy, and who are not absorbed in these gifts lest they fall away from the giver. These are they whom the day will not overtake as a thief unprepared.'[1] We must not, in criticizing Augustine for neo-Platonic elements in his thought, obscure the Christian elements which will be equally an

[1] *Comm. on Ps.* cxx, 3.

offence to modern men who regard the world as self-sufficing and self-explanatory, who reject as absurd the Christian faith that there is not only a mystery behind and above the world of observed phenomena and intelligible meanings, but that it is a mystery whose meaning has been disclosed as a love which elicits our answering love. This modern generation with its confidence in a world without mystery, and without meaning beyond simple intelligibility, will not be beguiled from its unbelief by a reminder that its emancipation from God has betrayed it into precisely those idolatries, the worship of false gods, the dedication of finite values as if they were ultimate, of which Augustine spoke. But it must be recorded nevertheless as a significant fact of modern history. While it is an offence to regard communism as the inevitable end-product of secularism, as some Christians would have us believe, it is only fair to point out that the vast evils of modern communism come ironically to a generation which thought it would be easy to invest all the spiritual capital of men, who mysteriously transcend the historical process, in some value or end without that process; and communism is merely the most pathetic and cruel of the idolatrous illusions of this generation.

We must be clear about the fact that all the illusions about man's character and history which made it so difficult for either the classical or the modern age to come to terms with the vexing problems of our togetherness, seem to stem from efforts to understand man in both his grandeur and his misery by 'integrating' him into some natural or rational system of coherence. Thereby they denied the mystery of his transcendence over every process which points to another mystery beyond himself without which man is not only a mystery to himself but a misunderstood being.

We cannot deny that from a Christian standpoint the world is like a 'river of Babylon', to use Augustine's symbol; and that Augustine is right in suggesting that ultimately we cannot find peace if we are merely tossed down the river of time. We must find security in that which is not carried down the river. 'Observe however,' declares Augustine in a simile which will seem strange to generations which have made the 'rivers of Babylon', the stream of temporal events, into forces of redemption; but which will not seem so strange as the modern experience proves history as such to be less redemptive than we had believed: 'the rivers of Babylon are all things which are here loved, and pass away. For example, one man loves to practise husbandry, to grow rich by it, to employ his mind on it, to get his pleasure from it. Let him observe the issue and see that what he has loved is not a foundation of Jerusalem, but a river of Babylon. Another says, it is a grand thing to be a soldier; all farmers fear those who are soldiers, are subservient to them, tremble at them. If I am a farmer, I shall fear soldiers; if a soldier, farmers will fear me. Madman! thou hast cast thyself headlong into another river of Babylon, and that still more turbulent and sweeping. Thou wishest to be feared by thy inferior; fear Him who is greater than thou. He who fears thee may on a sudden become greater than thou, but He whom thou oughtest to fear will never become less. To be an advocate, says another, is a grand thing; eloquence is most powerful; always to have clients hanging on the lips of their eloquent advocate, and from his words looking for loss or gain, death or life, ruin or security. Thou knowest not whither thou hast cast thyself. This too is another river of Babylon, and its roaring sound is the din of the waters dashing against the rocks. Mark that it flows, that it glides on; beware, for it carries things away with it. To sail the seas, says another, and to trade is a grand thing—to know many lands, to make gains from every quarter, never to be answerable to any powerful man in thy country, to be always travelling, and to feed thy mind with the diversity of the nations and the business met with, and to return enriched by the increase of thy gains. This too is a river of Babylon. When will the gains stop? When wilt thou have confidence and be secure in the gains thou makest? The richer thou art, the more fearful wilt thou be. Once shipwrecked, thou wilt come forth stripped of all, and rightly wilt bewail thy fate *in* the rivers of Babylon, because thou wouldest not sit down and weep *upon* the rivers of Babylon.

'But there are other citizens of the holy Jerusalem, understanding their captivity, who mark how human wishes and the diverse lusts of men, hurry and drag them hither and thither, and drive them into the sea. They see this, and do not throw themselves into the rivers of Babylon, but sit down upon the rivers of Babylon and upon the rivers of Babylon weep, either for those who are being carried away by them, or for themselves whose deserts have placed them in Babylon.'[1]

Whatever the defects of the Augustine approach may be, we must acknowledge his immense superiority both over those who preceded him and who came after him. A part of that superiority was due to his reliance upon biblical rather than idealistic or naturalistic conceptions

[1] *Comm. on Ps.* CXXXVI, 3, 4.

of selfhood. But that could not have been the only cause, else Christian systems before and after him would not have been so inferior. Or were they inferior either because they subordinated the biblical-dramatic conception of human selfhood too much to the rationalistic scheme, as was the case with medieval Christianity culminating in the thought of Thomas Aquinas? or because they did not understand that the corruption of human freedom could not destroy the original dignity of man, as was the case with the Reformation with its doctrines of sin, bordering on total depravity and resulting in Luther's too pessimistic approach to political problems? As for secular thought, it has difficulty in approaching Augustine's realism without falling into cynicism or in avoiding nihilism without falling into sentimentality. Hobbes' realism was based on an insight which he shared with Augustine, namely, that in all historical encounters the mind is the servant and not the master of the self. But he failed to recognize that the self which thus made the mind its instrument was a corrupted and not a 'normal' self. Modern 'realists' know the power of collective self-interest as Augustine did; but they do not understand its blindness. Modern pragmatists understood the irrelevance of fixed and detailed norms; but they do not understand that love must take the place as the final norm for these inadequate norms. Modern liberal Christians know that love is the final norm for man; but they fall into sentimentality because they fail to measure the power and persistence of self-love. Thus Augustine, whatever may be the defects of his approach to political reality, and whatever may be the dangers of a too slavish devotion to his insights, nevertheless proves himself a more reliable guide than any known thinker. A generation which finds its communities imperilled and in decay from the smallest and most primordial community, the family, to the largest and most recent, the potential world community, might well take counsel of Augustine in solving its perplexities.

[14]

ST. AUGUSTINE AND THE CHRISTIAN IDEA OF PROGRESS:

THE BACKGROUND OF THE CITY OF GOD *

By Theodor E. Mommsen

In the summer of the year 410 Rome fell to a Visigothic army under King Alaric. Since the city suffered relatively little external damage, modern historians have sometimes been inclined to regard that conquest or sack of Rome as a rather insignificant incident. We should be wary, however, of any tendency to belittle the event, remembering that it impelled Augustine to write *The City of God.* In view of the impact this work has had upon the development of Christian thought, it can certainly be said that the fall of Rome in the year 410, which motivated its composition, marks a momentous date in the intellectual history of the western world.

Moreover, Augustine was not the only contemporary to be profoundly impressed by that event, as several other writings show. It may suffice here to quote a few sentences from St. Jerome, who was at that time living in Bethlehem. When he received the news of " the havoc wrought in the West and, above all, in the city of Rome " (*Epist.* 126, 2), he expressed his feelings in the preface to the first book of the *Commentaries on Ezekiel,* which he was then writing: " When the brightest light on the whole earth was extinguished, when the Roman empire was deprived of its head and when, to speak more correctly, the whole world perished in one city, then ' I was dumb

* This article was already in the hands of the printer when I got a copy of the essay by J. Straub, " Christliche Geschichtsapologetik in der Krisis des römischen Reiches," *Historia* (1950), 52–81. Prof. Straub's article does not discuss the idea of progress and the other Christian and pagan conceptions of history which were current before and throughout the fourth century. His main objective is rather, for the period from 378 to the aftermath of the fall of Rome in 410, to deal " mit der Rolle, welche die christlichen Apologeten in jenem epochalen Umwandlungsprozess gespielt haben, in dem der römische Staat zugrundeging, aber die mit dem Staat aufs engste verbundene Kirche ihre eigene Existenz zu behaupten und sich für die Teilnahme an der neu zu bildenden Völkergemeinschaft der Welt des Mittelalters freizumachen suchte " (p. 54). Of particular value is Prof. Straub's clarification of the views which Augustine and Orosius had concerning the Christian attitude toward the Roman empire.—Unfortunately I was unable to consult the articles by H. v. Campenhausen, O. Herding, and W. Loewenich, all of which, according to Straub, *l.c.*, p. 52, n. 1, deal with Augustine's historical conceptions.

with silence, I held my peace, even from good, and my sorrow was stirred' (*Psalm* 39, 2)." And in the preface to the third book of the same work Jerome asked: "Who would believe that Rome, built up by the conquest of the whole world, has collapsed, that the mother of nations has also become their tomb?" [1]

To understand the profound consternation of Jerome and his contemporaries we must realize that the fate of Rome meant infinitely more to the people of late antiquity than the fate of any city, even the most renowned, would mean to the western world today. For many deeply rooted ideas and beliefs, and numerous superstitions, were connected with the very name and existence of that city. One need recall only the famous lines of Vergil's *Aeneid* (1, 278f.), in which Jupiter says: "To the Romans I assign limits neither to the extent nor to the duration of their empire; dominion have I given them without end." This notion of "the eternal city," the capital of a universal empire, "the golden Rome," we find reflected in the works of almost all the pagan writers and poets of the first centuries of our era, whether they were of Latin, Greek or Oriental origin.[2] Thus, at the end of the fourth century, the pagan general and historian Ammianus Marcellinus declared (*Histor.*, 14, 6, 3) that "as long as there are men, Rome will be victorious so that it will increase with lofty growth." And around the year 400 the Christian poet Claudianus wrote (*On the consulate of Stilicho*, 3, 159f.): "There will never be an end to the power of Rome, for luxury and pride resulting in vices and enmities have destroyed all other kingdoms."

During the same period the attitude of the Christians toward the Roman empire was divided. On the one hand there ran within early Christianity an undercurrent of strong hatred of the Roman state and of everything that state stood for. This hostility, nourished by Jewish traditions and strengthened by the persecutions, manifested itself in the apparently widespread expectation that some day the prediction of the angel in the *Book of Revelation* (14, 8) would be fulfilled: "Babylon [*i.e.*, Rome] is fallen, is fallen, that great city, because she made all nations drink of the wine of the wrath of her fornication."

[1] Throughout this article I have based the text of my quotations from the Church Fathers on the translations in the three series of *The Select Library of the Ante-Nicene Fathers*, and of the *Nicene and Post-Nicene Fathers* (1885–1900); very frequently, however, I have found it necessary to make changes in the translations, for which I have to take the responsibility.

[2] See E. K. Rand, *The Building of Eternal Rome* (1943).

On the other hand, the official spokesmen of the early Church always remembered that Jesus himself had ordered his disciples to "render unto Caesar the things which are Caesar's" (*Matthew,* 23, 21), and that St. Paul had demanded obedience to the Empire when he wrote in his *Epistle to the Romans* (13, 1): "Let every soul be subject unto the higher powers; for there is no power but of God: the powers that be, are ordained of God." In accordance, then, with these explicit orders of Christ and St. Paul, every adherent of the faith had to pay his outward respect, at least, to the established authorities of the state.

But many Christians showed themselves willing to go even farther and actually hoped and prayed for the continuance of the Roman empire. This affirmative attitude grew out of certain historical and eschatological ideas which went back to both pagan and Jewish traditions.[3] In the Hellenistic era there had developed in the East a theory which saw history take its course in a sequence of great or, rather, universal monarchies. Four of these empires were to follow one another, and the series was to conclude with a fifth monarchy which, it was believed, would last to the end of the world. This idea of the four or five monarchies was adopted by some of the Roman and Greek historians, and it appeared likewise in Jewish literature. For the great image seen in a dream by Nebuchadnezzar (*Daniel,* 2, 31ff.) and the four beasts seen by Daniel himself (7, 1ff.), were explained by the pre-Christian tradition in terms of an interpretation of world history: these visions were believed to signify symbolically that history takes its course through the succession of four universal monarchies; the disintegration of the last of the four empires was assumed to usher in the end of the world.

In the latter part of the second century and in the first part of the third century Christian theologians like Irenaeus of Lyons, Tertullian and Hippolytus adopted these pagan and Jewish traditions and expressed their opinion that the Roman empire "which now rules" (Irenaeus, *Against Heresies,* 5, 26, 1), should be considered to be the fourth monarchy.[4] All these Christian authors shared the belief that

[3] The most recent treatments of this question have been given by J. W. Swain, "The theory of the four monarchies: opposition history under the Roman empire," *Classical Philology* (1940), 1–21; H. L. Ginsberg, *Studies in Daniel* (1948), 5–23.

[4] See the list of authors who identified the fourth monarchy with the Roman empire, which has been compiled by H. H. Rowley, *Darius the Mede and the Four World Empires in the Book of Daniel* (1935), 73ff.

the fall of the last empire would be a most ominous event. Thus, Tertullian said in his treatise *On the Resurrection of the Flesh* (ch. 24), in which he interpreted a passage in St. Paul's *Second Epistle to the Thessalonians* (2, 7), that the Antichrist will appear after the Roman state has been scattered into ten kingdoms. On the basis of this eschatological belief Tertullian declared very emphatically in his *Apology* (ch. 32, 1): " There is also another and greater necessity for our praying in behalf of the emperors and the whole status of the empire and Roman affairs. For we know that only the continued existence of the Roman Empire retards the mighty power which threatens the whole earth, and postpones the very end of this world with its menace of horrible afflictions." In the early fourth century Lactantius stated even more explicitly in his *Divine Institutions* (7, 25, 6–8): " The fall and the ruin of the world will shortly take place, although it seems that nothing of that kind is to be feared as long as the city of Rome stands intact. But when the capital of the world has fallen . . . who can doubt that the end will have arrived for the affairs of men and the whole world? It is that city which still sustains all things. And the God of heaven is to be entreated by us and implored—if indeed His laws and decrees can be delayed—lest sooner than we think that detestable tyrant should come who will undertake so great a deed and tear out that eye by the destruction of which the world itself is about to fall."

During the fourth century a number of commentators on the *Book of Daniel,* including Eusebius and John Chrysostom in the East, Jerome and Sulpicius Severus (*Sacred Histories,* 2, 3) in the West, continued to identify the fourth monarchy with the Roman empire. Cyril of Jerusalem (*Catechetical Lectures,* 15, 12) followed even more closely the line of Irenaeus, Tertullian and Lactantius, by declaring: " The Antichrist is to come when the time of the Roman empire has been fulfilled and the end of the world is drawing near."

In view of the persistence of this concern for the continuance of Rome it seems safe to assume that in the year 410 many contemporaries regarded Alaric's conquest of Rome as the realization of the long-dreaded " fall of Rome " and considered the end of the world to be imminent. A reflection of this superstitious fear we find, I think, even in the words of Jerome, that " the whole world has perished in one city."

Augustine was, of course, well aware of both the pagan belief in "eternal Rome" and the eschatological speculations of his fellow-Christians. He rejected emphatically the one idea as well as the other. As to the pagan notion, he pointed out (*Sermon* 105, 9) that "the earthly kingdoms have their changes" and that only of the Kingdom of Christ it can be said: "There shall be no end" (*Luke*, 1, 33). He continued (*ibid.*, § 10): "They who have promised this to earthly kingdoms have not been guided by truth but have lied by flattery." He quoted the famous line from Vergil—whom he calls rather slightingly "a certain poet of theirs"—and remarked: "This kingdom which you [Jupiter] have given 'without limits to its duration,' is it on earth or in heaven? Certainly it is on earth. And even if it were in heaven, yet 'heaven and earth shall pass away' (*Matthew*, 24, 35). Those things shall pass away, which God Himself has made. How much more rapidly shall that pass away which Romulus founded?" As to the meaning of the passage in St. Paul's *Second Epistle to the Thessalonians* (2, 7): "Only he who now holdeth, let him hold until he be taken out of the way,"[5] Augustine was much less certain than Tertullian, who had concluded from these words that the duration of this world is bound up with the duration of the Roman empire. Augustine knew (*City of God*, 20, 19 E–F)[6] that "some think that this refers to the Roman empire," and he granted that such an interpretation, in contrast to some others, "is not absurd." But at the same time he felt obliged to state: "I frankly confess that I do not know what St. Paul meant."

In reply to those Christian thinkers who attempted to figure out the exact date of the end of the world and connected the coming of that event with concrete developments and with definite historical incidents like "the fall of Rome," Augustine declared (*City of God*, 18, 53 A–B)[6] that such a question "is entirely improper." For he pointed out that Christ himself told his disciples: "It is not for you to know the times and the seasons which the Father hath put in His own power" (*Acts*, 1, 7). "In vain, then," Augustine stated, "do we attempt to compute and determine the years which remain to this world." Whoever undertakes that kind of calculation, Augustine con-

[5] The above translation is based on the text of the *Itala* quoted by Augustine; the version in the *King James Bible* reads: "Only he who now letteth will let, until he be taken out of the way."

[6] My quotations from *De civitate Dei* are based on the Latin text edited by J. E. Welldon, 2 vols. (1924), and on the translation by M. Dods, *The City of God*, 2 vols. (1872); frequently, however, I have replaced Dods' translation with my own.

cluded, "uses human conjecture and brings forward nothing certain from the authority of the canonical Scriptures."

Another argument which in several of his sermons Augustine employed, though in a more incidental fashion, is the observation that, after all, Rome was still standing, in spite of the disaster of the year 410. For instance, in the *Sermon on the Ruin of the City* he said that Rome, unlike Sodom, was not completely destroyed, and in another discourse (*Sermon* 105, 9) he declared: "The city which has given us birth, according to the flesh, still abides, God be thanked." He added (§ 11): "An end there will be to all earthly kingdoms. If that end be now, God alone knows. Perhaps the end is not yet, and we, because of a certain weakness or mercifulness or anguish, wish that it may not yet be." Augustine confessed (§ 12) that he himself was "entreating the Lord for Rome," not because he believed the duration of that one city would guarantee the duration of the whole world, but simply because there were many fellow-Christians in Rome, dear to him as all other Christians were.[7]

Since Rome did, in fact, survive, the old belief in its eternity also survived for many centuries to come, and with it persisted the popular superstition, in spite of its rejection by Augustine, that the final "fall" of the city would signify the coming end of the world. Only one of many testimonials to that belief may be quoted. In a British text of the early eighth century, which was wrongly ascribed to the Venerable Bede, we find the following lines:

> As long as the Colosseum stands, Rome also stands.
> When the Colosseum falls, Rome also will fall.
> When Rome falls, the world also will fall.[8]

The denial of the pagan belief in the eternity of Rome and the rejection of any connection between Christian eschatology and specific historical events occupy, however, only a rather minor place in the whole context of *The City of God*. Augustine felt justified in making short shrift of these ideas because he regarded them as either mere superstitions or futile conjectures.

[7] Cf. also *Sermon* 81, 9; all three sermons mentioned were preached in the years 410 and 411: see A. Kunzelmann in *Miscellanea Agostiniana* (1931), II, 449f., 500. On these sermons see also M. Pontet, *L'exégèse de S. Augustin prédicateur* (1944), 454, 471–76.

[8] Pseudo-Bede, *Flores ex diversis, quaestiones et parabola*, ed. Migne, *Patrologia Latina*, 94, col. 543; cf. F. Schneider, *Rom und Romgedanke im Mittelalter* (1926), 66f., 251.

The real purpose of his great book he stated in a number of places but nowhere more concisely than in the work entitled *Retractations* (2, 68, 1), which he wrote after the completion of *The City of God* in the year 426. He defined his primary objective as follows: " In the meantime Rome had been overthrown by the invasion of the Goths under king Alaric and by the vehemence of a great defeat. The worshippers of the many and false gods, whom we commonly call pagans, attempted to attribute that overthrow to the Christian religion, and they began to blaspheme the true God with even more than their customary acrimony and bitterness. It was for that reason that I, kindled by zeal for the house of God, undertook to write the books on *The City of God* against their blasphemies and errors."

The accusation was very old that Christianity was responsible for the miseries of the world. The pagans claimed that the Christians, through their refusal to honor the traditional deities, were provoking the wrath of the very gods whose favor had raised Rome to her universal power. The Christian apologists found it easy to refute the charge. One of the most precise expressions of their customary reply is contained in Tertullian's *Apology* (40, 3, 5). Tertullian addressed the pagans as follows: " Pray, tell me, how many calamities befell the world as a whole, as well as individual cities, before Tiberius reigned, before the coming, that is, of Christ? " He asked: " Where were your gods in those days when a deluge effaced the whole earth or, as Plato believed, merely its plains? " And he concluded: " The truth is that the human race has always deserved ill at God's hand . . . . Therefore one ought to know that the very same God is angry now, as he always was, long before Christians were so much as spoken of."

Augustine used exactly the same kind of argument throughout the first five books of *The City of God,* only in a much more elaborate and detailed fashion than Tertullian, Arnobius, Lactantius and other apologists of the third century had done before him. He went still further and commissioned his younger friend Orosius to write an entire history of the world from a point of view which is best described by Orosius himself in the dedication to Augustine of his *Seven books of Histories against the Pagans:* "You bade me to discover from all the available data of histories and annals, whatever instances past ages have afforded of the burdens of war, the ravages of diseases, the horrors of famine, terrible earthquakes, extraordinary floods, dreadful eruptions of fire, thunderbolts and hailstorms, and also instances of the cruel miseries caused by murders and crimes against man's better self." [9] Orosius proved himself indeed " the true compiler of the evils of the world," as Petrarch (*Familiares,* 15, 9, 10) was to characterize him scornfully many centuries later. But in spite, or perhaps because, of their admitted prejudices and their preconceived ideas, Augustine's and Orosius's systematic expositions of the old apologist conceptions of world history in general and of Roman history in particular were to determine the historical outlook of most western writers to the time of the Italian Renaissance.

However, that traditional apology fills only one section in the first part of *The City of God.*[10] In the second half of the work (books XI to XXII) Augustine wanted to offer much more than a mere defense, as he stated himself in his *Retractations* (2, 68, 2): " In order that no one might raise the charge against me that I have merely refuted the opinions of other men but not stated my own, I devoted to this objective the second part of the work."

Of the vast number of ideas which Augustine set forth as his " own opinions," only one problem will be discussed here, that of " History ": how does history take its course and is there any meaning to be found in the sequence of events from the beginning of this world to the present age and to the day of the Last Judgment? [11]

How deeply Augustine was concerned with the question of the

[9] Quoted from J. W. Woodworth's translation of Orosius's *Seven Books* (1936), 1.

[10] The second section of the first part of the work, which consists of books VI to X, can be passed over in this article because Augustine did not deal in it with historical problems but set out to disprove the assertions of those philosophers who " maintain that polytheistic worship is advantageous for the life to come " (*Retractations,* 2, 68, 1).

[11] See the comprehensive analysis of the main body of ideas of Augustine's main work, which has been recently presented by W. J. Oates in his introduction to *Basic Writings of St. Augustine* (1948), I, ix–xl; and by E. Gilson in his introduction to D. B. Zema's and G. G. Walsh's translation of *The City of God* (1950), I, pp. XI–XCVIII.—Of the vast literature dealing with Augustine's historical ideas, I can list only some of the most recent treatments: R. J. Defferari and M. Keeler, " St. Augustine's City of God: its plan and development," *American Journal of Philology* (1929), L, 109–37; U. A. Padovano, " La Città di Dio: teologia e non filosofia della storia," *Rivista di Filosofia Neo-scolastica* (1931), supplem. vol. to vol. XXIII, 220–63; H. I. Marrou, *S. Augustin et la fin de la culture antique* (1938; see esp. 131–35, 417–19, 461–67); H. Fuchs, *Der geistige Widerstand gegen Rom in der antiken Welt* (1938); C. N. Cochrane, *Christianity and classical culture; a study of thought and action from Augustus to Augustine* (1944; esp. 397–516); W. M. Green, " Augustine on the teaching of history," *University of California Publications in Classical Philology* (1944), XII, 315–32; K. Löwith, *Meaning in History* (1949), 160–73.

philosophical or rather, from his point of view, the theological interpretation of the meaning and course of history, is shown by those chapters of *The City of God* in which he discussed the problems of the origin of the world and the uniqueness of its creation. He rejected the view that this world is eternal and without beginnings, and he stated that it was definitely created in time and will come to an end in another definite moment in time, a moment known to God alone. In connection with his discussion of " this controversy about the beginnings of things temporal " (12, 13 E) Augustine wrote (12, 14 A): " The philosophers of this world believed that they could or should not solve that controversy in any other way than by introducing cycles of time, in which they asserted that the revolving of coming and passing ages would always be renewed and repeated in the nature of things and would thus go on without cessation." In this sentence Augustine was obviously referring to the cyclical theory of history held by Platonists, Stoics and other Greek schools of philosophy.[12] But although he mentioned no name, it becomes evident from the context of the passage just quoted that he knew that this cyclical view was also maintained by Origen, who attempted to support it in a somewhat qualified fashion through quotations from the Scriptures, for instance the famous sentence in *Ecclesiastes* (1, 9): " There is no new thing under the sun." In his Latin translation of Origen's text Rufinus considerably modified these views, but this did not prevent Jerome from attacking them sharply. Augustine was even more emphatic in his refutation when he exclaimed in *The City of God* (12, 14 E): " Far be it from the right faith to believe that by these words of Solomon [*i.e., Ecclesiastes*] those cycles are meant in which [according to these philosophers] the revolving of the same periods and things is repeated." He found it logical that those thinkers " erroneously wandering around in cycles, find neither entrance nor exit," for he was convinced that " they do not know how the human race and this mortal condition of ours took its origin nor how it will be brought to an end " (12, 15 A). Those " false cycles which were discovered by false and deceitful sages," he believed, " can be avoided in the sound doctrine, through the path of the straight road (*tramite recti itineris*)." [13]

[12] Cf. K. Löwith, *l.c.*, 162–65, 248 n. 15; J. Baillie, *The Belief in Progress* (1951), 42–57.

[13] *City of God*, 12, 14 B.—C. N. Cochrane, *l.c.*, 245, stated that " we find Origen, for instance, protesting vigorously against the Platonic theory of cycles " But

To Augustine, then, history takes its course, not in cycles, but along a line. That line has a most definite beginning, the Creation, and a most definite end, the Last Judgment. Within this definite period of time the greatest single event was, of course, the appearance of Christ. "For," Augustine said (12, 14 F), "Once Christ died for our sins and 'raised from the dead dieth no more' (*Romans*, 6, 9); . . . and we ourselves, after the resurrection, 'shall ever be with the Lord' (*I Thessalon.*, 4, 17)." It seems that here Augustine was arguing again indirectly against Origen who, according to Jerome, "allowed himself to assert that Christ has often suffered and will often suffer, on the ground that what was beneficial once, will always be beneficial," and who also, "in his desire to confirm the most impious dogma of the Stoics through the authority of the Divine Scriptures, dared to write that man dies over and over again.[14]

From Augustine's conception of the course of history it follows that every particular event that takes place in time, every human life and human action, is a unique phenomenon which happens under the auspices of Divine Providence and must therefore have a definite meaning. The roots of this linear conception of history, as distinguished from the cyclical theories of the Greeks, went back to Hebrew ideas which had been further developed by the early Christian theologians.[15] But it was Augustine who elaborated those ideas most fully

Cochrane and, following him, R. Niebuhr, *Faith and History* (1949), 65, based their assertion exclusively on one passage in Origen's writings (*Against Celsus*, 4, 68) and neglected the much more detailed treatment of this problem in Origen's book *On first principles*, 2, 3, 1–5; 3, 5, 3; 4, 13. P. Koetschau, in his edition of Rufinus's translation and of the Greek fragments of *On first principles* (*Origenes Werke* [1913], V, 113f., 120), commented on Rufinus's modifications of the original text and printed the relevant remarks made by Jerome on Origen's belief in a series of many worlds: see the English translation of Koetschau's edition by G. W. Butterworth, *Origen, On first principles* (1935), 83–89, 238f.; J. Baillie, *l.c.*, 74ff., seems to overlook, too, the fact that Origen shared the cyclical theory, although in a modified form.

[14] See Butterworth, *l.c.*, 88 n. 4 (Jerome, *Apology*, 1, 20) and 83 n. 1 (Jerome, *Epist.*, 96, 9).

[15] On the Hebrew conceptions, see H. Butterfield, *Christianity and History* (1950), esp. 1–4, 57–62, 68–88; on the Christian views, see O. Cullmann, *Christus und die Zeit; die urchristliche Zeit- und Geschichtsauffassung* (1946); R. G. Collingwood, *The Idea of History* (1946), 46–52; J. Baillie, *l.c.*, 57–87; Th. Preiss, "The vision of history in the New Testament," *Papers of the Ecumenical Institute* (1950), V, 48–66; J. Daniélou, "The conception of history in the Christian tradition," *ibid.*, 67–79.

and consistently and thus determined the theology of history which prevailed throughout the Middle Ages and was to influence the philosophies of history of modern times.

When Augustine decided to combat the cyclical theories, he was probably motivated, as we have seen, by his knowledge that this pagan view was shared, to a certain extent at least, by a prominent, though suspect and even heretical, Christian thinker, Origen. But it appears that there existed still another philosophy of history at that time, which from Augustine's point of view was even more dangerous than the cyclical theory because it was very widespread among the Christians of his own as well as previous generations. To Augustine the truly problematic and the most objectionable theory of history must have been a conception which may be called " the Christian idea of progress."

When in 1920 J. B. Bury published his book on *The Idea of Progress,* he wrote (20f.) that " the idea of the universe which prevailed throughout the Middle Ages and the general orientation of men's thoughts were incompatible with some of the fundamental assumptions which are required by the idea of progress." But more recently, a number of scholars have pointed out that, to a certain degree, such an idea can actually be found among some of the early Christian thinkers.[16] A systematic treatment of this complex topic does not yet exist and it cannot be given in a brief essay. But in the following an attempt will be made at least to set forth some examples from early Christian writings, which may serve to illustrate the nature of that idea.

One might be inclined to find the first instance of the conception of progress in that part of Christian literature which dealt with the question of the Millennium. For some of the early theologians, including Justin, Irenaeus and Lactantius, interpreted the apocalyptic prediction of Christ's future reign of one thousand years in terms of a very material bliss. But this peculiar notion cannot be truly said to express a belief in " progress," because the Messianic kingdom of the future was not to come into existence through a gradual or evolutionary process but rather through the dramatically sudden second coming of Christ. Moreover, even before Augustine's time thinkers like Origen and Tychonius had successfully discredited that very

[16] See, *e.g.*, E. K. Rand, *Founders of the Middle Ages* (1929), 13–22, 291; Rand, *The Building of Eternal Rome* (1943), 72, 189ff.; C. N. Cochrane, *l.c.*, 242–47, 483f.; K. Löwith, *l.c.*, 60f., 84, 112f., 182ff.; J. Baillie, *l.c.*, 19–22, 94–96.

materialistic notion of the Millennium and had interpreted the conception in a primarily spiritual sense.[17] This became Augustine's own opinion also, because in the writings of the later period of his life, which dealt with eschatological speculations, he made it very clear that the question of the Millennium has nothing to do with any kind of earthly prosperity but has reference only to the necessarily imperfect realization of the divine in this world.

But apart from these speculations concerning the Millennium we find that some of the most prominent Christian apologists voiced views which implied the belief that under the auspices of Christianity the world had made concrete progress in historical time and that further progress could be expected. Those writers asserted that the new creed was bringing blessings to the whole of mankind, not merely to its own adherents. They pointed to the historically undeniable fact that the birth of Christ had taken place at the time of the foundation of the Roman empire by Augustus and the establishment of the *Pax Romana* on earth. As the appearance of Christ coincided with a marked improvement of all things secular, so, the early apologists argued, the growth of the new faith will be accompanied by further progress.[18]

The first testimony to this conception is to be found in the *Apology* which Bishop Melito of Sardis addressed to Emperor Antoninus Pius in the middle of the second century. According to Eusebius' *Ecclesiastical History* (4, 26, 7–8), Melito wrote: "Our philosophy [*i.e.*, Christianity] flourished first among the barbarians; then, during the great reign of your ancestor Augustus, it spread among your people and, above all, it has become to your own reign an auspicious blessing. For from that time the power of Rome has grown in greatness and splendor. To this power you have succeeded as the desired heir and you will continue it with your sons if you safeguard that philosophy which grew up with the empire and took its start under Augustus .... The best evidence that our doctrine has been flourishing for the good

[17] On the ideas concerning the Millennium, see, *e.g.*, E. Bernheim, *Mittelalterliche Zeitanschauungen in ihrem Einfluss auf Politik und Geschichtschreibung* (1918), esp. 63–109; A. Wikenhauser, "Das Problem des tausendjährigen Reiches in der Johannes-Apokalypse," *Römische Quartalschrift* (1932), XL, 13–36; Wikenhauser, "Die Herkunft der Idee des tausendjährigen Reiches in der Johannes-Apokalypse," *ibid.* (1937), XLV, 1–24; J. Baillie, *l.c.*, 60–64, 79–83.

[18] On the discussion of these arguments, see also E. Peterson, *Der Monotheismus als politisches Problem* (1935), 66–88; J. Geffcken, *Zwei griechische Apologeten* (1907), esp. 63, 92.

of an empire happily started in this: since the reign of Augustus no misfortune has befallen it; on the contrary, all things have been splendid and glorious, in accordance with the wishes of all."

Around the year 200, Tertullian expressed the same idea, though somewhat more cautiously. He wrote in his *Apology* (ch. 40, 13): "And for all that is said, if we compare the calamities of former times [with those of our own era], we find that they fall on us more lightly now, since the earth has received from God the believers of the Christian faith. For since that time innocence has put restraint on the wickedness of this world and men have begun to plead with God for the averting of His wrath."

These two apologists, then, did not merely content themselves with rejecting the pagan accusation that Christianity was responsible for the misfortunes of the era; on the contrary, they dared to take the offensive and claimed that their faith was making a positive contribution to the well-being of the Roman empire.

From this assertion there was but a single step to the expression of the belief that the universal acceptance of the Christian religion by the Roman world would lead to a still greater degree of security and prosperity. The pagan Celsus, in the middle of the third century, raised the question as to the consequences of such an event. Origen replied to Celsus' question with utmost confidence (*Against Celsus*, 4, 69): "If all the Romans were to pray together in full harmony, then they would be able to put to flight many more enemies than those who were discomfitted by the prayers of Moses when he cried to the Lord." Fifty years after Origen, around the year 300, Arnobius expressed the same belief in his treatise *Against the Pagans* (1, 6): "If all without exception, who consider themselves men, not in form of body, but in power of reason, were willing to lend, for a little while, an ear to [Christ's] salutary and peaceful prescriptions and were not, swollen with pride and arrogance, to trust to their own senses rather than to His admonitions, then the whole world, having turned the use of iron into more peaceful occupations, would live in the most placid tranquillity and would unite in blessed harmony, maintaining inviolate the sanctity of treaties."

This conviction that the appearance of Christ has led to a general improvement of the material conditions of the world and that its universal acceptance will lead to a still greater progress, was set forth by Melito and Tertullian, by Origen and Arnobius, during a period when their faith was suppressed by the official authorities of the Roman state. When, in the reign of Constantine, the great turning-point arrived and Christianity was not only tolerated but became the religion most favored by the emperor, it was natural that hope for progress rose still higher. Thus even Lactantius, once the champion of eschatological ideas in their most extreme and pessimistic form, dared to express rather optimistic expectations at the very end of his book *On the Death of the Persecutors* (ch. 52): "The Lord has destroyed and erased from the earth those proud names [of the anti-Christian rulers]. Let us therefore celebrate the triumph of God with joy. Let us frequently praise the victory of the Lord. Day and night let us offer our prayers to the Lord that He may establish for all time the peace which has been given to His people after [a warfare of] ten years."

Constantine showed himself most eager to adopt the idea that the worship of the true and omnipotent God was bound to benefit his empire in a material sense. In a letter written shortly after his decisive victory at the Milvian Bridge in the year 312, he declared (Eusebius, *Eccles. Hist.*, 10, 7, 1): "From many facts it appears . . . that the lawful recognition and observance [of the Christian faith] has bestowed the greatest success on the Roman name and singular prosperity on all affairs of mankind, blessings which were provided by the divine beneficence." Constantine's highly materialistic conception of his relationship with the Christian God was very much in accordance with the religious notions of the ancient Romans.[19] It was the old principle of *do ut des:* "I give that you may give." The emperor argued: I, Constantine, do something for you, God, so that you may do something for me; likewise, of course, God himself was assumed to expect gifts in return from those to whom he had extended favors. This idea of a commutative contract between God and man found reflection in the politico-ecclesiastical writings of quite a few of the Christian authors of the fourth century, beginning with Constantine's court-bishop, Eusebius of Caesarea. It was a complete ideological reversal: once the pagans had charged that the worship of the Christian God was the source of all the calamities of the empire; now, Constantine had the symbol of the cross displayed in the principal room of his new imperial palace in Constantinople; according to Eusebius' *Life of Constantine* (3, 49), "this symbol seemed to the

[19] On this point, see H. Berkhof, *Kirche und Kaiser; eine Untersuchung der Entstehung der byzantinischen und theokratischen Staatsauffassung im 4. Jahrhundert* (1947), esp. 14–18, 31–34, 55–59, 66, 70.

beloved of God [Constantine] to have been made as a safeguard of the empire itself."

The principle of *do ut des* was most emphatically rejected by Augustine, for it was wholly contrary to his conception of the relationship between God and man, even the great of this world.[20] Thus he stated in *The City of God* (4, 33) that in God's eyes earthly power and all similar things temporal are not important gifts and that therefore God "bestows them on both the good and the bad." In discussing the question of the *imperator felix*, Augustine admitted (*City of God*, 5, 25 A) that God "gave to the emperor Constantine, who was not a worshipper of demons but of the true God Himself, such fulness of earthly gifts as no one would even dare to wish for." But Augustine continued: "Lest, however, any emperor shall become a Christian in order to merit the blessed felicity of Constantine—when everyone ought to be a Christian for the sake of the eternal life—God took away [the Christian prince] Jovian far sooner than [his pagan brother, the emperor] Julian, and He allowed [the Christian emperor] Gratian to be slain by the sword of a tyrant."

These sentences in *The City of God* sound as if they were written expressly against Eusebius, who had declared in his *Life of Constantine* (1, 3, 3), with specific reference to the emperor: "God, that God who is the common Saviour of all, has treasured up with Himself, for those who love religion, far greater blessings than man can conceive, and He gives even here and now the first-fruits as a pledge of future rewards, thus assuring in some sort immortal hopes to mortal eyes."

Eusebius based his belief in the effectiveness of the principle of *do ut des* on a very definite interpretation and philosophy of history.[21] He emphasized (*Demonstratio Evangelica*, 3, 7, 139) even more strongly than Melito and other Christian thinkers during the previous centuries, that "it was not through human merit that at no other time but only since the time of Christ most of the nations were under the single rule of the Romans; for the period of His wonderful sojourn among men coincided with the period when the Romans reached their summit under Augustus, who was then the first monarch to rule over most of the nations." [22] This concurrence of the appearance of

[20] Cf. Berkhof, *l.c.*, 205–209.

[21] Cf. H. Berkhof, *Die Theologie des Eusebius von Caesarea* (1939), 45–50, 55f., 58f.; E. Peterson, *l.c.*, 66ff.

[22] See the similar passages in Eusebius' *Theophania*, 3, 2; *Praeparatio Evangelica*, 5, 1.

Christ on earth and the founding of the universal empire by Augustus "was not by mere human accident" but it was "of God's arrangement." Whereas the earlier interpreters of that concurrence had stated it simply as a historical fact, Eusebius believed himself capable of adducing proof from the Scriptures that those events were long before predicted by God. Thus he quoted in all the works in which he discussed the "synchronising" of the birth of Christ with the reign of Augustus, the following passages from the Old Testament: "In His days the righteous shall flourish and abundance of peace" (*Psalm* 72, 7); "He shall have dominion also from sea to sea, and from the river unto the ends of the earth" (*Psalm* 72, 8); "And they shall beat their swords into plowshares, and their spears into pruning-hooks: nation shall not lift up sword against nation, neither shall they learn war any more" (*Isaiah,* 2, 4).

These quotations are highly remarkable. For according to tradition these prophecies were to be understood as predictions of the future Messianic Kingdom, as we can learn from their interpretation by men like Irenaeus (*Against Heresies,* 4, 56, 3), Tertullian (*Against Marcion,* 3, 21) and Lactantius (*Divine Institutions,* 4, 16, 14). It seems that previous to Eusebius only Origen (*Against Celsus,* 2, 30) had ventured to refer the passage in *Psalm* 72, 7 to the *Pax Romana.*[23] But the full elaboration of Origen's suggestion was left to Eusebius, who gave the most bluntly secular interpretations to these scriptural texts. Witness the passage in Eusebius' *Praeparatio Evangelica* (1, 4): "In accordance with these predictions [*i.e.,* of *Psalm* 72 and of *Isaiah,* 2, 4], the actual events followed. Immediately after Augustus had established his sole rule, at the time of our Saviour's appearance, the rule by the many became abolished among the Romans. And from that time to the present you cannot see, as before, cities at war with cities, nor nation fighting with nation, nor life being worn away in the confusion of everything." Eusebius saw a close parallel between the victory of Christian monotheism and the growth of the Roman monarchy. Thus he stated in his *Theophania* (3, 2):[24] "Two great powers sprang up fully as out of one stream and they gave peace to all and brought all together to a state of friendship: the Roman

[23] It may be noted that Origen interpreted the passage in *Isaiah,* 2, 4 in an entirely spiritual sense; see *Against Celsus,* 5, 33; *Against Heresies,* 6, 16.

[24] Translated from the Syriac by S. Lee, *Eusebius on the Theophania* (1853), 156f.; cf. the very similar passage in Eusebius' *Praise of Constantine,* 16, 4–5.

empire, which from that time appeared as one kingdom, and the power of the Saviour of all, whose aid was at once extended to and established with everyone. For the divine superiority of our Saviour swept away the authority of the many demons and gods, so that the one Kingdom of God was preached to all men, Greeks and barbarians, and to those who resided in the extremities of the earth. The Roman empire, too—since those had been previously uprooted who had been the cause of the rule by many—soon subjugated all others and quickly brought together the whole race of man into one state of accordance and agreement."

To Eusebius the greatest gains made by mankind since the days of Christ and Augustus were the abolition of wars, foreign and civil, and the establishment of peace and security, the time-hallowed ideals of the *Pax Romana*. But he saw also other improvements. For instance, he declared in his *Praeparatio Evangelica* (1, 4): "Of the benefits resulting from God's doctrines which have become manifest on earth, you may see a clear proof if you consider that at no other time from the beginning until now, and not through the merits of any of the illustrious men of old but only through Christ's utterances and teachings, diffused throughout the whole world, the customs of all nations have been set aright, even those customs which before were savage and barbarous." Because of the strict discipline of the new faith men have learned to lead a moral life, to refrain from hostility toward others and to master their own emotions and passions. Eusebius concluded his enumeration of all the improvements made in the political, legal and moral spheres by asking: "How, then, can anyone . . . refuse to admit that our doctrine has brought to all men good tidings of very great and true blessings, and has supplied to human life that which is of immediate advantage toward happiness?"

There was no doubt in Eusebius' mind that mankind, under divine guidance, had made progress from the pre-Christian era through the three centuries of the gradual ascent of the new Church to the reign of Constantine in which he himself lived. He declared in his *Praise of Constantine* (16, 8): "As those predictions concerning our Saviour [*i.e.*, *Psalm* 72, 7–8, and *Isaiah*, 2, 4] were foretold and delivered in the Hebrew tongue many ages before, so in our own times they have become really fulfilled and the ancient testimonies of the prophets clearly confirmed." Great as the advances made by mankind were, still further progress was expected by Eusebius. For he asserted (*ibid.*, 6): "Although the object of the Roman empire to unite all nations in one harmonious whole has already been secured to a large degree, it is destined to be still more perfectly attained, even to the final conquest of the ends of the habitable world, by means of the salutary doctrine and through the aid of that Divine Providence which facilitates and smooths the way [of the Empire]."

In his recent essay on *The Idea of Progress,* G. H. Hildebrand stated[25] that this idea includes three principles: "First, the belief that history follows a continuous, necessary, and orderly course; second, the belief that this course is the effect of a regularly operating causal law; and third, the belief that the course of change has brought and will continue to bring improvement in the condition of mankind." The first two of these principles were always implied in the Christian belief that every single event and consequently also the course of historical events as a whole take place under God's will and in accordance with the plan of Divine Providence. But it remained for Eusebius to add the third principle, the optimistic belief in continuous improvement, and thus to develop a full-fledged Christian idea of progress.

Eusebius' idea was taken up by some of the most prominent theologians of the fourth and early fifth centuries, both in the eastern and the western parts of the Church.[26] This is shown by the interpretations which John Chrysostom, Ambrose, Jerome, Cyril of Alexandria and Theodoret of Cyprus gave in their various commentaries on *Psalm 72* and *Isaiah* (2, 4), and we may add, on the passage in *Psalm 46* (v. 9), which reads: "He maketh wars to cease unto the end of the earth." Like Eusebius all the writers just mentioned explained these passages in terms of the *Pax Romana* and its earthly achievements, and it seems that of the great theologians of the fourth century only Athanasius and Basil expounded them in a strictly spiritual sense.

When Augustine wrote his *Enarrations on the Psalms,* he replaced the explanations of the above passages with interpretations wholly different and entirely his own. For instance, Origen, Eusebius, John Chrysostom and Ambrose had declared that the words of *Psalm 46:* "He maketh wars to end," had been realized in the reign of Augustus; Basil alone had explained that passage in exclusively religious terms. But whereas Basil had contented himself with simply setting forth his personal exposition, Augustine accompanied the commentary which

[25] *The Idea of Progress; a Collection of Readings;* selected by F. J. Teggart; revised edition with an introduction by G. H. Hildebrand, 4.

[26] Cf. E. Peterson, *l.c.,* 71–88.

he wrote in 412, two years after the fall of Rome, with a polemic directed against the interpretation given by so many of his famous predecessors.[27] For although he did not mention any name, there seems to be no doubt that he was taking issue with the current view when he denied categorically that the prediction of a reign of peace had been fulfilled in any material or historical sense: " There are still wars, wars among nations for supremacy, wars among sects, wars among Jews, pagans, Christians, heretics, and these wars are becoming more frequent " (*Enarration on Psalm 45, 13* = 46, 9). In Augustine's opinion, external peace was not yet achieved and, in fact, it would not even matter if it actually had. Only that peace matters which, through divine grace, man finds in himself, by his complete submission to the will of God. " When man learns that in himself he is nothing and that he has no help from himself," Augustine said, " then arms in himself are broken in pieces, then wars in himself are ended. Such wars, then, destroyed that voice of the Most High out of His holy clouds whereby the earth was shaken and the kingdoms were bowed; these wars He has taken away unto the ends of the earth."

In his *Enarration on Psalm 71, 10* (= 72, 7), Augustine commented on the passage: " In His days righteousness (*iustitia*) shall arise and abundance of peace until the moon be exalted." [28] These words, Augustine declared, " ought to be understood as if it were said: there shall arise in His days righteousness to conquer the contradiction and the rebellion of the flesh, and there shall be made a peace so abundant and increasing ' until the moon be exalted,' that is until the Church be lifted up, through thc glory of the resurrection to reign with Him." Righteousness and peace in the words of the psalmist ought not to be confused, then, with the notions of *iustitia* and *pax* of the earthly state. Those highest Christian ideals have not yet been nor will they ever be embodied in the secular organization of the Roman empire, but they will be realized in the spiritual community of the eternal Church. The theologically untenable identification of the Messianic ideal with the historical reality of the *Imperium Romanum* could not have been rejected more radically than was done by Augustine in his commentary.

[27] Cf. E. Peterson, *l.c.*, 97f.; as to the date of *Enarration on Psalm 45*, cf. S. M. Zarb, " Chronologia enarrationum S. Augustini in Psalmos," in *Angelicum* (1947), XXIV, 275–83.

[28] The above translation of *Psalm* 72 is based on the text of the *Itala* used by Augustine.—This *Enarration* was written between 415 and 416; see S. M. Zarb, *op. cit.*, *Angelicum* (1935), XII, 77–81.

Augustine was fully aware of the fact that in his exegetical works he was frequently deviating from his predecessors on essential points. No less a man than Jerome had told him so very bluntly in two letters written in the year 404 (*Epist.* 105 and 112), that is, long before Augustine wrote his *Enarrations on Psalms 45 and 71.* It is interesting to note that Jerome specifically referred to Augustine's " little commentaries on some of the Psalms, which, if I were disposed to criticise them," Jerome said (*Epist.* 105, 2), " I could prove to be at variance, I shall not say with my own opinion, for ' I am nothing ' (*I Corinth.*, 13, 2), but with the interpretations of the older Greek commentators." [29] In his reply Augustine stated in unmistakable terms (*Epist.* 82, 3) that he felt justified in deviating from views held by previous commentators in any instance in which he considered himself to be in full accordance with the Scriptures; for he declared that " of only those books of the Scriptures, which are now called canonical, do I most firmly believe that their authors have made no error in their writing." He continued: " But the others I read in such a way that, however outstanding the authors are in sanctity and learning, I do not accept their teaching as true on the mere ground of the opinion held by them, but only because they have succeeded in convincing my judgment of its truth either by means of those canonical writings themselves or by arguments addressed to my reason." The definite nature of this statement entitles us to ascribe great significance to the fact that Augustine interpreted the Messianic predicions of the Old Testament in a fashion so fundamentally different from that of some of the most renowned earlier theologians, both Greek and Latin, who had found in those passages the promise of material well-being and progress to be achieved by man on earth and in the course of history.

Augustine's rejection of these conceptions appears even more noteworthy when we remember that it was during his own lifetime that the Christian idea of progress as developed by Eusebius became the crucial issue in a basic controversy. This was the famous affair of the Altar of Victory in Rome, the great conflict, the last one in history, between pagan traditionalism and Christian progressivism.[30] That

[29] We do not know to which of Augustine's " little commentaries " Jerome referred; Augustine started writing his *Enarrations* in the last decade of the fourth century; cf. Zarb, *op. cit.*

[30] On this affair, see esp. J. R. Palanque, *S. Ambroise et l'empire Romain* (1933), 131–36, 221f., 278f., 307, 358–64, 510, 536; J. Wytzes, *Der Streit um den*

incident, with its later repercussions, forms the immediate background of the composition of *The City of God.*

Ever since the days of the Republic the statue of Victory had stood in the building of the Roman Senate, and the meetings of the Senate used to be opened with the burning of incense at the altar of the goddess. In the mid-fourth century emperor Constantius ordered the removal of the statue, but Julian the Apostate had it restored to its old place. It was taken away once again in the year 382. The pagan members of the Roman Senate were naturally very much disturbed, and in the year 384 the most highly respected member of that group, Symmachus, submitted an impressive plea to the reigning emperors for the restoration of the Altar of Victory. Symmachus argued on the basis of the principle of *do ut des,* but he used the principle, of course, according to the pagan mode of thought. The ancient deities, he declared, have raised Rome to her great position, and for that reason Rome owes them gratitude (Symmachus' *Relatio,* §§ 3 and 8). Symmachus let the personification of Rome address herself to the emperors (§ 9): "Excellent princes, fathers of the country, respect my years to which pious rites have brought me. Let me use the ancestral ceremonies, for I do not repent of them. Let me live after my fashion, for I am free. This worship has subdued the world to my laws, these sacred rites repelled Hannibal from my walls and the Gauls from the Capitol." In the same spirit Symmachus sounded an emphatic warning (§ 4): "We are cautious as to what may happen in the future, and we shun portentous actions."

The leading Christian figure of that time, Bishop Ambrose of Milan took it upon himself to reply to the plea made by the great pagan statesman. In his refutation of Symmachus' assertion that Rome rose to power through the favor of the pagan gods, Ambrose employed, of course, the old arguments of the Christian apologists. But he went farther. He, too, let Rome speak for herself (*Epist.* 18, 7). But whereas Symmachus' *Roma* had pleaded for the preservation of the time-honored traditions of the past, Ambrose's *Roma* appealed to the idea of progress. "It is no disgrace," she declared, "to pass on to better things." And in answer to Symmachus' traditionalist argument that "the rites of our ancestors ought to be retained," Ambrose asked (§ 23): "Why should we do so? Has not everything

Altar der Viktoria (1936); L. Malunowicz, *De ara victoriae in curia Romana quomodo certatum sit* (1937); M. Lavarenne in his edition of the works of *Prudence* (1948), III, 85–90.

made advances in the course of time toward what is better?" In both the memoranda which he addressed to the then reigning emperors, Ambrose made it clear that he shared the current belief that Christianity was a progressive factor in history. It may be remarked in passing that Ambrose, like Eusebius and Symmachus, believed that the relationship between God and man is largely determined by the principle of merit and reward. For instance, in his treatise *On Faith* (2, 16), Ambrose did not hesitate to find the explanation for the defeat of the emperor Valens in the battle of Adrianople in 378 in the fact that Valens was an Arian heretic: on the other hand he predicted with full confidence the victory of the emperor Gratian over the Visigoths because the new ruler confessed the orthodox faith.[31]

In the year 384, the question of the Altar of Victory was settled in accordance with Ambrose's wishes, but during the next two decades the pagan faction of the Roman Senate continued to work, with varying success, for the restoration of the statue. Thus around the year 403, the poet Prudentius decided to present once more the Christian point of view in regard to that problem.[32] His poem entitled *Against Symmachus* was the greatest poetical expression the Christian idea of progress ever found in early western Christendom. According to Prudentius, God had assigned to the Romans the task of conquering the world and establishing a universal empire so as to pave the way for the spread of the universal religion. The mission of the Roman empire was to become finally the Christian empire. That great turn took place under Constantine who, in Prudentius' words (1, 539f.), "accustomed Romulus' state to be powerful for ever in a dominion derived from above." In his description of the universal and eternal Christian empire as it was established by Constantine, Prudentius used phrases (1, 541–43) which are almost identical with those which Vergil once had made Jupiter say: "[Constantine] did not set any boundaries nor did he fix limits of time; he taught an imperial power without end so that the Roman valor should no longer be senile nor the glory which Rome had won should ever know old age." This Christian Rome, Prudentius said (1, 587–90), which "has dedicated herself to Thee, O Christ, and has passed under Thy laws, and is willing now, with all her people and her greatest citizens, to extend her earthly rule beyond the lofty stars of the great heavens." Pru-

[31] Cf. H. Berkhof, *Kirche und Kaiser,* 90–94, 173–82.

[32] On the Date of Prudentius' *Contra Symmachum,* cf. L. Malunowicz, *l.c.,* 99f.; M. Lavarenne, *l.c.,* III, 89f.

dentius recalled Symmachus' assertion that it was only because of the help of the ancient gods that neither the Gauls nor Hannibal had succeeded in completely overwhelming Rome. He let his personification of the Christian *Roma* reply as follows (2, 690–95): "Whosoever tries to impress me again with the memories of past defeats and ancient calamities, he ought to see that in this age of yours [*i.e.*, that of the Christian emperors] I no longer suffer anything of that sort. No barbaric enemy shatters my walls with a javelin and no man with strange weapons, attire and hairdress wanders around the city he has conquered and carries off my young men into transalpine prisons."

These lines were written around the year 403. In 410 Rome fell to Alaric and Visigothic "strangers wandered around the city they had conquered." Under these circumstances many contemporaries, pagan as well as Christian, must have remembered the sombre warnings of Symmachus, which had been so recently discussed again and so optimistically rejected by Prudentius. In the year 410 Alaric had achieved that complete conquest of Rome which hundreds of years before Hannibal had failed to accomplish, and the long-dreaded "fall of Rome" had taken place almost immediately after a Christian poet had assured his listeners that it could not happen now and never would.

The reactions of the pagan and Christian contemporaries were profound and radical, as we learn from the *Sermon on the Fall of the City,* which Augustine preached shortly after the event.[33] The pagans said to the Christians (§ 9): "As long as we brought sacrifices to our Gods, Rome stood; now when the sacrifice to your God is triumphant and abounds and the sacrifices to our gods are prevented and forbidden, see what Rome is suffering." And the Christians, according to Augustine's sermon (§ 6), were shocked and bewildered by the fact that in spite of the many holy places in the city, in spite of the tombs of St. Peter and St. Paul and many other martyrs, "Rome is miserable and devastated, Rome is afflicted, laid waste and burnt." Augustine was naturally much more concerned about the reactions of the Christians than about those of the pagans. For in the aftermath of the year 410 it had become evident that Christianity included within its ranks many people who had been won over to the new faith simply because of its external triumph. To them Christianity meant primarily the belief in the effectiveness of the principle of *do ut des,*

[33] The Latin text of Sermon 296 has recently been re-edited by G. Morin, in *Miscellanea Agostiniana* (1930), I, 401–19.

which had been taught by Eusebius and his followers. Such a faith, based as it was on essentially materialistic foundations, and such a shallow optimism was of necessity badly shaken by the turn of events. How deeply conscious Augustine was of the problem presented by those worldly-minded Christians is revealed by another sermon which he preached after the fall of Rome. In bitter words he condemned (*Sermon* 105, 13) " those blasphemers who chase and long after things earthly and place their hopes in things earthly. When they have lost them, whether they will or not, what shall they hold and where shall they abide? Nothing within, nothing without; an empty coffer, an emptier conscience."

This was the situation, from the ideological point of view a very critical situation, which motivated Augustine to write *The City of God.* He realized that one single event, the " fall of Rome," had an impact upon the thinking and the feeling of his contemporaries which went far beyond its material importance. The significance attributed to the event resulted from the central position which the destiny and fate of " eternal " Rome occupied in the existing conceptions of history, whether they were pagan or Christian. If Augustine, then, wanted to combat in a truly fundamental fashion the interpretations of that " fall of Rome," he could do so only by setting forth his own ideas concerning the course and the meaning of history. Therefore he was willing to devote thirteen years of his life to the most comprehensive study of the problem of history, a problem which up to the year 410 had been of merely incidental interest to him.

In attempting to solve that problem, Augustine found, as we have seen, that he had to reject practically all the current conceptions of history. He did not share the sentiments of those among the early Christian writers to whom any concern about history was superfluous in view of the presumably imminent end of this world, and he had no interest in eschatological speculations and calculations regarding the future millennium. Neither could he, of course, accept the cyclical theory as it was held by some of the pagan schools of philosophy and, in a modified form, by Origen. And he saw most clearly how perilous it was for the Christian faith to proclaim, as Eusebius and others had done during the fourth century, a belief in " progress," if that notion was understood in any kind of materialistic sense. For under the existing circumstances it was inevitable that " most of the pagans," as Augustine said in his *Enarration on Psalm 136, 9,* asked the question: " Is it not true that since the coming of Christ the state of human affairs has been worse than it was before and that human affairs were once much more fortunate than they are now? "[34] Every emphasis on the idea of secular progress was bound to lay the Christian cause wide open to attacks by the pagans and to the disillusionment of the half-hearted Christians. Both groups could rightly find that all promises of worldly success were totally disproved by the catastrophe of the year 410—and there might be more and worse disasters to come.

In contradistinction to all these conceptions Augustine's own views concerning history represent a basic reiteration and systematic elaboration of Hebrew and early Christian ideas.[35] To him history was the *operatio Dei* in time, it was "a one-directional, teleological process, directed towards one goal—salvation," the salvation of individual men, not of any collective groups or organizations.[36] Ever since the creation of the world there have existed two cities, the city of God or the community of those who "wish to live after the spirit," and the earthly city or the community of those who "wish to live after the flesh" (*City of God,* 14, 1 C). Of the twelve books of the second part of *The City of God,* eight books deal with the origin (*exortus*) and the end (*finis*) of those two cities, that is with the Creation and the Last Judgment. Only the middle section (books XV to XVIII) deals with that period of time which is commonly considered to be the historical era, and even within that section Augustine gave his main attention to those men and events which belonged to "the heavenly city which is a pilgrim on earth" (18, 54 K). The fact that only one book of *The City of God* (b. XVIII) treats historical developments proper, shows clearly that Augustine regarded the purely secular aspects of the drama of mankind as relatively insignificant.

The content of that middle section of *The City of God* comprising books XV to XVIII has been defined by Augustine as follows (15, 1 C): "It now seems right to me to approach the account of the course [of the two cities] from the time when those two [*i.e.,* Adam and Eve] began to propagate the race to the time when men shall cease to

[34] This *Enarration* was written between 410 and 413; see Zarb, *l.c.* (1939), XVI, 289f.

[35] See above, note 15.

[36] See K. Löwith, *l.c.,* 170f.; E. Frank, "The role of history in Christian thought," *The Duke Divinity School Bulletin* (1949), XIV, 74.

propagate. For this whole time or world-age, in which the dying give place and those who are born succeed, is the course of the two cities which are under discussion." Twice in the passage just quoted, and in two other passages (11, 1 C and 18, 54 K), Augustine used the word *excursus* to define the historical process which is taking place between the Creation and the Last Judgment.[37] In other passages of *The City of God,* and more frequently, he employed the words *procursus* and *procurrere* for the development within the same span of time.[38] What is the meaning of these words? When we look in the translations of *The City of God* by John Healey and by Marcus Dods, we find that they translated the noun *procursus* most frequently with "progress," but also with "history," "proceedings" and "advance," the verb *procurrere* with "run its course," "run on," "proceed" and "progress," and the word *excursus* with "progress," "progression," "career" or "course." In their recent translation of *The City of God,* Fathers Demetrius B. Zema and Gerald G. Walsh translated the word *procursus* with "progress" and *excursus* with "development." Do we have to assume, then, that Augustine believed that the course of the two cities on earth takes place in some form of evolutionary progress? Such an assumption appears highly improbable. For not only were the two words *procursus* and *excursus* used interchangeably throughout *The City of God* and in the description of this work in Augustine's *Retractations* (2, 69, 2),[39] but in a letter which was written shortly after the completion of *The City of God,* Augustine said explicitly that the section under discussion "sets forth the *procursus* or, as we have preferred to say, the *excursus* [of the heavenly city]."[40] In retrospect, then, Augustine himself considered the term *excursus* more adequate. To equate that word with "progress" seems very questionable, both from the linguistic point of view and in consideration of the modern connotation of this term.

The best key to the right understanding of this particular ter-

[37] Cf. *City of God,* 15, 9 D: *praeterit saeculi excursus.*

[38] *E.g., City of God,* 1, 35 B; 10, 32 U; 15, 1 D; 16, 12 A, 35 A and 43 I; 17, 1 A, 4 A and 14 A; 18, 1 A, B, C and 2 G.

[39] M. Dods, *The City of God* (1872), I, p. VIII, and, following him, G. H. Hildebrand, *The Idea of Progress* (1949), 110, translated the words *excursum earum siue procursum* in *Retractat.* 69, 2, with "their history or progress."

[40] The text of this newly found letter to Firmus has been published by C. Lambot in *Revue Bénédictine* (1939), LI, 212; the passage reads: *procursum siue dicere maluimus excursum;* it has been translated by Zema and Walsh, *l.c.,* I, 400, with "its progress or, as we might choose to say, its development."

minology seems to be provided by a passage in *The City of God* (15, 21 E), in which Augustine said: " The reckoning of the times [in the Scripture] begins after the two cities have been set forth, the one founded in the business of this world, the other in the hope for God, but both coming out from the common gate of mortality, which is opened in Adam, so that they might run on and run out (*procurrant et excurrant*) to their separate proper and merited ends." The history of the two cities, according to this passage, has the same starting-point, the fall of Adam; from that point they follow each its own course to the terminal point in time, the Last Judgment. Thus Augustine conceived of the historical process in the form of two tracks the courses of which have been laid out by God and are to be followed by the successive generations of the citizens of the two communities. In the terms of that figure of speech it was possible for Augustine to use the words " run on " and " run out " as synonyms and to say that the city of God on earth " proceeded in running out its course." [41]

With regard to the course of the heavenly city it may be said that there is a " progress," not of any materialistic nature, but in the sense that there is a gradual revelation of the divine truth communicated by God to man, especially through the prophecies predicting the future Messiah (see, *e.g.*, 18, 27).[42] Augustine declared (10, 14 A): " Like the correct knowledge of an individual man, the correct knowledge of that part of mankind which belongs to the people of God, has advanced by approaches through certain epochs of time or, as it were, ages, so that it might be lifted from the temporal to the perception of the eternal and from the visible to that of the invisible." In the spiritual realm, therefore, according to Augustine, mankind has grown up from the time of its infancy through the phases of childhood, adolescence, young manhood and mature manhood to its old age (*senectus*) which has begun with the birth of Christ. That growth of the spiritual enlightenment of the human race found its clearest expression in the scheme of " the six ages," to which Augustine alluded in the passage just quoted and into which he divided the

[41] *City of God*, XIX, 5 A: . . . *ista Dei civitas . . . progrederetur excursu. . . .*

[42] Cf. K. Löwith, *l.c.*, p. 172: " . . . there is only one progress: the advance toward an ever sharper distinction between faith and unbelief, Christ and Antichrist . . ."; according to J. Daniélou, *l.c.*, 70, it was Irenæus of Lyons who first saw that " the reason for this progression is of a pedagogical nature."

course of the heavenly city on earth.[43] The summit has been reached with the appearance and the gospel of Christ, and no further fundamental change will take place in the spiritual realm to the end of time.

In regard to the developments in the sphere of the earthly city, Augustine emphasized repeatedly in his historical survey the mutability and the instability of human affairs. Cities, kingdoms and empires have risen and fallen throughout the course of history, and this will always be the case. For, Augustine declared (17, 13 C) "because of the mutability of things human no security will ever be given to any nation to such a degree that it should not have to fear invasions inimical to its very existence." Augustine admitted that the Roman empire had achieved more than any other state, and he granted that the pagan Romans had possessed certain qualities which might be called virtues, though not in the full and true sense of the word. At the same time Augustine, like his pupil Orosius, maintained that for many centuries the Roman empire was involved in a process of moral disintegration, in a decline which had started long before the times of Christ and Augustus.[44]

Eusebius and the other Christian progressivists of the fourth century had strongly stressed the coincidence of the birth of Christ and the reign of Augustus, for they saw the counter-part of the religious summit in the erection of the "eternal" Roman empire and in the establishment of the "universal" *Pax Romana.* Whereas that observation occupied a central position in their conceptions of history, Augustine passed over it in a single sentence, by simply stating (18, 46 A): "While Herod reigned in Judaea and, after the change of the republican government, Caesar Augustus was emperor in Rome and pacified the world, Christ, man manifest out of a human virgin, God hidden out of God the Father, was born of Judah in Bethlehem." Whereas according to Eusebius and his followers the history of man had taken a fresh start at that time and had "progressed" toward a new culminating-point under Constantine, when the Roman empire reached the fulfillment of its mission by becoming Christian, Augustine stopped his historical account precisely with the appearance of

[43] See *City of God,* 15 C A; 16, 24 F and 43 G; 22, 30 O–P; the most detailed exposition of that scheme is to be found in Augustine's treatise *De Genesi contra Manichaeos,* I, 23–24, in Migne, *Patrologia Latina,* XXXIV, 190–94; cf. W. M. Green, *l.c.*, 320–27.

[44] Besides many passages in *The City of God,* see a letter written by Augustine in the year 412 (*Epist.* 138).

Christ. To him the period following that event and extending to his own days and to the end to come, was not a modern era but it was "the *senectus* of the old man, the last age in which the new man is born who now lives according to the spirit."[45] God has revealed all the truth that is to be communicated to man in this world, and henceforth the history of both the heavenly and the earthly cities has no fundamentally new lessons to teach. Augustine did not share the optimism of Eusebius and others; on the contrary, he spoke of his own era as "this malignant world, these evil days" (18, 49 A), and he reckoned even with the possibility of future persecutions of the Church and the faith (18, 52). He reminded his readers (16, 24 H) that, according to Christ's own words, the terminal period of history will not be an era of secular peace and earthly prosperity but just the opposite: "About the end of this world the faithful shall be in great perturbation and tribulation, of which the Lord has said in the Gospel: 'For then shall be great tribulation, such as was not since the beginning of the world to this time, no, nor ever shall be' (*Matthew*, 24, 21)."

In Augustine's opinion, then, there is no true "progress" to be found in the course of human history. He was, of course, well aware of the fact that "the human genius has invented and put to practical use many and great arts . . . and that human industry has made wonderful and stupefying advances" (22, 24 K–L). But at the same time he pointed out a fact which has been overlooked all too often by believers in the blessings of material progress, the fact that the ingenuity and the inventiveness of man have also their destructive aspects: "And for the injury of men, how many kinds of poison, how many weapons and machines of destruction have been invented." This dual aspect of the development of human history results from the very nature of the forces determining its course. "In this river or torrent of the human race," Augustine said toward the end of *The City of God* (22, 24 A), "two things run the course together, the evil which is derived from the parent [Adam], and the good which is bestowed by the Creator."

Princeton University.

[45] Augustine, *De Genesi contra Manichaeos*, I, 23, 40, in Migne, *l.c.*, XXXIV, 192.

[15]

Augustine's Philosophy of History

Rüdiger Bittner

THE MEANING OF "HISTORIA"

To speak of Augustine's philosophy of history is anachronistic in more than one way. Not only was the expression "philosophy of history" coined by Voltaire in the 1760s only, and coined precisely to herald a treatment of history that has cast off the fetters of a Christian conception. What is more important, Augustine does not use the term "historia" in the modern sense of "history," which in the modern sense can refer to events rather than to reports of events and to a totality of events or even to *the* totality of events. Thus in the latter case "history" can be used absolutely: it need not be some person's or some institution's history, it can be history, period.[1] In fact it is this sense of "history" that first invites a philosophy of history. Take the standard question of a philosophy of history: whether there is meaning in history. Whatever may be meant by "meaning" here, it is clear that "history" in this question means the events rather than what people write and say about the events. And what is asked here is not whether the events, taken individually, have meaning but whether the whole of which they are parts does. Augustine's concept of historia is different. For him, historia is a narrative.[2] It is not what we call history, since we can refer by this term to events and indeed to a totality of events, which Augustine by his term cannot. Augustine's "historia" is not "history," it is "story."

"Historia," while not appearing very frequently in Augustine's writings, is a basic concept in Augustine's thought. According to *De vera religione* 7.13 the chief part to take in in Christian religion is "the narrative [historia] and prophecy of the temporal dispensations of divine providence for the salvation of mankind." Just because the dispensations of divine providence for the salvation of mankind are temporal, it takes historia, a narrative of things past, and prophecy, a narrative of things to come, to represent them. That means you cannot prove the heart of Christian doctrine by rational arguments; you have to tell a story to communicate it. Witness the Platonists: here are the best philosophers in the world, and they do get as far as to produce persuasive arguments for what is effectively the logos doctrine in John. Still, incarnation, crucifixion, and resurrection are beyond their reach, for these happened in time, and as philosophers they have knowledge only of what is timeless. To learn of what happens in time there is no way but to listen to stories.[3] For teaching Christian religion, accordingly, Augustine recommends giving the pupil "the full story" (narratio plena), running "from where it is written: 'In the beginning God made heaven and earth' up to the present times of the church" (*De catechizandis rudibus* 3.5). Here it is evident that the doctrine comes as a story: it is only in a story that you can continue right down to the present time. So while you can indeed reach truth by sheer rational argument and skepticism is out, you cannot reach all important truth by sheer rational argument. This is why philosophers are standardly said to suffer from pride (*Confessions* 7.9.13; *City of God* 2.7): they try to go it alone, renouncing the help that comes from things received through listening.[4] That philosophers trust their reasonings as far as they go is fine. That they trust their reasonings to give them all the truth they need is their mistake. Some truth we need is "storical."[5]

It may appear to be an invidious understatement to say that incarnation, crucifixion, and resurrection need to be represented in stories. It is not just a story to report these events, one may protest, it is an enunciation of an altogether higher dignity. This protest is justified insofar as our term "story" sometimes carries the connotation of "a mere story," something made up. Still, "story" can also be used in a neutral sense, without an implication of truth or falsity. Taken in that way, the term fits Augustine's use of "historia." It is historia to represent incarnation, crucifixion, and resurrection in speech, and it is in the same sense historia to indicate who was Roman consul in a given year.[6]

Indeed, it is historia in the same sense to tell some fable about the gods (*Epistulae* 17.1.3). The exposition of Christian doctrine for Augustine does not recede to a different literary genre. It is a story like the others people tell. It differs from pagan fables simply in being true. From reports on past human institutions it does not differ in truth, for these may be true, too, and in the same sense.[7] From them it differs, first, in importance: "What is contained in worldly writings, be it true or false, does not carry anything of weight whereby to live right and well."[8] It differs, second, in authority: "the wisdom of God, whereby everything was made, transfers itself into sacred souls, makes them friends of God and prophets and tells them silently in their inner self his works; . . . and one of these was he who said and wrote: 'In the beginning God created heaven and earth'" (*City of God* 10.4; also 11.3). Thus, if worldly books and the scripture contradict each other, the latter trumps the former by its immediate divine authority, for God himself told the writer his works. This is also why pagan fables, insofar as they are incompatible with what the scripture says, must be rejected as untrue. On the other hand, since worldly writings and the scripture are in the same field, both offering reports of things that happened, Christian doctrine can occasionally use the material provided by secular books for a clearer or more reliable chronology of the events of which it speaks (*De doctrina Christiana* 2.28.42). So to tell of Christ's incarnation, crucifixion, and resurrection is not different in kind from ordinary stories about what people did in various times and situations. It is the same sort of business, only the Christian story is better because it is more important and because it is authorized by him who is the origin of whatever any true story is about.[9] As Augustine puts it in *De libero arbitrio* (1.3.7) the Christian story (historia) excels by divine authority over other books. Yet if it excels, it must be in the same contest.

SACRED AND PROFANE HISTORY

There is a distinction in the literature between sacred and profane (or sacred and secular) history.[10] The foregoing considerations suggest that, for "historiae"—that is, stories—there is no distinction in kind between what sacred and secular books contain, only a difference in importance and a difference in reliability. Turning now and in the following from historia to history in the sense of what true stories report, what Augustine often calls "gestae" (things done),[11] the above considerations suggest that a distinction between sacred and secular history cannot be maintained at all.[12] Clearly the different degree of reliability of sacred and secular reports does not constitute a difference in kind between what these reports are about, since that is a difference that concerns only our access to events, not the events themselves. A similar point holds for the difference in importance of sacred and secular narratives. This difference derives, to be sure, from the difference in importance of the events narrated, but that difference is a difference only in what the events mean for us; it does not constitute a difference in kind among the events themselves. In itself history, the course of happenings, is homogeneous. There are not two strands,[13] the sacred and the secular, which, twisted together, form the rope of history. The whole of history is running from one spool. The fact that the Word became flesh and the fact that I had breakfast this morning do not belong to different realms of things or on different levels of events. The former fact is just more important than the latter, and better known. The reason for claiming that Augustine regards history as homogeneous is that otherwise sacred and profane narratives could not so much as contradict each other, which according to Augustine they sometimes do (see above), nor could the secular story support the chronology of the sacred one, as again according to Augustine it sometimes does (see above). You can only contradict or supplement what somebody else said if the two of you are talking about the same sort of things. Once you settle for different strands, levels, or something of the sort, the argument between the two of you is off.[14]

The teacher of Christian doctrine, then, is a "storian" as opposed to a mere reasoner: he offers a narrative. And he is a historian as opposed to a narrator of fables: he says what happened. Not all that happened, of course; no historian does that. He tells about some events. Augustine, it is true, rejected the idea of being a historian (*City of God* 3.18), and since he did consider himself a teacher of Christian doctrine there seems to be a contradiction here. In fact it is only apparent. When Augustine denies being a historian, this means only that he is not a historian whose attention is devoted to the things historians normally care about, like names of consuls, sizes of armies, results of battles. He is a historian whose concern is with other matters, namely those relevant for salvation. It may be objected that then there is a distinction between profane and sacred history after all; namely the distinction between the history ordinary historians are interested in and the history described by teachers of Christian doctrine. Indeed there is that distinction; and in this sense one can speak of sacred history as one strand of history. However, this is too weak a sense to support the use of the distinction in the literature. True, there is a strand of sacred history, but in no more interesting a sense than the one in which there is also a strand, say, of Norwegian history. That is to say, it is unexcitingly true that from all that happened in history a historian singles out one series of events and disregards the rest. So does the historian who is a teacher of Christian doctrine, and the events he singles out may well be called sacred history. This does not say anything, however, about what constitutes history; it does not say anything about history as such. It just says that there are these events in which these historians are interested, and that is boring news, since there are other events in which other historians are interested. The metaphor makes the point: though there can be said to be a strand of sacred history, there cannot really be said to be a strand of profane history, since profane history is just what remains when you subtract sacred history,[15] and that is not a strand because it lacks unity. To divide history into sacred and profane is as illuminating as to divide history into Norwegian and other. Such a distinction only serves to demarcate the field of interest of this or that historian.

GOD AND THE REASON THERE IS HISTORY

It is not my task to repeat the full story that, on Augustine's view, a teacher of Christian doctrine should tell. The task is to illuminate the basic conception of history that shapes it. This conception is what may be called Augustine's philosophy of history, in spite of the fact that he does not have such an expression.[16] The fundamental idea of this conception is that something is outside history; history is a limited field. To put the point more precisely, take a fact to be what is stated in a true statement; then the point is that history is not all the facts there are. This so far is just Platonism: conceptual and mathematical truths state facts that belong to a realm outside history. Augustine goes beyond traditional Platonism, though here perhaps not beyond Neoplatonism, in holding that what is outside history is not just the dead stuff investigated in conceptual analysis in the manner of Plato's dialogue *The Sophist* or in mathematics but a reality that is life and indeed mind. It is God who is beyond history. His is an unchangeable substance (*City of God* 11.2).

That he is good, for instance, is one of those facts outside history: it is a fact exempt from change (*City of God* 12.6).

History and what is outside history, however, are not on a par. Augustine was convinced from early to late that what is exempt from change is higher and better than what is not. This holds both metaphysically ("God is the highest being, i.e. he is most highly; and so he is unchangeable" [*City of God* 12.2; see also *Confessions* 12.28.38]) and morally ("to do evil is to neglect what is eternal and to pursue what is temporal" [*De libero arbitrio* 1.16.34; see also *Confessions* 12.11.11]). Given, then, that what is outside history is superior to history, the task is to understand what the place of history is below the eternal. We cannot leave it at saying that there is God unchangeable and then there is a changeable world. For someone convinced of the superiority of what is unchangeable it is hard to understand why there should be such a thing as history at all.

The answer is creation. There is history because God made it. There is even time because God made it. In fact they were made together, for an empty time is incomprehensible,[17] and the world, being changeable (*City of God* 11.4; *Confessions* 11.4.6), cannot be without time. God's will, then, is what makes the transition: eternal, it gives rise to the temporal. It is eternal, for it is itself God (*Confessions* 11.10.12; 12.15.18; 12.28.38): God did not change his mind in creating the world (*City of God* 11.4.2). For what reasons God's unchanging will made a beginning with time and world we do not know. We only know that he did it with reason, not for nothing (*City of God* 11.5). So we know that, even though temporal things are inferior to atemporal ones, this is no good reason to do without them altogether (*City of God* 12.4). To use again an anachronistic expression, there is in this sense reason in history: there is reason for there to be history. Consequently there is reason in history also in the sense that every particular event in history makes sense from God's point of view. Eternal himself, he understands everything temporal, since he gave rise to it. His understanding, however, like his will, does not involve change: "His thinking does not turn from one thing to another, but he sees things altogether invariably. Thus he comprehends what happens in time, things future, present and past, all in a stable and permanent presence" (*City of God* 11.21).[18] All changeable things, then, are willed by a will and understood by an intellect, both of which are changeless. History is owed to what is beyond history.

It may be wondered whether temporal things, having begun at a certain point, will come to an end at another, whether God is going to wipe the slate clean again. According to Augustine he will not. The world will be renewed, changing some of its qualities, and so will our bodies (*City of God* 20.16); but that is not their end, it is a transition (*City of God* 20.17). We will be living forever (*City of God* 19.20, 27) in bodily existence (*City of God* 22.4–21). Thus temporal things will stay. Time will stay.[19] Not that we see why. As little as we know God's reason for creating the world, as little do we know his reason for keeping it in existence. We just know from his word that he will. So it is in fact not the case that the world is just a big accident relative to eternity. Only for us it looks that way, insofar as we do not have a grasp of the reasons for its existence and continuation.

PREHUMAN AND HUMAN HISTORY

History, understood as comprising everything changeable, may be divided in two parts, one involving, the other not involving, humans. Augustine does not doubt that the extrahuman world is older than humanity, though he cannot say by how much (*City of God* 12.17). The prehuman world is a world of nature. Things change, indeed they perish, but in that there is nothing to complain about, given what they are. Eternal being they did not receive, and so in changing, deteriorating, and dying they fulfill "the order of transient things" (*City of God* 12.4, 5). Prehuman history is therefore running on the same spot. Things happen, but these happenings only implement the natural order, which is constant. So in another sense nothing happens in prehuman history. It is just the nature of things that is being realized in time here.

Human history differs in that humans have free will.[20] In human doings it is not just human nature that takes its course. If it were, humans could not have gone wrong: "God, author of natures and by no means of vices, created man right" (*City of God* 13.14; also 14.11). By implication, then, man's wrong act of disobeying God is not the realization of his nature. Speaking anachronistically again, it is "un acte gratuit," something he does not owe to his nature.[21] So with humans entering the scene the concept of nature loses the privilege of covering all that happens. Human history is not the mere display of what it is to be human. In this sense human history admits novelty; the novel being not just what has not been heard of but what does not lie in the order of things. In this respect human doings resemble God's creative act. "Something novel therefore happens in time," Augustine concludes in his attack against those who represent history as running in ever repeated circles (*City of God* 12.14), and he calls God's creation "a new work" (*City of God* 12.18). In the same way humans, making use of their freedom (*City of God* 13.14), bring about what was not there. There is that difference, though: what enables humans to bring about the novel, their will, is itself subject to change, whereas God's will is not (*City of God* 12.18). Some might say that only here, with novelty appearing in the world, the term "history" becomes appropriate. That is, they construe history and nature as opposites. This is only a terminological issue, though. Important is the material difference between human history and, as you prefer, all other history or nature: in human history what happens is no more the mere unfolding of what is.

What happens by nature may be defective, but what happens by will may be wrong: "Cattle and trees and other mutable and mortal things which lack intellect, sense or indeed life have their deficiencies which make their fragile natures perish, but it is ridiculous to consider these deficiencies damnable" (*City of God* 12.4). Damnable is only the voluntary, not the natural (*City of God* 12.3). Natures are better or less good, but no event in nature can be blamed. You may be worse off if your cow breaks a leg, but this is part of cowhood, and cowhood in general, with milk and broken legs and all, is a good thing, even if there are better ones (*City of God* 12.4, 5). That is to say, the goodness of a thing in the nonhuman world does not depend on particular events in its history. Its goodness is fixed once and for all by where its nature ranks in the overall order of entities (*City of God* 12.2). True, its goodness is limited, but it would hardly seem appropriate to complain that this nature is not another, better one instead. This is different with humans. They are good insofar as they have this nature, but they may still be evil insofar as they do evil (*City of God* 12.3). It is possible for them to do evil while being good in nature, because their doings do not merely explicate their nature. So a man is better or worse owing to what happens in his history, and some of these happenings accordingly can be blamed on him. Natural history displays, human history confers or fails to confer, goodness. Human history, unlike natural history, can go awry.

Thus, whereas nothing in nature can be contrary to God, things happening in human history can. Not that the evil deeds of humans could harm God or upset the order of the world as he created it. In fact God knows them and uses them to good purpose (*City of God* 14.26–27). Still, evil human deeds run counter to God's will (*City of God* 22.2); they offend God (*City of God* 22.22). Here it could be asked why it should be important for human history that parts of it offend God. He is in a different realm, beyond all history, so it is not clear why what we are doing *in* history should be any of his business. After all, if my neighbor is offended by my lawn, I do not care either. The answer to this query is that the eternal and the temporal do not stand beside each other; instead, the latter is subordinated to the former: "Reason proclaimed without any doubt that what cannot change is preferable to what can."[22] It is preferable not just in the sense that it serves our needs better but in the sense that in itself it is the higher reality. "That truly is which remains unchangeably" (*Confessions* 8.11.17).

With the phrase (from *De libero arbitrio* 1.3.7) used earlier the unchangeable excels over what is changeable and shows the latter to be falling short of true being. In this way God is the measure of everything, and of human history in particular. In its very being human history is subordinated to God's judgment, whereas my lawn is not subordinated in its being to my neighbor's feelings. For that reason Augustine understands and articulates human history basically in terms of how it is judged by God.

THE THREE STAGES OF HUMAN HISTORY

On this basis human history is divided into three parts. There was a time of faultless humanity, there is the time of sinful humanity, there will be a time of partly redeemed, partly damned humanity. Initially man lived fully in accordance with God's will (*City of God* 12.22; 14.11) and therefore happily as well. The act of disobedience brought a radical corruption of mankind and with it utter misery (*City *of God* 13.14). Only helped by God's grace can a human being escape that depravity (*City of God* 19.11). Those who do will, on the day of judgment, begin a life of untempted goodness and undiminished bliss without end. Those who do not will suffer unending punishment (*City of God* 21.12).

History would appear to be rather monotonous in the first and the last of the three stages. It is true that in the first stage, paradise, things do change in time. People eat, for example (*City of God* 13.20), people beget children (*City of God* 14.23–24), people work the fields (*De Genesi ad litteram* 8.9.18); or at any rate they would have done these things if paradise had lasted long enough. Still, while these things involve change, they do not change the basic condition in which humans live; they only realize it again and again in changing time. Nor is there any need to change it: people are happy, since neither death nor pain nor servitude oppresses them (*City of God* 14.10; *De Genesi ad litteram* 8.9.18). And they feel their happiness: they find life "sweet" (*De Genesi ad litteram* 8.16.35). There could have been a narrative of paradise history, but it would have resembled the reports on home news in *Neues Deutschland*, the official party organ of the GDR: this Friday, 29 August, our happy people finished the corn harvest. There is only one event in paradise history that changes things, and that is the end of paradise history, the fall. On the other end of things the third stage of human history is even more uniform than the first. Both the saints and the damned will continue to exist as bodies (*City of God* 13.22; 21.4), so presumably there will be physical movement, hence time. The saints, however, will be free from all bodily needs, and the damned will be unable to do anything about theirs (*City of God* 13.22; 19.28), so neither will, as we do, become active to relieve a need when it arises. The saints will be seeing God, the damned will be suffering: nothing novel will happen. Moreover, the last stage of human history differs from the first in that it cannot end. Like Thomas Hobbes,[23] Augustine thinks that to be insecure about whether one's happiness will last is to that extent to be unhappy (*City of God* 12.14). So the felicity of the saints would not be perfect, as it is supposed to be, if they could not be sure it is inalterable. History, then, does not come to a halt with the last judgment. Change is going to continue. Yet the change will be superficial only. If history is the realm of changing things, then in the literal sense there is no such thing as an end of history. However, history reaches a stable end state in which it runs on forever.

It must be admitted that there is evidence against this interpretation in Augustine's writings. Strikingly, he speaks in the treatise on John of our eventual liberation from time, and in the psalm exegesis he maintains that God's word calls those who are temporal and makes them eternal.[24] On the other hand he insists in *Confessions* on denying the predicate "eternal" to everything besides God.[25] So there is an apparent contradiction here: Augustine seems both to affirm and to deny that we can and will be eternal (i.e., exist without time). The natural solution to the difficulty is this: Augustine uses both "time" and "eternal" in a strict and a loose way. Strictly, we will not and cannot be eternal. We are, and will not cease to be, temporal creatures. However, in a loose sense time can be said to come to an end with the last judgment, since further changes, which do keep occurring, will be insignificant. One could put it this way: formal time does not end, destructive time does.[26] And as this state without significant change is going to continue forever, it can be called, loosely, "eternal."

Both the first and the last stages of human history, then, are similar to natural history: there is change, but it does not fundamentally affect the way in which humans live. "Real" history can only come in the second part of human history, that between fall and judgment, ours, which Augustine sometimes just calls "hoc saeculum" (this time of the world). Here indeed there is change: "Human affairs are so liable to change that no people at any time could be as secure as not to fear a hostile attack on their lives."[27] Security is lacking in this age, precisely that security that renders life in the last age of human history so uniform. Actually, however, our age, for all its instability, is pretty monotonous, too, in Augustine's view. True, human affairs are liable to change, but in another way nothing changes. The human condition was radically debased in the fall, and it cannot be improved by human efforts. It is a miserable condition, and so it will remain, with all historical changes, until the day of judgment. Augustine likes to describe this part of human history between fall and judgment with the traditional image of a river: "in this river, as it were, and torrent of mankind."[28] The image is appropriate. Think of watching a river or especially a torrent: this is enjoyable because there is change at every moment. Still, when you turn away you know that in another way nothing has changed since you came. So it is with the history of fallen humanity: there is much movement, but the basic character of human life, which is misery, does not change.[29] Stressing its pervasive character, Augustine occasionally speaks of these "evil days" (*City of God* 18.49, 51; *Sermo 25* 6): this time itself appears bad, because what is in it is thoroughly bad. Even the good, beautiful, or useful things in our lives that Augustine contemplates in a memorable chapter close to the end of *City of God* are said to be "filled in" into the misery of mankind (*City of God* 22.24): misery remains the fundamental condition. To be sure, human nature is still good and could not be anything else. Yet miserable we are nonetheless: that nature has been ruined by human action.

Thus historical changes that we should normally consider important turn out to be as insignificant as the events of human history before the fall or after judgment, since they change the human predicament as little as these do: "As far as this life of mortals is concerned, a life led and ended in a few days, what does it matter under whose command a man lives who is going to die, provided his rulers do not force him to do what is impious and unjust?" (*City of God* 5.17). This suggests that some historical changes are important, as when a ruler who forces his subjects to commit impiety is replaced by one who does not.[30] Still, this importance only concerns people's moral standing with respect to God. As far as it is a matter of bettering human life in this world, of providing for greater glory, greater comfort, or greater freedom, historical changes count for nothing. First, such attempts are bound to fail. There is in principle no way to improve the way humans live in this world. It is all rotten from the root up (*City of God* 13.14). Second, even if chances of success were better, why bother? The ills of our condition burden us only for these few days until we die, so, given the superiority of the eternal over the temporal, they do not deserve any attention. Thus, when Augustine compares the superhuman deeds of a Brutus who killed his own sons for Rome's sake to the easier tasks of the Christian, like alms-giving (*City of God* 5.18), there is admiration here for what Roman virtue could accomplish but also condescending pity for its having barked up the wrong tree and wasted its efforts on earth rather than on heaven.[31] For people who understand the true value of things there are no final aims of a political nature. They have, literally, better things to do: eternal life is the highest good for which one should be shooting in action (*City of God* 19.4). Augustine's standing image for this attitude toward politics is "peregrinari" (sojourning as a foreigner [e.g., *City of God* preface]). People who are heading for eternal life are not at home in this world of human politics, they are in exile here. Not that they are indifferent to what is around them; after all they do not know how long they will have to stay. They cannot but use the peace that it is the aim of political institutions to provide, since such peace is necessary for the mortal life in which they are dwelling temporarily (*City of God* 19.17). Accordingly they obey the laws of the relevant political community, provided that these do not interfere with their religious commitments (*City of God* 19.17). Even so, their heart is not in it. They are absent-minded citizens of this world: always waiting, though waiting patiently,[32] to reach the unseen but promised (*City of God* 19.14) country they feel to be theirs (*City of God* 5.17).

Augustine, sufficiently close to the classical tradition of political philosophy, insists that their life is still a social life (*City of God* 19.5). Foreigners in human politics, they belong to one another in a different community, God's city, which is in exile in this world for the time being and will come into its own in a renewed world on the day of judgment (*City of God* 20.16). Who is member of this city, however, and who is not cannot be ascertained in this age of human history. The division in question is between "those who live according to man and those who live according to God. These groups we also call, mystically speaking, two cities, i.e. two communities of humans. The one is predestinated to reign with God in eternity, the other to suffer eternal damnation with the devil" (*City of God* 15.1). The first is the city of God, the second is the earthly city. However, nobody knows of anyone, himself included, to what city he belongs, for nobody knows of anyone whether he is one of the elected saints or not. In particular to belong to the city of God it is neither necessary nor sufficient to be a member of the church (*City of God* 1.35). So the city of God is present in human history, but nowhere can it be identified. When Augustine says that "these two cities are interwoven in this world and mixed with each other, until the last judgment will separate them" (*City of God* 1.35), this does not only mean that it is difficult, it means that it is impossible for us to tell them apart. In this world the interwoven threads form one continuous cloth. Only at its end will the threads themselves show. Until the day of judgment God's city is not visible in the historical arena. In this respect the title *The City of God* may mislead. It may give the impression as if it were just another city like those we know. In fact it is a city "mystically speaking": no institution can claim to represent it. As H. Caton puts it, "a Christian state is a contradiction in terms."[33] The saints do enjoy a political existence in the city of God, but it is not a worldly political existence. In the political institutions of this world they remain foreigners.

The monotony of the second part of human history is broken only by the advent of Christ and by everything that points to or derives from it.[34] Here is change. It does not consist in human life ceasing to be miserable and human action ceasing to be sinful. The change is that a future and definitive liberation from this condition becomes possible (*City of God* 22.22; 14.11). Nobody can trust that he will be among those who are saved by God's free grace through Christ. Still, that grace has come. Thus while everything else that happens between fall and judgment only continues our misery, this event opens a door out of it, however many or few will walk through it in the end. This event changes the condition of human life once and for all: redemption has come.

Precisely for this reason it is important that incarnation, crucifixion, and resurrection do not belong to another, special history called sacred history but as historical events are on a par with everything else happening in human history. After all it is ordinary human history in which the misery of fallen humanity endures, and that misery is what needs to be met. Salvation only on the upper floor of history is no use. This is the point of incarnation: that grace arrive right in the middle of misery.

It is true, though, that incarnation, crucifixion, and resurrection are the only really interesting events in this part of human history between fall and judgment (disregarding here and in the following those events that are interesting derivatively, by their relation to that central event). The only interesting event in this age of human history is the appearance of what is beyond history: that "God's only son, remaining in himself unchangeably, puts on the clothes of humanity" (*City of God* 10.29; see also 10.20). It is true for all human history, indeed for all history, that God is its master, ruling and coordinating everything that happens.[35] Yet, as we never, or only very seldom (*City of God* 20.2), see why God directs things the way he does, history does not become transparent. We can only be confident in general that all history is in God's hands, but we cannot watch his hand at work. In incarnation, by contrast, God himself becomes visible, as directly as anything in human history. Bernard Williams not long ago wrote an essay on the tedium of immortality.[36] For Augustine the opposite is true: mortality is boring, boringly miserable, without the epiphany of the immortal. Peter Brown quotes from Augustine's *In Joannis evangelium* 9.6: "The centuries of past history would have rolled by like empty jars, if Christ had not been foretold by means of them."[37] But for Christ's coming all human history after the fall would have rolled by like empty jars.

CONCLUSION

So here is the overall Augustinian picture of history. It is a nested structure, like a Russian doll. First, beyond all history, and indeed beyond time, is God, existing timelessly. What the word "beyond" means in this sentence remains unexplained, given that it does not literally mean "prior to" or "outside of." The idea is, at any rate, that God encompasses everything that is not God. Second, there is the realm of temporal things, the realm of history, as this word has been used here. History has a beginning, creation, and so it has a certain age now, even if we do not know what it is; but it will go on indefinitely. There is a reason there is history, but we do not know that either. Third, within history there is human history. Later than and surrounded by a history that merely unfolds in time the stable nature of things, human history introduces free will and thus novelty: no nature is realized in the workings of free will. Fourth, within human history there is, surrounded by the uniform life in paradise and after judgment, the changing life of fallen humanity, which is unchanging, though, in its basic misery. Fifth, there is within this age of human misery that unique event in which God who is beyond all history enters history. This is the turning point of the whole structure. Thanks to it, a path is opened for humans to leave their misery and to enter a new life that is as much in accordance with the eternal God as is possible for a temporal creature of this kind.

So for Augustine there is not a great deal of important history after all. While history in the present sense of the word comprises everything that happens in the created world since its beginning, only very, very few of these happenings really change the course of things. Under nature, what happens merely unfolds what a thing is. Human history is as uniform in its initial and in its final part, except only for the fall. Even these our bad days, while full of change, are constant in their misery. Christ's coming, the first and the second, are within this age of mutability the only events that have significance. It is not that there are two histories, sacred and secular, or two strands of history. The point is that in the one history of the world there is so little that counts: creation, fall, redemption, judgment, that is all. The rest is waste. Moreover, the central event in all history, the pivot on which the whole structure turns, is the appearance of what is not in history, which promises the elimination of change as far as this is possible for temporal creatures. What Nietzsche's Zarathustra says about man[38] is Augustine's view about history: it is something that must be overcome.

This is reflected in Augustine's conception of peace as the final aim of all our efforts. Perfect peace, peace such that there cannot be any better and greater, is what the city of God expects to find at the end of its travels (*City of God* preface; 19.10). Indeed, "peace is such a great good that even in things of this world, mortal things, nothing more gratifying can be heard, nothing more desirable can be yearned for, simply nothing better can be found" (*City of God* 19.11). Peace in turn is understood in terms of order. True, peace is many different things, depending on the kind of thing whose peace it is. The general formula, though, is "peace is the tranquillity of order" (*City of God* 19.13). The idea is: when things are where they belong and do not move, then there is peace. Peace is to have arrived. Hence, conversely, to be moving is itself a bad thing. To be sure, any peace to which we aspire cannot but involve some change, given that we are temporal creatures. Such changes within peace, however, do not disturb the order. These are changes like that of day and night, changes that do not change anything. In the peace that is, according to Augustine, "devoutly to be wished" any movement has ceased to occur that gives things a new turn. The famous line in the opening chapter of *Confessions,* "you created us toward you and our heart is unquiet until it finds quiet in you," has been taken to express the essence of Augustinian thought. And so it does: it tells of the overwhelming desire to get rid of history, to the extent it is possible for a temporal being.

"Reason proclaimed without any doubt that what cannot change is preferable to what can" (*Confessions* 12.17.23). There are those whose reason does not proclaim any such thing. So what is the interest of Augustine's conception of history, given that it is built on this alleged declaration of reason and tries, in the various ways discussed, to frame history? The interest lies in the fact that with this conception those have been struggling who in more recent times recognized that nothing eternal is in sight and that we have to understand ourselves in terms of history alone. Not that Augustine has been frequently quoted by modern philosophers. His conception has been present all the more just because it had come to represent the traditional understanding rather than being seen as the view of a particular author. So it is largely the picture of history as represented in Augustine against which modern writers in the field implicitly have been arguing. To take just one example, when in his poem "Resignation" Schiller declares, "world history is the world's judgment,"[39] a formula immediately picked up by his contemporaries,[40] then his point is also, implicitly but no less significantly, that nothing other than world history is the world's judgment; that the world will not be judged by anything outside the world—which is what Augustine held. In failing to recognize in Schiller's slogan the challenge to an Augustinian view of history one would be missing a good part of what animates Schiller's thought here and gives it its power. And what holds for Schiller holds, often in more complicated ways than in this example, for a large part of modern philosophy of history. The aim has been, again and again, to cast off what came to be seen as the fetters of the Augustinian framework. The aim has been, against Augustine, to untie history from its transhistorical moorings.

And you do not get your opponents for free. You pay for them in coming to resemble them. So Augustinian ideas have shaped the very conceptions that were meant to replace them. Schiller's line again presents a clear example. Eager to establish that God's son will not come from heaven to judge the world, Schiller turns things around and has world history itself do the judging. However, in rejecting Augustine's doctrine he follows him at the same time, for he accepts the idea that there is such a thing as a judgment of the world. He just puts somebody else on the job rather than scrapping it entirely. Thus Augustine's idea stays in force. Indeed, people say to this day that history will judge what a person did or what a regulation effected. Apparently it is difficult to loosen the grip of the thought that at some point a balance will be struck and a reckoning be made, that the definitive truth about our doings will come out. Similarly for other elements of the Augustinian story: that history is intelligible, that it forms a whole, that it reaches a final stage, and so on—these ideas have dominated our thinking about history from Augustine's time to the present. Modern philosophy of history has been in this sense thoroughly Augustinian. Here lies the interest of Augustine's conception. For all our endeavors we have not yet left it behind.

NOTES

1. Koselleck speaks of "Geschichte überhaupt" and "Geschichte schlechthin." For the history and significance of this use of "history" see his contribution to the article "Geschichte" in O. Brunner, W. Conze, and R. Koselleck, eds., *Geschichtliche Grundbegriffe,* vol. 2 (Stuttgart: E. Klett, 1975).

2. See G. Amari, *Il concetto di storia in Sant' Agostino* (Ph.D. diss., Universitas Gregoriana, Rome, 1951), 17. Amari's view is disputed, though with little argument, by F.-M. Schmölz, "Historia sacra et profana bei Augustin," in H. Rahner, S.J., and E. V. Severus, O.S.B., eds., *Perennitas* (Münster: Aschendorf, 1963), 34. *De Genesi ad litteram* 9.12.22 supports Amari's view with an especially salient opposition between events ("res gestae") and "historia"; see also St. Augustine, *The City of God* 17.1. In fact there is one genuine counterexample to Amari's claim, which C. Meier, Art. "Geschichte," 600, pointed out: in *De doctrina Christiana* 2.28.44 Augustine distinguishes between historical narration, which reports on past human institutions, and history itself, "historia ipsa," which is not a human institution, because things past cannot be made undone and belong into the order of times that is founded and administrated by God. However, this is one of those exceptions that confirm the rule. True, "historia" does refer here to past events, but, given Augustine's standing usage of "historia" as "narrative," the added word "ipsa" here shows only his terminological embarrassment in referring to what "historia" is about; it should not be taken as suggesting that reference to events is the genuine function of "historia." (The division into chapters of *The City of God* is taken from the edition of Bernard Dombart and Alfons Kalb [Stuttgart: Teubner, 1981].) All translations, from Augustine and from other authors, are mine, except where stated otherwise.

3. The point here and some of the expressions are based on St. Augustine, *Confessions* 7.9.13–15; *De Trinitate* 4.16.21; 13.1.2; 8.19.24. Running together these chapters is justified by the evident parallels between them in substance and phrasing.

4. *City of God* 11.3: "things of which we should not be ignorant and which we are not capable of knowing by ourselves."

5. On this topic see the discussion in R. A. Markus, *Saeculum: History and Society in the Theology of St. Augustine* (Cambridge: Cambridge University Press, 1970), 7–9.

6. See *De doctrina Christiana* 2.28.42

7. See the phrase "historiae, quae res veraciter gestas continent" (*City of God* 18.13).

8. Ibid., 18.40. This is also why knowledge about Roman consuls and the like is "childish erudition" (*De doctrina Christiana* 2.28.42).

9. Vico's principle that you can know only what you made seems to be a humanized version of this idea. In sec. 349 of the *New Science* (trans. Thomas G. Bergin and Max H. Fisch [Ithaca: Cornell University Press, 1948]) he writes, "history cannot be more certain than when he who creates the things also narrates them." The telling word here is "creates." See on this topic Karl Löwith, *Vicos Grundsatz: Verum et factum convertuntur* (Heidelberg: C. Winter, 1968).

10. Karl Löwith, *Meaning in History* (Chicago: University of Chicago Press, 1949), chap. 9; Schmölz, "Historia sacra et profana"; Markus, *Saeculum,* chap. 1.

11. See, for instance, *De Genesi ad litteram* 8.1.2.

12. This is Markus's conclusion, too (*Saeculum,* 14f.), though he does not rigorously stick to this line in his text (see 9–11).

13. Markus's phrase (ibid., 9, 11).

14. *City of God* 18.43.46 tells of late Jewish history and of Christ's birth under the reign of Herod in one breath: no shift from profane to sacred history can be felt here.

15. Markus, *Saeculum,* 11.

16. If it is urged that this is, rather, Augustine's theology of history (see Alois Wachtel, *Beiträge zur Geschichtstheologie des Aurelius Augustinus* [Bonn: Rõhrscheid, 1960], chap. 1)—fine, let that title be used: there is no real difference here, since theology is philosophy by other means.

17. *City of God* 11.6; 12.26; *Confessions* 12.11.14. The compatibility of this conception of time with that in *Confessions* 11 may be questioned.

18. Kant's distinction between intuitive and discursive understanding (see, for instance, *The Critique of Pure Reason* B 135, 138f., 145) clearly stems from this tradition.

19. Augustine sometimes speaks of a "novum saeculum," a "new world-time" (*City of God* 22.10; 19) that is going to open after judgment.

20. Ibid., 22.1, *De Genesi ad litteram* 8.23.44.

21. In fact God set up man's nature in such a way that "if he offended the Lord, his God, by using his free will proudly and disobediently, then he would live like a beast, tied to death, dominated by lust, destined to eternal damnation after death" (ibid., 12.22). It is not man's nature to be disobedient; it is man's nature to be punished if disobedient.

22. *Confessions* 7.17.23. Metaphors of above and below, of superiority, and rise and ascent abound in Augustine; see especially the second half of *Confessions.*

23. Thomas Hobbes, *De homine,* chap. 10, sect. 3.

24. St. Augustine, *In Joannis evangelium* 31.5; idem, *Enarrationes in Psalmos* 101.2.10. On this topic see the discussion in Wachtel, *Beiträge,* 46f.

25. See *Confessions* 7.15.21; 12.9.9; 12.11.11; 12.11.12.

26. The passage in the treatise on John supports this interpretation by speaking of our arriving "where there is no mutability of time any more." So there may still be time, only no mutability; which is to say, no serious change.

27. *City of God* 17.13; see also 17.9; 19.4; 20.3.

28. Ibid., 22.24; also *De Trinitate* 4.16, 21; *Sermo 25* 6.

29. "Series calamitatis" in *City of God* 13.14 makes the same point with a different image.

30. Peter J. Burnell, "The Status of Politics in St. Augustine's *City of God*," *History of Political Thought* 13 (1992): 20, insists on this point against Markus, *Saeculum*, 70.

31. This alludes to Hegel's statement that "it was left to our days in particular to vindicate as human property, in theory at least, the treasures wasted on heaven" (*Hegels theologische Jugendschriften*, ed. H. Nohl [Tübingen: Mohr, 1907], 225).

32. *City of God* preface; 19.4; but cf. St. Augustine, *Epistulae* 27.1.

33. Hiram Caton, "St. Augustine's Critique of Politics," *New Scholasticism* 47 (1973): 453.

34. On the relevance of prophetic history see Peter Brown, *Augustine of Hippo* (Berkeley: University of California Press, 1967), 317–19.

35. *City of God* 4.33; see also 5.11; 22.2.

36. B. Williams, "The Macropulos Case: Reflections on the Tedium of Immortality," in *Problems of the Self* (Cambridge: Cambridge University Press, 1973).

37. Brown, *Augustine of Hippo*, 318.

38. Friedrich Nietzsche, *Also Sprach Zarathustra* 1.3, in *Sämtliche Werke: Kritische Studienausgabe*, 15 vols., ed. Giorgio Colli and Mazzimo Montimari (Berlin: De Gruyter, 1980).

39. "Die Weltgeschichte ist das Weltgericht."

40. Koselleck, "Geschichte," 667.

[16]

Augustine's Confessions and the Poetics of the Law

EUGENE VANCE

The last four books of Augustine's *Confessions* are a radical departure from the story of his life contained in the preceding nine books. Book X is an epistemological study of the functions of his memory, and Book XI is a commentary on the first chapter of the Book of Genesis. Since God knows everything, Augustine suddenly asks in Book XI, why should he address all these stories *(narrationes)* about himself to God? Rather than dwelling upon his "present" position as a Christian convert and priest, Augustine now elects priorities other than those of autobiography and philosophy to command the tongue of his pen *(lingua calami)*: above all, his burning desire to meditate upon God's Law—that is, upon the letter of the Old Testament—and to share his understanding "fraternally" with other men. As he abandons the *narratio* of his life story for the *enarratio* of the Law, Augustine undertakes to explicate only that part of Genesis which narrates the six days of the creation, the seventh day being God's sabbath.

This moment in Augustine's *Confessions* raises interesting problems for the modern reader, especially for the critic in search of a theory of "autobiography." Though I have dealt superficially in other studies with this strange substitution of goals in Augustine's *Confessions,*[1] much remains to be understood about Augustine's strategy of assuming the role of exegete before reaching the end of the story of his life, which is the "present" of enunciation. In particular, we need to explore Augustine's exegesis of the Old Testament as a discursive act subtended by a set of metaphysical and typological presuppositions not wholly apparent to us today. More importantly, we need to understand how this exegetical gesture is related to the composition of the *Confessions* as a whole. Although it has been surmised by reliable scholars that

[1] Eugene Vance, "Le moi comme langage: Saint Augustin et l'autobiographie," *Poétique* 14 (1973), p. 163-77; and "Augustine's *Confessions* and the Grammar of Selfhood," *Genre* 6 (1973), p. 1-28.

Augustine added his study of memory and the commentary on Genesis several years after he had finished the narrative portion of the *Confessions,* I shall take it for granted that Augustine undertook this addition with a lucid purpose in mind.

In his prayer inaugurating his exegesis of Genesis 1, Augustine employs what for us can only seem like a daring metaphor to describe his hermeneutical objectives, but it is a metaphor whose pre-history tells us a great deal about Augustine's gesture of passing from the narrative to the exegetical: "From all temerity and all lying curcumcise my lips," he writes, "both my interior and my exterior lips. May your Scriptures be my chaste delights!"[2] This metaphor is instructive for several reasons, among them, as we shall see, that it compels reflexion about metaphor itself, metaphor as both a repression and transformation of what is "literal." We should bear in mind that Augustine's metaphor inaugurates an exegesis whose dominant mode is figurative, which is to say that its purpose is to "vivify" the dead letter of the Law with the Spirit. Augustine undertook four different commentaries on Genesis, and since a "literal" commentary *(De Genese ad litteram)* was probably written about the same time as the allegorical commentary included in the *Confessions,* or shortly thereafter, we may safely infer that Augustine's choice of a cognitive mode in the latter commentary was deliberate. It will perhaps be instructive, therefore, if we dwell upon Augustine's metaphor for a moment, with the idea that it will help us better to perceive how Augustine's gesture of explicating Genesis relates to the narrative portions of the *Confessions* that precede it.

In pleading with God to circumcise his lips so that he may gain the chaste pleasures *(castae deliciae)* of reading God's text, Augustine is on the one hand conflating the tongue of his pen with his phallus, and on the other, conflating the hermeneutic performance with sexual love: as used by Augustine's classical forebears the word *deliciae* commonly connotes voluptuousness. The "outer" lies that must be circumcised from his lips are lies

[2] St. Augustine, *The Confessions* XI.ii.3. The English is based, with occasional modifications of my own, on the translation by John K. Ryan, *The Confessions of St. Augustine,* New York, 1960. Latin quotations are taken from the Skutella edition as published by A. Solignac, with the French translation by E. Tréhorel and G. Bouissou, with introduction an and notes by Solignac. I am heavily indebted to the scholarship and profound intelligence of A. Solignac in this edition: *Les Confessions,* in 2 vol, Paris, 1962. Future references to his notes will be to "Solignac."

uttered as verbal signs, while the "inner" lies pertain to the production of that inner, silent and non-verbal "language" of the soul which precedes the utterance of outward speech: the foreskin of these inner signs must also be trimmed in sacrifice before Augustine may enjoy, as he tells God, the "inside of your words" *(interiora sermonum tuorum)*. To possess and be possessed by the inner voice of the Law is to experience something "beyond the flood of voluptuous pleasure:" *ecce uox tua gaudium meum, uox tua super afluentiam uoluptatum* (XI. ii. 3). In expressing here his preference for spiritual over carnal climaxes, Augustine is echoing a previous moment in the Confessions when he condemned his "flood" *(fluctus)* of semen at puberty on the "shore" or "bank" of conjugality *(ad coniugale litus* II. ii. 2) and lamented not having become a eunuch of heaven *(abscisus propter regnum caelorum)* in order to enjoy more pleasurable *(felicior)* embraces.

Augustine's metaphor derives from St. Paul's Epistle to the Romans, a text devoted first to the sin of idolatry which God has punished by allowing its practitioners to become sexually perverted, and secondly, to the problems of a carnal observance of the Jewish Law:

> Circumcision, indeed, profits if thou keep the Law; but if thou be a transgressor of the Law, thy circumcision has become uncircumcision. Therefore if the uncircumcised keep the precepts of the Law, will not his uncircumcision be reckoned as circumcision? And he who is by nature uncircumcised, if he fulfills the Law, will judge thee who with the letter and circumcision art a transgressor of the Law. For he is not a Jew who is so outwardly; be he is a Jew is so inwardly, and circumcision is a matter of the heart in the spirit, not in the letter.[3]

St. Paul opposes the written Jewish Law to the "natural" law of the Gentiles, which is "written in their hearts." (Rom. 2: 12)

Augustine explored Paul's notion of "inner" circumcision in treatises of his own. In his treatise *On Lying (De mendacio)*, for example, Augustine considers as a type of lie the gesture of the Jew who tries to become a non-Jew by covering up "what has been made bare" with what remains of his foreskin *(De mendacio 7)*. In his *On the Spirit and the Letter,* however, Augustine elaborates on Paul's "circumcision of the heart" differently and in such a way as to accentuate Paul's equation of fleshy circumcision with the textuality of the Law itself and with the letter of that text of stone in which the

[3] Rom. 2:25-29. Because of its proximity to the Latin, I have used the Confraternity-Douay version of the Bible, New York, 1957.

Law was incised. At the time when the Law was first given, its text was written by God's finger, which is the Holy Ghost, in the tablets of stone; at the time of the Pentecost, by contrast, God's ghostly finger wrote the new Law not in stone, but in the living tables of the heart: "the Holy Ghost came upon them who were gathered together in expectation of his promised gift. *There* it was written on tables of stone that the finger of God operated; *here* it was on the hearts of men." (XXIX)[4] The circumcision of the heart—and of the lips that speak the heart—corresponds, then, to a text written by the Holy Ghost which abrogates the stony text of the Law which kills. In his other treatise on lying, Augustine defends spiritual interpretations of the letter of the Old Testament against the charge of lying, especially metaphor, "that is, the transfer of a word from a proper to an improper thing" (*hoc est, de re propria ad rem non propriam verbi alicujus usurpata translatio—Contra mendacium* x. 24).[5] By analogy, any person who transgresses, through sins, the eternally true natural law written in the hearts may be called a liar. Hence, Augustine's plea to be circumcised from both inward and outward lying *(mendacio)* in Book XI of the *Confessions* is as much a plea to be free of sin as it is to speak truly, that is, to comprehend and convey the spirit of the Law.[6]

The commentary on Genesis, understood as a "meditation on God's Law" (XI. ii. 2), may be seen, then, as the conclusion of a spiritual itinerary that involves the passage from an outward Law, the Law of the letter incised in stone and also of the circumcision of the flesh, to another inner Law, a universal Law "written" in the circumcised heart. Though this latter Law is now known through the Gospel as the work of the Holy Ghost, it is given also at birth as a "natural" Law which is therefore prior to Mosaic Law because it is universal. A. Solignac summarizes Augustine's conception of the two Laws thus: the natural Law is divine, and immutable, and it is written in the souls of the wise (*De Ordine* II. viii. 25); however, that Law can be obscured and perhaps even effaced by sin. As a consequence of man's sin, a second Law, opposed to the first, the Law of Sin (Rom. 7) was given to man *outwardly* as a written text.[7]

[4] St. Augustine, *On the Spirit and the Letter,* trans. by P. Holmes, as published in *Basic Writings of Saint Augustine,* ed. Whitney Oates, New York, 1948, p. 461-520.

[5] St. Augustine, *Contra mendacium*, as edited by G. Combès, Paris, 1948, in *Oeuvres de Saint Augustin, vol. 2, Ire série: opuscules II: Problèmes moraux,* p. 374-453. Translation into English my own.

[6] Solignac I, p. 663, n.8.

[7] Solignac XI, p. 664, no.8.

Yet this second Law kills not only because it condemns the carnally inclined sinner, but also because this Law begets the very carnal desire that it forbids. As St. Paul had put it, "I had not known lust unless the Law had said, 'Thou shalt not lust.' " (Rom. 7:7) The Law, then, instills in innocent men the unlawful and unnatural desire to desire, as Augustine aptly explains with another metaphor of flooding:

> Just as the rush of water which flows incessantly in a particular direction, becomes more violent when it meets with any impediment, and when it has overcome the stoppage, falls in greater bulk, and with increased inpetuosity hurries forward in its downward course. In some strange way the very object which we covet becomes all the more pleasant when it is forbidden. And this is the sin by which the commandment deceives and by it slays, whenever transgression is actually added, which occurs not where there is no law.[8]

Such, then, are the presuppositions that underlie Augustine's plea that God circumcise his lips as he undertakes his commentary on Genesis 1.

Obviously, here as elsewhere, Augustine's achievements in the *Confessions* are not to be measured by the "originality" of his ideas, since it is clear that the equations between Law, letter and lust had already been carefully asserted by St. Paul, but rather by the systematic dramatization of these ideas in what we commonly call, for lack of a better term, Augustine's "autobiography." Although space will oblige me to be very schematic, I shall now indicate a few important passages in Augustine's narrative which illustrate, first, the inculcation of the "Law of Sin" in his soul and secondly, the process by which he purges himself of that Law and its intellectual consequences; finally I shall speak of the commentary on Genesis itself as a re-wording of God's wording of the world and as a process of speech which is re-generative or re-creative, with regard to Augustine's soul, thanks to the relationship of homology that pertains between the structure of the soul and the structure of God's creation.

The parameters of Augustine's spiritual universe are already succinctly set forth in the *exordium* of the *Confessions,* though in the form of an insoluble logical problem, and not as narrative. The *exordium* begins with an exclamation of praise drawn from the Psalms, that is, from the Old Testament, followed by these seemingly unanswerable questions: how can a mere fragment

[8] *On the Spirit and the Letter* vi.

(portio) of the creation (and a sinning fragment besides), possibly presume to praise its uncreated creator? And should a mortal not first invoke God—call God inside him—before returning his love as praise? But how can he invoke God without *already* knowing the God he is invoking? Augustine's ontological and epistemological questions are answered by the Scriptures: if he seeks he will find, for God has been fore-spoken *(praedicatus)* by his Word and mediator. This debate serves at once as a beginning and as a conclusion to the *Confessions,* understood as the record of a spiritual journey: illuminated by the Gospel, a converted and redeemed Augustine now communicates successfully with the mind of God (and with himself) through the previously opaque letter of the Old Testament. However, this journey began by Augustine's alienation in the Law of Sin and of letters—as we shall presently see.

With regard to his earliest infancy, Augustine implies that, like all children, for a brief period he enjoyed a kind of tranquility that was possible because, as a newborn child, he was still close to that "natural" Law into which he was born and which was born in him. Hence, his existence was such that the basic dichotomies of human life—inner/outer (*intus/foris*), spiritual/corporeal, divine/mortal, etc.—did not yet divide and torment his consciousness:

> I myself do not remember this. Therefore, the comfort of human milk nourished me, but neither my mother nor my nurses filled their own breasts. Rather, through them you gave me an infant's food in accordance with your law, and out of the riches that you have distributed even down to the lowest level of things. You gave me to want no more than you gave, and you gave to those who nursed me the will to find what you gave to them . . . For at that time I knew how to seek the breast, to be satisfied with pleasant things, and to cry at my bodily hurts, but nothing more. (I. vi. 7)

However, not even infants are free of sin: not only did Augustine cry immoderately for the breast and, far worse, pale at the sight of other infants being suckled at the same breast (covetousness, despising of one's neighbor), but he even tried, as best he could, to strike and hurt those around him who would not obey his whims: "Thus it is not the infant's will that is harmless, but the weakness of infant limbs." (I. vii. 11) The acquisition of signs is the beginning of Augustine's subjection to the external Law, since by acquiring signs he allied his inner thoughts first to natural, corporeal signs (kicking and crying) and next to vocal signs: "Thus to those among whom I was I communicated the signs of what I wished to express. I entered more deeply into the stormy society of human life, although still dependent on my parents' authority *(auctoritas)* and the will of my elders." (I. viii. 13) Augustine's parents and elders express, it seems, the will of a vengeful God. Indeed, in Augustine's home it is by the whip that his father, not yet a Christian, kept peace among the servants of his household. His mother Monica, a Christian, was able to escape such beatings by her virtues of patience and meekness, and she regularly counseled other wives to accept their bondage to their husbands and masters: "From the time, she said, they heard what are termed marriage contracts read to them, they should regard those documents as legal instruments making them slaves." (IX. ix. 19)

The acquisition of language and the subsequent schooling of Augustine have attracted much interest among historians and educators, but what perhaps needs to be stressed is that Augustine considers his education as a systematic process of becoming subjugated to the Law in all of its diverse modes of manifestation in man's social and cultural institutions, especially Letters. Indeed, the schoolteacher is understood by Augustine as an especially stern temporal mediator of a wrathful God's retribution to fallen man, though we must bear in mind that the child by his sinning nature compels, himself, the dispensation of such justice as he acquires the arts of language:

> O God, my God, great was the misery and great the deception that I met with when it was impressed upon me that, to behave properly as a boy, I must obey my teachers. This was all that I might succeed in this world and excel in those arts of speech which would serve to bring honor among men and to gain deceitful riches. Hence I was sent to school to acquire learning, the utility of which, wretched child that I was, I did not know. Yet if I was slow at learning, I was beaten. This method was praised by our forbears, many of whom had passed through this life before us and had laid out the hard paths that we were forced to follow. Thus were both toil and sorrow multiplied for the sons of Adam. (I. ix. 14)

The labor of learning the arts of vain speech *(ut excellerem linguosis artibus)* is a consequence of God's curse following Adam's fall: "Cursed be the ground because of you; in toil shall you eat of it all the days of your life." (Gen. 3:17), and the only possible relationship of the fallen schoolboy to such a God is one of fear: "A little one, but with no little feeling, I prayed to you that I would not be beaten." (I. ix. 14) Learning writing (*grammatica*) and laws of grammar, and especially of Greek, seemed like a terrible punishment to the young child, yet the acquisition of these very laws also engendered lust in him which took the form of immoderate love of poetry, especially the story of Dido and Aeneas, two fictive fornicators for whom he wept: "I did not love you, and I committed fornication against you. . . ." (I. xiii 21) To master rhetoric and oratory is to idolize the purely arbitrary and conventional laws of language in such a way that mere errors in pronunciation will cause men to transgress the natural Law (and the second great commandment) that is written in their conscience, which is to love their neighbors as themselves:

> Thus if a man who accepts or teaches the ancient conventional forms of pronunciation violates the rules of grammar, and utters the word *homo* (man) without sounding the "h" in the first syllable, he will offend men more than if, contrary to your laws, he who is a man himself would hate another man . . . It is as if he thought an enemy more pernicious to him than his own hatred by which he is aroused against the other. Certainly, no knowledge of letters is more interior to us than that written in consciences, since he does to another what he himself does not want to suffer. (I. xviii. 29)

Moreover, pride in rhetoric makes the letter of the Scriptures opaque:

> When I first turned to that Scripture, I did not feel towards it as I am speaking now, but it seemed to me unworthy of comparison with the nobility of Cicero's writings. My swelling pride turned away from its humble style, and my sharp gaze did not penetrate into its inner meaning. (III. v. 9)

If the first two disciplines of what came to be institutionalized as the medieval *trivium* (grammar and rhetoric) burden the soul with sins that are obvious, far more subtle and tenacious are the sinful habits that third, logic, inculcates in the student's mind. This is what Augustine infers from his reading of Aristotle's *Categories*. One will recall that the purpose of Aristotle's text is to teach the laws of predicating properly, that is, of correctly asserting in propositions the reality of a created thing as we apprehend it. The *Categories* (and by extension, dialectics as a discipline) induces Augustine to believe that what his mind apprehends of God's substance (e.g., greatness, beauty) is *in* God in the same way that accidents are *in* substances as opposed to being *of* them. Now though, Augustine believes that however we, as creatures in time, apprehend God, his existence is not subject to such ontological differences with regard to itself:

> In this way, I attempted to understand even yourself, my God, who are most wonderfully simple and immutable, as if you were subject to your greatness and beauty in such wise that they would be in you as a subject, just as they are in bodies. But you yourself are your greatness and beauty. (IV. xvi. 29)

Augustine explains later that the whirlpool of contradictory phantasms (*turba phantasmatum* VII. xvii. 23) that his mind has created is inferior to the mental power to create phantasms in the first place, a power which is presumably to be compared with God's own power to create, since we are made in his image: the *Categories,* then, teaches mortals to love *figmenta* derived by the mind from its experience of the material world created on the *third* day, and not from the firmament, which was God's immaterial creation of the *second* day and which is a kind of sky that is immaterial and immutable, even though it is created. (XII. viii. 8) Augustine considers the labors of the Aristotelian logician as the intellectual consequences of Adam's sin and of God's curse (Gen. 3:17) condemning Adam's race to cultivating the ungrateful fields of this world, as opposed to those of Paradise or of the firmament:

> What I had conceived of you was falsity itself: it was not truth. It was a figment formed out of my own misery; it was not the firmament of your beatitude. For you had commanded it, and so it was done in me, that the earth should bring forth thorns and thistles for me and with labor should I eat my bread.

Indeed, Augustine's experiences as a student finally lead him to conclude that all of the books of the liberal arts *(artes liberales)* are anything but liberating and that as a student, Augustine is nothing but their slave *(seruus).* Only in the Gospel will his mind at last be freed of unlawful lust so that it may enjoy an intellectual sabbath. (*pax sabbati* X. xxxv. 50) Indeed, if Augustine tends to complement his accounts of intellectual servitude with accounts of his sexual extravagances, it is because he saw his desperate compulsion to fornicate as a consequence of that very literal Law in Sin to which his intellect is subject and by which he must also be judged and punished. (II. ii. 4) For this reason it is already easy for us to see why, at the end of the *Confessions,* a spiritual interpretation of the Letter of the creation which leads beyond to a knowledge of the creator might coincide with a victory of the commentator over his own desiring flesh. Just as the text incised in stone is abrogated by a new text that heals the living heart, so too circumcision of

Augustine's fleshly foreskin is superceded by an act of grace which is also an act of metaphorizing, that is, by a non-circumcision of the heart that heals as it does not cut. As Augustine writes in his treatise *On the Spirit and the Letter,* "He [the Apostle] calls, however, the circumcision of the heart the will that is pure from all unlawful desire; which comes not from the *letter,* inculcating and threatening, but from the *Spirit,* assisting and healing." (xiii)

Though the operations of the Holy Ghost are what make possible the repression of that obscure, lust-begetting, uncanny, killing letter of the Old Law and its re-vision in the New, the procedures by which these ghostly operations are perpetrated in Augustine's life and mind are as subtle and diverse as those by which the Law had earlier enslaved him. Space will permit only the most schematic outline of this process, and briefly, its principal phases are as follows: first, Augustine must overcome his carnal (hence false) intellections both of God and of his own soul; secondly, he must apprehend, in an emotion of terror and awe, the radical difference *(dissimilitudo)* not only between the creator and the creation, but also between the soul and the carnal world that it has sinfully loved; thirdly, after striving to communicate with God and discovering his ineffability, Augustine must discover for himself both the proper mediator and the language of mediation. Though we may easily glimpse in these phases the complementary operations of the Trinity as Augustine would more fully describe them later in his *De Trinitate,* once again, the peculiar interest of the *Confessions* as a work of art derives from Augustine's shrewdness in projecting these operations upon "real life" events.

The principal obstacles to Augustine's intellection of God as an immaterial substance are his Manicheism and the burden of Epicurean and Stoic materialism. Augustine's close personal proximity to the great Manichean professor, Faustus, portends very early his future disillusionment with that religion: for all his charm, humility and semblance of eloquence, Faustus proves to be a man of shallow learning in the liberal arts. However, Augustine is still unable to free himself either of a corporeal understanding of God (V. x. 19) or of a belief in evil as an autonomous principle:

> I wished to meditate upon my God, but I did not know how to think of him except as a vast corporeal mass, for I thought that anything not a body was nothing whatsoever. This was the greatest and almost sole cause of my inevitable error.

> As a result, I believed that evil is some such substance and that it possesses its own foul and hideous mass, either gross, which they styled the earth, or thin and subtle, as is the body of the air, which they imagine to be a malignant mind stealing through the earth. (V. x. 19)

Augustine's appointment to a chair in rhetoric at Milan led to his encounter with Ambrose, a decisive event in his liberation from the Law and from the sins that it begot. Not only was he dispelled of his fear that the New Testament had been falsified in a conspiracy to infiltrate Christian teaching with the Jewish Law (V. xi. 21), but through Ambrose's sermons he also acquired new respect for Christianity because it allowed him to understand certain problematical passages in the Old Testament allegorically, "by which passages I was killed when I had taken them literally." (V. xiv. 24) Moreover, certain aspects of Ambrose's personal conduct struck him: first, the man's celibacy, secondly, his ability to withdraw not only from other people, but even from the production of vocal signs in his reading: Ambrose is a living portrait of a man who is carnal yet capable of enjoying spiritual knowledge:

> When he read, his eyes moved down the pages and his heart sought out their meaning, while his voice and tongue remained silent. Often when we were present—for no one was forbidden to enter, and it was not his custom to have whoever came announced to him—we saw him reading to himself, and never otherwise. After sitting for a long time in silence—who would dare to annoy a man so occupied?—we would go away. (VI. iii. 3)

Through Ambrose, Augustine's literal understanding of the text of the Law continues to be overcome:

> I rejoiced also that the ancient scriptures of the law and the prophets were now set before me for reading, not with that eye which once looked on them as absurdities . . . I was glad when I often heard Ambrose speaking in his sermons to the people as though he most earnestly commended it as a rule that "the letter kills, but the spirit quickens." For he would draw aside the veil of mystery and spiritually lay open things that interpreted literally seemed to teach unsound doctrine. (VI. iv. 6)

By the same token, Augustine illustrates through a curious anecdote about his friend Nebridius how difficult it is for the solitary human soul to eliminate from itself that unlawful desire which is both cause and effect of original sin. Alypius was

Augustine's lifelong friend and a man of great integrity, but had a penchant for watching fights between gladiators. Augustine considered such fights as a paradigm of human society at its most decadent, as legal crimes where peace and love of neighbors are deliberately abhorred and where individuals, as they succumb to the tumult of the crowd, lose their inner harmony when they are swallowed up in the chaos of the multitude that erupts at the spilling of human blood. Though Alypius has renounced such spectacles, one day he meets some friends in the street who urge him to come along to the arena. Alypius boldly seizes the occasion as a challenge: he will go, but will prove his moral superiority and his wisdom by sitting through the entire spectacle with his eyes shut. When a gladiator finally falls, however, so great is the clamor at the spilling of human blood that Alypius is conquered by *curiositas* and opens his eyes: his spiritual fall is worse, Augustine says, than that of the gladiator in the ring. (VI. viii. 13)

However, Augustine illustrates by another episode in the life of this same Alypius that God, if he is wrathful toward fallen man, is just, and that a principle of justice subsists even within the institutions of pagan law. Once when Alypius was a student, he happened to arrive at the forum just as a thief with a hatchet, who had been chopping lead away from a trellis, dropped the hatchet and fled. Not knowing what had just occurred, Alypius innocently picked up the hatchet and was immediately apprehended and led off by the angry crowd to be judged. As if by chance, an inspector of public buildings passed by who recognized Alypius and extracted him from the grip of the crowd. The inspector had already suspected, moreover, another individual of previous crimes of this sort, and when he displayed the hatchet to a slave belonging to that individual, the slave revealed that his master was indeed its true owner: "For immediately you, O Lord, stood present to prove his innocence, of which you were the sole witness." (VI. ix. 15)

It is above all Augustine's encounter with the writings of the Neo-Platonists (translated into Latin) that leads him to discover the absolute ontological difference between the creation, which is the *regio dissimilitudinis*, and the creator. Consequently, he also discovers the need to understand spiritual things *(intelligibilia)*, hence, to surpass knowledge of things existing temporally, knowledge that clutters the soul with phantasms of its own making which must not be idolatrously predicated to God. Augustine now becomes capable of experiencing suprarational ecstasies in which his soul enjoys unmediated, yet fleeting, knowledge of God as the very principle of existence:

> Thus I gradually passed from bodies to the soul, which perceives by means of the body, and thence to its interior power, to which the bodily senses present exterior things—beasts too are capable of doing this much—and thence again to the reasoning power *(potentia ratiocinans),* to which what is apprehended by the bodily senses is referred for judgment *(iudicandum).* When this power found itself to be in me a variable thing, it raised itself up to its own understanding *(ad intelligentiam suam).* It removed its thought from the tyranny of habit, and withdrew itself from the throngs of contradictory phantasms. In this way it might find that light by which it was sprinkled, when it cried out . . . Thus in a flash of its trembling sight it came to that which is *(id quod est).* (VII. xvii. 23)

Although this Neo-Platonic mystical vision belongs to the narrative portion of the *Confessions,* its sequence of steps makes it obvious why Augustine would become dissatisfied with the narration of his personal life as a source of true wisdom and would consequently invite his soul (as he does in Book X) to reflect upon its own spiritual substance as opposed to reflecting upon external images of the creation that have threatened to corrupt his soul by infiltrating his memory.

What follows in the context of this same passage also leads us to anticipate why Augustine saw fit not to exalt, as might a Neo-Platonist, his unmediated, face-to-face knowledge of God as existence (even though in his famous vision at Ostia he does once again celebrate the mystical potential of the soul to encounter God), but rather to stress the sad but inevitable return of his vision to what is ordinary: Augustine requires, he tells us, a constant and trustworthy mediator to make fast his bond with God. That mediator is of course Christ, who as both the way and the truth, is a signifier co-substantial with its signified, hence a unique, yet perfect sign. Yet, in the *Confessions,* Augustine emphasizes his understanding of Christ more as an epistemological instrument than as a historical person in whose passion he might vicariously indulge. This Christological bias in the *Confessions* explains to a large extent, as we shall promptly see, why a commentary on Genesis 1 follows the soul's examinations of its own powers in Book X, and not a theophany through the *person* of Christ.

After reading St. Paul, who was himself deeply marked by Neo-Platonic teachings, Augustine came to identify the deep division within his own will as a conflict between the two Laws, the Old and the New: "In vain was I delighted with your law according to the inward man, when another law in my members fought against the law of my mind, and led me captive in the law of sin which was in my members." (VIII. vi. 12) Moreover, since the Old Law had come to dominate Augustine through the intimately related forms of an idolatrous love of letters and a passionate attachment to the creation, especially to women, who, through Eve, had wreaked so much havoc in the creation, obviously only through new experiences of language and of love may Augustine be redeemed from the Letter and the Law of Sin. Accordingly, in his readings of St. Paul and St. John, Augustine clings above all to the principle of Christ as Word *(Verbum)*, not only as Word fore-spoken in vocal signs to men by a God in and of the flesh, but also as Word "spoken" by God at the creation: "In the beginning was the Word, and the Word was with God; and the Word was God. He was in the beginning with God. All things were made through him, and without him was made nothing that has been made." (John 1:1-3) It is above all through an intellection of the Word of creation, as that Word is spoken in the Old Testament and respoken in the New, that Augustine will attempt to understand the creator through the creation.

Augustine's espousal of Christ as Word occurs in two distinct phases in the *Confessions*. First, through the Gospel, whose authenticity Augustine has, thanks to Ambrose, now come to accept, Augustine gains liberating knowledge of himself as a sinner when, in a moment of violent anguish, a mysteriously disembodied, childlike voice (a visitation of the Holy Ghost?) exhorts him to "take up and read" (*"tolle, lege"* VIII. xii. 29) the Scripture, whereupon Augustine's eyes fall providently upon a verse of St. Paul's commanding men to walk "not in revelry and drunkenness, not in debauchery and wantonness, not in strife and jealousy. But put on the Lord Jesus Christ, and as for the flesh take no thought for its lusts." (Rom. 13: 13-14) Augustine is now liberated from his sinful servitude of the Old Law as he fulfills the first and greatest commandment on which hangs the Law and Prophets, which is to love God with all his heart; and just as spontaneously, he fulfills the second, which is to love his neighbor as himself, when he runs to

Alypius to share his excitement, and Alypius too finds in the very next sentence of the Scripture his own liberating self-knowledge. As St. Paul puts it in that same chapter of Romans, "Love therefore is the fulfillment of the Law."

Augustine's choice of the life of the soul now necessitates his divesting himself not only of false doctrines, but of attachments to other people, including his friends, his mistresses, and even his mother, who, after pursuing her son doggedly through all of his wanderings, takes leave of the world. It is at this point in Augustine's text that he dispels any idea of his *Confessions* as an autobiographical venture whose goal might be to make him known among his fellow men through a process of intersubjective communication: "What have I to do with men, that they should hear my confessions, as if they were to 'heal all my diseases?' A race too curious to know about another man's life, but slothful to correct their own! Why do they seek to hear from me what I am, men who do not want to hear from you what they themselves are?" (X. iii. 3)

But the final operation by which Augustine repeals the Law of Sin in him is to undo the killing letter of the text in which that Law was first engraved, that is, to utter, with lips circumcised by the Holy Ghost, the spiritual meaning of the creation by the Word as that Word is written in the Old Testament. It is perfectly in character with Augustine's portrayal of his initiation into the Law of Sin, which is the law of the letter and of lust, that he should choose to approach and to "speak" the creator neither by contemplating the *visibilia* of the creation nor by intense meditation upon the personal passion of the Word made flesh, but rather through a hermeneutics of a text once veiled by sin, yet now made transparent through the Gospel and through the Holy Ghost as the principle of charitable metaphor, if we may adhere to the root sense of that term as a "carrying beyond" what is given in the letter and in the body of the sign.

However, Augustine's exegesis of Genesis 1 must be understood as more than a gesture of charitable pedagogy. Given the profound isomorphism between the hierarchy of faculties in the human soul and the hierarchy of the creation as the good work of the Word, Augustine's hermeneutic discourse is not simply a mimetic re-presentation of the Word that lies hidden under the "veil" of the Biblical *narratio:* Augustine's *enarratio* of the creation is a ritual of Augustine's own *re*-creation from the abyss of his sins through illumination by the spirit, through whom God let there be light in Augustine's soul. Since evil is nothing, but only annihilation of the soul, to understand God's creation *ex nihilo* is, for the sinner, to be re-made, to be made complete: "O Lord," he writes as he begins his exegesis, "per-fect me and reveal to me these things." (*o domine, perfice me et reuela mihi eas.* XI. ii. 3) During his writing, though, only the actions of prayer and confession protect his text from the darkness of the abyss: "O may it be the Truth, the light of my heart, not my own darkness *(tenebrae)* that speak to me. I fell away to those material things and I became darkened over, but from there, even from there, I loved you." (XII. x. 10) If there can be re-creation through writing, it is because the creation itself is a manifestation of textuality in a hierarchy of modes. The material world is that of temporal, mortal language and of the dead letter. However, stretched out as a scroll above this world is a kind of parchment which is God's Scripture: it is a firmament of writing which allows mortals to contemplate the heavenly bodies in such a way as to understand intuitively what lies beyond: "These things you, our God, wisely discuss with us in your book, your firmament, so that we may discern all things in wondrous contemplation, although as yet in signs and in times, and in days and in years." (XIII. xviii. 23) This parchment is a threshold which separates mortals from the "sky of the sky," where intellection is immediate, rather than dialectical or figurative or temporal:

> Meanwhile I interpret the sky of sky as the intellectual sky, were where it belongs to the intellect to know all at once, not in part, not in a dark manner, not through a glass, but as a whole, in plain sight, face to face, not this thing now and that thing then, but, as has been said, it knows all at once, without any passage of time. By the earth invisible and without form, I understand an earth without any change of time, which change is wont to have now this thing, now that. (XII. xiii. 16)

And in this sky of sky, the angelic and the blessed spend the non-time reading, but not reading as mortals do under the Law of Sin; they read a language without syllables that unfold in temporal sequence, and from a text that is unequivocal and eternal because it is the Word itself. And unlike mortals enslaved by the liberal arts, for whom servitude is a consequence of the Law of Sin, these celestial readers give themselves to a reading that they choose of their own free will, and which they love: *legunt, eligunt et diligunt*

(XIII. xv. 18), in contrast with the vexation of reading mortals beneath this spiritual firmament. The text in the sky of sky is a writing without difference: neither is it different from, or extrinsic to, what it means; nor is there difference within its own substance, the difference of syllables succeeding each other in time:

> Let the supercelestial peoples, who are your angels, praise you, they who have no need to look up at this firmament [of the Scripture], or by reading to know your Word. They always behold your face, and, without any syllables of time, they read upon it what your eternal will decrees. They read your will; they choose it; and they love it. They read forever, and what they read never passes away. For by choosing and loving, they read the actual immutability of your counsel. Their book is never closed, nor is their scroll folded up, because you yourself are this to them, and you are this for eternity. (XIII. xv. 18)

In contrast with those who are in bondage to the Mosaic Law and for whom the sabbath is a mere day of rest, St. Augustine considers the seventh day of the creation as the eternal rest of salvation for those whose good works please God just as the creation pleased him on the sixth day when he "saw that all he had made was very good." (Gen. 1:31) If Augustine's exegesis of the letter of the creation is a good work, a work of charity, it is not because he himself is its author; nor has it been written under God's authority: it is God's gift, as is the sabbath for those who do not turn away from God and his book, but who praise him:

> But the seventh day is without an evening, and it does not have a setting, because you have sanctified it to endure for all eternity, so that by the fact that you rested on the seventh day, having fulfilled all your works, which are very good, your book may proclaim to us beforehand that we also, after our works, which are very good because you have given them to us, may rest in you on the sabbath of eternal life. (XIII. xxxvi. 51)

[17]

AUGUSTINE AND THE PROBLEM OF CHRISTIAN RHETORIC

Ernest L. Fortin

It is surprising, particularly when one considers the importance which the Church Fathers attached to the transmission of the word of God, that so little should have been written on the art of preaching during the early Christian centuries. The one notable exception is, of course, Book IV of Augustine's *De doctrina christiana,* which has long been acclaimed as the first handbook of Christian rhetoric.[1] While no one to my knowledge has ever questioned the uniqueness of Augustine's treatise, the novelty of the views contained therein has been the subject of a good deal of discussion in recent years. With few dissenting voices, the trend among scholars has been to minimize Augustine's originality in favor of the once commonly held opinion that the core of his teaching is simply derived from Cicero's rhetorical works.

There are, to be sure, a number of features that set Augustine's treatise apart from those of his illustrious predecessor, not the least obvious of which is that the content of Christian rhetoric, which is drawn for the most part from sacred Scripture, differs significantly from that of pagan rhetoric. It is also true that Augustine regards the rules of the rhetorical art as being less important to the Christian orator than to the statesman or the lawyer in a civil court and even goes so far as to propose that they may be dispensed with altogether if the preacher has reached the age beyond which they can no longer be profitably acquired.[2] A greater simplicity would likewise seem to be required of the Christian orator than would normally be the case with his pagan counterpart, although it is not clear in this instance whether Augustine is taking issue with Cicero himself or merely reacting against the excessive formalism of the rhetors of his own time.[3]

All of these points nevertheless leave untouched the central issue of the nature and principles of the rhetorical art, and scholars are virtually unanimous in asserting that Augustine remains by and large faithful to the Ciceronian tradition. Thus, in his monumental study of the influence of the Latin classics on Augustine, Professor Harald Hagendahl is able to state that he has "followed the course of Augustine's exposition with a view to showing how much it tallies with Cicero's rhetorical treatises in the general conception of rhetoric and even in words: in the division, terminology and other technicalities, whether rendered literally or by paraphrase."[4] The conclusion at which he arrives is clear and peremptory: Augustine's teaching is based on the system of rhetoric introduced into the Roman world by Cicero. That teaching "follows . . . Cicero's views so closely, often even in the minutest particulars, that it cannot make a substantial claim to novelty and originality in the doctrinal system, at most to a slight modification on this or that point."[5]

Even Professor H.-I. Marrou, who has gone further than anyone else in defending the revolutionary character of the *De doctrina christiana,* concedes that as regards the fundamentals of rhetoric Augustine has been content to repeat the views developed by Cicero, the chief theorist as well as the greatest master of Roman eloquence.[6] The same basic position is adopted by J. Oroz, who agrees with Marrou that the themes of Christian and pagan rhetoric are worlds apart but finds that on all other important points the *De doctrina christiana* remains well within the boundaries defined by the Ciceronian tradition.[7] The new wine of the Gospel has simply been poured into the old pagan cask without in any way causing it to be altered in the process.

Yet, when all the evidence is sifted out, one wonders to what degree full justice has been done to the subtlety of Augustine's thought; for it is still conceivable that the cribbings from Cicero have been used to formulate a notion of rhetoric which resembles that of Cicero in outward appearance more than in inner substance. With the help newly provided by A. Hus's study of *docere* and its cognates in Cicero's rhetorical works,[8] one may be in a better position to review the merits of the case and determine more accurately the extent of Augustine's originality. That originality, as far as I can tell, is much greater than anyone has yet dared to maintain.

Like the *Orator* and the *De oratore,* the *De doctrina christiana* assigns to the orator the threefold duty of "teaching" (*docere*), of "pleasing" (*delectare*), and of "persuading" (*flectere*). To teach, Augustine adds, again quoting Cicero, is a matter of necessity: *docere necessitatis est.* To speak in a pleasing manner adds an element of charm to the orator's words: *delectare suavitatis.* Finally, to persuade pertains to the triumph that the orator seeks for his client or his cause: *flectere victoriae.*[9] The question is whether the "teaching" to which the *De doctrina christiana* refers has anything at all in common with what Cicero originally intended by that term. A fresh look at the relevant texts suggests that Augustine has in fact profoundly modified the Ciceronian doctrine on two major points at least: first, by asserting the priority of the teaching function of the orator over the two other functions, and, secondly, by investing the terms *docere* and *doctrina,* which best express that function, with a meaning that could never have been ascribed to them by Cicero. We shall gain a new insight into the matter if we begin by examining that "teaching" to which in Cicero's view a substantial portion of the orator's efforts must be devoted.

Cicero's remarks occur within the broad context of a discussion of the two leading forms of oratory, namely, deliberative or political and judicial oratory.[10] Before reaching any important decision in matters of public policy or rendering a verdict in a court of law, the assembly or the judges must be supplied with all of the necessary information pertaining to the issue before them. A judge, for example, should not only know what crime has been committed but, as much as possible, why and how it was committed, what the provisions of the law in regard to such a crime might be, and a host of other relevant data. The lawyer is thus faced with the initial task of apprizing his hearers of the facts of the case, or, if the facts are not contested, of establishing the validity of his case on the basis of commonly accepted principles of justice.[11] To that extent he may be said to teach. But the teaching with which he is concerned is clearly in the service of something else, which is to persuade the judge of the innocence of his client.[12] This and nothing else is the end to which all of his energies are directed. The criminal lawyer will not spare any effort to obtain a favorable verdict; the political orator, if he can help it, will not settle for anything less than a vote resulting in the adoption of the measure that he advocates. In either case, whatever teaching they may be called upon to do remains subordinate to the one goal on the attainment of which the success or failure of their respective endeavors hinges. Neither of them will have accomplished anything if the accused is convicted or if the proposal in behalf of which he pleads is defeated.

This is not to deny that the orator's teaching function is as much a part of the rhetorical art as either of the other two functions; for the outcome of the legal or juridical proceedings in which he is involved will be affected to a very large extent by the manner in which the case is presented in the first place. Not any kind of presentation will do. The speaker must see to it that his narration of the facts is not only clear but "credible."[13] This alone requires considerable skill on his part, and all the more so as the art which he brings to that "narration" must remain imperceptible to the listener.[14] The same rule applies to the *loci communes* or general principles which the orator has at his disposal and which are not all equally suitable to his needs. Attention must be drawn to those principles which support his case and away from those which could conceivably weaken it. One may argue, for example, that the particular law which the accused has violated needs to be reinterpreted in the light of a higher principle which it contravenes, or, inversely, that the higher principle in the light of which the accused would appear to stand convicted is itself in need of correction by some more precise law justifying its transgression in specific instances.

One gathers therefore that the "teaching" which the orator dispenses cannot be construed as a universal teaching in the strict sense, since it has to do either with the particulars of the issue at hand or with a series of more general arguments whose usefulness depends less on their intrinsic worth than on the opinion that people commonly entertain in regard to them. What is most important in all such cases is not that the argument be defensible on rational grounds but that it seem plausible to the hearer. The orator is of necessity less concerned with the truth than with its appearance. A plausible falsehood is infinitely more valuable to him than an unlikely truth.

It should not be inferred from these remarks that Cicero had no regard for the truth in political or judicial matters but only that he was aware of the frequent impossibility of arriving at any completely objective solution to the problems that they raise. The questions to which the orator addresses himself can rarely be decided on the basis of knowledge alone. If he speaks about them, it is less for the purpose of instructing his hearers than of persuading them, and passion rather than reason is the instrument par excellence of persuasion, the middle term as it were by which the orator seeks to win the assent of his audience and gain acceptance for such courses of action as practical wisdom may dictate given the nature of the case and the circumstances that surround it.[15] Hence the confidence that he inspires is as much a function of the opinion that others have formed of him as a man as it is of his competence or his ability to speak well. People will trust him if they are convinced that he is a good man and that he has their common good at heart.[16] In that regard, his own person is a better witness to the "truth" of his assertions than any of the arguments that he may be able to muster in support of them.

The deeper point of Cicero's observations could easily be missed, however, if one were to leave it at saying that opinion rather than true knowledge is the stuff of rhetoric or that the complexity of human affairs precludes any attempt to approach them with the detachment that characterizes rational or scientific discourse. One cannot point to the limitations of any rhetorical argument without at the same time raising the larger issue of the relation of rhetoric to philosophy and, more generally, of the political life to the philosophic life. What distinguishes Cicero's works from the common run of rhetorical treatises is precisely that they are guided by an awareness of philosophy and its ambiguous relationship to the city. For the orator that Cicero has in mind is not just the man who combines a natural talent for public speaking with a knowledge of the rules of rhetoric but a new type of orator in whose person the accomplishments of the statesman and the philosopher coalesce and are brought to a higher level of perfection.[17] The consequences of this important fact will come to light if we glance briefly at the attributes of the perfect orator as they are outlined in the *Orator* and the *De oratore.*

The highest form of oratory is political oratory, and political oratory deals with the greatest and best of human affairs: religion, death, piety, patriotism, right and wrong, the virtues and vices of men, the duties of citizens, their pleasures and pains, the passions by which they are moved, and the evils to which they succumb.[18] One cannot begin to speak wisely about such matters until one has achieved a true understanding of human nature; for only the man who has a thorough knowledge of the whole is the proper judge of the ends of human existence and of the means by which they are best attained. It follows that the orator must have mastered not only the art of persuasion but all of the theoretical sciences as well.[19]

Needless to say, few men have either the capacity, or the opportunity, or for that matter the desire to engage in such pursuits. Even the greatest orators of the past—Pericles, Demosthenes—did not conform to the proposed ideal and it is doubtful whether anyone could.[20] The crucial point, however, is not whether the perfect orator has ever existed or ever will but, assuming that the quest for theoretical wisdom has uncovered a dimension of reality that transcends the horizon of the political life, whether there is any common measure between the knowledge that is ideally demanded of him and the notions of justice by which most men are guided. If by justice one understands, as Cicero did, not simply the rules governing the distribution or the exchange of goods among fellow citizens but the perfect order of the soul or the perfectly just way of life, one may come to the conclusion that the degree of justice of which a particular society is capable at any given moment will fall considerably short of what a wise man would regard as truly just. To say nothing of other matters, it is doubtful whether Cicero seriously thought that belief in the gods of the Roman Pantheon was compatible with justice in this loftier sense. Yet any orator speaking in behalf of Rome would necessarily have to defer to such beliefs. Viewed in that perspective, the question is not only how much injustice a society can tolerate but how much justice it can bear without endangering its own existence.[21] Granted that all societies should strive for justice, a point is sooner or later reached at which it becomes impossible, without injustice, to enforce such measures as would be in perfect accord with the demands of theoretical reason. The counsels of the wise man will represent at best a compromise between what reason is capable of knowing about justice and the needs of the society for which they are intended.

But this can only mean that in addressing his fellow citizens, the orator is compelled to adopt an ironic posture. Although his teaching does not correspond fully to what he himself knows to be true, it is essential that it be perceived as a true teaching by his hearers. He will be successful to the extent to which others remain ignorant of the fact that what he does is the one thing that he cannot claim to be doing.[22] There is an element of high comedy in the highest form of oratory. Cicero's perfect orator is a liar, not because he wants to be, but because he has no choice in the matter. Between thought and speech or between theory and practice there is a necessary cleavage, of which Cicero himself, whose aim it was to bring about a fusion between Greek philosophy and Roman virtue,[23] seems to have been uniquely aware.

It is hardly surprising therefore that Cicero should have refrained from using the word *doctrina* to characterize the content of the orator's speech. As opposed to the older and more neutral *docere,* which designates the act by which knowledge or information of any kind is imparted to another person, *doctrina* refers specifically to the object of philosophic inquiry and functions most often as the equivalent of the Greek *epistêmê* in Cicero's own dialogues and treatises.[24] Philosophers qua philosophers speak to the educated for the purpose of instructing them and not for the purpose of swaying them: *docendi non capiendi causa.*[25] The proper mode of their discourses is dialectical rather than rhetorical. These discourses may have an eloquence all their own, but of a kind that is only remotely akin to that to which the typical orator is accustomed.

A vastly different picture emerges the moment we turn to Augustine's Christian adaptation of the Ciceronian doctrine. Augustine's preacher must also begin by instructing his audience, and this he does by laying before them the truths of the faith and, whenever necessary, by using arguments based on the proper authorities to clarify any difficulties that they may have in regard to them.[26] But, as might be expected, the kind of teaching in which he engages is no longer the object of the subtle depreciation that we encountered in Cicero. The substance of that teaching is the "sound doctrine" of which St. Paul had spoken and in which the preacher has steeped himself through the assiduous reading and study of the Scriptures.[27] Its cognitive status is therefore totally different from that of the pagan orator. Augustine's preacher teaches in a way in which even Cicero's perfect orator could never be said to teach. It is above all the superior dignity of that "teaching" which accounts for Augustine's inversion of the order of rank of the three functions performed by the orator. The duty to teach is not merely the Christian orator's first duty; it is his highest and in a sense his only duty.[28] The preacher will have accomplished all that is essentially required of him if what he teaches is the truth. If he is to be judged at all, it is on his ability to discharge that function rather than on any natural endowments or oratorical talents that he may or may not possess. He has no other title to be heard. Hence, departing from the canon of Ciceronian orthodoxy, Augustine takes it for granted that, regardless of the style in which the preacher expresses himself, whether it be the simple, the moderate, or the grand, his primary goal is still to instruct his audience. The *munus docendi* is no longer restricted to the simple style and vice versa; it pervades all three styles and is itself the end to which they are universally ordered.[29]

The same concern for the primacy of the truth is evinced by another less conspicuous but equally significant alteration that Augustine has introduced into the Ciceronian scheme. Contrary to what Hagendahl suggests, one observes that, in paraphrasing the text of the *De oratore,* Augustine has tacitly deleted all reference to what Cicero regarded as the chief merit of any rhetorical argument, namely, its plausibility. The word *verisimiliter* does appear in the *De doctrina christiana,* but only in connection with the teachers of false doctrines.[30] The suggestion is not that, for Augustine, the truths (*vera*) of the faith are implausible but only that it would be misleading to describe them as plausible truths. The contrast on which the whole discussion plays is precisely between the eminently truthful character of the Christian faith and the apparent truths or merely plausible teachings of the promoters of erroneous doctrines.

This does not mean that it is not to the preacher's advantage to cultivate the other qualities of a good orator if he has the ability to do so. There is surely no reason why the divine truth should not be rendered as appealing as possible to the hearer. Even a preacher has nothing to gain by boring his audience. It would be strange, to say the least, if error were to be clothed in an attractive garb by its proponents while truth is made to appear tedious and dull for lack of proper adornments.[31] Furthermore, it sometimes happens that the hearer is already familiar with the truths of the faith but cannot bring himself to act in accordance with them; in which case the preacher may be summoned to use whatever powers of persuasion he has at his command to induce him to reform his life.[32] For all of these reasons, then, one should not underestimate the benefits of eloquence. In general, the man who speaks both "wisely" and "well" will accomplish more than the one who speaks only wisely.[33]

Here again, however, the classic formula, *sapiens et eloquens,* which Augustine inherits this time from the *De inventione*,[34] partially masks a more profound disagreement with Cicero on the relation of teaching to persuading in rhetorical discourse. The truth which the Christian is "persuaded" to accept is not a truth in any ordinary sense of the word but, as we saw in chapter one, a beatifying or saving truth,[35] which is fully appropriated only when it issues in those deeds to which it points as its fulfillment.

It is hardly necessary to point out that such a doctrine is incommensurable with the "heartless doctrines"—*doctrinae sine corde*—of the philosophers.[36] The precise manner in which the two modes of thought are related is more complex than one might be tempted to assume on the basis of some of Augustine's well-known pronouncements on the subject.[37] The objection to philosophy from a religious point of view is not so much that its teachings are sometimes at odds with those of the faith, for in that case a measure of agreement could still be reached between the philosopher and the Christian, if not always on the solutions to the common problems with which they both deal, at least on the nature of those problems and the terms in which they might suitably be posed. The more serious difficulty arises from the philosopher's own inability to arrive at any firm conclusion concerning matters of the utmost interest for the whole of human life. The philosopher is compelled by his love of the truth to suspend his judgment about all such matters until the theoretical issues to which they give rise have been fully examined. The question is whether one can ever be satisfied that the necessary clarity about any of these fundamental issues has been reached. If the object of the investigation should prove to be more elusive than had been anticipated or the problems more readily accessible than the solutions to them, the philosopher may find it difficult to commit himself heart and soul to any position whatever. What had begun as an attempt on his part to set forth the truth about the good life has, it seems, transformed itself into an endless and hence unfulfilled quest for the nature of the good life.

It is precisely this radical character of philosophy, which refuses to take knowledge itself for granted, that constitutes the ultimate challenge to the Christian faith. The opposition in the final analysis is not so much between one set of doctrines and another but between the self-proclaimed ignorance of the philosopher and the firmly held beliefs of the religious thinker. The touchstone of one's attachment to the truth is one's willingness to die for it. But, even though philosophers have often been persecuted across the centuries, few of them have ever demonstrated any real appetite for martyrdom. It may be objected that Socrates was willing to sacrifice himself for the truth. Even this example, however, is not decisive; for there is no guarantee that what Socrates did at the age of seventy is exactly what he would have done had his trial taken place thirty years earlier.[38] The lesson that later philosophers learned from Socrates is not that they should be ready to lay down their lives for the truth but that, for their own protection, they would be well-advised to accommodate themselves to the prejudices of the society in which they happen to live. Philosophers may parade as lovers and teachers of moral virtue, but none of them seems to have been eager to place the service of his fellow men above the good of the mind.[39] Socrates's own "coldness" and aloofness from the affairs of the city is no doubt a better index of his fundamental disposition than his public declarations of piety or his professed concern for the welfare of his fellow Athenians.[40] The philosopher poses a threat to religion and society not because he knows too much but because he knows too little. By questioning all things, he undermines the consensus on which both religion and society depend for their well-being.

But even this is only half the story. If Socrates can boast of his ignorance, it is because he has learned what true knowledge is and is able to distinguish it from its opposite. His would-be ignorance is merely the obverse of a deep-seated pride which causes him to place himself above the rest of society. He speaks to his judges or to the citizens of Athens as one speaks to children, telling them only what is good for them, regardless of whether it is true or not.[41] His own speeches were more "persuasive" than genuinely truthful.[42] They were aimed as much at keeping the multitude away from the truth as they were at attracting to it the few who had proved themselves worthy of it by their ability to penetrate the disguise in which it is habitually cloaked. Between his arrogance (*praesumptio*) and the humble "confession" of the believer, it is difficult to see how any reconciliation could be effected.[43]

Even though Augustine could not accept Plato's and Cicero's views concerning the essential disproportion between theoretical reason and political reason, he was nevertheless very much aware of the need to speak differently to different audiences. It would obviously be foolish to think that everyone is capable of the same degree of understanding of the divine truth. The Scriptures themselves are often written in a manner that makes it hard for most people to grasp them without the aid of an interpreter.[44] Anyone who undertakes to explain them to the general public must first learn to express himself in a language that all men can understand and not in a language that is intelligible only to the learned.[45] Moreover, it is reasonable to suppose that there are depths of understanding to which the untrained multitude is incapable of acceding. One would perform a disservice to the simple faithful by burdening them with subtleties that exceed their powers of comprehension. Accordingly, the *De doctrina christiana* makes it clear that there are questions which "by their very nature are not understood or are barely understood no matter how much, how often, how clearly, or how well they are expounded, and these either should never be brought up before a popular audience or only rarely, when there is a special reason to do so."[46] By maintaining a prudent reserve on all such questions, the preacher does not commit an injustice toward anyone, since the doctrines that he passes over in silence would only be misunderstood and possibly misused by the majority of his hearers. The situation is different if one has the opportunity to deal in private conversation with individuals whose intelligence, degree of preparation, and willingness to learn can be assessed more easily and more accurately.[47]

But if the mode of presentation of the divine truth varies with each audience, its substance does not, and on this level all Christians are united in the knowledge of the same basic truth. There is only one truth, "which all men hear in the same measure when it is publicly spoken, but which each one appropriates in his own measure."[48] The wise preacher undoubtedly knows *more* than his less learned fellows, but what he knows is not something *other* than what every Christian knows.[49] To the extent to which he has achieved a more profound grasp of the divine mysteries, he can add to the knowledge that others already have of them, but the foundation on which he builds is the same in all cases. There can be no question of persuading the hearer to accept any doctrine to which the speaker has not previously given his own wholehearted assent. What one knows in one way "in the world at large" is not essentially different from what one knows "in the privacy of his chambers."[50] Embroidering on the metaphor that St. Paul had used in the First Letter to the Corinthians, Augustine explains that the milk with which the mother nourishes her suckling is the very food from which her own sustenance is derived and which has merely been transformed into a substance that is more easily absorbed by the child. It therefore makes no sense to speak, as others had done, of an "opposition" between the simple fare that is provided for beginners and the wisdom reserved for those who have attained a higher level of spiritual advancement.[51] The latter simply perceive more perfectly what the former strive to assimilate according to their own capacity.

What is even more important, however, is the conclusion regarding the need for absolute truthfulness which Augustine draws from these premises. The Christian's commitment to the truth is such that he can never publicly or privately betray it in speech even for the noblest of causes. There may be valid reasons for not revealing to others all of one's thoughts on some subjects; but it is one thing to withhold the truth from someone and quite another to lie to him.[52] The sacred writers themselves deliberately concealed certain doctrines from the multitude, but without ever lying about anything: *nonnulla obtegunt, sed nulla mentiuntur.*[53] The Christian orator can do no less. One can say without exaggeration that there is no moral principle which Augustine defended with greater vehemence and on which he was least willing to compromise. Never, even under the most extreme circumstances, is one allowed to speak an untruth. The question is, Why? For it is surely not self-evident that the true interests of one's fellow men are better served by the determination to speak the truth at all times than by an occasional breach of truthfulness. To take a simple example, one has a hard time imagining that a man who perpetrates a white lie in order to save, not indeed his own life, but the life of a loved one or perhaps some other innocent person is guilty of any sin whatever. Christian charity, to say nothing of plain common sense, would seem to prescribe as much. Yet Augustine, who was prepared to make allowances for what would appear to be the much more grievous crime of adultery,[54] is adamant in his refusal to make even the slightest concession on that point.

The reason, we discover, is not unrelated to the central task of preaching the word of God which has been entrusted to the Christian orator. That reason is best illustrated by Augustine's reaction to Jerome's commentary on Chapter Two of the Letter to the Galatians, in which Paul gives an account of his famous altercation with Peter at Antioch.[55] It may be recalled that on that occasion Paul publicly upbraided Peter for refusing to eat with the Gentiles in order to placate the circumcision party, headed by James. Following Origen's interpretation, Jerome had attempted to remove any trace of dissension among the apostles by contending that Peter was not guilty of wrongdoing but had merely sought to accommodate himself to the prejudices of the Judaizers. Had not Paul himself done as much by circumcising Timothy and, on James's advice, by providing for the offering of sacrifices in accordance with the prescriptions of the old law, thereby giving credence to the belief that Christian salvation was linked to these observances?[56] It is hardly likely, then, that he should have quarreled with Peter over a similar issue. Far from finding fault with Peter, Paul actually sided with him but feigned to rebuke him lest others should interpret his conduct as signifying that the Gentiles were to be subjected to the Jewish law.[57]

Augustine expresses utter astonishment at the fact that Jerome had chosen to endorse what would really amount to an *officiosum mendacium* on Paul's part.[53] For if what Peter did is what he was supposed to do, then Paul lied when he accused him of not being straightforward about the truth of the Gospel. That he should have done so for a good cause is beside the point. Nor does it matter that the enemies of the faith should seize upon the disagreement of which Paul speaks as a pretext for discrediting the New Testament. Nothing can justify the imputation of lies to the Bible. To suggest for one moment that the sacred writers indulged in falsehood is to jeopardize the authority of the whole of Scripture and open the door to every kind of malice. "If one were to admit in that supreme authority even one polite lie, nothing at all would be left of these books, because whenever anyone finds something difficult to practice or hard to achieve, he will follow this most dangerous precedent and explain it as the thought or practice of a lying author."[59] As long as the *veritas doctrinae* remains intact, one can always turn to it to rectify any error into which he may have fallen; but if that standard is itself subject to doubt, the very possibility of a return to the truth is destroyed forever.[60] It is therefore preferable to believe that, out of weakness, "Peter did so act as to compel the Gentiles to live like Jews."[61] Better a thousand times a cowardly Peter than a lying Paul. No immediate advantage could ever compensate for the unlimited harm that is done by calling into question even a single passage of Scripture.

What is said of the sacred writers applies, *mutatis mutandis,* to all Christian teachers as well; for what confidence could one have in a person who is of the opinion that it is sometimes permissible to lie? Could not he, too, by any chance be lying when he speaks to others about the mysteries of the faith?[62] Like everyone else, the Christian orator may unwittingly err in his interpretation of the sacred text; but if what he says is conducive to the love of God and neighbor, which is the principle in the light of which all of Scripture is to be interpreted, he leads no one astray and is not himself guilty of any wicked deed.[63] What is intolerable is to think that anyone could arrogate to himself the prerogative of using evil in order to bring about a greater good among men. One puts it mildly when one says that Cicero's ideal orator had no such qualms about lying to his hearers. The road leading from the *De oratore* to the *De doctrina christiana* may indeed be longer and more tortuous than the casual reader would ever have suspected.

It would be futile to deny that, in elaborating his views on Christian oratory, Augustine has relied extensively on the tradition of Roman rhetoric in which he had been trained. He himself certainly made no great effort to conceal his indebtedness to that tradition and to its foremost representative, Cicero. But it would be a grave misconception to think that one can give an adequate account of his thought merely by listing the numerous parallels between the two authors. One is reminded in this connection of Lord Acton's remark (to Mary Gladstone) that a disposition to detect resemblances is one of the greatest sources of error. The paradox of Book IV of the *De doctrina christiana* is that it is precisely when Augustine sounds most like Cicero, to the point of reproducing his own words, that he stands at the furthest remove from him. There are good reasons to believe that Augustine quoted Cicero the way Shakespeare's devil quotes the Bible—for his own purposes. The success with which he was able to do so is amply demonstrated by the difficulty that one experiences in trying to assess the originality of his thought.

Modern scholars have been guilty not so much of misreading Augustine as of rashly ascribing to Cicero what is in fact a profound albeit silent transformation of Cicero's basic teaching. The pitfall might have been avoided if, before attempting to second-guess Augustine, greater pains had been taken to arrive at a satisfactory interpretation of the original Ciceronian doctrine. It should probably be added that anyone embarking upon such an endeavor would have received little direct encouragement from Augustine himself. In defending what he considered to be the cause of truth, Augustine had much to gain and little to lose by stressing the similarity rather than the dissimilarity between his position and that of Cicero. Nor was there any "special reason" for calling attention to that strategy. To discuss openly the points on which at a deeper level the divergences between the Christian and the classical views of truth become truly significant would have necessitated the public disclosure of a whole gamut of problems that are of no interest to most Christians or, as far as that goes, to most preachers.

Like all the great books on rhetoric written in antiquity, whether it be the *Gorgias,* the *Phaedrus,* the *Orator,* or the *De oratore,* the *De doctrina christiana* is rhetorical in mode as well as in content. In this respect at least it remains remarkably faithful to the spirit of the classical tradition. The moderation in speech that it both advocates and displays may well be the most important lesson that Augustine learned from his revered pagan masters.

NOTES

1. Cf. Harald Hagendahl, *Augustine and the Latin Classics* (Göteborg: Universitetet, 1967), 558.

2. Augustine, *De doctrina christiana* (*On Christian Doctrine*) IV.3.4.

3. Cf. H.-I. Marrou, *Saint Augustin et la fin de la culture antique* (Paris: E. de Boccard, 1938), 524ff. C. Morhmann, *Études sur le latin des chrétiens* I (Rome: Edizioni Di Storia E Letteratura, 1958), 359.

4. H. Hagendahl, *Augustine and the Latin Classes*, 565.

5. Ibid., 567. For a somewhat more balanced view, cf. M. Testard, *Saint Augustin et Cicéron I* (Paris: Etudes Augustiniennes, 1958), 235-6, 261, 268-9, 279, 330. Also, among the older studies, C. S. Baldwin, *Medieval Rhetoric and Poetic* (New York: Macmillan, 1928), 52: ". . . and now scarcely an edition or translation of Augustine's works is published which, by cross references and footnotes, does not so stress the 'classical elements' in Augustine's rhetoric that the reader is led to believe that only minor differences distinguish the rhetorical doctrines of Cicero and Augustine." M. Comeau, *La rhétorique de saint Augustin d'après les Tractatus in*

Joannem (Paris: Beauchesne, 1930), 21: "Ainsi le livre du *De doctrina christiana,* en dépit de quelques vues personnelles à son auteur, se place-t-il naturellement dans la longue série de rhétoriques que les écrivains latins publièrent à l'envi jusqu'aux invasions barbares. La théorie du style et de l'éloquence n'y présente aucune nouveauté." Further references in H. Hagendahl, *Augustin and the Latin Classics*, 565, n. 1. A stronger emphasis on the newness of Augustine's position is to be found in L. D. McNew, "The Relation of Cicero's Rhetoric to Augustine," *Research Studies of the State College of Washington* 25, 1 (March, 1957): 5-13.

6. H.-I. Marrou, *Saint Augustin et la fin de la culture antique* (Paris: E. de Boccard, 1938), 520. See also Marrou's review of Hagendahl's book in *Gnomon* 41 (1969): 282-85.

7. J. Oroz, "El *De doctrina christiana* o la retorica cristiana," *Estudios Clasicos* 3 (1956): 452-59. Id., "La retorica augustiniana: Clasicismo y Cristianismo," *Studia Patristica* 6 (1962): 490: "Por lo dicho hasta ahora, podemos affirmar que la obra de san Augustin sobre la retorica es notamente clasicista, es decir sigue la linea ortodoxa de los autores clasicos, y sobre todo de Ciceron."

8. A. Hus, *Docere et les mots de la famille de docere: Étude de sémantique latine* (Paris: Presses Universitaires de France, 1965).

9. Augustine, *De doctr. christ.* IV.12.27. Cf. Cicero, *Orator* 69; *De oratore* II.310; also *Brutus* 185; *De optimo genere Or.* 3.

10. On the lesser importance of epideictic rhetoric, cf. Cicero, *Orator* 207; *De oratore* II, 43ff.

11. Cf. Cicero, *Orator* 120ff; *De oratore* II.307ff.

12. On persuasion as the goal of rhetoric, cf. Cicero, *Orator* 128; Cicero, *De oratore* I.60; II.214; Cicero, *Brutus* 279.

13. *Narrationes credibiles*: *Orator* 124. Cf. Aristotle, *Rhetoric* III.16.1417a.

14. Cf. *Orator* 78.208-9; *De oratore* II.153,156,177; *De doctr. christ.* IV.6.10.

15. Cf. *Orator* 15; *De oratore* II.185 ff, 201 ff.; *Tuscalanae disputationes* (*Tusculan Disputations*) IV.55.

16. On the orator as vir *bonus dicendi peritus*, cf. A. S. Wilkins's introduction to the *De oratore* (Oxford, 1888), 47.

17. Cf. *De oratore* I.48.60; II.337.

18. *Orator* 118.

19. *Orator* 14ff.

20. *Orator* 3,7,19,101.

21. On the whole question of the necessity and feasibility of justice, see esp. Cicero, *De re publica* Bk. III.

22. *De oratore* II.310-11.

23. *De oratore* III.137.

24. Cf. A. Hus, op. cit., 283ff.

25. *Orator* 63

26. *De doctr. christ.* IV.4.6.

27. *De doctr. christ.* IV.21.45; 27.59; 31.64.

28. *De doctr. christ.* IV.12.28.

29. *De doctr. christ.* IV.17.34; 25.55. Cicero, *Orator* 69 and 101.

30. Compare *De doctr. christ.* IV.2.3 with *De oratore* II.80. *Probabiliter* is substituted for *verisimilis* in *Orator* 122.

31. *De doctr. christ.* IV.2.3; 14.30.

32. *De doctr. christ.* IV.12.28.

33. *De doctr. christ.* IV.5.7; cf. IV.5.8; 6.9; 25.55; 26.56; 27.59. See Augustine's defense of his own use of rhetoric in *Contra Cresconium* (*Against Cresconius*) 1.1.

34. *De doctr. christ.* IV.5.7. Cicero, *De inventione* I.1.

35. *De doctr. christ.* IV.21.35: *rerum divinarum atque salubrium scientia.*

36. *Confessiones* (*Confessions*) VIII.8.19. See chapter one, pp. 7-8.

37. E. g., *De doctr. christ.* II.40.60.

38. Cf. *Crito* 53d.

39. Cf. *Apology of Socrates* 31b.

40. *Apol. of Socrates* 31d.

41. Cf. *Gorgias* 521e.

42. *Apol. of Socrates* 17a-b, 20d-e, 22b *et passim.*

43. Cf. *Confessions* VII.20.26.

44. *De doctr. christ.* IV.21.45.

45. Ibid., IV.8.22; cf. *De Genesi contra Manichaeos* (*On Genesis against the Manichaeans*) I.1.1; *De moribus ecclesiae catholicae et de moribus Manichaeorum* (*On the Way of Life of the Catholic Church*) I.1.

46. *De doctr. christ.* IV.9.23.

47. *De doctr. christ.* IV.9.23.

48. *Tractatus in Joannis evangelium* (*Tracts on the Gospel of John*) 98, 2 (Migne *Patrologia, Series Latina* or *PL* 35.1881).

49. *Tractatus in Joan. Ev.* 98.7 (*PL* 35.1884).

50. *Tractatus in Joan. Ev.* 98.2 (*PL* 35.1881).

51. *Tractatus in Joan. Ev.* 98.6 (*PL* 35.1883).

52. Cf. *Contra mendacium* (*Against Lying*) 10.23; *De mendacio* (*On Lying*) 10.17.

53. *De vera religione* (*On True Religion*) 28.51.

54. Cf. *De sermone Domini in monte* (*The Lord's Sermon on the Mount*) 1.16.

55. See especially Augustine, *Epistula* (*Letter*) 28.40, and 82.

56. Cf. Acts 16:3 and 21:17-26.

57. See Jerome's letter to Augustine in Augustine, *Epist.* 75.3.4 (*PL* 33.252).

58. *Officiosum mendacium*: *Epist.* 28.3.4; 40.3.3; 82.2.21.

59. *Epistula* (*Letter*) 28.3.3.

60. Cf. *De mendacio* 19.40.

61. *Epist.* 82.2.8.

62. Cf. *De mendacio* 8.11.

63. *De doctr. christ.* I.36.40.

Part V
Applications of Augustine's Thought to Selected Legal Topics

[18]

SAINT AUGUSTINE ON WAR AND KILLING: THE PROBLEM OF THE INNOCENT

By Richard Shelly Hartigan

With the advent of nuclear weapons and the ever-present possibility of a devastating third world war, many writers have turned their attention to available means of preventing such a holocaust. As a result there has occurred in recent years, along with much sophisticated speculation in arms control theory, a veritable renaissance in what may be simply described as "just war" theorizing. Unlike the arms controllers, who concentrate on the practical questions of weapons limitation, the just war theorists aim at delineating moral and ethical restraints on the use of nuclear force. Their goal is to construct a modern theoretical framework within which the use of nuclear weapons can be subjected to ethical calculation; inevitably their starting point is that body of norms collectively called the Christian doctrine of just war. Any elaboration of the traditional just war doctrine must consider at some point the pronouncements of St. Augustine on war and on the legitimacy of killing in war. This is due to the great influence which his authority had in shaping the traditional "just war" doctrine.

One of the long accepted premises of the Christian doctrine of just war has been that innocent or noncombatant civilians ought not to be slaughtered intentionally. In another form, this principle has been adopted and articulated as an operative norm of international law.[1] Given the present vulnerability of civilians to nuclear attack it is understandable that contemporary just war theorizing has emphasized the inviolability of this principle, and has employed the *auctoritas* of the Christian moral philosophy, originating with St. Augustine, to give weight to the arguments. It is most surprising, therefore, to turn to the actual statements of St. Augustine on the permissibility of killing innocents in war and to discover that he exhibited an unexpected degree of harshness and seeming indifference to the fate of the innocent. There is an ambivalence in the position of St. Augustine on this matter which has thus far not been sufficiently noted or appreciated. The following examination of his views is intended to clarify his position and perhaps make it more meaningful in contemporary discussion on the ethical relevance of noncombatant immunity.

[1] See, for example, the Hague Conventions of 1899 and 1907. More recent explication of this principle is embodied in the Geneva Convention Relative to the Protection of Civilian Persons in Time of War (Geneva Convention IV), 1949.

I. On Killing in Self-Defense

St. Augustine was, among many other things, a polemicist. In the majority of his works he set out to refute blatant heresies, false charges against the Christian religion, and erroneous teachings which had sprung up within his Christian Church. It is in this last respect that his statements on war and killing primarily fall: the pacifism of Origen, Lactantius, and Tertullian was not an explicit heresy nor was it criticism from without; rather, it was a tenaciously maintained position which orthodox Christians could support with ample New Testament authority and a substantial theological tradition. With characteristic verve Augustine sought to establish in various writings and within the context of his moral philosophy a base for justified war, and Christian participation in war, which would dissipate any scruples that Christian soldiers or citizens might have, while at the same time placing war within the Divine plan. None of these conclusions are anticipated, however, by Augustine's statements regarding the private taking of human life. In his very important text on free will, written characteristically to answer a Manichaean heresy concerning God as the author of good, he takes an unequivocal position of pacifism when only the individual's life is at stake.

Through his interlocutor, Evodius, Augustine explores the nature of evil, especially in relation to the act of murder. He argues that the act of murder will always be evil, regardless of the motive for which it is committed.[2] Next he inquires as to what acts of homicide may be classed as murder. Here he agrees that what the state prohibits as murder is equally prohibited by the moral law. Yet he is not satisfied that the legal prohibition is inclusive enough. Augustine is particularly concerned with the situation in which an individual is allowed by law to kill an unjust aggressor, that is, one who is directly attacking his person or property without moral or legal justification. He at first seems to question the justice of such a law, which would permit a traveller to kill an assailant who is about to attack him. The reason for this reservation is made explicit through the words of Evodius, who suggests that whatever it is that the unjust attacker might take away, whether life or property, it is not really very important because the individual does not wholly own these things anyway; rather God, the author of life and ultimate source of all authority through which possessions are conferred, is the real owner. The possibility of such loss does not justify the taking of a human life, even if this life belongs

[2] Augustine, *De Libero Arbitrio,* I, 4.9, trans. by Dom Mark Pontifex (Westminster, Md., 1955).

to an evil man.[3]

Augustine is exploring here something far more subtle than at first appears. He is not actually challenging the justice of a law which permits self-protection; instead he is distinguishing between two kinds of law—the temporal and the eternal. Hence, he concludes that "the law which is decreed to govern states seems . . . to permit much and leave it unpunished, though it is punished by Divine Providence. Rightly so. Because a law does not do everything, it does not follow that what it does do is to be blamed." [4]

The temporal law which allows the slaying of an attacker is therefore just law, though it is not adequate law for the Christian. To permit one to defend oneself, even to killing an assailant, is justifiable normal practice as the choice of a lesser instead of a greater evil, for "it is far more dreadful that an innocent person should suffer violence than that the assailant should be killed by the intended victim." [5] But, for the Christian, upon whom extraordinary demands are made, the law of love requires a literal turning of the other cheek. The Christian ought not to avail himself of his legal right to self-defense but should rather be guided by the divine law of love, which enshrines all human life as inviolate, even that of an enemy. Augustine later reaffirms this view in a letter to a friend: "In regard to killing men so as not to be killed by them, this view does not please me." [6]

Augustine's position on the matter of private self-defense was therefore unqualifiedly pacific: the Christian is never permitted to take a human life intentionally, even if the temporal (civil) law permits it; he is not allowed to do so because as a Christian the superior law of charity is his guide to action; hence, the life even of an unjust aggressor must not be jeopardized by any action which might accidentally result in death for the evil man, even though by abstaining from direct defensive action the innocent party may lose his life.[7]

[3] *Ibid.*, I, 5.11–5.13. "Some may perhaps doubt whether the soul's life is by any means taken away when the body perishes, but if it can be taken away it is of no value, while if it cannot, there is not reason for fear. . . . Whatever a man who is killed was going to take away is not wholly in our power, and so I do not understand how it can be called ours."

[4] *Ibid.* For a detailed exposition of Augustine's theory of law, see Anton-Hermann Chroust, "The Philosophy of Law of St. Augustine," *Philosophical Review,* LIII (March 1944), 195–202.

[5] *De Lib. Arbit., op. cit.*

[6] *Epistle* 47 (To Publicola). Cf. *St. Augustine: Letters,* trans. by Sister Wilfrid Parsons, S.N.D. (New York, 1951).

[7] For an excellent recent examination of this aspect of Augustine's moral philosophy see Paul Ramsey, *War and the Christian Conscience* (Durham, N. C., 1961), ch. 2.

II. Just War and Public Self-Defense

It is a mistake to assume that, because St. Augustine attempted to reconcile war to the Christian ethic of love, he embraced war and its bloodshed eagerly or without reservation. Quite the contrary is true. The pages of his *De Civitate Dei* abound with sympathetic references to the miseries inflicted by past wars, and in one place he remarks:

> Let every one, then, who thinks with pain on all these great evils, so horrible, so ruthless, acknowledge that this is misery. And if any one either endures or thinks of them without mental pain, this is a more miserable plight still.[8]

Yet Augustine did believe that some wars at least could be just and that as such they served as instruments of God's will. The elaboration of this theme is, of course, his familiar doctrine of just war.[9]

One of the fundamental axioms underlying St. Augustine's political thought is that all nations desire peace.[10] But in order that peace may be preserved it is sometimes necessary to employ force: "Peace is not sought for the purpose of stirring up war, but war is waged for the purpose of securing peace." [11] If war is sometimes a necessary means of attaining temporal peace, then why is it considered evil? To this question Augustine answers, with obvious allusion to his pacifist predecessors, that the evil in war is not the mere death of those who eventually will die anyway; rather, "the real evils in war are love of violence, revengeful cruelty, fierce and implacable enmity, wild resistance, and the lust of power." [12] It is clear that the physical evil of death is insignificant compared with the moral lapses which may occur because of war.

Given this proclivity of war to engender evil, a goal of temporal peace alone is not sufficient in Augustine's mind to justify resort to such violence. The peace which is the proper end of war must be a

[8] Augustine, *De Civitate Dei*, XIX, 7, trans. by Marcus Dods (New York, 1950).

[9] Perhaps the most balanced survey of the Christian just war doctrine is that by Robert Regout, *La doctrine de la guerre juste de Saint Augustin à nos jours* (Paris, 1935). The best and most recent examination of Augustine's entire political thought is that of Herbert A. Deane, *The Political and Social Ideas of St. Augustine* (New York, 1963). This work is valuable because it places Augustine's views on war in the broader context of his entire social thought.

[10] "For even they who make war desire nothing but victory—desire, that is to say, to attain to peace with glory. . . . It is therefore with the desire for peace that wars are waged, even by those who take pleasure in expressing their warlike nature." *De Civ. Dei, op. cit.*, XIX, 12.

[11] *Ep.* 138 (to Marcellinus).

[12] Augustine, *Contra Faustum*, XXII, 74, trans. in *A Select Library of the Nicene and Post-Nicene Fathers*, ed. by Philip Schaff (Grand Rapids, Mich., 1956).

true peace, which Augustine understands as involving more than a mere condition of tranquility: robbers maintain a kind of peace among themselves so as better to disturb the peace of others,[13] but this is not a true peace. For Augustine true peace is a condition of tranquility based upon justice, which in turn is seen as a harmonious ordering of rights and duties among men, and between men and God.[14] A war which seeks to achieve or restore true peace is therefore a just war.

Typically, a just war will result from the necessity

> to avenge injuries, when the nation or city against which warlike action is to be directed has neglected either to punish wrongs committed by its own citizens or to restore what has been unjustly taken by it.[15]

Because there exists for Augustine such an intimate connection between the juridical and moral orders a *delict* which occurs in the former necessarily involves a sin in the latter as well. Hence, if one nation violates the legal rights of another it has also broken the moral law. This is the essential fact which explains why for Augustine just war is action designed above all else to restore a violated moral order. It also explains his emphasis on the subjective guilt or *culpa* of the enemy, which not only justifies the use of force but indeed requires it.

The notion of punishment for wickedness is markedly strong in Augustine. He often stresses that it is to punish wrongdoing that force is justified and, most important, that the visitation of war on an enemy represents not the application of private vengeance or passion but the righteous wrath of those who would avenge in the name of justice a violation of God's sacred order. The end to be achieved is a true peace, but the means employed produce a suitable chastisement of those wicked and guilty persons who would presume to disturb the existing order.[16] Even though war under certain conditions [17] is just, and therefore worthy of the Christian citizen's support, the question still remains, "How shall this war be conducted?" Since even just war can hardly be prosecuted without killing, it is obvious that Augustine's views on just war admit some modification of the stringent proscriptions against killing which characterize his private ethics.

[13] *De Civ. Dei, op. cit.* [14] *Ibid.*, XIX, 13.

[15] Augustine, *Questiones in Heptateuchum,* VI, 10, J. P. Migne, *Patrologiae Latina* (Paris, 1854–66), vol. 34, p. 781. This and other not readily available texts are translated in John Eppstein, *The Catholic Tradition of the Law of Nations* (Washington, D.C., 1935).

[16] Cf. *Contra Faustum, op. cit.*, XXII, 74. See also on this point Regout, *op. cit.*, 43–44, and D. Beaufort, *La Guerre comme instrument de secours ou de punition* (The Hague, 1933).

[17] In addition to a just cause Augustine insists that the war must be declared by a proper authority. Cf. *Contra Faustum,* XII, 75.

Augustine consistently makes an exception to his general prohibition against taking human life when the situation is one involving the public good. When Evodius remarks that in his opinion a soldier who kills the enemy, and an executioner who carries out a sentence of death on a criminal, do not sin, Augustine agrees, adding that these persons are not usually called murderers.[18] In his discussion of that law which permits the killing of an assailant, which the Christian may not avail himself of, Augustine says that the law also orders a soldier to kill the enemy and "if he refuses to do so he is punished by the military authorities," [19] a fact which Augustine implicitly sanctions through the opinion of Evodius, who concludes that "when a soldier kills the enemy he is enforcing the law, and so has no difficulty in carrying out his duty without passion." [20] Finally, in the same letter to Publicola cited above Augustine points out that though the killing of men does not please him, it is certainly permissible in the case of a soldier or a public official, because "in this case, he does not do it for his own sake, but for others or for the state to which he belongs, having received the power lawfully and in accord with his public character." [21]

Perhaps the definitive expression of his position appears in Augustine's *De Civitate Dei.*

> However, there are some exceptions made by the divine authority to its own law, that men may not be put to death. These exceptions are of two kinds, being justified either by a general law, or by a special commission granted for a time to some individual. And in this latter case, he to whom authority is delegated, and who is but the sword in the hand of him who uses it, is not himself responsible for the death he deals. And, accordingly, they who have waged war in obedience to the divine command, or in conformity with His laws have represented in their persons the public justice or the wisdom of government, and in this capacity have put to death wicked men; such persons have by no means violated the commandment, "Thou shalt not kill." [22]

The important elements which are explicitly affirmed in this statement are that the soldier or public official is an agent of the public *jus,* "the wisdom of government," in which capacity he is merely an instrument of the public authority and hence not actually a morally free agent. He incurs no guilt when he kills the enemy who, it is assumed, are "wicked men." The soldier is like an automaton who performs his duties in the manner of an executioner. The requirement to vindicate justice in the public realm seems to supersede the demands of charity which should obtain in the Christian's private life.

[18] *De Lib. Arbit.,* I, 4.9. [19] *Ibid.,* 5.11–5.12. [20] *Ibid.*
[21] *Ep.* 47, *op. cit.* [22] *De Civ. Dei,* I, 21, p. 27.

Yet few writers have recounted with such obvious abhorrence the cruelties and atrocities which are common in war. The sacking of temples, the slaughter of infants and women, the killing of prisoners are all cruelties which should be avoided, even though they are in accordance with the customs of war.[23] The Christian soldier should always be prepared to temper the "stern and lasting necessities" of war with mercy, as Theodosius had done when he spared the sons of his enemies.[24] Augustine insists that necessity, not choice, should be the reason for killing an enemy: "Just as violence is meted out to him who rebels and resists, so mercy is due him who is defeated or captured, especially where no disturbance of peace is to be feared."[25] Hence, so long as the Christian kills without feelings of personal rancor or vengeance he not only does not violate God's law of charity but in reality obeys that law by participating in an act of retributive justice, which in Augustine's moral philosophy is an aspect of charity.[26]

It is at this point that St. Augustine's admirable effort to reconcile war and killing with the New Testament's ethic of love begins to falter in its consistency. There are several aspects of this question which might well be considered, but in the remainder of this essay I intend to concentrate on the ambivalence which his doctrine exhibits in regard to the concept of innocence and the category of innocent persons.

III. The Problem of the Innocent

Since war may only be justified as a punishment of wicked men who have incurred moral guilt by disturbance of a just peace, it seems at least incongruous that Augustine should insist that this enemy be treated mercifully when possible. The fact of the enemy's moral turpitude and the public nature of the sanction against him are the only factors which justify killing him in the first place. Given these presumptions of the enemy's guilt it would seem necessary, not to say consistent, to slay him wherever and whenever he might be found. Augustine says, however, that though enemy soldiers may be killed in a just war, this is permitted in order to restore justice, not because they are morally guilty, for it is likely that they may be completely innocent of injustice.

[23] *Ibid.*, I, 4 and 5; VII; V, 23; and *Ep.* 138 (to Marcellinus).

[24] *De Civ. Dei*, V, 26.

[25] *Ep.* 189 (to Boniface).

[26] Cf. Bernard Roland-Gosselin, *La Morale de Saint Augustin* (Paris, 1925), esp. 142–49; and Etienne Gilson, *The Christian Philosophy of Saint Augustine*, trans. by L. E. M. Lynch (New York, 1960).

A righteous man, serving it may be under an ungodly king, may do the duty belonging to his position in the State in fighting by the order of his sovereign, . . . it may be an unrighteous command on the part of the king, while the soldier is innocent because his position makes obedience a duty.[27]

This view is certainly in line with Augustine's view of the soldier as a passionless agent of the public authority, but it does raise the disturbing question of what protection is afforded the innocent among the enemy population. Furthermore, if there are innocents, as it is obvious there are, how can war be justly waged against them, since in the case of soldiers, who are merely doing their duty,[28] and of noncombatants, who are not actively engaged in prosecuting the unjust war, there has certainly been no volitional commitment to an injustice which alone would qualify them as guilty and as such proper objects of retribution.

The fact is that Augustine remains candidly oblivious of the inherent inconsistency in his doctrine. This is all the more remarkable when his great sensitivity and private pacifism are recalled. It seems as though the requirement to vindicate justice obviates all other considerations, and though he recognizes that the innocent may accidentally suffer in the process, he consigns this to necessity and is resigned to it. Thus, to a judge who through ignorance condemns an innocent man to death Augustine offers the advice that he not trouble himself but rather pray to God, "from my necessities deliver Thou me." [29] To Boniface, a military man who is faced with many difficult moral choices in the performance of his duty, he suggests that the soldier make his interior peace but by no means abandon that duty.[30]

There are two aspects of Augustine's thought which provide probable rationales for his position in this matter. The first is, while he admits that there may be innocent persons among the enemy population, he clearly does not believe that this will regularly be the case. For Augustine the extremely intimate relationship which exists between individual and social morality means that an unjust nation will not be characterized by the presence of a just citizenry. Just as Lot's family was an exceptional minority in the city of Sodom, so it seems that Augustine presumes that most often innocent men will be a small minority in the unjust state. In addition, the guilt with which Augus-

[27] *Contra Faustum*, XXII, 75.

[28] Augustine is quite explicit that soldiers need not investigate to determine the justice of the war they are required to fight. *Ibid.*, XII, 75.

[29] *De Civ. Dei*, XIX, 6.

[30] *Ep.* 220 (to Boniface). I have been unable to discover a single instance in Augustine's writings on war wherein he recommends that mercy replace justice in dealings with an enemy; when victory is secure and a just peace restored, then it is time enough to be merciful to captives.

tine is concerned is an interior spiritual condition; so too its obverse, innocence, will be an interior disposition, impossible to ascertain or to ascribe with certainty to any particular individuals or classes.

The second basis for Augustine's view is more explicit. It is his frequently expressed attitude that death is merely a physical evil and to suffer this fate is far better than to be guilty of bad motivation or vice.[31] It was noted earlier how Augustine maintained that death was not the evil to be shunned in war. If guiltless people are slain in a just war it is lamentable but not condemnable, for God often permits the innocent to be scourged with the guilty in this life, "though in eternity they quite escape punishment." [32] Those who kill while prosecuting a just war are condemned by Augustine only if they do so from a motive of private passion or vengeance, or if they continue to slay when it is no longer necessary to obtain victory. This fact is significant because it means that no moral guilt is attached to the slaughter of any particular persons. The innocence or guilt of those attacked is of no consequence in determining the guilt of the attacker; the only factors which constrain him are the subjective ones of his own intent and his estimation of military necessity. Any objective determination as to who are innocent or guilty among the enemy is not only impossible but is also irrelevant.

Given these views and the inferences which can be drawn from them, it must be concluded that Augustine presented no clear-cut argument for the protection of the innocent, especially for the civilian innocent or noncombatant, in time of war.[33] On the contrary, he indicates explicitly, often and in several contexts, that he is unconcerned with the fate of the innocent so far as the necessities of just war are concerned. His notion of just war is in one respect highly subjective in that knowledge of the enemy's moral guilt is required before war is justified; consistently adhered to, this strict requirement would severely limit the number of wars which could be considered just, since such a knowledge of interior guilt would be extremely difficult to obtain. Yet this salutary effect is largely dissipated by the corollary view that a violation of the natural order of things, i.e., a material, objective transgression of rights, constitutes by definition a violation of a just peace and hence of the moral order, a circumstance which automatically justifies punishment of the wicked enemy population.

[31] *Contra Faustum*, XXII, 74. [32] *De Civ. Dei*, I, 9. Cf. also, *De Lib. Arb.*, I, 5.12.

[33] See, e.g., Ramsey, *op. cit.* Ramsey purports to find in Augustine's position on private killing the basis for a theologically supported doctrine of innocent immunity. I admit to having looked in vain for such a position, finding only a highly subjective doctrine which in its rigid application by later writers retarded for many centuries the meaningful application of the Christian ethic to the *debitus modus* of war.

Just war has become a crusade of retribution in which the enemy population's guilt may be presumed. The death of the "innocents" is an accidental consequence of the just act of war.[34]

It is not surprising that with such a theologically sensitized doctrine of war as this, the crusader mentality proliferated among Christian writers who relied on Augustine as the final word in the matter of just war. Emphasizing as they did the causes of war and the conditions which would justify its initiation, theologians and philosophers demonstrated literally no concern to place limits on the acts of war, i.e., they never inquired as to what was proper conduct or what restraints on action should obtain in the prosecution of a just war.[35] Only in the later Middle Ages, with the emergence of spontaneous popular movements to control the effects of private feudal war, do we find an articulation of obligations incumbent upon belligerents to distinguish and protect innocent life, even in a just war.[36]

There are many plausible explanations of why Augustine held the views he did. Yet the fact remains that in his attempt to counter the Christian pacifism of his predecessors he obviously overstated his case. In the context of his moral philosophy, with its emphasis on order and justice, he is perfectly consistent. Yet a nagging incongruity remains between his private and public ethics, between the requirements of a charity so strong that in one sphere an evil man may not be slain and in the other an innocent man may be. It is an incongruity which remains to plague Christian ethics today.

College of St. Thomas.

[34] "The inwardness of Augustine's ethic served to justify outward violence, because right and wrong were seen to reside not in acts but in attitudes." Roland H. Bainton, *Christian Attitudes Toward War and Peace* (New York, 1960), 92.

[35] Followers of Augustine in this matter range from Isidore of Seville in the VIth century to Thomas Aquinas in the XIIIth. Aquinas not only quotes with approval the definitions and arguments of Augustine but adds as his own the observation that "true religion looks upon as peaceful those wars that are waged not for motives of aggrandisement, or cruelty, but with the object of securing peace, of punishing evil-doers, and of uplifting the good." Thomas Aquinas, *Summa Theologica,* II–II, 40, 1.

[36] In this respect the peace movements and legislation of the XIth to XIIIth centuries are remarkable instances in which popular zeal achieved a humanization of warfare without a dependence on formal moral reasoning.

[19]

COGE INTRARE: THE CHURCH AND POLITICAL POWER

R.A. Markus

To reconstruct the mind of a writer from his works is an activity in some ways very like formulating a hypothesis, working out its implications, and testing it by continual reference back to the texts. So far this procedure in the first five chapters of this study has yielded a remarkably consistent reconstruction of Augustine's reflection on history, society and the Church. The strands of his thought on these related subjects, always closely interwoven, produced a single, coherent body as it matured. At the risk of representing Augustine as a precursor of modern 'secularist' theology, it is not out of place to describe his mature thought in this sphere as a synthesis of three themes: first, the secularisation of history, in the sense that all history outside the scriptural canon was seen as homogeneous and, in terms of ultimate significance, ambivalent (Chapters 1 and 2); second, the secularisation of the Roman Empire (Chapters 2 and 3) and of the state and social institutions in general, in the sense that they had no immediate relation to ultimate purposes (Chapters 3 and 4); third, the secularisation of the Church in the sense that its social existence was conceived in sharp antithesis to an 'otherworldly' Church such as was envisaged by a theology of the Donatist type (Chapter 5). These three strands together constitute what we may call a theology of the *saeculum*. The *saeculum* for Augustine was the sphere of temporal realities in which the two 'cities' share an interest. In Augustine's language, the *saeculum* is the whole stretch of time in which the two cities are 'inextricably intertwined'; it is the sphere of human living, history, society and its institutions, characterised by the fact that in it the ultimate eschatological oppositions, though present, are not discernible:

SAECULUM

> ... the enchainment of past and future
> Woven in the weakness of the changing body,
> Protects mankind from heaven and damnation.
>
> (T. S. Eliot, *Burnt Norton*)

The coherence of this picture is disturbed, and the truth of the hypothesis threatened, by an aspect of Augustine's mind not so far considered: his readiness to endorse religious coercion by the authorities of the state. His statements on the duties of Christian rulers to enforce orthodoxy, above all his notorious defence of religious coercion with the aid of the Gospel text 'Compel them to come in' (Luke 14:23) have earned Augustine the reputation of being the first theorist of the Inquisition. Certainly, he deployed a massive argument for using the repressive machinery of the state in support of Christian orthodoxy against the Donatists' insistence on religious freedom and their denunciation of state interference in matters of religion.

These facts cannot be denied. Do they invalidate the interpretation of his theology of the *saeculum* which has disclosed a very different direction in his thought? It could be that at this point Augustine's mind appears like one of those drawings which can be read in two alternative ways, according to the way one looks at them. If so, it has at least been worth attempting to look at Augustine's theology from a point of view not often adopted, to see what sort of sense it makes considered as a critique of the 'establishment' of the Church in the Roman Empire. If we should now find that one side of his mind just makes no sense if looked at from this point of view, we should have to be content with leaving the matter there, and to concede either that Augustine faced in two irreconcilable directions or that the hypothesis in which we have interpreted him is unfounded. In the case of a man with Augustine's acute self-knowledge and reflectiveness the first option is not open. He was not the man to act on impulse, under pressure, or in defence of self-interest in flagrant denial of his principles and to disguise such action from himself. But it is too soon to abandon our hypothesis. With a highly differentiated personality like Augustine's, with his complex and subtle mind, it would be a counsel of despair to begin with the assumption that his thoughts and attitudes should have a simple, monolithic consistency about them. We must at least explore the possibility that Augustine's attitude to religious coercion is related in some way to the fundamentals of his theology, including among these the fundamentals of his theology of the *saeculum* as we have interpreted them, even if the relation is far from simple. In this chapter, then, I shall enquire whether and how far Augustine's views on religious coercion cohere with the theological reflection whose growth we have traced in the preceding chapters. The details of his views and arguments have been much studied.[1] They are of interest to us here only in so far as they affect the answer to the question: can they be reconciled with the other facets of his thought?

Augustine took the lead in the African Catholics' struggle against Donatism very early in his career. As a priest, he composed a work in the form of an extended jingle to state the case against Donatism in a popular form. He was already a leading figure in the African Church when he composed this, in 393, the year in which the first of the great series of African Councils was inaugurated with the Council held, significantly, in Hippo.[2] Two years later, he succeeded to the See of Hippo, and attended most of the Councils of Carthage held during his long episcopate. He became a close friend of Aurelius, the bishop of Carthage, and remained the centre of an intimate group of disciples several of whom had become bishops in neighbouring Sees. It will be as well to consider Augustine's attitude in relation to what the African episcopate thought about religious coercion.

The Catholic bishops were by no means averse to the use of repressive measures against pagans. Indeed, in 401, they asked for

[1] The most illuminating study, to which I owe much, is Brown, 'Saint Augustine's attitude'; cf. also Joly, 'Saint Augustin et l'intolérance', and Zepf, 'Zur Chronologie'. Among works covering a wider ground there are useful accounts in Frend, *The Donatist Church*, 227 f.; Willis, *Saint Augustine*, 36 f. The facts are exhaustively re-told in Grasmück, *Coercitio*. For the actual working of coercion in practice, Brown, 'Religious coercion' and Tengström, *Donatisten und Katholiken*.

[2] Cf. Ch. 5, above, p. 128.

their intensification. Encouraged, apparently, by the success of the previous two years, which had witnessed a feverish burst of repressive activity by the authorities in Africa, the bishops asked the government for further legislation to extirpate 'the last remnants of idolatry'.[1] Augustine must have been in full agreement with his colleagues at this time. Whether he actually advocated such policies at the two councils of 401 or not, he was certainly already prepared to endorse them on principle in works written about this time,[2] and later on, when justifying the use of coercion against Donatists, he would often write as if there had never been any doubt—in his own mind or anybody else's—about coercing pagans.[3] His agreement with the conciliar policy may even have been enthusiastic. His preaching and writing about the 'Christian times' rose to a great crescendo in the very years around the turn of the century. Around 399–401 he had no reservations about endorsing the Theodosian establishment, with its forcible methods of repressing paganism and heresy and its recourse to legislation to enforce Christian orthodoxy. This phase of the Empire's history seemed to him, in these years, to mark the climax of its role as the vehicle of divine purpose in history. Through the agency of the Roman Empire, God was fulfilling the promises made of old, the world was being brought to serve his name as the prophets had foretold.[4] In his theology of the 'Christian times' Augustine possessed a fully fledged justification for religious coercion. Theodosius and his successors were the instruments of a divine purpose in uprooting the idols and in subjugating their peoples to the worship of Christ. Augustine certainly had no grounds for disagreement with his fellow bishops in 401. He may even have been the chief theorist of their policies.

At this time, however, the Catholic bishops were still seeking peaceful means of converting Donatists,[5] and it was not until three years later that they changed their views in this respect.

[1] *C. Carth. V*, Can. 2; *VI*, Can. 18. [2] Cf. e.g. *C. ep. Parm.* I, 10.16.

[3] *Inter multa*, cf. *Epp.* 93.3.10; 97.2–3.

[4] Cf. Brown, 'Saint Augustine's attitude', and Ch. 2, above, pp. 30–7.

[5] Cf. *C. Carth. VI*, Can. 1–3.

THE CHURCH AND POLITICAL POWER

During these years the struggle between the two Churches grew in violence. Even so, however, the Catholic bishops wanted to conduct the struggle *more ecclesiastico*, by preaching, by discussion and in public debate. At their Council in 403 they still clung to this policy, and though they invoked the support of the Proconsul, it was only to the extent of asking him to have official archives opened to them for their search for documents to support their case in debate, and to have the schismatics summoned 'honourably' to appear in public to discuss the matters at issue under 'the friendly moderation of the law'.[1] But the Donatists, following the lead of their bishop in Carthage, refused the challenge, and would not appear for these public debates. During the following year the tension rose. At their Council in 404 the Catholic bishops decided to ask the government for repressive measures against Donatists. Even before the arrival of their emissaries in Ravenna, the Court had already decided to act. The 'Edict of Unity', together with some supporting legislation, was despatched to Africa in February and March 405.[2] This inaugurated a sustained attempt by the government to repress the schism.

But at this time Augustine's attitude did not amount to anything like full support of the policies advocated by his fellow bishops and adopted by the government. It may even be that the bishops' delay in adopting against the Donatists the coercive policies they had already advocated against pagans—though it can be explained by the situation they were faced with—was due, at least in part, to the restraint on them of Augustine's reluctance. For we have it on his own authority that he did not agree with the policy of coercion decided upon in 404, and that it was not until some time after the Edict of Unity (405) that he had embraced such a policy. Writing in 408 he explained the reasons for this inhibition: what, he had thought, was the use of legislation to convert heretics into 'feigned' (*ficti*) Catholics? He would have preferred at the time, he says, not to coerce the schismatics for fear of producing a mass of 'feigned' conversions, but to continue with preaching and discussion and to

[1] *Gesta Coll. Carth.* III, 174. [2] *Cod. Theod.* XVI, 5.37, 38; 6.4, 5; 11.2.

prevail by the force of reason. But subsequent events have reconciled him to coercive methods. In his own city of Hippo he had seen the success of the Edict of Unity in operation: multitudes who needed only this external impulse to abandon the error they had clung to from force of habit and prejudice were now grateful for having been helped to the truth by the Edict.[1] There is every reason for accepting Augustine's explanation of his reluctance at its face value. The multitude of semi-Christian converts ushered into the Church by the social pressures on pagans constituted a serious pastoral problem, one to which Augustine had been particularly sensitive in the early years of his priestly and episcopal ministry.[2] He was very apt to interpret the low standards of popular Christianity as the result of the hypocrisy of pagans whose conversion to Christianity was little more than outward conformity. He feared a worse corruption of standards as a consequence of a possible landslide of coerced Donatists. But he overcame his fears. Perhaps he had become less fastidious and learnt to accept the peculiarities of popular religion. At any rate within a year or two of the Edict of Unity, having seen its working, his doubts were dispelled. His own congregation had successfully absorbed the converts who had been 'brought over to the Catholic unity by fear of the imperial Edicts'.[3] With growing confidence in his Church's power to assimilate the masses, Augustine's chief inhibition about the policy of coercion now lost its force. Some time between 405 and 408 his consent followed, and thereafter he never wavered. At the end of his life he recalled that long ago—around 398—he had written a work *Contra partem Donati*, in which he had rejected recourse to the secular power to bring schismatics forcibly into communion. 'I rejected it at that time because I had not yet learnt from my experience either how much wickedness they could resort to if left unpunished, or how much they could benefit from the application of discipline.'[4]

[1] *Ep.* 93.5.17.
[2] Cf. Van der Meer, *Augustine the bishop*, 46 f.
[3] *Ep.* 93.5.17.
[4] *Retr.* II, 5.

THE CHURCH AND POLITICAL POWER

Augustine, then, did change his mind on the advisability of coercing Donatists, and we are in the comparatively rare position of having his own statement not only pin-pointing the change of mind, but also giving a convincing explanation for it. This change of mind gives no grounds for speaking of a 'conversion' of Augustine from previously 'liberal' ideas to the repressive policies of the African espiscopate and the Roman government. We have seen that he was probably in full agreement with coercing pagans in 401, and that his theology down to about 399–401 would have provided the support of principle for the policy. His 'conversion' to coercion against Donatists is no more than a delayed extension to their case of a policy already endorsed against pagans.

Within three or four years of the letter (*Ep.* 93) containing his apologia for sanctioning coercion Augustine had, however, come to reject decisively the views about the Theodosian establishment which he had held around the turn of the century[1] and which were one of the chief theoretical props of religious coercion. By the time of this famous letter (written in 408) the flow of positive statements about 'Christian times' and indeed about the scope of political action in religious matters had dried up. This loss of enthusiasm did not turn into explicit repudiation until a few years later, the early years of the second decade of the century, when he began elaborating a theology cast in a very different mould. But although the chief theoretical foundation of religious coercion built into his theology had thus disappeared, Augustine never repudiated the policies which had been based on it. This is the central paradox of Augustine's attitude to religious coercion when placed in relation to his fundamental theological development. To solve it, if it can be solved, we need to enquire into two things: what were the theoretical foundations, if any, for Augustine's *continued* approval of coercion? and if these principles did not lie in the sphere of his theology of the *saeculum*, but elsewhere, how were they compatible with his thought in that sphere?

[1] Cf. Ch. 2, above, pp. 37–41.

SAECULUM

This study is concerned with theological reflection, and therefore confined to abstract, general ideas. But a man's attitude to an issue such as that of religious coercion is something too complex, and something that operates on too many levels, to be treated exclusively in this abstract dimension.[1] Only a part of it will be captured in the net of a 'doctrine' of coercion. In Augustine's Africa, coercion was one of the facts of life, and a provincial bishop was deeply involved in its exercise. Administrative routine, if nothing else, made the distinction between Church and State inapplicable in this context. An African bishop was not faced with the question whether coercion was justifiable or not; in innumerable ways his position in society, even his episcopal functions, involved him in a repressive régime.[2] We are not here concerned with the working of religious coercion in Augustine's Africa, or even with the way in which Augustine participated in its working. But it is as well to keep these administrative, social and human complexities in mind as a permanent backdrop to define the middle distance. We confine our attention to the chosen foreground, the ideas involved.

Augustine's 'theory' of coercion was, from beginning to end, part of a pastoral strategy.[3] As a young priest he explained his mind to his elderly bishop on how to curb sinners: 'abuses are to be cut off "in a spirit of gentleness" [Gal. 6:1], as it is written... These things are not to be removed, it seems to me, by harshness or in a sharp, imperious way (*non ergo aspere...non duriter, non modo imperioso*): but by teaching rather than commanding, by admonition rather than with threats. This is how to proceed with the majority; severity is best kept for dealing with the sins of the few.'[4] Harshness, fear, threats, coercion are not, even at this early stage, rejected on principle. They are modes of the exercise of pastoral office, but modes which must be kept in reserve, not to be

[1] Brown, 'Saint Augustine's attitude', has some penetrating remarks on this.

[2] For its workings, see Brown, 'Religious coercion'.

[3] Berkhof, *Kirche und Kaiser*, 105–22, on the strength of a very cursory investigation, asserts, rightly, that this is where the novelty of Augustine's position lies in relation to earlier theories of coercion. Cf. Crespin, *Ministère*, esp. 162–8, 174–5.

[4] *Ep.* 22.5.

used indiscriminately. Episcopal office seems, however, to have weakened Augustine's resolve to keep pastoral 'severity' within such narrow bounds. His confidence in his ability, and that of his congregation, to cope with 'corrected' sinners, pagans and schismatics in large numbers overcame his reluctance to sanction large-scale coercion. The change of his mind after 405 concerned only the scale on which he envisaged that coercive measures could be applied. They remained, for him, primarily an application of pastoral *severitas*.

The importance of pastoral considerations in sanctioning the use of force is evident from Augustine's Letter 93. He had never doubted that violence should be controlled by the public authority and that Donatist terrorists should be punished; and before now he had spoken of the government's competence to 'persecute schismatics'.[1] But these considerations had not, up to now, tilted the scales in favour of his sanctioning coercion. That, evidently, was done by the 'pastoral' arguments deployed in Letter 93. The key-note is struck in the opening paragraph: 'We see many who have renounced their former blindness; how could I begrudge them their salvation, by dissuading my colleagues from exercising their fatherly care, by which this has been brought about?'[2] Throughout this long letter Augustine considers religious coercion from this perspective. It is likened to medicine administered to an unwilling patient for his own good;[3] it is a true work of love, for 'it is better to love with severity than to deceive with indulgence';[4] even God—and no one can love men more than He does—is always scourging those whom He loves. Can we doubt that people should be compelled to righteousness when we read that the master of the house commanded his servants: 'whomever you find, compel them to come in' (Luke 14:23)?[5] Throughout the Bible we read of punishment being administered as a remedy.[6] After some paragraphs in defence of religious coercion by the secular power, Augustine returns to the gratitude shown by ex-Donatists

[1] *Ep.* 87.7. [2] *Ep.* 93.1.1; cf. *ibid.* 5.19. [3] *Ibid.* 1.3.
[4] *Ibid.* 2.4. [5] *Ibid.* 2.5. [6] *Ibid.* 2.6–8.

for having had the imperial edicts to break them from procrastination, to help them overcome the force of habit and prejudice, for having brought them to an unclouded vision of the truth previously obscured by rumour; for making them do, in short, what they would have wanted to do had they known better.[1]

This kind of argumentation is the kernel, not only of this most self-conscious of Augustine's writings on this question, but of his whole attitude to coercion of schismatics from the moment he endorsed it. The case for coercive measures against the Donatists was fundamentally different from the case—which Augustine never actually deployed in full and whose basis he came to reject—for coercing pagans. With pagans it had been a question of forcing them to accept a truth to which they were blind and to accept a historical destiny expressed in the Christian Church and its alliance with the Roman Empire. With the Donatist schismatics it was a matter of *recalling* them to the flock to which they rightfully belonged and from which they had strayed. Coercing schismatics was, in a sense in which coercing pagans could never be, part of the Church's pastoral activity among its own flock. When preaching on the shepherds of Chapter 34 of Ezechiel, Augustine's mind turns quite naturally to bringing the strayed sheep—the Donatists—back to the one sheepfold;[2] even with the help of inflicted pain, if need be, this is part of *diligentia pastoralis*.[3] In the last of his anti-Donatist tracts, written some thirteen years after Letter 93, he would write, still in the same vein, to a Donatist bishop who had barricaded himself in his splendid cathedral against the imperial official sent against him, and was threatening to burn himself and his congregation in it: 'the tribune sent against you is not your persecutor; he is persecuting your persecutor, that is, your error...'[4]

This horrible doctrine, with all its potentialities for being insidiously and cynically generalised, derives from Augustine's notion of *disciplina*. This was the seed from which his theory of

[1] *Ibid.* 5.18.
[2] *Sermo* 46, *De pastoribus*; cf. also *Sermo* 47, *De ovibus*.
[3] *Ep.* 185.6.23.
[4] *C. Gaudent.* 1, 18.19.

persecution grew. Its beneficial value, as we know from his own statement,[1] Augustine realised only late. But once he had come to accept it, Augustine, characteristically, found many threads linking the idea of *disciplina* to the basic texture of his theology. Especially from his late fifties on, he considered freedom of choice less and less as something incompatible with constraint and fear. God had made use of constraint and fear in the long education to which he subjected his chosen people. The divine *disciplina* uses external pressure to bring about an internal moral development. In his justification of religious coercion Augustine would often quote from the Book of Proverbs: 'Give occasion to a wise man, and he will become wiser' (9: 9).[2] To the notion—deeply enough established in Christian tradition, even to the extent of finding an echo in Constantine's 'Edict of toleration'—that belief is a matter of free decision, not of compulsion, Augustine replied by rejecting the dichotomy. Free choice and compulsion were not incompatible: 'It is not true that nothing is accomplished by external pressure. For not only is the wall of hardened habit breached by human terrors, but the mind's faith and understanding is at the same time strengthened by divine authority and reason.'[3] A sermon Augustine once preached—his only one actually on the text of the parable of the wedding feast—closed with the reminder that the Lord did not just invite the willing; he gave instructions for the unwilling to be compelled to come in: 'Let constraint be found outside: the will is born within.'[4]

This remained Augustine's settled response to the objection that 'the unwilling are not to be brought forcibly to the truth',[5] urged frequently especially by his Donatist opponents. The notion of *disciplina*, with its cognates—*correctio*, *per molestias eruditio*—remained the kernel of his 'theory' of coercion. Indeed the power of these ideas increased in his mind with the development of his views on grace, on predestination and on man's freedom, from the

[1] *Retr.* II, 5; cf. above, p. 138, n. 4.

[2] E.g. *Ep.* 93.5.17; much later, *C. Gaudent.* I, 33.43.

[3] *Ep.* 89.7.

[4] *Foris inveniatur necessitas, nascitur intus voluntas*—*Sermo* 112.8; cf. also *C. litt. Pet.* II, 84.186.

[5] *C. Gaudent.* I, 25.28.

time of his conflict with Pelagianism, around 410. As a young philosopher, recently converted to Christianity, Augustine had defended the freedom of the will against Manichaean determinism. But long before his encounter with the teaching of Pelagius he had been deeply conscious of the difficulty of achieving the good life in one's conduct. The force of habit (*consuetudo*; apt to become *consuetudo carnalis*) held a man's freedom of action in the grip of his own past. For Pelagius, the grip of past habit on the personality could be broken. In his 'theology of discontinuity' baptism and conversion marked the Christian's emancipation from the power of his own past over him.[1] For Augustine, the man reborn in the Spirit was not so free from the power of the past. For him, the force of habit was not something external to the personality and capable of being discarded in conversion, but something that entered deeply into a man's make-up. This 'wall of hardened habit' was the barrier Augustine saw between the schismatic communities and the unity of the one fold.[2]

To summarise: it seems that Augustine's ideas on religious coercion sprang from several different contexts. First, it is clear that he was never entirely opposed to *severitas* as a pastoral method. His later statements, especially from Letter 93 onwards, place most weight on the notion of coercion as an exercise of this *severitas*, as an infliction of *disciplina* for the education and the ultimate benefit of the coerced. In this sense his later ideas are substantially in line with his earliest, and only constitute a development from them in two respects: first, in the scale on which he was later prepared to sanction the use of methods which he had at first envisaged as applicable only to a few; and second, in the wider resonances his ideas on *disciplina* acquired in the course of his reflection on grace, freedom and predestination during his controversy with Pelagianism. There is, however, another source, of quite a different kind,

[1] Cf. Brown, 'Pelagius'. It is one of the singular merits of this deeply impressive paper to have thrown this aspect of the difference between the two men into clear relief. On the importance of Augustine's teaching on grace and freedom for his ideas on coercion, see Brown, 'Saint Augustine's attitude'.

[2] *Ep*. 89.7; cf. above, p. 143, n. 3.

which also nourished his readiness to endorse coercion: his theology of the Roman Empire as a divinely willed instrument of the Gospel. This was a phase of his thought which rose to a climax around 399–401, thereafter declined in importance, and was decisively repudiated soon after 410. It must have played some part in his agreement with his fellow bishops in 401 over coercing pagans, but probably none in securing his consent to coercing Donatists around 406–8, and soon after 410 Augustine must have been conscious that this reason for the policy of coercion was gone. But it made no difference in practice: there were other, equally strong reasons which remained, and could serve to justify continued adherence to the policy. Moreover, Augustine was being increasingly drawn into meditating on the deep mysteries of human freedom and on God's ways with the wills of men. He could equate God's action on human will with external impingement: 'God himself is doing this [recalling you to the fold] through us—whether by pleading, by threats, by rebukes, by punishment and by troubles; whether through his own secret admonitions and visitations, or through the power of the temporal law.'[1] His last anti-Donatist work, *Against Gaudentius* (421), compared with the anti-Donatist writings of 400–11, shows clear traces of enrichment from this more recently developed context of Augustine's thought.[2] The role of rebuke, punishment, fear and all salutary constraint did not cease to preoccupy Augustine. One of his last works was devoted to these very problems.[3] Grounds for approving coercion were therefore well embedded in other spheres of Augustine's thought than in a relatively short phase of his reflection on politics and the Roman Empire.

We may then conclude that Augustine's views on coercion need not be taken as part only of his reflection on history and on politics, indeed that this reflection would have supported them only during a relatively short period and would not have done so at any rate during the last twenty years of his life. The theoretical

[1] *Ep.* 105.4.13. [2] See for instance *C. Gaudent.* 1, 19.20.

[3] *De corr. et gratia* (426–7); cf. also *Ep.* 210.

background of his views on coercion was a changing constellation of ideas belonging to different realms of thought, and the views themselves are part of a complex set of attitudes rather than implications drawn with rigorous logic from any theory.[1] It does, however, remain true that there is an unresolved tension between Augustine's mature theology of the *saeculum* and his views on coercion. His endorsement of official enforcement of Christian orthodoxy, whatever its theoretical foundations, is not well at home in the repudiation of the Theodosian 'Christian times', nor in the setting of his scepticism about a Christian Roman Empire and about legal and institutional means of christianisation.

Augustine was assisted in concealing this tension from himself by a habit of mind which is revealed in his customary manner of dealing with the theme of the 'Christian ruler'. In discussing this theme, Augustine came up against the central problem of the intersection of two spheres of discourse: the Christian ruler or magistrate can be thought of either as a member of the Church, or as part of a system of governmental institutions; either as a servant of God or of the *res publica*. In his earliest pronouncements on this subject Augustine tends to by-pass the problem of relating these two spheres. Thus in a work written soon after his conversion to Christianity he apostrophises the Church as the guardian of all the virtues distinctive of all stations in life. Among the several kinds and conditions of men taught their proper place in the world are rulers and their subjects: 'You (the Church) teach kings to care for their people, you admonish peoples to be subject to their rulers.'[2] Here the Church appears as the guardian of all established order and of all proper human relationships, and in the passage as a whole there is an implicit but effective rhetorical identification of the existing with an ideal order. At this stage, of course, Augustine

[1] This is well brought out by Brown, 'Saint Augustine's attitude', 107–8. It is for this reason, too, that one cannot in the end, as a historian, identify Augustine with some of the caricatures to which his teaching easily lends itself. Cf. the concluding paragraphs of Brown's paper: 'But remove the foundation of honesty for one moment from this attitude, and Augustine's phrases become fallacious, horrible and insidious...', *ibid.* 115.

[2] *De mor. eccl.* I, 30.63.

would not have rejected such an identification.[1] Rulers were the agents of founding an order among men grounded upon the universal order established by God in the world. The tasks and interests of Church and State necessarily coincided in the person of the ruler.

This coincidence was further strengthened by the Eusebian type of theology of the Empire, from whose sway Augustine only learnt to free himself after 400. The Empire was the instrument of a divine purpose, the Emperor a quasi-messianic figure with a transcendent mission; Church and State were only provisionally distinct aspects of a single Christian 'polity'. Although Augustine never wholly identified himself with the more extreme forms of such a theology, it did, as we saw (Chapter 2), shape his thinking about the Empire for some years. In the context of such a conception the problem of defining the respective spheres of Church and State was again by-passed, for the two were, at root, identical. It is in the later period of his thought, when he had rejected both the idea of the political order as part of a universal, cosmic order, and the idea of a Christian Roman Empire, that we might expect to find traces of a consciousness of this problem in Augustine's writings. But in fact Augustine continued to speak of Christian rulers and officials owing specific service to God in their public, official capacity. In 405 he wrote: 'Uprooting the idols from the face of the earth—promised so long ago—is not something any private citizen can command. Kings thus have their own status in human society in virtue of which they can serve the Lord in ways not open to those who are not kings.'[2] 'When we ask something of our rulers for the benefit of the Church, we are not placing our hope in them: we are admonishing them to place their hope in God.'[3] The same thoughts are expressed twelve years later, in a letter to the Roman commander Boniface concerning 'the correction of the Donatists'.[4] Kings' specific service of God, as kings, consists in 'commanding what is good, prohibiting what is wicked, not only in matters pertaining to social relations between

[1] Cf. Ch. 4, above, pp. 75–80.
[2] *C. litt. Pet.* II, 92.210.
[3] *Ibid.* II, 97.224.
[4] *Ep.* 185.5.19.

men, but also in those pertaining to divine religion'.[1] Augustine sums it all up in the famous 'mirror for princes': Christian emperors achieve their true felicity if, among other things, 'they make their power serve God's majesty by using it to the utmost to spread his worship'.[2]

There is no trace of any reservation about the scope of imperial or royal authority in such statements, no suggestion that it is in any way restricted to 'temporal' matters. If there was a tension between Augustine's views about the function of the state or of the Roman Empire, as they were developing at this time, and his views on the duties of Christian kings and emperors (including the duty to enforce true religion),[3] Augustine seems not to have been aware of it. Once he remarked, in a letter to the Proconsul of Africa, that the 'business of a province is one thing, that of the Church another';[4] but this was no attempt to define distinct spheres of authority. On the contrary: the purpose of this distinction of spheres was to persuade the Proconsul to deal leniently with Donatists, so that through his mercy, the mercy of his mother, the Church, might be made manifest. 'For when you act, the Church acts, for whose sake and as whose son you act.'[5]

Here is the clue to the reason why Augustine could write as he did about the duties of Christian rulers and about religious coercion by the public authorities long after he had ceased to believe that the state had any religious purpose or function. Neither in his dealings with imperial officials nor in his writings in defence of religious coercion did he ever consider Christian rulers and civil servants as parts of a governmental machinery, of the 'state'. He thought of them as members of the Church. Through them, it is the Church that 'uses power'.[6] Once he even spoke of coercion *by* the Church.[7] The concept of the 'state' is conspicuous by its absence from all Augustine's discussions of this theme. When, on a rare occasion,

[1] *C. Cresc.* III, 51.56. [2] *De civ. Dei*, V, 24. Cf. above, p. 57, n. 1.

[3] The quotations in the previous paragraph cover the years *c.* 405 to 417; the same thoughts still occur in 421, *C. Gaudent.* I, 35.45.

[4] *Ep.* 134.3. [5] *Ibid.* 4. [6] *Ep.* 173.10.

[7] *Ep.* 185.6.23. It was no slip of the pen, for the thought is implicit *ibid.* 2.11.

he recalled that there was something wrong—as his own principles must have suggested—with the whole coercive establishment of the Theodosian Empire, he formulated the objection not in terms of the state's proper function, but from the point of view of the Church's well-being: through the service rendered to it by kings the Church is exposed 'to greater and more serious temptation'.[1] The reason why it did not occur to Augustine to restrict the scope of the state's proper sphere of action when he was thinking about religious coercion is simple: it did not occur to him to think in terms of the 'state' at all in this context. It is striking that when Augustine defends the exercise of coercive power by the secular authority in the religious sphere, he always does so in a vocabulary of persons rather than of institutions. Although he did have at his disposal words such as *imperium* or *res publica*, which may suitably be rendered in abstract political terminology, these are not the words he uses for this purpose. He will speak of emperors rather than of empire, of kings and magistrates rather than of state or government. Thus he could continue to speak without inhibition of Christian emperors long after he had abandoned all talk about a Christian empire.[2]

This is no accident of linguistic habit. Augustine's linguistic preferences here are an index of some of the profoundest preoccupations of his mind. The reasons for his choice of vocabulary are embedded in the perpetual liability of his conception of the state to dissolve into a kind of atomistic personalism. 'A city consists of its citizens, not of its walls.'[3] Especially when he wished

1 *De perf. iust.* 15.35. Cf. Ch. 2 above, p. 40, n. 6.

2 There are signs, however, that even in his speech about Christian emperors Augustine was deliberately reserved. A meticulous recent study, Duval, 'L'éloge de Théodose', has disclosed the extent of the independence of Augustine's judgement from that of the writers on whose work he drew for information. In his eulogy of Theodosius (*De civ. Dei*, v, 26.1) he drew heavily on Rufinus's recently completed translation and continuation of Eusebius's *Ecclesiastical history*. But there is no trace in Augustine's presentation of the emperor of any of the quasi-messianic features which Rufinus, in the Eusebian tradition, had projected onto his hero. On the contrary: Augustine prefers to single out the typically private virtues for special praise in Christian emperors: their humility in the face of the seductions offered by high office, their submission to God and their grateful recognition of his gifts.

3 *De urb. exc.* 6. For further passages of this kind, cf. Ch. 3 above, p. 61, n. 2.

to comment on the moral quality—the piety or turpitude—of a society, Augustine liked to dismember it in this fashion into its constituent, personal atoms. 'Where a king, a council, officials, people are to be found, there is the *civitas*'; wickedness is not something to be found disembodied in 'cities', it does not exist in institutions but in individuals who are 'the constituent elements and atoms of cities'.[1] This somewhat simple-minded approach to political morality, with its exclusive interest in persons and neglect of structures, does not, of course, represent the whole of Augustine's mind on the matter. He could give much weight to the quality of a society's institutions, traditions, and its collectively upheld ideals.[2] But the protest against objectifying the mixed ultimate personal allegiances current in any social group into a collective entity capable of simple moral assessment was a vital part of his rejection both of pagan Roman and of Christian Eusebian ideology.

It was this protest that was at the roots of his insistence that in any human grouping the two eschatological 'cities' always coexist and overlap.[3] Once he had embarked on the writing of the *City of God*, and on the sustained meditation on God's purposes in history which lie behind it, what interested Augustine increasingly were the eschatological ultimates as they were interwoven in the *saeculum*. Terms such as the 'state' disguised the fact that, from this point of view, the entity designated by them was a composite one, consisting of the two 'cities' in their overlap. But this was precisely what Augustine had to stress in order to empty the 'state' of eschatological significance. To preserve its neutrality between the two 'cities' and to transfer to them the whole burden of being the exclusive bearers of all ultimate significance, what was required

[1] *elementa et semina civitatum*—*Enarr. in Ps.* 9.8. The tendency of the abstract political concepts to dissolve into 'personalistic' terms is, of course, very much in line with the development of late Roman government. The 'patriarchal' situation of the great estate was becoming increasingly characteristic of the social and administrative life of the Empire. The 'state' was becoming increasingly eclipsed as an abstraction only dimly visible behind the peculiarly personal and quasi-feudal authority of the senatorial governors of the Western provinces.

[2] Cf. above, pp. 66 f., 96 f.

[3] Cf. Ch. 3, above, pp. 64–71. What follows summarises the argument there given in full.

was a kind of invisible re-grouping of the state's citizens into the two mutually exclusive bodies of the citizens of the earthly and of the heavenly cities: Rome could not have any ultimate, eternal destiny because it was—as is any other actual body of men—necessarily a mixed body. Only the two 'cities' are in the relevant sense 'unmixed'—but in their historical existence they can never be discerned in their unmixed state. This invisibility of the presence of eschatological categories in historical realities is the foundation of Augustine's theology of the *saeculum*. In order to insist on the ultimate eschatological ambivalence of all empirical human groupings and institutions Augustine had to by-pass their collective, institutional character, and to break them down (though with the rider that this could never in fact be carried out with assignable named individuals) into terms of individuals with their personal loyalties to different, and very mixed, ultimate values. This is why his habit of reducing political institutions into their component personal atoms is linked with some of his most fundamental concerns, at a fundamental level.

We come thus to the paradoxical conclusion that both Augustine's 'desacralisation' of the Roman Empire, with the 'secular' theology of society implied in it, and his defence of religious coercion spring from a single root. More precisely, although his views on coercion sprang from another context, it was the fundamentals of his theology of the *saeculum* which, on the one hand, pointed in a very different direction, and, on the other, by virtue of their formulation, disguised from Augustine this divergence. The main lines of his thinking about history, society and human institutions in general (the *saeculum*) point towards a political order to which we may not unreasonably apply the anachronistic epithet 'pluralist', in that it is neutral in respect of ultimate beliefs and values. On the other hand, it was this very reflection itself, and its terminology, that undermined the solidity of Augustine's political vocabulary, with the effect that concepts such as that of the 'state' tended to dissolve in his hands. The concept of the Church was less susceptible to this 'atomisation'. It was, for obvious reasons, less easy to dissolve into its members, whereas the idea of the 'state' could not so easily survive the tendency to break down into terms of the individuals who compose it. In consequence it ceased to be a concept which engaged the centre of Augustine's interests, or in terms of which he discussed other related questions in which he was interested. Among such questions is the one we have been considering in this chapter, that of religious coercion. Perhaps, had Augustine thought of this issue in terms of the proper function of the 'state', he might have come to take another view of the matter than he did; perhaps he would at least have been more conscious of an unresolved tension than he appears to have been. These are conjectures. At any rate, we may say that the fact that he did not think of this problem in terms of the state, but in terms of individual members of the Church who held secular office, disguised from Augustine the acute tension between his consent to coercion and the implications of his theology of history and society. The 'atomistic personalism' bound up with the latter is what, in large part, made it possible for him to elaborate a 'theory' of coercion of the type he did.

That this was a theory of coercion by the Church, not by the state, is of vital importance for understanding Augustine's mind on the matter, though the difference is, of course, irrelevant in practice. There was, indeed, little foothold for such a distinction in the actual circumstances of Augustine's Africa. In the course of the early middle ages, with the increasing difficulty of applying the concept of the 'state' to anything that could be found in Western Europe, the categories of Augustine's 'atomistic personalism' found more ready application than ever. For centuries it was much easier to think of political realities in terms of rulers, officials, their duties and ideals, than in terms of abstract political concepts such as the 'state', 'government', or 'public authority'. Hence that 'political Augustinianism' so characteristic of the middle ages which, though scarcely in line with the grain of Augustine's own thought, has been aptly defined as 'a tendency to absorb natural law in supernatural justice, the right of the state in that of the

Church'.[1] Not for nothing was the *genre* of Augustine's 'mirror for princes'[2] one of the favourite forms of medieval political writing. For all that, the argument of this book is that if we wish to understand the political bearings of the fundamental theological structures of Augustine's thought, we do better to pursue the implications of the hypothesis in which we have reconstructed the shape of that thought than to remain content with what he actually said about the duties of Christian rulers and subjects.

[1] Arquillière, *L'augustinisme politique*, 4.

[2] *De civ. Dei*, v, 24.

[20]

Augustine on Justifying Coercion

John R. Bowlin

ABSTRACT

Augustine encouraged Christian bishops and magistrates to coerce and constrain religious dissenters, he participated in these activities almost from the start of his career as presbyter under Valerius, and he offered justifications for what he did. Robert Markus and John Milbank consider Augustine's justifications inconsistent with the aspect of his social thought each admires most. Their conclusions are unwarranted and unnecessary. Augustine's justifications are neither inconsistent with the rest of his social thought, nor dependent upon judgments about just and unjust coercion that are fundamentally different from our own.

Introduction

The well known facts, in brief outline, are these: Augustine encouraged Christian bishops and magistrates to coerce and constrain religious dissenters; he participated in these activities almost from the start of his career as presbyter under Valerius; and he offered justifications for what he did.[1] Famous for his

---

[1] I use "coercion" as Augustine does, rather loosely. Some precision can be had here, but not much. In the most general sense you are coerced when force is deliberately brought to bear *contra voluntatem tuam*, against your will (*Ep.*173.4), either against what you want generally or intend specifically. This can be done with more or less severity, with more or less guarantee of compliance. You can be given an incentive to refrain from doing what you want or intend. Taxes and fines are a good example (*Ep.*93.i.2). You can be restrained from doing what you want or intend, as the physician does to the madman (*Ep.*185.ii.7). You can be compelled to do what you do not want or intend to do, as the father does to his undisciplined son (Ibid.) By the time he writes his letter to Count Boniface (417) the Donatists suffer all three and he defends each (*Ep.*185.ii.7,

changes of heart and mind, in this he never wavered, although he did reconsider the aims that the church might seek by coercive means. At first he thought that pagans and heretics should be suppressed but not compelled, their exercise constrained but never their freedom to believe this or that. In his 392 letter to Maximinus the Donatist bishop of Hippo (*Ep.*23.7) and again in his 396 letter to Eusebius he insists that no one "should against his will be coerced into the Catholic communion" (*Ep.*34.1).[2] (The unity of Christ can be forged by argument alone. Twelve years later, in a letter to Vincentius, he tells us why. At the time he was convinced that Donatists forced into the church would remain heretics at heart, while "feigning themselves to be Catholics" (*Ep.*93.17, v., *Ep.*185.25–6). Now his mind has changed, in part because the intervening years have brought a new understanding of "the ruts of habit" in thought and action (*Conf.*VII.xvi.22), in part because he now has evidence of efficacy. Sincere belief, he now contends, has in fact been coercion's yield, while without it, many are cut off from the truth by "some indescribable bondage of custom" (*Ep.*93.1).

In recent years the response of critics and exegetes has been largely uniform, both denouncing Augustine's intolerance in word and deed and doubting the merit and the sincerity of the justifications he offers. Oddly enough, most of Augustine's contemporaries would have found the first complaint unusual and the second misplaced. In the rough and tumble North African church of the late forth and early fifth centuries, resort to force against heretics, schismatics, and pagans was common, indeed hardly worth mentioning. Toleration of religious minorities was infrequent, and reflection upon the merits of restraint unusual, normally an accidental consequence of persecution and weakness. Indeed,

---

vi.22). Finally, throughout his Donatist writings Augustine uses *cogere* and *compellere*, both of which mean to force or to compel, but also to drive together, to unite, to condense. This bears on intention, for Augustine hoped that coercion might yield common knowledge and shared desire within the church.

2 I consulted the following translations, modifying them infrequently through reference to J.–P. Migne, *Patrologiae Latina* (Paris, 1844–) and only to improve clarity and bite: *The City of God Against the Pagans*, trans. G.E. McCracken, 7 vols. (Cambridge: Harvard University Press, 1957); *Confessions*, trans. Henry Chadwick (Oxford: Oxford University Press, 1991); *The Letters of Saint Augustine*, trans. J.A.G. Cunningham, 2 vols. (Edinburgh: T&T Clark, 1872, 1875); *Letters*, trans. Wilfred Parsons, 5 vols. (New York: Fathers of the Church, Inc., 1951–1956); *Sermons on Selected Lessons of the New Testament* (Oxford: John Henry Parker, 1894); *Three Books in Answer to the Letters of Petilian*, trans. J.R. King, rev.ed. C.D. Hartranft, in *The Writings Against the Manichaeans and Against the Donatist*, volume iv in *Nicene and Post–Nicene Fathers*, ed. Philip Schaff (Buffalo: The Christian Literature Company, 1887); *A Treatise Concerning the Correction of the Donatists*, trans. J.R. King, rev.ed. C.D. Hartranft, in *The Writings Against the Manichaeans and Against the Donatists*, volume iv in *Nicene and Post–Nicene Fathers*, ed. Philip Schaff (Buffalo: The Christian Literature Company, 1887).

throughout the ancient world, with perhaps Tertullian's efforts offering the one exception, scattered appeals to religious liberty were always ad hoc and local.[3] Most considered universal appeals reckless precisely because political fortunes can change and the persecuted may find themselves in a position to appeal to imperial authority in order to advance their own purposes.

It follows that "coercion, in some form, was one of the 'facts of life' for a provincial bishop."[4] For the most part, the clergy came from the upper classes and the bureaucratic elites of a largely military culture, and most considered coercion a customary, indeed a morally unproblematic, means of structuring human relations. They appreciated power and expected obedience in their spheres of authority, and they were men who were willing to use discipline to secure order.[5] No doubt, this attitude had its origin in the command and submission that obtained between provincial governors and their subjects, and yet its influence was ubiquitous. In business and in family life, and eventually in the relations between a bishop and his flock, coercion was an ordinary feature of the North African moral landscape.[6]

Nevertheless, after Honorius issued the Edict of Unity in June of 405, most North African bishops discovered that this ordinary feature demanded frequent attention. We tend to suppose that they pursued their cause against the Donatists by calling in the imperial troops to shut down churches, confiscate property, and flog the intransigent. In fact, Rome dispatched neither army nor police, and for the most part provided only "a lofty tone of intolerance" and proper legal authority.[7] Of course, provincial governments did bring the force of law to bear upon Donatists from the upper classes, preventing these privileged few from protecting their wealth, making contracts, pursuing litigation, and the like, but unmediated state coercion of this sort touched very few.[8] Upon the rest, fines were imposed, but the details of crime and punishment were left to the discretion

---

[3] Peter Garnsey, "Religious Toleration in Classical Antiquity," in *Persecution and Toleration*, ed. W. J. Sheils (Oxford: Blackwell, 1984), 16–25.

[4] Peter Brown, "St. Augustine's Attitude to Religious Coercion," in *Religion and Society in the Age of Saint Augustine* (New York: Harper & Row, 1972), 261.

[5] Peter Brown, *Authority and the Sacred: Aspects of the Christianisation of the Roman World* (Cambridge: Cambridge University Press, 1995), 38–39.

[6] Peter Brown, *The Body and Society: Men, Women, and Sexual Renunciation in Early Christianity* (New York: Columbia University Press, 1988), 398.

[7] Peter Brown, "Religious Coercion in the Later Roman Empire: The Case of North Africa," in *Religion and Society in the Age of Saint Augustine* (New York: Harper & Row, 1972), 308.

[8] Brown, "Religious Coercion," p. 312 and John Rist, *Augustine: Ancient Thought Baptized* (Cambridge: Cambridge University Press, 1994), 240.

of the bishops, who were, of course, the only reliable sources of information about church affiliation in their towns and districts. Add to this the fact that Catholic bishops inherited the property of suppressed churches, and it is easy to conclude that state power was mediated through church authority, and that coercion and constraint of religious dissent was therefore an enterprise left largely to the bishops themselves.[9]

It follows that few of Augustine's contemporaries would have found his participation in these activities troubling or surprising. However, they may have been puzzled by his willingness to offer justifications: frequent, forceful, and public. If coercion was common in late Roman society, then it remained unremarkable at least in part because force was normally exercised with a certain dignity, a certain decorum. Rarely accompanied by an account of motives or warrants, indeed, rarely accompanied by threats of violence, this quiet coercion was designed to preserve the unquestioned authority of those in power and the natural dependence of those coerced. As Peter Brown remarks, "(W)e must remember that it is a 'period eye'—an unmistakably late Roman eye, that does not ask, first, whether a powerful bishop is intolerant, but rather, whether or not he will set about being intolerant in an acceptable manner."[10] Arguments that challenge and provoke, sermons that call upon imperial power in the same breath that they denounce one's opponent, letters that expound motives, and pamphlets that justify the use of force for this purpose in that circumstance—all of these noisy efforts tempt the charge of unmannerly conduct precisely because they make the power to coerce appear something less than natural and the authority to structure social relations appear something less than given. Naked force dissipates the self-deception that is needed on both sides for coercion to proceed unnoticed, while more often than not justifications generate doubt about the legitimacy of the force employed even as they work to dispel it.

Augustine senses this from the start. When, as a newly minted presbyter (392 CE), he encourages Aurelius to suppress "the drunken revels and luxurious feasts in the cemeteries" on the feast days of the martyrs, he recommends "the most gentle" (*lenissimis*) means. Aurelius, he contends, should proceed, not by "harshness, severity, and an imperious mode of dealing," but "rather by teaching than by commanding, rather by advice than by denunciation." Threats and severity must be last resorts, used only against those few who do not yield. Moreover, these rougher magics should be delivered sorrowfully and accompanied by the relevant scriptural warrants, so that, as Augustine insists, "the fear

---

[9] Brown, "Religious Coercion," 327–328.

[10] Brown, *Authority*, 45.

that men feel through our words may not be of us in our authority, but of God himself" (*Ep*.22.5–6).

Here is a refined intolerance if ever there was one, and when it becomes ill-mannered it does not taint the bishop's authority, for the violence employed is referred to God whose authority is beyond taint. Yet, in slightly less than seven years (399 CE) Augustine preaches a sermon in Carthage that gives explicit support to Theodosius's suppression of paganism in North Africa. Here there is no refinement. Indeed, the tone turns ugly, at times vulgar.[11] A few years after that (402–404 CE) in his second reply to Petilianus, the Donatist bishop of Cirta, Augustine endorses similar treatment of heretics and schismatics and pushes toward a thorough-going justification for compelling them back into the church with the aid of Christian magistrates. No doubt his hand is forced. Petilianus's powerful case against Christian participation in coercive practices of all kinds, his assiduous use of biblical warrants[12] and philosophical argument,[13] and the facility with which he yokes the Donatist church, hunted and persecuted, to the blessed church of the martyrs,[14] compel Augustine's reply. Nevertheless, there it is, and as the years pass other justifications, other failures in good taste, follow.

Indeed, it is this reason-giving enterprise, this attempt to make sense of a practice that most of his contemporaries consider morally unproblematic, that distinguishes Augustine, not his participation in this or that persecution. Without his persistent efforts he would have been just another thoughtlessly intolerant North African bishop. Of course, our troubles with Augustine go beyond the ancient indignation with force that proceeds without the right kind of deportment. Nevertheless, I do think that more often than not our complaints begin here, with provoked offense. Augustine's efforts to defend state action against pagans and heretics do in fact lay bare the inequalities of power and authority that frequently obtain in social relations, whether in the fifth century or in our own. They expose coercion and discipline as rather ordinary means of structuring our lives and perfecting our activities. In short, they provide a raw experience of certain aspects of our social world that we would prefer not to recognize, let alone endorse.

Thus when Robert Markus insists that Augustine's account of ecclesiastical discipline is "horrible doctrine," I suspect it is the raw experience of what Markus

---

[11] "Heretics, Jews, and Heathens have made a unity against our Unity." *Sermo* 62.18.

[12] *C. litt. Petil.*II.xix.31; xv.34; xvii.38; xix.42; lxxiv.163; lxxxi.177; xciii.202.

[13] *C. litt. Petil.*II.lxxxiv.183; lxxxv.185.

[14] *C. litt. Petil.*II.xxiii.51.

considers fundamentally unjustifiable that provokes his modern indignation.[15] Indeed, I suspect that it is precisely because Augustine's efforts on behalf of coercion and constraint are so prominent and so unapologetic that modern critics—even cautious critics like Peter Brown—cannot help but conclude that here we confront an attitude that is truly "oppressive."[16] Nor is it a surprise that moral complaint leads to the conclusion that Augustine's justifications are offered cynically, as mere "debating points." Indeed, many of his critics suspect that he does not believe his own "threadbare arguments," or at the very least should not, given that his efforts to justify coercion are inconsistent with his more settled views about virtue, freedom, and the limits of political authority in the *saeculum.*[17]

In what follows, I consider some of these criticisms and complaints; in particular, two charges of inconsistency brought against Augustine in recent years and the moral criticisms that invariably accompany them. Why invariably? Because the most interesting charges of inconsistency come from Augustine's friends, from those sympathetic with his social thought. In order to safeguard their sympathies from moral taint they decry Augustine's defense of coercion and then find it inconsistent with the aspect of his thought they admire most. My suspicion is that separating wheat from chaff in Augustine's social thought is more difficult than his friendly critics imagine. My exegetical hopes are straightforward: on the one hand, to make better sense of Augustine's justifications and their place within the rest of his social thought; on the other, to say more precisely where our moral disagreements with him in fact lie. The critics howl and most of us join in chorus, and yet little effort has been made to say why Augustine's views are in fact horrible and oppressive, at least not in recent years.[18] Perhaps this is understandable. Not every moral judgment requires support from reasons. Surely our most basic judgments do not. The fact that we cannot imagine sharing Augustine's conclusions about the use of coercion against religious dissent may in fact excuse our refusal to justify our complaints. Still, my hunch is that Augustine's assessments are closer to our own than we imagine, closer than the flick-of-the-wrist response of the critics would lead us to believe. Indeed, I suspect the differences that divide us to be subtle, more accidents of history and

---

15 Robert Markus, *Saeculum: History and Society in the Theology of St. Augustine* (Cambridge: Cambridge University Press, 1970), 142.

16 Peter Brown, *Augustine of Hippo* (Berkeley: University of California Press, 1967), 239.

17 Brown, "St. Augustine's Attitude," 262.

18 Exceptions include: Robert Joly, "St. Augustin et l'intolerance religieuse," *Revue belge daphilosophie et d'histoire* 33 (1955) 263–294 and Emilien Lamirande, *Church, State, and Toleration: An Intriguing Change of Mind in Augustine* (Villanova: Villanova University Press, 1975.)

circumstance than significant departures in moral judgment about just and unjust coercion.

Augustinian Liberalism

The aspect of Augustine's social thought that Markus most admires is the secular, pluralist, and autonomous politics that he finds in Augustine's mature theology of the *saeculum*. And of course, it is this politics that Markus finds inconsistent with Augustine's defense of state sponsored coercion of religious dissent. The argument, highly compressed, goes something like this.[19]

Early in his career no such inconsistency threatened. Like most of his contemporaries Augustine welcomed the prospect of paganism's quick collapse under Theodosius's thumb (398–400 CE), and he interpreted these events prophetically. With a Christian empire established and the gospel now preached to all nations, he saw ancient prophesies fulfilled. These were "Christian times," when Rome's sacred place in sacred history was laid bare for all to see, when Roman power was used to complete Christ's saving work (29–35), and when salvation, the ultimate good, was unthinkable apart from Roman citizenship (94–97). With these assumptions in hand, Augustine had little trouble justifying Rome's efforts against pagans and heretics (36).

This naïve view did not last. As the years pass Augustine resists every attempt to give sacred significance to any slice of history after the incarnation, even the slice that includes the Christianization of the empire. Indeed, he eventually regards all extra-biblical history as homogeneously secular, precisely because the character and pattern of God's redemptive work between ascension and parousia remains unknown (10–25). As a result of this agnosticism about history Augustine resists every effort to regard any particular political regime as sacred or as profane. Both Eusebian and Donatist political theologies are refused. In their place Augustine offers a theologically neutral account of public life and political association (51–55, 122–123). Neither can be regarded as having anything to do with first things or final ends. Neither can be considered the place where our ultimate longings find fulfillment. Rather, politics is a limited enterprise, designed to remedy at least some of the conflict and disorder in human relations east of Eden. Its goals are modest: restraining human rapaciousness and securing the temporal needs of human life, all in the hope that

19 All references are to Markus, *Saeculum*, hereafter cited in the text. For an excellent summary of Markus's treatment of Augustine's political thought see his discussion of the Latin Fathers in *The Cambridge History of Medieval Political Thought*, ed. J.H. Burns (Cambridge: Cambridge University Press, 1988), 92–122.

some measure of order, some hint of peace, might come to our social interactions (94–97). Since all human beings have an interest in these less than ultimate goods, whatever their final loves might be, all have a stake in the modest order that politics secures. And yet, because politics is limited to the pursuit of penultimate goods, no human beings, no human communities, should be permitted to direct the apparatus of political authority to the service of the goods they consider ultimate.

Call this Augustinian liberalism, where desacralization is thought to imply a certain autonomy within the restricted sphere of politics and a certain plurality of final loves among those who participate in a common civic life (67–9, 100–104, 151, 173). Disestablishment is its natural consequence (134). In fact, Markus maintains that the very idea of a Christian state would have struck the mature Augustine as odd, as oxymoronic (126). So indeed should have the idea of state sponsored coercion of religious dissent, but paradoxically it did not (139). This, according to Markus, is the "unresolved tension" in Augustine's mature social thought (146) and the fundamental challenge for exegetes, who must explain how it was possible for Augustine to justify such illiberal activities when the desacralization of politics has such liberal implications. For example, they must explain how it was possible for Augustine to write his famous letter to Boniface concerning the correction of the Donatists (*Ep.*185), and just two years later (419 CE) to write an equally famous statement of the bland secularity and the theological homogeneity of extra-biblical history in his letter to Hesychius (*Ep.*199).

Confident that the inference from desacralization to something that resembles liberal politics is sound, and undeterred by a conclusion that he admits is anachronistic (151), Markus leaves this tension unresolved. Instead he argues that certain aspects of Augustine's thought disguise these troubles and thus make it possible for still other aspects—principally his understanding of pastoral discipline—to provide the warrants needed to justify coercion without regarding the state that coerces as God's chosen (133–153). Of course, there is another possibility here, indeed an obvious one. If the inference to liberal politics is in fact anachronistic, then perhaps it is false. The argument might go something like this.

When Augustine resists every effort to sacralize political life he is not providing a prescriptive account of politics, liberal or otherwise. He is not telling us what a legitimate political community looks like. He is not telling us what the limits of political authority should be. Rather, his intentions are strictly negative. God's salvific purposes do not depend upon the fate of any earthly society, and therefore the goods that can be achieved within any political association outside of the city of God cannot be regarded as ultimate. They cannot be regarded as ends in themselves, at least not simply. Rather, the goods of political life and the mechanisms of political authority are mixed goods, neither strictly final ends nor merely instrumental means. They are proximate ends that are pursued and achieved, at least in part, so that they might be put to use for the sake of achieving those ends that are in fact regarded as final. Whether this or that final end is pursued with the assistance of the mixed goods of this or that political community largely depends upon the vicissitudes of political fortune.[20] Indeed, it is *this* initial neutrality with respect to final ends, transformed as princes come and go, that is the consequence of Augustine's desacralization of politics, not nascent liberalism.

It follows that we should find it perfectly ordinary when Augustine encourages Christian magistrates to regard their efforts against the Donatists as politics transformed by the right kind of final ends. Thus, to Macedonius he writes (414):

> If . . . any administrative act of yours . . . is limited to this end and aim, that men may suffer no undue distress according to the flesh, if you think it is not incumbent on you that they should make a return for that tranquillity which you try to secure for them, that is, not to speak in riddles, that they would worship the true God in whom is all the fruition of the peaceful life, such effort on your part will bring you no return in true happiness (*Ep.*155.10; v., *Ep.*204).

Similarly, we should not be surprised when Augustine concedes that the early church did not resort to state power in order to bring sheep to its fold, and then in the next breath argues that these are different times. In many places Christians rule, and as a result we should expect them to direct the goods of political association to the service of the one true God (*Ep.*185.v.19–20; v., *C.litt.Petil.* II.xciii.202–213).

To these remarks Markus would no doubt reply that here Augustine contradicts his more settled convictions on the limits of political authority and the unavoidable pluralism of civic life that are found in book xix of the *City of God* (68–69, 97). There Markus finds Augustine confining politics to concern with temporal tranquillity and material advantage (*de civ. Dei*, xix.14–15), precisely because all human beings take interest in these goods whatever their final loves happen to be. All can put them to use, all should be allowed to do so, and thus politics—that is, the pursuit of these temporal goods—should proceed quite independent of any particular scheme of final loves.

But note, in the very same chapter of book xix to which Markus appeals in order to make his case about "the restricted sphere to which the earthly city

[20] Somewhat indignant, Augustine writes: "But how unreasonable it is not to consider that the Church, which bears fruit and grows through the whole world, may suffer persecution from kings in some nations even when she does not suffer it in others!" (*de civ. Dei*.xviii.52). See also, *C. litt. Petil.* II.xciii.204–205.

confines its concerns" (68), Augustine argues something quite different. When members of the heavenly city, sojourning on this earth, find themselves sharing the benefits of political community with those who do not worship the one true God, and when, as a result, agreement cannot be reached regarding "common laws of religion," it will come to pass that they will be "compelled in this matter to dissent, and to become a tiresome burden to those who think differently." They will avail themselves of the temporal advantages of political life and make them "bear upon the peace of heaven," which is nothing other than "the perfectly ordered and harmonious enjoyment of God and of one another in God." Of course, in its earthly pilgrimage, the heavenly city possesses this peace only by faith, and yet by this faith it lives justly in this life "when it makes the attainment of that peace the goal of every good action towards God and man" (*de civ. Dei*, xix.17).

It appears then, *pace* Markus, that even in his mature political theology Augustine resists secular limitations upon the use of the temporal goods of political association. Indeed, if there are constraints upon conduct that Augustine does in fact prescribe here, they do not refer to the use of earthly peace but rather to the kind of diversity that the heavenly city should bear on its earthly sojourn. The city of God is pluralist. It calls together pilgrims of all nations and languages, normally without abolishing their diversities. And yet, when some local belief or practice "impedes the worship of the one supreme and true God," the heavenly city must do what it can to abolish the hindrance (*de civ.Dei*, xix.17). If it happens that civil authority is at its disposal, then the heavenly city is obliged to make use of it. It follows that Augustine tempts no inconsistency when in 414 he encourages Macedonius to, "rouse the men subject to your authority and lead them to worship God, both by the example of your own devout life and by your zeal for their welfare, whether you rule them by love or by fear . . ."(*Ep*155).

We must conclude then, that the tension Markus locates in Augustine political theology is the fabrication of a false inference, while the exegetical puzzle, if there is one here at all, regards Markus's eagerness to believe that desacralizing extra-biblical history implies a liberal politics of one sort or another. Here we can only guess, and yet I suspect that his assent to the inference has something to do with the emphasis he places upon Augustine's eschatological rethinking of the two cities (122–126). The heavenly city, formally defined, is made up of those whose final love is God. For them all other ends are referred to this last end. By contrast, the earthly city is made up of those whose last end and final love is something other than God (*de civ. Dei*, xiv.28; xix.14). Membership in each city is exclusive, and yet neither will be in fact what they are by definition until Christ comes to separate wheat from chaff. Until then each is a *corpus permixtum* (*de civ. Dei*, i.35; xi.1; xviii.54), each a society that embodies fundamentally contradictory loves until the final winnowing (*de civ.Dei*, xviii.48). Still, from the vantage point of the threshing floor, wheat and chaff do indeed exclude one another, and it is this eschatological distinction between heavenly and earthly cities that I suspect Markus has in mind when he offers his sociological prescription. Because the two cities are distinct in principle and will be actually distinct at the final winnowing, it follows that they should remain largely autonomous now.

But notice this inference commits Markus to the same kind of mistake that Augustine finds the Donatists making, the kind of mistake Markus himself laments. The Donatists infer an eschatological distinction from sociological realities. Markus infers sociological distinctions from eschatological realities. Both inferences assume a necessary connection between sociological and eschatological treatments of the two cities. Both should be resisted. If sociological treatments of the two cities have no necessary eschatological significance, then why should we think that eschatological distinctions yield sociological prescriptions? In fact, contra Markus, it is the inference to autonomy in politics that Augustine would find odd, precisely because it implies that the ends of politics are in principle ultimate in their own sphere. To insist that the citizens of the heavenly city think in these terms is equivalent to asking them to refuse to refer a particular class of proximate ends to the final end of the heavenly city. It is, in effect, asking them to forego the very activity that distinguishes their citizenship.

Put another way, the inference to autonomy in politics implies that God's grace, which establishes membership in the heavenly city on its earthly sojourn, can have no concrete consequence for earthly politics. Augustine, I suggest, would have found *this* unthinkable. Indeed, there is ample evidence that he considered God's grace diminishing the autonomy of politics through the efforts of Christian magistrates. In his letter to Apringius, proconsul of Africa, he concedes that Christian rulers must restrain the violent excesses of savage men, and yet they must do so "showing forth the mildness" (*mansuetudo*) of the church, "for whose sake and as whose son" they act. Interrogations should proceed "without the use of hooks or fire." Punishments should be prudent and lenient, always displaying God's mercy, never resorting to violence against life or limb (*Ep.*134; v., *Ep.*133, 204). No doubt, politics transformed by grace remains politics. It remains concerned with the proximate ends of temporal life, it still operates with often tragic ignorance of human motivation and conduct (*de civ.Dei*, xix.6), and far too often it must resort to means of governance that elicit regret, if not remorse. Hooks and fire must be put aside, but the rod remains indispensable (*Ep.*134; v., *Ep.*133.2). Yet Augustine is convinced that without an infusion of grace these ordinary realities of political life will be put to use for the sake of ends that fall short of the good and the just (*de civ. Dei*, xix.21, 24–25). It follows that politics for Augustine is never autonomous. It abhors a vacuum. If it is not transformed by grace, then more often than not it will be transformed by vice. If the proximate ends of temporal life that politics are designed to secure do not serve the just peace of God, then they will invariably serve the perverted peace of those consumed by lust for domination and love for private gain (*de civ. Dei*, xix.12). Indeed, without the gracious transformation of politics and without obedience to "the command of God . . . (to) offer no sacrifice save to Him alone," the difference between Athens and Babylon is no difference at all (*de civ. Dei*, xix.24).

Given this possibility there is little room to wonder why Augustine encouraged Christian magistrates. Indeed, he considered them the only members of the earthly community who are able to offer hope of securing a temporal peace worthy of the name. Nor should it surprise us that he sought warrants for the use of state power against religious dissent. Indeed, by his lights, a city that does not give due worship to the one true God can neither expect justice to obtain among its citizens, nor enjoy those temporal advantages that are the fruit of just political association.

Augustinian Supernaturalism

John Milbank is sympathetic with these doubts about Markus's interpretation of Augustine's political theology (402–408).[21] He recognizes that Augustine's desacralization of politics implies the autonomy of the church, not the autonomy of the state, and he quite rightly concludes that for Augustine this means that the church reduces the scope of the political (419) insofar as it makes good use of those temporal goods and activities, those penultimate pursuits, that are too often considered the exclusive business of the city of man (406). It follows that, for Milbank, it is not Augustine's nascent liberalism that is inconsistent with state sponsored coercion of religious dissent and the eager pursuit of justifying reasons. Rather, the resort to coercive methods by the church is inconsistent with "the ontological priority of peace over conflict" that Augustine believes should be exhibited in both the church and in Christian virtue (363, 390). Or, put somewhat differently, Milbank finds coercion by the church inconsistent with the "supernaturalism" that marks every other aspect of Augustine's social thought (415). The argument, again significantly abridged, goes something like this.

Unlike Aquinas, Augustine does not distinguish the natural and the supernatural. He refuses to believe that there are activities and powers, practices and virtues common to us because of our common human nature (381). More precisely, he refuses to believe that there is a natural sphere—distorted by sin

[21] All page references in the text are to John Milbank, *Theology and Social Theory: Beyond Secular Reason* (Oxford: Blackwell, 1990).

and desperate for grace—that nevertheless instantiates genuine, if not imperfect, goods and virtues. Instead he insists that the perfections of this so-called "natural sphere" are in fact illusions. Its goods bear no real value at all. Its virtues are vices in disguise (406–409). It follows that earthly politics is not an imperfect example of the real thing, a distorted enterprise that grace might restore. It is, rather, an exercise in sin unrestrained, in self-love and self-assertion, in arbitrary violence and lust for domination (390). By the same token, its peace is nothing but a temporary cessation of war (392), its virtue, nothing but a hero's victory over rivals, a vice cloaked in garlands (410).

By Milbank's lights, *this* is the admirable aspect of Augustine's thought: the refusal to regard the ordinary features of our social world as anything but the shadowy products of human sinfulness, the insistence that value cannot be found in a world destined to pass away as God's kingdom comes (400–1). It is the peaceableness of that Kingdom, of the realized city of God at heavenly rest, that is the standard of criticism here. In that city there will be real peace—not the peace found in the balance of competing interests, not the peace achieved by the violent dominion of one over another, not the peace forged in conflict—but the peace of harmonious agreement and common love that Adam once knew and that the angels and saints will one day enjoy (390–2). In that same city there will be real virtue, real justice—not the virtue of sin resisted and passion restrained (363, 391), not the justice that adjudicates conflicts over punishment, ownership, and equitable exchange (406)—but virtue that stands apart from all psychic struggle, all need for self-control (363), and justice that crafts consensus without agonistic conflict (390), without "chaotic remainder" that must be disciplined or suppressed (410), indeed without "tragic profundity" (422). Milbank thinks that worldly prescriptions follow from this supernatural moral criticism, that the ontology of peace generates obligations for the heavenly city on its earthly sojourn. On the one hand, the city of God in exile should act as the earthly city does not: forgiving sinners, caring for the defeated, refusing vengeance, and remembering the victims of this world. On the other hand, it should, more often than not, refuse to act as the earthly city does. In particular, it should resist every temptation to compromise with earthly accounts of virtue and peace, accounts that are, quite literally, unimaginable apart from a secret foundation of violence and conflict (393).

It is here that Milbank thinks we can see Augustine's mistake most clearly. In his willingness to use force against religious dissent and to justify coercion, Augustine ignores the moral consequences of his own ontology. When he recommends peace pursued through the subordination of rivals and justice secured in a context of conflict, he foregoes his uniform supernaturalism and finds real value in the peace and justice of this world. Similarly, when he imagines God willing discipline and punishment for the sake of the good, he gives worldly violence real presence among the saints and angels in the heavenly city (417–418). All of these steps, according to Milbank, are missteps. All are inconsistent with the moral prescriptions that follow from the ontological priority of peace. All are at odds with Augustine's refusal to find value of any measure in the moral practices that are ordinary features of our earthly sojourn and yet unimaginable in that other city.

Confident that his exegetical conclusions are sound, Milbank does little to diffuse this tension in Augustine's social thought. Instead he scolds. Augustine should not have compromised the ontological priority of peace. He should not have back-slided into the thoroughly un-Augustinian distinction between the natural and the supernatural (419–421). If, despite all that, it is agreed that force must be used in this life to curb sin and protect the innocent, then at the very least Augustine should have insisted that the heavenly city on its earthly sojourn make this last resort remorsefully. He should have made it plain that a real obligation is transgressed in this tragic necessity (422). He should have, in other words, recognized the problematic character of his own efforts (406).

As before, there is another possibility here. Perhaps Milbank's exegetical conclusions are misleading. Perhaps the inconsistency he finds in Augustine's social thought is in fact more apparent than real. The argument might go something like this.

If the heavenly standards of peace and virtue in fact oblige the city of God in exile, then the resort to coercion is not the only earthly activity that falls short. Other moral practices will as well, even practices that distinguish the church, and yet it is unlikely that the church can forego them simply because they are unimaginable among the saints and angels. Consider the marks of the church according to Milbank. It should be an asylum, a house of refuge, where forgiveness and restitution are pursued (422), where burdens are shared (397), where truly just economic exchanges occur (422), where sin is met with reconciliation, not offense, and where atonement is progressively realized (411). Surely there is little to complain with here. Yet these are neither the moral practices nor the virtues that will be found in the city of God at heavenly rest, if only because the citizens of that city will not lead a kind of life that we could recognize as our own. In that city there will be no refugees to comfort, no harms to forgive, no property to restore, no sins to transform with reconciliation, no exchanges to make right. Indeed, in that city there will be no scope for virtue at all, at least not the kind of virtue that we could recognize and admire.

Of course, Milbank realizes that habits, however described, become recognizable as virtues only in certain contexts and only among creatures of one kind or another (411). He knows that the virtues of one sort of life may well be strange, indeed, unimaginable or undesirable in another. The point is an ancient one and has received many useful treatments: in Plato's *Statesman* (268d–274e), in Aquinas's discussion of virtue in Eden and among the blessed in heaven (ST I.95.1–3; I–II.67.1–6), and in Hume's account of the utility of justice (*Enquiry*

145–153). Milbank does not appear to take it seriously enough, despite the fact that his explicit intent is to show the strangeness of supernatural virtue (381). If resort to coercion by the church must be refused precisely because the conditions that make it imaginable in this life are absent in the house of the blessed, then the forgiveness and refuge the church offers in this life must also be refused, for they are equally unimaginable in that heavenly form of life. If discipline within the church gives ontological purchase to a world that stands apart from the heavenly city, if its necessity compels recognition of the *saeculum*, then so too does restitution, so too does justice. If the church in exile is obliged to avoid this ontological *faux pas* by refusing all but supernatural virtue, all but heavenly moral practices, then it must also forgo most of those habits and practices that distinguish it.

If this conclusion seems preposterous, then perhaps we should refuse to believe that Augustine's attitude toward our life in the *saeculum* is as unambiguous as Milbank contends. Perhaps, contra Milbank, Augustine does indeed assume something like the distinction between the natural and the supernatural, if only provisionally.[22] Better still, in language more appropriate to Augustine, perhaps he does assume a significant distinction between the temporal life of God's city in exile and the eternal life of the blessed. And although Milbank is surely correct to argue that Augustine uses his account of virtue and peace in the heavenly city to muster critical leverage against the virtue and peace we manage to secure in this world, perhaps he is mistaken to believe that Augustinian social criticism concludes in an obligation to act with the saints and angels and in unambiguous remorse over failure to do so.

Consider Augustine's remarks that conclude chapter 19 of the City of God, where he speaks of that *perfecta tranquillitas i hac temporali vita non potest adprehendi* (*de civ. Dei*, xix.27). With the supernatural perspective providing the point of contrast, he insists that temporal peace is more solace to misery than a positive enjoyment of blessedness and temporal justice more a matter of the

[22] Perhaps there is another possibility, one that Milbank does not consider but could have. Perhaps Augustinian supernaturalism concludes in the rejection of the incompatible not the unimaginable. Perhaps human justice and earthly compassion are unimaginable in the heavenly city, but neither are incompatible with its reign of charity. Coercion is. However, this suggestion implies that Augustine considers acts of coercion incompatible with charity *simpliciter*, like theft or murder, and there is no evidence that he does. If the reply is that he should have given his supernatural assumptions about the character of blessed life, then we will want to know how those assumptions and that life generate this conclusion. This returns us to the problem, at least as Milbank's exegesis frames it. For how can we get from, "there will be no coercion there" to "there should be none here" without sacrificing either consistency or many of the virtues and actions we cannot imagine doing without? In fact, he appears to treat just coercion like compassion: the blessed find no place for it in their lives while conceding its place in ours.

remission of sin and struggle against vice than the perfection of virtue. Nevertheless, the conclusion he draws at the close of critique is not that the citizens of God's city in exile are obliged to meet heavenly standards of virtue, for in fact temporal righteousness is the best that they can manage. Nor does he suggest that they should feel remorse for failing to measure up to a kind of virtue that they can only glimpse in the deficiencies of their own. Indeed, the consequence of his criticism is not prescription, at least not principally. It is, rather, a collection of sentiments and practices shaped by the theological virtues, a mixture of discontent and longing tempered by patience and hope; discontent with even the greatest virtue and the surest peace and longing for a different kind of life altogether, a life they can only faintly imagine, where virtue exists apart from "dangers, toils, and woes" (*de civ. Dei*, xix.4) and where peace is not "the solace of our misery" but rather "the positive enjoyment of felicity" (*de civ. Dei*, xix,27). Add to this an ambiguous sentiment that accompanies their longing, a feeling that stands somewhere between regret and remorse over their inability to meet the standards of that strange virtue in that different life.

Bernard Williams calls this odd sentiment agent-regret, and it seems to capture the curious yearning that Augustinian social criticism seeks to elicit.[23] Remorse, of course, is the proper response to one's own wrong-doing. Regret, by contrast, need not be preceded by moral failure. Something undesirable happens, perhaps quite by accident, and one simply regrets its occurrence. But how should the citizens of the city of God in exile feel when they inevitably fail to live up to a standard of justice embedded in a heavenly form of life? Should they feel remorse for failing to act as the saints and angels do in a life that they cannot imagine themselves inhabiting, a life without property or want, illness or death, disobedient passion or disordered social arrangements? Indeed, how could they? And yet Augustine insists that by faith they know that they are made for this strange life, this other virtue, and thus regret alone is an equally insufficient response. Something that stands between these two sentiments is needed—something that recognizes that the moral standard missed cannot be reached in a human form of life, and yet something that encourages even those who consistently meet ordinary standards to cry with the rest of the city of God in its pilgrim state, "Forgive us our debts as we forgive our debtors" (*de civ. Dei*, xix.27). The virtuous in exile must not only regret that earthly virtue is indispensable for human flourishing, they must also feel some responsibility for the kind of life that needs virtue of this kind.

---

[23] Bernard Williams, "Moral Luck," in *Moral Luck*, (Cambridge: Cambridge University Press, 1981), 20–39.

It follows that just coercion within the church—if there could be such a thing—would elicit this kind of response; not remorse over failure to measure up to a supernatural moral standard, but agent-regret over the necessity of acting justly in a sinful world. Moreover, we can now see that it is a mistake to conclude, as Milbank and others do, that Augustine's defense of coercion assumes a lamentable kind of political consequentialism.[24] For indeed it is one thing to say that earthly standards of justice can be sacrificed for the sake of some other good, whether other-worldly or not, quite another thing to concede that the citizens of the city of God in exile cannot measure up to the moral life of the blessed, which of course does not include anything like earthly justice. Thus if we assume that Augustine believes that just coercion is in fact possible, then we have no reason to conclude that his justifications amount to nothing more than consequentialist calculations. Rather, we find Augustine insisting that justice sets a standard that cannot be transgressed, at least not when it comes to the use of force against religious dissent. At the same time we find him conceding that the justice we know in this sinful world is a wretched business, an awful necessity. With God's gracious assistance we pursue it as best we can, while at the same time admitting that success brings misery (*de civ. Dei.*,xix.6) and that the just, more than the rest, long to flee to a life where temporal justice has no place (*Ep.*95.4).

Of course, it is not exactly clear what it means to long for a form of life significantly different from our own. As Wittgenstein put it in his doubts about the *Tractatus*, the limits of our life and world cannot be mapped without assuming that we can stand outside of each, and it is not exactly clear what this entails.[25] Nevertheless, Augustine assumes that with the assistance of faith supernatural moral criticism can in fact generate hope for a kind of virtue and a kind of peace unimaginable in our own life, with its own standards, its own demands.

Justifications: Augustine's and Our Own

If these exegetical judgments are sound, then we cannot conclude with Milbank that Augustine's efforts to justify coercion are inconsistent with the

---

[24] Milbank, *Theology and Social Theory*, 419; Rist, *Augustine*, 193–199, 254–255

[25] Ludwig Wittgenstein, *Philosophical Investigations*, trans. G.E.M. Anscombe (New York: Macmillan, 1953), 97-98. In defense of the younger Wittgenstein against the older we can point out that he does admit that knowledge of the world as a limited whole is not exactly ordinary knowledge. It is mystical knowledge. It is contemplation of the world *sub specie aeterni* (v. *Tractatus Logico-Philosophicus*, trans. C.K. Ogden (London: Routledge & Kegan Paul, 1983), 6.45; cf., 5.61).

most obvious moral consequences of his social criticism. Rather, we must conclude that if there is to be room for forgiveness in the church, then there may well be room for coercion. Both are earthly moral practices. Both will be absent in the heavenly city, and yet surely a community that fails to forgive cannot be the church. Of course, about coercion we cannot be so certain. Before *it* can be included among the moral practices of the church we shall have to see how the arguments go, and as I have already noted, most recent critics and exegetes are confident that they don't go very far.

Nevertheless, it is not at all clear that their confidence is warranted, at least not without remainder. Their most common complaint is that Augustine's justifications cannot succeed because the resort to coercion in this matter, or in any other, threatens human freedom. The conclusion is thought to be so obvious, and the value of freedom so great, that little else is said or considered. This is unfortunate, in part because Augustine's most thoughtful efforts—in the second reply to Petilianus and in the letters to Boniface (*Ep.*185) and Donatus (*Ep.*173)—are designed to respond to precisely this worry, and in part because (as I mentioned at the start) it appears that the moral sentiments about coercion that Augustine draws upon as he makes his case are closer to our own than the critics allow. Consider the following.

Augustine concedes that coercion constrains *liberum arbitrium*, the freedom to believe this or that, or to choose this or that course of action (*Ep.*173.2; *Ep.*185.vi.22; vi. 22). He also insists that in certain instances coercion's yield is "a somewhat freer sense of liberty" (*Ep.*185. iv.17). Here he has in mind what we would no doubt call positive freedom; the liberty (*libertas*) to participate in this or that activity and secure the goods that accompany participation (*Ep.*173.3–4). Nevertheless, because he believes that negative liberty is a genuine good he refuses to conclude that every negative liberty lost can be justified by this or that positive liberty gained. Instead he assumes a rough collection of criteria that must be met for coercion to proceed justly and for negative liberty to be sacrificed for the sake of positive. There are, I believe, at least three such criteria that can be distilled from his remarks.

First, coercion must be confined to certain role specific relationships (*Ep.*185.ii.7). This seems perfectly ordinary. Parents can constrain a son or daughter and an attending physician can discipline an intern precisely because of the roles that each party inhabits. Apart from these roles coercion would be inappropriate. Indeed, constraining my neighbor's children as I do my own would no doubt bring censure, not only because I have assumed authority that I do not have but also because negative liberty—something truly valuable—has been threatened by my arbitrary force.

Second, coercion must track the truth, its methods must be deployed for the sake of genuine human goods (*Ep.*185.ii.9–11; *C. litt. Petil.* xix.42–43; *Ep.*93.vi.20). For the most part, Augustine has in mind goods that accrue through participation in human activities that are in fact worth caring about, activities that offer their initiates some real chance at human flourishing. Again, this seems perfectly ordinary. It is this that distinguishes baseball, ballet, and brick-laying from, say, thieving. And it is this that explains why we can admire the tough and wise hitting coach while at the same time despising those parents who initiate their children, by force or persuasion, into the intricacies of crimes and cons. Put another way, our hope is that coercion and constraint come to an end in love for the activity, in choice that follows redirected desire. Of course, belief and desire cannot be compelled (*C.litt. Petil.* II.184), but Augustine is convinced that habits of knowledge and affection can be challenged, that the mind can be coerced to earnest study of the truth (*Ep.*93.1, 16). Once the truth is known the will's consent can follow, and when it does the action that was once resisted can be freely chosen. Indeed, Augustine maintains that it is this hope and this choice that make the loss of negative freedom bearable (*C. litt. Petil.* II.186). Nevertheless, this hope turns false if the activity turns out to be less than truly lovable (*Ep.*185.ii.8–9, 11). Again, this is what distinguishes thieving from baseball. One may come to love thieving, but insofar as it is an activity that falls short of the good, it is not truly lovable. The coercion and constraint that bring one to love it are therefore unjustified, just as the negative freedom lost along the way is never recouped in the freedom to act for the sake of the good. By contrast, the external pressures that are needed in order to hit a curve ball well and to love baseball as it should be loved can be harmless, even praiseworthy, precisely because their yield is voluntary participation in an activity that instantiates genuine human goods.

Lastly, coercion must be tempered with charity, with care for the coerced, and with worry about the negative freedom lost (*Ep.*185.i.2; ii.7, 11;). The goods achieved must in fact benefit the coerced. The activity must be one that they can come to love. Thus, the hitting coach must not love baseball so much that he fails to love those he is trying to initiate into the craft. Nor must he regard those in his care as mere means to some other end, at least not simply. Rather, his principal desire must be their good. His intention must be to better their lot by bringing them to secure the goods of a truly lovable activity, goods that would escape them without his aid. Those who—by habit or nature—cannot have their lot bettered in this way should not be coerced, at least not to secure the goods of this activity.

Now imagine that you regard citizenship in the city of God on its earthly sojourn as a truly lovable activity of just this kind. Imagine further, that you consider human beings disposed by Adam's sin to flee from difficult and desirable activities, and from the goods that participation yields. Finally, imagine you observe that failure to flee rarely results in participation precisely because our habitual delight in false goods too often prevents us from disciplining ourselves as we know we should (*Conf.* vi.22; *Ep.*93.i.3; *Ep.*185.vii.29).

Given these assumptions, you may well be favorably disposed to make use of coercion for the sake of the good. Like a parent or a surgeon (*Ep*.93.i.1; *C. litt. Petil.* III.iv.5), you may well consider external constraint of the will useful, perhaps even indispensable, for securing the good of another. You may well come to believe that many will refuse participation in that most lovable of activities—fellowship in the heavenly city—without fraternal correction of one kind or another. Indeed, you may well regard coercion as a kind of pastoral strategy.

Of course, it is hardly news that Augustine regards coercion as pastoral, but it *is* novel to note that his sentiments about just and unjust coercion are pretty much our own. And it *is* worth pointing out that the bulk of Augustine's remarks are designed to show that the acts of coercion he endorses are justified precisely because they satisfy these sentiments. So for example, he struggles to display Donatist confusions in ecclesiology (*Ep*.185.v.19–20; *C. litt. Petil.* II.xiv.33; xv.35), in sacramental theology (*C. litt. Petil.*III. passim; *C. litt. Petil.* II.xviii.41; xxx.69), in eschatology (*C. litt. Petil.* II.xxvi.6; xlvi.108; *Ep*.108), in morals (*C. litt. Petil.* II.lxxix.174), and in Christology (*Ep*.185.vi..22–24; *Ep*.93.ii.5), precisely because he knows that coercion used on behalf of falsehood is nothing but unjust persecution (*Ep*.185.ii.8–11; *Ep*.93.ii.6; *C. litt. Petil.* II.xciii.212; civ.237). It is for this reason that he repeatedly insists that the whole question of just and unjust coercion comes down to the distinction between truth and falsehood (*C. litt. Petil.* II.xix. 43; *Ep*.87.1, 7; *Ep*.93.ii.8; v.16). This no doubt overstates the point. And yet, once we realize that coercion deployed in order to secure participation in a false practice cannot possibly be just, we can no longer conclude that Augustine's anxious efforts to pointout Donatist confusions are the clever moves of a cynical debater. Quite the contrary, they are signs of his moral seriousness.

Similarly, Augustine insists repeatedly that coercing *certain kinds* of heretics is in fact a role specific duty of Christian magistrates.[26] The argument comes in two steps. First, just as parents are obliged to direct the conduct of their children, often by force and fear, so too magistrates are obliged to direct the conduct of their citizens, frequently with fatherly diligence (*Ep*.133). This is what law does beyond Eden's gardens: it coerces, and thus by definition law-makers have a paternal relationship with their citizens, a relationship that would no doubt be unjust apart from these established roles (*Ep*.185.v.20). Second, insofar as coercion is the ordinary enterprise of magistrates, their role specific right and obligation, there is, according to Augustine, little reason to complain when

[26] Only schismatics. Sinners and heretics already in the church can either be tolerated with love or disciplined with gentleness (*C. litt. Petil.* III.iv.5).

Christian magistrates use their coercive powers in God's service. Indeed, by his lights, when Christians rule with the assistance of God's grace we should be relieved that state power is put to use for the sake of the good. For, of course, it is only the good that can justify the coercion that magistrates everywhere bring to bear upon citizens (*Ep.*185.v.19).

Finally, Augustine contends that at least some acts of coercion may be acts of love. Surely when the proximate end intended is the correction of dangerously false beliefs (*Ep.*173.1) and the restraint of gravely disordered conduct (*Ep.*87.8), when the final end is fellowship with God and the blessed in the heavenly city, and when external pressures are applied in the hope that with God's assistance the coerced will turn toward these ends, recognize their goodness, and choose them because they are known to be good (*C. litt. Petil.* II.lxxxv.186)—surely when these conditions obtain, even coercion can be love (*C. litt. Petil.* II.lxix.154; Ep.93.ii.4). Indeed, Augustine insists, and I suspect we would agree, that failure to compel another to the good can be negligent, even cruel (*Ep.*173.2). By the same token, coercing those who cannot or should not be brought to participate in this or that activity can be a grave departure from charity. Only those who can know and love the good should be encouraged to do so. Thus Augustine contends that schismatics are to be compelled to return (*Ep.*93.5), while pagans are to be merely restrained from practicing their impiety (*Ep.*93.10).

Conclusion

If Augustine's moral sentiments about just and unjust coercion are neither inconsistent with the rest of his social thought, nor fundamentally different from our own, and if, as a result, we must think twice before finding his justifications perverse, then where do we dissent? Here I use the "we" of invitation cautiously, for some of us might not, and those that do will surely dissent for different reasons. Still, most of us do dissent, and most, I suspect, because of a number of features on the moral landscape that have accompanied the emergence of liberal societies. The features I have in mind are familiar, and obvious: suspicion of explicit and substantial ecclesiastical and political paternalism, resistance to most attempts to sacrifice negative freedom for the sake of positive, inability to fear alienation from the good more than physical cruelty,[27] preference for

[27] Augustine. quite plainly, does not. To Petilianus he writes: "You would be acting less cruelly in piercing the bodies of the prophets with a sword, than in endeavoring to destroy the words of the prophets with your tongue (*C. litt. Petil.* II.xiv.33; cf., II.lxvii.150 and *C. litt. Petil.* III.xxx.35).

sincerity over truth, unwillingness to believe that theological differences matter, and so on.

Not all of us find these features welcome or unavoidable. Foes of liberalism's moral consequences abound. Nevertheless, it is worth noting that the moral landscape of liberal society, like its more literal counter parts, is largely the product of chance and circumstance, its features the consequence of history's twists and turns in the modern period. It follows that even those who are content with these features and confident about their dissents must concede that their differences with Augustine are more accidents of history and circumstance than inferences from fundamentally different moral principles.[28]

[28] I would like to thank Scott Davis, Russell Hittinger, Travis Kroeker, John Kelsay, Charles Mathewes, Sumner Twiss, and the anonymous reviewers from *The Annual* for their helpful comments on earlier drafts of this essay. The usual disclaimers apply.

[21]

ST. AUGUSTINE'S ATTITUDE TO RELIGIOUS COERCION

By P. R. L. BROWN *

Augustine had to face the issue of religious coercion throughout his episcopate, and especially in his dealings with the Donatist schism. As far as I know, he is the only writer in the Early Church to discuss the subject at length. He even changed his mind on the issue, and he has told us of this ' conversion ' with characteristic disarming frankness. It is a change which cannot fail to interest us, for whom the problem remains acutely relevant. He went on to justify religious coercion with a thoroughness and coherence which is quite as much part of his character as is his candour : and so Augustine has appeared to generations of religious liberals as ' le prince et patriarche des persécuteurs ' [1]

Augustine's attitude to coercion is typical of the general quality of his thought. This thought never appears as a ' doctrine ' in a state of rest : it is marked by a painful and protracted attempt to embrace and resolve tensions. As a result of this quality, Augustine's thought on coercion, like many of his other opinions, has been regarded, throughout the centuries, with profound ambivalence. The historian who wishes to understand Augustine's evolution on this issue must resign himself, as best he can, to living with this ambivalence. It will not help his understanding if he cuts the Gordian knot. He cannot simply erect Augustine's ' attitude ' into a ' doctrine '—a fleshless abstraction that may be demolished, modified or justified (as has been done since the Reformation).[2] Nor can he avoid this ambivalence by following the more recent historical fashion, by dismissing Augustine's attitude as a mere *ex post facto* rationalization of inevitable circumstances: as the expression of an ' age of intolerance ',[3] or as the natural reaction of a Roman bishop to movements which, it is said, had threatened to disrupt the social order with which he was identified.[4]

For this reason, I should like to abandon the word ' doctrine ' and substitute the word ' attitude '. We may make some progress in understanding Augustine's ideas if we treat them as an ' attitude '—that is, as placed a little lower than the angels of pure Augustinian theology, and a little higher than the beasts of the social and political necessities of the North African provinces.

In the later Roman Empire, religious coercion, in some form, was one of the ' facts of life ' for a provincial bishop. Even if contemporaries did not wish to deplore or justify what was going on around them, they had to take up some attitude towards it : and this attitude would, at least, allow them to impose shape and meaning on the ' blooming, buzzing confusion ' of the events in which they were so deeply implicated. The ecclesiastical sources of the Latin Empire contain many fragments of just such attitudes to the problem of coercion. One need expect very little from these in terms of intellectual content : attitudes are moulded less by abstract thought than by the unconscious and unreflective selection of certain prejudices. But it is possible to trace in them the rudiments of what—to adapt, and limit, the excellent term of Lucien Febvre [5]—we might call an ' outillage moral ', a ' moral equipment '. Each writer has a slightly different ' outillage moral '. He draws upon a wide, yet distinctive, field of thought and experience : and we can see how it is the nature and

* This paper was given at the Fourth International Congress on Patristic Studies, in September, 1963. I owe a particular debt to the challenging treatments of W. H. C. Frend, *The Donatist Church* (Oxford 1952) and R. Joly, ' S. Augustin et l'intolérance religieuse,' *Rev. belge de philol. et d'histoire* XXXIII (1955), 263–94 ; and to the helpful remarks of Dr. Frend and le R. P. M. F. Berrouard, O.P. at the time of the Congress.

[1] E. Lamirande, ' Un siècle et demi d'études sur l'ecclésiologie de S. Augustin : Essai bibliographique,' *Rev. des études aug.* VIII (1962), 1–124, contains extensive references to the literature on this subject. All references accompanied simply by volume number and page are from the *Corpus Scriptorum Ecclesiae Latinorum* of Vienna.

[2] v. J. Lecler, *Histoire de la Tolérance au siècle de la Réforme* vols. I, II (1955) (transl. Weston, *Toleration and the Reformation*, 1960). P. Bayle, *Commentaire philosophique* . . . (revised ed. Amsterdam, 1713), remains the classic demolition of Augustine's arguments.

[3] v. references and criticisms in Joly, art. cit. (note *), 263–6.

[4] For reserves on such an interpretation of the problem of coercion in the Later Empire v. P. R. L. Brown, ' Religious Coercion in the Later Roman Empire : the case of North Africa,' *History* XLVIII (1963), 283–306. The best exponents of this view, Frend, o.c. (note *), 227–43, and J.-P. Brisson, *Autonomisme et christianisme dans l'Afrique romaine* (1958) 269–88, contain shrewd judgements on Augustine's final attitude to coercion, but pay insufficient attention to its sources and evolution.

[5] L. Febvre, *Le problème de l'incroyance au XVIe siècle* : *La religion de Rabelais* (Évolution de l'Humanité, 1942), 157.

source of his ' outillage ' that moulds his attitude. We can appreciate that he is arguing under different stars from Augustine, that he reflects a different climate of opinion, and, in certain cases, that his assumptions would lead him to very different conclusions from those of the Bishop of Hippo. Thus, when Bishop Porphyry of Gaza is confronted, in 402, with a situation similar to that which will confront Augustine after the suppression of the Donatist church in 405—that is, with a whole new congregation converted by coercive measures—he will turn instinctively to a different world of experience from that of Augustine. He can justify his reception of such men by appealing to the fact that there are sorts of virtues that come from circumstances—that is, περιστατικαὶ ἀρεταί.[6] This term takes us into what is distinctive in Porphyry's world, and unknown in Augustine's : the problem of monks who had been forced to flee the world, not through religious impulse, but merely by the force of overwhelming circumstances. Such a monk was Macarius, the Murderer, who had originally become a hermit because he had committed a murder and, so, had been forced to flee to the desert. Palladius had told this story in his ' Lausiac History ' to show that there could be such things as περιστατικαὶ ἀρεταί ; [7] and for Porphyry and the readers of his biography, such a little anecdote of the devious ways of human beings in the Egyptian desert, would provide a reassuring analogy to grapple with the more sinister problems of religious coercion.

So, when we study Augustine, we must go behind the somewhat threadbare arguments contained in his justification of the coercion of the Donatists, and attempt to reconstruct, on a deeper level, the sources and shape of his own, distinctive, ' outillage moral '. This can be a rash undertaking. It must involve speculating about the possible relation of different planes of thought and experience ; and it is in danger of appearing, perhaps, too sophisticated an instrument of research when applied to the blunt and unambiguous language of Augustine's pamphlets against the Donatists. But, just as the modern psychologist can perceive significant patterns and relations in the apparently unrelated and somewhat trite remarks of a patient, so the historian must use refined tools to seize the full implication of Augustine's explicit statements ; and so we may use these pamphlets as a door into the moral climate of this crucial age, which saw the final establishment of Christianity as the official religion of the Roman Empire.

Another danger to be avoided, at all costs, is the temptation to impose an academic consistency on Augustine, a man of mysterious discontinuities, wielding authority in a complex and violent situation. But it is one thing to see a man's thought as a whole ; and quite another to attempt to make it seem consistent. The historian must risk a task of integration if he is to understand any attitude, and especially an attitude to a subject such as this. For example : when Augustine wrote his *Retractationes*, he modified a quite innocuous remark in his *De Vera Religione*, in which he had said of Christ that : ' He did nothing by force, but all things by persuading and admonishing '. He felt obliged to add another dimension : he now adds that Christ had driven the money-changers from the Temple, and that demons are exorcised by the ' force of his power '.[8] A remark such as this shows the extent to which issues of constraint and, even, of violence, that are usually extrapolated in isolation as a ' doctrine ' of religious coercion, principally directed against the Donatists, had continued, throughout his life, to exercise Augustine on very many levels.

It has become usual to isolate Augustine's attitude to coercion by treating it purely in terms of his ' conversion ' to such a policy—a conversion which, it is sometimes said, was largely forced upon him by the violence of the Donatists. It is said that, until 405, Augustine had expressed purely ' liberal ' principles, by advocating a solution of the schism through free discussion ; that he was disillusioned by the unwillingness of the Donatists to listen to reason ; and that the unexpected success of the severe Imperial ' Edict of Unity ' of 405, had caused him to change his mind.[9] This interpretation is insufficient for many reasons.

[6] Marc le Diacre, *Vie de Porphyre*, c. 73, ed. Grégoire-Kugener (Association G. Budé, 1930), 57–9.
[7] Palladius. *Historia Lausiaca*, c. xv.
[8] *De Vera Religione* xvi, 31 ; *Retract* i, 12, 6.
[9] A well-known summary of this view is G. O. Willis, *St. Augustine and the Donatist Controversy* (1950), 127–35, which seems to be accepted in A. H. M. Jones, *The Later Roman Empire* (1964) ii, 935. For the wider aspects of the problem (the supposed anti-social nature of the Donatist movement, v. n. 4 above). Two points should be noted. First, that the violence of the Donatists, alone, cannot explain Augustine's change of attitude. The Rogatist sect had no record of violence, yet Augustine would not exempt them from the laws against heretics : *Ep.* 93, iii, 11 (34, 2, p. 455) : ' sed nulla bestia, si

It throws no light on the nature and sources of Augustine's attitude. In the hands of less differentiated exponents, this aspect of Augustine's life is reduced to a trite catena of citations, designed to show the essential reasonableness of Augustine's views on the repression of religious error.[10] Above all, such an interpretation claims to be able to impose a simple and schematic explanation on this notoriously complex man. We may be dealing less with a *volte-face* provoked by external circumstances, than with a phenomenon common to many aspects of the thought of Augustine—that is, with a sudden precipitation, under external pressures, of ideas which, previously, had evolved slowly and imperceptibly over a long time.[11]

I doubt whether the essentially diplomatic letters which Augustine addressed to neighbouring Donatist bishops, and local notables, between 392 and 402, can bear the interpretation usually put upon them.[12] In his early years in Hippo, Augustine was confronted with a situation similar to a Cold War. He wished to take the initiative in this situation without incurring the odium of appearing as an aggressor. So his early letters to individual Donatist bishops are marked by all the ponderous courtesy of Great Powers in a Cold War. They follow a fixed form : Augustine waits until provoked by some incident committed against his own flock ; setting this grievance aside, he offers to meet the bishop responsible in a pacific conference ; and he goes on to imply that, if his offer is refused, he will feel justified in letting the world know of his side of the case. In such small negotiations, explosive issues would, inevitably, be shelved ; and, for the Donatists, the most explosive issue of all had been the use of force by the Catholics. Such attempts at local conferences plainly suited Augustine's temperament, as well as his circumstances. He had been intimately involved with the Manichees, and the Manichees seem to have used the public religious debate as a usual means of propagating their ideas [13] (a fact which would have made Augustine's application of such tactics to the Donatists seem, perhaps, more revolutionary than we now appreciate). But such letters cannot be expected to exhaust Augustine's attitude to coercion. Indeed, if we are to see this attitude forming rapidly, we should look outside the immediate problem of the Donatist schism altogether.

The historian of the Later Roman church is in constant danger of taking the end of paganism for granted. Yet the fate of paganism filled the imagination of the Christian congregations ; and the place of a bishop in Roman society, indeed, the whole sense of direction of his church, was intimately linked with the fortunes of his traditional enemies—the pagan gods.

The period between 399 and 401 marks one of the climaxes of the official suppression of paganism in Africa. In 399, a special mission had arrived in Carthage to close temples.[14] Religious riots, leading to at least sixty deaths, may have broken out in the same year.[15] By 401, the Catholic Council of Carthage, in one of its busiest sessions, had sent a legation to appeal for yet more legislation against the ' remnants of idolatry '.[16] It is hardly surprising, therefore, that Augustine may have first taken up a firm stand on the issue of coercion, not in the local politics of Hippo, but in his visits to Carthage in these exciting years.

Indeed, if it is possible to date Augustine's sermons, especially his sermons 24 and 62,

neminem vulneret, propterea mansueta dicitur.' Second, that Augustine's statements cannot be treated as being all of equal value, or as reflecting a single viewpoint. Thus, in his later works, the violence of the Donatists comes to predominate, to the exclusion of other elements : *Contra Julianum* III, 5 (421) : *Retractationes* II, 5 (426/7) ; *C. Julianum op. imperf.* I, 10 (420/30), and Possidius, *Vita Augustini* cc. IX and X. This later perspective unduly simplifies the more differentiated account in *Ep.* 93 of 408 (34, 2, 445 f.).

[10] Most recently : H. Jans, ' De Verantwoording van geloofsdwang tegenover Ketters volgens Augustinus' correspondentie,' *Bijdragen* XXII, 2 (1961), 133–63.

[11] e.g. the evolution of the central ideas of the ' *City of God* ' : v. J.-C. Guy, *Unité et structure logique de la ' Cité de Dieu '* (1961), 5–10.

[12] These are : *Epp.* 23 (34, 2, 63 sq.)—Maximin bishop of Sinitum : 33 (34, 2, 18 f.)—Proculeianus bishop of Hippo ; 34 and 35 (34, 2, 23 f.)—on the same subject : 43 and 44 (34, 2, 85 f.)—debate with Fortunius bishop of Tubursicubure : 49 (34, 2, 140 f.)—bishop Honoratus : 51 (32, 2, 144 f.) and 66 (34, 2, 235 f.)—Crispinus of Calama.

[13] v. Andreas-Henning, ' Mitteliranische Manichaica,' M. 2. *S.P.A.W. Phil.-Hist. Kl.* VII (1933), 301 (Mission of Addas) : Philostorgius III, 15, ed. Bides, 461 (Challenge to debate by Apthonius to Aetius of Antioch) ; Marc le Diacre, *Vie de Porphyre* c. 85 f., ed. cit. (n. 6), 66 f. (debate of Julia with Porphyry); *Contra Fortunatum* and *Contra Felicem* (25, 81 f. and 801 f.)—debates with Augustine in Hippo ; *De Duabus Animabus* IX, 16 (25, 65)—Augustine's debates as a Manichee.

[14] *De Civ. Dei.* XVIII, 54.

[15] *Ep.* 50 (34, 2, 143).

[16] *Conc. Carth.* V can. 15.

to the years 399 to 401,[17] we can see in them nothing less than a dress-rehearsal of his justification of the coercion of the Donatists after 405. In one sermon of great charm, he had even defended the politic conformity of one leading pagan by referring to the forcible conversion of St. Paul—Paul also, had been converted *ex necessitate*, by being knocked down and blinded on the road to Damascus.[18] This scene of divine violence had begun to exercise Augustine: [19] he would later use it extensively in his writings after 405, both *ad hominem* [20] and applied to the Donatists in general.[21] Thus, in Augustine's first public work against the Donatists—the *Contra Epistolam Parmeniani*, which appeared in late 400—half of his attitude to coercion is already fully formed. The Christian Roman Emperors have an unquestioned right of *cohercitio*, in the strict legal sense, to punish, restrain and repress, those impious cults over which God's providence had given them dominion.[22] This is a deliberately provocative work, written 'pour épater les bourgeois'. In it the storm-cloud of the Imperial severity may still be distant; but its outline, in principle, is quite distinct.

What had enabled Augustine to take up so firm an attitude? Perhaps the most profound reason is that he and his colleagues were in the enviable position of knowing why history was happening. In his *Trattato di storia romana*, Professor Mazzarino has recently characterized the Later Roman period in terms of attitudes to authority current at the time: he has headed his chapter on the fourth and fifth centuries, 'La prospettiva carismatica,' 'The Charismatic viewpoint'. We might enter even deeper into the outlook of the Christian bishops if we substituted the title: 'La prospettiva profetica', 'The Prophetic viewpoint'. What was happening around them happened *secundum propheticam veritatem.*[23] It was a prophetic truth that the Church should be diffused among all nations: this was Augustine's main contention against the Donatists. But it was a prophetic truth on exactly the same level that the Kings of the Earth should serve Christ in fear and trembling; that the gods of the nations should be uprooted from the face of the earth,[24] and that what had been sung, centuries before by King David, should now become manifest, as a public command,[25] in the repression of pagans, Jews and heretics throughout the Roman Empire.

It is difficult for a historian who is accustomed to seeing the Later Roman Empire in terms of a slow evolution, over a long period of time, to enter into the 'mirages' of one generation within it, the generation of Augustine. But, in these early works of Augustine we can still sense the mood of heady optimism which the sudden collapse of paganism had induced, for a moment, before the disasters of the next decade: it had all happened, as Augustine said in a sermon, 'valde velociter'.[26]

For this reason, I think that it is not unimportant that these events should have coincided with the culmination of Augustine's attempts to unravel the prophetic truths of Biblical history. We see this in all the levels of his work at this time: from the *De Consensu Evangelistarum* [27] to the simple historical 'narratio' which he regarded as essential for his model catechism, in the *De Cathecizandis Rudibus.*[28] Thus, Augustine's reaction to the suppression of paganism and to the possibility of suppressing other forms of religious dissent, is, in part, determined by the deeper change which had led him from the purely allegorical exegesis of ten years previously to a concrete vision of the fulfilment of prophecy in history.[29]

But we have still to understand the final phase of Augustine's attitude: that is, the way in which his conviction that the Emperors could punish impieties shifted to a belief that such punishment could be coercive in the full sense of the word—that external pressures could provoke changes of allegiance in whole congregations. We will gain nothing by

[17] *Sermo* 24: 16th June, 401: v. *Sermones de Vetere Testamento*, ed. Lambot, *Corpus Christianorum*, 41, 1961, 234. *Sermo* 62: 399 or later: O. Perler, *Rech. augustin.* I (1958), 12. For an earlier dating—398–9, v. Tillemont, *Mémoires Ecclésiastiques* vol. XIII, 318–20.

[18] Morin I, c. I. *Sermones post Maurinos Reperti*, Miscellanea Agostiniana, 1930, 590; 23rd June, 401.

[19] *Serm.* 24, 7; 169, 10; 279, 4. All in reference to *Deut.* XXXII, 39: 'Ego percutiam et ego sanabo: ego occidam et ego vivere faciam.'

[20] *Ep.* 173, 3 (44, 641).

[21] e.g., *inter multa*, *Ep.* 93, ii, 5 (I, 342, 449).

[22] esp. *Contra Epistulam Parmeniani* VIII, 15 (51, 35).

[23] e.g. *Contra Cresconium* III, xlvii, 51 (52, 458).

[24] See the references and remarks of A. Mandouze, 'S. Augustin et la religion romaine,' *Rech. augustin.* I (1958), 218–22.

[25] *Con. Ep. Parm.* VIII, 15 (51, 35).

[26] *Enn. in Ps.* VI, c. 13.

[27] *De Cons. Evang.* I, xxvi, 40 f. (43, 39 f.).

[28] *De Cath. Rud.* XXVII, 53.

[29] v. B. Lohse, 'Augustins Wandlung i. seiner Beurteilung d. Staates,' Studia Patristica VI, *Texte u. Unters.* LXXXI (1962), 447–75, for the reflection of this attitude in his early evaluation of the State, and his later change of view.

setting aside Augustine's frequent admissions that, at a crucial stage in the Catholic campaign against the Donatists, between 403 and 405, he had been unwilling to impose such full coercive measures against the Donatists.[30]

This was a genuine inhibition. It concentrated effectively on one point: the problem of the *ficti*—of the landslide of feigned conversions which such a measure would have provoked.[31] Indeed, similar concerns remained as a constant braking-force on religious coercion throughout the Later Roman period. When the Christian church was still only one religious group among many in an ' open ' society, responsible bishops felt that they could not absorb too great an influx of bad Christians.[32] Augustine's early letters and sermons on the rowdy celebrations of the *Parentalia* in Africa and of the *Laetitia* of S. Leontius in Hippo show how he regarded the low standards of his own congregation as having arisen, largely, from the ' hypocrisy ' of pagans who had joined the church in masses after its official establishment by the Emperors.[33] So, we would be going against the evidence of Augustine's pastoral experience if we suggested that he regarded with anything less than genuine reluctance, the prospect of seeing the steady trickle of semi-pagans turned into a flood of resentful Donatists, used to being solemnly drunk on the feast of St. Leontius.

Yet Augustine seems to have accepted the new situation with surprising ease. This confidence in the absorptive powers of the Catholic Church calls for some explanation. Part of this explanation would, of course, take us into the details of Augustine's pastoral activity. Unfortunately, the measures which Augustine and his colleagues took to absorb the congregations that had rallied to the Catholic Church are insufficiently documented.[34] But, for Augustine, this work of absorption may well have been a landmark in a long and subtle process of symbiosis with the common, popular religion of African Christians: the congregations which Augustine had to take over, after 405, may no longer have appeared so alien and, hence, so ' indigestible ', as they had first appeared to him when he had returned to Africa as a Catholic.

But we must not forget another reason for this confidence: the development of Augustine's doctrine of grace and predestination. This doctrine, after all, was posed in terms of the disparity between the bewildering discontinuity of human actions and circumstances, and the invincible purposes of an omnipotent God. Briefly, such a deeply-ingrained attitude would lead Augustine to leave the crucial problem of the *ficti* to God. To object to the Catholic policy because it produced such feigned conversions came to appear as tantamount to denying the ' Virtus Dei '—the Power of God, Who could seek out His own among the multitude who had conformed with a bad grace to the Catholic Church.[35]

Augustine's reaction to the problem of the *ficti* reveals a distinctive feature of his attitude to coercion as a whole: his tendency to think in terms of processes rather than of isolated acts. Seen in this perspective, the individual act of free self-determination—the *liberum arbitrium*—is not denied: but it is mysteriously incorporated in an order which lies outside the range of such self-determination. This preoccupation had led Augustine to circumvent the previous tradition of thought available to Christians on the subject of coercion. It had appeared self-evident that freedom of choice—*voluntas* or *liberum arbitrium*—was the essence of religion; that adherence to a religion could be obtained only by such free choice; and that a religious institution which resorted to force must be a *figmentum*,[36] a merely human ' artifice ', since only an institution resting on human custom could resort to such all-too-human means of securing obedience. This tradition was articulate and respectable in the Latin world: it was shared in various ways by Christian apologists, Tertullian and Lactantius, and by Donatist writers, Petilian [37] and Gaudentius.[38]

[30] v. esp. *Ep.* 93, v, 17 (34, 2, 461/2).

[31] v. esp. *Ep.* 93, v, 17 (34, 2, 461). This anxiety is confirmed by the *Commonitorium* of the Council of 404. The laws affecting the testamentary powers of heretics were to be applied: ' His sane exceptis, qui lite pulsati putaverint ad Catholicam transeundum, quia de talibus credibile est, non metu coelestis judicii potius quod terreni commodi aviditatem unitatem catholicam praeoptasse.'

[32] e.g. Jean de Nikiou, *Chronique*, c. XCIX, ed. Zotenberg, *Extraits des manuscrits de la Bibliothèque Nationale* XXIV, 1, 535, on Domitian of Mitylene: ' Domitien . . . ordonna que l'on forçât, par contrainte, les Juifs et les Samaritains à recevoir le baptême et à devenir chrétiens. Mais ce furent de faux chrétiens. . . .'

[33] *Enn. in Ps.* VII, c. 7. *Ep.* 29, 9 (34, 1, 120).

[34] v. P. R. L. Brown, art. cit. (n. 4), 293.

[35] e.g. *Contra Gaudentium* XXV, 28 (53, 226).

[36] *Contra Gaudentium* XXXIII, 42 (53, 241).

[37] *Contra Litteras Petiliani* II, lxxxiv, 185 (52, 115), cf. II, lxxxiii, 183 (52, 112), and *Gesta Collationis Carthag.* iii die. no. 258 (*Patrol. Latina* XI, 1413C), that the Catholics were distinguished in their policy of forcing men to believe against their wills.

[38] *Contra Gaudentium* XIX, 20 (53, 215).

But it would be a brave man who could challenge Augustine on the *liberum arbitrium*. He made his own position clear in an answer to Petilian. Petilian had said ' For the Lord Christ says, " No man can come to me except the Father draw him ". But why do you not permit each several person to follow his free will, since the Lord God Himself has given free will to men, showing to them, however, the way of righteousness, lest any one by chance perish from ignorance of it.' And Augustine answered : ' If I were to propose to you the question how God the Father draws men to the Son, when He has left them to themselves in freedom of action, you would perhaps find it difficult of solution. For how does He draw them to Him if He leaves them to themselves, so that each should choose as he pleases ? And yet both these facts are true ; but it is a truth which few have intellect enough to penetrate. So, therefore, it is possible that those warnings which you have been given by the correction of the laws do not take away free will.'[39]

An answer such as this cannot be divorced from the main body of Augustine's thought. In this thought, the final, spontaneous act of the will could be preceded by a long process—of *eruditio* and *admonitio*—in which elements of fear, of constraint, of external inconvenience are never, at any time, excluded. This attitude is epitomized by two words which recur constantly in Augustine's writings on coercion : *disciplina* and *occasio*. The meaning of both words are moulded by Biblical usage. *Disciplina* is always used to describe a process of divinely-ordained impingements, *per molestias eruditio*, such as had marked the relations of God with the people of Israel.[40] *Occasio* derives from the Book of Proverbs : ' Da sapienti occasionem et sapentior erit.' Thus it is used to communicate the pressures of the Imperial laws as no more than one indirect impingement among many in the *eruditio* of the wise religious man.[41]

The acceptance of external impingement as a factor in moral evolution is particularly associated with Augustine's analysis of the force of habit, of the *vis consuetudinis*, an analysis which is one of his most profound and original contributions to ethical thought. From his earliest works, morally neutral impingements, such as the fear of death or the inconveniences of the life of the senses, are accepted as part of the 'pulchritudo justitiae ' of a universe in which this force of habit may be broken in men.[42] And from his works against the Donatists, one can see how it is this precise area of Augustine's thought—the force of habit and its sharp remedies—which overlaps with his judgement on the ' wall of hard habit ' which, in his opinion, had protected the schismatic congregations.[43] Therefore, what is common to Augustine's attitude to coercion and his thought in general is the acceptance of moral processes which admit an acute polarity—a polarity of external impingement and inner evolution, of fear and love, of constraint and freedom. It is summed up in the last sentence of the only surviving sermon which Augustine preached on the notorious text ' Compelle eos intrare '—of the Gospel of St. Luke : ' Foris inveniatur necessitas, nascitur intus voluntas '.[44]

Yet, it is undeniable that, in order to make religious coercion merge unobtrusively into this wider background, Augustine has applied a certain amount of intellectual camouflage. A coercive policy, in imposing a series of direct physical restraints and penalties on the individual, would seem to lead to a sudden debasement of motives : purely physical fear would come to predominate stripped of the religious implications which usually surround Augustine's concept of ' fear and trembling '.[45]

Therefore, it is difficult to enter fully into Augustine's acceptance of this polarity if we do not consider some of the nuances of his attitude to the Old Testament. The concrete events of the Old Testament were very much alive to Augustine and his contemporaries, and

[39] *Contra Lit. Pet.* II, lxxxiv, 185 (52, 115), transl. Dods, *The Works of Aurelius Augustine* vol. III (1872), 354–5.

[40] v. H. I. Marrou, ' *Doctrina* et *disciplina* dans la langue des Pères de l'Eglise,' *Bull. du Cange* IX (1934), esp. XII, 21–5.

[41] e.g., *inter multa, Ep.* 93, V, 17 (34, 2, 462–8). It is used for the indirect pressure to adopt Christianity brought to bear on the sons of the pagan rebel, Nicomachus Flavianus : *De Civ. Dei.* V, 26, 36 *Corpus Christianorum* 47, 162). For the nature of these pressures on the individual—which did in fact include the use of direct force against *coloni*—v. Brown, art. cit. (n. 4), 286.

[42] e.g. *De Genesi contra Manichaeos* II, c. 42, and *De Vera Religione*, c. 29.

[43] e.g., *inter multa, Ep.* 89, 7 (34, 2, 424).

[44] *Sermo* 112, 8.

[45] For a formal analysis of Augustine's general doctrine v. R. Rimml, 'Das Furchtproblem i.d. Lehre d. Hl. Augustins,' *Zeitschr. f. kath. Theol.* XLV (1921), 43–65, 229–59.

the attitude which they adopted to the present was, in large part, moulded and defined by their attitude to this distant past. It is noticeable that many of the *exempla* which Augustine uses in his arguments with the Donatists—Elias, Nebuchadnezzar, Paul—are not cited merely as precedents for severity : they are deliberately chosen as symbols of the polarity we have just mentioned. They are, in fact, crucial examples of the deeper polarity which marked the Christian scriptures as a whole : a polarity of severity and mildness, of fear and love, which approximated to, without ever coinciding with, the division of the Old and New Testament. They were thought of as the ' duae voces ' of the Scriptures of the one God. Now, it is revealing that Optatus of Milevis, when discussing the coercion of the Donatists by Count Macarius,[46] and Augustine, in his early sermons against the pagans [47] should both see the coercive measures of their time against the background of these ' duae voces '. The issue is, also, taken up by the Donatists : they wished to ' Separate the Times ',[48] to claim that coercive measures were suited only to the severity of the Old Testament, and, so, were inapplicable in the *tempora Christiana*, a time marked by *mansuetudo*.[49]

On this subject, Augustine had, yet again, by-passed the attitude of his opponents. He had been a Manichee, and had developed his early Catholicism in opposition to the Manichees. Thus, for ten years before the problem of the coercion of the Donatists had arisen, Augustine had been defending the polarity of the Scriptures against Manichaean criticisms. As a result, all the examples of legitimate severity cited by Augustine against the Donatists occur in his earlier works whenever it is necessary to deal with prevalent Manichaean criticisms : they are handled in detail and justified *con brio* in works as different in tone as the *De Sermone Domini in Monte*,[50] the *Contra Adimantum* [51] and the *Contra Faustum*.[52] This is a good example of the way in which subjects which, if seen in isolation in Augustine's anti-Donatist writings, appear as mere debating-points, have, in fact, a considerable previous history as part of the genuine preoccupations of Augustine in his early years.

It is tempting to risk a further speculation. In justifying the Old Testament to the Manichees, Augustine was well aware that he had to justify a coercive situation : the profoundly meaningful institutions of Israel had been imposed on the majority of Israelites frankly by fear ; the Law was a *paedagogus*—it had acted, coercively, by threats.[53] So, in dealing with the concrete institutions of Israel, Augustine could not avoid dealing with the wider problem of the *utilitas timoris* [54]—the rôle of fear as a necessary element in enforcing a religious establishment.

Augustine's justification of the Old Testament against the Manichees is one of his most ingenious excursions into the field of concrete historical reconstruction. The extent to which he had accepted as necessary this régime of fear is often effaced by his emphasis on the antithesis of Law and Grace in the anti-Pelagian writings.[55] But, far from abandoning this concrete view of the Old Testament, certain changes in Augustine's historical perspective may even have brought it a stage closer to his own times. He had ceased to think of the Old Testament as a distinct ' stage ' in the moral development of the human race—valuable and inevitable in its own time, but a stage that had now been transcended.[56] His later perspective of history did not admit such an irreversible moral ascent. Because of this, perhaps, Augustine could see the *utilitas timoris* of the Old Law, not as a remote ' period ', reflecting an alien ' *gradus morum* ',[57] so much as a continuous and necessary complement of the grace of the New dispensation. The Old Law, with its coercive qualities, was, of course, always doomed to remain incomplete, and it was certainly less predominant than in the time

[46] Optatus, *De Schismate Donatistarum* III, 5 (P. L. XI, 1013 B) : ' Unus Deus et duae diversae voces.'

[47] *Sermo* 24, 4.

[48] Optatus, *De Schism. Don.* III, 7 (P. L. XI, 1017A) : ' Sed video vos hoc loco tempora separantes.'

[49] Implied in *Contra Cresconium* IV, xlvi, 56 (52, 553–4).

[50] *De Sermone Domini in Monte* I, cc. 63–5.

[51] *Contra Adimantum* c. 17 f. (25, 166 f.).

[52] *Contra Faustum* XXII, 20 (25, 608 f.).

[53] e.g. *De Utilitate Credendi* c. 9 (25, 12) ; cf. *Sermo* 62, 8, where the image of a *Paedagogus* is used of the Imperial legislation against Jews, heretics and pagans.

[54] *Contra Faustum* XXII, 21 (25, 611, 7).

[55] e.g. B. Blumencranz, *Die Judenpredigt Augustins* (1946), 144–5.

[56] v. Edw. Cranz, ' The development of Augustine's ideas on Society before the Donatist controversy,' *Harv. Theol. Rev.* XLVII (1954), esp. 273–6 and 279–81, for Augustine's early ' periodisation ' of history, and its gradual abandonment.

[57] e.g. *Contra Faustum* XXII, 23 (25, 618).

of Moses : but in an incomplete existence, its permanent utility could not be denied. And so, the concrete example of the people of Israel, with their enforced laws, could come very close indeed to the ecclesiastical realities of Augustine's North Africa.

This nuance in Augustine's attitude to the Law had coincided with a profound change in the imagination of his contemporaries. For the first time, the events of the Old Testament had become the true *gesta maiorum* of a large body of the Roman governing class. The Emperor Theodosius might claim to be descended from Trajan ; but he was more aware of his resemblance to King David. The contemporary relations of Church and State were only fully comprehensible in terms of the relations of Kings and Prophets, relations for which no precedent could be found in the actions of the Apostles.[58] And with this, there came the inevitable undertone of harshness : it is perhaps no coincidence that the ' Zeal of Phineas ', that grisly incident of righteous violence, is mentioned by Optatus in connection with the coercive measures of Count Macarius [59] and also appears, in an almost contemporary fresco, of the newly discovered catacombs of the *Via Latina*.[60] It is in such subtle changes as these that we can trace the beginning of a Double Image of the Old Testament—at one and the same time the symbol of an outmoded dispensation and the ever-present precedent for an established religion, enforced by law. It is a Double Image which, from the time of Augustine to that of Spinoza [61] will be very near the root of every controversy on religious tolerance.

In practice, however, there is no question, with Augustine, of a reversion to the harshness of the Old Testament. Instead, one cannot help but be struck by the way in which his view of the coercive process seems to have been deliberately modelled upon the disciplinary processes of the church. Even his usual term for ' coercion ' is not *cohercitio*—root of our own word—which had retained its purely negative, legal meaning of ' restraint ' and ' punishment ' : it is *correptio*—' rebuke '—defined by its aim, *correctio*, ' setting right '. *Correptio—Correctio* : this is a doublet of deep meaning in Augustine's ecclesiastical vocabulary : and it may be that the words are chosen, here, to ensure that his attitude to coercion should not be construed as purely punitive, but that it should appear as a positive process of corrective treatment—a treatment, therefore, subjected to the same inner checks and inspired by the same spirit, by the same *modus dilectionis*, as formal ecclesiastical sanctions.

Augustine's choice of language may have been partly determined by his position as a bishop, writing to justify his position to other bishops. In this context one should remember that the Donatists had claimed complete spiritual and disciplinary autonomy for their church : ' that . . . in the church alone should the commands of the Law to the people of God be taught '.[62] Thus, for Augustine's Donatist readers, his extension of such disciplinary powers to the Emperor was the measure of his departure from the previous Christian tradition. One may hazard that Augustine's choice of language was dictated, in part, by a need to allay the misgivings of such readers by assimilating the exercise of the Imperial authority as much as possible to the traditional authority of a Christian bishop. In any case, it is a choice of language of momentous importance in the evolution of ideas in a Christian society.

As a bishop, Augustine was, also, in a strong position to impose his concept of authority on the execution of the Imperial laws.[63] In his many letters to lay officials, we can see how he was determined to ensure that the work of suppressing the Donatist church should be carried out according to the norms of corrective discipline current in the Catholic Church, and, hence, according to norms which he, himself, was in the habit of exercising with such

[58] v. esp. *Ep.* 93, III, 9 (34, 2, 453).

[59] Optatus, *De Schism. Don.* III, 5 (*P.L.* XI, 1013–14). cf. Jerome, *Ep.* 109, 2–3, with remarks of H. Silvestre, *Rev. d'Hist. ecclès.* LVIII (1963), 532–6.

[60] A. Ferrua, *Le pitture della nuova catacomba di Via Latina* (1960), tav. XCII, and 48–9.

[61] v. H. Liebeschutz, ' Die politische Interpretation d. Alten Testaments bei Thomas v. Aquino u. Spinoza,' *Antike u. Abendland* IX (1960), 39–62.

[62] *Contra Cresconium* I, x, 13 (52, 335). cf. the most illuminating reconstruction of part of this attitude by W. H. C. Frend, ' The Roman Empire in the eyes of Western Schismatics during the 4th century,' *Miscellanea Historiae Ecclesiasticae*, Stockholm, 1960 (1961), 9–22.

[63] The administrative circumstances of North Africa gave a bishop extensive powers to intervene in the application of the laws on religious dissent : v. Brown, art. cit. (n. 4), 302–4. Augustine's interventions by letter, therefore, should be treated as exceptions to the usual routine of suppression : they reflect circumstances where the application of the laws had passed beyond his immediate control and, so, called for correspondence.

scrupulous care.[64] This last aspect of Augustine's attitude should not be taken for granted. Anyone who has followed modern debates on penal reform will realize the extent to which the issues which Augustine had to handle, the infliction of punishment and the exercise of power, tend to conjure up attitudes in a particularly incoherent, semi-conscious and primitive form. It is only too true, in this field, that ' he goes farthest who knows not whither he is going '.

Augustine lived in a violent and authoritarian age. The death penalty and brutal tortures were imposed indiscriminately. At least it can be said of Augustine that, in this situation, he kept his head. In justifying religious coercion, he also thought about it : he had reflected on why he was advocating such a policy, and, so, he knew to what extent he was prepared to go in putting it into effect. Plainly, the Spanish bishops who had hounded Priscillian to his death in 386, had not been as certain as Augustine as to when they should have stopped. It would be naïve to maintain that in the Latin Empire Augustine's *mansuetudo Christiana* was a Christian monopoly. Ambrose speaks of pagan governors who were proud of never having inflicted the death penalty during their administration.[65] But the most effective guarantee of the quality of authority is not only that those who wield it should be sensitive and scrupulous men ; but that they should be in the habit of wielding it. Here the long record of the undisturbed exercise of authority which a Christian bishop such as Augustine could enjoy is a most impressive guarantee of quality.

We have seen how much of the attitude to coercion which Augustine finally took up after 405 can be traced back for a decade, at least ; and so we can conclude that this harsh policy was grafted on to a living and mature organism, so that its application was subjected to a whole series of inner checks and balances which more hurried or less experienced men might not have been able to take into account. Seen in this perspective, the months which Augustine spent in his first year as a priest in Hippo, reading his Bible for *saluberrima consilia* [66] that would enable him to adapt himself to a new life as a public figure, are quite as important, for his biographer, as are his readings in the *Libri Platonicorum*. For this reading laid the foundations of an ideal of authority which would dominate Augustine for the rest of his life. We should never underestimate the extent of the reorientation which this change of ideal had involved, nor the exacting standards of self-examination on which this ideal rested. Phrases which seem to drop tritely enough from Augustine as an old man are often built upon massive foundations : the notorious epigram by which he justifies the coercion of the Donatists in a sermon of 413—' Dilige et quod vis fac ' [67]—is first formed, twenty years earlier, in his *Expositio epistulae ad Galatas*, in a passage in which Augustine had turned over the general problem of administering a sharp rebuke with scrupulous sensitivity and honesty.[68]

But remove the foundation of honesty for one moment from this attitude, and Augustine's phrases become fallacious, horrible and insidious. In the excuses which the members of the congregation of Caesarius of Arles gave their bishop for having robbed the Jews, we can see a grim caricature of the subject we have just been discussing :

> ' Et tamen hic forte respondebis : Ego non ex aliquo odio poenam ingero, sed de dilectione potius disciplinam ; ideo exspolio judaeum, ut per hanc asperam et salubrem disciplinam faciam Christianum '.[69]

The historian must face this challenge honestly. He cannot merely circumvent it by defining, justifying or palliating a ' doctrine ' which he reads of in the pages of Augustine. He must undertake the long and exacting task of assessing the quality of the man who wrote these pages. Augustine does not emerge from such an examination as an entirely simple figure. His charity seems to vary greatly with the degree to which he was personally involved

[64] v. esp. the correspondence between Augustine and Macedonius, *Epp.* 152–5 (44, 393 f.), where the doctrinal basis of Augustine's attitude is made explicit. I regret that I have been unable to consult G. Keating, *The Moral problems of fraternal, paternal and judicial correction*, Diss. fac. theol. Pontif. Univ. Gregor. (Rome, 1958).

[65] Ambrose, *Ep.* 25, 3.

[66] *Ep.* 21, 6 (34, 1 ; 54, 5).

[67] In *I Ep. Joh.* VII, 8. v. J. Gallay, ' *Dilige et quod vis fac* : Notes d'éxegèse augustinienne,' *Rech. de sc. relig.* XLIII (1955), 545–55.

[68] *Ep. ad Gal. Expos.* c. 57.

[69] *Caes Arelat. Sermo* 183, 6 (*Corpus Christianorum* 104, 748).

in the suppression of a powerful rival. He is a sensitive and conscientious pastor up to his victory over the Donatists ; but, in 420, he can appear, for an instant, as a harsh and cold victor. The whole weight of his doctrine of predestination is turned, with horrible emphasis, on the broken remnants of a great church : the Donatist bishop of Timgad had threatened to burn himself with his flock in his basilica. Augustine can write :

> sed quoniam deus occulta satis dispositione sed tamen iusta nonnullos eorum poenis praedestinavit extremis, procul dubio melius incomparabili numerositate plurimis ab illa pestifera divisione et dispersione redintegratis atque collectis, quidam suis ignibus pereunt . . .[70]

Yet in a letter which he wrote to Paulinus of Nola, in 408, at a time when the bearer, Possidius, was on his way to the court to ask for more laws against heretics and pagans, we can glimpse the paradox by which Augustine can appear both as ' le prince et patriarche des persécuteurs ', and, at the same time, as an eloquent exponent of the ideal of corrective punishment, an ideal whose realization is still so painfully incomplete in our own ' civilized ' societies :

> ' What shall I say as to the infliction and remission of punishment in cases in which we only desire to forward the spiritual welfare of those we are deciding whether or not to punish ? . . . What trembling we feel in these things, my brother Paulinus, O holy man of God ! What trembling, what a darkness ! May we not think that with reference to these things it was said : " Fearfulness and trembling are come upon me, and horror hath overwhelmed me. And I said, O that I had wings like a dove, for then I should fly away and be at rest." '[71]

All Souls College, Oxford

[70] *Ep.* 204, 2 (57, 318). [71] *Ep.* 95, 3 (34, 2, 508–9).

[22]

THE COERCION OF HERETICS

John von Heyking

IT IS NECESSARY to examine Augustine's arguments for the coercion of heretics because these arguments appear to undermine his general understanding of love of God and of neighbor as virtue. This understanding allows expressions of love that differ from those of the Catholic Church. It is notable that Augustine even made an argument to justify coercion instead of assuming that it should be used simply as a matter of course. However, the mode and premises of Augustine's argument do raise concerns. His justification of having heretics "compelled to enter" appears to undermine this view and instead appears to constitute an imposition of orthodoxy. This chapter provides evidence that Augustine's justification of coercion does not undermine his concept of virtue because he did not conclude that nonviolent heretics should be deprived of their political rights. This chapter focuses on Augustine's justification of the coercion of the Donatists, which was a specific case that required his constant attention.[1] Although it is extremely difficult to derive general principles from political activities, this chapter provides evidence that Augustine justified coercion inasmuch as he saw it as a last resort for a sect that expressed its principles through violence. His general principles do not necessitate coercion, nor is it fully accurate to state that his "horrible doctrine"

1. Augustine's fullest justification for coercing heretics is found in *Ep.* 93 (written in 408). I focus on Augustine's arguments for coercing Donatist heretics instead of others such as the Pelagians (who denied original sin and the need for grace) or Rogatists (a Donatist faction) because these arguments reflect his most sustained justification of his position. He supported banning the Pelagian heresy because of false worship, and possibly because the Pelagians were associated with violent activity (Brown, *Augustine of Hippo,* 361). He also suspected the Rogatist heretics of plotting to commit acts of violence (*Ep.* 93.3.11).

(as Markus termed it) constitutes a "tragic" exception to his political thought that would otherwise admit of pluralism.[2]

Greater attention is instead given to Augustine's nuanced justification of the coercion of violent heretics and their leaders. In the disintegrating Roman empire, the distinction between belief and actions appeared to have dissolved, and it appears that Augustine thought the Donatist beliefs undermined the physical security of the empire. Furthermore, his justification of coercion is based on his view that the means of coercion must fit the end.[3] His position is usually interpreted as denying the heretic the knowledge of how the good that is enforced upon him actually shares with the proximate good the heretic loves. Rather, Augustine's view is that coercion takes the form of demonstrating to the heretic the insufficiency of that proximate good, while acknowledging that the proximate good intimates or shares in the highest good. Augustine's position on this affects his political theory, inasmuch as his position indicates reasons for the use of force to maintain civil peace.

According to Augustine, the purpose of coercion is not to enforce moral and religious conformity. He justified using coercion against Donatist heretics in order to curb their violence. He supported the banning of the Donatist heresy because he thought its doctrines were expressed in violence. He supported the banning of other, not always violent, heresies, because they had apparently emerged in North Africa, which could not be easily defined as either violent or nonviolent. Augustine's change of mind, from his initial advocacy of persuasion to his allowance of coercion, indicates that he first opposed the imperial policy in the *Theodosian Code,* which carried the pagan practice of enforcement of religion over to the Christian religion (see below for specifics on imperial law). That Augustine initially opposed this policy and the efforts of his Catholic colleagues to coerce heretics indicates his greater tolerance toward heretics. The

2. Those who view a direct link between Augustine's political views and coercion include: Deane, *Political and Social Ideas,* 215; Connolly, *Augustinian Imperative,* 66–73; William H. C. Frend, "Augustine and State Authority: The Example of the Donatists," 72; and Brian Tierney, who wrote that Augustine's theory of coercion shaped Church policy on the suppression of religious dissent ("Religious Rights: An Historical Perspective," 20–21). For the "tragic" view, see Markus, *Saeculum,* 134–46; Fortin, "St. Augustine," 198; and Thomas Heilke, "On Being Ethical without Moral Sadism: Two Readings of Augustine and the Beginnings of the Anabaptist Revolution." Milbank argues that Augustine's "ontology of peace" collapses at this point on the rocks of a "moment of 'pure violence' " between the Church and the heretic. For him, Augustine ends up presenting coercion not as a matter of persuasion or education, but as a battle of wills based on a "moment of 'pure violence,' externally and arbitrarily related to the end one has in mind" (*Theology and Social Theory,* 420). Markus's interpretation has been challenged by John R. Bowlin ("Augustine on Justifying Coercion").

3. A point that Bowlin argues but that is ultimately lost when he says that depriving one of freedom does not fit the end of coercion ("Augustine on Justifying Coercion," 66–67).

imperial policy of coercion, which caused chaos and dissent, put Augustine into the situation of having to justify the use of coercion as a last resort. His final position, however, placed him in a tenuous situation. On the one hand, he often had to exhort reluctant imperial officials (who themselves feared Donatist violence) to apply imperial law. On the other hand, evidence indicates that they used excessive, and even unlawful, violence when they finally applied the law (see *Ep.* 114.1). Augustine, therefore, was caught in the position of having to diffuse a situation in which it was difficult to have the law applied in a moderate and just way. He negotiated this dilemma by urging imperial officials to be clement, and, to heretics themselves, by utilizing the rhetoric of Roman authority, a mode of discourse in Roman culture that took an authoritative and prosecutorial tone.[4] As a result of his letters to the latter, his name would forever after be associated with the kind of immoderate persecution that he himself attempted to restrain.

Augustine changed his position when he saw that the laws could bring heretics to act virtuously. Coercion, he thought, can give people the opportunity, but only the opportunity, to live more virtuous lives. What really convinced Augustine of the efficacy of coercion is that it "liberated" people who stayed in the Donatist Church, due to their ignorance of the principles of the Catholic Church. As well, coercion enabled them to overcome the fear they had of leaving the Donatist Church, which coerced many of its members to stay. According to Augustine, therefore, coercion and law have an educative function. However, the scope of this function is limited; Augustine thought that law can force people only to *act* virtuously. *It cannot make them virtuous.* He did not think that coercion constitutes a sufficient cause of conversion.

DEFINITION OF HERESY

A heretic is a professed member of the Church who obstinately rejects Church teaching by asserting an insufficient, proximate good as the proper object of worship: "So those in the church of Christ who have a taste *(sapiunt)* for something morbid and depraved, if they receive correction, so that they may

4. This dilemma was due, in part, to the relative ease with which parties manipulated the imperial law to their own advantage. The ability of the powerful in the late Roman empire to use their patronage to "use" the law made the law difficult to enforce. According to Jill Harries, "'[U]sing' the law was all-important [for Augustine], enforcing it, to the letter, was not" (*Law and Empire in Late Antiquity,* 92). This meant that Augustine, like other Roman patrons, reinterpreted and applied the law to help their clients. In the case of Augustine and other bishops, however, such "use" had the effect of checking the abuses of power by imperial officials.

know (*sapiant*, or relish) something sound and right, stubbornly resist and are unwilling to emend their pestilent and deadly dogmas, but persist in defending them, become heretics and leave the church and are counted among the enemies who exercise the church" (*CD* 18.51).[5] Augustine calls lower goods "morbid and depraved," which appears to suggest that they absolutely oppose the good. Augustine appears to invoke a kind of Manichaean dualism by dismissing these things in this way, in that his language suggests that those objects do not in any way share in the good. However, Augustine actually considered them proximate goods insofar as he thought that everything participates in the good. Heretics make the mistake of replacing the good with a proximate good, and stubbornly continue to worship that proximate good despite having its nature as a proximate good pointed out to them. Augustine does not use the language of "proximate" or "insufficient" goods, but he does treat the objects of Donatist worship in this way.

This definition indicates that only those in the Church of Christ can ever be heretics. The category does not include Jews, atheists, or children of heretics. In this sense, the category finds its political analogy in the traitor who betrays the principles of his or her country and acts seditiously (see *Ep.* 93.1.2, 185.6.23, 10.43). Furthermore, the heretic is not merely one who is incorrect about Church teaching. Because heretics are said to relish something morbid and depraved, they are said to persist in worshiping a good that is not appropriately worshiped. For example, heretics might be those who seek salvation exclusively through ritual observation, as in the case of the Donatists (as shown below). Augustine considered the Donatists as puritanical legalists who sought perfection exclusively through ritual and group membership. Ritual or legal purity "satisfies" their desire for perfection, whereas group membership "satisfies" their desire for the fruits of community. Ritual or legal purity and group membership combine to fulfill their desire to "see" the fruits of God. They sought the fruits of grace by law rather than through habits of virtue.

HISTORICAL BACKGROUND AND DONATIST PRINCIPLES

Donatist principles expressed themselves in violence, and contributed to the disintegration of the western Roman empire. Before turning to the principles

5. "Qui ergo in ecclesia Christi morbidum aliquid pravumque sapiunt, si correpti, ut sanum rectumque sapiant, resistunt contumaciter suaque pestifera et mortifera dogmata emendare nolunt, sed defensare persistunt, haeretici fiunt et foras exeuntes habentur in exercentibus inimicis."

of Donatism, it is first necessary to examine the historical background to the Donatist controversy in order to show how Augustine found himself in a situation in which he finally had to admit that the distinction between violent and nonviolent heretics was insignificant.

The historical and political situation in which Augustine found himself was one episode in Rome's long, bloody history of religious persecution among pagans, Christians, and other groups.[6] Emperor Diocletian persecuted Christian sects until 305 A.D., at which time some of the bishops and priests surrendered sacred Scriptures rather than die as martyrs. They were branded *traditores* for having "handed over" the Scriptures. These *traditores* were considered traitorous by various Christians and deemed by some unsuitable to hold Church office. The event that sparked the Donatist scandal was the appointment by *traditores* of Caecilianus as bishop of Carthage. The Donatists, whose input in the decision was ignored and who opposed the tainted choice of the *traditores,* appealed to the emperor who then rejected their appeal, partly because he thought it inappropriate for him to handle the affairs of the Church.[7] The African bishops held more synods, and each one maintained the original decision; the Donatists persisted and then finally broke with the Church. Their subsequent violent activity (such as the attacks by the Circumcellions and the Battle of Bagai in 347) and the fact that they disobeyed the emperor led to their suppression, which involved the exile of bishops and confiscation of Church property.[8] The Donatists' invocation of imperial authority to settle the dispute later provided Augustine with a weapon to remind them, when they complained about coercion, that they were the first to appeal (repeatedly) to the emperors, including Constantine, to hear their case against the appointment of Caecilianus (see *Ep.* 43.2.4, written in 397). Augustine also reminded them of their attempts to use imperial authority to punish their own dissidents (*Ep.* 51.3, written in 399 or 400).[9] The dispute set Catholics and Donatists against one another, but they eventually reached a modus vivendi between 321 and 346, which ended when Julian the Apostate became emperor. He tolerated Donatism partly in order to weaken Christianity, which he opposed. Julian persecuted Catholics

6. See the following accounts of the suppression of Donatism: W. H. C. Frend, "Donatism-Donatists" and *The Donatist Church: A Movement of Protest in North Africa;* Peter Brown, "St. Augustine's Attitude to Religious Coercion"; Geoffrey Grimshaw Willis, *Saint Augustine and the Donatist Controversy;* Maureen A. Tilley, *Donatist Martyr Stories: The Church in Conflict in Roman North Africa,* x–xvii; and Deane, *Political and Social Ideas,* chap. 6.

7. Roman law generally allowed the Church to conduct its own affairs, especially to define doctrine (Tony Honoré, *Law and the Crisis of Empire, 379–455* A.D., 3).

8. Tilley, *Donatist Martyr Stories,* xv. See also *Ep.* 185.1.4, written in 417.

9. See Willis, *Augustine and the Donatist Controversy,* 34.

by transferring Catholic churches to the Donatists.[10] In 373, Emperor Valentian I banned Donatism again; nevertheless, the Donatist Church expanded in Africa. Around 374, under Optatus of Thamugadi in Numidia, they became allied with Gildo, an African count who rebelled against Emperor Honorius and his regent Stilicho with a view to transferring Africa to the eastern empire. Donatism was useful for Gildo's political ambitions because it was a conduit for African nationalist agitation against Rome. The revolt was serious, particularly since Gildo cut off corn supplies to Italy; this was considered an act of war, as Africa was Italy's sole source for corn. In response, Donatist property was confiscated.[11] Donatism, which had already attracted local resentment against Rome, became allied with forces intent on the disintegration of the Roman Empire. About this time, and until 390 when it was led by Parmenius, the Donatist Church grew to be as popular as Catholicism in North Africa. By the time Augustine began fighting it in the 390s, it had become a major force that threatened the security of the Roman Empire.

By the time Augustine turned his attention to the controversy, Catholic Christianity had been declared the official religion: "We command that those persons who follow this law shall embrace the name of Catholic Christians. The rest, however, whom We adjudge demented and insane, shall sustain the infamy of heretical dogmas, their meeting places shall not receive the name of churches, and they shall be smitten first by divine vengeance and secondly by the retribution of Our own initiative."[12] The imperial laws suppressing heresy also need to be seen in light of one of the political purposes of the *Theodosian Code*—an attempt to prevent the disintegration of the western empire.[13] This explains the imperial readiness to persecute heretics, who would have been seen as threats to imperial unity. The empire suppressed heretics by removing heretical priests from their churches (*CT* 16.1.3, proclaimed in 381), confiscating their property (*CT* 16.5.7–8, May 8, 381), forbidding them from holding assembly (*CT* 16.5.6.3, January 10, 381), fining people ten pounds of gold for permitting heretical groups to meet on their property (or beating them with clubs and deporting them if they could not afford to pay) (*CT* 16.5.21, June 15, 392), deporting those who threatened Catholics (*CT* 16.4.3, July 18, 392; explicated below), fining any heretic ten pounds of gold for securing ordination

10. Augustine, *Against the Letters of Petilian, the Donatist*, in *Writings against the Manichaeans and Donatists*, 2.84.184, written ca. 400. See also F. Van der Meer, *Augustine the Bishop*, 83.

11. Willis, *Augustine and the Donatist Controversy*, 62.

12. Clyde Parr, trans., *The Theodosian Code and Novels and Sirmordian Constitutions*, 16.1.2 (proclaimed in 380). Hereinafter *CT (Codex Theodosianus)*.

13. Honoré, *Law and the Crisis of Empire*, 97.

(*CT* 165.21, June 15, 392), and requiring everyone to hold the Catholic faith in every detail (*CT* 16.5.28, September 3, 395). Most historians argue that despite these laws against Donatists and heretics in general, they were laxly enforced, and the imperial government was powerless to impose its will. As Tony Honoré argues, provincial governors often failed to execute the laws because doing so would have caused unrest. Any magistrate who tried "would have been a fool."[14] Changes in imperial law, the Church's position, and Augustine's position are considered in greater detail below.

Donatist doctrine lent itself to being expressed through violence, and its hardness led its leaders and followers to believe that God had given them special authority to cleanse the world through means that otherwise would be morally wrong. Donatist doctrines and beliefs derived from a set of writings called the *Acts*, which provided descriptions of persecution by Catholics. Peter Brown reports that these "martyr stories" reflect the Donatists' dedication to ritual and legal purity:

> In the Acts, the Donatists admired an attitude such as the orthodox Jew had to the Torah. Their religion also was thought of as a "Law." Like the Macabees, whose example moved them profoundly, their martyrs died for "their holy laws." "I care for nothing but the Law of God, which I have learnt. This I guard, for this I die; in this I shall be burnt up. There is nothing in life other than this Law." The feeling of having defended something precious, of preserving a "Law" that had maintained the identity of a group in a hostile world, these are potent emotions. . . . Such a church was *"catholic"* in what the Donatists regarded as the most profound sense of the word: for it was the only church that had preserved the *"total"* Christian Law. A church could only preserve the Christian "Law" in its entirety by remaining "pure."[15]

The Donatists maintained ritual purity and understood their religion as Law. They saw themselves as the true keepers of virtue in a hostile world. Brown indicates that they saw the source of their own purity as different from that of Augustine and the Catholics: "It was the purity of the group in its relationship to God, that mattered. This group, like the ancient Israel, enjoyed a special relationship with God: for its prayers only were heard by Him. The anxiety, that genuinely haunted the Donatist bishops, was that, by tolerating any breach in a narrow and clearly defined order of ritual behavior, they might alienate

14. Ibid., 26, 133; see also Willis, *Augustine and the Donatist Controversy*, 30.

15. Brown, *Augustine of Hippo*, 218. He quotes from various Donatist sources and Augustine's own observations found in his letter against Pettilian (2.8.17, 2.38.90). Brown refers to *Monumenta ad Donatistarum historiam pertinentia*, P.L. viii, 673–784.

God from His church." This communal desire for purity demanded that rituals be followed precisely, and asserted that any breach of ritual would result in losing God's favor. Despite this, Donatist basilicas were often scenes of drunkenness and dancing, which frequently led Augustine to express doubts that the Donatists truly believed what they preached (*Ep.* 23.6–7, written in 392; 29.2, ca. 395 [on the feast called "Laetitia, vainly attempting to disguise their revels under a fair name"]; 35.2 [sexual licence]; 43.8.24; 108.5.14; 134.2).[16]

Augustine criticizes Donatist legalism and inordinate ritual purity, which (in his view) led to absurd consequences for liturgical practice. The Donatists exhibited the characteristics of a legalistic morality in their claim that only those who are part of the true Church can be saved. Membership, as they saw it, entailed following the Church's precepts to the letter:

> You think that you make a very acute remark when you affirm the name catholic to mean universal, not in respect to the communion as embracing the whole world, but in respect to the observance of all Divine precepts and of all the sacraments as if we (even accepting the position that the church is called catholic because it honestly holds the whole truth, of which parts here and there are found in some heresies) relied upon the testimony of this name *(huius nominis testimonio nitamur)*, and not upon the promises of God, and so many indisputable testimonies of the truth itself, our demonstration of the existence of the church of God in all nations. (*Ep.* 93.7.23)

The term *catholic,* that is, universal, meant different things to Catholics and Donatists (who considered themselves truly catholic). For the Donatists, being catholic entailed perfect observance of ritual and the Law, which guaranteed one's purity. For the Catholics, being catholic entailed worldwide communion, which includes the virtuous and depraved. For Augustine, rituals express, rather than constitute, virtue.

The Donatist claim that salvation comes through ritual observation of Law led them to believe that salvation could be gained only by communion with Donatist bishops and clergy, such as Vincentius in his hometown of Cartenna: "Meanwhile do all you can to proclaim and to maintain, that even though the gospel be published in Persia and India, as indeed it has been for a long time, no one who hears it can be in any degree cleansed from his sins, unless he come to Cartenna, or to the neighborhood of Cartenna! If you have not expressly said this, it is evidently through fear lest men should laugh at you" (*Ep.* 93.7.22; see

16. Willis, *Augustine and the Donatist Controversy,* 29.

also 93.6.21). Ritual purity required communion with pure bishops in their hometowns. The sacredness of locale combined with their African nationalism and anti-Roman sentiment, and Augustine criticizes them for restricting God's church to Africa alone (see *Ep.* 185.1.3). Donatist legalism, combined with their insistence that communion with God take place in the bishops' hometowns, led them to reject other forms of worship. For Augustine, this meant that they broke themselves off from the worldwide Christian communion: "[H]ow do you know that in the Christian society, which is spread so far and wide, there may not have been some in a very remote place, from which the fame of their righteousness could not reach you, who had already, before the date of your separation, separated themselves for some just cause from the communion of the whole world? How could the church in that case be found in your sect, rather than in those who were separated before you?" (*Ep.* 93.8.25). This statement indicates that the Donatists, by insisting on their own purity, separated themselves from the worldwide communion. For instance, they acted like a separate society, forbidding members from meeting with Catholics, sharing the same space (as in a room), intermarrying, answering their letters, responding to their letters, or letting them into their churches.[17]

Like a late Roman version of *Billy Budd*, this communal desire for purity appears to have resulted in violent acts, intended to cleanse the impure Catholics whom they saw polluted by the world: "The Donatist enthusiasts carried clubs called 'Israels'; they would 'purify' Catholic basilicas with coats of whitewash; they would destroy the altars of others."[18] Augustine reports various violent acts such as murder and the destruction of houses; he used these reports to argue for the need to restrain the Donatists (*Ep.* 88.7, written in 406; see also 133.1, written in 412).[19] He tells of the violence suffered by Maximianus, the Catholic bishop of Bagai, after one of the trials against the Donatists:

> [T]hey rushed upon him as he was standing at the altar, with fearful violence and cruel fury, beat him savagely with cudgels and weapons of every kind, and at last with the very boards of the broken altar. They also wounded him with a dagger in the groin so severely, that the effusion of blood would have soon put an end to his life, had not their further cruelty proved of service for his preservation; for, as they were dragging him along the ground thus severely wounded, the dust forced into the spouting vein stanched

17. Ibid., 28–29.

18. Brown, *Augustine of Hippo*, 219. See *EnP* 10.5; *Ep.* 29.12.

19. For other examples of Donatist violence, see *Ep.* 51.3, 88.6, 89.1, 133.1, 185.3–4, 185.7, 185.13, 185.27, 185.30). See also Brown, *Augustine of Hippo*, 241.

> with blood, whose effusion was rapidly on the way to cause his death. (*Ep.* 185.7.27, written in 417)

The Donatists also used violence to dissuade their own members from becoming Catholics. For example, Augustine reports of Donatists who beat a presbyter who had left them for the Catholics (*Ep.* 88.6, written in 406) and later of the intimidation of members: "[T]hey were living among men among whom those who wished to be Catholics could not be so through the infirmity of fear, seeing that if anyone there said a single word in favor of the Catholic church, he and his house were utterly destroyed at once" (*Ep.* 185.4.13, written in 417).[20]

The Donatists' violence was often meant to bait authorities into persecuting them, which would enable them to view themselves as martyrs, thus solidifying their own position as the pure who are persecuted by an impure world. One of the reasons Augustine rejected the death penalty is that it provided the Donatists with even more martyrs (*Ep.* 139.2, written in 412). He mentions that Donatists often threatened authorities with violence if those authorities did not put them to death. If threats did not work, Donatists would often commit suicide (*Ep.* 185.3.12).

Leaders played a crucial role in Donatist ecclesiology, and Augustine's advocacy of coercion targets them. Augustine also suspected that Donatist leaders, though feigning a belief in moderation, actually encouraged Donatist violence.[21] In Donatist ecclesiology, the bishops and priests constituted an unbroken line of martyrs and the pure that originated in the handing over *(traditio)*, or the sacrificing, of the Christian Law:

> [The Donatist] caste of "pure" bishops were often eminent men in Roman towns that had maintained their prestige. In the eyes of their congregations, these bishops stood for the uninterrupted succession of the "church of the Martyrs": a Donatist priest would be told by an angel the precise "line of descent of Christianity" that culminated in the bishop of his town. In a society that valued sheer physical continuity in life and death, these bishops were thought of as the "sons of the martyrs" as surely as the despised Catholics were the "sons of Caecilian [the original *traditore*]."[22]

The Donatist Church, then, appears to have been centered on the symbol of the procession of the martyrs, represented by the bishops and priests.

20. Brown, *Augustine of Hippo*, 223; see also *Ep.* 83.1, 85.29, 93.1.3, 3.10; *EnP* 54.16.

21. See Peter Iver Kaufman, *Redeeming Politics*, 139–40. Augustine elsewhere complains about intellectual elites who stir up crowds to attack Christians (*CD* 4.1, 6.pref., 18.51; see also 2.1, 5.26).

22. Brown, *Augustine of Hippo*, 220.

The fruits of community and grace were sought by the ritual purity of the priests. However, this ritual purity did not extend to the general congregation. The Donatist Church was based on a core of pure elites who constituted the procession of the martyrs; the general congregation would have been purified by observing the rituals conducted by the bishops and priests. In Augustine's view, because the Donatists advocated the purity of the Church as opposed to the Catholic "impurity," they sought the fruits of God prematurely. The Donatists sought the fruits of God with an insufficient good. They sought a perfect good through ritual observance and through their ecclesiology, but according to Augustine, those are only proximate and insufficient goods (my terms). For Augustine, loving an insufficient good as if it were a perfect good produces ill effects. It forces individuals to grasp the insufficient good, which leads them to lash out and destroy either it or other things, when the insufficient good fails to produce the good for which the heretics hope. The Donatists turned to violence in order to "purify" worldly objects, because they themselves sought purification from their attachment to worldly things.

As was shown in the previous chapter, Augustine understood that love of God or worship *(latreia)* is possible outside the sacramental order of the Church. The Catholic Church differed most significantly from the Donatists in that it sought the fruits of God not in ritual purity or in the procession of the martyrs, but in the vision of God that can be seen only "through an enigma" or mixed in with sins while the Catholic Church maintains temporal existence. This theory is reflected most directly in Augustine's view that the city of God and the earthly city exist intermingled in this life, that the Church will be filled with both the virtuous and the sinful who seek salvation (*CD* 1.35, 10.32, 11.1, 14.28, 15.1, 18.1). For example, he calls these two cities "mystical *(mystice)*," meaning that they must be interpreted figuratively (*CD* 15.1; *DDC* 2.62). In practice, this means that they seek the fruits of God in the actual virtues of their members (inside and outside the official sacramental order). Augustine states this principle when he explains the success of the early Church:

> [I]t is incredible that a very few men, of mean birth and the lowest rank, and no education, should have been able so effectually to persuade the world, and even its learned men, of so incredible a thing. . . . But if [skeptics] do not believe that these miracles were wrought by Christ's apostles to gain credence to their preaching of His resurrection and ascension, this one grand miracle suffices for us, that the whole world has believed without any miracles. (*CD* 22.5; see also 16.2)

Augustine's understanding of unity is governed by the Matthean idea that "By their fruits ye shall know them" (*CD* 16.2 [Matt. 7:20]; see also *CD* 5.15). The Catholic Church is united by the ability of its members to observe and practice virtue, and to see the miraculous in the unexpected and mundane, in the way that the apostles miraculously converted people to Christianity without the use of miracles. Adherence to this principle would have required great virtue and patience among Catholics because it required them to seek the fruits of God in unexpected places. Contrary to the views of the Donatists, the virtue required of the Catholics may have been even greater than that required of the Donatists themselves, who sought the fruits of God in the "physical" continuation of the martyrs, in the ritual and legal purity of their Church, and in their lust for persecution and martyrdom.

LAW AND PUNISHMENTS

The year 408 A.D. marks a major break in Augustine's thinking. Before that, he had supported the use of imperial power only inasmuch as it could prevent Donatist violence against the Catholics. As we shall see, this included suppressing their activities, since these religious activities were linked to violence. Political instability had prevented both Augustine and the imperial powers from distinguishing the sect from the violence that it engendered. Until 408, Augustine rejected imperial laws compelling Donatists to become Catholic (for example, see *CT* 16.5.28), but he changed his mind once he appreciated the efficacy of these laws. Augustine's position changed in response to the changes in imperial and ecclesiastical policy. As shown below, he was reluctant to agree with the increasing tendency of the Church and the empire to compel Donatists to enter the Church; however, he consistently supported them once he agreed with their positions. The one exception to this is his rejection of the death penalty and his ambiguous rhetoric exhorting imperial officials to apply the law. Changes in imperial and Church policy can be divided into three periods: (1) the years 395 to 400, marked by the Church's appeal to the empire to protect it from Donatist attack, (2) the years 400 to 405, marked by the Church's declaration that the Donatists were heretics, and imperial suppression, and (3) the years 405 to 411, marked by the move toward coercing Donatists into the Catholic Church.

The Years 395 to 400

As shown above, the period up to 390 was marked by imperial efforts to suppress Donatism and its accompanying violence; by 380, membership in the

Catholic Church was compulsory. The Church until then generally appealed to the emperor only to protect it from Donatist violence, and to enforce unity. This was the prevailing attitude of the Church until the period following the Edict of Unity of 405 (see below).[23] The Church differed from the emperor, who had declared all non-Catholics as heretics as early as 395 (*CT* 16.5.28). During this period Augustine, like other churchmen, was willing to appeal to the emperor to protect the Catholics from Donatist violence, but not to coerce them into communion with the Catholics.[24] That being the case, it has been noted that the "germ" of Augustine's idea of coercion lay in the writings of this period.[25] For instance, he appears to consider heresy in the same class as violent and sinful activities, as defined by Paul and punishable by imperial authorities (Gal. 5:19–21): "iniquity, fornication, moral corruption *(immunditiae)*, contentiousness, ambition, animosity, dissension, heresy, envy, drunkenness, and offenses."[26] Drawing on the words of Paul, Augustine understood heresy as a species of moral corruption that accompanied other kinds of moral pollution, particularly violence, of which the Donatists were guilty. Nevertheless, Augustine did not at this time advocate coercing the Donatists into becoming Catholics, but instead urged the use of imperial power to prevent them from attacking the Catholics.

The Years 400 to 405

The period between 400 and 405 is characterized by increased persecution of the Donatists by the empire, and by appeals by the Church. At the Synod of Carthage in June 405, the Church pressured the empire to enforce its antiheretical laws by declaring the Donatists heretics.[27] Although the Church moved to categorize the Donatists as heretics, it stopped short of calling for enforced unity, although some bishops (not yet including Augustine) did.[28] The empire continued to consider the Donatists heretical and actually exceeded the Church's demands by declaring (in advance of the Church's appeal to the emperor) that all must become Catholic, and by disbanding Donatist churches (*CT* 16.5.37–38). *CT* 16.5.38, decreed on February 12, 405, is generally known as the "Edict

23. Ibid., 234; Willis, *Augustine and the Donatist Controversy*, 23–24.

24. Augustine, *The Retractions*, 2.31, commenting on (the lost work) *Contra partem Donati libri duo*, written about 397–400; "Against the Letter of Parmenian," in *Works of Saint Augustine*, ed. John E. Rotelle, O.S.A., vol. 18 (New York: New City Press, 1990), 8.15 (51, 35); see also Brown, "Augustine's Attitude," 265–66.

25. Brown, "Augustine's Attitude," 266.

26. Augustine, "Against the Letter of Parmenian," 1.10.16.

27. Willis, *Augustine and the Donatist Controversy*, 130.

28. Van der Meer, *Augustine the Bishop*, 88–89.

of Unity"; it transferred churches over to the Catholics, forbade rebaptism and other Donatist practices, and, even though it declared that all must be Catholic, stopped short of coercing heretics into their communion. As Brown argues, "For all its bombast, this Edict was faithful to the general principle of Roman legislation on religion. It touched only externals. No Donatist, as yet, was forced to join the Catholic church. Rather, the Donatist church was 'disbanded,' like a modern political party that has been declared illegal."[29]

During this period, Augustine supported the use of exile and fines to suppress Donatists. He does not appear to have supported the Church's position on the Edict of Unity. He maintained the pre-405 position by appealing merely for protection:

> Our brethren indeed demand help from the powers which are ordained, not to persecute you, but to protect themselves against the lawless acts of violence perpetrated by individuals of your party, which you yourselves, who refrain from such things, bewail and deplore; just as before the Roman Empire became Christian, the Apostle Paul took measures to secure that the protection of armed Roman soldiers should be granted him against the Jews who had conspired to kill him. (*Ep.* 87.8, written in 405)

Markus observes that Augustine's reluctance to adopt a policy of coercion may have played a part in delaying the African bishops from adopting such a strategy.[30] Indeed, that there was a problem of overzealous enforcement that exceeded Church policy is evidenced by Augustine's subsequent expressions of displeasure at actual enforcement as well as that advocated by some of his fellow Catholics: "Finally, if some of our party transgress the bounds of Christian moderation in this matter, it displeases us" (*Ep.* 87.8). Augustine's support of the Edict of Unity must have been lukewarm at best, since he consented to its principles only sometime in the subsequent three-year period, prior to his writing a letter recording his justification for his change of mind in 408.[31]

As shown above, Augustine thought that the Donatists had separated themselves from the worldwide Christian communion and believed, therefore, that the most appropriate punishment would be exile rather than corporal punishment: "But what shall I say against those whose fatal obstinacy is such that

29. Brown, *Augustine of Hippo*, 234.

30. Markus, *Saeculum*, 137.

31. According to Markus, the evidence is only sufficient to identify his change of mind sometime between 405 and 408: "At any rate within a year or two of the Edict of Unity, having seen its working, his doubts were dispelled. . . . Some time between 405 and 408 his consent followed, and thereafter he never wavered" (ibid., 138).

it is either coerced only by fear of losses, or is taught by exile *(vel damnorum terrore coercetur, vel docetur exsilio)* how universal (as had been foretold) is the diffusion of the church which they prefer to attack rather than to acknowledge?" (*Ep.* 89.2 (written in 406); see also 185.7.26 (written in 417).[32] Exile would make that removal concrete, since heresy is an expression of one's rejection of communion (with God and neighbor). Thus, the proper punishment is to deprive the heretic, whose physical violence can no longer be tolerated, of communal life (a punishment that his actions intend to achieve anyway). Such a justification is consistent with Augustine's theory of virtue. Just as being virtuous is enjoyable and being vicious unenjoyable, entailing as it does separation from God, so too is heresy punished by making concrete what the heretic has already chosen. What is crucial for this idea of exile is that, for Augustine, it is intended for leaders of movements whose violent activities have become impossible for others to tolerate. It is not, for Augustine (as it was for imperial law), a tool simply to ensure orthodoxy. We shall see presently, however, that Augustine found himself in a situation in which even exile was insufficient to maintain physical security.

Augustine's writings do not clarify the location to which the Donatists would be exiled. His failure to specify a location indicates that he assumed his readers would know that the Donatists would be exiled according to imperial law (although not completely, as shown presently). The *Theodosian Code* arranged to have heretics merely removed from cities and sent into the surrounding country, but it also decreed that more dangerous heretics be sent to outer provinces and islands; its authors presumably thought that the exile should fit the crime. For instance, the support of subversive hermits, who often entered town from their desert caves and engaged in political agitation, was punished by expulsion into the country to those same caves, which was another way of forcing them to adhere to their own self-proclaimed principles (*CT* 16.4.3, September 2, 390). Similarly, the code expels the Manichaean heretic Jovinian, who had engaged in heretical rites outside the city:

> Therefore, We command that the aforesaid person shall be arrested and beaten with leaden whips and that he shall be forced into exile along with the remaining adherents and ministers. He himself, as the instigator, shall be transported with all haste to the island of Boa; the rest, as seems best, provided only that the band of superstitious conspirators shall be dissolved

32. *Damnare* in classical and early medieval Latin means passing judgment, to sentence to pay. It derives from *damnum*, which is a loss of money or other possessions (Souter, *Glossary of Later Latin*, 87). Only later did it come to mean exclusively eternal damnation.

> by the separation of exile, shall be deported for life to solitary islands situated at a great distance from each other. (*CT* 16.5.53, March 6, 412 [although the editor argues it was proclaimed in 398])

The author of this law thought it appropriate for Jovinian's heretical activities, which took place outside of Rome, to be punished with exile and beatings. The law goes further than Augustine's principles in calling for harsh beatings, and in exiling Jovinian's followers. Augustine, on the other hand, advocated exile only for leaders, and only pecuniary fines for violent followers. Earlier laws against the Donatists were more lenient than later ones. For example, one law (*CT* 16.5.34, March 4, 398) sent them into the country, and sent them farther only when they persisted in reentering Rome. In 407, a proclamation declared that Donatists and other heretics "shall have no customs and no laws in common with the rest of mankind" (*CT* 16.5.40, February 22, 407). The law itself does not specify location or conditions of exile, but lists a host of ways the heretics were to be deprived of their rights. This law reflects the general principles of punishment of heretics, and also reflects the chaotic condition of the western empire; the eastern empire continued to permit heretics to take offices such as that of a local councillor (*CT* 16.5.48, February 21, 410).[33] In 414, a severe proclamation was issued exiling Donatist bishops and priests to separate islands and provinces (*CT* 16.5.54.1, January 17, 414). That it lists outer provinces indicates that exile did not entail physical removal from the empire as a whole, which may have been impossible in any case, given its size. However, the principle behind the exile was to remove heretics from communion with others; exile to outer islands and provinces effectively cut them off from the empire. Imperial policy on heretics in general, therefore, gave Augustine a spectrum of types of exile to advocate for violent heretics: from mere banishment from the city, to expulsion to the outer limits of the empire. However, he does not appear to have advocated exile for followers. Furthermore, imperial policy understood exile as appropriate to the crime of heresy, which is consistent with Augustine's theory of punishment.

Augustine also advocated fines for heretical leaders and violent heretics. Heretics most commonly found themselves fined under the *Theodosian Code*. Social elites in particular were often fined ten pounds of gold (*CT* 16.5.21, proclaimed in 392),[34] and Circumcellions were fined ten pounds of silver

33. Honoré, *Law and the Crisis of Empire*, 131.

34. The translator considers this amount exceedingly high (454 n. 48), although Deane considers it "extraordinarily mild," considering the enormity of the crime (*Political and Social Ideas*, 188).

(*CT* 16.5.52, January 30, 412). Augustine warned a Donatist bishop, Crispinus, for instance, that he would be fined ten pounds of gold by the empire for rebaptizing people (*Ep.* 66.1, written in 402). His case was prosecuted by Augustine's friend Possidius, and Crispinus was found guilty; however, the fine was remitted at Possidius's behest (*Ep.* 88.7, written in 406). Augustine thought such fines were appropriate for heretics who committed acts of violence (see below), but that elites should be the only nonviolent heretics who should be fined. For example, he argued that heretical bishops or clergymen should be fined ten pounds of gold in those districts where the Catholic Church suffered violence from their clergy, Circumcellions, or "at the hands of any of their people" (*Ep.* 185.7.25, written in 417; see also 88.7). Augustine instead recommended fining such heretics the amount that would prevent them from leading wicked lives (*Ep.* 91.9, written in 408). The principle behind this was to prevent heretics from supporting their sect, but Augustine adamantly states that this should not involve their poverty, destitution, or dependence on others for their daily bread: "Neither was there any ground for your apprehending our inflicting a life of indigence and of dependence upon others for daily bread on those regarding whom I had said that we desired to secure to them the second of the possessions named above, vis., the means of supporting life" (*Ep.* 104.2.5, written in 409; see also 104.1.4). Such deprivation does not entail dependence on others for basic subsistence. Augustine contrasts this deprivation with the much more extreme poverty of the Roman dictators Cincinnatus and Fabricius. For example, he advocates fining a group of heretics ten pounds of silver for burning down a Catholic church: "But as to their third possession, viz. the means and opportunities of living wickedly, that is to say—passing over other things—their silver with which they constructed those images of their false gods, in whose protection or adoration or unhallowed worship an attempt was made even to destroy the church of God by fire" (*Ep.* 104.2.5). He thought the fine of ten pounds of silver was appropriate because it prevented the heretics who had burned down a Catholic church from furthering their impiety.

However, Augustine's optimal solution to violent heresy was not practical in the end because the threat of political dissolution in North Africa was too high and because Donatist leaders retained their followers by habit and by intimidation. He describes, in 417, the failure of the Edict of Unity to preserve the peace after 405:

> For a law had already been published, that the heresy of the Donatists, being of so savage a description that mercy towards it really involved a greater cruelty than its very madness wrought, should for the future be prevented

> not only from being violent, but from existing with impunity at all; but yet no capital punishment was imposed upon it, that even in dealing with those who were unworthy, Christian gentleness might be observed, but a pecuniary fine was ordained, and sentence of exile was pronounced against their bishops or ministers.[35] (*Ep.* 185.7.26, written in 417)

Ultimately, Donatist numbers were too high, and their violence too severe, for exile and fines to be sufficiently effective penalties. The emperor reissued many decrees, which, as mentioned above, reflected the inability of magistrates to enforce the laws.[36] Thus, the empire, the Church, and Augustine lagging not far behind moved to eliminate the sect outright and use imperial power to incorporate it into the Church. This process culminated in the Synod of Carthage of 411, which was meant to conclude the century-old problem by allowing each side to compare each other's claims, in order to identify the true Catholic Church.[37]

The Years 405 to 411

This period sees Augustine's final acceptance of coercion against the Donatists, and his support of the Edict of Unity of 405. Magistrates were too weak to enforce the edict; the Donatist Church grew and its violence intensified. Further, imperial decrees were issued, such as one proscribing the partisans of Gildo (which was an attempt to prevent sedition against Roman rule in North Africa) (*CT* 9.40.19, November 11, 408), forbidding heretical assemblies (*CT* 16.5.45, November 27, 408), punishing those who destroyed basilicas (*CT* 16.2.31, January 13, 409), and removing magistrates who neglected to carry out imperial orders (*CT* 16.5.46, 16.5.47, January 15 and June 26, 409). At the same time, the African proconsul punished heretics with death, which Augustine opposed (*Ep.* 100, written in 409; see below). Under earlier imperial law, heretics had received capital punishment for attacking Catholic churches and priests (*CT* 16.2.31, August 25, 398; 16.4.1, January 13, 386) and for disobeying their sentence of exile (*CT* 16.5.34, March 4, 398). After the Synod of Carthage in 409, however, heresy by itself (whether or not it involved violent acts) became a capital crime (*CT* 16.5.51, August 25, 410; 16.5.56, August 25, 410, and repeated in 415).

35. See Markus, *Saeculum*, 138; and Brown, *Augustine of Hippo*, 334. Capital punishment was proclaimed in 410 and again in 415 (*CT* 16.5.51, 16.5.56) (see below).

36. Willis, *Augustine and the Donatist Controversy*, 131; Honoré, *Law and the Crisis of Empire*, 26, 133.

37. Brown, *Augustine of Hippo*, 330–34.

The Synod of Carthage, chaired by Augustine's friend Marcellinus, lasted for three days and concluded with a proclamation to ban the Donatist heresy. The Donatists, as expected, rejected its conclusion and increased their violent activity, and were answered by increased imperial suppression. The ensuing violence was so widespread that Augustine commented on the fear that civil authorities had of the Donatist influence (*Ep.* 185.4.15). For instance, his friend Marcellinus, to whom the *City of God* is dedicated, appears to have been condemned to death and executed as a result of Donatist plots or pressure to avenge his role in the conference.[38] This fear was further justified: Augustine himself barely escaped assassination on one occasion.[39] The widespread influence of Donatism and the violence associated with it indicate that the optimal punishment for heretics, banishment, was unavailable to Augustine and the Church at the time.[40]

This account of efforts by the Church and the empire to suppress Donatism provides the background for Augustine's change of mind from initially rejecting to finally advocating coercion, as documented in Epistle 93. In the letter, he compares the compulsion of heretics to Christ's commanding the apostles to enter the house of his feast: "[C]ompel them to enter *(Quoscomque inveneritis cogite intrare)*" (*Ep.* 93.2.5, citing Luke 14:23). He states that he opposed coercion because he thought it would result in feigned conversions (*Ep.* 93.5.17). His rejection of coercion was the result of underestimating heretical violence and wickedness if left unpunished, and the extent to which heretics could benefit from the application of discipline. He also underestimated the ability of coercion to bring Donatists into the Catholic fold. The picture we have of Augustine's justifications, in their political context, is one of him facing a strong and violent sect that posed a threat not only to Catholics, but also to the physical integrity of the Roman Empire. His justification cannot be taken as a sanction to impose orthodoxy for its own sake, but rather because this sect held principles that expressed themselves in violence. Augustine was faced with the further difficulty of exhorting reluctant Roman authorities to carry out the imperial laws, but then having to restrain their violence when the application of the law became excessive. He wanted the authorities to enforce most of the imperial laws, but tried, often vainly, to make them stop short of capital punishment (permitted by law) and other excessively violent punishments.

38. T. D. Barnes, "Aspects of the Background of the *City of God*," 65 n. 6.
39. Brown, *Augustine of Hippo*, 330; Van der Meer, *Augustine the Bishop*, 88.
40. Brown, *Augustine of Hippo*, 240; Van der Meer, *Augustine the Bishop*, 80.

Augustine justified different types of coercion in this period. He maintained that exile and fines for leaders (when effective) were justified but changed his mind in advocating the coercion of Donatists to join the Catholic Church (instead of merely preventing Donatists from attacking Catholics), and in assenting to corporal punishment for violent heretics (but not for nonviolent ones). I have not found evidence that he advocated punishment for nonviolent Donatist followers, other than small fines (see *Ep.* 104.1–2, written in 409). He judged that the success of the Edict of Unity of 405 was based on the fact that most Donatist followers remained in the Church due to sloth, habit, and intimidation by their leaders. For these people, he provides a somewhat Aristotelian account of why coercion appears to have successfully effected "conversions": "Yet these same persons, under force of custom *(vi consuetudinis)*, would in no way have thought of being changed to a better condition, had they not, under the terror of this danger *(nisi hoc terrore perculisi)*, directed their minds earnestly to the study of truth" (*Ep.* 93.1.1). He reiterates this point later in the same letter:

> How many were bound, not by truth—for you [Vincentius, Donatist bishop] never pretended to that as yours—but by the chains of inveterate custom *(obduratae consuetudinis)* . . . ! How many supposed the sect of Donatus to be the true church, merely because ease had made them too listless, or conceited, or sluggish, to take pains to examine Catholic truth! How many would have entered earlier had not the calumnies of slanderers, who declared that we offered something else than we do upon the altar of God, shut them out! How many, believing that it mattered not to which party a Christian might belong, remained in the schism of Donatus only because they had been born into it, and no one was compelling them to forsake it and pass over into the Catholic church! (*Ep.* 93.5.17)

This statement reflects Augustine's view that law may force a certain number of people to change their actions and habits, in order to give them the opportunity to act virtuously. He observes that such people were held to heresy out of old habits and by misunderstanding the practices of the Catholic Church. As mentioned above, Donatists and Catholics had little contact with one another, since Donatists strove to separate themselves from "impure" Catholics. Their views of one another were incomplete, and followers in both camps were ignorant of one another, and, therefore, easily misled. Some Donatists remained because of intimidation by their leaders (see *Ep.* 83.1, 85.29, 93.1.3, 3.10). Thus, according to Augustine, the chains of bad habit developed because Donatist followers were ignorant of Catholics, and removing their leaders was the only way to convert them.

Augustine's understanding of the coercive aspect of law, as shown here, is similar to Aristotle's account of how law forces wicked people to act virtuously so that at least some of them will then become virtuous. Coercion in these circumstances is a necessary but not a sufficient cause of conversion. The role of bad habit in sin is a constant theme, especially in Augustine's *Confessions* where he narrates the ways in which his bad habits prevented him from fully loving God. Elsewhere, he points out the extent to which habits shape our perspectives: "For it is not for nothing that custom is called a sort of second and fitted-on nature. But we see new senses in the judging of these kinds of corporeal things, built by custom, by another custom disappear" (*DM* 6.7.19). Custom, as a kind of second nature, shapes our perceptions of right and wrong in ways that we may forget what is natural and not according to custom. Thus, Augustine uses terms such as *terror* and *shock* to indicate the means of breaking these habits in people's minds.

Augustine uses violent language in his rhetoric toward the Donatist bishop, and this harshness gives the impression of a gap between the habits of the heretic and the purposes of punishment. In other words, it gives the impression that coercion is detached from persuasion, since the means of coercion are disconnected from the understanding of the coerced. Coercion appears as a battle of wills, containing "a moment of 'pure violence.' " Augustine's rhetoric toward the Donatist bishops certainly includes an element of coercion. But is this his final view on the matter? Evidence indicates that it is not. A more substantive account of coercion lies beneath Augustine's excessive rhetoric directed toward Vincentius, the Donatist bishop and recipient of the infamous letter. However, Augustine was unsuccessful in ensuring that his substantive teaching was influential.

It is not surprising that Augustine's rhetoric veils a deeper meaning. His antipolitical rhetoric in the *City of God,* for example, covers his substantive political teaching. He did not wish to make this teaching explicit because he did not want to give his audience any reason to think that they could gain salvation through political means. The Donatists would certainly have been targeted by this rhetoric because they, like the pagans who constituted part of Augustine's audience in the *City of God,* sought perfect blessedness in this life. As with his strategy in the *City of God,* in his letters to the Donatists Augustine uses rhetoric to belittle worldly ambition and pride.

Peter Brown, in an essay called "The Limits of Intolerance," has recently explained that modern readers often overestimate the intolerance and "pure violence" of Christian apologists such as Augustine. He points out that, in the late empire, moral and religious order was preserved through a distinctive "style of command," such as unchallenged authority, fear, and force, which was accepted by the upper classes (to govern both themselves and the lower classes):

> For modern persons, it is not an altogether pleasant glimpse. If authority was to work without overt violence, it had to seem "natural"; it had to relay commands with quiet certainty from a position of unchallenged superiority to persons whose inferiority, also, was to be taken for granted. As a result of the religious changes of the age, the social hierarchy became even more high pitched. . . . Among the upper classes, a combination of browbeating and cajolery was the stuff of late Roman politics.[41]

Elites in the late Roman empire governed themselves through a network of patronage and honor. It was socially dangerous to overstep the bounds of what was permissible in these kinds of debates. Thus, Brown notes, it is a mistake to assert straightforwardly that the persecutions in which Augustine participated provided the principles of later persecutions: "In this manner, the opening of the modern debate on religious tolerance was fueled by a characteristically late Roman betrayal of a breach in decorum." Brown alerts the reader of the unspoken social conventions that structured Augustine's rhetoric. Historical scholarship on Roman legal rhetoric confirms Brown's thesis by comparing the rhetoric of religious disputes to the tone of legal battles: "Repeatedly, orators 'used' the law to wrong-foot opponents, not only in real life, as Augustine did, but also in leading a case, as it were a case at law. In this quasi-courtroom, 'they,' the enemy, were the law-breakers, while the speaker, invariably, was the champion of right, justice and the lawful authority of emperors." It was common to imitate the rhetorical style of command of the emperor, as well as to portray themselves as "victims" of their more "powerful" opponents.[42] According to this view, Augustine used the rhetoric of Roman law and of aristocratic manner to shame Vincentius and the Donatists for their base actions. Such shaming also belittles the shamed, and portrays them as incapable of reasoning and amenable to persuasion, which explains his imitation of the emperor's rhetoric that utilizes command rather than persuasion. Such a relationship between "shamer" and "shamed" would contain the aforementioned "moment of 'pure violence.' " However, the scholarship of Brown and Harries indicates that this

41. Brown, "The Limits of Intolerance," in *Authority and the Sacred: Aspects of Christianisation of the Roman World*, 44–45.

42. Ibid., 46; Harries, *Law and Empire*, 96, 2–5.

moment is rooted in the rhetoric of social decorum and not necessarily in the substance of Augustine's argument.

Since fines and exile of heretics did not appear to be working, a certain kind of violent coercion was required. This necessity, however, presented a conflict for Augustine. He felt compelled to exhort imperial authorities to enforce laws, but those authorities were often prone to excessive violence in their enforcement of those laws. Augustine's letters show that he strove to convince civil authorities to be more lenient. For example, he outlines the above principles for removing property in a letter (*Ep.* 104, written in 409) responding to Nectarius of Calama, a pagan philosopher, who had charged him with being responsible for the violent measures used by imperial authorities against a population in which there were religious riots (*Ep.* 103.4). Augustine denies responsibility and further states his opposition to violent measures; he advocates instead removal of property: "Far be it from us to demand the infliction, either by ourselves or by anyone, of such hardships upon any of our enemies . . . ! Examine more carefully my letter, to which you have so reluctantly sent a reply, for I have in it made my views sufficiently plain" (*Ep.* 104.1–2, referring to 93). That imperial authorities used violence in this way indicates that Augustine was unable to restrain them. It also shows his awareness that people misinterpreted his views. As Brown observes, Augustine's "interventions by letter, therefore, should be treated as exceptions to the usual routine of suppression: they reflect circumstances where the application of the laws had passed beyond his immediate control and, so, called for correspondence."[43]

Augustine's attempt to restrain officials is seen in a letter in which he asks Apringius, proconsul of Africa and Marcellinus's brother: "[W]hy do you not commute your sentence to a more prudent and more lenient one, as judges have the liberty of doing even in non-ecclesiastical cases?" (*Ep.* 134, written in 412). Even after his notorious change of heart in 408 when he stated that compulsion is rightful, Augustine always opposed the death penalty.[44] He told Donatus (a civil authority unrelated to the founder of Donatism) that the Catholics would stop bringing cases to his tribunal if he used capital punishment. In one letter, Augustine objects to the capital punishment of a murderous heretic and reminds his friend Marcellinus that the purpose of punishment is to turn men "from their insane disquiet to the quietness of men in their sound judgment, and

43. Brown, "Augustine's Attitude," 275 n. 2.

44. Brown observes Augustine was unable to prevent many executions (*Augustine of Hippo*, 242). Augustine opposed the death penalty because it prevents repentance (see *Ep.* 153.18, written ca. 414; see also 139.2 [written in 412], where he argues that capital punishment dishonors the blood of the martyrs). The Donatists claimed to be martyrs on account of their being persecuted.

betake themselves to some useful labour. This is indeed called a penal sentence" (*Ep.* 133.1, written in 412). Augustine argues that murderers' lives should be spared, and, further, that they should be tortured "not by stretching them on the rack, not by furrowing their flesh with iron claws, not by scorching them with flames, but by beating them with wooden rods *(sed virgarum verberibus eruisti)*—a mode of correction used by schoolmasters *(magistris artium liberalium)*, and by parents themselves in chastising children, and often by bishops in the sentences awarded by them" (*Ep.* 133.1–2). Although people today might wince at Augustine's general acceptance of torture as a method of discovering the perpetrator of a crime (he and other Romans thought it worked), it should be noted that he states that the actual punishment should be lighter. He also advocates beating the murderers with wooden rods, a method of discipline used by teachers, parents, and bishops. In its cultural context, Augustine's view of punishment was relatively mild; for instance, imperial law called for the use of leaden whips (*CT* 16.5.53, March 6, 412). In other words, the maximum penalty that a heretic who committed murder could expect, in Augustine's doctrine of compulsion, would be the same that a schoolboy would receive from his teachers.[45]

At one point Augustine appears to advocate violent methods for coercing heretics who had not engaged in violent activities; however, this is misleading. It should be noted that he uses a double-voice rhetoric to exhort Boniface, an imperial official, to apply the law. He uses violent and figurative language to exhort the official to keep the Donatists in awe of the law, but he fails to give a specific recommendation on the type of punishment; despite Augustine's intention, however, he failed to restrain the official. In a letter that has come down to us as a treatise titled "On the Correction of Donatists," he apparently asserts that beating heretics with rods is appropriate (*Ep.* 185.6.22–23, written in 417). He advocates this course after arguing that the persistence of Donatist violence shows that verbal persuasion, which up until then had failed, must be supplemented by coercion. This is the case because heretics lack the fear that one has of being separate from God (*Ep.* 185.6.21); instead, they fear only temporal punishments. However, Augustine's apparent advocacy of violent coercion constitutes an example of what Brown has called his "two voices *(duos voces)*" that reflect the scriptural polarities of "severity and mildness, of fear and love";[46] closer examination of the letter shows that he treats punishment by

45. This is a punishment that Augustine himself received from his schoolmasters. See *Conf.* 1.9–10; *CD* 22.22.

46. Brown, "Augustine's Attitude," 272.

rods as a figurative representation of the awe of imperial authority that heretics should fear. The *Theodosian Code* itself provided Augustine with a precedent for using figurative language. For instance, one law proclaims that heretics would be punished *(urere)* by deportation (*CT* 16.2.40). *Urere* means literally "to brand" or "to burn," as in "to be branded a traitor." However, the term is used figuratively here, since the punishment referred to is deportation rather than burning or branding.

Augustine speaks literally of using rods only for heretics who have committed violent acts. He invokes a passage from Proverbs to justify violent methods: "'You will beat him with the rod *(percutis eum virga)*, and will free his soul from death' (Prov. 23:14); and elsewhere he says, 'He who spares the rod *(parcit baculo)* hates his son' (Prov. 23:24)" (*Ep.* 185.6.21). However, here again he speaks in a double voice. His rhetoric seems to encourage the authority to use violence to coerce all heretics to return to the fold. After having made his case, however, he concludes that he has been discussing heretics who have used violence (*Ep.* 185.6.23). He uses the example of Paul (which I discuss again below) to illustrate his point. Christ compelled Paul to love Christ by striking him down and by afterward consoling him:

> Let them recognize in his case Christ first compelling *(prius cogentem)*, and afterwards teaching *(postea docentem)*; first striking *(prius ferientem)*, and afterwards consoling *(postea consolantem)*. For it is wonderful how he who entered the service of the gospel in the first instance under the compulsion of bodily punishment *(poena corporis)*, afterwards labored more in the gospel than all they who were called by word only; and he who was compelled by the greater influence of fear to love, displayed that perfect love which casts out fear. (*Ep.* 185.6.22)

Augustine concludes from the example of Paul that the Church should use force in compelling violent heretics to return to the fold: "Why, therefore *(ergo)*, should not the church use force in compelling *(cogeret)* her lost sons to return, if the lost sons compelled *(coegerunt)* others to their destruction?" (*Ep.* 185.6.23). The Latin *ergo* indicates that Augustine considers this statement a conclusion based on the previous passage. The lesson he draws from Christ striking Paul is that those who persecute the Church, as did Paul, and who violently coerced others to remain Donatist, deserve to be coerced with violence.

Augustine reiterates this point when he compares the Church to a shepherd who brings sheep back to the fold "by fear or even the pain of the whip *(flagellorum terroribus)*, if [sheep and heretics] show symptoms of resistance; especially since, if they multiply with growing abundance among the fugitive slaves and robbers *(praesertim quoniam si apud fugitivos servos et praedones fecunditate multiplicentur)*, he has the more right in that the mark of the master is recognized on them, who is not outraged in those whom we receive but do not rebaptise." The term *especially (praesertim)* in this quote reflects Augustine's emphasis on curbing the violence of heretics. In general, *praesertim* means "especially" or "above all," which makes it possible to interpret Augustine here as making a comparison of degree instead of kind. He may be arguing that all heretics deserve violent methods of coercion but that heretics who commit violent atrocities deserve it especially. However, *praesertim* here needs to be interpreted in the context he has previously established. This context involves the recommendation to Boniface, the Roman official and recipient of this letter, that imperial law must stop the violence of the heretics, and that this be achieved only by banning the sect. Augustine emphasizes the awe engendered by the violence of the imperial law. He then hints, however, that he is referring to violent methods for perpetrators of violence, and that lesser penalties are suitable for heretics not engaged in violent acts. *Praesertim*, therefore, means not so much the comparative "especially" or "above all," but, rather, constitutes the rhetorical hammer with which Augustine emphasizes the necessity of having Roman law instill awe in order to dissuade violent and nonviolent heretics, even though he believed that nonviolent heretics do not deserve violent punishments. Unfortunately, this kind of rhetoric was taken literally, and thus it failed to restrain imperial authorities and future generations of inquisitors.

Finally, Augustine's understanding of coercion as educative is illuminated in his discussion of the way the trials of heretics should be conducted:

> You will, however, most effectively help us to secure the fruit of our labours and dangers, if you take care that the imperial laws for the restraining of their sect, which is full of conceit and of impious pride, be so used that they may not appear either to themselves or to others to be suffering hardship in any form for the sake of truth and righteousness; but suffer them, when this is requested at your hands, to be convinced and instructed *(convinci atque instrui)* of certain things by the most manifest documentation *(rerum certarum manifestissimis documentis)* in the presence of your Excellency or of inferior judges, in order that those who are arrested by your command may themselves incline their stubborn will to the better part, and may read these things profitably to others in their party. (*Ep.* 100.2)

The proceedings of the trial should be public so that the individual understands clearly the purpose of the charges. Since the Donatists were making what he saw as false claims to martyrdom, Augustine thought that the purpose of the charges ought to be made public. This would prevent the Donatists from claiming that they had been falsely accused, and thus from portraying themselves as victims, a portrayal that would otherwise support their martyrology. Making the charges public also had the effect of explaining the purpose of the charges to others in the sect, which would act both as a clarification and as a warning. The public nature of the trial is important for a right-by-nature theory of punishment, since the form of the trial requires that the prosecutors attempt to convince and instruct the accused that the criminal charge is based on reasonable grounds, and not on reasons of political convenience for the authorities. This quotation alone does not prove that the trial aims to convince and instruct the accused on reasonable grounds. However, Augustine's theory of the purpose of punishment—to educate and to form virtue—indicates that the trial would have to speak to the accused's intellect in order for punishment, in the case of established guilt, to harmonize with its purpose. The requirement for the proceedings to be recorded and given to the sect at large is consistent with this general purpose of punishment, in that it attempts to teach others in the sect about the purpose of the accusation.

PRINCIPLES OF COERCION

One of the purposes of coercing heretics is to preserve the physical security of church members. Augustine thought that one of the duties of a ruler is preserving the safety of the city (or church in Augustine's case) as a place in which citizens can, to an extent, fulfill their particular perfections. He draws from the example of Paul who sought assistance from the emperor when he discovered there were conspiracies against his life: "He sought assistance, therefore, not so much with any desire of revenging himself, as with the view of defending the church entrusted to his charge. And if he had omitted to do this, he would have deserved not to be praised for his patience *(patientia)*, but to be blamed for negligence *(negligentia)*" (*Ep.* 185.7.28, citing Acts 23:17–32). This passage shows that the ruler shirks his duty when he neglects to defend his city or church. The precarious position of the Church in North Africa made this concern paramount. A common criticism of this kind of reasoning is that it appears to apply the standards of the world to the life of the Church. For instance, would it not have been saintly for Paul to have been martyred? Does Christ not teach one to reject the ways of emperors and soldiers, and instead entrust oneself and one's church to God? This view is critical of

Augustine's apparent impatience, which led him to distrust God's providence and, consequently, to intervene in God's plan. Augustine might be accused of failing to trust that God's work will be done regardless of one's actions. The above passage, however, indicates that he considered this to be negligence because, as a ruler or bishop, one would neglect those entrusted to one's charge. He would have neglected those for whose souls he is in some way (although not completely) responsible. It would be unjust to keep faith at the expense of safety in this instance. In this sense, the case of Augustine's justification of coercion is comparable to his discussion of whether it was rightful for the city of Sagentum to keep faith with the gods and the Romans and cause its own destruction (*CD* 22.6; discussed in Chapter 2 of this study). In that instance, it was shown that Augustine hints that Sagentum would have been justified in preserving itself. It is not that Augustine chooses the safety of the Church at the expense of virtue or keeping faith, but rather that he understands the love of God and of neighbor as being expressed in the cultivation of the virtue of those under the governor.

The main principle animating Augustine's understanding of coercion is reflected in his statement that the heretic should be threatened with deprivation of the proximate or inferior good that masquerades as the greatest good: "[O]ffenders must be deprived of that which they most fear to lose" (*Ep.* 104.1.2). What the heretic most fears to lose is that which he falsely thinks will bring salvation:

> [T]he thing to be considered when any one is coerced *(cogitur)*, is not the mere fact of the coercion, but the nature of that to which he is coerced, whether it be good or bad: not that any one can be good in spite of his own will, but that, through fear of suffering what he does not desire *(sed timendo quod non vult pati)*, he either renounces his hostile prejudices *(impedientem animositatem)*, or is compelled to examine truth of which he had been contentedly ignorant; so that through fearing, repudiate falsehood that he had contended, or seek truth of which he had been ignorant, and desiring to hold now what he had rejected *(ut timens vel respuat falsam de quo contendebat, vel quaerat verum quod nesciebat, et volens teneat jam quod nolebat)*. (*Ep.* 93.5.16)

These passages appear to reflect the "moment of 'pure violence,' " as described by Milbank. Augustine seems merely to state that the heretic will lose that which he most fears losing; if this is all he says, then the relation between the authority and the heretic is merely a battle of wills, since Augustine does not explain how the miserable heretic is then to love the real good and not just his proximate good. One suspects that Brown's comments on the Roman "style of command" are applicable here; Augustine had previously stated that the purpose of coercion is not to return evil for evil (*Ep.* 93.1.2). If coercion entails merely depriving a heretic of what he most fears to lose, then coercion would in fact be a return of evil for evil. Augustine does not appear to explain what to be the necessary next step. Neglecting to do this does not necessarily indicate that his theory of coercion contains this "moment of 'pure violence,'" however. Rather, neglecting to do this is consistent with Brown's view of the style of command among Roman elites. Authority does not need to justify itself to those it commands, and Augustine incorporates this idea into his rhetoric.

Furthermore, the second passage quoted above implies an Aristotelian understanding of punishment and law that transcends this moment of pure violence. The purpose of law is to enable citizens to choose the right and the good. Whether they do so lies beyond the power of the law. This is reflected in Augustine's statement that coercion puts the heretic into the position of either renouncing his "hostile prejudices" or actively turning to the search for truth. The purpose of coercion is to clarify Church doctrine to the heretic. After having done so, the individual heretic, freed from his initial ignorance, would have to decide whether to love the truth (and enter the Church). Force, in this circumstance, is a necessary but not a sufficient cause of conversion. The purpose of coercion, according to this passage, is to show the heretic the insufficiency of his object of worship and to teach him about the Church in order to prevent his hostility toward it. To use a popular metaphor, the heretic is brought to water but is not forced to drink.

COERCION AS HEALING

Augustine's method of relating means to ends is explained more completely in his discussion of Christian healing. Spiritual healing parallels God's way of healing the sins of human beings. God's healing is based on what Augustine calls the principles of contrariety and similarity (*DDC* 1.27), which work in the following way. The principle of contrariety shows the heretic how opposed his proximate cause is to his proper end. The principle is insufficient because, taken by itself, it contains the "moment of 'pure violence.'" This principle is seen in Augustine's dictum of "removing that which the heretic fears most to lose." This is why Augustine adds the principle of similarity, by which the heretic learns that his proximate good masquerading as the highest good actually intimates the highest good.

Augustine compares these principles to those a doctor follows in healing a wound: "A doctor treating a physical wound applies some medications that are contrary—a cold one to a hot wound, a dry one to a wet wound, and so on—and also some that are similar, such as a round bandage to a round wound and a rectangular bandage to a rectangular wound, and he does not apply the same ligature to all wounds, but matches like with like" (*DDC* 1.28). The principle of contrariety is applied in order to moderate the extremes of a wound. The principle of similarity is applied so as to suit the wound. He uses this analogy in explaining how the principle of contrariety is present in God's healing activity:

> Because human beings fell through pride, [God's wisdom] used humility in healing them. We were deceived by the wisdom of the serpent; we are freed by the foolishness of God. But just as that was called wisdom yet was foolishness to those who despise God, so this so-called foolishness is wisdom to those who overcome the devil. We made base use of immortality, and so we died; Christ made good use of mortality, so we live. The disease entered through a corrupted female mind; healing emerged from an intact female body. Also relevant to the principle of contrariety is the fact that our vices too are treated by the example of his virtues. (*DDC* 1.29)

God applies the contrary aspects of our vice to bring that extreme to a condition of health: God's humility heals pride; God's "foolishness" heals false wisdom. Each contrary element opposes the extreme of the particular vice.

Augustine proposes that the principle of similarity prevents the vice from lapsing into its opposite vice. He then explains the principle of similarity in God's healing activity: "Examples of similarity in the kinds of bandages (as it were) applied to our limbs and wounds are these: it was one born of a woman that freed those deceived by a woman; it was a mortal man that freed mortals; and it was by death that he freed the dead" (*DDC* 1.30). The principle of similarity complements the principle of contrariety by showing the heretic how his proximate good actually intimates the highest good, even though he actually opposes the highest good in his obstinate and inordinate love of the proximate good. This is seen in Augustine's suggestions that Donatist heretics should lose only enough property to prevent them from harming Catholics. Augustine also applies the principle of similarity in his acknowledgment that Donatist criticisms of Catholic corruption contain an element of truth, and that these criticisms reflect the way that both sides share in truth (see *Ep.* 43.8.23). The operation of this principle is illustrated in the context of Augustine's strategy of internal Church reformation below.

In this context, Augustine's principles of similarity and contrariety compare with Aristotle's understanding of forming desires by finding the mean between extremes. For Aristotle, sometimes an inordinate desire can find the mean by applying its opposite (for example, forcing a coward to commit rash deeds), but the individual must also recognize that the opposing action, and its accompanying desire, also shares in the mean. Therefore, Augustine's theory of coercion lacks the "moment of 'pure violence' " by which the greatest good is completely alien to the good loved by the heretic. The principles of similarity and contrariety show sinful human beings how to reach the final goal that their sins purport to achieve, and also demonstrate how far their sins are from reaching their goal. The principles can be related to Augustine's statement, in Epistle 93, that the heretic is coerced by losing what he most fears losing. One loses one's greatest possession by understanding how short it falls in securing happiness (the principle of contrariety), but one is possibly led to see how that possession intimates the greater principle that needs to be fulfilled for happiness (the principle of similarity). For instance, exile is appropriate for one whose own purported purity alienates him from other human beings (thus showing how such purity is false); one has one's silver idols taken away and thus sees how one's reliance on those idols is misplaced.

These principles are reflected in Augustine's example of the conversion of Paul, used in order to demonstrate the principle of coercion:

> You also read how he who was at first Saul, and afterwards Paul, was compelled by the great violence *(magna violentia . . . compulsum)* with which Christ coerced him, to know and to embrace the truth; for you cannot but think that the light which your eyes enjoy is more precious to men than money or any other possession *(quamlemlibet possessionem)*. This light, lost suddenly by him when he was cast to the ground by the heavenly voice, he did not recover until he became a member of the Holy church. (*Ep.* 93.1.5)

This example shows that Augustine's principle of coercion involves the punishment of deprivation of one's proximate good, which still shares with the highest good. The Lord blinded Saul, but the Lord also gave him a vision of the "third heaven," which convinced him to enter the Church. Saul's blindness in sight enabled him to focus on what the Lord wanted him to see in his mind. Paul suffered the opposite (or contrariety) of sight, blindness, and was healed through similarity by the light of the third heaven of his spiritual vision. The agent who coerces does not return sight, as this example might suggest; rather, he teaches the heretic about the insufficiency of his proximate good, and attempts to convince him of the goodness of the highest good, by showing him that his previous understanding of the highest good was false. At this point, coercion must end and the heretic must be left to himself to decide whether to enter the Church or, at the very least, refrain from attacking it. Both principles, contrariety and similarity, are important for Augustine's theory; the principle of contrariety, applied by depriving the heretic of his possession, is insufficient if taken by itself, since, unless the heretic is taught, through the principle of similarity, to move beyond his possession, he will not know how his possession can be fulfilled.

REFORMATION STRATEGY

Augustine's strategy of coercing heretics is not entirely one-sided, but it is accompanied by a reformation strategy on the part of the Church. The problem of maintaining virtue within the Church, and specifically of preventing scandal, was a paramount concern for Augustine. This in part explains his reluctance to embrace coercion because he was afraid of the effect of false conversions.[47]

In his letters, Augustine emphasizes the necessity for heretics to reform. This makes a certain amount of sense given the nature of his rhetoric, as discussed above. His reformation strategy, though not explicitly addressed in his polemical letters to the Donatists, is presented in his theoretical *City of God*. For example, there he discloses his concern for scandal when he emphasizes that Christians must truly be Christians and not just be Christians in name only: "Where therefore who are, and are called, Christians *(qui sumus vocamurque Christiani)* believe not in Peter, but in him in whom Peter believed" (*CD* 18.54; see also 1.35). Augustine's ecclesiology is based on the view that the Church will consist of reprobates as well as Christians, since it will experience the intermingling of the cities of God and of man:

> In this evil world, therefore, in these evil days, when amid present humiliation the church is preparing for her future high estate, and is schooled by the goads of fear, the tortures of sorrow, the vexations of toil and the dangers of temptation, rejoicing only in hope, in so far as her joy is wholesome, many reprobates are mingled with the good, and both kinds are gathered together as it were into the dragnet of the gospel. And in this world, as it were in a sea, both swim indiscriminately enclosed in nets until shore is reached, where the evil are to be separated from the good, and "God is to be all in all" (1 Cor. 15:28). (*CD* 18.49)

47. Markus, *Saeculum*, 138.

Augustine rejects the view that one can be saved merely by partaking in the sacrament; he maintains that one must also steadfastly practice virtue (*CD* 21.20). Those who sin and persist in sinning without asking forgiveness actually separate themselves from the body of Christ: "[Christ] shows what it is to eat the body of Christ and drink His blood, not only in the sacrament, but in reality, for to remain in Christ is to have Christ also remaining in him. For this is the same as if He said: 'He who does not remain in me, and in whom I do not remain, may not say or think that he is eating my body or drinking my blood.' So those who are not his members do not remain in Christ" (*CD* 21.25; citing John 6:56). These sins include not only explicit heresy such as that of the Donatists, but also other iniquities. The key is that one separates oneself from the body of Christ when one perseveres in sin: "For if they persevere in these sins until the end of this life, they cannot be said to persevere in Christ till the end." Such sins can be committed both by heretics and by those who, being Christians in name only, merely engage in ritual observance rather than attempt to be virtuous, thus bringing scandal to the Church. Such people are heretics inasmuch as they persevere in cutting themselves off from the body of Christ while calling themselves Christians. This requires that the Church reform itself by cultivating the virtues of its members, rather than by persecuting them (as the Donatists did with their own) when they do not cause scandal by leading others astray. If it does not reform itself in this way, then the Donatist charge that the Catholic Church is irreparably corrupt is justified. Although Augustine does not appear explicitly to grant the Donatists this point in the letters, he implicitly grants it when he points to the danger that merely nominal Christians pose to the Church. His reformation strategy requires that the Church experience the intermingling of heavenly and earthly cities, without succumbing either to Donatist-type legalism and hypermoralism or to an earthly organization of *traditores.*

Augustine points out that the success of the Church in satisfying the longings of human beings has led to the entry into the Church of many people who have only feigned love. He states this only to prevent Christians from becoming prideful about their identity and about the success of the Church: "But the devil, seeing the temples of the demons deserted and the human race running to the name of the Mediator who sets men free, stirred up heretics to resist the Christian doctrine under Christian guise *(sub vocabulo Christiano)*, as if they could be kept indifferently in the city of God without any reproof, even as the city of confusion kept indifferently the philosophers who held diverse and conflicting beliefs" (*CD* 18.51). Later in the chapter he reiterates: "For [heretics] are the cause of railing against the Christian and catholic name *(nomen)*; and the dearer this name is to those who wish to live a godly life in Christ, the more they grieve that evildoers within the church make it less attractive than the minds of the godly desire" (*CD* 18.51). The success of the Church creates a new danger; whereas before it was persecuted by outsiders, it is now persecuted from within by those who seek to destroy it by giving it a bad name.

Augustine argues that the existence of heretics is important if weaker members of the Church are to recognize true Church doctrine, and thus virtue. Defending the Church against heresies provides leaders of the Church with the opportunity to clarify doctrine and to instruct: "No doubt many matters pertaining to the catholic faith are not only more diligently investigated when they are attacked by the feverish restlessness of the heretics, but are more clearly understood and more fervently expounded for the sake of defending them against these enemies. Thus the controversy stirred up by the adversary affords an opportunity for instruction" (*CD* 16.2; see also *Conf.* 7.9; *DDC* 3.104–5; *DVR* 8.15). Defending the ecclesiastical body against heretics is useful because it enables its members to understand virtue. This situation is analogous to the political situation in which citizens gain deeper insight into the principles of their regime when they are faced by a political crisis or enemy. For example, one possible explanation for the current "malaise" or dilemma in Western constitutional republics is that their citizens now lack an ideological enemy, communism, against which to organize. Augustine makes a similar point when he observes that Scipio opposed the destruction of Carthage, because such destruction would eventually undermine Rome: "He feared security, that enemy of weak minds, and he perceived that a wholesome fear would be a fit guardian for the citizens" (*CD* 1.30). Augustine's account of group identity is not reducible to hostility to the enemy; he points out, rather, that heresies help to clarify Church doctrine. In other words, the initial premise of the Church remains constant, but heretics or a crisis can provide members of the Church with deeper understanding of that premise.

This strategy of using heresy to reform the Church with its internal "heretics" illuminates Augustine's general use of *exempla*. Chapters 1, 5, and 6 showed that Augustine treats the *exempla* of the city of God and the city of man in two ways. On the one hand, the Church represents the perfect virtue of the city of God, whereas earthly cities filled with the reprobate represent the city of man. On the other hand, the world, which includes the political city and the Church, experiences these two cities as intermingled and intermixed, just as most human beings experience their wills as divided. As a result, Augustine also treats these *exempla* as models for each other, and treats the Church and heretics in an analogous manner.

According to Augustine, the principles of similarity and contrariety teach the heretic that the object of his love is insufficient, but that this object nevertheless shares with the highest good. He argues also that an intra-Church reformation strategy complements the coercion of heretics. Although Augustine does not appear to have admitted explicitly to the Donatists that the Catholic Church was filled with heretics, he insists in his theoretical treatise, the *City of God*, that it was disrupted by those who called themselves Catholic but whose perseverance in sin had caused them to separate from the body of Christ. This implicitly constitutes a partial agreement with the Donatist charge that some Catholics were corrupt (see *Ep.* 43). The difference between the Catholics and the Donatists was, however, that the Catholic Church, as viewed by Augustine, consists of the intermingling of the cities of God and of man, and that the body of Christ is more than the sum total of its members' virtues.

Augustine's theory of coercion is situated to some extent within a historical context. He changed his mind to justify coercion only after long holding the hope that the Donatists could be persuaded to join the Catholic Church and to cease their violent activities. In addition, he hoped that virtue could be instilled by persuasion; however, a combination of Donatist principles and Roman politics made that impossible. Coercion is a last resort to be applied only after the possibility of persuasion is exhausted. Augustine's insistence on an internal reformation strategy on the part of the Church indicates that he believed such violence involved corruption within the Church. Such reformation does not end even when the possibility of persuading heretics (which includes showing the heretics how much the Church has reformed) has been exhausted. Once it has been exhausted, Augustine considered that exile and fines become the optimal forms of coercion, and then only for leaders.

The exile of Donatist leaders from the community makes heresy concrete, since heresy entails spiritual separation. This means that the optimal form of coercion entails depriving heretics of the fruits of community. In Augustine's case, exile was not practical because the Donatists constituted the majority of the population in North Africa. The second-best form of coercion was to deprive the heretics of property, but only to the extent of depriving them of the means of false worship and of harming Catholics. Augustine opposed depriving heretics of the means of sustenance, since he did not want to make them dependent on others. From the evidence I have found, Augustine advocated physical punishments only for heretics who murdered; he does not appear to have prescribed beatings for those who did not commit acts of violence.[48] Augustine opposed the death penalty, believing, rather, that murderers deserved only the kind of beatings that schoolboys received. The important point here is that Augustine insisted that coercion be educative, even for murderers, and that he shared this view with the ancient world in general, and certainly with the Roman world. Unfortunately, Augustine's rhetoric, intended to exhort reluctant authorities to apply the law, albeit without excess, was taken in later ages to justify ruthless persecution.

48. See Deane, *Political and Social Ideas,* 206.

[23]

MARRIAGE IN ITS PROCREATIVE DIMENSION: THE MEANING OF THE INSTITUTION OF MARRIAGE THROUGHOUT THE AGES*

DR. CHARLES J. REID, JR.**

The word "institution" is one of those open-ended words that could mean many things to many different audiences. I intend to use the word in much the same manner as it has been employed by Douglass North in his studies of Western economic history. Institutions, North has written, define "the rules of the game; . . . they structure incentives in exchange, whether political, social, or economic."[1] Institutions, in other words, embrace rules of law and other norms governing human interaction. They help us to channel human behavior in certain ways and not in others. Necessarily, they also embrace the belief systems that stand behind and animate the rules. They help to define social expectations and to set standards.

I shall take the position that the institutional weight of marriage, for most of the last two thousand years, has been in favor of seeing marriage as the appropriate vehicle in which to give birth to and raise children. The procreative dimension of marriage has been the central core organizing principle of the institutional—that is, the legal—understanding of marriage from the time of pre-Christian Roman law to the present, although it is currently endangered by various shifts in legal norms and public philosophies. But, for most of its history, it can fairly be said that the legal order of the West has dedicated itself, through a variety of rules and understandings, incentives and disincentives, to preserving marriage as a principal means of bringing into being the next generation. To have made this sort of claim even as recently as two or three decades ago might have appeared as stating

---

* An earlier version of this article was presented at a conference on family law and policy held in Banff National Park, Alberta.

** Associate Professor of Law, University of St. Thomas School of Law (Minn.).

1. Douglass C. North, *Institutions, Ideology, and Economic Performance*, *in* THE REVOLUTION IN DEVELOPMENT ECONOMICS 95 (James A. Dorn, Steve H. Hanke & Alan A. Walters eds., 1989).

the obvious. But in light of recent arguments about the nature and function of marriage—recently accepted by courts in the United States and Canada—reviewing the history of the procreative dimension of marriage seems like a worthwhile undertaking.

In this paper, I shall consider four societies that have existed over the course of western history. These include pre-Christian classical Rome, the early medieval West of the sixth through eleventh centuries, the High Middle Ages of the twelfth through fifteenth centuries, and the Anglican high church and theological culture of the early modern period. There is, in each of these societies, a great emphasis placed on marriage as the legitimate means of bringing into being the next generation. Indeed, the procreative dimension of marriage was, in each of these societies, the central organizing principle of legal analysis and social life.

I. Pre-Christian Roman Law

Let us begin with pre-Christian Roman law. The popular opinion, shaped probably by pulp novels and television and film representation, would have one believe that the Romans did not hold marriage in high regard. The morals of Petronius and Nero are likely what most people would think of should they be asked to focus on pre-Christian Roman sexual behaviors and expectations. The law, however, did not reflect or condone this code of conduct. There were steady efforts by lawmakers to provide institutional support for marriage and to recognize marriage as the means by which the next generation should come into being and be trained to accept its responsibilities.

We might consider the Augustan marriage reforms. Emperor Octavian, who took the name "Augustus"—"the Great" or "the Exalted One"—sought to restore order to a Roman Empire that had experienced decades of turmoil.[2] He understood marriage to be under grave threat in his day (he reigned from 31 BC to AD 14), and was especially concerned with the failure of the Roman elites to have children and thus to produce the next generation of leading citizens. Rome, in the century before Augustus ascended to the imperial throne, had undergone wrenching social and economic change. Over the course of one hundred years, Rome expanded its imperial reach over large parts of the Mediterranean basin and also over areas of the far North—northern Gaul and even Britain. Rome had also undergone a series of bloody civil wars. The old republican forms of government lost their real significance and were replaced by the principate—government by an emperor who preserved, on behalf of the elites, the old republican titles but who ruled on his own accord. In the course of these

2. One of Augustus's most recent English-language biographers begins by describing him, then Octavian, as "[t]he man who can justifiably be called the founder of the Roman Empire." Pat Southern, Augustus 1 (1998).

upheavals, the elites stopped having children. Indeed, one sees the emergence in the course of the first century BC of a kind of contraceptive mentality that favored present-centered hedonism over the foresight and sacrifice that fecund married life necessarily entailed.[3]

Augustus sought to counter these trends and to encourage the growth and fostering of families through a series of inducements and penalties.[4] At least two laws were promulgated, one in 17 BC known as the *Lex Iulia de Maritandis Ordinibus* and the other in AD 9 known as the *Lex Iulia et Papia Poppaea*. Taken as a whole, this legislation is commonly known today as the *Lex Papia Poppaea* after the names of the men who were counsels at the time of the latter law's promulgation. The texts survive only in partial and derivative form, culled from a variety of ancient sources.[5]

The Hungarian scholar Pál Csillag has painstakingly identified the basic categories of thought behind this legislation. Csillag notes that the law divided all men between roughly the ages of twenty-five and sixty and all women between roughly the ages of twenty and fifty into two basic types—the married and the celibate (*caelibes*).[6] The law expected all those who fell between the specified age limitations to marry or to face certain penalties, chief among them being the loss of the capacity to inherit.[7] By marrying within one hundred days of receiving notice of a bequest, however, a celibate man or woman might remove the incapacity imposed by the statute.[8] Failure to comply caused the gift to lapse and to become the property of the state.[9] *Orbi*—childless couples[10]—were permitted to take one-half of the

3. The ancient writer Aulus Gellius recorded a speech delivered by a public censor, Metellus Numidicus, around the year 102 BC on the necessity of marriage. Metellus warned his audience that "it was impossible for the City to survive without frequent marriage" ("*civitatem salvam esse sine matrimoniorum frequentia non posse*"). AULUS GELLIUS, NOCTES ATTICAE, bk. I, VI.6. Suetonius records that Augustus used this speech, or one like it, in his own arguments before the Senate when seeking approval for his marriage legislation; the title of the speech was "*De Prole Augenda*" ("On the Increase of Children"). C. SUETONI TRANQUILLI, DIVUS AUGUSTUS 89.2 (1979).

4. The idea of legislative reform of morals and marriage was something that was current in late Republican thought. Thus, Karl Galinsky calls attention to Cicero's efforts to encourage Julius Caesar to embark upon a similar program. *See* Karl Galinsky, *Augustus' Legislation on Morals and Marriage*, 125 PHILOLOGUS 126, 132 (1981). There is also indirect evidence that Augustus may have commenced his legislative activity almost as soon as he became princeps, prior to the year 27 BC. *See* PETER BRUNT, ITALIAN MANPOWER 225 B.C.–A.D. 14, at 558 (1971).

5. The best source for these documents remains SALVATORE RICCOBONO, JR., 1 ACTA DIVI AUGUSTI 166–97 (1945).

6. PÁL CSILLAG, THE AUGUSTAN LAWS ON FAMILY RELATIONS 81–82 (1976).

7. Gaius's *Institutes* obliquely preserves the legislation on the incapacity of *caelibes* to take under a will when it acknowledges an exception for soldiers' wills: "Celibates . . . are forbidden to take an inheritance and legacies by the lex Iulia . . . ." ("*Caelibes . . . lege Iulia hereditates legataque capere uetantur . . . .*"). GAIUS, INSTITUTES, bk. II, 111.

8. CSILLAG, *supra* note 6, at 86.

9. *Id.*

10. *Orbi* (masculine singular *orbus*) is a richly nuanced word that carries with it the sense of both deprivation and barrenness. It may mean a parent who has lost a child, a child who has lost

estates bequeathed to them.[11] Those who failed to marry or to reproduce might incur still other civil penalties, including the loss of political office.[12] In practice, the harshness of the law was mitigated by juristic commentary which taught that "inheritance from ascendants or descendants within three degrees was excepted."[13]

The ancient historians noted that Augustus's legislation enjoyed at best a mixed reception. Suetonius recorded that Augustus's marriage legislation was met with a "tumult of refusal" (*tumultu recusantium*) at the time of its promulgation and was accordingly "softened" (*lenita*).[14] Tacitus indicated that Augustus intended to rely on a general public duty to report those who might have received suspicious inheritances. As a practical matter, this enforcement mechanism evolved into a system of informers-for-profit that grew to be intensely disliked by the general population because, if the commentators are to be believed, it was a thoroughly corrupt process.[15]

While Augustus's approach emphasized penalties, subsequent emperors stressed inducements. Again, the law of succession proved the vehicle by which childbirth was encouraged. By a decree of the second-century emperor Hadrian, freeborn mothers of three children and freedwomen mothers of four children received the preferential right to inherit from children who predeceased them even where the children were in the power of a relative—including the father.[16] This rule represented a notable exception to the legally dominant position the father occupied in the Roman household.[17] Further, the Emperor Septimius Severus, around the year 203, decreed "that one may be excused from the onerous duty of being a guardian or curator by having a certain number of children: three in Rome, four in the rest of Italy, five in the provinces."[18]

Philosophers lent much-needed intellectual support to the proclaimed policy objectives of the Roman law. One might consider the teaching of Musonius Rufus, a Stoic philosopher who wrote in the latter half of the first century AD. Musonius understood marriage to serve two fundamental

---

his or her parents, those unable to reproduce, or those left alone and desolate in the world. *See* OXFORD LATIN DICTIONARY 1264–65 (1982).

11. CSILLAG, *supra* note 6, at 85.

12. JOHN T. NOONAN, JR., CONTRACEPTION: A HISTORY OF ITS TREATMENT BY THE CATHOLIC THEOLOGIANS AND CANONISTS 21 (1965).

13. *Id.*; *see also* Andrew Wallace-Hadrill, *Family and Inheritance in the Augustan Marriage Laws*, PROC. OF THE CAMBRIDGE PHILOLOGICAL SOC'Y 58 (1981) (exploring the implications of the Augustan legislation for families and estate planning).

14. C. SUETONI TRANQUILLI, *supra* note 3, at 34.

15. TACITUS, ANNALES 3.28; *see also* CSILLAG, *supra* note 6, at 163–64 (reviewing Tacitus and other sources).

16. GAIUS, *supra* note 7, at 3.3.2.

17. *See* CHARLES J. REID, JR., POWER OVER THE BODY, EQUALITY IN THE FAMILY: RIGHTS AND DOMESTIC RELATIONS IN MEDIEVAL CANON LAW 69–72 (2004) (describing the scope and nature of the Roman legal doctrine of paternal power).

18. NOONAN, *supra* note 12, at 23 (summarizing CODEX 5.66.1).

goals—the procreation of children and the formation of a union that reflected the most intimate sorts of friendship and love. In this context, Musonius asserted, marriage was a coming together by husband and wife for the purposes of rearing the next generation. Such a goal, he asserted, was best achieved in a family filled with mutual love:

> The husband and wife . . . should come together for the purpose of making a life in common and of procreating children, and furthermore of regarding all things in common between them, and nothing peculiar or private to one or the other, not even their own bodies. The birth of a human being which results from such a union is to be sure something marvelous, but it is not yet enough for the relation of husband and wife, inasmuch as quite apart from marriage it could result from any other sexual union, just as in the case of animals. But in marriage there must be above all perfect companionship and mutual love of husband and wife, both in health and in sickness and under all conditions, since it was with this desire as well as for having children that both entered upon marriage.[19]

The procreative and companionate ideals embodied in these legislative enactments and reflected in the writings of philosophers like Musonius Rufus, although resisted by some among the elites, must have had an effect. A review of recent scholarship, not on Roman marriage but on Roman concubinage, reveals that Roman social practice recognized that marriage, where it was available, should serve as the legitimate means of procreation.

In Roman practice, concubinage often involved a relationship of unequals; it might thus involve men too young for marriage but who lived for a while with a partner of lesser social status, as St. Augustine recorded he personally did in his *Confessions*.[20] It might also involve older men, whose wives had died and whose children were grown, living with women of unequal status. Finally, it might involve relationships where one party was forbidden by law to marry—for instance, where one party was a slave or of servile birth.[21] What is significant, according to scholars who have studied the evidence of inscriptions, is how rarely children are acknowledged as being produced from such unions. Susan Treggiari, in her study of concubinage, could find evidence among the inscriptions she studied that only three

19. Cora Lutz, Musonius Rufus: The Roman Socrates 89 (1947); Some Stoics also advocated the development of a strong bond between parents and offspring. Thus, one often finds Stoic writers arguing on behalf of maternal breast-feeding of children, against the Roman custom of sending children out to wet-nurses. *See* Gretchen Reydams-Schils, The Roman Stoics: Self, Responsibility, and Affection 126–28 (2005).

20. Thomas A.J. McGinn, *Concubinage and the Lex Iulia on Adultery*, 121 Transactions of the Am. Philological Ass'n 335, 338 (1991).

21. Beryl Rawson, *Roman Concubinage and Other De Facto Marriages*, 104 Transactions of the Am. Philological Ass'n 279, 304 (1974).

couples had children.[22] Marriage, it seems, was considered by all involved to be the proper venue for the raising of children.[23]

Procreation, of course, was not an absolute ideal in pre-Christian Rome. Throughout the history of pre-Christian Rome, the *paterfamilias*—the head of the household—retained the power of life and death over infants born into his family. The odious practice of exposure thus remained a regular feature of pre-Christian life. One has a sense of how deeply entrenched this practice must have been when one reads a document like Seneca the Younger's *De Ira*. Well regarded by many modern readers for his humaneness, Seneca spoke warmly about the need to destroy "weak and deformed" (*debiles monstrosique*) children.[24] Addressing the general need to avoid anger, Seneca opined that we are sometimes called to perform violent acts, but we must nevertheless retain our composure even under these circumstances. We must beat rabid dogs to death.[25] We kill wild oxen and slay sickly sheep lest they infect the entire flock. Just so, we "extinguish" (*enxstinguimus*) unnatural offspring and drown sick children. We do these things, Seneca counseled his reader, not from a heart filled with rage, but moved by reason and the rightful desire to remove the "useless" (*inutilia*) from the healthy and the sound. Seneca's concern was not with the moral problems associated with the taking of human life, but rather with encouraging that such unpleasant tasks be carried out with equanimity and the assurance that they are in accord with reason.[26]

If the procreative ideal did not trump the paternal power to expose unwanted young, neither could it serve to open up the institution of marriage to those who were legally excluded from it. As alluded to above, slaves were excluded from the possibility of marriage, although they were allowed to form stable if not entirely permanent relations under the rubric of *contubernia*.[27] Realizing the utility in promoting affectionate relations

22. Susan Treggiari, *Concubinae*, 49 PAPERS OF THE BRIT. SCH. AT ROME 59, 67 (1981).

23. "[M]arriage," Beryl Rawson concluded, "remained the norm." Rawson, *supra* note 21, at 304.

24. SENECA, DE IRA I.XV.2.

25. *Id.*

26. Exposure was used not only as a means of eliminating children deemed unfit to live on account of birth defects, but also as a means of limiting family size or of dealing with suspected cases of infidelity. Mireille Corbier, *Child Exposure and Abandonment*, *in* CHILDHOOD, CLASS AND KIN IN THE ROMAN WORLD 52, 72 (Suzanne Dixon ed., 2001).

27. Adolf Berger defines *contubernium* as "[a] permanent, marriage-like union between slaves. Masters favored the maintenance of slave families. Children of such unions were *liberi naturales*." *See* ADOLF BERGER, ENCYCLOPEDIC DICTIONARY OF ROMAN LAW 415 (1953) (*Liberi naturales* means "natural children" as opposed to the legitimate children of legally married couples.). In addition to the status of the children, Buckland notes other consequences of *contubernia*—because the parties were slaves and hence incapable of marriage, neither could commit adultery. Slaves were also incapable of inheriting from one another. *See* W.W. BUCKLAND, THE ROMAN LAW OF SLAVERY: THE CONDITION OF THE SLAVE IN PRIVATE LAW FROM AUGUSTUS TO JUSTINIAN 76–77 (2000).

among the persons they owned, slave owners often permitted if not encouraged marriage-like unions that frequently produced children.[28]

Despite these qualifications, however, it is clear that the central organizing principle supporting the Roman conception of marriage was the idea of procreation. To say that Roman marriage was all about the conservation of property, inheritance strategies, or the transmissibility of estates, or to observe that it was formed by the free consent of the parties and dissoluble in the same manner it was formed is all beside the point. None of this is comprehensible without keeping in mind the procreative dimension of marriage. After all, arrangements regarding property and inheritance only make sense when there is a succeeding generation to benefit from such planning. This was emphasized by Emperor Augustus and reiterated by succeeding generations of emperors. It was justified by the Stoic philosophers and can also be found in Ulpian's explication of natural law, which teaches "the joining of male and female that we call marriage, and the procreation and education of children."[29]

II. The Christian Experience of the Early Middle Ages

Christianity represented a reordering of the way in which marriage was conceived. Most fundamentally, marriage was no longer seen as the highest or best life for persons committed to following Christ. Pride of place belonged, rather, to those who, in accord with the "counsels of perfection," chose instead to follow a life of perfect continence.[30]

Virginity had existed as a religiously motivated phenomenon in the ancient world prior to the rise of Christianity. For example, the ancient Rome of Emperor Augustus preserved and revered the cult of the Vestal Virgins who were women selected before attaining puberty from among the

---

28.
> [B]ecause slaves were technically not permitted to marry and could thus not produce legally recognisable families, the relationships which are attested in the sources must be considered concessions to the slaves from their owners: it cannot be imagined, in light of owners' omnipotence over their slaves, that servile marriages occurred and lasted, or that children were born to married slaves, without the connivance if not express permission of [their] masters.

K.R. Bradley, Slaves and Masters in the Roman Empire: A Study in Social Control 50 (1984). Establishing the fullness of masters' control over slaves' reproductive capabilities, Bradley goes on to note that slave owners frequently sold mothers and children but almost never sold family groupings that included a husband, wife, and children. *Id.* at 52–55.

29. Justinian, Digest 1.1.1 § 3 ("hinc descendit maris atque feminae coniunctio, quam nos matrimonium appellamus, hinc liberorum procreatio, hinc educatio").

30. In speaking of the "counsels of perfection," I am borrowing the classical term for the three great vows those entering the religious life would customarily undertake—chastity, obedience, and poverty. The classical distinction drawn by generations of scholastic writers was between "counsels," which one is free to accept or reject, and "precepts," which one is obliged to follow. All Christians are obliged to follow the evangelical precepts—the positive commandments of the Scripture—but are free to accept or reject those admonitions—"counsels"—intended to help us achieve a high level of perfection. One can still consult productively classic works like Bishop Charles Gay, The Religious Life and the Vows 1–15 (1942) (exploring the differences between the evangelical precepts and the counsels of perfection).

Roman aristocracy and given the task of serving at the altar of Vesta, the goddess of the Roman hearth.[31] Vestal Virgins played a crucially important political role in ensuring the health of the state.[32] Their continued virginity symbolized Roman stability, but the loss of virginity consequent upon an individual's moral lapse was feared as a threat to the state's very survival.[33] (Vestal Virgins, it should be added, did not maintain a commitment to perpetual virginity but rather were allowed to marry and engage in sexual intercourse late in life, after the possibility of procreation had passed by.)

While the purity of Vestal Virgins was essential to political right order, their way of life was not intended to represent the Roman ideal. Procreation remained the fundamental value of family life,[34] and Roman religion did not hold out the Vestal Virgin as a model for emulation or exalt the virgin to a special place in the afterlife. Peter Brown has captured these ideas well: "[Vestal Virgins] fitted into a clearly demarcated space in civic society. Though eminent and admired, they were not thought to stand for human nature at its peak."[35]

The Church Fathers who wrote in the fourth and fifth centuries changed the premises on which religiously inspired virginity was constructed. They were emphatic on the transcendent significance of the virginal life. Methodius, a Greek writer active around the year 300, argued that virginity mirrored the divine form of life. It was necessary, on this account, that Jesus Christ remain virginal and that his life should constitute a pattern for those who would be perfect: "What then did the Lord, the Truth and the Light, accomplish on coming down to the world? He preserved His flesh incorrupt in virginity with which he had adorned it. And so let us too, if we are to come to the likeness of God, endeavor to banish corruptibility."[36]

St. Ambrose, bishop of Milan, doctor of the Church, and teacher of St. Augustine, stressed the close connection between virginity and the promise of immortal life. Jesus Christ, by rising from the dead, offered to all the promise of resurrection of the body and life everlasting in glorified form. Jesus had also stated that in heaven they neither marry nor are given in

31. On the selection, training, and expectations of Vestal Virgins, see Mary Beard, *The Sexual Status of Vestal Virgins*, 70 J. ROMAN STUD. 12, 12–27 (1980). Beard has more recently reconsidered and modified her larger anthropological claims about the sexually ambiguous nature of the Vestal Virgins. *See* Mary Beard, *Re-reading (Vestal) Virginity*, *in* WOMEN IN ANTIQUITY: NEW ASSESSMENTS 166–77 (Richard Hawley & Barbara Levick eds., 1995).

32. ARIADNE STAPLES, FROM GOOD GODDESS TO VESTAL VIRGINS: SEX AND CATEGORY IN ROMAN RELIGION 135 (1998).

33. *Id.* ("A single lapse by a single priestess threatened the very existence of the state."). The sanction for such a lapse was terrifying—burial alive with token amounts of food and drink.

34. *Id.* at 130.

35. PETER BROWN, THE BODY AND SOCIETY: MEN, WOMEN, AND SEXUAL RENUNCIATION IN EARLY CHRISTIANITY 8 (1st ed. 1988).

36. ST. METHODIUS, THE SYMPOSIUM: A TREATISE ON CHASTITY 47 (Herbert Musurillo trans., Longmans, Green & Co. 1958).

marriage.[37] St. Ambrose construed these and other teachings to justify virginity in this life as a foretaste and intimation of the life of the world to come:

> "When the dead rise again there is no marrying or giving in marriage; they are as the angels in heaven are." He who condemns virginity condemns our desire for that resurrection. Resurrection can hardly be counted wrong if it is assigned as the final reward for mankind; and its likeness, virginity, can hardly be offensive if its model is approved both by present desire and by future enjoyment.[38]

Virginity, St. Ambrose stressed repeatedly, imitates the life of the angels themselves. It is not a naturally occurring phenomenon, and the mind focused only on the things of this world will not appreciate its foundation in a transcendent order.[39] It is not a practice found among "the nations" (*gentilibus*) nor among the "barbarians" (*barbaris*).[40] Animals do not practice virginity.[41] "Virginity," St. Ambrose asserted, "quite rightly looks to heaven for its manner of life."[42] It is, indeed, a gift from heaven, but one which can be imitated on Earth by those gifted with grace and filled with a firm disposition to follow the highest counsels of Christ. St. Ambrose also contrasted virginity practiced by Christians with the pagan practices of classical Rome. Vestal Virgins do not take a vow of perpetual continence, but rather practice chastity only for a few years. They maintain a youthful integrity only to be corrupted in advanced age.[43] St. Ambrose was both perplexed and dismayed at such a strange practice.

St. Augustine offered a similar theological defense of virginity. There are many natural duties that arise from our human nature, St. Augustine wrote, chief among them the requirement that we bring about the next generation. Virginity, however, is something set apart: virginal integrity, practiced through devoted continence, and the consequent freedom from sexual relations that those under vows enjoy, does not belong to this world; rather, it is the "angelic portion" (*angelica portio*)—the form of life led by celestial beings.[44]

St. Augustine went so far as to assert that a special place has been reserved in heaven for those who observe virginal continence. In making

37. *Matthew* 22:30.

38. St. Ambrose, *De virginitate*, *in* Given to Love para. 27, at 87 (James Shiel trans., Scepter Publishers 1963). St. Ambrose is quoting *Matthew* 22:30.

39. St. Ambrose, *De virginibus*, bk. I, 11, 16 Patrologia Latina 191 (Jacques-Paul Migne ed., 1844–55).

40. *Id.* bk. I, 14.

41. *Id.*

42. *Id.* bk. I, 14, *in* Given to Love 21–22 (James Shiel trans., Scepter Publishers 1963).

43. St. Ambrose, *De virginibus*, *supra* note 39, bk. I, 15.

44. St. Augustine, *De sancta virginitate*, *in* De bono coniugali, De sancta virginitate 78, para. 12 (P.G. Walsh ed. & trans., 2001).

this point, he chose to reflect on the text in the Gospel of Matthew that compares our eternal reward to the householder who has hired some laborers: Some labor all day long, others for a few hours, and some only for one hour at the very end of the day. Yet the householder gave to each one a single denarius as their wage.[45]

Fearing, perhaps, that this text stood against his contentions, St. Augustine responded:

> [E]ternal life will itself be shared alike by all the saints, and so the denarius has been allotted equally to all. But because in that eternal life the lights of their merits will shine differently, "There are many dwelling places in the Father's house." Accordingly, since the value of the denarius remains the same, one of us will not live longer than another, but in those numerous dwelling-places one will obtain brighter glory than another.[46]

Virginity thus led to munificent eternal rewards. Even in this life, however, virginity was not to be understood as barrenness. A central feature of the case made on behalf of virginity was its procreative capacity. This was not procreation in a terrestrial, physical sense. Virginity, rather, was rich with the possibility of reproduction in a deeply transcendent, spiritual sense. By its witness to the perfection of human life in God, it won souls for the Church.

St. Augustine stressed that there were two kinds of birth: physical birth and spiritual birth. The latter was the more important since what mattered in this life was our salvation—our acceptance into the kingdom of God at the end of our days. Virgins were the ones responsible for the spiritual birth of souls within the Church; through the perfect lives they led, they modeled for the rest of us the way to salvation. They are, St. Augustine writes, "both virgins and mothers of Christ in the faith" (*virgines matresque Christi sunt in fide*).[47] They may have renounced the possibility of bearing children physically, but their cooperation in the birth of Christians to eternal life was indispensable to the survival and success of the faith.[48] Virginity was a form of motherhood—indeed, the highest form of motherhood—by which all are brought home to God's mansions.

St. Ambrose made similar claims for virginity. Jesus Christ was both born of a virgin and has taken as his bride the virgin Church.[49] Mary's marriage with Joseph, though virginal, was uniquely fecund. Similarly, Christ's marriage to the Church has produced nothing less than salvation for all humankind.[50] Those who take a vow of virginity under the Church's

45. *Matthew* 20:1–16.
46. St. Augustine, *De sancta virginitate*, *supra* note 44, at 101.
47. *See id.* at 78, para. 7. Translation is author's own.
48. *Id.*
49. St. Ambrose, *De virginibus*, *supra* note 39, paras. 21–22.
50. *Id.*

supervising authority have themselves agreed to take Christ as their spouse and they share in Christ's fruitfulness.

In making these claims for virginity, the theologians of the fourth and fifth century exalted the ideal of fecundity to a spiritual plane. They did not reject marriage; indeed, as will become clear, they viewed marriage as a great good. Rather, they made use of the image of a sound and fruitful marriage to explain the religious significance of virginity: Mary and Joseph enjoyed a virginal but fruitful relationship. Indeed, the fruit of their marriage brought salvation to the world. Christ enjoys the same sort of relationship with the Church; indeed, Christ is considered the Church's bridegroom. Extending the analogy, virgins were understood to have entered into a relationship with Christ and the Church that will win converts for Christ and thereby give birth to the next generation of Christians. Virgins have thus married Christ in a special way and can expect their unions to be fruitful. In this way, not only virginity, but also marriage, acquired institutional strength.

Not surprisingly, the fourth- and fifth-century theologians also explained and explored carnal marriage in terms of its fecundity. One might consider in particular the writing of St. Augustine, whose theology of the "goods of marriage" deeply influenced not only the shape of Christian doctrine but the concept of marriage as it was understood by secular lawyers until very nearly our own day.[51]

These goods of marriage were threefold: procreation, fidelity, and sacramental unity.[52] Connecting the three goods into a single unity was the role of friendship between the parties. All persons, male or female, St. Augustine wrote, are members of the same human race and are capable of friendship.[53] God created all persons from one archetype—Adam—so as to enhance our natural capacity for friendship.[54] And marriage, which represented the natural unity that should prevail between man and woman, joins the couple together in unity and friendship.[55] Indeed, this friendship is so tight and so all-encompassing that it has caused some scholars to argue that

51. *See* Charles J. Reid, Jr., *The Augustinian Goods of Marriage: The Disappearing Cornerstone of the American Law of Marriage*, 18 BYU J. PUB. L. 449 (2003).

52. *Id.* at 455.

53. ST. AUGUSTINE, *De bono coniugali*, *supra* note 44, at 2–3, para. 1.1.

54. *Id.*

55. *Id.* It has been observed that friendship is a fundamental organizing principle of St. Augustine's thought regarding human relations. "[F]riendship, sustained over time, brings such a rich, deep intimacy and unity to the friends that the friends become one in spirit and soul." PAUL J. WADELL, BECOMING FRIENDS: WORSHIP, JUSTICE, AND THE PRACTICE OF CHRISTIAN FRIENDSHIP 86 (2002). St. Augustine was borrowing from classical models in his analysis of friendship, but applied these classical models in startlingly new ways to the relationship between the spouses that is marriage.

there is a structural unity to St. Augustine's goods of marriage that can be usefully compared to the Trinity.[56]

We shall concentrate on one of these goods—the good of procreation. For St. Augustine, sexual passions were inherently unruly and needed firm guidance and control. Marriage provided both the sole and proper outlet for sexual urges and also channeled human sexuality toward the fulfillment of a great social need—the reproduction of the next generation.[57] Especially when we are young, he stressed, we "burn with the passion of the flesh" (*aestuat concupiscentia carnis*).[58] Childbirth, the requirement that we look after the welfare of our children, places a brake on our ardor. As St. Augustine put it, "parental affection tempers [concupiscence]."[59]

Affirmatively, St. Augustine made the case that all marriages must be open to the possibility of children. This was so even among elderly couples who were not expected to have children and married principally to give each other companionship in old age.[60] St. Augustine added, however, that one did not need to marry out of an express desire to have children: a couple might therefore marry solely for the purpose of sexual satisfaction. So long as the two agreed to remain together until death and did not affirmatively take steps to frustrate procreation, their union can legitimately be called "marriage."[61] Their sexual intimacy might exceed proper limits, but, so long as they were married, they sinned only venially, and their offense was pardoned by reason of their marriage.[62] In this way, St. Augustine drew an unbreakable connection between procreation and marriage. St. Augustine made this case both affirmatively, by insisting that openness to procreation be a feature of every marriage, and negatively, by stressing that couples may not exclude the possibility of children from their union. A couple, St. Augustine taught, must not actively avoid procreation, nor should they make use of "some evil means" (*opere aliquo malo*) to frustrate childbirth.[63] "I do not see how we can call such a thing a marriage," St. Augustine wrote dismissively.[64]

Like the pre-Christian Romans, St. Augustine did not view procreation as an absolute value. Permanence in marriage, like procreation, was one of the fundamental goods. St. Augustine stressed that one could not abandon a

56. *See* Perry J. Cahall, *The Trinitarian Structure of St. Augustine's Good of Marriage*, 34 Augustinian Stud. 223 (2003).

57. St. Augustine, De bono coniugali, *supra* note 44, at 7–9, III.3.

58. *Id.* at 8.

59. *Id.*

60. *Id.* at 8, III.3.

61. *Id.* at 11, V.5.

62. St. Augustine, De bono coniugali, *supra* note 44, at 11, V.5.

63. *Id.* at 10–11.

64. *See id.* at 10 ("non invenio quemadmodum has nuptias appellare possimus"). The word *quemadmodum* carries intensifying force when used in the sort of question St. Augustine has posed. I have used the word "thing" to carry this force. One might also more colloquially translate the passage as: "I do not know how in the devil we can call this marriage."

marriage that had failed to produce offspring in order to move to another one that held out the promise of procreation.[65] Similarly, St. Augustine counseled that even married couples should consider sexual abstinence, although he stressed that it was mandatory that such a decision be mutual.[66] He made it clear that he did not value a high birth rate for its own sake.[67] What mattered, rather, was the number of new inhabitants in the spiritual City of God.

Despite these qualifications to the good of procreation, it should be obvious that procreation was a fundamental organizing principle for Augustine's analysis of the marital relationship. It was this principle that allowed not only his marital theory but also his concept of sacred virginity to cohere logically. Fecundity in a real and physical sense was a principal justification for marriage, and fecundity in an extended, spiritual sense was a key justification for virginity.

St. Augustine's basic framework for analyzing marriage would prove to be enduring. A millennium and a half after St. Augustine wrote and flourished, one can still find early American lawyers analyzing marriage in terms of the Augustinian goods, even when Augustine's name is never invoked.[68] There were, of course, multiple lines of transmission between the fifth and nineteenth centuries. I would like to consider briefly one such line—the Irish penitential literature of the early Middle Ages (roughly the seventh through ninth centuries). This line of transmission represents perhaps the logic of the procreative ideal taken to its most extreme form in the history of the West.

The penitential literature of Ireland was a product of a Church whose view of the world was shaped by an Irish monastic culture that observed an extreme asceticism.[69] The goal was nothing less than triumphant spiritual warfare against the devil.[70] Seen in this light, it was natural for the Irish monastics to teach an austere and demanding sexual ethic. Taming the desires of the flesh was a means of combating Satan and a sign of his ultimate defeat. An austere sexual ethic, inculcated in the population at large, was thus nothing more than an extension of the spiritual warfare and self-denial of monastic existence.

65. *Id.* at 16–17, VII.7.

66. *Id.* at 14–15, VI.6–VII.6.

67. *Id.* at 21–23.

68. Reid, *supra* note 51, at 459–70.

69. Dáibhí Ó Crónín has written about St. Columbanus, one of the greatest of the Irish monks, and his Rule for the monastic settlement he established on the Continent at Luxeuil: "[It prescribed] a harsh and unremittingly severe existence for the monks with no concessions to the frailties of body and soul. 'Let him come weary to his bed and sleep walking, and let him be forced to rise while his sleep is not yet finished.'" Dáibhí Ó Crónín, Early Medieval Ireland, 400–1200, at 197 (1995) (quoting the Rule of St. Columbanus).

70. "The founding fathers of Irish monasticism . . . appealed to the native bellicose instinct of the Irish and sought to transform it into the service of Christian ideals." Hugh Connolly, The Irish Penitentials and Their Significance for the Sacrament of Penance Today 9 (1995).

The monastic authors of the penitentials had a keen sense of the many ways one might sin sexually. "Sexual offenses constituted the largest single category of behavior that the penitentials treated."[71] This suspicion of human sexuality fueled the penitentials' effort to minimize the possibility of sexual intercourse even among laypersons. With a single-minded logic and intensity, the penitentials insisted that sexual relations between persons could take place only within marriage and then only for the sake of procreation.[72]

One might briefly consider some leading penitential texts. The *Penitential of Finnian* declared as a general rule that "marriage is to be continent," although it permitted couples to have sexual relations, not to satisfy lustful desires, but for the sake of children.[73] Driving the point home, the *Penitential* added that where it was clear that a wife was sterile, the parties should practice continence "until God passes true and just judgment" upon them.[74] In more abbreviated form, this rule is repeated in the *Penitential of Cummean*.[75]

The penitentials made the point that sexual intercourse was solely for procreation through other, less extreme, rules as well. Thus it was frequently legislated that married men and women should refrain from sexual intercourse after the woman learned that she was pregnant.[76] The penitentials also generally forbade sexual contact with a woman during her menstrual periods, but this prohibition seems to have been motivated largely out of concerns over ritual impurity.[77]

As with the other sources that have been considered, procreation was not the ultimate value before which all other rules were subordinated. Like St. Augustine, the penitential writers stressed that one could not abandon one's spouse and move to another for the sake of procreation. Indeed, as noted above, the penitential writers insisted upon mutual continence in such circumstances.[78] And the penitential writers also prescribed long periods of time, corresponding to periods in the Church calendar, during which couples were expected to refrain from intercourse. These periods included Lent, Advent, and a period of time following the feast of Pentecost.[79] During these times, couples were expected to be preoccupied with the things of the next world, not the sordid affairs of our shattered and sinful universe.

71. JAMES A. BRUNDAGE, LAW, SEX, AND CHRISTIAN SOCIETY IN MEDIEVAL EUROPE 153 (1987).

72. PIERRE PAYER, SEX AND THE PENITENTIALS: THE DEVELOPMENT OF A SEXUAL CODE, 550-1150, at 115 (1984).

73. THE IRISH PENITENTIALS para. 46, at 90–92 (Ludwig Bieler ed. & trans., 1975).

74. *Id.* at paras. 41, 88.

75. *Id.* at paras. 28, 116.

76. *See* the references collected by BRUNDAGE, *supra* note 71, at 156.

77. *Id.* at 155–56.

78. *Supra* notes 71–73 and accompanying text.

79. BRUNDAGE, *supra* note 71, at 158.

But with these exceptions, it is clear that procreation was a central organizing principle of the penitential literature. This collection of norms and principles, teachings and expectations in turn "helped shape the mentality, the ethic, of western Europe."[80]

III. Sacred Sex, the Good of Children, and Marital Permanence: Theologians and Canonists in the High Middle Ages

The early Middle Ages were a time of chaos. Kingdoms and principalities rose and fell with dreary regularity. Even the papacy became the plaything of the competing dynastic interests of the leading families of central Italy. It is fair to describe the period of the fifth through eleventh centuries as a time of widespread institutional failure. Christian sensibilities gradually gained a foothold among the Germanic tribes that settled Western Europe following the fall of the Roman Empire, but the Christianization of Europe was a gradual process, accomplished in fits and starts amidst a great deal of political and social turmoil.

By the end of the eleventh century, however, a certain stability was achieved. The papacy, thanks to the great reform movement led by the likes of Nicholas II and Gregory VII, established itself as an independent, effective, and powerful player on the European stage.[81] Indeed, the Church took on the trappings of a transnational state, with papal representatives (legates) and courts in every country. The nation-states of Europe also took their first fledgling steps toward consolidation, much of it accomplished through the adoption of systematized law codes. Universities, whose purposes were to inquire into fundamental issues of philosophy, theology, and law, arose throughout Europe.[82]

A major line of inquiry among the scholastic writers who peopled the faculties of the new universities was the nature of the sacraments, including the sacrament of marriage. In a previous paper, I explored the question of the marital rights of non-Christians.[83] That paper considered the sacramental theology of early scholastic writers like Hugh of St. Victor and Anselm of Laon who asserted that it was possible that Christians and non-Christians alike enjoyed marital rights deserving of at least some respect at law. The next several paragraphs will build on these earlier findings to consider "sacred sex": the sacral dimension of the sex act in symbolizing the sacramental nature of marriage.

80. Noonan, *supra* note 12, at 153.

81. For a good review of these developments, see generally Harold J. Berman, Law and Revolution: The Making of the Western Legal Tradition (1983).

82. For a classic treatment of the rise of the universities, see generally Hastings Rashdall, The Universities of Europe in the Middle Ages (F.M. Powicke & A.B. Emden eds., 1936).

83. Charles J. Reid, Jr., *Toward an Understanding of Medieval Universal Rights: The Marital Rights of Non-Christians in Early Scholastic and Canonistic Writings*, 3 Ave Maria L. Rev. 95 (2005).

In the twelfth century it became established among canon lawyers and theologians that consent made a marriage while consummation conferred on a Christian marriage a special firmness.[84] In essence, consummation created a bond that was so tight that no earthly power could dissolve it.[85] But what was it about consummation that gave it such power? That is the question that shall next be considered.

The term "sacrament" (*sacramentum*) carried a variety of nontheological meanings. It carried the sense of an oath taken in judicial proceedings, as well as the oath taken upon entry into the military.[86] By extension, it conveyed the sense of a solemn undertaking[87] or the rites of initiation into a secret society.[88] The term was eventually taken up by Christian writers who imparted to it a technical, theological meaning. In early theological writing, *sacramentum* could carry the meaning of a theological mystery, such as the Incarnation.[89] It could also convey the sense of an outward sign of some sacred thing.[90] Finally, it might simply mean some visible sign of God's presence in the world.[91]

St. Augustine made extensive use of the term in this final sense. "Sacraments, to St. Augustine, were signs of God's presence and promise in the world, of His gifts to His creation, and of salvation through His Word."[92] A wide variety of events, natural phenomena, and human actions could convey the divine presence—everything from gestures of reverence, the liturgical calendar, or prayers for mercy.[93]

This broad Augustinian understanding of the word sacrament continued to influence writers in the twelfth century, although one sees in this latter period a sustained—and ultimately successful—effort to confine its technical meaning to efficacious signs that were understood to confer grace upon the believers who made use of them. During the twelfth century, the Latin word *sacramentum* was narrowed and given greater precision—it now signified not any sign of God's presence but, as the formula put it, "a sign of some sacred thing."[94] It also came to represent a channel by which believers might come to acquire the grace necessary for salvation.

84. James Brundage traces this idea to the work of the twelfth-century canonist Gratian. *See* BRUNDAGE, *supra* note 71, at 235–42.

85. JOHN T. NOONAN, JR., POWER TO DISSOLVE: LAWYERS AND MARRIAGES IN THE COURTS OF THE ROMAN CURIA 81–82 (1972).

86. OXFORD LATIN DICTIONARY, *supra* note 10, at 1674–75.

87. *Id.* at 1675.

88. *Id.*

89. CHARLES DU CANGE, GLOSSARIUM MEDIAE ET INFIMAE LATINITATIS 257 (Léopold Favre ed., 1886).

90. *Id.*

91. Reid, *supra* note 83, at 103.

92. *Id.*

93. *Id.*

94. SEAMUS P. HEANEY, THE DEVELOPMENT OF THE SACRAMENTALITY OF MARRIAGE FROM ANSELM OF LAON TO THOMAS AQUINAS 3 (1963).

We are concerned in particular with the symbolism that came to be associated with marriage. What was it about marriage that signaled and represented the divine? What was uniquely sacred to marriage that elevated it to the level of a sacrament, not in the old Augustinian sense, but in the newer, more restricted, scholastic understanding of a grace-conferring, efficacious symbol? To answer this question will require us to examine the symbolic significance of the sex act, and in particular, the act of consummating a union.

Let us consider some of the scholastic treatises of the early and middle twelfth century. This period includes the first formative writings of the scholastic theology that would become the foundation of the Catholic Church's understanding of God and the sacraments for centuries to come. At the very beginning of this period, the anonymous treatise *Deus de cuius principio et fine tacetur* sought to compare and contrast the marriages of Christians and non-Christians.[95] All marriages have this much in common, the author asserted: parties enter into them to avoid fornication.[96] But consummated Christian marriages add to this minimalist understanding a symbolic significance: they reveal a fundamental truth about the relationship of Christ and His Church. This truth is revealed by the joining of the parties: Christ has married His Church and has become one body with the Church in the same way that a man becomes one body with his wife.[97]

Honorius of Autun, active in the first half of the twelfth century, wrote a large number of works including the *Elucidarium*, intended as a summary of Catholic theology put in dialogue format. In the course of his dialogue, his interlocutors ask why it is impossible for close relatives to marry one another.[98] The answer, Honorius suggested, lay in the sacramental nature of marriage: earthly marriage among Christians represents the transcendent union of Christ and the Church. Jesus Christ and the Church are of different natures—divine and human—but have come together to form a single unbreakable body. So also, male and female should be of different natures—they should come from different bloodlines (*parentelae*) in order to represent the union of the divine and the human, that is, the joining together of Christ and His Church.[99] As Seamus Heaney put it in his analysis of this

95. This text appears as *Le recueil des sentences 'Deus de cuius principio et fine tacetur' et son remaniement*, in 5 Recherches de Théologie ancienne et médiévale 245–74 (H. Weisweiler ed., 1933).

96. *Id.* at 272–73.

97. *Id.* at 273 ("Nam nuptias Christi et ecclesie significat, quia Christus et ecclesia unum corpus sunt. Christus tamen preest et regit. Sic vir cum sit unum corpus cum uxore . . . tamen preest ei et regit . . . [T]alis coniunctio dicitur sanctitas sacramenti."); *cf.* Heaney, *supra* note 94, at 6.

98. 172 Honorius of Autun, Elucidarium, Patrologia Latina 1147 (n.d.).

99. *Id.*

text, "It is clearly not the state of marriage which is the sacrament, but the sexual union."[100]

A twelfth-century Bible commentary went into even greater detail: "The copulation of male and female is said to be a great sacrament," containing in itself Christ and the Church.[101] Marriage, the author repeated for emphasis, represents the joining of Christ and his Church. Paraphrasing Scripture, the author noted that just as a man leaves his mother and father to join himself to his wife, so Jesus left his mother and father to join his bride—the Church.[102] When we marry, furthermore, we partake in the virtues that Christ displayed in his earthly ministry.[103] Marriage is thus a means of achieving personal sanctity as well as symbolizing Christ's salvific love for all humankind.

Rufinus, author of an important early commentary on Gratian's *Decretum*, the founding document of the systematic study of canon law, accepted the framework laid down by the theologians.[104] There were, Rufinus asserted, really two sacraments of marriage. The first, which represented the soul's union with God, consisted of the exchange of consent to marry—even before consummation.[105] But the relationship of the soul to God is inherently unstable—people fall into heresy or apostasy every day. Something more was needed, and that was consummation. Consummation, Rufinus asserted, has within itself the whole symbolism of Christ and his Church.[106] The Church and Christ enjoyed a relationship that was unbreakable, and consummation permitted human persons to represent that transcendent relationship in their own marital relations.

In this way, theologians and canonists developed the positive attributes of human sexuality within marriage. Sexual intercourse was no longer seen—as it had been understood in the Penitentials—as a narrow concession in a relationship that should normally be governed by continence. Indeed, in the writings of these twelfth-century thinkers, intercourse became a necessary feature of the symbolism of Christian marriage and was necessary to give marriage its sacramental stability and unity. Christ and the Church had forged an unbreakable bond of different but compatible natures; so also do man and woman at the time they consummate their union. Consummation, and the joining of bodies that thereby occurred, was a sign

100. HEANEY, *supra* note 94, at 9.

101. ARTUR LANDGRAF, COMMENTARIUS CANTABRIGIENSIS IN EPISTOLAS PAULI E SCHOLA PETRI ABELARDI: 2. IN EPISTOLAM AD CORINTHIOS IAM ET IIAM, AD GALATAS ET AD EPHESIOS 431 (Philip S. Moore ed., University of Notre Dame 1939). "'Sacramentum'. Hanc copulationem maris et femine dicit esse sacramentum magnum, in Christo videlicet et ecclesia." *Id.*

102. *Id.*

103. *Id.*

104. RUFINUS, SUMMA DECRETORUM 442–43 (Heinrich Singer ed., 1963).

105. *Id.*; *cf.* Reid, *supra* note 83, at 116–17.

106. "Quod habeat in se Christi et ecclesiae sacramentum." RUFINUS, *supra* note 104, at 443.

pointing to a sacred reality—the promise of salvation through the mystery of Christ's union with His Church.

If sexual relations had in some sense been sanctified, the theologians of the twelfth and thirteenth centuries also had important and original things to say about other aspects of marriage. In the process, they made it clear that marriage served the fundamental good of procreation. They built up a set of rules and doctrines that ensured that, ordinarily, marriages should be directed toward this great social good. In particular, the scholastic writers came to articulate the Augustinian goods of marriage in terms that would support the proposition that marriage existed to serve procreative ends.

Peter Lombard (c. 1100–c. 1161) was the most influential of these early theological writers. A professor at the University of Paris, Peter's work would prove to be of enduring significance to the intellectual life of the Church. His *Sentences* became the foundational text of subsequent scholastic writing through the remainder of the Middle Ages—all doctoral candidates in theology were expected to write a dissertation on the *Sentences*.[107] His understanding of the sacraments as seven outward manifestations of sacred things that not only symbolize divine reality but confer grace on those who partake in them would become generally accepted by the Church and canonized as ecclesiastical doctrine at the Council of Trent in the sixteenth century.[108]

With this as background, one can consider Peter's treatment of the Augustinian goods of marriage. Peter, like the other medieval writers who have been reviewed, made productive use of St. Augustine where he was able to do so. He commenced his analysis of marriage by noting that sexual relations were a duty incumbent on persons even before the Fall: while Adam and Eve were still in Paradise, God enjoined on them the duty "to increase and multiply."[109] Citing St. Augustine as support, Peter continued: When Adam and Eve sinned, they brought sin into the world and marriage assumed a double aspect. It was both a duty upon those able to use it properly and a remedy for those who suffered from illness (*aegrotis*), by which Peter meant clearly disordered human sexual urges.[110] By providing a proper outlet for these impulses, marriage furnished a means by which to

107. On the gradual acceptance of Peter Lombard's text as foundational to medieval theology, see Nancy Spatz, *Approaches and Attitudes to a New Theology Textbook: The Sentences of Peter Lombard*, *in* The Intellectual Climate of the Early University: Essays in Honor of Otto Gründler 27, 27–52 (Nancy Van Deusen ed., 1997).

108. For further information on Peter Lombard and the sacrament of marriage, see 2 Marcia Colish, Peter Lombard 628–98 (1994), and compare Charles J. Reid, Jr., *Marriage in the Western Legal Tradition: A Product of Natural Law or a Creature of the State?*, *in* Family in the Third Millennium: Selected Scholarship Submitted to the Doha Conference on Marriage and the Family (2007).

109. Peter Lombard, Sententiarum Libri Quatuor 656 (Paris 1892).

110. *Id.*

direct them to a good purpose.[111] Attacking those whom he labeled heretics, Peter defended marriage as something that had been blessed twice by God—at the creation of the world and again by Jesus at the marriage feast at Cana.[112] Marriage, he concluded, is therefore a sacrament, a sacred symbol, and a channel of divine grace.[113]

Following what was rapidly becoming the received scholastic tradition, Peter asserted that it was consummation that constituted the visible sacramental sign of marriage, signifying the union of Christ and the Church.[114] The consent that persons exchange in order to bring about marriage, Peter asserted, signifies the spiritual union of Christ and the Church, while the physical coupling of bodies represented the joining of human and divine natures in the Church.[115]

Peter in particular developed the significance of the Augustinian goods. Where the "three goods" have not been made part of the marriage contract, there is no marriage.[116] Regarding the good of children, Peter acknowledged that it was impossible to expect every married couple to have children. A couple might have chosen to renounce the conjugal debt, or they may be aged or infertile.[117] But so long as they do not exclude the "hope of children" (*prolis spes*), they contract marriage validly.[118] Peter condemned both the use of "poisons of sterility" (the standard medieval term for contraceptives) and recourse to abortion as destructive of the good of children.[119]

Finally, St. Bonaventure, the thirteenth-century Franciscan theologian,[120] drew connections between fidelity and sacramental stability, on the one hand, and the good of children, on the other. In a disputation meant to respond to those who defended the concubinage of the ancient world, St. Bonaventure declared that the good of children was thereby offended.[121] "Right reason," St. Bonaventure argued, taught that a married couple is made "one flesh." Their coming together is a kind of exercise of "genera-

---

111. *Id.*

112. Colish tends to read Peter as presenting a more optimistic account of marital sexuality than St. Augustine, especially in discussing sexual relations undertaken to prevent fornication. Where St. Augustine saw such relations as at least venially sinful, Colish notes that Peter Lombard understood "this type of sex in marriage not as a means of preventing sin but as a means of strengthening the couple's mutual commitment." COLISH, *supra* note 108, at 661.

113. *Id.* at 657.

114. *Id.*

115. *Id.*

116. *Id.* at 673.

117. *Id.*

118. COLISH, *supra* note 108, at 657.

119. *Id.*

120. St. Bonaventure (1221–1274), along with St. Thomas Aquinas, was one of the giants of thirteenth-century theology. He was a colleague of Thomas Aquinas at the University of Paris and authored a large number of theological treatises.

121. St. Bonaventure, *Commentaria in Quatuor Libros Sententiarum*, *in* OPERA OMNIA 747 (1889).

tive power" (*vis generativa*).[122] This much, however, St. Bonaventure conceded, was true of any sexual relationship, even of those engaged in concubinage. He made this last point not in order to denigrate marriage but in order to stress that marriage was the divinely appointed means of achieving the procreation and education of the next generation. Because of the importance of sexual relations to procreation, St. Bonaventure believed two conclusions followed from his argument—all extramarital sexual relations were illicit; and, within marriage, the goods of sacramental unity and permanence served to effectuate the good of procreation.

Thus if a man and wife have children, "both parents" (*parentes ambo*) are required to see to the education of their children.[123] When the parents age and can no longer care for themselves, children must see to their parents' needs. Concubinage shatters these obligations and expectations. Parents, especially fathers, will not be attentive to their children, preferring instead the attention of their paramours; and children will neglect their parents' needs. Indeed, parentage itself would be made uncertain. It is always possible that a man will have a child by his concubine. Mingling the sublime with the intensely practical, St. Bonaventure noted that such a possibility shattered the natural order of marriage by gravely disrupting its sacramental stability, and by overturning the father's carefully contrived estate planning.[124]

What is significant for our purposes in this argument is the way in which St. Bonaventure has connected procreation with the other Augustinian goods. He has effectively united them in the course of his argument and thereby made procreation the chief bulwark against claims that concubinage should be permitted. Procreation has become the great social end toward which marriage is directed. To be sure, sacramental unity served as a symbol of Christ's unbreakable union, but it also ensured the proper rearing of children; the same might also be said for permanence. Thus, these other Augustinian goods are now seen not only as good in their own right but as a means of facilitating this larger end of procreation.

IV. English Theology and Law: The Fruitful Marriage

The Act of Supremacy of 1534, by which Henry VIII declared himself head of both church and state in England and broke off ecclesiastical allegiance to Rome, was one of the great transformative events in the history of the European Church (not to mention the modern unitary state).[125] By the terms of the Act, King Henry VIII henceforth became entitled to "enjoy, annexed and united to the imperial crown of this realm . . . all honours,

122. *Id.*
123. *Id.*
124. *Id.*
125. Mark A. Noll, Turning Points: Decisive Moments in the History of Christianity 177–79 (2d ed. 2000).

dignities, pre-eminences, jurisdictions, privileges, authorities, immunities, profits, and commodities" previously belonging to the Roman pontiff in England.[126]

Significant for our purposes was the claim over the jurisdictions and authorities exercised by the Roman pontiff. Henceforward, there could be no appeal of marriage cases to Rome. Rather, the law of marriage and all that belonged to it—divorce, annulment, child support, sexual crimes—belonged to the English ecclesiastical courts whose supreme head was the English monarch. The ecclesiastical courts would retain their jurisdiction over matrimonial causes until the mid-nineteenth century.[127] However, in spite of new jurisdictional lines of authority, English canon law held tenaciously to the law of the medieval Catholic Church in many respects.[128]

While English canon law maintained fidelity to its medieval roots, the Protestant Reformation led to the introduction of some fundamental changes in the theology of marriage. The idea that marriage was a sacrament, instituted by Christ during His earthly ministry and conferring grace upon His followers, was rejected in favor of conception of marriage as a sacramental—a holy estate implanted in nature by God to channel the human person's reproductive urges and to assist all who partake in it.[129] Marriage was a great social good and it continued to retain a spiritual dimension, but it ceased to be described as a grace-conferring sign and symbol of Christ's union with the Church. Thus, John Witte has argued persuasively that the English reformers of the sixteenth and seventeenth centuries successfully replaced the Catholic conception of marriage as a sacrament with a new conception of marriage as a "commonwealth," an entity that served "the common good—of the couple, the children, the church, and the state."[130] Finally, the connection between virginity and marriage—indeed, the whole theology of virginity that had grown up since

---

126. *Id.* at 178 (quoting the Act of Supremacy).

127. In 1857, Parliament enacted a law greatly simplifying the procedures to be used in obtaining a divorce and removing the ecclesiastical courts from the process. Prior to 1857, a petitioner had to obtain a divorce *a mensa et thoro* (from bed and board) from an ecclesiastical court and subsequently petition Parliament for approval to remarry. The 1857 Act moved to the secular courts the power to grant divorce with the right to remarry. *See* STEPHEN CRETNEY, FAMILY LAW IN THE TWENTIETH CENTURY 161–62 (2003); Sybil Wolfram, *Divorce in England, 1700–1857*, 5 OXFORD J. LEGAL STUD. 155, 155–86 (1985); Margaret K. Woodhouse, *The Marriage and Divorce Bill of 1857*, 3 AM. J. LEGAL HIST. 260, 260–75 (1959).

128. Richard Helmholz states that "[t]he law of marriage presents the paradoxical case in which the English Church clung to a part of the medieval Roman canon law which the Roman Catholic Church itself discarded." RICHARD H. HELMHOLZ, ROMAN CANON LAW IN REFORMATION ENGLAND 69 (1990). Helmholz is specifically referring to the practice of clandestine marriage, which was practically abolished by the Council of Trent.

129. E. GARTH MOORE, AN INTRODUCTION TO ENGLISH CANON LAW 82 (1967).

130. JOHN WITTE, JR., FROM SACRAMENT TO CONTRACT: MARRIAGE, RELIGION, AND LAW IN THE WESTERN TRADITION 131 (1997).

patristic days—was rejected in favor of a strong Protestant commitment to marriage as the ideal form of Christian life.[131]

One area of remarkable continuity with the medieval tradition in both theology and canon law was the centrality of the procreative dimension of marriage. One might consider theological developments first. The *Encyclopedia of Christianity* has compared the English Book of Common Prayer to the Bible in stating that "[a]long with the Bible, it has something of a standard of faith among Anglicans."[132] It was first published in 1549 under the direction of King Edward VI and revised and republished periodically since that year.[133] In its various editions, it has helped to condition several hundred years of Anglican thought and devotion.

The Prayer Book of 1549 referred back to medieval Catholic theology in declaring that marriage "signif[ied] unto us the misticall union that is betwixte Christe and his Church."[134] God, the Prayer Book stressed, had instituted marriage "in the time of mannes innocencie," before the Fall from grace in the Garden of Eden.[135] Its importance to humankind was renewed by Jesus Christ at the wedding feast at Cana.[136] Its continued existence was intended to serve three great ends, the first of which was procreation. The Prayer Book stated, "Duely consideryng the cuases for the whiche matrimonie was ordeined. One cause was the procreation of children, to be brought up in the feare and nurture of the Lord, and the prayse of God."[137]

After pronouncing the couple man and wife, a blessing, adapted from Psalm 128, was then to be pronounced, stressing the importance of fruitfulness:

> Thy wife shall bee as the fruitful vine, upon the walles of thy house.
> Thy children like the olife braunches rounde about thy table.
> Loe, thus shal the man be blessed, that feareth the Lord.
> The Lord from out of Sion shall so blesse thee: that thou shalt see Hierusalem in prosperitie al thy life long.

131. John Witte, Jr., Law and Protestantism: The Legal Teachings of the Lutheran Reformation 17 (2002). Witte speaks for the entire Protestant Reformation, continental and English, when he states that "[a]ll adult persons, preachers and others alike, should pursue the calling of marriage, for all were in need of the comforts of marital love and the protection from sexual sin." *Id.*

132. Thaddeus A. Schnitker, *Book of Common Prayer*, *in* 3 Encyclopedia of Christianity 285 (Erwin Fahlbusch et al. eds., Geoffrey William Bromiley trans., 1999).

133. G.J. Cuming, A History of Anglican Liturgy 66–95 (1969) (reviewing the drafting and promulgation of the first English prayerbook of 1549).

134. Church of England, The First and Second Prayer Books of Edward the Sixth 252 (1913) [hereinafter The First and Second Prayer Books].

135. *Id.*

136. *Id.*

137. *Id.* The other two causes included: marriage as "a remedie agaynst sinne, and to avoide fornicacion" and marriage for the sake of "the mutuall societie, helpe, and coumfort, that the one oughte to have of thother, both in prosperitie and adversitie." *Id.*

> Yea, that thou shalt see thy childers children; and peace be upon Israel.[138]

Thus, themes of fecundity, earthly prosperity, and ultimate transcendence through the survival of the next generation were blended together as a way of seeking divine favor upon the newly married couple.

The second Prayer Book of Edward VI, promulgated in 1552, proved to be excessively Protestant for the English public and met ultimate popular disapproval for this reason.[139] This short-lived Prayer Book nevertheless retained the language reviewed above. Marriage still served first the purpose of procreation,[140] and the same blessing was still pronounced.[141] When Queen Elizabeth I revived the Book of Common Prayer following Queen Mary's short-lived attempt to return the English realm to Catholicism, she removed from the 1552 version its more extreme Protestant elements.[142] Elizabeth, however, retained the teachings on marriage. The same purposes ascribed to marriage in the earlier prayer books, and the same Psalm pronounced over the married couple, continued to be prescribed by Elizabeth's new Prayer Book of 1559.[143]

The seventeenth century was a time of revolutionary ferment. Puritans, advocates of an austere Christianity harshly critical of the adornments and trappings of Anglicanism, gained power in the mid-seventeenth century and embarked upon a campaign of religious reform intended to purge the vestiges of "popery" from English lands.[144] Oliver Cromwell, however, who had declared himself Lord Protector in the 1650s, governed with a harshness that caused people to yearn for the old royal house. Eventually, with the death of Cromwell, Charles II, the exiled son of the first King Charles, was invited back to England in a Restoration of Monarchy. This Restoration was accompanied by a renewal of Anglican sensibilities, now tempered but not obliterated by Puritan theology.[145]

An important exposition of the theological foundations of marriage and its centrality in the procreation of the next generation was Thomas

138. *Id.* at 255.

139. The 1552 Prayer Book was quickly rescinded with the accession to the throne of Queen Mary. When Elizabeth I succeeded Mary, she did not turn to the 1552 Prayer Book but set to work on a new version. *See* Schnitker, *supra* note 132, at 285; *see also* WILLIAM SYDNOR, THE STORY OF THE REAL PRAYER BOOK 16–19 (1989).

140. THE FIRST AND SECOND PRAYER BOOKS, *supra* note 134, at 410.

141. *Id.* at 413.

142. SYDNOR, *supra* note 139, at 20–24.

143. CHURCH OF ENGLAND, THE BOOK OF COMMON PRAYER, 1559: THE ELIZABETHAN PRAYER BOOK 290–91 (John E. Booty ed., University Press of Virginia 1976) (setting forth the purposes of marriage); *see also id.* at 294 (reiterating the Psalm).

144. A good summary of these developments can be found in HAROLD J. BERMAN, LAW AND REVOLUTION II: THE IMPACT OF THE PROTESTANT REFORMATIONS ON THE WESTERN LEGAL TRADITION 216–22 (2003).

145. *Id.* at 222–24, 228–30.

Comber's *The Occasional Offices of Matrimony*.[146] Published at the height of the Restoration, this work set forth—in greater detail than any of the official documents—the theology behind marriage and childbirth. Rejecting the Catholic doctrine of the sacramentality of marriage, Comber nevertheless repeated much of the medieval theology used to justify the Catholic stance. Marriage was "instituted by God the Father, vindicated by God the son, and explicated by God the Holy Ghoste, to signifie the mysterious Love of Jesus to his Church; For our Lord forsook his Heavenly Father, and did cleave to our Nature, becoming one flesh with us."[147]

Marriage, Comber continued, was instituted first of all for procreation.[148] Comber turned to Jewish theology to stress the transcendent significance of childbirth: Jewish writers, Comber declared, consider the biblical injunction to be fruitful and multiply "an indispensable precept, affirming that those who do neglect it, are Murtherers, and shall have no part in the world to come."[149] Comber acknowledged that Christianity did not hold to the same position, but even Christians believe that "God designed Marriage to replenish the world; and therefore all who enter into that estate are bound to aim principally at the Procreation and Education of Children."[150] In support of this proposition, Comber reviewed a veritable parade of classical Christian writers—St. Ignatius of Antioch, St. Augustine, and St. Isidore of Seville, among others.[151] He concluded,

> [T]hus matrimony becomes the preserver of the world, and the continuer of Mankind, being a never-failing Foundation which always sends forth new streams . . . And yet still Marriage hath a higher end than barely to produce Children, for it is designed also for the Education of Children in the fear and nurture of the Lord, and to his praise and glory.[152]

Comber's commentary on a related Anglican rite, "The Churching of Women," also bears analysis. A medieval rite,[153] retained by the successive

146. Thomas Comber, The Occasional Offices of Matrimony, Visitation of the Sick, Burial of the Dead, Churching of Women, and Commination (1679).

147. *Id.* at 25–26.

148. *Id.* at 31–36.

149. *Id.* at 32.

150. *Id.* In support of this proposition, Comber looked not only to Christian sources but also to the Augustan marriage laws reviewed above. *Id.* at 32–33.

151. Comber, *supra* note 146, at 33–34.

152. *Id.* at 34–35. Comber continues by writing that,

> [t]he Parents work is not half done when they have brought Children into this world, they must feed them and attend them, cloath and instruct them, preserve them from dangers, warn them against all evil things, and labour to make them truly fear God. Parents therefore, must not only desire to have Children, but resolve to bring them up well and vertuously.

Id.

153. On medieval antecedents to the "churching of women" ritual, see Joanne M. Pierce, 'Green Women' and Blood Pollution: Some Medieval Rituals for the Churching of Women After Childbirth 191–215 (1999).

versions of the English Book of Common Prayer,[154] this ritual called down God's blessings on women who have undergone childbirth. Comber offered an extended explication of the significance of this rite.[155] Concerning the purpose of the ceremony, Comber wrote,

> The Birth of Man is so truly wonderful, that it seems to be designed for a constant demonstration of the Omnipotence of our Creator; and if the frequency did not abate of our admiration, it could be esteemed no less than a perpetual miracle. However it is not a meaner act of God's power and mercy in it self, because he often repeats it; and therefore that the number of these Providences may not diminish our sense of their true worth, Holy Church ordains a publick and solemn acknowledgement by the Party most concerned; that is, the Woman, who still feels the bruises of our first Parents most deplorable fall . . . .[156]

Every childbirth, Comber thus asserted, is sacred; none shall be taken for granted. Every child is a small miracle revealing divine power and an event worthy of the most solemn thanksgiving.

As with his citation to Augustus's marriage legislation,[157] Comber chose to justify Christian celebration by considering pagan wisdom. Galen is thus quoted as seeing in the birth of a child "the power of its Maker."[158] Comber continued: "And shall not we Christians be as just to our Creator? Shall we not acknowledge every instance he gives us of this kind? especially since he not only makes us in our Mothers Womb, but brings us also wonderfully from thence."[159]

Anglican theology thus made procreation and education the chief purpose and responsibility of marriage. It was declaimed in the marriage ceremony and celebrated in the recitation of the Psalms that followed. It was also celebrated in the ritual known as the Churching of Women which was justified as a thanksgiving for the daily miracle of childbirth. The procreative dimension of marriage was thus advanced in a comprehensive form by Anglican teaching.

Anglican canon law also stressed the procreative dimension of marriage. Henry Swinburne, the author of a sixteenth-century treatise on marriage contracts, explained that parties become free to consent to marriage at the age of puberty because that is the age at which God Himself equipped

154. The rite appeared in the 1549 Prayer Book as a rite of purification. It became a rite of Thanksgiving in the 1552 Prayer Book and remained so characterized through subsequent editions of the Book of Common Prayer. *See* DAVID CRESSY, PURIFICATION, THANKSGIVING AND THE CHURCHING OF WOMEN IN POST-REFORMATION ENGLAND 106, 118–19 (1993).

155. COMBER, *supra* note 146, at 505–38.

156. *Id.* at 505.

157. *See* discussion, *supra* note 150.

158. COMBER, *supra* note 146 at 512.

159. *Id.*

the human person to reproduce.[160] A man at the age of fourteen and a woman at the age of twelve "have Natural and Corporal Ability to perform the duty of Marriage."[161] They have achieved the age at which,

> the Lord and Maker of all Creatures in the beginning of the World, hath by Divine Providence, for the propagation of his Church, proclaimed an universal Liberty, *Crescite et Multiplicamini* [Increase and Multiply]. And therefore this Liberty is to be denied to none, whom otherwise the Almighty hath naturally disposed and enabled to encreate and multiply.[162]

Elsewhere in his work, Swinburne reiterated and dressed in legal garb the classic Augustinian argument that the affirmative exclusion of the good of children resulted in the invalidity of the marriage contract. Swinburne condemned as contrary to marriage itself the placement in the contract of certain "unhonest conditions."[163] By this term, Swinburne meant to include conditions against "the Substance of Matrimony," which included the three Augustinian goods: "*bonum prolis, bonum fidei, et vinculum individuum*—the good of Issue, the good of Faithfulness, and the Bond inseparable."[164] Such conditions, Swinburne reiterated, were "opposed to those things without which true Matrimony cannot consist."[165] A condition against the good of children, Swinburne asserted, was especially destructive of the matrimonial contract because the good of children was "the first and principal good of Matrimony."[166] Echoing his medieval forebears, Swinburne rejected the claims of those who would point to the marriage of Mary and Joseph as not a true marriage. To be sure, they did not avail themselves of the marital rights, but they were open to the possibility of procreation, and the birth of the Lord Jesus fulfilled the procreative good of marriage.[167]

Subsequent generations of English canonists expanded upon these claims. John Ayliffe (1676–1732) echoed the writings of the fourth- and fifth-century patristic authors in declaring that marriage came into being even before the Fall for the sake of "the Propagation of Mankind."[168] Neither approving or disapproving of the categories, Ayliffe noted that "among the papists, there is a threefold matrionial Good, *viz.*, what they in Latin call *Fides, Proles* and *Sacramentum*."[169]

160. Henry Swinburne, A Treatise of Spousals, or Matrimonial Contracts 47 (London 2d ed. 1711).

161. *Id.*

162. *Id.*

163. *Id.* at 134.

164. *Id.*

165. *Id.* at 135.

166. Swinburne, *supra* note 160, at 135.

167. *Id.* at 135–36.

168. John Ayliffe, Parergon Juris Canonici Anglicani 359–60 (London 1726).

169. *Id.* at 360.

This manner of thinking and talking about marriage persisted into nineteenth-century English ecclesiastical law. One can consider the work of Thomas Poynter who published a treatise on marriage and divorce in 1824. He asked why impotence or frigidity invalidated marital consent. In the process of resolving this question, he reviewed what the legal tradition had to say on the subject.[170] The eighteenth-century Anglican canonist Thomas Oughton, Poynter noted, had asserted that impotence and frigidity were "natural impediments" to marriage because they prevented the parties from fulfilling the good of children.[171] Poynter also looked to the eighteenth-century continental jurist Samuel Pufendorf for guidance on this subject. Pufendorf had asked how it was that men and women who were beyond their reproductive years might be allowed to marry. Pufendorf concluded that such couples might be considered "as honorary members of the matrimonial state, enjoying a title without an office."[172] Poynter was inclined to agree with these commentators that procreation must be the central organizing principle of marriage.[173]

The English Protestant writers tended to emphasize the procreative dimension of marriage to an even greater extent than their medieval forebears. Medieval Catholic writers, of course, were always required to recognize virginity as the ideal form of life. They thus moved intellectually back and forth between the spiritual fecundity of the virgin's vows to God and the spouses' physical fecundity in the here and now. Protestant theology had largely discarded such a belief in the sanctifying power of virginity. Greater emphasis was placed on carnal marriage, and its procreative dimension was thereby expected to carry greater weight.

Thus, in the English ecclesiastical law which would come to form the backbone of the American law of marriage, procreation remained the central organizing principle. This was the case whether one regarded the principles laid down by generations of theological writers—whose works informed and guided the work of the English canonists—or whether one considered the writings of the canonists themselves. A marriage contract that excluded the good of children contained a dishonest condition that resulted in the contract's invalidity. A true marriage contained within its terms the three-fold Augustinian goods of procreation, fidelity, and indissolubility. Natural impediments such as impotence or frigidity, which served to frustrate procreation, also frustrated the possibility of bringing a marriage into being. This was the tradition that would inform American

170. THOMAS POYNTER, A CONCISE VIEW OF THE DOCTRINE AND PRACTICE OF THE ECCLESIASTICAL COURTS IN DOCTORS COMMONS ON VARIOUS POINTS RELATIVE TO THE SUBJECT OF MARRIAGE AND DIVORCE 123–26 (London, J. & W.T. Clarke 1824).

171. *Id.* at 123.

172. *Id.* at 124.

173. *Id.* at 123–24.

judicial writing on marriage in the nineteenth century and, indeed, for much of the twentieth century.

V. Concluding Observations

American marriage law continued to reflect these basic presuppositions until well into the twentieth century. *Skinner v. Oklahoma*, decided by the United States Supreme Court in 1942, six months after the United States entered World War II, involved a constitutional challenge to an Oklahoma law compelling the sterilization of those determined to be habitual criminals.[174] William Orville Douglas, writing for a unanimous court, opened his opinion by stressing that what was involved was the right to procreate: "This case touches a sensitive and important area of human rights. Oklahoma deprives certain individuals of a right which is basic to the perpetuation of a race—the right to have offspring."[175]

In these opening lines, personal rights and public purposes were linked: procreation was a fundamental human right, but it was also necessary for group survival. Later in the opinion, Douglas drove home the point that it was within the institution of marriage that this right was to be exercised: "We are dealing here with legislation which involves one of the basic civil rights of man. Marriage and procreation are fundamental to the very existence and survival of the race."[176]

In 1965, *Griswold v. Connecticut*, known widely as the case that struck down legislation outlawing the sale of contraceptives to married persons, did not repudiate this fundamental purpose to marriage.[177] Rather, the *Griswold* Court understood its decision as protecting and enhancing the marital relationship. Once again, Justice Douglas—who can hardly be said to have respected marriage in his private life[178]—offered a defense of marriage as "a coming together for better or for worse, hopefully enduring, and intimate to the degree of being sacred."[179] Justice John Marshall Harlan, in his concurrence, developed the kind of respect the Court continued to harbor for the institution of marriage. Harlan declared that the Court did not mean by the decision to depreciate the State's professed policy behind the statute—the prevention of "all forms of promiscuous or illicit sexual relation-

174. Skinner v. Oklahoma, 316 U.S. 535 (1942). Habitual criminal for the purposes of the statute was defined as a person who was convicted of two or more crimes "amounting to felonies involving moral turpitude." *Id.* at 536.

175. *Id.*

176. *Id.* at 541.

177. Griswold v. Connecticut, 381 U.S. 479 (1965).

178. Douglas was married and divorced several times. One might get a sense of how Douglas comported himself in his private life by reading chapter thirty-two of Bruce Murphy's new biography of Douglas, entitled "A Tale of Two Women." *See* Bruce Allen Murphy, Wild Bill: The Legend and Life of William O. Douglas 392–401 (2003).

179. *Griswold*, 381 U.S. at 486.

ships."[180] Harlan noted that the Court's judgment extended only to the prohibition on the sale of contraceptives to married persons. There may be legitimate reasons, Harlan asserted, for marital use of contraceptives—whether out of a desire for family planning or out of a concern for the well-being and even the lives of those involved.[181]

Only in the mid-1980s, in the academic reception given to the case of *Turner v. Safley*,[182] does one see the definitive severing of procreation from its place of pride as the central organizing principle of American marriage law.[183] *Turner v. Safley* involved a challenge to prison regulations that prevented inmates from marrying. The Court, in unanimously striking down the regulations, noted that marriage served not only the purposes of sexual intimacy and procreation but also acted as a means of providing emotional or spiritual support for those who might be separated by distance.[184] Marriages, the *Turner* Court added, could serve as outward evidence of ongoing personal commitment.[185] Marriages might even serve as "a pre-condition to the receipt of government benefits."[186] All of these purposes—all of these marital goods, to borrow the language of the theologians—were legitimate.

The *Turner v. Safley* Court did not intend to distinguish among these various marital purposes, nor did it see these purposes as somehow competing for primacy. The *Turner* Court, finally, did not view these purposes as somehow divisible. Indeed, it recognized that in most prison marriages, the inmate spouse will eventually be released and the union will be "fully consummated."[187] Scholars and courts, however, "have now removed this list of marital goods from the penological context and relied upon them to argue against the traditional linkage between marriage and heterosexual reproduction."[188] In the process, marriage came to be understood and explicated as serving the purposes of emotional fulfillment, or even the economic pooling of resources.

---

180. *Id.* at 505 (Harlan, J., concurring).

181. *Id.* at 503. Justice Arthur Goldberg, concurring in the Court's judgment, quoted a prior Harlan opinion in *Poe v. Ullman*, 367 U.S. 497, 551–52 (1961), to emphasize the centrality of family life to the *Griswold* Court:

> Certainly the safeguarding of the home does not follow merely from the sanctity of property rights. The home derives its pre-eminence as the seat of family life. And the integrity of that life is something so fundamental that it has been found to draw to its protection the principles of more than one explicitly granted Constitutional right. . . . Of this whole 'private realm of family life' it is difficult to imagine what is more private or intimate than a husband and wife's marital relations.

Griswold, 381 U.S. at 495 (Goldberg, J., concurring).

182. Turner v. Safley, 482 U.S. 78 (1987).

183. The academic reception given to *Turner v. Safley* has been traced in Charles J. Reid, Jr., *The Gingerbread Man Thirty Years On: The Parlous State of Marital Theory*, 1 U. ST. THOMAS L.J. 656, 677–86 (2003).

184. *Turner*, 482 U.S. at 95–96.

185. *Id.* at 95.

186. *Id.* at 96.

187. *Id.*

188. Reid, *supra* note 183, at 683.

The American same-sex marriage decisions were the beneficiaries of the nominalistic treatment accorded *Turner v. Safley*. The Hawaii Supreme Court's decision in favor of same-sex marriage, *Baehr v. Lewin*,[189] understood the goods of marriage as chiefly economic in nature. Community property, spousal support, and access to a variety of state welfare programs were the goods of marriage, according to *Baehr*.[190]

The Vermont Supreme Court in *Baker v. Vermont*[191] explicitly rejected the State's assertion that its interest in the procreative dimension of marriage precluded it from recognizing same-sex marriage.[192] Such a claim, the court concluded, was both under- and over-inclusive. Many heterosexual couples marry with no intention of having children, while many homosexual couples would seek to procreate through various artificial means.[193] Having diminished the linkage between procreation and marriage, the *Baker* court engaged in the same sort of economic reductionism found in *Baehr*: inheritance rights, pension and insurance rights, the right to sue for loss of consortium, and rights of joint tenancy and survivorship. These were among the fundamental rights and privileges of the marital relationship, according to *Baker*.[194]

The Massachusetts case of *Goodridge v. Department of Public Health* recognized that marriage served emotional and economic ends.[195] The right to choose whether or not to marry was fundamental because only through its exercise or nonexercise might one truly have access to "the full range of human experience and [the] full protection of the laws for one's 'avowed commitment to an intimate and lasting human relationship.'"[196] But marriage did not exist solely to further human emotional needs, according to *Goodridge*. It also provided access to economic benefits, "touching nearly every aspect of life and death."[197] Marriage, on this analysis, primarily served these two ends—the emotional and the economic.

There is a certain radicalism to these decisions. They represent a drastic departure from a western legal tradition that can be traced back to pre-Christian sources, to the Rome of Emperor Augustus. On the analysis of *Baehr*, *Baker*, and *Goodridge*, procreation no longer serves as the central organizing principle of the law. In a sense, then, these cases have ceased to connect marriage to the natural processes of fecundity and reproduction.

189. Baehr v. Lewin, 852 P.2d 44 (Haw. 1993).
190. *Id.* at 59.
191. Baker v. Vermont, 744 A.2d 864 (Vt. 1999).
192. *Id.* at 881.
193. *Id.*
194. *Id.* at 883–84.
195. Goodridge v. Dep't of Pub. Health, 798 N.E.2d 941 (Mass. 2003).
196. *Id.* at 957 (quoting Baker v. State, 744 A.2d 864, 889 (1999)).
197. *Id.* at 955.

The central reference point by which not only marriage—but even virginity—was understood in western theology and law has been taken away. One is left to wonder what comes next.

Name Index

For Product Safety Concerns and Information please contact our EU
representative GPSR@taylorandfrancis.com
Taylor & Francis Verlag GmbH, Kaufingerstraße 24, 80331 München, Germany

www.ingramcontent.com/pod-product-compliance
Lightning Source LLC
LaVergne TN
LVHW080801011026
849160LV00015B/1497

9781138378568